Developments in American Sociological Theory, 1915–1950

Developments in American Sociological Theory, 1915–1950

Roscoe C. Hinkle

STATE UNIVERSITY OF NEW YORK PRESS

Published by
State University of New York Press, Albany

© 1994   State University of New York

For information, address State University of New York
Press, State University Plaza, Albany, N.Y., 12246

Production by E. Moore
Marketing by Theresa A. Swierzowski

Library of Congress Cataloging-in-Publication Data

Hinkle, Roscoe C.
    Developments in American sociological theory, 1915–1950 /
Roscoe C. Hinkle.
        p.   cm.
    Includes bibliographical references and index.
    ISBN 0-7914-1931-2 (HC   :   alk. paper). — ISBN 0-7914-1932-0 (pbk.
: alk. paper)
    1. Sociology—United States—History.   2. Sociology—Philosophy.
I. Title.
HM22.U5H48   1994
301'.0973—dc20   93-26776
                                                                           CIP

10 9 8 7 6 5 4 3 2 1

To J. H. U., F. J. S., and G. J. H.
all of whom have crucially contributed in diverse ways
to making potentiality actuality

Contents

Preface   ix

Acknowledgments   xiii

PART I: ORIENTATION

1   Confronting Problems in the Study of Theory
    in American Sociology (1915/18–1945/50)   3

2   Three Epistemological-Methodological Stances   29

PART II: CONTINUITIES (WITH FIRST-PERIOD THEORY)

3   Social Evolutionism, Social Origins, and Social Structure   65

4   Critique of Earlier Social Evolutionism and
    Its Legacy in the Second Period   94

5   Fragmentation and Demise of Social
    Evolutionary Change Theories   118

PART III: DISCONTINUITIES (IN RELATION TO FIRST PERIOD THEORY)

6   Discontinuities Arising within American Sociology   151

7   Theory, Anthropology, and History   172

8   Theory, Psychiatry, and Psychology   200

9   Philosophy, Psychology, Sociology,
    and Symbolic Interactionism   232

10 Possible European Influences on American Theory   273

PART IV: SUMMARY RETROSPECTIVE
AND PROSPECTIVE

11   The Concept of the Group: An Analytical Summary   303

12   An Overview in Context: Past, Present, and Future   322

       Appendix   349

       Notes   351

       Selected Reference List   391

       Index   419

Preface

Although the study undergirding this volume actually began in a somewhat unsystematic and desultory fashion during the 1960s, it was undertaken continuously and systematically about two years after publication of *Founding Theory of American Sociology 1881–1915* (i.e., 1980). Undoubtedly, this work is a sequel to the prior inquiry in several senses: in its objectives, major inspiration, organization, and contents. Like its predecessor, it takes its point of departure from two basic objectives: (1) elaboration of the same classificatory and periodizing scheme, and (2) application of the scheme to the study of American sociological theory within a particular interval of time.

Two sociologists have been especially important as sources of inspiration of this volume. To the first, Professor (F.) Joseph Schneider, the author is indebted for an introduction (during his early years as a graduate student) to the approach of F. J. Teggart to the history of methodological ideas of the social sciences. To the second, Professor John H. Useem, the author is indebted for the development (during his later years as a graduate student) of an abiding interest in the history of American sociology. And to the latter, he is also indebted for a critical, yet sympathetic, reading of one of the later versions of the text of this book.

And surely those who have read the earlier *Founding Theory* will notice that the present undertaking includes—like the earlier—chapters on the socio-intellectual context, epistemology-methodology, and especially an emphasis on substantive or social ontological theory (dealing with the problem-domains of social origins, social structure, and social change) that is identifiable with social evolution.

However, this work involves the second period of American sociological theory, which follows that of the founding period and precedes that of structural functionalism. Broadly speaking, it spans the time between World Wars I and II, some thirty to thirty-five years. It treats a period of theory that has generally been ignored except for a too-casual identification with the views of a few notable Chicagoans. Accordingly, this book differs from the earlier one by virtue of the time period and thus the specific controversies and contents of theory.

This is a period in which (general) theory—at least in the view of many—more or less loses the prestige it had during the founding years. Unlike in the first period, fewer distinctive personal formulations of (general) theory appear. General theory is identifiable with what otherwise has often been termed "general sociology." Yet this general sociology, some versions of which are of high and demanding intellectual caliber, is substantially being transformed over the years into introductory sociology with its numerous texts. True, the well-known Park and Burgess text from the 1920s can be cited. Certain others, such as Ellwood 1925, Hankins 1928, Reuter and Hart 1933, Lundberg 1939, Sutherland and Woodward (1937) 1940, and Ogburn and Nimkoff 1940—to mention only a few—provide much of the data for chapters 3 through 6.

However, neither the fragmenting residual social evolutionism nor the (Parkian) social processualism was able to dominate the terrain of general theory. Based on both book and periodical publications, chapters 7 through 10 reveal that efforts to invoke culture (using the resources of either anthropology or history), the premises of Freudian psychiatry, behaviorist psychology, an emergent symbolic interactionist social psychology, or a largely Weberian-derived social actionist frame of reference were not susceptible to reformulation as the bases of a general theory.

Group became the crucial or pivotal concept through which a general sociological theory was to be reconstructed. Chapter 11 explores just how the different theoretical stances from chapters 3 through 10 were analyzable as variants of social nominalism or social realism (as noted in the analytical classificatory schema).

Chapter 12 provides a detailed summary of the results of the analysis of chapters 2 through 11 and their implications. It also suggests the relevance of the postmodern critique of foundationalism for the inquiry into theory between World Wars I and II. Thus, second-period theory might be characterized as involving a series of contested foundations, yet with essentially no intimation (except for Teggart's views) of the contestability of foundationalism itself.

This version of the book is the outcome of numerous drafts and revisions. Basic research began with a professional leave granted by the Ohio State University for the first six months of 1982. Within less than a year, initial drafts of about half the planned chapters were complete. They and others were the beneficiaries of the reactions of graduate students in classes and seminars in sociological theory at Ohio State University (1982–86) and at Texas A&M University (1988–89). Certainly, the author wishes to express his gratitude for the warm and hospitable atmosphere of the sociology department at the latter institution during his stay as visiting professor. He is especially indebted to Professors Mary Zey, Alex McIntosh, Jim Burk, and Ben Aguirre for cordial and stimulating intellectual exchanges. A first full draft of fifteen chapters was completed within several months following return to Ohio. (Professor David Sciulli, who had just joined the Texas A&M faculty, and Professor Danny Jorgensen, at the University of South Florida, also kindly provided critical reactions to portions of that larger version.) In turn, it was subjected to revision and reduction to twelve chapters, out of which the present version has emerged. The author must, of course, accept responsibility for difficulties and problems that remain.

Ten years surely represent an extended period of gestation even for a manuscript dealing with a period in the history of sociological theory with essentially no substantial precedents. Thus, the author recognizes that any expression of gratitude to Gisela J. Hinkle—no matter how elaborate—may pale into insignificance in the realization that his almost single-minded devotion to completion of this manuscript has at times impacted negatively on her own professional career and threatened to exceed the limits of her patience and forbearance.

Last, as readers turn to the text proper of this study, they must be aware that the age of the relevant primary literature created a distinctive problem. Because it was impossible, within a reasonable interval of time, to ascertain the identities of current copyright holders to some of the books and articles published anywhere from fifty to seventy years ago, it also became impossible, in these instances, to secure legal consent (or authorization) for quotation (or republication) beyond the limits of "fair use." Thus, the only acceptable alternative open to the author—irrespective of his preference for quotation—was a resort to extensive paraphrasing.

Acknowledgments

The author wishes to express his appreciation to Professor Werner W. Landecker, University of Michigan, Ann Arbor, Michigan, and to Professor William H. Sewell, University of Wisconsin, Madison, Wisconsin, for providing essential documents on the histories of the Departments of Sociology at these two institutions.

He is especially grateful for the generosity of Professor E. L. Quarentelli, formerly a member of the Department of Sociology at Ohio State University but currently Research Professor at the Disaster Research Center of the University of Delaware, Newark, for making available his notes from Sociology 321 in Advanced Social Psychology, which Professor Herbert Blumer offered at the University of Chicago during winter quarter 1951 (and prior to his departure for the University of California, Berkeley, in 1952).

He is also appreciative of the kindness of Professor Kurt H. Wolff, who is Professor Emeritus of Sociology, Brandeis University, Waltham, Massachusetts, and now holder of the copyright to, and former editor of, *Emile Durkheim, 1858–1917: A Collection of Essays, with Translations and a Bibliography,* which was originally published by the Ohio State University Press in 1960 (and later reprinted under an altered title by Harper Torchbooks in 1964) for permission to quote selectively from the author's chapter "Durkheim in American Sociology," pp. 267–95.

Finally, the author gratefully acknowledges his indebtedness for permission to make selected quotations:

Reprinted from *Social Forces* 7 (3) March, 1919. Notes on [House's] Timeless Sociology by Frederick J. Teggart. Copyright © The University of North Carolina Press.

Reprinted from *Social Forces* 8 (2) December, 1929. Concerning the Distinction between the Social and the Cultural by Bernhard J. Stern. Copyright © The University of North Carolina Press.

Reprinted from *Mind, Self, and Society*, "From the Standpoint of a Social Behaviorist" by George H. Mead; edited, with an introduction, by Charles W. Morris. Copyright 1934 © by The University of Chicago.

PART I: ORIENTATION

Chapter 1

Confronting Problems in the Study of Theory in American Sociology (1915/18–1945/50)

An adequate account of how contemporary sociological theory in the United States has come to be as it is will probably elude us for some time to come. Certainly, the task becomes even more problematic, or formidable, if the usual textbook-like chronological sequence of masters/mistresses, exemplars, or chief representatives of major orientations across the years is rejected. To demand an analysis of major and minor, dominant, minority, and/or coordinate competing orientations, divided and arranged in appropriate time periods, compounds the difficulties, because this approach requires the assessment of the rise and fall, intellectual defenses and critiques, expansions and contractions, displacements and replacements, of the stances. Most emphatically, the delineation of the background period immediately preceding the present is not sufficient for present purposes. Demarcation of periods back to the beginning of theory in American sociology, along with their sequential interrelations, becomes a required task. (The possible contribution of each and every period to the present state of theory must be considered and not excluded a priori simply because of its apparent temporal-historical "distance.") Though preparatory studies have begun, much remains to be done.

One of the more conspicuous lacunae is to be found between World Wars I and II. To be sure, the ideas of a few sociologists (e.g., Park, Thomas, Mead) have been investigated. But a comprehensive, extended, systematic analysis of general theory—beyond an isolated chapter or specialized article—simply does not exist. Precisely such an inquiry is contemplated here and holds the promise of extending knowledge about

1. the circumstances under which conflict occurred within (epistemological-) methodological theory and between it and substantive (or ontological) theory so that the two were differentiated and largely separated in the period in question;
2. what befell the legacy of social evolutionism from the pre-World War I years;
3. new theoretical orientations and their sources, especially in the 1930s and 1940s;
4. the displacement of earlier exemplars of classical European theory (e.g., Comte, Spencer, Gumplowicz) by somewhat later Europeans (e.g., Durkheim, Simmel, M. Weber) in the late 1930s and 1940s;[1] and
5. what permitted, if not facilitated, the rapid ascent and dominance of Parsonsian structural functionalism in so few years after the mid 1940s.[2]

Certainly, each of these questions has a major importance for the subsequent development of theory in American sociology. Each demands attention. But before inquiry can profitably begin, several major (and logically prior) problems must be recognized and addressed:

1. A critic may claim that in the above concerns, theory is merely assumed to exist. Thus, the question of evidence for a basic and continuous interest in theory in American sociology from 1915 to 1945 must be examined and assessed.
2. If such interest can be shown to exist, it must presumably be associated with one or more conceptions of theory, including their relations to present views.
3. Further, a conception may be defined abstractly or formally without a specific referent, exemplification, or content. If the latter is absent, some means of linkage must be found or devised.
4. Because the content of theory at any point in time may involve continuity with, as well as discontinuity from, the past, an analytic classifi-

catory scheme that encompasses the basic problems of theory and the possible bases of answers will have to be introduced. It must become possible analytically to state comparisons and contrasts, similarities and dissimilarities, between one particular theory and another at a given time and at different points in time (e.g., between those of 1881–1915 and those of 1915–45).

5.   Nevertheless, special precautions must be taken to assure that potential sources of discontinuity and dissimilarity are acknowledged and accorded their due weight. Such precaution will entail, among other things, attention to the possible intellectual influence of theoretical stances in other fields of knowledge in the United States and from Europe.

The first three problems (and a portion of the fourth) will be examined in some detail in the remainder of this chapter. Pursuit of the implications of a portion of the fourth and of the fifth, and the required analyses, will govern the organization of inquiry throughout most of the remaining chapters (except for chapter 2).

INDICATORS OF INTEREST IN THEORY

Undeniably, the most fundamental of all of the problems concerns evidence for a basic and continuous interest in theory throughout the years 1915–45 in American sociology. Fortunately, three major types of data are available for dealing with this issue.

The first type concerns the nature of the topical sessions in terms of which the annual meetings of the American Sociological Society or ASS were organized from 1921 on. Significantly, a "Social Theory and Social Evolution" division was included in 1921 but dropped in subsequent years. In 1931 a "Theory of Sociology" division was made a part of the program, but this was then omitted for two years. A "General Sociology: Sociological Theory and Social Planning" division was introduced in 1934. Finally, in 1935 a "Social Theory" division was instituted and included in the annual meetings (and in the plans for two meetings canceled during World War II) up to the end of the Second World War. Undeniably, the sporadic inclusion of the theory sessions up to 1935 in the annual American Sociological Society programs raises a basic question about the continuity of interest in the field.

The second type of data is afforded by the references to theory in the classificatory scheme for abstracting periodical literature in the *American Journal of Sociology* (AJS), beginning in 1921/22. Although the terms of reference varied, it is clear that an interest was present in 1921/22 through 1928/29, 1933/34 and 1934/35, 1939, 1939/40, 1940/41, and 1941/42 (i.e., until the onset of World War II). Because the years just noted are also the years in which abstracting occurred in the *AJS,* an interest in theory is thus continuous for the years indicated.

In 1929 the Census of Current Research Projects was reported in the *AJS* for the first time (based, presumably, on the categories employed in *Social Science Abstracts*). Theory appeared under "Social Theory and Its History" from this time until 1934. In 1934 and 1935 the category was "Theory and Methods," with the subdivisions "Methods of Research" and "Sociological Theory and History." In 1936, it became "Sociological Theory and History." For the next three years (1937–1939), the designation "History and Theory" was used. In 1940, the category was altered to "History and Theory of Sociology," and this persisted through 1945.

Among the sixteen categories that Ethel Shanas used in the analysis of space (by articles) in the *AJS* for 1895–1945 is "Theory and History" (i.e., not merely theory), in her article as published in that journal in May 1945. Shanas used five-year intervals, and the percentage varied from 35.9 (for 1920–24) to 7.1 (in 1935–39).[3] Unfortunately, she provided no specific criteria for inclusion in the category. If the category is limited to theory only and, further, requires explicit use of the word *theory* in article titles, the number of includable articles (as I calculate it) is drastically reduced for the years 1915–44 from an overall percentage of 13.04 down to 0.04.[4] (Indeed, no articles, so defined, could be found for the period from 1921 through 1937.)

Application of this restrictive notion of theory to the study of the *American Sociological Review* (*ASR*) yields only a bare minimum of articles for the period 1936 (when this journal began) to 1945. A total of 12 (or 1.9 percent of the 652 articles) is indicated.[5]

If the journals *Sociology and Social Research* (*S&SR*) and *Social Forces* (*SF*) are examined in terms of their contributions of theory articles (as just construed) for the time period 1915–44, only a few appear. (Seven can be identified in the former and only three for the latter.[6]

A search of book and monograph publications employing the word *theory* in their titles or subtitles provides a third indication of interest in theory. The resulting list includes L.M. Bristol's *Social Adaptation* (via subtitle, 1915); J.P. Lichtenberger's *Development of Social Theory* (1923); H. E. Barnes's *Sociology and Political Theory* (1924); C. A. Ellwood's *The Psychology of Human Society* [1925] 1929); N. J. Spykman's *The Social Theory of Georg Simmel* (1925); P. A. Sorokin's *Contemporary Sociological Theories* (1928); F. N. House's *The Range of Social Theory* (1929); "Recent Theoretic Sociology in Europe and America," part 4 of House's *Development of Sociology* (1936); and *Contemporary Social Theory* (1940), edited by H. E. Barnes, H. P. Becker, and F. B. Becker.

Just how much is missed by requiring the explicit reference to theory in the title or subtitle is now apparent. Certainly, E. S. Bogardus's *History of Social Thought* (1922), T. Abel's *Systematic Sociology in Germany* (1929), T. Parsons's *The Structure of Social Action* (1937), H. E. Barnes's and H. P. Becker's *Social Thought from Lore to Science* (1938), and much of *Twentieth Century Sociology* (1945), edited by Gurvitch and Moore, are clearly classifiable under the rubric "theory." The use of such an "objective" criterion manifestly underestimates the extent of the interest in theory.

Accordingly, it is clearly evident that interest in sociological theory existed across the years 1915–45. Evidence for that interest can be documented in the titles of divisions or sections at the ASS annual meetings, especially from 1935 onward, as a category in the classification of abstracted literature and current research in progress, as one of the categories in the classification of articles studied by Shanas in the *AJS,* and as part of the actual titles of articles, books, and monographs. Admittedly, the evidence of interest is scarcely overwhelming, but it still constitutes at least an undeniable minimum.

CONCEPTIONS OF THEORY

Certainly, it is also basically important to know what conceptions were held of theory—and not just that sociologists were interested in theory. Eight generalizations can be drawn.

1. Actual definitions of theory, that is, social and sociological theory, are conspicuously missing over the three decades in question. No one specifically and systematically offered an actual definition—or even extended commentary—about the nature of social or sociological theory, until Merton's famous 1945 essay, "Sociological Theory," which discussed sociological theory in general. It is not that it is impossible to infer what theory meant, but that, interestingly, sociologists during these years did not feel obliged to provide definitions.

One might, of course, speculate that only with the very considerable intellectual change in the discipline throughout the 1920s and 1930s, which substantially affected the way that theory might be construed, was there a need to offer explicit definitions. The concerns about "sound" (or acceptable) sociological theory in Read Bain's "Trends in American Sociological Theory" (1929b), in Chapin's "Social Theory and Social Action" (1936), and in Lundberg's "The Thoughtways of Contemporary Sociology" (1936b) are suggestive of the importance of intellectual change in occasioning actual definitions of theory.

2. The terms *social theory* and *sociological theory* seem to have been used with about the same frequency throughout the years under consideration. *Social theory* was the designation employed in the census of current

research in the early 1930s and the term used in the annual meetings of the ASS up to and including 1945. By contrast, *sociological theory* was used in the vast majority of instances in article titles from 1936 to 1945.

Some sense of what may be involved can be gained from an examination of the meaning of the term *social theory* in Thomas and Znaniecki's *The Polish Peasant in Europe and America* (1918–20) at the very beginning of the period, and in Floyd H. House's *The Range of Social Theory* (1929) at about the midpoint of the period. As will become evident, the meanings seem to suggest that many sociologists and theorists apparently did not believe that a genuine, relatively complete, and independent discipline or science had as yet been achieved before the 1930s. The term *social theory* was sufficiently broad to include the intellectual resources of the other social sciences, which many sociologists wanted to be able to appropriate in the course of the changes and controversies in their discipline. Interestingly, in their "Methodological Note," Thomas and Znaniecki (1918–20 1:33) note that both social psychology and sociology are "to be embraced under the general term of social theory, as they are both concerned with the relation between the individual and the concrete social group." The "social" is apparently both attitude and "value," "subjective" and "objective," "part" and "whole," "individual" and "collective." Clearly, Thomas and Znaniecki do not want to forego the possible use of social psychology and its connections with general psychology in favor of an exclusive interest in sociology (and social structure).

House's *The Range of Social Theory* (1929) is considerably more encompassing. It envisages theory as including contributions to solving problems about people and their physical environment (e.g., human geography, population, race, and nationality); community and the organization of economic markets (economics); human nature and personality (social psychology); collective action (collective behavior); organizations, cultures, and cultural change (cultural anthropology); and social conflict, order, law, government, and politics (political science). *The Range of Social Theory* seems to reflect the importance of the contributions of other disciplines in the resolution of the controversies of the 1920s over the nature of social phenomena, the character of the instincts and original nature in the conception of social forces, the significance of culture, and the tenability of social evolution as a grand theory of social change—in all of which psychology and cultural anthropology were especially significant. Understandably, then, social theory was to be construed as encompassing and synthetic.[7]

Certainly by the mid 1930s, the professionalization of the discipline had advanced substantially, and the newer generation of sociologists, with perhaps more methodological rigor and confidence, no longer sought to avoid disciplinary self-reliance or autonomy. And so it might be conjectured that the term *sociological theory* has tended to become prevalent in the literature.

3. During the 1920s and 1930s, theory was commonly conceived to be general (or, as might more recently be said, grand, comprehensive, or macro) in nature, and was equated with general sociology. Admittedly, this view persisted from the pre–World War I era. Both Giddings at Columbia and Small at Chicago subscribed to this view differentiating a general from a special (or specialized) sociology or sociologies. Gehlke, who was one of Giddings's doctoral students, equates "sociological theory . . . [with] what is usually denominated 'general sociology'" in the preface of his 1915 doctoral dissertation (Gehlke 1915). According to Giddings (1896, 31–33), the term *general sociology* designates "the scientific study of society as a whole," social elements, first principles, essential fact, causes or laws, the fundamental phenomena of social life under its varied forms. It involves what is universal and fundamental to all societies at all times (32–33; Giddings 1901, 8). In Small's (1912, 200) view, general sociology is the "study of the conditions (physical and psychical), elements, forms, processes, results (at given stages), and implications of human association." And whether focused on structure or process in association, such a general sociology is to reveal the general, common, invariant, or universal in social life—including, presumably, its foundations.

And the association of theory with general sociology persists. At one point, Floyd House (1929, 287) refers to the "task of social theory, or general sociology." It is also evident that Becker associates his systematic theory with general sociology in his *Systematic Sociology* (1932b, 15), for he alludes to "the general sociology here expounded."

4. Theory during the period under review also came to mean the sets of explanatory ideas of the great figures of the past, the classical masters of sociology. Thus, theory came to have a historical dimension (which many sociologists in the later years of the period attempted to redefine, reject, or even extirpate; e.g., Lundberg 1945, 504). Interestingly, many of the presentations were thus temporal, historical, or developmental. Bristol's *Social Adaptation* (1915), Bogardus's *A History of Social Thought* (1922), Lichtenberger's *Development of Social Theory* (1923), Ellwood's *A History of Social Philosophy* (1938), and Barnes's and Becker's *Social Thought from Lore to Science* (1938) are illustrative.

Accordingly, a curious association between theory and historical sociology developed, with the latter being construed in part as the "history of sociology." (Howard Becker, [1934, 18] objected to this "lamentable error" of identifying "historical sociology" with the "history of sociology," but he conceded that it was one that a "great many American sociologists" have made.) This linkage is also evident in the designations used to refer to theory in the schemes for classification of abstracted periodical literature and research projects in the censuses as reported in the *AJS*.

5. The term *theory* in sociology was also invoked during the years under review to signify the general intellectual sociological orientations of sociologists. The considerable number of references in titles of articles to theories of particular sociologists (e.g., Giddings, Small, Howe, Sumner, and Tocqueville) is illustrative. Three were in *S&SR,* two in the *AJS,* and one in *SF* from 1918 to 1942.

6. In this period, too, theory was conceived to mean a coherent, logically developed, and integrated system. Both the European and the American masters of the past (i.e., before World War I) were systematists and their sociologies systems. Certainly, many American sociologists during the 1920s found it difficult to conceive of theory apart from a rational whole or a logical system. Giddings (1896) referred to his book *The Principles of Sociology* as combining "the principles of sociology in a coherent theory" that is "avowedly and without apology deductive as well as inductive" (v, xvi). One of his last graduate students, Theodore Abel, published *Systematic Sociology in Germany* in 1929.

However, Giddings's graduate students were by no means primarily responsible for the revival, in the 1930s and 1940s, of theory as general, deductive, systematic theory. Sociologists of very different intellectual persuasions were also involved, including Znaniecki, MacIver, Becker, and Parsons. Although Znaniecki and MacIver did not explicitly comment about sociological theory as being general and systematic, their works of the 1930s and 1940s indicate their adherence to that view (see Znaniecki 1934, 1936; MacIver 1931c, 1942). Becker's views as first formulated in his *Systematic Sociology* are also more implicit than explicit (Becker 1932b, 61, 62, 39).[8] These views seem to still persist in Becker's 1945 essay.

Parsons is—irrepressibly—a systematic theorist from *The Structure of Social Action* (1937) onward. In that work, he envisages theory as a system based on a unified frame of reference. Theory is a system or a "body of interrelated 'general concepts' of empirical reference" (6). The frame of reference in terms of which the theory is to be developed is designated as the (voluntaristic) action frame of reference (by way of the unit-act). His paper "The Present Position and Prospects of Systematic Theory in Sociology" (1945) reiterates his notion of theory as a system , a "body of logically interdependent generalized concepts of empirical reference" that tend ideally "to reach a state of logical integration such that every logical implication of any combination of propositions in the system is explicitly stated in some other propositions in the same system."

Lundberg—a student of Chapin, who was a student of Giddings—regards his *Foundations of Sociology* (1939b) as a contribution to "a more comprehensive and mature system of scientific theory in terms of specific formal postulates and theories subject to rigorous test" (x). Certainly it is predicated on the desirability of systematicity. It endeavors to begin with a frame of reference (based on Dodd's S-theory). It does seek to select out the major components of the sociological universe (116). It does contemplate the (deductive) organization of (general) scientific laws "into a system compatible with each other" (116).

Clearly, theory was also seen as ultimately being a logically integrated and closed system. Becker and Parsons, on the one hand, and Lundberg, on the other, are exemplary protagonists of the notion.

7. At least some of the views on theory also reflect the central position that scientific research methodology and epistemology had come to occupy in the 1930s and later. Such is reflected above in Lundberg's reference to "scientific theory" and Parsons's insistence that the core of theory is comprised of "logically interdependent generalized concepts of *empirical reference*" (emphasis added). It is also evident in the earlier statements of Bain (1929b, 73–74), in which acceptable or sound theory is restricted to confirmed generalizations as subjected to tests.[9]

Chapin (1936, 1–11) adopts an apparently more systematic notion of theory. But he insists that sound social theory is based on concepts that are operationally defined, and issue from an explicitly stated frame of reference. Theory involved a "logical system of relations among concepts, postulates, and hypotheses" in terms of which experience can be interpreted meaningfully. It begins with the more concrete symbolic substitutes for reality and ascends to the more abstract symbolic substitutes. Chapin would apparently agree with Bain's contention that "all theory is relative, tentative, partial."

Published in 1936 in the *ASR,* like Chapin's paper, Lundberg's article "Thoughtways of Contemporary Sociology" proposes a conception of sound theory substantially resembling Chapin's. In Lundberg's view a theory is sound if it satisfies certain requirements: (1) The definition of terms must be clear and unambiguous; (2) the postulates upon which the theory proceeds must be explicitly stated in these terms; (3) the deductions from the postulates, and their implications, must be worked out and exhibited step by step; (4) the theorems should be specifically formulated so that they can be stated as the outcome of empirical observations and experiments; and (5) the theorems must be susceptible of empirical test and not be metaphysical in nature (708). Presumably, these constitute the foundation for his natural-science theory of human society as represented by *Foundations of Sociology* (1939b).

Beginning thus with the difference between social and sociological theory, this résumé has noted the increasing use of the term *sociological* as opposed to *social theory* in American sociology after 1936. Such theory is still conceived to be general, grand, comprehensive, or macro in nature (and so is equatable with general sociology), as tending to become a coherent, logically developed, and integrated system, and as being compatible with and responsive to the requirements of scientific method and the results of empirical research. A change in the notion of theory has thus been detected. The possible broader context or contexts in which this change and others can become meaningful now warrant examination.

THE CONTEXTS OF THEORY

On the whole, it is difficult to specify in advance just what constitutes the context or setting of social or sociological theory. It might be assumed, a priori, that the most consequential settings of theory would be the developments in the larger society, academia (or higher education), certain allied domains of knowledge (e.g., anthropology, psychology), sociology itself as a discipline and (emergent) profession, and perhaps a related more substantive or abstract field within sociology.

The Societal Setting

Certainly, it is not readily apparent that the character of general theory would be affected by details of the declining position of agriculture, the expanding and improving state of American urban and industrial life (including aspects of urban decentralization), the near cessation of legal immigration after 1924, the bureaucratization of the economy, the separation of ownership and control of businesses and industries, and the rise of a white-collar middle class. However, it does appear that World War I, on the one hand, and the Great Depression, some fifteen years later, on the other, were consequential in undermining the tenability of the idea of progress as a rationale of the discipline that theories could continue to invoke or elaborate. The massive violence of the war contradicted beliefs in progress, some argued. In the 1920s, awareness of the data of cross-cultural variability and ideas about moral relativity articulated by cultural anthropology provided further problems for proponents of progress. Younger theorists were also left to ponder the implications of the popularity of science as affirmed by research, especially the results of quantitative research. By World War II, few theorists could or would claim a justification for the discipline other than some variation of instrumentalism.

Sociology Itself As a Setting

On the whole, the fate of theory depended largely on the changing fortunes of the discipline at large, especially the state of membership in the American Sociological Society and undergraduate and graduate enrollments in academia. During 1919–29, membership of the ASS expanded from 852 to 1,812, an increase of 113 percent. Membership peaked at 1,567 in 1932, after which it declined to 997 in 1939. It increased gradually during World War II, reaching 1,651 in 1946.[10]

Total student enrollment in higher education in 1920 was just under 600,000. It rose markedly during the 1920s to just over 1,000,000 in 1930, with a slight further increase up to 1932. In 1934 enrollment dropped by almost 100,000 students (presumably in response to the depression). But it then expanded constantly up to 1940, when aggregate enrollment amounted to just under 1,500,000. The figures registered a slight decline in 1942 and a more precipitous drop in 1944, to just over 1,100,000—apparently under the impact of the draft and World War II.[11]

The number of graduate students trebled in the decade 1920–1930 from 15,612 to 47,255. A decline occurred from 1932 to 1934, but a substantial increase to 106,119 was registered in 1940. During the next four years, enrollment declined sharply to just under 60,000. The total number of doctorates awarded quadrupled from 1920 to 1930 (going from 432 to 2,078) and burst upward to 3,459 in 1941, with no intervening decreases. It dropped off each year thereafter, to a low point of 1,515 in 1945, but rose slightly in 1946 and then dramatically to 4,671 in 1949.[12]

In the decades of the 1930s and 1940s, sociology had, respectively, 447 and 591 doctorates. During the 1930s, its maximum was 60 (in 1930) and its minimum was 36 (in 1935). In the 1940s, its maximum was 99 (in 1949) and its minimum 30 (in 1945).[13]

A variety of characteristics of sociology and sociologists seem to be involved, directly and indirectly, and to have implications for theory:[14]

1. Sociology in the United States became primarily a field or discipline in higher education and aligned with the liberal arts in the period after World War I.

2. Sociology in the United States developed as a distinctively American discipline and increasingly separated from its European precedents and counterparts.

3. Sociologists in the United States were no longer self-educated, part-time, or substantially European-trained, as were the pre-World War I generations. They did not come from elite private colleges, but, rather, had small denominational or public university backgrounds. Their graduate degrees in sociology were awarded by American universities. (During the 1930s and 1940s, Chicago, Columbia, Wisconsin, Harvard, and Ohio State Universities were among the top six institutions in the number of doctoral degrees awarded in sociology.) Theory and research methods were commonly demanded as part of their programs. Sociologists no longer knew as much about their European intellectual antecedents, or had as substantial foreign language competencies, as their predecessors did.

4. Sociologists were virtually all male, white, Anglo-Saxon, and Protestant. (But a small number of females, Jews, Southern and Eastern European ethnics, and blacks gained admittance to the field). Overwhelmingly, they became academics, for whom teaching was an important part of their lives.

5. In addition, the increasing size of undergraduate enrollments and faculty appointments presumably played some part in sociology's achievement of administrative autonomy in the 1920s and later. A study of 152 colleges and universities from 1880 to 1928 revealed that 69 departments had gained autonomy by 1928; 31 had achieved some form of recognition in a joint departmental name; 52 cases indicated no departmental recognition.[15] By 1928, sociology had won some departmental autonomy in all major institutions in the Midwest, though the dates varied considerably. Sociology had increasingly detached itself from political economy and economics and was linked with anthropology.

Even in the larger institutions, the senior departmental ranks of sociologists were still numerically small. Up to the end of World War II, no more than five or six sociologists and one or two anthropologists were represented in these departments.[16]

6. This is also the period in which the department at the University of Chicago was preeminent. Its top position is indicated in the two published rankings of sociology departments, in the number of doctorates awarded, in the number of presidents of the ASS it provided from 1920 to 1950, and by the professional prestige of its individual faculty members.[17]

7. Over the years, considerable field differentiation and interest specialization occurred. By the 1930 annual meeting, nine sections were formed and accorded access to the annual program of the ASS (but theory was not one of these). Regional associations and specialized multidisciplinary organizations also developed in the 1920s and 1930s.[18]

8. Nevertheless, sociologists were also active in major national organizations involving broad interdisciplinary interests (e.g., the Social Science Research Council formed in 1923), in joint or collaborative publication enterprises on either their own or others' initiatives (e.g., *Encyclopaedia of the Social Sciences; An American Dilemma*), and in roundtable discussions at the ASS annual meetings.

9. Two organizations, one in New York City and the other in Chicago, set the precedents for the development of funded research and research institutions in sociology during the period. One was the Institute for Social and Religious Research (ISSR), which was created in 1922 as the successor to the Committee on Social and Religious Surveys of the Interchurch World Movement (and involved sociologists or persons who became sociologists, such as Robert Lynd). The other was the University of Chicago's Local Community Research Committee (LCRC), formed in 1923 with representa-

tives drawn from the philosophy and social science departments. Both the ISSR and the LCRC received major (or exclusive) funding from Rockefeller sources, the termination of which brought their demise.[19]

Academic social science research was established under similar Rockefeller arrangements, albeit with less-generous funding, at other universities (e.g., North Carolina, Columbia, Harvard, Stanford, Yale, Texas, and Virginia).[20]

10. During the years of the Great Depression and World War II, a considerable number of sociologists were employed by the federal government (by the Works Project Administration, the Department of Agriculture, the Office of Strategic Services, the Office of Price Administration, etc.).[21] Such positions also brought a measure of added prestige to sociologists on their return to academia.

11. A final feature of significance both generally to sociology and particularly to theory throughout most of the thirty-year interwar period is what is loosely termed the "preoccupation with methods," including disputes over method and its relationship to theory. By the end of the 1920s, two (or, more accurately, three) fundamental stances, emerged, with rather distinctive and contrasting features. The first, and the one that eventually became predominant, accepted a qualified empiricist epistemology and neo-positivist methodology, with quantification, statistics, and measurement as hallmarks of its approach. The other two are similar in having a commitment to a qualitative case-study approach inclined to idealism. Still, it is more accurate to distinguish one as an American equivalent of German neo-idealism (with similarities to Dilthey) and another as an American equivalent of German Neo-Kantianism (with similarities to Windelband and Rickert). (See chapter 2.)

These eleven features certainly comprise the most basic and dominant aspects of the organizational, disciplinary, and intellectual contexts of general theory in American sociology. Without them, an understanding of the peculiarities of the history of theory in the approximately thirty years from 1915/18 to 1945/50 cannot be understood. Yet any explanatory or interpretive account must await a detailed inquiry into the actual content of the nature of general theory in this period. (Significantly, the shifting meanings examined just prior to the above section all entailed formal characteristics without any actual content.) "Data" or evidence is required, but there looms a basic problem about locating sources.

SOURCES OF DATA ON SOCIOLOGICAL THEORY

To the careful reader, the suggestion that sources of data on the character of theory are relatively inaccessible (or even nonexistent) surely must seem to contradict my contention that an interest in theory was relatively continuous throughout the years of the period. Certainly, no problem exists in the literature for the years after 1935. Though they are few, articles can be found in the *ASR, S&SR,* and *SF.* Monographs, such as Parsons's *The Structure of Social Action* (1937) can be cited. *Contemporary Social Theory* (1940), edited by Barnes, Becker, and Becker, was published as a graduate text and reference work.

The problem seems to lie in the years prior to 1935. Virtually no sessions on theory were part of the annual programs of the ASS. A rigorous, restrictive criterion, requiring an occurrence of the word *theory* in title, produced no articles in the *AJS* from 1921 to 1937. Most disturbing of all, the genre of published personalized statements of theoretical stances, so common among the founding fathers prior to World War I, seemed to have disappeared. (Specifically, then: What had happened to the pre-World War I majoritarian position on social evolutionism?)

The key to the sources of data on theory was found accidentally by a scrutiny of Ellwood's *The Psychology of Human Society* (1925), the subtitle of which, "An Introduction to Sociological Theory," provoked immediate attention. In both its subtitle and its actual contents, Ellwood's book is, indeed, an "introduction" to general sociological theory or, as it was also termed (e.g., by Small and Giddings), "general sociology." Further, its format basically coincides with the major divisions of general sociological theory before World War I. Chapter 1 begins with an account of its author's conception of the nature of social science and ends with an examination of the scientific methods of studying human society (e.g., the comparative method, the historical method, the social survey method, and the method of deduction from biology and psychology). Thus, it deals rudimentarily with what might be termed social "epistemological-methodological" theory. Chapter 1 also indicates the "group" as the point of departure for the author's conception or theory of the social. The contents of chapters 2 and 3, entitled "Group Life and Organic Evolution" and "Group Life and Mental Evolution," include his theory of social genesis or origins. Chapters 4, 5, and 6 (which deal with unity of the group, the continuity of the group, and forms of human association) provide Ellwood's theory of social structure. Chapters 6 and 7, on changes within the group, contain some, though not all, of the ingredients of his theory of social change (which apparently undergoes alteration in his subsequent *Cultural Evolution*).

Put simply, the importance of the Ellwood volume resides in its revelation of the connection between general sociology, sociological theory, and an intellectually demanding level of introduction to the field as such. The volume was designed as a text and suggested the possibility of similar others, which were quick to come into print. These included: Frank H. Hankins's *An Introduction to the Study of Society* (1928), Robert M. MacIver's

Society (1931c), E. B. Reuter and C. W. Hart's *Introduction to Sociology* (1933) (and if this one is admitted, certainly one of its major antecedent inspirations cannot be ignored, i.e., Robert E. Park and Ernest W. Burgess's *Introduction to the Science of Sociology* (1921)), E. T. Hiller's *Principles of Sociology* (1933), Kimball Young's *Introductory Sociology* (1934 and its revision in 1942), George A. Lundberg's *Foundations of Sociology* (1939b), and L. L. Bernard's *An Introduction to Sociology* (1942). To provide additional balance, C. M. Case's *Outlines of Introductory Sociology* (1924), F. E. Lumley's *Principles of Sociology* (1928) R. L. Sutherland and J. L. Woodward's *Introductory Sociology* (1937), and W. F. Ogburn and M. F. Nimkoff's *Sociology* (1940) were also analyzed. (Illuminatingly, Hiller [1933, xix] and Bernard [1942, 8, 9, 10] both link their texts to "general sociology." Reuter and Hart [1933, v] claim that their aim "is to give an introductory, but consistent and integrated presentation of sociological theory.") Admittedly, the intellectual demands made by the texts did vary as the shift occurred in the 1920s and 1930s from primarily "general" sociology to primarily "introductory" sociology.

At the time of their authorships, Hankins was associated with Smith, Lundberg with Bennington, MacIver with Columbia, Woodward with Cornell, Nimkoff with Bucknell—all part of the East. Park and Burgess and Ogburn held positions at Chicago, Hiller at Illinois, Bernard at Washington University (St. Louis), Ellwood at Missouri, Reuter and Hart at Iowa, Young at Wisconsin, and Lumley at Ohio State—all part of the Midwest. Sutherland was at Texas in the Southwest and Case at Southern California in the Far West (or Pacific Coast).

In terms of doctorates awarded, Chicago had the largest number (seven): Burgess, Ellwood, Bernard, Reuter, Hart, Hiller, and Sutherland. Two (Hankins and Ogburn) had been awarded their doctorates by Columbia. One each (Lumley, Woodward, Lundberg, Case, Young, and Nimkoff, respectively) had taken his Ph. D. at Yale, Cornell, Minnesota, Wisconsin, Stanford, and Southern California. Park and MacIver had been awarded doctorates abroad (at Heidelberg and Edinburgh).

Considerable diversity is evident in the institutions awarding the authors' doctorates and providing employment at the time of the authorships. Thus, the chances for discovering theoretical diversity among these sociologists should be substantial. (Furthermore, it is by no means to be assumed that analysis is to be restricted exclusively to them.)

To those who might object to this list of authors as involving many who were not especially notably identified with theory, the following response is offered: (1) The list does include MacIver, Bernard, Ellwood, and Lundberg, who can strongly claim the mantle of theory, though whether all of them would have done so is another matter. Admittedly, the thirty years from 1915 to 1945 may represent a period in which a claim to be a theorist would scarcely bring encomiums. MacIver may well have been the only president of the ASS during this period whose professional reputation was predominantly gained in theory. Virtually all others had professional reputations won substantially, and perhaps in most cases predominantly, in other fields, such as social psychology. Hence, (2) any acceptance of the desirability of an expanded range of views about theory must reckon with the possible inclusion of many who are not exclusively theorists. And (3) it must be emphasized (as above) that intellectual stances to be considered in this study are not to be limited only to the seventeen sociologists just noted.

Let us turn now, finally, to an examination of the texts themselves. It is noteworthy that they do indeed seem to exhibit considerable variation in certain basic characteristics (e.g., dates of publication, number of chapters and pages). The earliest date of publication (within the period) is the Park and Burgess text in 1921, followed by Case in 1924. The latest was the L. L. Bernard volume, which appeared in 1942 but seems to have been basically written much earlier. Most of the texts seem to have been published during the 1930s. The one with the fewest number of chapters (thirteen) was Lundberg's, and the one with the fewest number of pages (479) was Ellwood's. The text with the greatest number of chapters (forty-one) and pages (1,023) was Bernard's.

INTELLECTUAL STRUCTURE OF TEXTS IN GENERAL SOCIOLOGY AND SOCIOLOGICAL THEORY

Paradoxically, perhaps, the intellectual content and organization of the texts seem to exhibit much more similarity than dissimilarity, much more convergence in a common pattern than divergence among many. Generally, they involve an introductory overview chapter, several chapters on the major factors in human social life, some chapters on the several social processes, still others on major social institutions, and concluding chapters on social control and/or social change. Given the considerable intellectual controversy in sociology across the several decades of the period, such apparent continuity in a basic common structure is striking.

Most commonly, the introductory chapter sets forth what the distinctive object of sociology's study is, its relations to other social sciences, what kind of knowledge it aims at, or, indeed, already claims to be, and, in a few cases, the common or distinctive methods, procedures, or techniques used in inquiry, and the justifications for including the book in an academic curriculum. Each of these aspects requires preliminary comment, though the necessary detailed analysis will have to be deferred until later chapters.

Certainly no issue was of more significance initially than what sociology, as a discipline, studies. One author (MacIver) defined its subject matter as essentially inter- and/or multi personal relationships. Two others (Reuter and Hart) opted for social processes. But for the great majority in the 1920s, it had become the study of human groups—though the precise qualifications might vary. For one earlier author (Ellwood 1925, 14), sociology was the science of the origins, development, structuring, and functioning of groups. For another (Hankins 1928, 167), it was the synthetic explanation of the origins and evolutionary changes in the forms and activities of human groups. Still later authors (e.g., K. Young 1934, xiii, 6–7) endeavored to interrelate the character of interaction with group, process, culture, and personality.

Generally, too, these textbook sociologists were concerned with the interrelations of their own discipline with others. Thus, they often attempted to characterize their own field as like or unlike history, anthropology, psychology, economics, or political science. In turn, this concern raised more abstract issues, especially what kind of discipline sociology is and what kind of knowledge it aspires to. Hankins's view of sociology as a science requires the acceptance of objectivity and naturalism and the rejection of religion, theology, supernaturalism, mysticism, and parochial bias. For others (e.g., Park and Burgess), it required confronting arguments about basic classifications of the basic fields of knowledge, such as Windelband's Neo-Kantian history/science (or idiographic/nomothetic) dichotomy. History was conceived to study the nonrecurrent, unique, concrete, particular, and variable, and sited and dated, whereas science investigates the recurrent, general, uniform, or common, the nonsited and nondated in phenomena.

Some sociologists regarded the acceptance of certain requirements of a common method as central to sociology's claim to be a science or, rather, scientific. Only two texts (those of Ellwood and of Reuter and Hart) briefly reviewed the specific, distinguishing methods, procedures, or techniques of sociology. And only the texts of the two major antagonists (MacIver, along with his *Social Causation,* and Lundberg, along with his *Social Research*) actually dealt with the basic epistemological-methodological issues in connection with the debate over sociology as a science that virtually polarized the discipline at some points in time.

It is important to note here that the text, or "public" presentation of the argument for sociology's status as a science, thus almost entirely concealed the vigorous "private" (professional) controversy in the periodicals of the discipline. Perhaps such professional "reserve" in the writing of the texts might be expected, but it does point to difficulties in any unquestioning assumption that the texts will faithfully represent the state of the discipline and its assumptions.

In turning to the first major section of the texts following their introductory chapters, a reader frequently confronts several chapters that concern the main factors (or causes) in human social life. These chapters ordinarily deal with the physical, geographical environment; the hierarchy of organisms, both plants and animals; the so-called higher forms of life that evidence rudimentary consciousness, culminating in the human species, and that incorporate psychological factors; and finally societal structure and culture as factors themselves in social life. Hankins, Ellwood, Bernard, and even Ogburn and Nimkoff more or less involve and accept this kind of formulation. Without exception, the major sociologists and theorists adhering to this conception of basic factors or causes were also committed to evolution—physical, organic, psychic (or psychological), social, and cultural—as is embodied in the term *evolutionary naturalism* and expounded below.

However, the Ogburn and Nimkoff text (1940) reveals that by the time of its publication, a major intellectual alteration had already occurred. Although substantial intellectual vestiges of social and cultural evolutionism remain in their chapter on the role of culture, the other chapters on the natural environment or geography, and on the nature of the "higher" organisms and the human organism, seem to be devoid of major allusions to the processes of physical, organic, and psychic (or psychological) evolution. Most of the texts appearing in the 1920s were written by sociologists who had completed their graduate work and received their doctorates before World War I. They accepted the doctrine of parallel evolution and applied evolutionary ideas to the problems of social and cultural origins and to social and cultural structure. But professional dispute as registered in the periodicals had already begun in the 1920s. Admittedly, organic evolution does not seem to be prominent in the Park and Burgess text, though its presence can be readily detected in the subsection of chapter 8 on competition, "The Struggle for Existence," and in the acknowledgment of the relationship of adaptation and accommodation at the beginning of chapter 10, on accommodation. But by the time Reuter and Hart had published their text (1933), which followed the basic structure of the Park and Burgess text, the authors sharply separated organic change (as selective and evolutionary) and socio-cultural change (as nonselective and accumulative). Kimball Young's text (1934) confirms the rejection of parallel physical, organic, psychic, and sociocultural evolutionism. But by then physical environment, organisms (especially the human), the psychic (now in the form of personality), and the sociocultural had come to stand in a different and perhaps unsteady relationship. They were no longer integrated in a theoretical unity by a pervasive general evolutionism, which had been widely abandoned by younger sociologists (e.g., Young, Reuter and Hart, Hiller, Lundberg, Sutherland and Woodward). Only Ellwood, Bernard, and Lumley were overt adherents, and Ogburn was perhaps a covert one, but these were all from the pre-World War I generation.

The next section, and perhaps the most extended major section, of the texts was devoted to the exposition of a variety of social institutions. Interestingly, the section on institutions has a direct connection with the prior one on basic factors of social life. Institutions are often conceived to have their origins in the common human-nature needs of an aggregate of human beings adapting or adjusting to the problems of a common environment. Ogburn and Nimkoff remark (1940, 555), "Social institutions are organized, established ways of satisfying" such basic needs as "security, food and shelter, sex expression, and training of the young." Most frequently discussed were the family, religion, the political state or government, and then the economic and technological. Science, recreation, social welfare, and health tend to be regarded as newly emergent institutions.

Institutions reveal just how sociologists conceive structure in relation to change. Frequently, chapters would culminate with an analysis of the particular institutions in modern (and ordinarily American) society. However, some of the texts by older authors of this period (e.g., Hankins, Ogburn and Nimkoff, Bernard) also presented institutions in terms of evolutionary stages or forms—even if the unilinear stages theory of social evolution was explicitly rejected. By contrast, younger theorists (e.g., Young, Sutherland and Woodward) tended to envisage modern institutional forms within cross-cultural perspectives.

Most of the texts also included a major section on social processes as the major forms of social interaction. Although the social processes were undoubtedly a part of the sociology of the founding fathers of the pre–World War I period, the Park and Burgess formulation provides the basic inspiration and model. Initially, Park had construed the term *social process* as "the name for all changes . . . in the life of the group" (Park and Burgess [1921] 1924, 51). He devotes an entire chapter to isolation, another to social contacts, one to social interaction, followed by one chapter each to competition, conflict, accommodation, and assimilation. Lumley, Reuter and Hart, Young, Ogburn and Nimkoff, and Sutherland and Woodward tend, more or less, to follow Park's lead in their view of the social processes. Lumley, Hiller, Young, Sutherland and Woodward, and Ogburn and Nimkoff also include a chapter (or a part of a chapter) on cooperation. Young devotes two chapters to differentiation, and Young and Ogburn and Nimkoff offer a chapter on stratification or status and classes.

Clearly, not all of those who included analyses of the social processes in their texts followed Park in construing the social processes as providing a cyclical explanation of social change in opposition to the older unilinear sociocultural evolutionism. Such younger sociologists as Reuter and Hart, Hiller, Young (perhaps Lundberg), and the older Ogburn were less certain of the adequacy of an abstract social-process interpretation of change under the impact of the emphasis on culture and the data on cultural variation from cultural anthropology. All of these sociologists had sections on both the social processes and social change.

Manifestly, the detail in, and number of, chapters concerned with social change varied considerably. Most authors devoted more than two chapters to the subject—MacIver, Reuter and Hart, and Hiller offered six each, Bernard eight, and Young eleven in his 1942 edition. Change theory commonly began with a consideration of certain terminological distinctions, such as mere change versus social evolution, social evolution versus revolution, social evolution versus social progress. Nevertheless, the meanings attributed to the terms seemed to vary greatly.

In view of the considerable prevalence of social evolutionism as a theory of social change during the founding period, the interest of the second period in that theory is scarcely surprising. But almost unanimously, authors disagreed with the assumption of universal successive stages signifying unilinear (irreversible) directionality. Nevertheless, many of them (Ellwood, Bernard, Lumley, Hankins, MacIver, and even Ogburn to some extent) still adhered to some version of social evolutionism. Park and his students (e.g., Reuter and Hart, Hiller and K. Young) dissented. They subscribed to what might be characterized as (cyclical) "social process theory."

Nonetheless, the major ideas involved in explaining the processes of social and cultural change were basically the same and considerably more complex than those of the previous period. The impact of cultural anthropology was unmistakable. Such notions as material and nonmaterial culture, invention, discovery, diffusion or borrowing, accumulation, culture base, isolation versus accessibility, parallels, survivals, differential rates of change, (cultural) leads and lags, run of attention, disorganization and reorganization entered the terminology of change. Irrespective of whether the theory was evolutionary or nonevolutionary (e.g., a cyclical social process), the explanatory concepts were substantially the same. Indeed, a kind of eclecticism seemed evident.

Admittedly, the chapters on social change are not the only evidence of intellectual change in the texts from the 1920s to the 1930s and early 1940s. In the later years of the period, chapters appeared on the community, sometimes linked to human ecology (MacIver, Sutherland and Woodward, Ogburn and Nimkoff); population (Young, Lundberg, Ogburn and Nimkoff, Bernard); crowds, publics, and collective behavior (MacIver, Reuter and Hart, Sutherland and Woodward, Ogburn and Nimkoff); and personality (Young, Reuter and Hart, Hiller, Sutherland and Woodward, Ogburn and Nimkoff).

A CLASSIFICATORY-PERIODIZING SCHEME

Even though the summary exposition of general sociology and socio-logical theory in the texts indicates considerable similarity and convergence, it is still impossible to gauge just how well founded this characterization is—or whether major differences are actually concealed beneath surface similarities. Therefore, the detailed study of general theory involving text-books and other relevant literature from the discipline during the thirty-year period will make its point of departure from a classificatory periodizing scheme that was employed in a previous study of founding theory of the prior period in American sociology, 1881–1915.[22]

The development of the scheme derives from a conviction that any extended historical study of the content of American sociological theory can be successfully pursued only if it is envisaged rigorously in terms of what sociological theory in its broadest sense has meant in the past and present. Accordingly, a both extensive and intensive scrutiny of early literature (dat-ing from the founding fathers) on the meanings of the terms was undertaken. (Undeniably, some concern with etymology was involved, and some attempt was made to pursue the intellectual leads of the major relevant sociological and philosophical literature, e.g., Sorokin's *Social and Cultural Dynamics,* vol. 2, and Radnitzky's *Contemporary Schools of Metascience.*)[23]

General Nature of the Scheme

Out of this analysis came a conclusion about the most fundamental general problem-domains of sociological theory, which could be further par-ticularized as a series of additional and increasingly more specific questions or issues and their related answers or positions definable in certain terminol-ogy. Such was the procedure for constituting the framework for the classifi-catory-periodizing scheme. It does imply a departure from the traditional Western subject/object or knower/known (or /to be known) dualism. But it does also assume that various monisms and pluralisms (both epistemically and ontically) are also derivable in terms of how questions are posed histori-cally.

Put as simply as possible, two basic problem-domains were identified: (1) the nature of sociological knowledge and methods of study (social episte-mology-methodology or the theories of social epistemology-methodology), and (2) the nature of the social or social reality (social ontology, or the theory or theories of social ontology). Each problem-domain entails subsidiary or related questions; and if posed basically, each implies the possibility of deriving additional questions *and* linked answers or positions not stated below (see the Appendix) or in the scheme in *Founding Theory* (Hinkle 1980, 60–64).

For instance, theory about knowing or studying the social (i.e., social epistemology-methodology) identifies the following possible bases of knowing the social: sensation (empiricism), as opposed to reason (rationalism), as opposed to feeling and lived experience (e.g., empathy and the German *nacherleben*). These have implications for the methods of studying the social and for epistemologically-methodologically implementing the formulation of theory as such.

The same approach is followed in the domain of theory about the (known) social (i.e., social ontology). This domain proposes that the major conceptions of the social are inter- and/or multipersonal relationships, inter- and/or multipersonal activities, out of which arise the persisting (structured) group. But these can be understood only in the relation of the social to other phenomena and/or realities and by recognition that the social has its bases (ontically in materialism and idealism and in part/whole controversies over [social] nominalism and [social] realism).

Furthermore, three major problems in the study of the social can be identified as genesis or origins, stasis or structure, and dynamis or change. Each also has its distinctive questions and answers or positions. (See the Appendix and Hinkle 1980, 62–64, for further details and explanation.)

Use of the Scheme in Periodization (and Historiography)

The scheme is to be used to facilitate the analysis and characterization of the intellectual positions of a plurality of theorists across time, but not to force them willy-nilly into some category. The scheme is to aid in identification and typification of similarities and dissimilarities and thus (technically) enables both comparison and contrasts to be drawn. The scheme directs attention to certain (social) epistemological-methodological and (social) ontological issues and related (potential) answers or positions, or demands an answer to why the issue could or could not be raised or answered.

Employment of the scheme can aid in delimiting common intellectual positions or orientations, some or one of which becomes dominant during a particular interval of time and for which particular theorists become crucial expositors or representative figures. Allusions to particular theorists in terms of such general and dominant orientations become justifiable in terms of their significance in the orientation. Presumably, their statements are important in the development of characterizations and generalizations about the nature of general or macrotheory within a particular time interval. However, it is also necessary to recognize that dominant orientations (or even important subordinate orientations) ordinarily are not monolithically uniform. Knowing just how much internal variation exists within a stance can be significant for subsequent theoretical development. (It is also possible to identify basic assumptions of a stance.[24]) What may seem to be minor differences at one point in time may under different circumstances become major and consequential.

By virtue of the identification and characterization of such common and general intellectual orientations, one or more of which are dominant, periodization can be effected. The history of theory is no longer merely the chronological arrangement of prominent theorists. Instead, it becomes a succession of periods, in which a dominant orientation, perhaps achieving the status of an orthodoxy, may be followed in turn by a transition involving controversy (and heterodoxy) among several contending stances, out of which may be generated other dominant orientations, and so on.

Founding Theory (Hinkle 1980) endeavored to provide an example of the application of the scheme to one particular period, the first, of American sociology and sociological theory. It clearly implies that the demarcation of periods (i.e., periodization) is in a basic sense a response to fundamental social shifts in the structure of American society itself. That is, the emergence of sociology represents a *delayed* response to social changes associated with the Civil War and the aftermath of industrialization, urbanization, and so on. The initial temporal boundary was stated in terms of the onset of relatively continuously published theoretical views in the discipline (e.g., Sumner's article in the *Princeton Review* in 1881, preceding by two years Ward's *Dynamic Sociology* in two volumes). The terminal temporal boundary was set to coincide with the social dislocations associated with World War I, that is, c. 1915. (Ultimately, *Founding Theory,* 327–28, proposed an explanatory "mechanism" to account for periodization in the history of American sociological theory.)

Founding Theory had noted that early Americna theory (prior to 1915) was more concerned with social ontological than with epistemological-methodological theory. Further, its basic ontological theory could be characterized as "evolutionary naturalism," especially in its concerns with origins and change.

If World War I does roughly coincide with the terminal boundary of early founding theory, some new innovative development should be identifiable about then. It does in fact occur with the publication of Thomas and Znaniecki's *The Polish Peasant in Europe and America* (1918–20), for that book marks the beginning of the concern with research and research methods to which theory was eventually expected to accommodate itself. Simultaneously, a change in substantive or ontological theory would necessarily have to occur after 1915 to warrant in part the designation of a "new period" of theory.

Use of the Scheme in the Periodizing of Theory between World Wars I and II

Tentatively, the boundaries of the period are set for 1915/18 and 1945/50. In actuality, the first volume of Thomas and Znaniecki's *The Polish Peasant* was published in 1918 and the last in 1920. (Admittedly, Thomas had relevant articles before 1918, but not before 1915.) During the five terminal years of 1945–50, Parsons's turn to functionlism is evident, but that orientation is distinctive of the next period in theory and is thus not subject to inquiry in this work.

As just argued, (social) epistemological-methodological and (social) ontological theory are both relevant in establishing the character of second-period theory, though not necessarily equally so. Founding theory indicated that epistemological-methodological theory was of less consequence than ontological theory in the first period. A priori, it might be expected that a reversal of the significance of the two might occur in the second period. And, indeed, such seems to have increasingly occurred as the years passed. Although the dominant epistemological-methodological theory represents a continuation from the first period, the peculiar blend of rationalism and empiricism is supplanted by what might be considered a qualified empiricism. The positivistic methodology of the second period is also a continuation of the first, but with a decisively different resort to the quantitative, statistical, and mensurative. (In addition, two minority epistemological-methodological positions are identified in chapter 2.)

Because other historical accounts of the some thirty years after World War I have tended to emphasize the epistemological and especially methodological developments, this study by contrast endeavors to focus on the unique features of social ontological theory. Such a stress can result from the pursuit of one or both of two alternatives—that is, continuities with and discontinuities from the first period.

Continuities are exhibited in the persistence of social evolutionism as a theory of social origins, social structure, and social change—yet with some unique feature in each of the three subtypes. Perhaps the major difference lies in the considerable diversity in the formulation of the directional sequence of stages in change theory. Significantly, social evolutionism seems to experience a rapid decline, then demise, after about 1930.

Discontinuities appear in the possible efforts to renovate and reconstitute theory by resort to intellectual resources from within American sociology (e.g., Park and his students) and from outside of sociology but still within American academia (i.e., the influences from anthropology, history, psychiatry, and psychology, and from a peculiar amalgam of philosophy, psychology, and sociology.) In addition, European social science also provided innovative stimuli (e.g., Pareto for a short period of time, and Durkheim and M. Weber more enduringly). (Admittedly, the scheme was not conspicuously useful in the analyses of the discontinuities.)

Significantly, the notion of the group was substantially invoked during the second period. It provided a unique opportunity for drawing comparisons and contrasts with the first period of theory using a combined analysis (drawing on the scheme) of materialist and idealist assumptions and those of nominalism and realism.

With but one exception—the section on discontinuities—the scheme has played a major role in the analysis and periodization of theory in the period between the two world wars. Important though the scheme is, the parts and their interconnection in a whole must be made explicit.

OVERVIEW OF THE STRUCTURE OF THE INQUIRY

This study has four major parts. Part I, "Orientation," is comprised of the first two chapters. In this chapter we have noted the major and distinctive problems of theory during the thirty or so years between World Wars I and II. In chapter 2, the emergence of relatively new epistemological-methodological stances is analyzed. Such an inquiry is demanded because substantive or social ontological theory cannot ordinarily be characterized in isolation and because, paradoxically, epistemological-methodological concerns seemed to acquire an intellectual autonomy that eventually had a profound impact on the nature of the conception of theory itself during the later years of the second period.

Part II, "Continuities," and part III, "Discontinuities," involve the relationship between the substantive or social ontological theory of the earlier period and that of the period under study. Chapters 3, 4, and 5 inquire into the various manifestations of continuity in social evolutionary theory from before World War I through the next three decades. Chapter 3 compares the tenets of social evolutionism in the theories of social origins and social structure both before and after World War I. Chapters 4 and 5 assume a similarly comparative interest in the features and forms of social evolutionism as a theory of change prior and subsequent to World War I. The five chapters of part III consider sources of theoretical innovation in American sociology, in fields outside of sociology but still part of American academia, and in European (especially French, Italian, and German) social science, versus their actual impact on general sociological theory in the United States between World Wars I and II.

Part IV provides a summary and integration of the analyses from chapters 2 through 10 and assesses continuities and discontinuities in general theory. Chapter 11 uses the interest in the concept of the group during this period, in conjunction with the analytical classificatory scheme proposed in chapter 1, to state the results of the inquiry in more general terms. Invoking the materialist/idealist and nominalist/realist polarities, it summarizes the various positions of theorists to indicate just what continuities and discontinuities exist with earlier and later periods in the history of theory. Chapter 12 seeks to account for the major findings of the study, including the apparently weakened intellectual state of theory in the last decade of the period. It examines the indicators of the terminal temporal boundary of the period and what they contribute to an understanding of how it was possible for Parsonsian structural functionalism to achieve intellectual preeminence so rapidly in the 1950s. And it argues for the significance of the study of theoretical heterogeneity in the interwar decades for the more recent period since the mid 1970s.

We now turn to chapter 2, which provides extensive details on consequential developments in the shifting relationship between social epistemological-methodological and substantive or social ontological theories during the second period in the history of social and sociological theory in the United States.

Chapter 2

Three Epistemological-
Methodological Stances

RESEARCH, RESEARCH METHODS, AND DIVERGING
EPISTEMOLOGICAL-METHODOLOGICAL POSITIONS

Manifestly, the changing character of sociological theory across different intervals of time can be indicated by the varying emphasis on either one
of its two main divisions, social ontological or social epistemological-
methodological theory. During the first or founding period of American theory (1881–1915), the stress was placed on social ontological theory, though
by no means to the complete exclusion of the other division. But during the
second period, 1915–45/50, the predominant preoccupation was epistemological-methodological theory. In actuality, the kind of systematic exposition
of a personal view of substantive theory that had characterized the years
before World War I almost ceased. Only a very few major figures developed
comprehensive statements of their theoretical stances (e.g., Park and Burgess
[1921] 1924; Lundberg, 1939b; Sorokin 1947). (Admittedly, general sociology
and sociological theory texts were published and do, in part, substitute for

such statements.) Still, it is obvious to the researcher in the history of sociology that the prestige of general (substantive or ontological) theory declined almost in direct proportion to the rise of interest in research methods and techniques, which became a specialized area within the larger field differentiation and specialization of sociology in the 1920s and 1930s. (Indeed, a commitment to expertise in research also seems to have been an important feature of a trend toward professionalization in post–World War I sociology.)

Perhaps, the most characteristic concern of the second period was to make sociology a genuine science through a devotion to inductive, empirical research. And for many sociologists this entailed a repudiation of the systematic deductive formulations of theory and the major epistemological-methodological premises on which it had rested before World War I. Among others, Ogburn attacked theory with an almost extirpative zeal. Little wonder that the now-conventional dichotomies between theory and research or theory and methods arose during these years when the two enterprises seemed to be so antagonistic and mutually exclusive. The character of the epistemological-methodological stances of pre-World War I theory clearly warrants summary. (For more details, consult Hinkle 1980, chap. 4.)

Epistemological-Methodological Stances of Early Theory

Except for Cooley, all the founding theorists claimed the mantle of science for their discipline. Nevertheless, they were pervasively epistemological dualists, with some (e.g., Giddings, Sumner and Keller) seeming to emphasize sensory experience and others (e.g., Ward and Small) reason and logic. Undeniably, they accepted the basic significance of sensation (in the form of observation), description, and fact. But they all agreed that induction could not be relied upon exclusively. Deduction was also necessary. Reason or mind is imperative to achieve the abstract generality of generalization and law that they believed science demands. For Sumner and Keller, Ward, Giddings, Ross, and Small, science involves a Cartesian concern with the study of what happens normally and naturally, generally, commonly, for the most part, recurrently, or persistently. Reason is important in separating out and excluding the individual, concrete, particular, peculiar, abnormal, accidental, exceptional, or unique.

Although casual explanation was of central concern to them (the terms *cause* and *effect* occur frequently in their writings), no one of them offered systematic, detailed accounts of the technical criteria of causation in sociology. Naturalistic in outlook, they agreed that the causes in which they were interested were secondary (as opposed to primary) causes. Such distinctions as Ward's between efficient, conative, and telic causes and Giddings's between independent or original and dependent or derived secondary causes reflect their ontological or substantive conceptions much more than their epistemological notions.

But it was this combination of general, abstract, and abstruse systematic formulations of knowledge by the first-generation theorists, together with their doctrine of causes, that eventually evoked such negative reaction from many of the second-generation sociologists. The earlier theorists invoked various conceptions of the doctrine of social forces that had ramifications throughout their notions of human society and group, social origins, social structure, and social change. Early theory was thus envisaged (and criticized) by those of the second generation as deductive, speculative, abstruse, and subjective. Necessarily, first-generation theorists sought comprehensive conceptualizations and, perforce, were compelled to employ indirectly acquired (secondary) data from a mass of sources such as geology, paleontology, biology, physical anthropology, psychology, cultural anthropology, history, political science, and economics. They could point to virtually no data that their own discipline had provided. Accordingly, sociology could not vouch for its own trustworthiness.

Still, except for Cooley, major theorists of the first period were more or less favorably disposed to a postivistic methodological stance. Giddings, Ross, Sumner and Keller, possibly Ward, and perhaps even Small tended to hold (though with varying emphasis) that the methods, procedures, and techniques of the physical and biological sciences can and should become the basis for the study of social phenomena without major qualification or supplement. Perhaps the most conspicuous common indicator of this positivism was their resort to the comparative method, which, as Comte had noted much earlier, derived from biology.

Although positivistic methodology gained rather than lost adherents in sociology after World War I, many sociologists urged a reconsideration of the basic features of a common scientific method and were more favorable to physics and its methods and techniques than to biology as a model science. And their colleagues in anthropology made them aware of how vulnerable the comparative method was to criticisms.

Sociologists before World War I made cases for objectivity, detachment, or impersonality in the discipline. But their successors were not impressed.

Such earlier figures as Ross and Giddings had urged the desirability of a resort to quantification, measurement, and statistics. Those who followed after the war demanded actual application in research. For them, the hallmarks of science were, in addition, induction, empiricism, objectivity, observability, and verifiability, with primary (directly acquired) data. Just how an interest in a research-oriented sociology eventuated in the emergence of two divergent epistemological-methodological stances is the question to which an answer must now be sought.

Rise of a Social Research Movement

Interestingly, both Thomas and Znaniecki's *The Polish Peasant in Europe and America,* as a major example of research, and a committee of the American Sociological Society, as the focus of a research movement, appeared just at the end of the second decade of this century. (Thomas received a University of Chicago Ph.D. and was then a member of its sociology department. Gillin, who was the first chairman of the committee, was at the University of Wisconsin. Along with the majority of his successors, he had been one of Giddings's graduate students at Columbia University.) It seems evident that research had become a major intellectual and professional desidertum for at least some members of the most important centers of graduate training in American sociology.

Under the chairmanship of Gillin, the Committee on the Standardization of Research (later simply the Committee on Social Research) was constituted in 1917 (Eaves 1917, 248). This committee was unable to fulfill its charge in 1918, and its life was extended. It offered reports in 1919, 1920, and 1921. In 1923, the committee was finally able to fulfill its mandate, including a short report and an extensive document, "Social Research in Progress in the United States" (Gillin 1923, 155–81). In part, the document apparently became a precedent for and a precursor of the annual census of research in progress that was published in the *American Journal of Sociology,* volumes 34–41 (1928/29–1935/36), and in the *American Sociological Review* beginning with volume 1 (1936).

Gillin's reports on the Committee on Social Research are illuminating in revealing that many sociologists before, and even more after, 1921 were sensitive to the charge that sociology as a discipline was not genuinely scientific. His reports conceded that the founding sociologies of Comte and Spencer had arisen out of social philosophy (Gillin 1920, 231; Gillin, 247). Despite disclaimers, many sociologists were distressed by the scorn bordering on contempt that natural scientists, on the one hand, and economists, historians, and psychologists, on the other, frequently directed toward their field (Gillin 1920, 231; Gillin 1921, 243). And most of them seemed to agree that the increasing pursuit of research by increasing numbers of their members was indispensable to improving the image of their field, although they might not have been clear about what constitutes research (as opposed to the kinds of inquiries reported earlier at the annual meetings and included in *PASS*).

Some sociologists did insist that research entailed a study initiated in respect of certain kinds of problems and using certain kinds of data, methods, procedures, and techniques. Although Gillin's reports are somewhat suggestive (–1920, 230; –1923, 156), more clearly indicative were the papers of Gehlke (1926), Chapin, and Lundberg (two of whom had chaired the Committee on Social Research, one of whom [Chapin] had presented a paper at its division on social research, and all of whom had been students of Giddings or students of his students [Lundberg]). It is abundantly clear for Chapin (1920) and Lundberg (1929b) that research is characteristically oriented to a relatively contemporary problem, involves data from the present, or has been collected firsthand (e.g., from case study, social survey, statistics) and so might be said to be more or less empirical, and entails inductive generalizations through which laws might develop and prediction eventually occur. Indeed, such might be said to be the case for the majority of the papers in the sessions on social research in the later 1920s.

General Scientific Method and Specific Methods in Sociology

Curiously, the sessions in the division on social research seem to have been largely devoid of arguments about the scientific method in general. But Chapin's paper in the society's division on the organization of social research in 1922 was an exception (Chapin 1922, 168–72). Though the paper's title might seem to suggest a primarily pedagogical interest, its content was directly oriented to the character of scientific method. The paper permitted Chapin to refer back to his exposition of the scientific method as an inductive method (169) and to the historical, field, and statistical methods as specific forms or types of inductive method (175–77) on the basis of his earlier (1920) work. (Admittedly, a relatively extended exposition of scientific method, along with specific procedures and techniques, did not occur until the publication of Lundberg's *Social Research* in 1929.)

Other papers on scientific method in general had been published just before and after Chapin's article. The number was rather small—only five or six in the *American Journal of Sociology* and the *Publications of the ASS* from 1919 to 1928.

Most noteworthy about the more succinct accounts of scientific method (Ogburn 1922, 1929; Chapin 1920, 1922; Meroney 1925; and Lundberg 1929a) is their considerable consensus on the five or so basic procedural steps or stages involved. (Indeed, their views are supported in the textbooks of Ellwood, Hankins, Lumley, and Reuter and Hart.)

In addition, both the professional literature and the textbooks indicate that a variety of more specific methods and techniques that were particularly associated with other disciplines were useful to sociologists in their inquiries. These included the comparative method (from anthropology), the historical method (from history), and the social survey method, case method, and statistical method (especially associated with social work in the years just before and after World War I). Each was considered in the Ellwood, Lumley, and Reuter and Hart texts.[1] Except for Lundberg's 1939 *Foundations of Sociology,* the theory texts after 1933 (e.g., Hiller 1933, Young 1934, Bernard 1942) tended to ignore science and scientific method in any sociologically relevant sense.

It is illuminating to note, however, that the professional literature tended to focus especially on case studies and statistics, which were often construed as being in an antagonistic relationship. Among the several relevant papers, Jocher's (1928) comments on the case study are especially illuminating. Giddings's *The Scientific Study of Human Society* (1924) provided the most complete exposition of elementary statistical operations during the 1920s. Ogburn and Goldenweiser's *The Social Sciences and Their Interrelations* (1927) afforded sociologists and specialists of related disciplines an unusual perspective on the role of statistics in the social sciences. Burgess's article comparing statistics and case studies is very enlightening (Burgess 1927, 104–20).

It is evident that by the end of the 1920s, two major and antagonistic conceptions of science and scientific method are beginning to crystallize, one centering on statistics and the other on case study. Lundberg (1929b, 1939b) was the most vocal figure in articulating a statistics-oriented, qualified empiricist, and neo-positivist epistemological-methodological stance. His major allies included Chapin, Ogburn, Rice, Bernard, and Bain—to cite only the most prominent protagonists, who (except for the last two) were drawn especially from the ranks of Giddings's students or who were students of Giddings's students.[2]

Their major opponents, who essentially espoused case-study and qualitative research, included Park, Howard P. Becker, MacIver, Znaniecki, Parsons, and Sorokin. They all seem to have been substantially influenced by European epistemological-methodological arguments, particularly those arising from the German *Methodenstreit* of the late nineteenth century. At least one can be characterized as an American counterpart or exponent of neo-idealism, and the others can be identified with a Neo-Kantian epistemological-methodological stance.[3]

A STATISTICALLY-CENTERED, NEO-EMPIRICIST, NEO-POSITIVIST EPISTEMOLOGY-METHODOLOGY

Introduction

The dominant epistemological-methodological stance of the period arose during the 1920s. It can be characterized more precisely as a qualified empiricism and neo-positivism. The terms *empiricism* and *positivism* were used in an earlier study of the founding fathers of American sociological theory (Hinkle 1980). *Empiricism,* of course, designates the view that sensory experience is the legitimate foundation of tenable (i.e., naturalistic or scientific) knowledge. The term *positivism* was used to indicate the view that the methods, techniques, and procedures of the natural sciences constitute the most useful methodological basis of the social sciences and sociology. Admittedly, both terms have had varied usages and meanings in philosophy, social science, and sociology. In philosophy, *positivism* has been employed to, among other things, signify encompassing orientations or systems (e.g., Comtian positivism, logical positivism). Clearly, intellectual movements in philosophy have had their impact on the social sciences and sociology. C. G. A. Bryant (1985, 1–10) has reviewed these influences on sociology (e.g., Lezak Kolakowski's *The Alienation of Reason,* 1968) and Giddens's contribution to sociology (e.g., Giddens's "Positivism and Its Critics," 1977).

Bryant's review and analysis have been useful in formulating the dominant features in the changing character of empiricism and positivism in the 1920s and later, as opposed to those before 1915. In actuality, the characterization "qualified empiricism and neopositivism" involves a variety of features that pertain not only to epistemology and methodology but also to ontology and a vocabulary appropriate to a natural science sociology. (See below.)

Influenced especially by Pearson, Giddings was the initial expositor of the stance.[4] As noted, most of the sociologists who adopted the position had been Giddings's (and Mayo-Smith's) graduate students at Columbia or students of their students. They included Gillin, Chapin, Ogburn, Gehlke, and Rice; also Lundberg (perhaps the most famous of Chapin's students) and McCormick and Stouffer (prominent among Ogburn's students). Two other non-Columbia students were Bernard and Bain (Ph.D's from Chicago and Michigan, respectively).

Probably the most complete and systematic formulations of the position can be found in the publications of Bain, Rice, Chapin, and especially Lundberg.

Main Features of This Epistemological-Methodological Stance

Because this investigation of the nature of social and sociological theory is concerned primarily with the continuities and discontinuities in social ontological theory, and because historically so much attention has been devoted to the study of methodology during this period, only a minimal and basic consideration of the major features of this social epistemological-methodological stance can be offered. It is, of course, necessary to keep constantly in mind that this stance and the other two arose more or less in a polemical relationship. Thus, each of the major points of this stance tends to presuppose negative or opposite ones on the part of the other two positions.

   Basic (Ontological) Differences between the Physical and Organic and the Social Realms Are Denied. To assert, as positivism does, that social phenomena can and should be studied by the same basic methods as the physical and organic sciences employ is, in effect, to argue that no fundamental differences exist between the two domains that would legitimately bar the studies of the former from invoking the methods of the latter. Lundberg and Rice exemplify such arguments, the former in his *Social Research* (1929b) and the latter on the basis of his *Quantitative Methods in Politics* (1928a).
   Lundberg (1929b, 13, 15, 17–20) advances four major points. First, he claims that the alleged complexity of the social is more apparent than real, simply because social phenomena are unfamiliar or strange by virtue of not having been studied closely. Complexity is thus largely a derivative of ignorance. Second, he disputes the allegation that social data are known symbolically in contrast to physical data as known directly through the senses. Both are actually known through symbolic behavior, or language mechanisms. third, social phemena are not unpredictable by virture of the operations of will and mind. The seeming unpredictability of group behavior arises because present knowledge of the stimuli and responses operative in such groups is limited. Finally, he insists that the qualitative nature of social phenomena is a barrier only at present and will eventually be translatable into quantitative terms, just as has occurred in other fields.
   Rice (1928a, 25, 27, 30, 33). claims a similar position, though he seems to argue from a reverse stance. In some instances, he contends that careful examination will show social phenomena and natural phenomena to have heretofore unnoted resemblances. For example, natural phenomena do not exhibit exact repetition and precise identity; individual variation also exists. Furthermore, laws in natural phenomena are only probable rather than exact. Nor is the social intrinsically intractable to experimentation, though more practical difficulties may be involved. Moreover, complete control even in the natural world is impossible, and some margin of error exists. And in neither domain is causation to be sought—all that is possible is correlation and concomitant variation. Basically, the nature of existence, whether natural or social, is derived from sense impressions and is thus inferential. Otherwise put, all data from perceptions have the character of indexes (29).
   Lundberg and Rice concur that no fundamental dissimilarities between biophysical and social data can be shown. All that is required for any field to become a science is its resort to the common methods of science.

A Behaviorist, Externalist, Objectivist, Physicalist, or Materialist Notion of Reality is Presupposed. If no basic difference between the physical and organic and the social domains can be demonstrated, it follows that one is being assimilated to or reduced to the other, either the physical and organic to the human social or the latter to the former. And it was indeed the second alternative that was ordinarily taken. Reality is then what is physical or material—external, objective, observable, and verifiable—not what is psychic (internal, subjective, covert, and not publicly verifiable). In effect, then, what is real is overt, observable, and measurable behavior (Bain 1928, 941; Bernard 1919, 298–325).

Illuminatingly, Lundberg (1939b, 178). acknowledges that symbols may represent relatively easily verifiable or nonverifiable referents. But it is clear that he wishes to exclude anthropomorphic, animistic, theological, volitional, motivational, and causal assumptions as metaphysical.

What is real is what is and not what ought to be, what is descriptive and not what is normative (Bain 1928, 941; Lundberg 1939b, 29–31; Rice 1932, 323, 324, 325).

Lundberg (1939b) in particular is inclined to reductionism and physicalism. Note his plea for parsimony in science, for the unity underlying disparate phenomena, and his resort to a variety of physicalist notions (203–13), concluding with the claim that social phenomena are finally only a form of electron-proton system or a form of energy transformation (203, 204, 210).

A Qualified Empiricist Epistemology Is Adopted by the Position. Sometimes, empiricism as a theory of knowledge based on sensory experience is explicitly asserted. Endorsing Pearson, Gehlke (1926, 143) remarks that we can know only a succession of sense impressions. Lundberg (1929b, 26) and Bain (1929, 947) both agree that our knowledge of the world is derived from our sensory organs, that is, from sense data that are the same for all competent individuals.

But both Bain and Lundberg had reservations about sensation as the unqualified basis of knowledge. They warned (Bain 1935, 482–82; and Lundberg 1939b, 89) that because our sensory equipment restricts our experience to only limited aspects of objects and events at any given instant, our knowledge of anything in the universe is less than complete. Thus, the study of anything in the known universe requires restriction by abstraction (Lundberg 1939b, 89).

Most importantly, Lundberg recognized that the accuracy and reliability of sensory reports depend on certain conditions. Organs must be physically sound and unaffected by possible adverse physiological and environmental conditions (e.g., fatigue, age, temperature). Furthermore, past training and past and present circumstances, such as bias, prejudice (strong value commitments, such as religion and supernaturalism) are relevant (Rice 1928a, 169, 172; Lundberg 1929b, 22–29, 34, 35).

But the major qualification to an empiricist theory of knowledge lay in the recognition that human perceptions are mediated by and through language symbols. So Lundberg (1929b) cautions that we do not know things directly through our sensory responses but only because others respond to the same stimuli in approximately the same way and use common language symbols (26 n. 2). Bain (1935) adds that we can know only sensory experiences that have become objective as they have become communicated, that is, that involve use of the same system of verbal symbols (482). Clearly, an empiricist notion of the basis of knowledge has been qualified by the intervention of the symbol between perception and response. Moreover, language symbols do not necessarily have to presuppose adaptation to the physical conditions of social existence as their crucial requirement, which Lundberg's arguments seem to assume. Unfortunately, the implications of this qualification were not seriously pursued. Equivocation was a more common response.

Methodological Individualism (Atomism) Tends to Be Accepted. Because the locus of sensory experience as the major epistemological key lies in specific, concrete individuals, the group as a whole can be studied and known only through perceptible, perceiving, discrete individuals. Stated more fully, this methodological tenet presupposed implicitly or asserts explicitly that the group as a type of whole can be investigated (adequately? reliably? representatively? necessarily?) as the sum or aggregate of individual, atom-like units. The group is, therefore, to be conceived as a plurality, multiplicity, or aggregation involving individual differences (differentiation, individualization, individuality) and possibly their ranking or differential evaluation (as inequality). Necessarily, the group in activity is actually, invariably, or finally the actions, reactions, and interactions of particular individuals. Because numerousness and (calculable) centrality and dispersion are also assumed, the potential resort to mathematics, particularly statistics, becomes evident. Giddings, Chapin, Ogburn, Lundberg, and Bain are illustrative. (See also Hinkle 1980, 60).

An Initial Concern with a Common Scientific Method Is Accommodated to an Acceptance of Sound Theory. Positivists generally agreed that a common scientific method undergirded all of the natural sciences and that the social sciences, especially sociology, should follow the mandates of this common method. (At least initially, the previous tenet had emphasized induction.) Yet positivists seemed to exhibit little interest in the nature of that method as presented by some of the founders of European sociology (e.g., Durkheim and his *Rules of Sociological Method,* which was not translated into English until 1938) or method in general (e.g., John Stuart Mill's exposition). They offered no analysis of the merits and demerits of the comparative method (from biology) versus the experimental method (from physics and chemistry), but Chapin did examine the nature of experimentation itself as early as 1917. Karl Pearson's *The Grammar of Science* (1900) was often cited in their papers.

Ogburn, Chapin, and Lundberg were especially important in outlining the nature of a general or common scientific method. (Hankins and other textbook authors—some of whom could scarcely be associated with positivism—basically concurred with the views of the three positivists.) Clearly inductive in its early formulations, their account involved the following tenets:

1. Inquiry must be initiated with a problem.[5]
2. There must be accurate collection, recording, and classification of the facts of observation.[6]
3. Formulation of a hypothesis is critical.[7]
4. There must be further research culminating in the verification of the hypothesis as an explanatory generalization and a potential law.[8]

Curiously, neither the 1929 nor the 1942 edition of Lundberg's *Social Research* carries the neophyte social investigator substantially into the last steps. Lundberg notes only that his present volumes are concerned with the methods of collecting data as opposed to the methods of manipulating, summarizing, or generalizing data already gathered.

In 1936, both Chapin and Lundberg suddenly abandoned their notion that scientific method is primarily inductive rather than deductive for one that interrelates induction and deduction in recognition of the intellectual changes that apparently had occurred in both physics (Bridgman) and psychology (Hull). This acceptance of the role of deduction was expressed as a new respect for "sound theory" (cf. Chapin 1936, 1–11; Lundberg 1936b, 703–23, 708).

Understandably, then, Lundberg's *Foundations of Sociology* (1939b) exhibits a sharp break with his *Social Research* of 1929. No elaborate exposition of inductive method is included. Instead, Lundberg is concerned with the development of a satisfactory frame of reference, derived from natural science, and the requirements for achieving reliable generalizations or laws. Methods per se have receded into the background to become an assumed necessary feature of a natural science or positivistic sociology, with induction and deduction construed to be interrelated and complementary in function (49). Indeed, *Foundations of Sociology* is itself conceived to be a contribution

to a more complete and mature system of scientific theory comprised of specific formal postulates and theories that have been subjected to rigorous test
(x). It contemplates the deductive organization of general scientific laws into
a mutually consistent system (116; cf. Lundberg 1945, 503–4).

In the 1942 edition of *Social Research,* Lundberg conceives scientific
inquiry to be pursued at four different levels: (1) mere random observation;
(2) systematic investigation; (3) testing, by either experiment or statistical
methods, of well-defined but isolated hypotheses (p. 7); and (4) consistent
derivation of hypotheses from a systematic and integrated theory. The fourth
involves (a) a "set of rigorous and unambiguous terms to be used," (b) a "set
of postulates or hypothetical statements and their corollaries (inferences
from the postulates) which are tentatively assumed to be true for the purposes of investigation," (c) theorems stated "as formal propositions which
could or should be true if the postulates, the corollaries and the reasoning
[about] the theorems are sound. These theorems are really hypothetical generalizations," which stipulate the kind of (d) "empirical observations [to be]
undertaken to test the validity of the entire explicit theoretical structure outlined" (p. 7). Lundberg's footnotes suggest that physics has been his model
for this conception. However, the immediate inspiration was apparently
Hull's work in psychology (Lundberg [1929b] 1942, 9).

*Natural Science Generalizations and Laws Are Held to Be Possible in
Sociology.* Clearly, positivists in sociology have generally held that adoption
of a natural-science method in general, and especially a resort to quantification, statistics, measurement, and scalar devices in particular, will allow
sociology to achieve natural-science-like generalizations and laws. Again,
Chapin and Lundberg are illustrative.

When Chapin published his *Field Work and Social Reserach* in 1920,
his fourth or concluding step in the scientific method was the discovery of
"some sort of formula or law to explain the sequence of facts and to express
their relationship" (7). Established in this way, the deductions from inductive generalizations form the reliable predictions of science (7, cf. 17).

In Lundberg's *Social Research* and his *Foundations of Sociology,* generalizations and laws are the culmination of the scientific method. This last
step entails the formulation of a "brief statement or description of these
sequences in such a form as to apply to all similar phenomena in the universe studied under given conditions" (Lundberg 1929b, 5; Lundberg
[1929b] 1942, 10–11). Following Pearson, he also argues that causation is
replaced by association and correlation, just as certainty is replaced by probability and approximation. *Foundations of Sociology* characterizes a generalization as a statement, determined "from less than all the relevant data," of
"the probable prevalence in a universe of a given datum or configuration of

data" (54). It becomes a scientific law if the generalization about the occurrence of "events . . . under stated conditions" is verifiable and stipulates the measurable degree of accuracy (133). Ideally, it is stated in terms of a set of verbal or mathematical symbols.

Such laws then are the basis of prediction. They "provide norms from which individual, actual occurrences can be predicted within measurable probability-expectations" by virtue of the carefully defined (measured) abstract and standardized circumstances under which these laws hold (115, 138–39).

Natural Scientific (or Positivistic) Inquiry Is Identified with Quantitative, Statistical, Mensurative, and Scalar Techniques. In this feature (as in the prior ones), Giddings has played an historically important mediating role in transmitting the ideas of Pearson. According to Turner and Turner (1990, 27), he in essence resurrected Comte's law of the three stages of knowledge (i.e., the theological, metaphysical, and positive) but followed their transformation by Pearson into the speculative, observational, and metrical.[9] Thus, the supreme form of knowledge is stated in terms of quantitative units subject to statistical manipulation and analysis. In addition, Giddings offers an illuminating substantive justification for a resort to statistics. Committed as he was to selection as the mechanism of organic, psychic, and social evolution, he concurred with Pearson's advocacy of statistics as a device for displaying the distribution (dispersion) of individuals around a statistical norm (or mean) and thus represents the more extreme deviations as probabilistically destined for elimination (Ross 1991, 227–28; Pearson 1990 chaps. 10 and 11, esp. pp. 418–19, 502–3).

Significantly, too, Chapin, one of Giddings's students, developed a justification for a resort to statistics in sociology that analogized its function to that of the experimental method in physical science. By the use of correlation and sampling techniques, the sociologist can isolate the effects of different factors and so overcome or resolve the problematic heterogeneity of human aggregates (Chapin 1917, 133–38, 238–47, esp. 133, 135, 240, 244, 247).

It is interesting to note that twelve years later Lundberg (Chapin's student) noted that the statistical method allows an "escape from the seemingly insurmountable obstacles to precise methods of experimentation in sociology" (Lundberg 1929b, 47). By use of sampling and averages, it "disposes of the apparently insuperable difficulties of the enormous number and variability of social phenomena. By the method of correlation it provides a technique of measuring the degree of contingency between social phenomena" (47). Generalizations and causal inference become possible through "sampling, averaging, and correlation" (49). Eventually, correlation displaces causation. But, broadly speaking, quantification and mensuration acquire a significance, if not indispensability, that comes to permeate the view of scientific method.

Statistics came to occupy a peculiarly crucial and central place in the advocacy of the empiricist-positivist epistemological-methodological stance. Although the earliest use of statistics in sociology may well have occurred by virtue of the discipline's early association with social work (and particularly the social survey), the primary reason for the major expanded adoption of statistics during the 1920s and later seems to have been its identification with the natural sciences. The adherents of an empiricist-positivistic epistemological stance were convinced that a natural-science approach would yield scientific knowledge involving generalizations that are empirical, inductive, precise, reliable, verifiable, and predictive, because the method is characteristically quantitative and mensurative. In particular, a quantitative approach means focusing on data in terms of quantities: They can be counted, enumerated, or reckoned numerically. The exponents of this stance concurred with Chapin (1935, 480) that a numerical symbol possesses such fundamental advantages as being more standardized, objective, and interchangeable, or uniform from time to time and place to place, and being more confirmable or verifiable, than any other symbol.

Beginning around the time of World War I and more rapidly in the years afterward, sociologists, especially the students of Giddings and Mayo-Smith at Columbia University, came to appreciate statistics. Giddings himself, Gehlke, Chaddock, Ogburn and Goldenweiser, and Burgess were among those who published relevant books or articles.

Interestingly, the major textbooks and treatises cited were in mathematical or economic statistics. Apparently, academic resistance occurred as "newcomer" disciplines, like sociology, attempted to introduce their own statistics courses into college and university curricula. In part, then, the failure of textbooks in social and sociological research (e.g., Lundberg 1929b) to include chapters on statistics becomes explicable. Not until 1941 were textbooks in elementary social statistics published: Thomas C. McCormick's *Elementary Social Statistics* (1941) and Margaret Jarman Hagood's *Statistical for Sociologists* (1941). McCormick was a student of Ogburn after the latter had moved from Columbia to Chicago in the later 1920s.

For the empiricist-positivists, quantification is a necessary basis for measurement, though initially in the 1920s confusion existed over the question of equating enumeration with measurement. Chapin (1929, 94) denied flatly that counting is measurement. (He differentiated between that which is to be compared, as the unit of observation, and that in terms of which it is to be compared, the unit of reference.) Later, Chapin (1935, 479) claimed that measurement occurs when something (a unit of observation) can be related to some external feature that comprises a scale of units on a continuum from low and lower to high and higher values, with the units so standardized as to be approximately equal and to represent equal degrees of the observed trait.

For Lundberg (1939b, 66) measurement involves a characterization of more or less particular items in terms of an abstract variable exhibited on a (scalar) continuum comprised of units that are additive and interchangeable with one another. Measurement requires an objective device for standardizing responses in accordance with an abstract, calibrated, graduated unit of magnitude as designated by certain verbal symbls (67). But Lundberg opposed Kirkpatrick's argument for an objective or physical counterpart of the unit of magnitude, such as a brass gram weight to correspond to the idea of a gram as a unit (71).

Clearly, then, the dissemination of statistics in sociology seems to have been predicated on the premise that it could confer the presumed characteristic assets of the natural sciences. Empiricalness, induction, objectivity, precision, reliability, verifiability, and prediction seem to be linked with statistics because it was quantitative and presumably a requisite for measurement, which became a reality with the adoption of scales (for which again psychology in particular provided a model). Yet it is the character of the conclusions deriving from the statistical methods (i.e., generalizations or laws) that had a special significance for the sociological adherents of positivism.

A Rigorously Objective and Finally Operationalized Scientific Terminology Is Sought. Positivists in sociology were thoroughly aware of the necessity to develop a scientific terminology that would not itself distort the natural science approach to sociological inquiry, social data, analysis, and generalization. Bain (1931, 10–11) and Lundberg (1929b, 54–74) addressed some of the initial problems. Of the two main options for securing a sociological terminology, Bain preferred the development of a new professionally specialized terminology to the reconstitution of old lay notions.

Lundberg (1929b, 63) proposed that sociology follow the lead of psychological behaviorism in redefining its notions and concepts in terms of objectively observable and measurable behavior. Terms not susceptible to such redefinition must be abandoned. Eventually, he believed appropriate terms would come to be associated with mathematical symbols. In general, he proposed certain requirements for a term or unit: appropriateness (utility for a purpose), clarity (commonness of meaning and use by different people), measurability (permitting similarity of responses), comparability (the symbol representing units to be compared must describe the same objective realities similarly in all significant respects) (68–72). And he also set forth criteria for categories employed in classificatory schemes: exclusivity of one another, exhaustiveness, and appropriateness (suitability to ends sought) (73–74).

By the mid 1930s, the adherents of positivism had found a new mode of defining concepts—operationalization—which they adopted enthusiastically. Major proponents included Chapin, Alpert, and Lundberg. Chapin (1935, 476–80) had suggested that his reconceptualization of socioeconomic status in terms of the objective attributes of observable living-room furnishings provides an illuminating example of how sociological terminology might be made more scientifically acceptable by what came to be regarded as operationalization. Following Bridgeman's *The Logic of Modern Physics,* Lundberg (1936a, 44) insisted that a concept be defined in terms of the operations by which it is arrived at. Indeed, for Lundberg (1936b, 711), the definition of a phenomenon and its measurement are actually the same operation. Interestingly, Lundberg (1936a, 38) is explicit in his insistence that the precision afforded by measurement in an operational definition facilitates adjustment to the conditions of life and thus reflects the sanction for science in assumptions about evolution.

Harry Alpert (1938b, 850–61) expressed major misgivings about Lundberg's formulation of operationalism. Clearly, Alpert was concerned about an inclination to erect operationalism into a kind of metaphysics with an exclusive claim to legitimacy in sociology and to possible solipsistic, subjective-idealist, or (raw) empiricist epistemological tendencies, or to any reductive or atomistic ontological inclinations. For Alpert, social phenomena should be defined in terms of both operations and probability—that is, in "terms of the probability of occurrences and in terms of socio-meaningful verifiable operations" (858).

Lundberg's *Foundations of Sociology* (1939b) confirms his commitment to the operationalization of concepts. As a preliminary, Lundberg remarks that definition means "(a) the selection of significant behavior-segments and (b) their representation by symbols which lend themselves to operational representation of relationships" (58). He advocates following the forward strides of physics in defining a term as "that which evokes a certain type of human response, represented by measurement symbols" (60). Clearly, some—perhaps many—sociological terms will have to be redefined or abandoned and new ones invented for those important behavior segments not at present symbolized.

Operationalism played a significant part in the recommendations of the report of the subcommittee on definition of definition of the Committee on Conceptual Integration (1943). Using the species-genus-differentiae type as its basic point of departure, it distinguished the genetic, identifying, and analytical types. It concluded that all real definitions are both verbal and operational, and elaborated on the latter (340).

For Many Positivists, Sociological Advance, Which Is Primarily Dependent on Improving Research Instrumentation, Can Assure Enhanced Social Adaptation and the Possibility of a Positive Social Order. In the years immediately following World War I, the advance of science was justified by increasing utility or, in the terms of organic evolution, by increasing adaptation. In his earlier writings, Chapin claimed in effect that statistical analysis in sociology can and will aid society in rationally selecting among alternatives under changing conditions of social existence so that social adaptation and evolution may continue. About a decade later, Lundberg (1929a, 390) contended that research methods are forms of adjustment techniques that have survived because they have utility. Employed so successfully in relation to the physical environment, the method of physical science can be applied to other aspects of our environment. It can be used especially in the social domain, in which, Lundberg believed an increasing development of the quantitative approach was called for (Lundberg 1929a, 401, 404).

But by the time of the publication of his *Foundations of Sociology,* the resort to such directly adaptive arguments drawn from organic evolution had become more suspect. Lundberg's terminology became more oblique. He simply characterized science as the most evidently successful of adjustment techniques in the fields in which it has been tried (Lundberg 1939b, 5).

Manifestly, positivists regarded an increasingly more efficient research instrumentation as crucial to the development of reliable generalizations and laws and thus to the use of sociology and its acceptance by the public. Although science cannot determine "what ought to be," it can "determine the immediate and remote costs and consequences of alternative courses of action, and . . . make them known to the public" (Lundberg 1947, 33; cf. Lundberg 1939b, 402–3).

In the pursuit of such a determination, Lundberg could never genuinely envisage the possibility of irresolvable value conflict. Whatever men and women have valued in the course of evolution is consistent with the conditions of human existence and is therefore right. For Lundberg, such values apparently reflected the pursuit of a set of universal human needs (and desires?) that are so abstract and devoid of cultural content as to be unwittingly subject to the same criticisms as the old social forces. These ends are, furthermore, so timeless that, Lundberg claims, to say that any others should be pursued amounts simply "to saying that man should be different than he is, that he should have [had] a different evolutionary history than he has had" (Lundberg 1947, 13).

Accordingly, Bryant (1985) urges that Lundberg "perpetuates the teleological fallacy that what has been, is, and is becoming, must be" as well as "ignores the scarcity of all valued things and benefits" (149). So, in effect, science must support the status quo but cannot be held responsible. In calculating the best means to these broad, even vacuous, ends, science "leaves no room for conflicting interpretations once the facts about past practices, present means and future costs are known to all" (149). Thus, science can provide knowledge about which "of our aspirations are achievable" and which "ones mutually incompatible" (Lundberg 1947, 103). Science can save us!

Rejecting the contentions of cultural relativism, Lundberg (1947) urges "the possibility that there are 'natural processes' in the social as in the physical world and that there may be limits to the liberties man can take with these processes if he wishes to achieve a successful organization and peace" (109). In effect, Lundberg seems to be suggesting a universal abstract and natural social order to which any particular form of human organization must become an ever-closer approximation, in the same sense that the seventeenth century thought of a natural physical order. Indeed, one may even suspect endorsement of Comte's notion that a secure social order is ultimately possible only with the universal prevalence of scientific principles of knowledge, which requires development of a natural-science (and thus, in this case, an instrumentally effective) sociology, that is, a positivistic society.

With almost no modifications, these features of a qualified empiricism and neo-positivism were transmitted to the post-World War II period to become the orthodox, foundational, epistemological-methodological stance of American sociology. Admittedly, two features may seem disputable. Perhaps, the pursuit of a positivist social order may appear almost shrilly utopian or even messianic, but in its more respectable form of the (asserted) advancing instrumental utility of science, it is hardly questioned. The "behaviorist-physicalist" ontological implications of empiricism may also cause some uneasiness, but they are generally suppressed as part of a necessary optimistic naturalism. Certainly, the "data" of the field are generally construed to be externally given "observations." Conversely, few sociologists appear to be exercised by, or even aware of, the "linguistic turn" of contemporary philosophy. The notion of a common scientific method is nowhere seriously challenged—nor are the possibility of natural-science generalizations and laws and the indispensability of statistical operations and measurement for a natural-science sociology.

DENIAL AND REJECTION BY OPPOSING THEORETICAL STANCES

However, the orthodoxy of the post-World War II period was not always unquestioned and uncontested. During the 1930s and early 1940s, it did evoke considerable opposition, some of which was partial and fragmentary and some of which was relatively unified and comprehensive. It is clear, for instance, that sociologists of such disparate positions as Robert Lynd and Herbert Blumer were part of that opposition from time to time. However, other sociologists argued their positions much more systematically and comprehensively. Among the latter were MacIver, Znaniecki, H. P. Becker, and Bierstedt (who was exposed to the professorial influence of both MacIver and Lundberg during his years as a graduate student at Columbia). Only a few years after his arrival at Columbia, MacIver became involved in intellectual controversy with the adherents of neo-empiricism and positivism in general and with Lundberg in particular.

Each of the four figures published his views in reviews, articles, and books. MacIver's arguments are contained in his 1930, 1931, and 1940 papers, which are summarized in his *Social Causation* (1942); Znaniecki's in his 1927 and 1931 papers and his *Method of Sociology* (1934) and *Social Actions* (1936); and Becker's in his 1940 and 1941 papers and his *Through Values to Social Interpretation* (1950). Bierstedt's incisive critiques were apparently first developed as part of his Columbia Ph.D. dissertation in 1946 and substantially reproduced in his *Power and Progress* (1975) and his *American Sociological Theory* (1981). Certainly, too, Sorokin is to be counted among the critics.

The more systematically developed objections to the empiricist-positivist epistemological-methodological stance center on six major points:

1. The character of method depends on what is being studied.[10]
2. Knowledge of the social is not to be acquired simply and exclusively by collecting similar, discrete sensory experiences or observations as occur in relation to physical phenomena, and as empiricism holds. (Consult especially MacIver 1930, 28, 29.)
3. Statistically-oriented empiricist-positivists pit induction simplistically against deduction and regard induction as a simple, easily understood, all-sufficing, and alone legitimate process of passing from particulars to the general (MacIver 1930, 25).
4. The notion of science as concerned only with similarities or identities of particulars, with description, with statements of (statistical) association or correlation, is unacceptable. Instead, the objective of scientific inquiry is to relate a phenomenon to a system of relationships, to offer an explanation or interpretation, and to specify causation. (Refer to MacIver 1930, 32; and MacIver [1942] 1964, 91–92.)
5. Counting or enumeration (and thus quantification) and measurement are not indispensable for inductive generalization and science. (See MacIver 1931b, 30, 31, 35; Znaniecki 1934, 233, 234; MacIver [1942] 1964, 53, 54; Bierstedt 1975, 62, 63, 68; also Blumer 1931, 194.
6. The effort to construct the units or concepts of sociological terminology by resort to operationalization is unsatisfactory. (Perhaps the most incisive critique was offered by Bierstedt in his doctoral dissertation. Consult Bierstadt 1975, 7–8, 41–72.)

However, in all cases these contentions are part of much more encompassing stances, which require analysis on their own. Two such stances are discussed in the next section.

AMERICAN VERSIONS OF GERMAN NEO-IDEALIST AND NEO-KANTIAN EPISTEMOLOGICAL-METHODOLOGICAL STANCES

Case Study and Epistemological-Methodological Positions

Just as statistics was the core identifying feature of a neo-empiricist and positivistic stance, so the case study became the core of related opposing epistemological-methodological positions that can perhaps be most accurately characterized as American versions of German neo-idealism (as represented by Dilthey) and Neo-Kantianism (as represented by Windelband, Rickert, and Weber). The word *became* in the previous sentence is important. Unlike the relatively immediate association between statistics and empiricism-positivism, the linkage between the case study and neo-idealism and Neo-Kantianism developed only after some time and never was as clearly evident. Consequently, it is now important to examine how the case-study method was initially conceived, apart from and before it became linked (at least in part) to distinctive epistemological-methodological positions.

Four articles (Burgess 1927; Shaw 1927; Bernard 1928; Jocher 1928) are especially useful in summarizing the major features distinguishing the case study during the mid to late 1920s. Back then, apparently no one anticipated that the case study would become central to the neo-idealist and Neo-Kantian epistemological-methodological stances of the 1930s. Nine distinguishing features of the case study can be identified:

1. The case study should begin with a well-defined problem, the unit or units of which are carefully specified, selected, and intensively studied. (Admittedly, some insisted that the problem became explicit and definite only as relevant cases were themselves carefully considered.)
2. It involves the informal acquisition of data (e.g., from diaries, autobiographies, personal letters, confidential interviews, participant observation).
3. The phenomena comprising the case or cases are viewed contextually or situationally.
4. A case constitutes a whole or totality (parts or aspects of which are to be examined in relation to others and to the whole).
5. Sometimes the case-study method was argued to require adoption of the perspective of the person or social unit or units under inquiry: But others also claimed that subjectivity and bias resulted from this perspective.
6. Some proponents insisted that a dramatic sense and sympathetic attitude on the part of the investigator are indispensable.
7. Data of the case (and the case study) are thus characteristically and distinctively qualitative rather than quantitative.

8. Cases will tend to assume a narrative form, though the kind of language and terminology to be used was open to debate.
9. The case-study approach may lead both to discerning the typical, categorical, or universal and to ascertaining social causation (in time).

Burgess's 1927 article is significant because it alludes to some of the personalities linked to neo-idealism and Neo-Kantianism. In discussing feature 6 above, Burgess had referred to Cooley's sympathetic introspection, which was central to Cooley's humanistic methodology and linked to his epistemological idealism. Burgess also cited Park (along with Thomas) as one of his contemporaries in sociology most active in advocating case study. (Many of the monographs of the University of Chicago Sociological Series of the 1920s and 1930s made their point of departure from Park's construction of general types or universals by abstraction and analysis of cases as particulars.)

But Burgess did not explicitly indicate any connection between Park's advocacy of case study and his acceptance (through Windelband) of a German Neo-Kantian epistemology-methodology. Becker, Znaniecki, and Parsons, in addition to Park made significant use of aspects of a Neo-Kantian epistemology-methodology as represented in the works of Windelband, Rickert, and Max Weber. Becker and Znaniecki explicitly endorsed case study as a necessary aspect of typological construction. Parsons's early position is not entirely clear.

What all of this points to is the emergence of two separate, though somewhat interconnected, epistemological-methodological stances in American sociology during the 1930s and 1940s. Both seem to represent American versions of, or at least congruencies with, positions arising somewhat earlier in German philosophy and social science. One is what might be termed a "neo-idealist-humanistic" position involving major similarities between the German Wilhelm Dilthey and Cooley and MacIver. The second is a related but separate version of Neo-Kantianism entailing major similarities between the positions of Wilhelm Windelband and Heinrich Rickert, on the one hand, and Park, Becker, Znaniecki, and Parsons, on the other. (Admittedly, some of the Americans are much more silent or vague about the sources of their views than is desirable for this kind of analysis.[11]

American Versions of German Neo-Idealism

Interestingly, Cooley is the main mediating figure between the first and second periods of American sociology for transmitting an anti-empiricist-positivist and antiquantitative stance, just as Giddings was the main mediating figure for transmitting an empiricist-positivist and quantitative orientation from the first to the second period. The linkage between a distinctive general epistemological-methodological stance and the espousal of a particular method is revealed in several of Cooley's last papers, all of which were posthumously published in *Sociological Theory and Social Research* (Cooley 1930, 289–309, 313–22, 331–39).[12]

Because Dilthey (1833–1911) was substantially Cooley's and MacIver's senior, Dilthey will be used as the point of comparative departure. Most importantly, the three agree on three major points: (a) The domains of external biophysical nature and human consciousness and experience are basically different; (b) that difference is crucially important in the methods of study of the appropriate fields of knowledge; and (c) the distinctive method in studying human interpersonal relations must include, if not begin with, human consciousness and involve "understanding."

Dilthey (1883) was primarily responsible for the differentiation of two fundamentally different realms of knowledge, the *Naturwissenschaften* and the *Geisteswissenschaften* (i.e., the natural sciences, and the mental or human or humanistic disciplines).[13] Each branch of knowledge has its characteristic object, approach, and method corresponding to the dualism of matter and mind. The characteristic marks of "outer experience" with external nature are spatial extension and mechanistic determinism. Cooley similarly separated the domains of natural sciences and humanistic disciplines, one yielding "spatial-material knowledge" and the other "personal-social knowledge." In distinguishing major realms of causality in his *Social Causation,* MacIver implies a separation of the physical-chemical and organic (concerned with invariant sequence and concomitance and functional interdependence) from that of conscious being (involving the whys of objective, motivation and patterning).

Dilthey was very explicit about the two realms of knowledge differing in their objectives, whereas Cooley and MacIver only—yet surely—implied a basic difference in objectives. The objective of the natural sciences was to provide (causal) explanation, and that of the humanistic disciplines was to offer (interpretive) understanding. In the former, the objective was accomplished by construction of deductive theories to account for what has been observed in terms of unobservables. In the latter, understanding, especially understanding of motivation, is achieved, through the methods of (mental, emotional) reliving and reconstruction (*Nacherleben* and *Nachbilden*) of other persons. Cooley's "instructed imagination" or "sympathetic introspection" and MacIver's "imaginative or sympathetic reconstruction" are essentially similar. (Interestingly, all three agree on the construction of types to aid in the process.)

Dilthey noted that one uses one's own imagination, in relation to one's past experiences, to try to relive and reconstruct the feelings and experiences of others. First in the reproduction or reconstruction is the development of a feeling of the same kind that the other is believed to have had (*nachfühlen*) and then a feeling about the feeling ascribed to the other (of *Sympathie* or *Mitgefühl*). As the sense of likeness between the situations the investigator knows and the feelings she or he has and those which the other seems to be experiencing increases, it becomes possible for her or him to transpose herself or himself into the life of the other and to empathize with that other. So mental or imaginative reliving and reconstruction are eventually held to produce an understanding of the other.

Cooley (1927, 157) proposes similarly that the social inquirer embrace the situation of a particular subject within his own mind and, by an act of creative intelligence, anticipate the outcome—as "you would anticipate the conduct of an individual by putting yourself wholeheartedly in his place." According to Cooley (1930), one understands another's consciousness by the aid of one's own (300). The conduct of other persons, including their language, is interpreted by ascribing to them thoughts and sentiments similar to one's own (300). When we observe overt activities and hear others' words, we understand them by recalling in our own consciousnesses how we thought and felt under similar circumstances of word and deed. We impute the same thoughts and feelings to others and thus gain an insight into their minds (Cooley 1930, 298).

Although MacIver does not use the term *interpretation* to characterize his own position, he employs the term *imaginative reconstruction,* which bears a marked similarity to Dilthey's *Nachbild* and in the elucidation of which he introduces the word *interpret.* He insists that such imaginative reconstruction (or interpretation) derives from what occurs in the course of ordinary interpersonal action and experience of laypersons.

More particularly, MacIver claims, entering into effective interpersonal relations requires that each of us attempt to reconstruct, often on the basis of subtle evidence, concealed but crucial "thoughts, attitudes, desires, and motivations" of other participants in the situation. Presumably, social experience itself has taught us to seek out the "meaningful design" not evident to the senses as such, and to do it as readily as we interpret the "linguistic symbols by means of which" persons "partly reveal and partly conceal their thoughts." Mediated by symbols, all "communication is indirect or semantic." The success or failure of our efforts "to interpret these symbols" is governed largely by the degree and kind of experience we have had. Even if an attempt is made to be rigorously behavioristic, it will fail. We can never entirely ignore "the subjective evidences" of the "experiences," "problems," "desires," and "feelings" that are provided in the communication of those whose conduct is under investigation. Imaginative reconstruction must be invoked (MacIver [1942] 1964, 264, 332fn).

It must also be acknowledged that Diltheyan "understanding" extended beyond (a) empathic identification and virtual reenactment of another person's mental processes. It also entailed (b) the "grasping of meaning" through a sign representing something common and shared among members of a community or group and (c) the ascertaining of the significance of a statement, action, or event in light of a larger context. This last aspect led eventually to "interpretation" of complex, permanent expressions and the methodology of hermenuetics, which fundamentally depended on the "to-and-fro [intellectual] movement [of mind] from part to whole and back to part again" as demanded by the hermeneutical circle (Ermarth 1978, 251, 252–53).

Dilthey's neo-idealism thus involved a peculiar kind of methodological holism. Undeniably, Cooley's and MacIver's neo-idealisms also entailed holisms, though it can hardly be argued that an explicit hermeneutics was entailed in either case.

American Versions of German Neo-Kantianism

Either explicitly or implicitly, Park, Becker, Znaniecki, and Parsons accepted the basic views of the German Southwestern (or Baden) school of Neo-Kantianism, whose main exponents were Wilhelm Windelband (1848–1915) and Heinrich Rickert (1863–1936). (Max Weber, of course, also expressed his agreement with the views of Rickert, and Weber in turn basically affected Becker's and Parsons's stances.)

Windelband and Rickert stated their own position directly in opposition to Dilthey. Basically, they objected to Dilthey's separation of the fields of knowledge (into the natural sciences and mental or humanistic disciplines) because it was predicated on an ontic division of reality into external nature or matter and an internal sphere of (human) mind or consciousness, with essentially two kinds of experience, one outer and the other inner. Windelband and Rickert contended that all empirical knowledge is founded on experience that is substantially one.

Hence, they developed another classification of the fields of knowledge. Windelband advanced a history/(natural) science or idiographic/nomothetic distinction in his rectoral address at the University of Strasbourg in 1894.[14] This distinction was further extended, analyzed, and refined by Windelband's student and successor, Rickert, in *The Limits of Concept Formation in the Natural Sciences,* published in part in 1896 and in its entirety in 1902.[15] First expounded in 1898, Rickert's somewhat more elaborate classification was published in his *Science and History* in 1902. All four of the Americans reveal a commitment to various features of the Windelband-Rickert Neo-Kantianism, as will be analyzed below.

A full study of the epistemological-methodological views of Park,

Becker, Znaniecki, and Parsons will involve their notions about three topics: the nature and acquisition of knowledge generally, the classification of the basic fields of knowledge and sociology's place in that classification, and methodology generally and especially typology and "understanding."

Ideas about the Nature and Acquisition of Knowledge Generally. Because the question is ultimately whether or not the four Americans' ideas are derived from or basically coincide with those of the German Neo-Kantians, the latters' notions about the nature and acquisition of knowledge must be the point of departure. Kant and the Neo-Kantians rejected the empiricists' notion that knowledge is a mere reproduction or picture of experience or experiential reality. What that reality gives us is only single entities or objects that are unique, indeterminate, heterogeneous, and changing manifolds (Rickert [1896] 1902, 36, 37, 38). The orderliness of knowledge thus cannot be a direct reflex of sensory experience with the (phenomenal) world of nature. Knowledge is selectively formed, constructed, and organized by the mind by means of concepts that simplify, select, and abstract from reality. Indeed, reality cannot be known directly, but only indirectly as a construction of mind.

Park argues that only as words, concepts, and a logical order are imposed on and substituted for the actual course of events can stability be established in the general flux of things and events. For him, science is knowledge having some degree of exactness and precision by virtue of the substitution of ideas for concrete reality and of words for things. Ideas are the logical framework of all systematic knowledge (Park 1955, 74, 75).

Both Becker and Znaniecki adopted a similar position. Becker claimed that concepts are needed to master the tangled skein of the senses, the empirical chaos (Becker 1932b, 534).[16] Znaniecki (1934) similarly refers to concrete reality as (descriptively) inexhaustible or infinite (8–11). Only by adopting the principle (concept?) of the closed system (of a limited number of interrelated elements) can the bewildering mass of empirical data be confronted and investigated (11–14).

In Parsons's case, Neo-Kantianism remains more implicit than explicit. Parsons rejects empiricism and positivism, as do the Neo-Kantians. Though he does not allude to the chaos of concrete reality, he denies that knowledge can be based on "pure sense data," "raw experience" apart from a conceptual scheme or theory. Through the use of certain adjectives, Parsons ([1937] 1968, 18–30, 732) goes back beyond Rickert to suggest that he is making claims bearing a strong resemblance to those Kant made for his a priori categories—that they are "indispensable [and universal?] principles" underlying all knowledge.[17]

In sum, Park, Becker, and Znaniecki adopt a stance about reality and knowledge akin to that of the Neo-Kantians. Parsons is similar, but with a difference.

Conceptions of the Fields of Knowledge and of Sociology's Place. Park and Becker both used Windelband's history/science dichotomy as their point of departure. Park's first chapter in his and Burgess's *Introduction to the Science of Sociology* contains extensive selections from Windelband's 1894 University of Strasbourg rectoral address, parts of which Park translated into English. According to Windelband, history endeavors to portray events as individual and unique; they are revived by the historian in all of their particularity, individuality, and vividness. By contrast, science seeks to formulate laws. It is interested in the repeated and recurrent, the class or general from which a type may be deduced. It searches for universal laws that the timeless changes of events embody as rules. It creates a system of abstract concepts in which the true nature of things is conceived to exist.

In this classification, then, Park infers that sociology is to be construed as a natural science, in contrast to history. As such, it will deal with things or objects that as natural phenomena (according to Rickert) will be characterized by a certain rule or law in terms of which they change. It will classify its objects (e.g., human nature, groups, institutions) and devise general categories, classes, types, along with their subvarieties. What is unique and unclassifiable must be disregarded (Park 1952, 202). Comparison inevitably reveals that the individual as a case is an example of a class (Park 1952, 239).

In both the Barnes, Becker, and Becker 1940 and Becker 1950 volumes, Becker acknowledges that his conception of sociology is based on the Windelband-Rickert nomothetic/idiographic dichotomy. Thus, history deals with events in all their uniqueness, "thisness," nonrepeatability (Becker 1950, 95). But science studies the general. For Becker, sociology is committed to the study of the general in social phenomena through the construction of types as based on (specific) culture case studies. (Admittedly, Becker's adoption of prediction as the goal of his science reveals an accommodation with positivism.[18] Nevertheless, Becker is basically a Neo-Kantian, and by acknowledging that his generalizing discipline entails interpretation ("understanding"), it implicitly accepts a place as one of Rickert's intermediate or mixed types of disciplines.[19]

Although Znaniecki's volume on method curiously attacks the very distinction between the idiographic and the nomothetic (Znaniecki 1934, 21–22), it still assumes that any science is generalizing in character and deals with a particular subject matter, reality, or type of data as a type of closed system. Earlier anticipated in Rickert's second major book (Rickert 1902), the two types of such system, natural and cultural, presuppose a distinction between (natural) objects (which exist independently of human experience) and values (which can exist only in the active experience of some particular people).[20]

Znaniecki holds that each science, whether in the natural or in the cultural realm, will discern an order—in part from empirical evidence and in part in relation to the development of logical classes, categories, or types. His interest in their logical elaboration and refinement testifies to his conception of science as a study of the general and abstract and to his indebtedness to, or amazing congruence with, Neo-Kantianism.

To cast this in different terms, Parsons's position is congruent with, if not derived from, a Neo-Kantian stance. His rejection of empiricism and positivism is unmistakably explicit in his 1937 treatise. He acknowledges the historical significance of Windelband and Rickert in German epistemological-methodological disputes, but without any suggestion of their relevance for his own views (Parsons 1937, 476, 580, 595).

His basic conception of the sciences involves a division between the historical and the analytical sciences. His interest lies in the second, which are subdivided into three general theoretical systems: those of nature, action, and culture. Each is distinctly defined in relation to space and time. Manifestly, Parsons is primarily concerned with action that is not distinctively spatial but involves time in relation to means and ends.[21] Certainly, Parsons's general conceptions are compatible with, if not indusputably derivable from, Neo-Kantian premises.

Finally, Sorokin's conception of sociology as a generalizing social science is predicated on the tenability of Rickert's distinction between generalizing and individualizing disciplines or sciences. The distinction is fundamental to Sorokin's arguments in *Society, Culture, and Personality* (7).

Thus, Neo-Kantianism or its American counterpart has had a heretofore unrecognized impact on the conception of sociology in American sociology.

Notions of a Specifically Sociological Method or Methods. In accordance with his notion of sociology as a generalizing science, Park held that sociology would have its distinctive general objects, such as personalities, groups, societies, and institutions, each with its major species or types and minor subtypes. Each such social object-type would be established by comparative study. The distinctiveness of each such object would be revealed, as Rickert had claimed, in the rule or law by which it moves or changes. It would exhibit an inherent tendency to change—as a series of stages of growth, or what Greek philosophers called its *physis*. Thus, comparison and abstraction will divulge, for a gang, a sect, a plantation, a strike, a revolution, or race relations, an intrinsic pattern of successive and irreversible stages. Presumably, therefore, it should be possible, given knowledge of the actual circumstances, to predict the typical next stage or stages. (However, Park's awareness of arguments about external versus internal social change theories might have disposed him to have less than complete confidence at the end of his career in the notion of change just presented. (See Park 1952, 224, 229.)

During the mid to late 1920s, Park also acknowledged that interpretation and understanding had a legitimate methodological role in accounting for inter- and multipersonal relations in addition to the explanation of a generalizing natural-scientific sociology.[22]

A former student of Park at Chicago who later played an important part in introducing Max Weber to American sociology, Howard P. Becker was the only one of the American Neo-Kantians who accepted Weber's notion of the ideal type (but recast as the constructed type) in his conception of the logic of method or procedure. According to Becker (1950, 127), the type is "a conscious, planned selection, combination, and accentuation of the 'empirically given,' relatively free from value-judgment." Based on the culture case study, the type is a generalizing device, the scope of which depends on comparisons in terms of increasing numbers of (varied) cases. Clearly, Becker envisages the use of types in relation to actors, social structures, social change, values, and the sociocultural context, of varying generality. It is entirely evident that he regarded typology as intrinsically interrelated with interpretation, but, curiously, he never genuinely defined "interpretation." But it is inextricably connected with "understanding" in the several senses of VERSTEHEN in Dilthey and Weber.[23]

By contrast, Parsons, the most famous exponent of Weberian social action sociology, rejects Weber's ideal types for the analytical element, which he contrasts with class universals. He contends that the appropriate categories of his action frame of reference (e.g., means, ends, conditions, norms) are to be conceived as analytical elements, because each refers to a general property. What is observed in a concrete case or instance is only a particular value (a single variation) in such case or instance (Parsons [1937] 1968, 34–35). In contrast, analytical elements are universal in that they refer to properties or qualities of objects rather than to a class of objects.

Parsons ([1937] 1968) especially objects to type concepts, because a separate type is required, he claims, "for every possible combination of relations between the values of the relevant elements" (618, 621). As additional empirical cases are studied, more and more sharply and narrowly defined types are demanded. Ultimately, a methodological atomism may result. What are needed are not types but analytical elements and laws (628).

Znaniecki represents still another variation in the use of a method to achieve a generalizing science of sociology. Unlike Parsons, he accepts the type, but not the Weberian ideal type, and rejects any resort to understanding (or *verstehen*). He proposes to devise types as concepts in the sociocultural realm using a procedure he terms "analytic induction."

As opposed to enumerative induction, analytic induction abstracts out only those general, generic features that are essential (in this case, to the type). Such a type derives from a typical or eidetic case serving "to determine a class" and "to define it comprehensively" (Znaniecki 1934, 251). The types or classes are of varying generality. Eventually, they will be related to one another and arranged in a hierarchy in a comprehensive system of classification. That system will in turn involve static laws of functional dependence and dynamic laws of genesis, as are yielded by empirical research.

Although Znaniecki accepts vicarious experience, he rejects "understanding" and "interpretation" because they are to be identified with subjectivity. He even insists that observation is appropriate in the cultural sciences. It is objective, though not sensory, because it deals with objective systems (of values).[24]

Conclusions and Implications. Briefly, then, the construction of types represents the form of conceptualization advocated by the American exponents of Neo-Kantianism, even though they display considerable variation. Such type construction must ultimately be viewed from the Kantian premise that knowledge is selectively formed, constructed, and organized by the mind. Empirical reality is a heterogeneous amalgam in constant flux. Thus, Park's types are types of natural social objects significant to his notion of sociology as a generalizing or nomothetic discipline. Becker's constructed types are of varying generality based on values explicit or implicit in the culture case studies. Both he and Znaniecki in effect followed Rickert in associating sociology as a nomothetic discipline with a domain of values (i.e., culture) rather than with things or objects (i.e., biophysical nature). Znaniecki used typical or eidetic cases to select the features common to, distinctive of, and thus essential to classes or categories of a closed system. Parsons alone rejects typology (or at least that based on Weber's ideal types) but divides the sciences into the analytical and the historical. Sociology, one of the analytical sciences, studies action, which is formulable as a theoretical system.

Put very simply, the Neo-Kantian notion of sociology as a nomothetic generalizing discipline renders sociology more like a natural science and less at odds with the prevailing qualified empiricist and neo-positivist stance in American sociology than the neo-idealist view. This latter view tended to link sociology with the humanities and with a divergent emphasis on subjectivity, consciousness, and interpretive understanding versus objective explanation and prediction. However, both stances can be understood only in relation to the rise of a dominant, statistics-oriented, qualified empiricist and neo-positivist epistemology-methodology, which itself emerged as a response to the earlier concern with research at the end of World War I.

SUMMARY OF
EPISTEMOLOGICAL-METHODOLOGICAL DEVELOPMENTS

Background Considerations

Two major indications of this preoccupation with research at the end of the second decade of the twentieth century can be cited. One is Thomas and Znaniecki's *The Polish Peasant in Europe and America* (1918–20), which is often regarded as the first major piece of empirical research in American sociology. The second is the American Sociological Society's Committee on Social Research, which under its chairman, John L. Gillin, was on the verge of issuing several reports. When these appeared, they disclosed, among other things, sociologists' alarm at the low esteem in which their field was held by several of the natural sciences and certain of the more established social sciences. And some sociologists apparently concluded that the low status was due especially to the failure of their field to produce research.

The ensuing preoccupation with research had many ramifications. It provoked an effort to define research as a particular kind of inquiry or study. It stimulated an interest in science and its method in general, as well as in more specialized procedures or techniques that were particularly applicable to the problems and data of sociology and allied fields (e.g., the comparative method of anthropology; the historical method of history; the social survey, case method, and statistics from social work). Ultimately, it generated a basic epistemological-methodological dispute.

Indeed, by the early 1930s, controversy over the advantages and disadvantages, the assets and liabilities, of statistics and case study had so intensified and expanded that the outlines of several distinctive epistemological-methodological stances could be discerned. The protagonists of the first stance, which we have characterized as a statistically oriented, qualified empiricist, and neo-positivist epistemological-methodological position, included Lundberg, along with Chapin, Ogburn, Rice, Bain, and Bernard. This position became the predominant one, though it was especially contested by Park, Howard P. Becker, MacIver, Znaniecki, Parsons, and Sorokin. But their opposition actually embraces two other related and yet distinctive orientations, which were anticipated in earlier German philosophy and social science. One involves what we have characterized as an American counterpart of German neo-idealism, as articulated by Dilthey and as represented here by Cooley and MacIver. The other is an American counterpart of German Neo-Kantianism, as articulated by Windelband and Rickert and as represented here by Park, Becker, Znaniecki, the early Parsons, and possibly even Sorokin. (Caveat: None of the three positions just noted is characterized by intricate and logically elaborated expositions as might now be expected.)

Similarities and Dissimilarities in the Three Epistemological-Methodological Stances

To a considerable extent, the three positions—and especially the first versus the other two—arose in a more or less polemical relationship. On some questions or issues, the neo-idealists and Neo-Kantians held the same positions, whereas they differed on others. Both stances pervasively opposed the dominant statistically oriented, qualified empiricist, and neo-positivist stance.[25] Their positions can be summarized in relation to the following six basic issues.

1. Neo-positivists, neo-idealists, and Neo-Kantians disagreed over the implications of the differences between natural and social realities for the study of the latter. The neo-positivists argued that whatever the differences may be, they are not sufficient to bar the studies of the latter from using the methods and techniques of the former. Lundberg contends that the alleged basic differences of the social from the biophysical are actually only apparent. Rice argues, conversely, that social phenomena have heretofore unnoted resemblances with natural phenomena, and vice versa. Accordingly, they minimize the significance of differences and thus deny the propriety of any basic classificatory separation of the sciences of the two domains.

Contrarily, Cooley and MacIver adhere to Dilthey's neo-idealist views, emphasizing the differences between the (nonconscious, materal) sphere of nature and the (conscious, mental) sphere of human inter- and multipersonal relationships. Dilthey bifurcated knowledge into the two domains of the natural sciences and the mental or humanistic studies. Cooley similarly separated two realms of knowledge, one yielding "spatial-material knowledge," and the other "personal-social knowledge." In MacIver's case, a demarcation of the physical, chemical, and organic (concerned with invariant sequence, concomitance, and functional interdependence) from that of conscious being (involving the whys of objective, motivation, and patterning) is implied. Epistemological and methodological differences follow for Cooley and MacIver, as for Dilthey.

Park, Becker, Znaniecki, and Parsons more or less concur in the Neo-Kantianism of Windelband and Rickert, which arose especially in reaction to Dilthey's neo-idealism. Park accepted Windelband's history/natural science (idiographic/nomothetic) dichotomy, allocating sociology to science. Becker also regarded sociology as a generalizing or nomothetic discipline, but he further specified that it studies both (human) action and values (thus agreeing with Dilthey, on the one hand, and Rickert, on the other). Znaniecki adhered to a notion of social science and sociology as nomothetic. He also accepted Rickert's distinction between natural objects and (human) values, with sociology thus falling into the cultural, rather than the natural, realm of closed systems. Finally, Parsons differentiated the historical from the analytical sciences. The latter involve those closed theoretical systems dealing with nature, action, and culture, each apparently to be studied separately. Although all four sociologists concurred in construing sociology as a generalizing or nomothetic discipline, they disagreed over the issue of whether the nature of the social domain implied or required a distinctive epistemology-methodology. Two (Park and Znaniecki) argued negatively, whereas Becker and Parsons argued positively (by way of *verstehen,* or understanding).

2. Nevertheless, both the neo-idealists and the Neo-Kantians were disinclined to accept the possibility or desirability of any reduction of all reality to a (monistic) unity. Some of the extreme positivists were disposed to endorse a basic physicalist-notion of all reality, including the social. Neo-idealists and Neo-Kantians rejected any such disposition.

3. From their disagreements over the implications of the differences between natural and social reality, it follows that the several stances also differed over how knowledge of social reality might be obtained. Neo-positivists held that reliable knowledge of the social domain is to be secured in the same way as knowledge of the natural domain is, by sensory experience, albeit a qualified empiricism. (The most important qualification involved the mediation of human perceptions by and through language symbols.) But the neo-idealists and Neo-Kantians rejected empiricism as an adequte theory for gaining knowledge of nature or human interpersonal relations.

Clearly, Cooley and MacIver essentially invoke equivalents of Dilthey's neo-idealist epistemology, which argues that one knows others only as one understands them. Such understanding is gained by the use of one's own imagination, in relation to one's past experience, to try to relive and reconstruct the feelings and experiences of others. Dilthey had used such German phrases as *sich übertragen* (to transpose oneself), *sich hineinversetzen* (to put oneself in the place of another), *nacherleben* (to relive an experience), and *nachbilden* (to reconstruct imaginatively). Only as the life position of another is adopted—as empathic identification and a virtual reenactment of his or her mental processes are achieved—is such understanding acquired. Manifestly, Cooley's "instructed imagination" or "sympathetic introspection" and MacIver's "imaginative or sympathetic reconstruction" are substantially equivalent.

4. Within the context of American sociology, the American version of Neo-Kantianism seems to have had a major advantage over neo-idealism. It explicitly promoted the comparative case study as a qualitative inductive means of generalization (e.g., by Park, Becker, and Znaniecki, though Coo-

ley had set the precedent). More precisely, the comparative study of cases in conjunction with the construction of types permitted generalization, though the terms *law* and *universal* were hardly conspicuous. At the same time, at least some of the American Neo-Kantians (e.g., Becker and Parsons) also could invoke Dilthey's "understanding" (*verstehen*) by way of Weber. By implication, at least, most Neo-Kantians conceived of sociology as a generalizing discipline devoted to the study of a cultural and historical subject matter. But perhaps only Znaniecki, in *The Method of Sociology,* approached the kind of logically integrated notion of sociology that a Neo-Kantian such as Rickert would have endorsed.

5. The several positions have different views of the nature and role of concepts. The neo-positivists envisage sociological concepts as stable, objective, operationalized terms akin to those in the physical sciences. For the neo-idealists and Neo-Kantians (except for Znaniecki), concepts are much more temporary and immediately relevant to particular and specific inquiries. The type was apparently the model concept—whether ideal, constructed, or eidetic. Becker, for instance, used Weber's ideal type as his point of departure, but recast as the constructed type for generalizing culture case studies. For Znaniecki, the typical or eidetic case incorporates the common and distinctive as the essential of a given class or category; the categories could be arranged in various grades of generality and specificity in a comprehensive system of classification.

6. For neo-positivists, research procedure became crucially significant in the conception of science. Research was to be conducted in accordance with a prescribed, standardized model. Induction, quantification, statistics, mensurative and scalar techniques, and the elaboration of increasingly complex instrumentation were demanded. Objectivity, precision, reliability, verifiability, predictability, and especially utility were held to be the characteristic assets of research conducted in accordance with the model of scientific method.

With all of this and the supporting assumptions, the neo-idealists and Neo-Kantians disagreed vigorously. Most of them would have concurred with Cooley, for instance, in his declaration that the "sooner we [in the social sciences] cease circumscribing and testing ourselves by the canons of physical and psychological science the better" (Cooley [1902] 1964, 121; Cooley [1918] 1966, 397). Exact "prediction or control" is a "false ideal inconsiderately borrowed from the provinces of physical science" (Cooley [1918] 1966, 398). The true aim of social science is "not . . . to bring society within the sphere of arithmetic," however important precision may be in preparing data (Cooley 1966, 398). As indicated earlier in this chapter, MacIver rejected the view that induction is the sole, legitimate process of passing from particulars to the general. He decried any notion of science as concerned only with statements of association or correlation. Rather, the objective of science is to relate a phenomenon to a system of relations, to offer explanation or interpretation, and to specify causation. He and Znaniecki denied that quantification and measurement were crucial and indispensable for inductive generalization and science. Certainly, then, it follows that neo-idealists and Neo-Kantians would have rejected what the neo-positivists regarded as concomitant assets of research pursued by their model of science.

Manifestly, then, basic and major differences existed over the central issues of epistemology and methodology in American sociology during the 1930s and 1940s. Dominant and minority viewpoints have been differentiated, with the dominant represented by a statistically-oriented, qualified empiricist neo-positivism[26] and the minority by American versions or counterparts of German neo-idealism and German Neo-Kantianism.

It is important to note that all three of these epistemological-methodological stances concurred in the significance of research for sociological knowledge. After 1940, research was assumed to be a requisite of any "sound theory." Such an assumption henceforth distinctively sets theory apart from what it had been during the earlier or founding period.

By the late 1930s and early 1940s, the dominant stance had acquired such hegemony in the field that it set the legitimating criteria (or norms) for undertaking valid sociological research. And surely during the 1940s it was becoming, if it had not already become, epistemologically-methodologically foundational. The two minority stances were overwhelmingly ignored and consigned to a pariah status.

With this background as context, it is now feasible to examine the nature of social ontological theory as it can be inferred from the texts and other evidence in the decade or so immediately following World War I. Manifestly, the most conspicuous continuity is to be found in social evolutionary theory. Our analysis of this stance extends through the next three chapters, each treating a separate problematic subdomain. The sequence does involve a "logic," but one that the passage of time and the change in both popular and scientific assumptions have now tended to obscure. Readers who experience difficulties with the early portions of chapter 3 may find that a careful reading of the section "The Pre–World War I Theory of Social Evolution of American Sociologists" in chapter 4 helps them reestablish contact with the more common features of social evolution and also provides a helpful overview of social evolution generally.

PART II: CONTINUITIES (WITH FIRST-PERIOD THEORY)

Chapter 3

Social Evolutionism, Social Origins, and Social Structure

Although the term *social evolution* is especially associated with social change, it applies equally to social origins and social structure. Its continuity from the first to the second period is evident in all three problem-domains, albeit with differences in its form and elaboration in the two periods. Indeed, the social evolutionary accounts of the second period are substantially more oblique, fragmentary, qualified, and diffuse, even residual, than those of the first period.

The following six textbooks by sociologists can be characterized as being more or less social evolutionary in character: Ellwood's *The Psychology of Human Society* (1925), Lumley's *Principles of Sociology* (1928), MacIver's *Society* (1931c), Hankins's *An Introduction to the Study of Society* (1928), Bernard's *An Introduction to Sociology* (1942), and Ogburn and Nimkoff's *Sociology* (1940). It is important to point out that the social evolutionism of Bernard and Ogburn began in articles or books in the early to mid 1920s. Essentially, then, social evolutionary theory continued only up to the early 1930s.

Basically, the inquiry of this chapter will center on what exactly constituted the social evolutionary theories of social origins and social structure of the first period and what the evidence is for their continuity into the second, using data especially from the volumes just cited. But because theories of social origins and structure were predicated on, and essentially derived from, a more general and generic conception of evolutionary process, the tenets of evolutionary naturalism will first be briefly outlined, with examples. The last half of this chapter will examine the circumstances undermining the tenability of the two (sub-) theories, with those about social origins considered last by virtue of their greater complexity.

Evolutionary Naturalism, Social Forces, and Social Origins

Because it is important to know to what extent the social evolutionism of the second period is genuinely similar to that of the first, it is appropriate to begin by a study of the commitment to evolutionary naturalism, which had been the intellectual foundation of the social evolutionism of the first period.[1] It appears that evolutionary naturalism as a generic ontological stance—with its three basic tenets—continued to exercise considerable influence throughout the 1920s, 1930s, and 1940s. Ellwood, Hankins, and Bernard are three well-known theorists who adhered to all three tenets. But a number of theorists did not. The first tenet continued to enjoy widespread acceptance throughout the field, but the second received somewhat less support, and the third least.

The first tenet asserts that it is possible and desirable to offer a naturalistic rather than a supernaturalistic explanation of social or societal phenomena. Humankind and social phenomena are construed as a domain in and of nature, just as the inorganic and organic generally were. The domains are somewhat separable from each other, each constituted by its own distinctive forces and each with its own regularities and laws. Each domain has become the object of study of a distinct science. Each can be approached, studied, and explained naturalistically rather than supernaturalistically.

Hankins (1928, 18–19) declares that the scientific stance relies characteristically on "natural or efficient causes" as opposed to magical or spiritual forces or entities. It repudiates any quest for first causes or origins as contrary to its (naturalistic) conception of the "universe as a self-regulating system of interacting bodies and forces." Assuming also that social phenomena are a separate domain within nature, society should be explicable in terms of its own internal forces rather than those that are external. Furthermore, given the same kind of regularity and uniformity of causes prevailing in other domains, the social domain should eventually be susceptible to a formulation of its own scientific laws (18–19).

Very different in their sociological stances, Ellwood (1925) and Bernard (1942) apparently endorse the same position. In restricting science to the study of conditions under which a phenomenon appears in experience, Ellwood (1925) clearly seems to be implying naturalism rather than supernaturalism (1–2). And he insists that a science of social phenomena is as legitimate as a science of physical phenomena (2). Bernard (1942) also alludes to nature as comprised of different realms of phenomena, the cosmic, organic, mental, and social. Each presumably has its own regularities and modes of evolution, implying a naturalistic approach and explanation.

Reuter and Hart (1933) do hold that the various sciences have their own domains of natural process within which and about which they seek to formulate scientific laws (87, 8–12, 6). For its part, sociology "undertakes to isolate and define the processes of social interaction" and seeks "to explain personality, social behavior, and the evolution of social organization" (12). Presumably, it too seeks to formulate distinctive naturalistic laws.[2]

Admittedly, the examples of adherence to the first tenet are fragmentary. However, these defects are mitigated by additional data below.

Though their numbers are apparently fewer, some sociologists explicitly (and some implicitly) committed themselves to the second tenet, the doctrine of continuity and, more precisely, the notion of genetic filiation, which asserts that each domain in the hierarchy of phenomena is derivable from the previous one, up to and including the human social and cultural domain. Hankins, Ellwood, and Bernard are so committed.

Hankins (1928, 33) noted that when the hierarchy of phenomena is viewed from top to bottom (from the psychic, social, and cultural down to the physical and chemical), each domain is more comprehensive and "more elementary" than the prior one. Conversely, as the levels are ascended, the phenomena become less simple, less general, and "more complex and more specific" (33). More importantly, each level can be conceived as the basis of the one above it and as deriving from the one beneath it (33).

For Ellwood, each level is affected by all the prior domains, but most importantly by the one immediately below it. Geographic factors play the major part in organic evolution, which in turn plays the major part in psychic evolution (though in conjunction with geographic conditions). As Ellwood (1925, 42) notes, "organic evolution must affect social evolution, but . . . these forces are modified by mental evolution, or mental life." Indeed, organic evolution affects the cultural traits of human society only indirectly, because it affects mainly "the physical and hereditary traits of human society only indirectly" by way of "the physical and hereditary traits of man" (42). In contrast, cultural evolution primarily concerns the mental and acquired traits of human beings (42).

Bernard (1942) is relatively direct in his acceptance of continuity and genetic filiation across the various domains of evolution. He remarks that the "general line of evolutionary development has been from the cosmic through the organic or biological to the mental and the social types," all of which are "closely interrelated" (351). If living forms "have evolved from non-living forms of matter," organic evolution must be a "continuation of cosmic evolution, or a special division or aspect of cosmic evolution" (36). In turn, mental evolution "is a continuation of organic evolution and a higher form of it" (360). Finally, "social evolution is a natural and continuous growth of both organic and mental evolution" (360). Bernard, in effect, denies the absence of major continuity between any two levels of phenomena or types of evolution. "So far as we can ascertain, all phenomena of whatever type have grown out of the same general evolutionary process, and homo sapiens and his culture are the highest products that have so far appeared on earth" (360).

Note that the related sciences in the hierarchies are not all of equal import, irrespective of the immediate genetic (or engendering) proximity of the related phenomena. Biology was of major consequence for sociology.

Following Darwinian (and Spencerian) views of organic evolution, the third tenet held that human association (in any aggregate in a given environment) is to be explained ultimately as an effective adaptation to the conditions of existence. This idea is manifested in the theories of social origins, social structure or organization, and social change. Its presence is likely to be signaled by the use of certain characteristic words that are to be found in the texts of Lumley, Bernard, Ellwood, and Hankins.

Some of the more common of these terms are *adaptation, struggle for existence, survival,* and *selection.* So Lumley (1928) declares that "society, social processes, social institutions, social organizations . . . are man's method of survival, of adaptation" (429). The various components of culture evolve through three processes, one of which is selection. Bernard (1942) holds similarly that culture—whether mechanically (overtly or performatively) behavioral, symbolically behavioral, or social organizational—is a distinctively man-made adjustment (727, 729–31). Like organic traits, it is subject to selection (751). According to Ellwood (1925), interaction among members of a group must lead to coadaptation and coordination of their activities so that a common aim is achievable (147). Persisting coordinations or coadaptations are the social organization (150). All social evolution must operate within the limits of heredity and selection as set by organic evolution, which, if they are exceeded, will eliminate sociocultural forms just as surely as an unadapted species of plant or animal will fail to survive (65). For Hankins (1928), the various aspects of culture represent different modes of an aggregate's behavioral adaptation to aspects of its physical and social environment (380–81). Just as the environment of particular animals subjects them to a struggle for existence and requires adaptation, so the habitat of society sets conditions to which its customs must "facilitate" (or positively provide) adaptation. If its customs fail in this task, they "and the people who practice them perish" (29).

Clearly, then, the authors' commitments to the various features of evolutionary naturalism vary. Similarly, an adherence to social evolutionism does not mean that each of its three problem domains is treated, or, if they are, that they are treated in equal detail or complexity of formulation. Lumley includes a chapter entitled "Social Origins." Ellwood's text has a section entitled "The Origins of Human Society," and Hankins's text a section entitled "Gregariousness in Man, Consciousness of Kind, and Group Formation." MacIver's *Society* contains an account of human social and societal genesis, but without explicit designation as such, and MacIver later denies the legitimacy of the problem. Reuter and Hart's text, which is not committed to social evolutionism, includes a section called "The Basis of Group Life."[3]

Other textbooks not explicitly included as part of this study also deal with origins. Case devoted all of part 2 (twelve chapters) of his *Outlines of Introductory Sociology* (1924) to social origins. Blackmar and Gillin's *Outlines of Sociology* (1915) had a chapter entitled "Social Origins."

Certainly, a problem as basic and important as origins would likely be included at least in the more differentiated academic curricula of the larger universities in the period. Lee Harvey's listing "Courses Offered in Sociology by the Department of Sociology and Anthropology," regarding the University of Chicago, in appendix 4 of his *Myths of the Chicago School of Sociology* (1987, 256) indicates that a course called "Social Origins" was introduced in 1913. It was taught by Thomas from 1914 to 1917; for 1918 and 1919, no instructor was specified. Faris offered the course from 1920 to 1924, when it was last listed.

Thus, interest in social origins is manifestly evident. It is undeniably present in second-period American sociology and sociological theory.

Social Origins Theory of the First Period

Because continuity between the first and second periods is at issue, it becomes necessary to indicate just how the evolutionary account of social origins was envisaged generally during the first. *Founding Theory of American Sociology* (Hinkle 1980) advises that a social evolutionary theory of origins was an intrinsic part of a comprehensive naturalistic ontology, otherwise characterized as "evolutionary naturalism" with its three major tenets. Each of the three tenets has continued into the second period, as noted above.

But the notion that each domain of nature is a domain of forces and the application of the notion of forces to the social domain as "social forces" have not yet been explained. As biopsychic human-nature forces, the social forces are of the utmost significance. They are an indispensable link between humankind as one kind of organism with organisms generally, on the one hand, and with what is peculiar and distinctive about human association, on the other.

In actuality, the conceptualization of social forces was more complex in early American sociology than has just been indicated. According to Hinkle 1980, three varieties of social forces—as the factors, causes, determinants, conditions, variables, or influences affecting human association, social existence, and society—can be identified (68–69). One is the "largely, (though not entirely) extra-human (or sub-psychic) and essentially *biophysical* forces, determinants, or conditions" (69). Another (a second, and by far the most common) variety is constituted of "the pan-human, universal and more or less original (human) nature or *biopsychic* forces" (69). The third is a set of forces also human but "interactionally or societally engendered (or derived) as *(personal) incentives and (impersonal) mechanisms*" maintaining "association in general and a specific set or structure of social relations in particular" (69). Of these three varieties, the second was most commonly regarded as *the* set of social forces.[4]

Ward, Sumner, Keller, Ross, and Small had notions of social forces or their equivalent. Neither Giddings nor Cooley invoked a conventional doctrine of social forces, though Cooley's primary ideals and sentiments seem similar.

For early American sociology, the paramount question was whether the social forces prompted permanent human association (i.e., the formation of societies) before or after hominoids had become hominids. Two types of origins theories emerged. One, propounded by Sumner, Ward, and Ross, claimed that hominoids had become organically human first, and that a state of permanent association developed only later out of the evolutionary relation of the social forces to the existing conditions of existence. This earlier majority position might be characterized as a "post-organic" social origins stance (i.e., social origins occurred after the hominoid stock had definitely become organically [genetically] human or hominid).

The second kind of origins theory, argued by Giddings, Small, and Cooley, held that humankind had organically descended from animal (primate?) ancestors who had already existed in a state of more or less permanent association. This position might be characterized as a "pre-organic" social origins stance. According to its views, humankind had always lived in a state of permanent association or society.

Social Origins Theory of the Second Period

Among second-period theorists, Keller, Lumley, and Blackmar and Gillen represent the post-organic social origins theory position. As a follower and protagonist of Sumner after World War I, Keller (in Sumner and Keller 1927) contended that human hunger and sex-love (two of Sumner's four socializing forces) "jointly impel to association" or produce "original association" (1:24, 26). (Man was not "outfitted with any innate quality of sociability implanted in his germ-plasm." The "tendency to associate is acquired rather than [being] inherited" or "hereditary in the race" from the outset (1:11, 13).

Keller's notion of the social (or socializing) forces derives entirely from Sumner's conception presented in the latter's *Folkways* (1907). In contrast to Ellwood, Keller's notion excludes the non-human physical and organic. The original or primary forces are hunger and sex (-love), both of which are regarded as instinctive. Vanity and (ghost-) fear are derived or secondary; they are not instinctive or primordial, for they do not produce association or society. Rather, they sustain or hold society together (Sumner and Keller 1927, 25, 26).

Lumley basically borrowed his conception of a division of social forces into original factors and derived factors from Ellwood (1925, 71–78). But Ellwood's treatment of original factors has been subject to some condensation and simplification. Lumley introduced additions to the analysis of derivative factors, using Sumner's classification of socializing forces to categorize desires, Thomas's schema of the four wishes to classify the latter, Park and Burgess's notion of attitude to implement the idea of sentiment as an enduring attitude, Small's six types of interests, and Bougle's notion of value (Lumley 1928, 75–76).

Blackmar and Gillin ([1915] 1923) also accept the view that permanent human association evolved after the humanoid stock had become organically human. They refer to "the various forces influencing the formation and development of society" in connection with their exposition of their conception of the social (or socializing) forces (310).

Their typology of social forces, which is also a comprehensive notion, includes four major varieties (309–40). Their category 1 is equatable with the domain of the extrahuman variety from above (e.g., climate, soil, topography, flora, fauna); their category 3, with the biopsychic (human nature) social forces, some of which (e.g., the appetitive) are instinctive, some of which [e.g., the egotic] are instinctive-social, and still others of which [e.g., the religious] are instinctive-cultural; and their category 4, with the interactively developed and engendered social forces (e.g., the economic). Blackmar and Gillin appear to be substantially indebted to Ross for their subclassifications of categories 3 and 4. Their category 2 refers to external social factors, such as the presence or absence of other groups, and their attitudes.

However, it is very clear that Keller's, Lumley's, and Blackmar and Gillin's use of the social forces in conjunction with a post-organic theory of

social origins was not widely shared after 1920. Apparently, even more theorists of the second period accepted the pre-organic social origins stance: that
permanent association, social relations, society had existed before our prehuman ancestors had become organically human. They concurred with Bernard
(1942) that "man has always lived in groups" (129; cf. Hankins 1928, 351,
168). Particularly "in all higher forms of animal life, the isolated and solitary
individual has been an exception" (Ellwood 1925, 51; cf. Reuter and Hart
1933, 115). Indeed, as Barnes ([1927] 1931) remarks, "the isolated individual
as separate from society . . . is not to be discovered anywhere in the world of
actual fact" (41). Reuter and Hart (1933) comment that the "prehuman ancestors of man lived an associated life" and the "immediate ancestors of the modern races of man lived in groups" (115). Certainly, modern humans—Hankins
(1928) insists—but also prehistoric and even paleolithic humans "have always
lived in groups" (168, 351). A "developed form of human association" which
is thus strictly speaking "without an independent origin," human society "must
be regarded as an inheritance from man's prehuman progenitors" (Ellwood
1925, 57). MacIver's (1931c, 20) insistence that "men did not become individuals first and then members of society" has its equivalent in Ellwood's (1925,
51) declaration that any assumption that human social groups originated
"through the coming together of individuals who developed in isolation or separateness" is in error. Hankins (1928, 351) avers that the human "tendency
toward association" arose from the "necessities of life"—not from anything
accidental or intentional. Barnes ([1927] 1931, 42) holds that human society is
based on organic impulses related to sex that "long antedate man himself,"
"inherent sociability," and the recognition of advantage of cooperation after
birth. Even Thomas (1923, 42) declared that "men have always lived together
in groups," though his scheme of the four wishes seems to have arisen from
different assumptions. And Reuter and Hart (1933, 115) assert categorically
that "all human life is group life." It appears, then, that most theorists of the
second period accepted the pre-organic social origins stance—that is, that permanent association, social relations, and society had existed before our prehuman ancestors had become organically human.

Conception of Social Structure in the Second Period

Manifestly, the problems of origins and structure were not arbitrarily
separated. Indeed, pursuit of the problem of sociocultural origins up to and
including persistent, continuous, permanent social existence is finally to
broach the problem of social structure. Of necessity, it involves the nature of
human society and its constituent groups or, perhaps more appropriately, the
group, one of whose varieties is society. Interestingly, the notion of a group
became central during the second period.

What most distinctively makes a human group a group (or a society a society) is its possession of a modicum of organization. It is not the plurality or numerousness of units, their aggregation in space, or their being conceived to belong together because they have one or more common characteristics, a common culture, or ability to communicate—all of these are prerequisites—but it is their organization that seems most decisive. Organization means that their "relations" and "interactions" are defined, regularized, reciprocally ordered, and predictable. It means order and orderliness. It means that the group is a whole, or a unity of parts that are interrelated, coordinated, or coadapted to one another and the external world. For first-period social evolutionism, organization meant enhanced adaptation and chances of social survival.

Only five of the second-period textbooks contain what might be regarded as at least preliminary definitions of social organization. Two of the authors, Ellwood and Lumley, are social evolutionists. According to Ellwood (1925, 150), social organization is the persistent coordinations or coadaptations "among the members of a group, looked at collectively and as forming a system." It is envisaged by Lumley ([1928] 1935, 143) as a social whole or unity composed of cooperating specialized parts fulfilling specialized functions. The remaining authors, Hiller, Young, and Reuter and Hart, are not identified with social evolutionism. Hiller (1933, 27) invokes Sumner's notion of social structure as a set of fixed positions of individuals and subgroups deriving from past interactions and serving the interests of all members of the group. Young (1934, 398) conceives of social organization as the "standard and more or less persistent and continuous forms of interaction by which men living in groups find ways of satisfying their fundamental and acquired needs." Reuter and Hart (1933, 161) are also illuminating when they say that social organization includes "not only the various folk practices, social rules, and institutional structures but also the manner in which they are integrated into a coherent system . . . It is the totality of the social groupings which develop from the interactions of persons and from the interactions of persons and groups." Significantly, except for the last, all of the definitions seem to reflect evolutionary inspirations or derivations.

More detail is now needed. And because this present study is interested in the continuities and discontinuities between first- and second-period American sociological theory, the major features of social structure from the first or founding period warrant consideration as a point of departure. Six features were involved from the first period (Hinkle 1980, 133–46):

1.   Any aggregate of individuals in communication can become organized or structured only as a sense or conception of a larger whole or entity

is engendered—that is, as it has acquired a definite, distinguishable social identity.

2.   Organization tends to entail the emergence of certain common interests, ends, or values with which the group is associated, as well as the definition of certain more concrete or specific ends that are to be sought collectively in given situations.

3.   Although the term *organization* is employed to refer to common ideas, ideals, and notions, feelings, values, and so on, it is more commonly applied to activities, behavior, actions, or interactions of members of groups. Four such meanings can be identified: (a) definiteness, uniformity, stability, and regularity; (b) consistency, compatability, and supportiveness (or complementarity); (c) division of labor, differentiation, and specialization of tasks; and (d) leadership and followership, hierarchy, stratification, and so forth.

4.   Organization also entails rules (implying values) that reflect or embody a notion of general goodwill, good of the whole, commonweal, or societal welfare. These rules include folkways, mores, laws, and institutions.

5.   If organization or structure is to be persistent (and effective), it must be supported by some minimum of conformity with the rules (i.e., social control) and exhibit some minimum of cohesiveness, solidarity, and integration.

6.   And, finally, structure implies a readiness for mobilization of action in the peculiar circumstances of the group's situations.

Of course, these features represent generalizations from the relatively systematically developed notions of first-period theorists as presented in their major works. The textbooks being used as sources of data from the second period were undergoing a transformation from general sociology and sociological theory to introductory texts, with simplification and condensation often occurring. It thus comes as no surprise to discover that the features of organization are presented and discussed much less systematically and coherently, and more simplistically and cryptically, in some instances, in the texts. Two textbooks, Lumley's and Reuter and Hart's, offer comments on five of the six major characteristics of organization. Hiller was next with contributions to three of the six. Other authors were also involved but to a lesser extent. It is noteworthy that Lumley is classifiable as a social evolutionist (as of 1928) but Reuter and Hart and Hiller (as of 1933) are not. Apparently, more minimal contributions were made by those authors associated with social evolutionism.

Of major significance is the fact that a pronounced interest in the classification or typology of groups emerged during the second period. The classifications most commonly invoked in the textbooks were in-groups versus out-groups, primary versus secondary groups, crowds versus publics, types of communities, varieties of social strata (especially castes and classes), and kinds of societies, i.e., nine classes or types. Only in the case of the societal typology were the social evolutionists (i.e., Hankins and Bernard) exclusively involved. And only in the case of the delineation of the characteristics of primary and secondary groups were the contributions of the social evolutionist and non-social-evolutionist authors relatively equal. Otherwise, the non-social-evolutionist authors predominated in the discussion of the characteristics of the remaining seven categories of groups. Still, it is true that Ogburn (who was identified with social evolutionism to some extent) and Nimkoff contributed to a discussion of eight of the nine categories of groups. Among the nonevolutionists, Reuter and Hart contributed to the analysis of the characteristics of nine of the nine categories of groups, Hiller and Sutherland and Woodward to six of the nine, and Young to five of the nine. It is also important to note that a major disparity existed, within the ranks of the evolutionary authors, between the top contribution of Ogburn and Nimkoff (eight of the nine categories) and the next-largest contributions (two each by Ellwood, Bernard, Lumley, and MacIver).

Paradoxically, the sociologists who were explicitly associated with a general theoretical stance were not those substantially involved in explicating the features of social organization and elaborating the social dichotomies and typologies. Indeed, Hankins, Bernard, Lumley, and Ellwood are the only participants whose comments clearly acknowledge a theoretical stance on organization. Lumley, for instance, declared that "society, social processes, social institutions, social organizations . . . are man's method of survival, of adaptation" (Lumley 1928, 429). The various components of culture evolved through three processes, one of which is selection. Bernard (1942, 717, 729–31) held that social organizational culture is a distinctive human adjustment. Like organic traits, it is subject to selection (751). According to Ellwood (1925, 150), persisting coadaptations and coordinations of groups are the social organization. For Hankins (1928, 380–81), the various aspects of culture represent so many different modes of aggregate behavioral adaptation to the physical and social environment of humankind. And Hankins (1928, 29) and Ellwood (1925, 65) agree that social and cultural forms must facilitate adaptation to society's habitat or fail and imperil the survival of those who practice them. Manifestly, Hankins, Bernard, Lumley, and Ellwood accepted an evolutionary (adaptational) notion of social organization or structure.

Conversely, the textbook authors who were most involved in the effort to develop intrasocietal social classifications and typologies were those former students of Park who did not formally endorse or assume a particular theoretical stance. Some evidence thus exists to infer that social evolutionism had become, or was becoming, a stance unwilling or unable generally to encompass the increasing complexity and differentiation of modern social stucture and then-contemporary sociological analysis.

But dissatisfaction with social evolutionism was not confined to its account of social structure. The attack on the evolutionary theory of socio-cultural origins was more direct, extensive, basic, and compelling.

THE DEMISE OF SOCIOCULTURAL ORIGINS AS CONCEIVED BY SOCIOCULTURAL EVOLUTIONISM

After the mid 1930s, the problem of social origins is raised much less frequently in the textbooks. Neither of Hiller's books (1933, 1947) makes explicit refernce to the problem. Young's *An Introductory Sociology* (1934) offers a factual account of "pre-human social life" (3–5), which is repro-duced in his *Sociology: A Study of Society and Culture* (1942, 16–17). But Lumley's second edition ([1928] 1935) and Lundberg's *Foundations of Sociology* (1939b) ignore the problem. Ogburn and Nimkoff's *Sociology* (1940) and Bernard's *An Introduction to Sociology* (1942) either only vaguely allude to the problem or treat it conjecturally. Sutherland and Woodward's *Introductory Sociology* ([1937] 1940) testifies to the increasing recognition of the relation of the cultural to the social in its chapter "The Origins of Culture," which avoids any explicit theoretical commitment. Accordingly, it seems appropriate to raise the problem of how the apparent shift in professional opinion about social origins can be accounted for.

Research on Humankind's Closest Primate Relatives

From the mid 1920s to the early 1930s, research was published on the conditions and characteristics of one category of humankind's nonhuman primate "relatives," the great apes (especially Kohler 1926; Yerkes 1925; Yerkes and Yerkes 1929; Zukerman 1932; and implications from Kellogg and Kellogg 1933). Hankins (1928, 365–66, 383) was the first sociologist to examine the psychological and sociological implications of the similarities between apes and humans as developed in Kohler's and Yerkes's (first) books. Young 1934 provides the first extensive quotation and commentary. Young (1942, 18) remarks that the "apes present us with the basic forms of our own social relations." Young emphasizes the significance of learning and habit formation. Furthermore, the

> dependency of the infant on his group is itself beneficial since this transmission of habits makes it possible for him to short-cut the time

needed to adapt himself to his society. This continuity of habits becomes the most important factor in human social life, making possible new learning as well as furnishing a foundation for adaptation to the environment. (Young 1942, 18)

In view of the enhanced prestige attaching to rigorously established observations such as those in the Kohler, Zuckerman, and Yerkes volumes, along with the general acceptance of a broad organic evolutionism, it would appear that the argument for primate and mammalian derivation of human association could only have become more acceptable in the eyes of sociologists. Certainly this research would have made sociologists' adherence to the pre-organic social origins theory more likely. And by virtue of the increasing acceptance of the pre-organic theory of social origins, which held that humankind had descended from animal ancestors already leading a social existence, the importance of social forces to account for origins at the human level was diminished.

Implications of the Instinct Controversy for Social Origins

It was precisely the alleged interconnection between the organic and the psychic that the controversy over the instincts eventually undermined. This controversy occurred throughout the 1920s but perhaps most intensely from about 1921–25. Actually, the dispute was multidisciplinary, including especially psychologists, some sociologists, and some philosophers.[5] In sociology, it seems to have begun with the publication of L. L. Bernard's paper "The Misuse of Instinct in the Social Sciences" (1921) and Ellsworth Faris's paper "Are Instincts Data or Hypotheses?" (1921). Public debate issued at the session "Psychic Factors in Social Causation," which Ellwood chaired, at the American Sociological Society's annual meeting in 1923. The three main papers were all presented by psychologists: McDougal, Kantor, and F. Allport. Three of the four discussants were sociologists: Bernard, Ogburn, and Bogardus. The fourth was the anthropologist Alexander Goldenweiser. However, the four sociologists especially associated with the dispute for over a decade were Ellwood, Bernard, Hankins, and Faris, each the author of a number of relevant papers.[6]

By virtue of the intellectually and pedagogically important role of the Department of Sociology at the University of Chicago in the discipline in the 1920s through the 1940s, it seems significant that three of the four persons in the long-term dispute had been associated with Chicago at some point in their careers. The one exception was Hankins, one of Giddings's students at Columbia before World War I. (See also Cooley [1920], 1922, 3–34.)

The debate over the instincts had a twofold significance. On the one hand, it demanded that attention be directed to the relations between instincts and the other components of original and acquired human nature, and to possible implications for the nature of the domains of the (human) psychic, social, and cultural. Presumably, concern with any other of the major components of biopsychic (original) human nature, such as innate appetites, needs, wants, cravings, impulses, inclinations, feelings, sentiments, desires, and wishes, might have had similar consequences. But the fact that heredity was regarded as being so important to the character of organic structure and functioning in the general process of organic evolution and especially to speciation would have been especially likely to center attention eventually on the instincts as an important key in human organic and social evolution.

On the other hand, the debate had a major impact on the continuation (and eventual discontinuation) of the effort at, as Read Bain (1929, 101) put it, "explanation from below"—that is, at what would now be termed "reductive" explanations. Put positively, the outcome of the debate was to accentuate the demand for explanation of the social on the level of the social or the psychic and social. In effect, it separated the social from the other domains of phenomena and had major consequences for evolutionary naturalism.

The following is a set of summary conclusions about the positions of the four main contenders in the debate:

1. Only a modicum of consensus existed about the meaning of instinct.
    a. Ellwood, for example, asserts that human behavior is based on certain hereditary or instinctive reaction elements, which
       i.   are universally present in the behavior, under all environmental conditions, of species closely related to humans;
       ii. occur universally in behavior among human beings;
       iii. appear early in childhood before the individual has accumulated experience or been subject to prolonged pressure of the environment; and
       iv. are associated with primary human emotions (e.g., anger, joy, grief, fear), which are universal among all humankind, regardless of culture or specific environment. (Ellwood 1925, 282–83).
    b. By contrast, Bernard argues that a conception of instinct must begin rigorously at the subhuman level. Thus, an instinct
       i.   is a definite and apparently inherited response to a stimulus, a neural behavior mechanism by means of which a "specific and definite response" is elicited by a specific stimulus;
       ii. is differentiated from a reflex by its greater degree of complexity;
       iii. serves "a definite function in the adjustment process";

       iv. is not conscious or purposive and thus cannot involve in its own organization any foresight of ends and cannot control its own organization and functioning in the interest of these ends;

       v. cannot entail any moral or prudential judgment about the worth or value of associated behavior; and

      vi. involves inheritance of a "unit organization of the neurons, the physiological and neurological bases of which lie back of and give form to the activity or resulting behavior." Only the structural organization can be inherited, and be inherited as a unity, and so be an instinct. (See Bernard 1926b, 114, 115, 116, 117, 134.)

Conversely, he contends that fixity, automaticity, unpremeditativeness, vagueness, and impulsiveness do not guarantee that behavior is instinctive. He objects particularly (in contrast to Ellwood 1925, 283) to conceiving of instincts in terms of categories, for they involve a variety of specific behavior from different situations and thus never occur in action together. They "never function as a unit behavior process" as is required for a unit organization of the neurons to be inherited. (Consult Bernard 1926b, 125, 127–28, 133.)

   c. Hankins declares that instincts

       i. are based on innate urges or impulses;

      ii. involve an overt activity that is genetically transmitted;

     iii. are both like and unlike reflexes (like in being like a link in a chain, series, or set, each of which sets off the next, and unlike in the sense of being active rather than passive in seeking its stimulus); and

      iv. are only minimally modifiable or adjustable to new situations. (See Hankins 1928, 335, 334–35.)

   d. Faris also agrees that the model for instincts at the human level is provided by lower animals. Instincts must thus be innate or genetically transmissible complex mechanisms of behavior that are specific and uniform within a given species of organism. (Consult Faris [1937a] 1976, 152, 70, 16; cf. Cooley [1918] 1966, 24.)

2.   Three of the four figures seem to concur that the past loose usage of the notion of instinct undermines its tenability in psychology and sociology. Only Ellwood refuses to indict past usage. (See Bernard 1924; Bernard 1926b esp. 129–32.) Both Hankins (1928, 333–34) and Faris ([1937a] 1976, 141, 61–65) cite Bernard's study of the instincts and agree with the implications he draws.

3.   All four, including Ellwood, deny that human social behavior can be substantially and characteristically attributed to the unqualified (or exclusive) operation of the instincts. (Ellwood 1925, 79, 285; Bernard

1926b, 128–29, 135, 137; Hankins 1928, 336–37, 382; Faris [1937a] 1976, 70, 152.)

4. All four have critically examined the term as applied to human social behavior, and redefine it, or propose a substitute, or argue for its abandonment. Ellwood (1925, 281, 288) advocates the terms *instinctive tendencies* or *native impulses.* Hankins (1928, 337) contends that *internal urges* (or drives), *predispositions,* and *aptitudes* are more appropriate. For his part, Bernard (1926b) insists that instinct must be redefined so that it is virtually inapplicable to the human domain (114–117, 134; Bernard 1942, 559–78), whereas Faris ([1937a] 1976) in effect demands its abandonment (16, 17, 70, 106–7, 152).

5. Three of the four (Ellwood, Bernard, and Hankins) agree that the acquired or the learned predominates in human social behavior. (Consult Ellwood 1925, 281; Bernard 1926b, 28–29, 118, 135, 137; Bernard 1942, 549, 559–78; Hankins 1928, 336–37). But only Faris ([1937a] 1976, 159, 161) seems ready entirely to reject the role of the instinctive or innate at the human level. Still, even he remarked once that "some of our mechanisms are inherited but most are acquired" (205).

6. Nevertheless, Ellwood, Bernard, and Hankins also appear unwilling to restrict the human biopsychic domain exclusively to plasticity, teachability, or a capacity for learning (Ellwood 1925, 279, 280, 282; Bernard 1926b, 57–58, 61–62, 67, 159–62; Bernard 1942, 549–50, 604–22; Hankins 1928, 337). They seem to believe that some ultimately universal directive or motivational resource remains in the nature of biopsychic human nature, and that sociologists need to invoke it in the explanation of the domain of the social. Faris ([1937a] 1976, 159, 161) thus stands in stark contrast to the other three.

Significantly, it was Faris—the only one of the sociological social psychologists who had had cross-cultural experience—who rigorously pursued the question of the relation of instincts to the origins of modern behavior, earlier customs, and primordial institutions. Most significantly, he recognized the connection of human instincts with the doctrine of parallel physico-biopsychic and sociocultural evolutionism. (See below.)

It is especially noteworthy that the aftermath of the instincts controversy was characterized by a marked decline in the use of the notion of social forces. True, Ellwood used the term in his *The Psychology of Human Society,* as including "physical factors" (geographical and organic), original human nature or biopsychic forces (his "psychic factors" from his "original social forces"), and societally engendered (and culturally defined) forces (his "derivative social forces"). But what is most interesting is that Thomas's doctrine of the four "wishes" is used as the social-forces notion by Park and Burgess (1921) and by Reuter and Hart (1933). These wishes or desires for new experience, security, response, and recognition are "forces which impel to action . . . and [which] correspond in general with the nervous mechanism" (Thomas 1923, 4). They have their foundation in emotions, which have an instinctive basis in the preservation of the individual or species.

Importantly, too, it was Faris, at Chicago, who apparently explicitly directed criticism at the instinctivism he discerned as the basis of the four wishes. Fay Berger Karpf, who completed her Ph.D. dissertation under Faris's direction, noted in her *American Social Psychology* (1932, 381–82) that Faris claimed that the four wishes represent "a hold-over of his [i.e., Thomas's] earlier instinct approach."

Sometime in the later 1930s, American sociological theory, and American sociology generally, concluded that the model for instincts at the human level is to be found at the animal level, that instinct at the human level, if it is applicable, involves an inherited mechanism with an explicit and specific behavior or behaviors, but that empirical evidence, especially cross-cultural evidence, tends to deny that human beings possess instincts as so conceived. The implications for the tenability of physico-biopsychic and sociocultural evolutionism were of the utmost significance: The absence of instinct at the human level thus meant that the direct connecting link with animal behavior was severed. Evolutionary naturalism was itself imperiled as a tenable doctrine accounting for specific, concrete human social behaviors. The prevalent acceptance of the anthropologists' notion of culture only provided further support for separating humankind from the rest of nature.

However, this account has not been carried to its final conclusion, for the rejection of instincts at the human level apparently led to a comprehensive critique of the doctrine of social forces as a whole. One of Faris's doctoral students, Eyler Newton Simpson, subjected the notion of social forces to a searching critique at the end of the first chapter of his dissertation (Simpson 1926): He raised six major objections to the social forces notion:

1. The notion of social forces is definitionally flawed, because it confuses causes of the social (i.e., features of the physical and organic that cause and affect association) with social causes having social effects (i.e., those existing at the psychic level and operating to produce or maintain association). Simpson directly refers (233) to a footnote in Blackmar and Gillin's *Outlines of Sociology* ([1915], 1923, 287) regarding the quarrel over the definition of the social forces.

2. The social forces are empirically and methodologically defective. No cases or materials have been studied, no facts observed, no explicit methodological principles or procedures involved; thus they have not

been formulated in terms such that they can be tested scientifically and inductively (Simpson 1926, 46, 51).

3. The social forces doctrine is based on a discredited and untenable procedure of explanation once followed, but now rejected, by physical science. Those in the physical sciences came to realize that their so-called forces "were only the phenomena over again translated from a specific and concrete form (in which they were at least actual) into a generalized form in which they were verbal" (Simpson 1926, 54–55). Their "alleged causal forces were only names which condensed into a duplicate form a variety of . . . occurrences" (Dewey 1922, 149–50). Forces are such only by virtue of the activity in the situation "and hence cannot be used to account for this activity" (Simpson 1926, 56). They are "functions of the situation, and [are] not independent of the situation" (56). Therefore, any notion of "independent, original instincts, or predispositions, interests, or forces of whatever sort, which manifest themselves in specific facts in a one-to-one correspondence" involves the same error in sociology that "physical scientists have long since repudiated" (56).

4. The assumption that a set of social forces, which are regarded as elemental, original, common to the whole human species, can explain "the diversity of behavior in human groups" as known to modern anthropology is simply not true (60). Both the procedure of explanation and the conception of original nature as revealed in the newborn are not tenable. It is not a process of abstracting out, from what is concretely given, a set of universal categories that are elemental, original, and common to the whole of the species (like for instance, instincts) and that in their combinations and permutations can account for the diversity of cultural behavior (62). And the newborn infant at best reveals a number of relatively inchoate and vague impulses that are given meaning only as the individual acts and interacts within his or her social environment (63).

5. The social forces notion oversimplifies the problem and inhibits the actual study of human actions (60). Social forces are only labels.

6. The social forces formulation presupposes a conception of the "normal" and "natural" ends of individual and collective behavior. The "natural" is assumed to be the "good," and thus in effect "norms of behavior" or "ethical measuring rods" are being established. In Simpson's view, the ethical assumptions of the formulators of the social forces, therefore, vitiate their scientificity (48).

Manifestly, now, the doctrine of social forces has been subjected implicitly (via the instincts) and explicitly (as by Simpson, above) to severe and, some might say, disabling criticisms. Indeed, to the extent that a naturalistic conception of social phenomena and sociology require a generalized notion of social forces akin to other forces in nature, sociology's commitment to evolutionary naturalism as a theory of origins might well be said to have been questioned.

But at least one other major intellectual development in sociology demands scrutiny before any generalized conclusion about the character of sociology as a discipline or the problem of social origins theory can be drawn. That development concerns the introduction of the notion of culture, especially as envisaged by cultural anthropology during the 1920s.

A Concern with Culture, Cultural Origins, and the Theory of Cultural Origins

Concurrent with the increasing rejection of instinctivism came an increasing acceptance in sociological theory and in sociology generally, of the view that socially shared experience, or culture, is the primary basis of a distinctive feature of human association. Ellwood (1925, 171), Hankins (1928, 381), Bernard (1942, 750), and Reuter and Hart (1933, 125) were all convinced that it was culture that distinctively differentiated human society from animal association. In contradistinction to the patterning of activities determined instinctively or genetically among other organisms, culture at the human level is an acquired or learned phenomenon characteristic of human social life. Presumably, most of their colleagues from the 1920s would have agreed with Reuter and Hart (1933, 117) in construing culture as "the organized result of group experience [up] to the present moment." It is typically accumulative across generations and subject to change apart from the biopsychic features of those human beings who are its carriers. This fact eventually has dramatic consequences for the problem of explaining social origins in accordance with the tenet of genetic filiation in evolutionary naturalism (with its implications of parallel physico-biopsychic and sociocultural change).

Once the view that the human social was distinctively and inextricably associated with culture had become relatively widely disseminated and accepted, the problem of social origins was translated into (or replaced by) the problem of cultural origins. Part 2 of Case's 1924 textbook substantially concerns the so-called stages of culture, along with the emergence of various social institutions (language, education, technology, economy, government and law, religion, art, and social organization). Ellwood's *Sociology in Its Psychological Aspects* (1912) contained a chapter on "the origins of society," the major contents of which were incorporated in his chapter "Organic and Social Evolution" in his *Introduction to Social Psychology* (1917) and in a similar chapter of his *The Psychology of Human Society* (1925). Both the 1917 volume (38*ff.*) and the 1925 volume (60*ff.*) note that what distinguishes human society from mere animal association is culture. Blackmar and Gillin's 1915 *Outlines of Sociology* includes a chapter entitled "Social Origins," which became "Social Origins and Evolution" in the 1923 edition and "Culture and Social Evolution" in their 1930 edition. The chapter "Social Origins" in Lumley's 1928 *Principles of Sociology* is apparently replaced by the chapter "The Social and Cultural" in the 1935 edition.

Initially, at least, the attempt was made to envisage the cultural in terms of evolutionary theory, that is, to construe cultural origins gradualistically as part of a series of stages akin to those of social evolution. Cultural origins theory also implicates a parallel physico-biopsychic and sociocultural evolution that interconnects a changing physical environment of geological epochs or ages with the evolutionary origins of humanoid and human species, as discovered by modern paleontology (and the survival of one species as a modern common human organic base with a common human nature [i.e., biopsychic unity]) along with their adaptive material culture remains. The texts by Hankins, Ogburn and Nimkoff, and Bernard are illustrative. Hankins's chapter "The Evolution of Material Culture," with its table showing alleged relationships between geological epochs, human or human-like types, and the apparent material-culture remains, offers the most detailed summary presentation. The table shows the later part of the Tertiary Period and all of the Quaternary Period, with its divisions into Pleistocene or Glacial, the Postglacial, and the recent stages. It indicates the linkage of Neanderthals with Mousterian culture (of the Middle Paleolithic) arising in the third interglacial phase and perhaps extending into the fourth glacial phase. The Cro-Magnon type is associated with Aurignacian culture (of the Upper Paleolithic). Connections are made between particular human types and Neolithic, Copper, Bronze, and Iron Ages. Hankins also evidences a willingness to connect this prehistoric and premodern evolution with the development of modern civilizations, holding that most, if not all, the peoples who have reared great civilizations have passed through certain broad types of material cultures: (1) the collectional, (2) the pastoral, (3) the horticultural, (4) settled agriculture, and (5) commercial and industrial stages (Hankins 1928, 487; cf. Lumley 1928, 448–52).[7] In addition, Hankins tends (as do Ogburn and Nimkoff and Bernard) to separate the whole of concrete cultures into different domains or spheres in accordance with modern differentiation in order to facilitate an abstract, simplified portrayal of evolutionary developments that minimizes the possibility of cross-sectional variations. Each such cultural or institutional domain begins with a first, most primitive, or primordial stage.

Most importantly, the mechanisms by which culture has originated, are given in the third tenet of evolutionary naturalism, expressed in the terms of the Darwinian-Spencerian view of organic evolution, such as the struggle for existence, survival of the fittest, selection, and adaptation. Keller insists that his formulation of the mechanisms as (individual) variation, selection, transmission, and adaptation is decisively Darwinian (cf. Lumley 1928, 429–43). Ellwood (1925, 65) acknowledges that social and cultural evolution must operate within the limits set by heredity and selection; otherwise, elimination of the cultural feature, group, society, or culture as a whole may be occasioned. Hankins (1928, 29, 380–81) regards the different aspects of culture as modes of aggregate adaptive behavior by which human wants in relation to given environmental conditions can be, and are, more or less effectively satisfied. Bernard (1942) construes culture as a "by-product of man's efforts to make a successful adjustment to his environment," which in turn transforms the natural environment or portions of it (727, 728, 728–31). Whether natural or cultural, the environment nonpurposively selects out cultural or acquired traits as adaptive (751). For Keller (and others of the first period), individual variation is the source of adaptive behaviors that the struggle for existence selects out both at the inter-individual and inter-species levels (see Hinkle 1980, 186–87).

Like Keller, Ellwood conceives of culture in terms of a notion of social forces grounded in a conception of the evolving nature of human nature and the human organism in relation to physical, organic conditions of existence. Culture thus reveals both continuity and discontinuity with the prior hierarchy of life. It reflects humankind's prolonged immaturity (associated with organic plasticity and the possible formation of habits), erect posture, free hands (facilitating the making and using of tools), a superior brain (entailing the power of abstract thought or of forming general notions of independent ideas), and the power of articulate speech or of vocalizing sounds (and so of being able to symbolize ideas and feelings and to communicate with others). By means of intercommunication, individuals in the human group can reciprocally adjust through more or less conscious interstimulation and response. Patterns of action in the mind can be symbolized and communicated and thus become social patterns. A group tradition is formed accordingly, and each generation transmits ideas, standards, values, and knowledge to its successors. Manifestly, culture has now arisen, with the possibility of exercising intelligence and reason in adjusting to the natural and social environment. Language, toolmaking, invention and discovery, moral ideas and ideals—with such regulative institutions as government, religion, morality, and education— are all part of culture.

Interestingly, Bernard (1942) does not explicitly refer to human nature as such as part of organic and psychic evolution. But, like Ellwood, he does allude to certain distinctive features that human organisms possess: upright posture, manipulative hands, a large brain, and vocalizing apparatus (554). Most human behavior is learned and not instinctive (580). Infant dependence on adults means that the young of the species do not need instincts to survive. Conditioning, or habit formation, is the major alternative to instincts at the human level, and it is evidenced in both overt, or neuromuscular, and covert, or neuropsychic and symbolic, behaviors; the latter are the basis for (objective) communication and (subjective) thinking as (symbolic) trial-and-error behavior. Bernard makes no reference to needs, urges, predispositions, and such. Emotions, both primary and secondary, are treated in relation to conditioning and learning in making adjustments. Culture is itself a result of inventions incidental to an adjustment process of human beings in relation to the natural environment (551).

Both Bernard and Hankins—the former implicitly, and the latter explicitly—conceive of humankind as having organically, or genetically, evolved a distinctive biopsychic nature as a foundation for culture and its evolution. Hankins alludes to certain basic needs and wants as part of that human nature, but Bernard does not. Both emphasize the development of consciousness, intelligence, or rationality and an unparalleled capacity to learn or acquire behavior. Neither theorist invokes the notion of social forces. Both contrast inherited or instinctive behavior with acquired or learned behavior as exemplified by habit. Both differentiate the various stimulus-response activities of organisms into random or impulsive movements, tropisms, reflexes (unconditioned versus conditioned), and instincts versus habits and intellectual or rational responses (Bernard 1942, 580–84, 601; Hankins 1928, 328–45).

They construe culture itself as founded on sets of adaptive habits, the origins of which presumably lie in the response of talented individuals in aggregates of human individuals. Interestingly, both sociologists tend to adhere to a moderate stimulus-response or conditioned-response behaviorism as the basis of culture as a set of shared adaptations or adjustments of that aggregate to its common conditions of existence. Imitation and suggestion are invoked to account for the transmission, dissemination, and adoption of the forms of behavior (e.g., Bernard 1942, 633–71; Hankins 1928, 360–63).

Both theorists envisage culture as structurally differentiatable into a variety of social institutions. Both examine the economic, the domestic (marriage and family), the religious or magico-religious, and the political (Bernard, chaps. 4–6, 8, 39, 40; Hankins, chaps. 11–14).

Most significantly, neither sociologist accepts the view that the emergence of culture in any way abrogates or basically qualifies the importance of organic factors of evolution in social change. Both are opposed to any notion of culture as explicable in and of itself, as sui generis and thus independent of individuals as organisms constantly involved in a struggle for survival in a common environment (Bernard 1942, 800; Hankins 1928, 402, 409–11). Both do envisage the emergence of culture as part of parallel physico-biopsychic and sociocultural evolutionism.

Objections to Parallel Evolutionism as a Theory of Cultural Origins

However, the effort to construe cultural origins as part of an evolution akin to the earlier social evolution encountered major opposition. The concept of culture itself had been substantially borrowed from American cultural anthropology, and many sociologists could hardly ignore its criticisms of parallel physico-biopsychic and sociocultural evolutionism. (Put simply, if not also simplistically, this conception held that changes in the physical environment altered the conditions of existence and so affected the physical characteristics (i.e., the anatomy, morphology) of the human population surviving in a given habitat, modifying also its biopsychic human nature, and eventually its behavioral adaptations (i.e., the character of its social and cultural features.) Both sociologists (who were conversant with accumulating field research of cultural anthropology) and anthropologists (who were known to sociologists as colleagues, as participants at sociology conventions, and as authors in sociological periodicals) elaborated arguments seriously opposing components of parallel evolutionism and even the very conception of cultural origins.[8]

The objections to the notion of parallel evolutionism were these:

1. The basic assumption that culture change is a response to the character of (i.e., to changes in) the geography or environment is fallacious. The anthropologist Wallis (1926) cited evidence of drastic cultural change in an area over the years while the geography or the environment remained constant. Conversely, Goldenweiser (1916, 630–31) referred to many instances of primitive peoples in similar environments with different cultures (e.g., the Eskimos in North America versus the Chukchee in Siberia, the Pacific Northwest Coast Indians versus the California Indians, who are surrounded by forests but do not engage in woodworking).

2. Evidence does not support the more precise claim that culture change is a response to change in human anatomy, which is in turn a response to environmental or geographic change. Ogburn ([1922] 1950) noted that external measurements of human fossil remains since the last ice age "make it seem probable that there has been no significant evolution in these characteristics in man, and certainly do not prove it conclusively." Furthermore, organic changes in humans over the last two

thousand years must be exceeding slight, if they have "occurred at all."
But culture change in these two millenia (especially in the rise of civilizations) "has been extraordinarily great." Manifestly, culture change
is not correlated with organic change in this period. Indeed, vast cultural change since the last ice age has apparently occurred without any
significant organic evolution in humankind (141).

3.   Perhaps, the most important culminating claim of sociocultural evolution was the assertion that culture change is the product of a change in
biopsychic human nature, which has altered along with the physical
structure of humankind in relation to shifts in the environment. The
sociological social psychologist Faris rejected this assertion with a
variety of arguments, including the following.

a. The doctrine of instincts was a common feature of the broader
claim.

   i.   Faris ([1937a] 1976) notes that instincts in the animal world are
uniform throughout a single species. If instincts at the human
level produce customs, and different tribes have different customs, then it must follow that "every tribe or race . . . must
have different instincts" and the human race must disappear as
a single organic species (16). The only other alternatives are
either to ignore the cultural diversity or to argue that certain
tribes (e.g., those that are not warlike) are hereditarily deviant
(106–7). (See also Faris's argument about instinct and changing customs, [17].)

  ii. The evolutionary explanation for the presence of instincts
involves a resort to both a discredited biology and a defective
methodology. To argue that the current behaviors of moderns
or (contemporary) primitives "are the result of the stamping in,
through age-long experience, of some reaction which is inherited by each succeeding generation" is to resort, to what some
would claim (Faris himself is not specific) to be the discredited
Lamarckianism of the inheritance of acquired characteristics
(66). It also involves, on the other, a resort to fanciful and
imaginary accounts in the absence of factual data and direct
observation (67). No acceptable method can be invoked (152).

b. A conception of a culture as the simple and exclusive result of a
people's biopsychic human nature is inaccurate.

   i.   As Faris remarks, the possibility that "many or even most of
the elements of a culture of a people may have been borrowed"
would seem to question the use of that culture—as in the case
of primitives—as the unaided or unstimulated ability of its carriers (259).

     ii. Furthermore, Faris points to six fundamental errors in the information possessed about the mental abilities of primitive peoples and uses his own experience of several years with the Bantu tribes of the Upper Congo River to argue that the savage child has on the average the same capacity as the child of civilized races (223–26).

The objections to the possibility of inferring sociocultural origins were these:

1.   Faris ([1937a] 1976) denies that it is possible with any degree of scientific confidence to separate primitive cultures, given their considerable variations, "into higher and lower" categories of any degree of objectivity and consistency (261). For instance, the use of the bow and arrow is often regarded as a considerable intellectual and technical achievement. However:
   a. The Andaman Islanders, who have no agriculture, no pastoral life, live off native pigs, fish, and turtles, and have only the simplest form of social organization, possess the bow and arrow and use them very proficiently.
   b. Certain Polynesians who have a complex social organization, along with chiefs and kings, are ignorant of the bow and arrow (257).

2.   Faris explicitly denied that contemporary primitive peoples "represent earlier stages of the [sociocultural] life which we are now living" (46). Indeed, primitive man "who is really primitive [i.e., aboriginal and primordial] is gone and gone forever" (221; cf. 249). Clearly, then, the effort to find a modern representative of human social and cultural life in its most pristine original form was and is doomed to failure.

3.   Social and cultural origins as a generic problem is insoluble. "The ultimate origin of any of our basic activities is lost in the unrecorded past" (46).

Interestingly, Faris did not categorically reject all possible forms of sociocultural evolutionism. His arguments do seem to deny evolutionary naturalism, with its tenet of genetic filiation (with the possibility of inferring sociocultural origins via social forces), and sociocultural evolution as an outgrowth of parallel physico-biopsychic evolution.

Others, such as Reuter and Hart (1933), contended that the organic and sociocultural realms differ and that change in one is different from change in the other. Change in the organic is "always selective" and thus evolutionary; but in the sociocultural, it is "cumulative rather than selective" and is thus nonevolutionary (164). "The new generally is an addition to the old rather than a substitute that displaces the old" (164). Basically, Reuter and Hart's text is contemporary and analytical rather than historical and developmental in its interest and orientation. These same traits are exhibited in even more accentuated form in the Hiller volume, which is also pervasively conceptual in its emphasis. (Admittedly, all of these authors had been students of Park, who was strongly committed to the Windelband-Rickert science/history dichotomy.)

Significantly, only one of the texts published between the mid-1930s and mid-1940s (and whose authors received their doctorates after World War I) deals with social or cultural origins. That was Sutherland and Woodward 1937, which includes a chapter on (but not a theory of) cultural origins.

Unfortunately, none of these later texts refers to Faris's views on sociocultural origins. Neither is the topic discussed at any of the sessions of the American Sociological Society in the late 1930s or early 1940s. The published record is devoid of any references. Perhaps the depression and the onset of World War II became the paramount concerns for professional sociologists, or the texts became oriented to introductory as opposed to general theoretical interests (including origins) in order to appeal effectively to the undergraduate student; either would be difficult to establish. It may also be that the kind of social background that generated a secularized response to a religious interest in origins among at least some of the generation of sociologists entering the field immediately before and after World War I was substantially different from the background of the generation entering just before and after World War II.

SUMMARY AND IMPLICATIONS

The problem of social and cultural origins remained a major concern in sociological theory at least during the first half of the second period (1915–30). Social origins theories were initially cast in terms of evolutionary naturalism from the prior period. Fundamentally, these theories especially departed from the second tenet of genetic filiation and the doctrine of social forces, which might be conceived comprehensively or restrictively. But in either case the social forces tended to include pan-human biopsychic needs, wants, and desires. Ellwood and Blackmar and Gillin are illustrative of the more comprehensive view, in contrast to Keller (who adopted Sumner's restrictive formulation) and to Park and Burgess and Reuter and Hart (who relied on Thomas's notion of the four wishes).

Nevertheless, the problem and theories of social origins substantially altered during the second period. Whereas during the earlier period, the post-organic and pre-organic theories of social origins enjoyed approximately equal numbers of supporters, during the second period opinion shifted markedly in favor of the pre-organic stance (i.e., that permanent human association, social relations, society, had occurred before rather than after our prehuman ancestors became organically human). Just what prompted this shift in positions cannot be determined with certainty. But at the minimum the change was certainly supported by the publication of research on our nonhuman primate relatives by Kohler, Yerkes, and Zuckerman. (Clearly, then, it would seem logical that the social forces in their more narrow biopsychic sense had evoked association before the final organic, genetic appearance of humankind itself.)

Irrespective of whether social forces were regarded as the basis of association at the (later) human level or the (earlier) prehuman level, or even as a comprehensive formulation of social causation or as fundamental sources of motivation, they became intellectually suspect because they were linked with instincts, about which conflict raged during the 1920s and later. Ellwood, Bernard, Hankins, and Faris were major figures in the dispute over the instincts in sociology. The first three qualified the applicability of the notion to humankind. They redefined it or proposed substitutes, concurring that acquired or learned behavior predominates in the human domain. By contrast, Faris entirely rejected the role of the innate or instinctive behavior at the human level, which is also to say that the others were unwilling to restrict the distinctiveness of the human biopsychic realm to plasticity, teachability, or a capacity for learning. They resisted rejection or abandonment of species-wide bases of universal human motivation (e.g., Thomas's four wishes), as Faris urged.

Almost simultaneously, the doctrine of social forces was itself subjected to a major critique by E. N. Simpson, one of Faris's former students at Chicago. He indicted the social forces for their definitional flaws (confusing causes of the social with social causes having social effects), for methodological and empirical defects, for redundant abstractionism, for the assumption that they can account for the facts of social diversity, and for the presupposition that individual and collective behavior has certain normal, natural, and universal ends.

Concurrent with the attack on instincts specifically and the social forces generally, the notion of culture diffused from anthropology into sociology and sociological theory. Sociology had concluded that association at the human level was not distinctive, but that association based on culture was. The interest in social origins was translated into a concern with cultural origins. The former was cast in terms of evolutionary naturalism, as was the latter, including a resort to the third (Darwinian-Spencerian) tenet of struggle for existence, survival of the fittest, selection, and adaptation (e.g., Keller, Ellwood, Hankins, Bernard). In actuality, the general orientation was not only that of evolutionary naturalism but also that of parallel physico-biopsy-chic and sociocultural evolutionism, in which the linkage between the organic and the mental and the conscious with the social and cultural is absolutely indispensable.

But certain sociologists (who were thoroughly conversant with the accumulating field research of cultural anthropology) and anthropologists (who were well known to sociologists both by their presence at sociology meetings and by their journal articles) elaborated arguments seriously con-tradicting components of the notion of parallel evolutionism. Admittedly, the arguments were not always unambiguously identified, rigorously logical, or systematically expounded. But their consequences for parallel evolutionism and sociocultural origins as a problem were unmistakable.

First, inductive generalizations on the basis of the newer anthropology and paleontology were shown to be incompatible with basic assumptions of parallel evolutionism such as those of similar physical environments, human physical types, and similar cultures. A uniform and consistent relationship between a given type of physical environment and a type or stage of culture (Wallis and Goldenweiser) or between a change in physical environment, human fossil remains, and culture (Ogburn) cannot be demonstrated.

Second, the effort to argue that features of a culture derive from com-ponents of biopsychic human nature that have altered in response to changes in the physical environment or organisms is untenable. For instance, if instincts produce customs on the human level, and different tribes have dif-ferent customs, it must follow that the different tribes or races have different instincts, and thus the human race must disappear as a single organic whole or species (Faris). Furthermore, the evolutionary explanation for the pres-ence of instincts involves a resort to both discredited Lamarckian biology and a defective methodology (Faris). So, too, the notion of culture as the simple and exclusive result of a people's biopsychic human nature is defec-tive, because it ignores the operation of widespread diffusion (Faris). And in the case of primitive peoples, the common view that their mental abilities are inferior is based on misinformation (Faris).

Thirdly, there are formidable difficulties with the assumptions involved in the evolutionary endeavor to derive cultural origins from con-temporary primitive peoples. For instance, it is impossible that primitive peoples in the modern world possess a culture that is consistently and entirely in accordance with all cultural indicators of the lowest (or simplest) forms of primitive social and cultural life and thus approximate the stage of human sociocultural origins. Most importantly, it is not tenable to declare that contemporary primitives may be regarded as representatives of "earlier stages of the life we are now living" (Faris). As Faris remarks, "primitive man who is really primitive [aboriginal and primordial] is gone and gone forever." Accordingly, social and cultural origins as a generic problem is insoluble.

Interestingly, only one of the texts published in the late 1930s by authors who had received their doctorates *after* World War I deals with social or cultural origins. That text was written by Sutherland and Woodward. It discusses cultural origins, but offers no theory as such.

Unfortunately, none of the texts in the last ten years of the period actually refers to problems in treating social or cultural origins or to Faris's arguments in particular. The topic is not discussed at any of the sessions of the American Sociological Society in the late 1930s or early 1940s. Indeed, the published record is devoid of any references to the problem, except for the original publication of Faris's main arguments as a chapter in an edited volume by the theologian Shailer Mathews in 1924 and its republication in Faris's *The Nature of Human Nature* in 1937. As in other instances, shifts in intellectual problematics may occasion no comment. Subsequent commentators and analysts are then compelled to ponder and conjecture as best they can.

Chapter 4

Critique of Earlier Social Evolutionism and Its Legacy in the Second Period

Social change remained a basic and central problem in general or macrotheory during the period after World War I. And at least immediately after the war, social evolutionism, in some variant, was the major mode of theoretical formulation. Social change continued to be explored in the general sociology textbooks and became a more or less specialized research field. Some sociologists were involved in both of these undertakings.

In the textbooks, the treatments ranged from two to eleven chapters in length. Ellwood's, Lumleys, and Lundberg's books devoted two chapters to change. Hankins's volume included four-plus relevant chapters. Hiller's, MacIver's, and Reuter and Hart's texts each offered six chapters. Bernard's and Young's books provided, respectively, eight and eleven chapters.

At least nine sociologists can be identified with the development of social change as a specialized field for research and theory: Thomas and Znaniecki, Ogburn, Chapin, Ellwood, MacIver, Park, Sorokin, and Howard

P. Becker. Evidently, then, change research and theory had exponents at most of the major graduate departments, including Chicago (initially with Thomas, Park, and later Ogburn), Columbia (initially Ogburn and later MacIver), Minnesota (Chapin and Sorokin at first), Wisconsin (Becker after 1937), Missouri (Ellwood before 1930), Duke (Ellwood after 1930), and Harvard (Sorokin after 1930).

Accordingly, then, the macrodynamics theory of the second period involves two categories of sociologists: the textbook authors and the specialists in the field of research and theory about social change. Evidence from the views of both will enter into our arguments about the continuity of second-period change theory with that of the first period.

PHASES IN THE INQUIRY OF THIS CHAPTER

In order to determine whether second-period macrochange theory is substantially continuous with that of the first period as a type of social evolutionism, the subsequent sections of this chapter will cover the following steps of inquiry:

1. A review of change terminology among second-period theorists
2. An examination of the evidence that second-period theorists (especially those in the research and theory of change specialty) were basically concerned with social evolutionism as a type of macrodynamics theory
3. A brief summary of the features of social evolution in first-period theory, as a prerequisite for eventually judging the evolutionary character of macrodynamics theory in the second period
4. A critique of social evolution as advanced by cultural anthropologists in the then-contemporary sociological literature, especially the periodicals of the 1920s
5. An assessment of second-period change theorists' reactions to the critique mounted by the cultural anthropologists

The sections covering steps 3, 4, and 5 all use as a point of departure a subsection of the general analytical classificatory scheme for organizing the relevant analyses (Appendix, also Hinkle 1980, 191). The same portion of the analytical classificatory scheme is also crucial to chapter 5.

On the basis of the analysis developed in this chapter, a determination can be made of the predominant types of change theories in the second period, and this will provide the basis for, in chapter 5, confirming or denying the continuity of social evolution between the first and second periods.

TERMINOLOGICAL DISTINCTIONS

Terminological distinctions are important in initially conceiving the nature of change and the subsequent development of theory. The writings of Ellwood, Hankins, Bernard, Lumley, MacIver, and Young are illustrative. Sometimes they distinguished between mere (social) change and (social) evolution, and sometimes they failed to do so. Occasionally they distinguished between (social) evolution and (social) revolution. And most frequently, they differentiated (social) evolution from (social) progress. Admittedly, they failed to offer the kind of rigorous and comprehensive terminological distinctions that would surely have been regarded as desirable, if not necessary, after World War II.

MacIver (1931c) provides the most explicit set of terminological differentiations departing from mere change itself. The term *change* he remarks, "is wholly neutral, implying nothing but a difference through time in the object to which it is applied." So, for instance the term *social change* suggests "no law, no theory, no meaning, no direction, no continuity even" (399, 400).

However curious it may now seem, many of the early theorists essentially equated change with evolution, or rather evolution with change, and thus, presumably, social evolution with social change. In Hankins's (1928, 429) view, the term *evolution* is so comprehensive that "all changes" are included. Presumably, then, social evolution must also include all social changes. And it was apparently Ellwood's (1925, 20) intention to equate social change and social evolution. He defines social evolution as a "scientific theory of social origins and of social change or development of all sorts."

Others did qualify the kind of social change comprehended in social evolution. In Bernard's (1942, 343) case, "evolution [in general] is orderly change" and thus social evolution is orderly social change. Lumley ([1928] 1935, 467) envisaged evolution in general as "continuous, connected changed in any direction." Apparently, the same definition follows for social evolution.

Young (1942, 923) uses a notion of organic evolution as a "gradual, somewhat stepwise development of organisms from rudimentary and simple to complex and diverse forms." Accordingly, sociocultural evolution entails the passage of societies and cultures "step-wise through more or less regular stages from simple to complex" (Young 1934, 99). But Hankins (1928, 29) denies that evolution means change of increasing complexity. Among societies, institutions may become more complex for an extended and considerable period of time "and then fall into decay."

MacIver (1931c) offers the most complex delineation of social evolution, which is compared with, and contrasted to, change, process, growth, and progress. As noted above, *change,* for MacIver, is a neutral term "implying nothing but a difference through time in the object to which it is applied (399). The term *process* introduces the idea of continuity, in the sense of a definite "operation of forces present from the first within the situation." It signifies, further, a "series of transitions between one state of being and another." In a word, it means a "determinate continuous change." If such change entails specific direction, it may be quantitatively or qualitatively defined. Growth is such quantitatively defined change "with respect to size." Evolution, for MacIver, also connotes "a direction of change but only one of qualitative character" involving structural or functional differentiation. (He cautions that progress differs from evolution in involving not merely direction "but direction towards some final goal" as determined by "the value-judgment of the spectator." More particularly, evolution is a process in which "the variety of aspects belonging to the nature of the changing object" are (literally "unrolled" or) unfolded so that the potential is made actual. Such change or changes must be internal: They must be a manifestation of forces operative within the entity. The core criterion is differentiation, "a process in which latent or rudimentary characters take on distinct and variable forms within the unity of the organism" so that "new and more complex types of life" appear. So social evolution means more than the appearance of mere novelty or increasing complexity. For such novelty or complexity to entail differentiation, it must be accompanied by "the interrelation of function between the whole and the parts," that is, integration (400, 401, 402, 403, 405).

Admittedly, few of the change theorists of the second period were as specific as MacIver in delineating their notions of social evolution. But apparently most of them construed social evolution as prevailingly involving slow, gradual, continuous, orderly social change of a prevailingly linear directionality.

SOCIAL EVOLUTION AS A FUNDAMENTAL CONCERN

Although the main theorists and theories of social change reflect the newer features of American sociology in general after 1915 (and thus exhibit discontinuity with the past), they also display a major continuity with that past and especially the earlier theories of social change. They are oriented to and by the theory of social evolution, though it must also be simultaneously acknowledged that few, if any, of them can be designated as unqualified exponents of social evolution in its earlier sense. The evidence of the significance of social evolution as a point of departure for the special field of change theorists after World War I seems substantial and impressive, with perhaps two major exceptions.

The first is that Thomas and Znaniecki's *The Polish Peasant in Europe and America* is curiously lacking in the documentation that seems to be so readily citable after 1922, the publication date of Ogburn's *Social Change.* True, they do seem to suppose the legitimacy of an interest in macrochange and in its generally linear directionality. On occasion, they do use the term *social evolution.*" But they do not explicitly invoke social evolution as their basic point of departure.

This apparent failure must be viewed in light of other revealing information. On the one hand, Thomas's *Source Book for Social Origins* (from almost a decade earlier) contians a number of major objections to many of the basic features of social evolution (see Hinkle 1980, 219–21, 223–24, 228.) Indeed, Thomas seems to have rejected the doctrine of social evolution. Conversely, Znaniecki's *The Method of Sociology* (1934) actually proposes a method for establishing differentiation that is explicitly associated with social evolution (283–95 passim). Thus, the social evolution that Thomas seems to have rejected Znaniecki accepted. Clearly, a disinclintion to deal explicitly with social evolution as such is one way at least in part to prevent the two authors' differences from coming to the fore. Understandably, then, *The Polish Peasant in Europe and America* has an oblique relationship to social evolutionism.

The second exception is that Park's publications also have an ambiguous relationship to social evolution. The term scarcely appears in Park's works. Nevertheless, a peculiar congruity obtains with features of social evolution. The emergence of the realm of society, with a social, moral, and cultural order, from the realm of community, with its biotic and ecological order, through the several social processes has a distinctive evolutionary affinity. Competition, conflict, accommodation, and assimilation arise in a natural, serial, and evolutionary order with their related accompaniments.[1]

When Ogburn published his *Social Change* in 1922, it was, by contrast, substantially oriented to an interest in and conception of social evolution. He noted in his preface that the "vast social changes which characterize our age raise to a plane of great importance for sociology theories of social evolution and practical programmes" (v). He was basically preoccupied with the legacy of evolutionary naturalism and especially with the differentiation of the domain of original (or biopsychic) human nature from that of the superorganic, or of culture, and their respective parts played in social evolution. He acknowledged that just as society and culture are not the same, so social and cultural evolution are also different. Cultural evolution is clearly a more inclusive notion than social evolution (60) and affects it. (See also Ogburn [1922] 1950, part 4.)

Although Ellwood's *Cultural Evolution* was not published until 1927, its intellectual foundations are evident in his writings and in his courses at least a decade earlier. Clearly, Ellwood is committed to a conception of evolutionary naturalism, with organic evolution as the basis for social evolution and social evolution as the foundation for cultural evolution (11). It is culture that distinguishes the "group behavior of human beings" from the group behavior of (subhuman) animals (3), and thus cultural evolution is the distinctively human component in social evolution (4).

Published in 1928, Chapin's *Cultural Change* entails major departures from his earlier conception of social evolution presented in his *An Introduction to the Study of Social Evolution* of 1913. His later work involves major modifications of his earlier views. He does accept the notion of a "main or central stream of human culture" involving cultural continuity (202). But he warns that "the facts of concrete similarities in different areas at different times are "not illustrations of universal cultural stages in one continuous worldwide stream of unified cultural evolution" (202). Indeed, "they are really examples of similar cyclical changes in independent culture groups" (201). His 1928 book appears to be an effort to combine both the traditional notion of linear evolution with an oscillatory or cyclical conception—perhaps under the stimulus of Sorokin in the department at Minnesota.

MacIver's *Society* (1931c) contains the most explicit and detailed analysis of the relation between social change and social evolution to be found in any of the texts of the period. It clearly reflects the context of sociological controversy in the 1920s and 1930s. Manifestly, MacIver regards himself as a social evolutionist, but not a unilinear one. Insisting that differentiation "as the emergence of more distinct organs to fulfill more distinct functions . . .may take a myriad forms" (423), he may be intimating the espousal of a multilinear evolutionism. For MacIver, the crucial feature of the process of evolution as "the emergence of a variety of more specific forms from the less specific" remains unchallenged, though it must be dissociated from the concerns with social origins as unknowable (424).

From the earliest preliminaries in his study of social change, Sorokin was concerned with the tenability of the doctrine of social evolutionism. His 1927 article in *Social Forces* denied that either "the ever-repeating identical cycles" or a "definite, steady, and eternal trend in historical and social change" has been proved (39). His 1931 paper in the *Publications of the American Sociological Society* argues, among other things, that most of "the theories of progress and of linear evolution (in rectilinear, spiral, or oscillatory form with a perpetual trend) are based upon" the controvertible "assumption that a social process can go on indefinitely in the same direction and sense, and that there is no limit for such a movement in a given direction" (19, 25–27). At least two of the four volumes of Sorokin's *Social and Cultural Dynamics* (vol. 1, 1937, 182–83; vol. 4, 1941, 718–19) are concerned at length with the question of the acceptability of various forms of linear directionality of social change. His chapter "Sociocultural Dynamics and Evolutionism" (Sorokin 1945) is an elaborate summary of his position.

Certainly, Howard Becker's concerns in the field of social change were from the very outset focused substantially on the acceptability of the assumptions of social evolutionism. Becker 1934b and Becker 1940b take as their points of departure various aspects of social evolutionism (e.g., determination of trend in the total process of sociation, determination of stages in social evolution, and the study of social origins). The earlier paper is schematic (only sixteen pages), whereas the latter is elaborate (fifty-one pages).

In sum, of the nine figures in the specialized research and theory field of social change, four were apparently social evolutionists, and two more (Sorokin and Becker) were critics of social evolution. Park was surely cognizant of social evolution, but he had his own version of social process theory. As represented in *The Polish Peasant,* Thomas and Znaniecki's stance seems to be an accommodation to their individually divergent positions, though the term *social evolution* is often used in this joint work. Social evolution is thus an important part of the inteelectual life in the change specialty and in the textbooks.

THE PRE–WORLD WAR I THEORY OF SOCIAL EVOLUTION OF AMERICAN SOCIOLOGISTS

Indispensable to the determination of continuity between an alleged social evolutionism of the second period with that of the first is an unambiguous statement of just what the social evolutionism of the first period entails. It is one of the two dominant conceptions of social change during the period in American sociology before World War I. It is the theory of social (macro) change espoused by Ward, Giddings, and Keller (though not by his mentor Sumner; see Smith and Hinkle 1979.) As a macro theory, social evolution adopts certain answers to certain of the basic questions within the general domain of social dynamics. It has accepted a particular unit or subject as undergoing change, a certain kind of analogy or model, a distinctive method, a particular notion of rate and magnitude of change, a certain kind of direction (or directionality), along with particular features associated with the causal mechanism or modus operandi of change.[2]

The Social Unit

Like their counterparts in Europe, the social evolutionists in the founding generation of American sociology assumed that the ultimate social unit undergoing change is human society, humankind, the human species, or the human race. Giddings's view is evident from the comprehensiveness of the titles of his major books. Keller's notion is repeatedly stated (Sumner and Keller 1927). And Ward also endorses the same conception, though certain of his statements are readily subject to misinterpretation. Basically, all social change is to be approached as fundamentally one common process, because all humankind is assumed to be one, organically and psychically, and the conditions of human existence substantially similar everywhere. Just as biology endeavored to explain life as a whole and humankind as a whole organically, so sociology attempted to account for all human association and social existence in terms of a similar evolutionary naturalism.

The Analogy or Model

Although the three early American social evolutionists in sociology did not use the growth model or analogy (which is, of course, an aspect of the more encompassing organismic model or analogy) as conspicuously or frequently as their European predecessors and colleagues did, they still occasionally employed the notion. In a sense, this feature of social evolutionism is perhaps the most significant of all the features, because the others can be derived from it. It reinforces the unity of all humankind, or society in general, undergoing a vast change, with its empirical particulars finding their places in that whole through resort to the comparative method. But perhaps the most evident feature is the stages notion, which is fundamental to the directionality of evolutionary change. Human society is thus characterized by a series of stages of growth like the stages of growth in the life cycle of the organism. In the history of the transmission of the organismic growth analogy from medieval and classical sources to modern thought, Blaise Pascal's aphorism is a crucial link. Yet, curiously, Ward ([1930] 1970, 34–35) is the only early American theorist who quoted Pascal. All three social evolutionary theorists (Ward, Giddings, and Keller) used the organismic growth model, with Keller providing the most conspicuous and frequent use.

The Method

The comparative method is an indispensable methodological adjunct of social evolutionism. It assumes that all humankind is to be comprehended in a vast single developmental unity whose general course and component stages in sequence can and should be reconstructed by modern social science. Comparison is to be used to abstract out a graduated series of resemblances in a continuum (more or less from simplicity to complexity, which was believed to be both temporal and developmental. Simplicity was generally equated with temporal developmental earliness (or relatively undifferentiated primitivity), and complexity with temporal developmental lateness (or differentiated modernity). Actual historical (or chronological sequence) and geographical (or spatial) differences are ignored in the assumption of the unity of humankind.

Basically, two kinds of stages were proposed with the use of the comparative method. One involved total societal stages (e.g., Ward's "protosocial, metasocial, and social" stages; and Giddings's "ethnic or ethnogenic" and "demotic or demogenic" stages). The other kind of stage is labeled in terms of the development of a given institution (e.g., technological, economic, governmental, religious, familial, as illustrated by Ward and Keller).

One of the difficulties in the use of the comparative method is the absence of complete social and cultural data in sequence in specific societies. Accordingly, Keller, Giddings, and Ward resort to the use of "parallels," "parallelisms," and "survivals" to aid in the reconstruction of developmental sequences.

Rate and Magnitude

In accordance with a growth model of change, early American social evolutionists tended to conceive of the rate of change as being naturally slow, gradual, continuous, and by degrees, and the magnitude as being relatively imperceptible, or infinitesimal. Ward, Giddings, and Keller equally concur, with Keller providing most elaboration.

Although only Ward explicitly accepted the dictum "Natura non facit saltum" (Ward 1906, 232), the insistence that nature does not jump or leap (i.e., change sharply, spasmodically, or disruptively) seems to have been assumed widely by early American theorists. American sociologists' constant struggle with a still-powerful supernaturalism tended to confirm their equation of naturalism and a slow, gradual rate of change. Catastrophic change was unnatural, because it was associated either with providential intervention in human affairs or with an antiprogressive irrationality and violence of political revolutions. Saltigrade change is thus unnatural, whereas pedigrade change is natural.

Directionality

Humankind or human society is conceived to experience growth through several stages, of increasing differentiation and complexity, and so to manifest directionality, just as does the individual in passing through the stages of growth in his or her life cycle. Social stages in sequence imply a direction, whether the unit is an institution, a more or less concrete society, human society, or humanity as an abstract whole. Stages were assumed to exist in some general sequence, even if then-current knowledge of their distinguishing features, precise order of succession, or laws of transformation might still have been in dispute (cf. Small 1905, 222–23). Change evidenced a linear (i.e., unilinear or rectilinear) directionality, although cyclical or repetitive features might be present in the form of repeated processes in the overall linear trend.

The terminological differences in the identification of societal stages in Ward's and Giddings's writings should not be misconstrued. Ward (1903) proposed protosocial, metasocial, and social stages, which appear to be only adaptations of Morgan's savagery, barbarism, and civilization, through a terminology deriving from a geological analogy (237–40). Giddings distinguished an ethnic, ethnogenic, or predominantly kinship-oriented stage of human society and a civic, demotic, or demogenic, or prevailingly territorially and politically oriented stage of human society. Yet consanguinity, kinship, and descent are as much a part of Ward's first stage as they are of Giddings's ethnic stage. In turn, this earliest stage of Giddings's scheme implies relative social homogeneity or lack of differentiation. Ward's metasocial stage signifies the emergence of civilization, political bonds, territoriality, the state, and citizenship as much as does Giddings's demotic stage. Conversely, Giddings's own description of his second stage testifies to the appearance of social differentiation and complexity as much as does Ward's metasocial stage. Both characterizations of stages signify a shift from small, relatively homogeneous or undifferentiated, blood-related, kinship-organized social units to larger, more heterogeneous, differentiated, territorially and politically organized social units.

Keller proposed a relatively elaborate sequence of stages for each of the major institutions (i.e., the economy, government, property, marriage, and religion).

Finally, Ward, Giddings, and Keller construe social evolution as associated with increasing structural and functional differentiation or complexity as adaptation and survival are enhanced. The Spencerian-Darwinian legacy is evident.

Casual Mechanisms or Modus Operandi

For early American theorists, as for the Europeans, change was a consequence of causes, factors, or processes that were natural, necessary, internal, and uniform (or consistent through time). In the view of the American theorists, social change was natural because humanity was basically enmeshed in the processes of nature, and thus its behaviors were subject (naturally) to modifications as the conditions of existence altered. And although the precipitant of social change may reside in alterations in the conditions of aggregate existence (including contact with and incursions by external societies), the source of change is primarily internal, that is, in the biopsychic makeup of members. And for all of them, as Keller (Sumner and Keller 1927, 2189) declared, the "same forces remain always at work": They are constantly or uniformly in operation.

The Genesis of Social Innovation. All of these early sociologists are among the more materialistically and Darwinianly inclined of the early American theorists. They approach change in terms of (1) alterations in the biophysical and social conditions of existence, especially regarding the scarcity or abundance of resources for satisfying the needs, wants, and desires of the human aggregate; (2) the emergence of conflict and struggle; (3) the presence of biopsychic variations among the members of a human population (e.g., differential talents, intelligence, imagination, initiative) out of which an effective adaptive response can emerge; and (4) the testing and selection of such behavioral variations so associated with biopsychic differences through struggle in relation to altered conditions of existence so that only the most adaptive one remains. Ward was unique in his unswerving faith in the Lamarckian thesis of use and disuse (or exercise and nonexercise) of biopsychic characteristics, the accumulating enhancement of acquired capabilities and their hereditary transmission to offspring, that is, the inheritance of acquired characteristics. Still, Ward did subscribe to some minimal operation of Darwinian selection, or elimination of the unfit.

Acceptance, Adoption, and Dissemination of Social Innovation. Ward, Giddings, and Keller do hold that a particular idea, belief, sentiment, or behavior is in effect tested and confirmed by extensive acceptance, adoption, and dissemination within a society. Giddings sees certain dynamic individuals as models; their choices are spontaneously copied and uncritically followed by the masses. Repetition of an innovation constitutes a wave of imitation (Tarde) and will presumably continue until it meets a wave of equal force. Keller presumably agreed with Sumner's view that an innovation will be accepted and adopted as it decreases the hazards in the conditions of existence, increases the certainty of efficiency of survival, reduces pain (or increases pleasure), and is in accord with the strain of the folkways and mores toward consistency (Sumner [1907] 1959, 5, 94–95). Such new forms diffuse not only among members of the same generation but also among succeeding generations. Ward ([1903] 1970, 34, 214) and Keller both emphasize continuity and accumulation in the process of change.

THE ANTHROPOLOGICAL CRITIQUE OF SOCIOCULTURAL
EVOLUTIONISM

Just what the responses of the post-World War I macrotheorists were to the legacy of the older social evolutionism was surely conditioned by a knowledge of the developing criticism offered by Boas and a number of his students in American anthropology. As indicated above, sociologists in the years after 1918 had frequent and direct contacts with anthropologists. Often anthropologists were members of join departments with sociologists. They participated in presenting papers at the annual meetings of the American Sociological Society, and they contributed articles and reviews to sociological periodicals. In the emerging work in macrochange theory of the second period, sociologists often referred to the research and critiques of their anthropology colleagues. Boas was, of course, a major figure, but so also were Kroeber, Lowie, Wissler, Goldenweiser, Herskovits, and Wallis in disseminating the criticisms of the unilinear stages theory of social and cultural evolution.

The anthropological attack was both empirical and theoretical. As early as 1914, Lowie published an article in the *AJS* that summarized the empirical data for rejecting many of the features of Lewis Henry Morgan's formulation of the unilinear stages theory of social evolution. On the basis of extensive research of many anthropologists, Lowie (1914, 93) contended that (1) unilateral kin groups are not found universally among all primitives, (2) proof of the development of North American Indian gentes from clans has not been established, (3) marriage restrictions are not primarily determined by unilateral kin groups, (4) exogamous kin groups are not the sole foundation of the social fabric among primitive tribes, and (5) kin groups are phenomena of variable significance.

In both 1920 and 1921 Barnes admonished his sociology colleages for their ignorance of the work of the Boasian school and its implications for the theory of unilinear social evolution (Barnes 1920, 197–98; Barnes 1921, 26, 34). He noted that his colleagues almost unvaryingly predicated "their theories of social evolution on the old Morganian ethnology," adhered to the doctrine of independent origins and development, and used the comparative method (Barnes 1921, 36, 43). "But they have done so for the most part unconsciously and without deliberate consideration of the problem" (36). They have not "acquainted themselves to any degree with the problem of cultural evolution" (36).

Accordingly, Barnes also calls attention to the results of the research of the critical historico-analytical anthropology of Boas and his disciples. They "have proved that the assumption of a universal law of evolution from the simple to the complex is not invariably true with respect to culture or social institutions." Parallelisms "of culture and social organization in different areas do not imply identical antecedents or necessitate similar subsequent developments. Similarities may grow out of 'cultural convergences,' proceeding from widely varied antecedents or they may be produced by imitation of a common pattern." Gentile society is not universal and where it does exist, no general tendency to shift from a matrilineal to a patrilineal system obtains. Furthermore, matrilineal societies are not correlated with a simpler material culture or patrilineal societies with more complex material culture. Totemism has been dissociated from exogamy (Barnes 1921, 42, 43).

But throughout the mid 1920s—and even earlier—anthropologists contributed articles controverting many of the basic tenets of social evolution in major sociological periodicals. Goldenweiser was the author of articles in *PASS* in 1921 and *AJS* in 1916 and 1925, and of a chapter in *The History and Prospects of the Social Sciences* (Barnes 1925); Herskovits and Willey of an article in *AJS* in 1923, and Wallis of one in *SF* in 1926. On the basis of the findings of anthropology, these articles raised major objections to the social evolutionary legacy of earlier sociology and anthropology.

First, awareness of the tremendous range in the variability of human cultures may well raise the question as to whether it is useful to think of humankind as a common social unit in and behind all particular changes. Different civilizations exhibit many individual and specific peculiarities in their transformations (Goldenweiser 1925b, 19).

Second, although anthropologists did not refer to the organismic growth analogy as such, they did allude to, and deny, the implication that the parts of a culture or society in cross-section are necessarily harmoniously interrelated, interconnected, and interdependent. (See Barnes's reference to the absence of a correlation between matrilineal societies and simpler material culture or patrilineal societies and more complex material culture (Barnes 1920, 197–8).)

Third, the comparative method as used by evolutionists is conspicuously objectionable. Goldenweiser notes that as early as 1896 Boas had attcked the comparative method because it ignored the "difficulty of estimating the extent and significance of culture similarities," it assumed that errors in dealing with large numbers of imperfectly circumscribed facts will cancel themselves out, and it failed to envisage "cultural features in their realistic historical settings" (Goldenweiser 1925b, 28). But its basic defect, he contended, was the fact that the very possibility of substituting a cultural datum from one culture "into a loophole left by a missing corresponding stage [elsewhere] . . . was based on the assumption that the processes were throughout parallel" (Goldenweiser 1921, 61). Thus, the comparative method only illustrates; it does not provide proof.

Fourth, the assumption that the rate of change must be slow, gradual, and orderly in nature is unwarranted. He holds that culture change may occur suddenly, cataclysmically, saltatorily (Goldenweiser 1925b, 19–20).

Fifth, a simple, uniform, orderly, and fixed sequence of stages in the development of human cultures (and thus rectilinear directionality, e.g., from simplicity to complexity) cannot be demonstrated. (Consult Barnes 1920, 197–8.) Moreover, the technique of using survivals to argue successive stage development is logically defective. To designate a cultural feature as a survival "presupposes the assumption of a particular preceding stage" that existence of the survival is to prove. "But if doubt is thrown on the reality or identity of this preceding stage, then the first question to be asked is whether the so-called survival actually is one or of what it is the survival, or whether it does not represent an incipient stage of development still to come rather than a survival of a past stage" (Goldenweiser 1921, 61).

Sixth, the conventional conception of evolutionary causal mechanisms that emphasizes independent inventions as responses of a common biopsychic human nature to problems presented by the environment is comprehensively criticized. The extensive evidence of diffusion contradicts the evolutionary view that the alleged parallel development of cultures stems from internal independent origins. Indeed, such independent origins are far more rare than was believed formerly (Herskovits and Willey 1923, 195). Realistically, too, the notion of a given culture as a self-contained expression of a people's biopsychic traits is denied (Herskovits and Willey 1923, 190–91). So, too, the notion that any culture is an individualistic, rationalistic, and intellectualistic adaptation of a common human nature to a certain kind of physical setting is indictable. On the one hand, Goldenweiser (1925a, 220) denies that "the task of mechanical and ideational adjustment to nature" is solved "by means of a rational process" resembling "the solution of a problem." Noting the widespread character of diffusion, on the other hand, Goldenweiser (1916, 632) held that borrowed traits "are obviously independent of the environment of the recipient cultures." Indeed, much of the content and all of the formal elements of culture—such as "the shapes and techniques of material objects, the ritualistic content and spiritual aspect of religion, the plots and magic of myths, the principles underlying social and political structure"—"must, by and large, be declared immune from environmental influences" (Goldenweiser 1925b, 31). For his part, Wallis (1926, 702–8) cites evidence of the drastic change in the culture of an area over the years while the geography remained constant. If anything, culture determines the definition, response to, and use of the environment. And the more elaborate and complex the technology, the freer individuals are from the limits of their environment.

SOCIOLOGISTS' OWN ASSESSMENT OF SOCIAL EVOLUTIONISM

When an effort is made to assemble and compare the reactions of sociologists to the criticisms of sociocultural evolutionism that cultural anthropologists had mounted, a startling fact becomes evident. Only three systematic critiques as such by sociologists can be discovered in the period after World War I. Faris published a substantially critical paper, "Social Evolutionism," that was printed initially as part of a symposium edited by the theologian Shailer Mathews in 1924 and subsequently included as a chapter in Faris's *The Nature of Human Nature* (1937a).[3] Just how many sociologists would have seen and read Faris's original chapter in 1924 is open to dispute, but probably not many. On the other hand, certain papers by Sorokin in the late 1920s and in the 1930s did critically assess sociocultural evolutionism. And manifestly the same can be said for many of Howard Becker's publications in the 1930s and early 1940s. But the data themselves are the ultimate exhibit, and so attention must now be turned to what the textbook authors and dynamics specialists have written about each of the major characteristics of social evolutionary change theory after World War I.

More precisely, the objective is to ascertain their assessment of the features of social evolutionism. This task can be accomplished by direct reference to either their statements about the character of alleged empirical social change and or their own views on the specific tenets of social evolutionism itself as previously presented. (Clearly, this undertaking differs from inferences drawn from the study of their own theories of social change, which is problematic, as discussed in the next chapter.)

The Social Unit or Entity Undergoing Change

Concepts of the unit or subject of social change of second period sociologists diverge very little from their pre-World War I predecessors. In alluding to the "importance of culture in human social life" generically, Ellwood's *Cultural Evolution* (1927) suggests essential continuity with the earlier generation of dynamics theorists. Ogburn's use of the terms *human society, society, social evolution, the social heritage, culture, cultural evolution,* and *cultural change* as his point of departure in his *Social Change* (1922) reflects a similar position. Faris recognizes that older, orthodox social evolutionism was concerned with the "sort of path" which the "race of men" has traversed, "the stages through which society has everywhere passed" (Faris [1937a] 1976, 252, 254). MacIver's references to "society as process" and to "the reality of social evolution" (rather than to "societies" or to "social evolutions") in part 4 of his *Society* (1931c) apparently represents another instance of similar agreement with the pre–World War I notion of the social unit or subject experiencing change. Howard Becker's various publications from about 1930 to 1960 accept the existence of a "total historical process" and the possibility of working out "an acceptable theory of the general trend of historical development" (Becker 1934b, 28–29; Barnes and Becker 1938, 789–90; Becker 1950, 159; Becker 1960, 804).

Among the textbook authors, continuity with the pre-World War I position is also evident. Unfortunately, Lumley did not write explicitly, but his commitment (in 1928) to evolutionary naturalism generally and to the views of Keller would certainly seem to identify him with the pre-World War I social evolutionists regarding the unit undergoing change. Hankins's rejection of the idea of unique (separate) social evolutions, his endorsement of the doctrine of psychic unity and the notion of cultural parallelism, and his view of "widely manifested phases" in a general arborescent social evolutionism are surely indicative of his acceptance of human society as the fundamental unit in social change (Hankins 1928, 395, 398, 680). Bernard (1942) is relatively explicit. He refers unqualifiedly to "human society" (cf. titles of his first chapter and of part 1 of his text), and he adheres to evolutionary naturalism to account universally for humankind organically, psychically, and socioculturally.

However, divergence was also evident. Chapin's *Cultural Change* (1928, 201) accepts a "main stream of human culture" undergoing change (primarily accumulation), but also "separate streams of group [especially national] cultures" also experiencing change, albeit of a more limited character. Although Thomas and Znaniecki (1918–20) frequently refer pluralistically to human societies and to specific kinds of such societies (e.g., savage and primitive societies, peasant society, and modern urban civilized societies), they allude to "human society" in an abstract generic sense (1:6). Most importantly, they selected the Polish peasantry for study because the social changes that the peasants experienced were more or less representative of a general trend of change culminating in modern social organization (4:9). The subject of Sorokin's *Social and Cultural Dynamics* (1937–41) is Western European civilization, or culture from its relatively early Greek and Roman origins (c. 580 B.C.) to its modern variants (c. 1920). Sorokin avoids any implication that his subject is typical of all human societies or cultures. Certainly, the later Park, who accepted anthropology's claim to study primitive peoples and apparently envisaged sociology's role as predominantly the investigation of modern civilized urban societies, can scarcely be viewed in continuity with the older evolutionism.

The Organismic Growth Model

Many of the dynamics theorists after World War I do invoke organismic growth as a model or an analogy of change, which might seem to indicate fur-

ther continuity with their earlier evolutionary predecessors. Yet others explicitly repudiate the analogy. Though explicitly disavowing social evolutionism,
Sorokin (1937–41) does invoke the ancient Greek philosophical claim that
natural objects (or systems, in this case) possess a natural, or internal, tendency to change as growth, that is, a *physis* (4:603, 604). For Park (1950);
each identifiable type or species of natural social object (e.g., plantations,
gangs, sects, revolutions) has its own natural history or typical mode of
change. In each type a given stage tends to follow another in an orderly and
irreversible way (224, 225). Park explicitly expresses his indebtedness to
Rickert for the view that a natural object has a nature that is disclosed by the
"rule or law by which it moves or changes" (178). Chapin (1928), for his part,
referred to identifiable social or cultural forms (or types), each with its own
law of change or "law of its life cycle" (210, 211) that is (as in Park's notion)
recurrent in its empirical instances and thus can be termed "cyclical." For
MacIver (1931c), differentiation within organisms has been a model for his
social evolutionary change, though he refuses to accept the organism in general as a model for society in general (400, 404, 405). Specialization is also
construed to occur by virtue of the operation of forces inherent [or internal] to
the situation—presumably akin to *physis* (400).

Importantly, some sociologists invoked a derivative premise from the
organismic analogy, which asserts that the parts of a social or cultural structure are intrinsically interconnected, interrelated, and interdependent, as are
the parts of an organism in cross-section. Both Chapin and Ogburn employ
the notion of culture lag, with its implications of strain, which become
meaningful only if the parts of a culture are organismically interrelated.[4]

Yet it is this very premise that such sociologists as Barnes and Faris in
effect controverted in their ethnographically based arguments. Barnes
(1921), for instance, notes that "matrilineal societies are not correlated with
a simpler material culture or patrilineal societies with more complex material culture" (43). Nor is there a general tendency to shift from a matrilineal
to a patrilineal system with the advent of gentile society (43). Faris ([1937a]
1976) declared similarly that the classic theory of social evolution has been
criticized for the failure of a given economic organization or stage to be
found in association with "a corresponding political, moral, and religious
stage of ideas and institutions" (259–60).

Interestingly, both Sorokin and Ellwood seem to assume that sociocultural change operates akin to a domain of mind, reason, or logos. For
Sorokin, in its simplest form, change may be said to occur rationally or logically by the increasing or decreasing integration of meanings, by deductive
elaboration, and by elimination of what Sorokin terms (unrelated) "congeries." Ellwood (1927) seems to presuppose an analogy between the development of mind as a set of stages in learning and the stages in social or cul-

tural change (19. 22). He evidences no awareness of Blaise Pascal's aphorism from the seventeenth century that the entire sequence of individuals throughout the ages can be regarded as a single individual existing always and learning continuously (Teggart 1949, 167).

The Comparative Method

The comparative method also had its protagonists and some antagonists after World War I. It seems to be presupposed in Ellwood's *Cultural Evolution,* both for change in culture in general and for change in the specific divisions of culture (equivalent to the developmental sequences in different social institutions.) And to the extent that Ogburn, Chapin, and MacIver assume a mainline, mainstream basic or general social life, society, or culture undergoing change naturally and normally (from primitivity to modernity), they appear to be committed to the comparative method. True, they all attempt to avoid any complex delineation of stages, but they invoke the general outline of an abstract human society in change from which temporal and spatial specifics and particulars have been excluded by the use of comparison.

The same charge can be directed against such textbook authors as Bernard, Lumley, MacIver, and Hankins. In effect, Bernard (1942, 347) simply ignored the critics of sociocultural evolutionism. MacIver (1931c, 432) endorsed the use of survivals, and Hankins (1928, 398) advocated the resort to the idea of cultural parallels, both of which are associated with or derivatives of the comparative method.

Curiously, even Chapin's small-scale cycles of national cultures and Park's social objects, with their natural succession of changes, entail a notion of a (generalized, via comparison and abstraction) life cycle or natural history of development from which specifics and particulars have been abstracted and excluded. Each one is a type or species of a universal established in effect by a resort to something very akin to the old comparative method.

Still, a few of the macrodynamics theorists did disavow the comparative method, either explicity or in effect. For instance, although Ogburn ([1922] 1950) cited the similarity between the material cultures of prehistoric Cro-Magnon peoples and the contemporary Eskimo, he explicitly denied the legitimacy of inferring a similar nonmaterial culture for Cro-Magnons from known Eskimo features (72). Faris ([1937a] 1976) objected to the assumption, associated with the use of the comparative method, that contemporary primitive peoples "represent earlier stages of the life which we are now living" (46). Faris insists that primitive man "who is really primitive [aboriginal and primordial] is gone and gone forever" (221). By implication, therefore, the use of data from contemporary primitives to fill in missing details of the earlier stages of European peoples' development is unwarranted.

Accordingly, Becker (in Barnes and Becker, 1938) had insisted that the comparative method is not genuinely comparative but only illustrative. In the reconstruction of the record of human social change, it had been valid practice "to link together a series of isolated examples of any type [or stage] or culture. These examples were taken from the most diverse regions and periods of time, irrespective of the totality of the cultural complex from which each was lifted, and were forced into a prearranged scheme of evolution" (748).

Earlier Thomas and Znaniecki (1918–20) had warned against the acontextual comparison of which Spencer was guilty and insisted that any moral norm, institution, and the like must be studied in relation to the "whole meaning which it has in a particular society" as against the "whole meaning which it has in . . . various [other] societies" (1:19, 18). Unlike their classical predecessors, such as Comte and Spencer, they insisted that knowledge of our present, civilized social life must be the point of departure for, and basis of, comparison (1:18). Thus, they eschewed the use of the acontextual classical comparison of coexisting civilized societies as indispensable "to distinguish the essential from the accidental, the simple from the complex, the primary from the derived" (1:17).

Appraisal of the Problem of Rate

The macrodynamics theorists' views about rate diverged substantially from those of the pre–World War I social evolutionists, who had construed social change as being normally and naturally slow, gradual, step by step, or pedigrade. Ellwood, MacIver, Thomas and Znaniecki, Faris, Chapin, and Ogburn all concluded that the rate of change among primitive peoples is relatively slow and gradual but becomes increasingly rapid in civilized, and especially modern industrial, societies. Thomas and Znaniecki (1918–20) noted the "imperceptible, almost continuous changes" or the "small changes . . . not noticed at once" in Polish villages (2:89; 3:67). They alluded to "more rapid" social change now, to a more rapid pace of social evolution, to "periods" or "moments of social crisis," to "crises become more frequent and varied" (1:10; 3:64, 63). In our time, Faris ([1937a 1976) remarks, "the most salient features of the culture life . . . is the rapidly increasing tempo of alteration" at a "geometrical ratio" 271, 272. But it was Chapin and Ogburn who were most conspicuously associated with the argument that cultural change is occurring at an increasingly rapid or "ever-increasing rate" (Chapin 1928, 51, 202). According to Ogburn ([1922] 1950) such change is especially evident in material culture and particularly in the mechanical and technological sphere in which the criterion of increasing utility or efficiency is operative (76–77). Because material culture is accumulative and the culture base is ever-expanding, its rate of expansion roughly resembles an exponential growth curve (105–10). Chapin (1928, 210) remarks that the cycles of change at the level of material culture are "relatively rapid," whereas the cycles of change for nonmaterial culture forms are slower, though not as slow as those for groups or nations as wholes. Ogburn's notions of culture "leads" (in material and especially technological culture) and "lags" (in nonmaterial culture) achieved considerable popularity before World War II. The various institutional spheres of modern societies can be arranged in a hierarchy of susceptability or proclivity to change, beginning with science and technology, the economy next, then the political domain, followed by the family, and finally religion (Ogburn and Nimkoff 1940, 870–71, 873). This culture-lag interpretation of social change became the most prominent feature of Ogburn's conception of sociocultural change and, indeed, eventually became a convenient designation for his entire theory. (Even MacIver [1931c, 135] noted that technology and science seem to change constantly and most rapidly, the economic system next most rapidly, and the political system the slowest.)

In Hankins's (1928) view, the rate of change in cultural evolution is highly variable. It may increase rapidly, remain constant, decline, or "regress more or less sharply" (426). In general, the rate of change has been slowest in the earliest stages of sociocultural evolution and increasingly more rapid as culture has developed (425–26).

In contrast to other theorists of social change, Sorokin (1937–41) critically examined the notion of rate or tempo as applicable to different domains of culture. He insisted that the concept of tempo or its equivalent is inapplicable to all cases of comparison of qualitative changes or rhythms of different sociocultural processes or systems (4:555). Because the rates (or tempi) of qualitative changes of qualitatively different sociocultural systems are incommensurable, the very idea of tempo is inapplicable (4:556).

Linear Directionality (Stages in Sequence)

With but few exceptions, textbook authors and dynamics specialists after World War I rejected the irreversible, unilinear (stages) directionality of social evolutionary theory. As noted above, Barnes had initiated the discussion in his papers of 1920 and 1921 at the American Sociological Society annual meetings, in which he referred to the objections of cultural anthropologists.

In his *Social Change*, Ogburn (1922, 57)) declared that the "inevitable series of stages in the development of social institutions has not only not been proven but has been disproven." Such an evolutionary notion of sequence in various social institutions had failed empirically, he suggested later (Ogburn and Nimkoff 1940, 741–42), because diffusion disturbs endogenous development in any culture area and because institutions tend to be interdependent with one another. Faris remarked in a chapter in a 1924 book, which perhaps few sociologists would have seen, but which was republished in his own *The Nature of Human Nature,* that the idea of universal stages through which human societies have everywhere passed—"formulated again and again and correlated with economic organization, familial schemes, moral concepts, religious views and practices"—has "been regretfully abandoned under the strain of accumulated facts which have revealed exceptions, anomalies, and lacunae too serious for the theory to incorporate" (Faris [1937a] 1976, 254). Sorokin (1927) observed that the "existence of a definite, steady, and eternal trend in historical and social change has not been proven" (39). Chapin's *Cultural Change* (1928) declared simply that the "classical theory of universal and inevitable stages of social evolution" has collapsed. Concrete cultural similarities "in different times and places . . . are . . . not illustrations of universal stages in one continuous world-wide stream of unified cultural evolution" (202). And Becker (1934b) rejected "the idea of stages as describing general trends of social development in mankind taken as a whole" because it relied on the "uncritical illustrative method" (28).

With so many specialists or experts in the field of macrochange holding this preponderantly negative view, it would seem that the textbook authors could scarcely disagree. Reuter and Hart (1933, 164) declared that "there is no given series of steps or stages through which [all] cultures pass in evolutionary fashion." To assume that because "many peoples have passed through these stages, have developed in this way" and that, therefore, "all must do so," cautions Lumley ([1928] 1935, 448), is "an unproved and misleading assumption." Hankins, Hiller, and Young all concur with Reuter and Hart that the common idea of a uniform succession of economic and technological stages through which all peoples must pass does not correspond "with the known facts" or with the character of cultural dynamics (Hankins 1928, 164–65; (Hiller 1933, 415; Young 1934, 99). Hankins and Young agree with Hiller that a society may shift directly from a hunting to an agricultural stage (Hankins 1928, 397; Young 1934; 99; Hiller 1933, 415). Hankins and Hiller both held that any assumption of a certain typical institutional arrangement associated with a given stage of economic evolution is incorrect (Hankins 1928, 398; Hiller 1933, 415). In Young's (1934) view, "the static concept of step-wise evolution gave way" as "more adequate material on the life and history of native tribes and civilized peoples came to hand, and the whole culture of any society was seen in its dynamic relationships" (33, 34, 99). And Hankins (1928, 398) acknowledged that the antagonists of classical evolutionism have been successful in denying the universality of an uncomplicated and unambiguous "series of stages."

Causal Mechanisms or Modus Operandi

Interestingly, few sociologists directly and critically examined the nature of the causal mechanisms of social evolution. But Faris did so, and did so perceptively, in *The Nature of Human Nature* ([1937a] 1976).

In general, according to Faris, social evolution is a part of the comprehensive conception of evolutionary naturalism, which invokes the doctrine of parallel biopsychic and sociocultural evolution and its mechanism of adaptation. Put more precisely,

> The orthodox theory of social evolution is a corollary of the theory of psychological evolution. As the body can be traced from the very simple forms to a climax in the relatively large brain of man, so mental capacity was assumed to consist of separate states, the lower ones being those occupied by primitive man.

Culture and social organization are the result of an interaction between the human mind and its surrounding environment. The mind is "assumed to be uniform and constant for a given situation" (this is the doctrine of psychic unity), whereas the environment to which adaptation is required varies with the climate and physical situation. The product of the adaptation of a (talented?) individual or individuals, culture is regarded as high or low in accordance with the higher or lower order of mind involved in the adaptation.

Modern societies and cultures are alleged to be more effectively or efficiently adapted to their conditions of existence, and primitive societies and cultures less so, with the former representative of greater, and the latter of lesser, mental capacities. The survivals (i.e., survivors) of aboriginal, undeveloped societies and cultures (i.e., of earlier biopsychic evolution) can be found in geographically remote, marginal, or isolated sections of Australia, Patagonia, Greenland, and similar regions (255). They are simpler and inferior because the minds of their creators and carriers are inferior.

But Faris is at pains to point out that this form of argument essentially assumes the independent, internal origins of culture, which he critiques in relation to diffusion generally and in particular by specific instances of persons who have originated in primitive cultures, have had subsequent contact with, and have assimilated, modern forms of culture without evidence of mental inferiority (255–60).

Illuminatingly, Faris proposes his own version of social evolution of folkways to mores, mores to conscience and institutions, and their possible disorganization and reorganization, in such a way as to repudiate the typical features of the naturalness, necessity, uniformity, and internality of the evolutionary process of the older formulation (271). Change does "not necessarily take this [linear, sequential] direction" (271). Usages may remain indefinitely in the form of folkways. "Likewise, the mores undergo constant modification, decay, intensification, or substitution, without necessarily ever becoming institutionalized" (271). Indeed, "some institutions pass back into the life of a people" and so revert to being "mere customs" (271). In effect, Faris denies typical unidirectionality and irreversibility. But if naturalness, necessity, and (constant) uniformity (along with irreversibility and exclusive internality) are denied, social evolution might itself be questioned. So Faris's own formulation of social evolution appears to contain its own contradiction.

SUMMARY

Viewed retrospectively in relation to the previous features, the overwhelming rejection of linear directionality as the most central and basic feature of social evolutionism seems to be the culmination of an increasingly negative verdict on each of the other five characteristics of the theory. Certainly, many of the textbook writers and the dynamics specialists seemed to accept a comprehensive notion of human society as the subject undergoing social change, though Thomas and Znaniecki, Chapin, and Sorokin were inclined to adopt a more circumscribed subject. Some of them continued to invoke certain implications of the organismic growth analogy, though in this instance, too, a minority dissented (e.g., Faris, Case [1924, xxv] by inference, and the sociologically oriented historian Barnes). More of them accepted than rejected the resort to the comparative method. Apparently, a majority rejected the conventional social evolutionary pre–World War I notion that the rate of change is naturally and normally slow, gradual, step by step, or pedigrade. Ellwood, MacIver, Thomas and Znaniecki, and Ogburn concuded that change among primitive peoples might be relatively slow and gradual but becomes increasingly rapid among civilized and especially industrialized societies. (Only Sorokin claimed categorically that any comparative concern with rate or tempo is inappropriate and invalid for qualitative data.) And apparently Faris stood alone in denying that the human mind is naturally disposed to adapt creatively to the sensed needs of a biopsychic human nature in relation to changing biophysical conditions.

Now, of course, the central problem is to be confronted: What are the actual prevailing theories of social change? Do they indeed represent forms or types of social evolutionism continuing in the macrochange theory of the textbooks and in the articles and books of the specialized field of change after World War I? This is one of the questions the next chapter seeks to answer.

Chapter 5

Fragmentation and Demise of Social Evolutionary Change Theories

Interestingly, a preliminary reassessment of the character of the change theories after World War I discloses that a majority were still versions of social evolutionism. In addition to Keller (as noted in the previous chapter), Ellwood, Bernard, Lumley, MacIver, Ogburn and Chapin, Thomas and Znaniecki, and Hankins subscribed to some variant of social evolutionary theory as specified below. If the inquiry to be undertaken in this chapter confirms this preliminary assessment, their theories will evidence some degree of continuity with the predominant pre–World War I macrochange theory.

The objective, then, is to ascertain if and to what extent the characteristics of their change theories represent incorporations of, and extensions of, social evolutionism. In contrast to the previous chapter, which sought to assess the acceptance or rejection of social evolutionism in general, this one is concerned with the social evolutionary character of the stated macrochange theories of these theorists.

Accordingly, it will be necessary to focus on the nature of the operative assumptions of these theories themselves and to discern or infer the applicability of these theorists' assessments of social evolution in general to particular aspects of their own theories. But again, the point of departure is the typical core social evolutionary conceptions of the unit undergoing change, the model, method, rate, directionality, and mechanisms of change.

FEATURES OF SECOND-PERIOD SOCIAL EVOLUTIONISM

Theories of the second period predominantly endorse the view of their first-period predecessors that human society or culture is the unit, entity, or subject of social change. Ellwood's preoccupation with the importance of culture in human social life generically, Lumley's commitment to evolutionary naturalism generally and to the views of Keller specifically, Bernard's references to human society and his adherence to evolutionary naturalism, MacIver's allusions to society and to social evolution (in the singular), Ogburn's similar adoption of society, social evolution, and cultural evolution, and Hankins's acceptance of the doctrine of psychic unity, cultural parallelism, and a general arborescent social evolution reflect essential continuity with the pre–World War I comprehensive view of human society or humankind as the social entity undergoing change. But a modification of position is at least suggested in Chapin's acceptance of a "main stream of human culture" as well as "separate streams of group cultures" and in Thomas and Znaniecki's references to human societies pluralistically and to specific kinds of such societies as well as to human society in an abstract generic sense. (See chapter 4.)

Interestingly, acknowledgment of organismic growth as a general analogy or model of social evolutionism is more difficult to document during the second period of American sociology. True, the prevalent acceptance of evolutionary naturalism, with its tendency to envisage sociocultural evolution as continuous with organic evolution, points at least to a congruency with organic growth and adaptation. In MacIver's case, differentiation within organisms has been a model for his social evolutionary change, though he refuses to accept the organism in general as an analogy for society in general. Ellwood seems to presuppose an analogy between the development of mind as a set of stages in learning, with the adaptive growth of the organism, on the one hand, and with the stages in social or cultural change, on the other. Chapin refers to identifiable social or cultural forms (or types), each with its own law of change or "law of the life cycle," as presumably applicable to his own theory. In addition, some sociologists (e.g., Ogburn and Chapin) invoke a derivative premise from the organismic analogy (in connection with their cultural lag notion), which asserts that the parts of a social or cultural structure (or stage) are intrinsically interconnected, interrelated, and interdependent, as are the parts of an organism in cross-section. (See chapter 4.)

The comparative method seems to have been pervasively assumed and yet only infrequently directly acknowledged. It is presupposed in Ellwood's notion of evolution in culture in general and in its specific divisions or realms (i.e., equivalent to developmental sequences in different social institutions). And to the extent that Ogburn, Chapin, MacIver, Bernard, Lumley, and Hankins assume a mainline, mainstream basic or general social life, society, or culture undergoing change naturally and normally (from primitivity to modernity), they appear to be committed to the use of the comparative method in their own theories. (Note also MacIver's endorsement of the use of survivals and Hankin's and Ellwood's resort to the idea of cultural parallels, both of which are linked with the comparative method. See also Ogburn's reservations and Thomas and Znaniecki's concern with comparison in context. (See chapter 4.)

But it is in their views about rate that the post–World War I sociocultural evolutionists diverged most substantially from their pre–World War I predecessors, who had construed social change as being normally and naturally slow, gradual, step-by-step, or pedigrade. Ellwood, MacIver, Ogburn and Chapin, Thomas and Znaniecki, and Hankins all conclude that the rate of change among primitive peoples is relatively slow and gradual but becomes increasingly rapid in civilized and especially modern industrial societies. As is well known, Ogburn and Chapin were most conspicuously associated with the argument that cultural change is occurring in the modern world at an ever-increasing rate. Though Hankins (1928, 426) generally concurred, he also warned that cultural evolution occurs at a varying rate. It may increase rapidly, remain constant, decline or "regress more or less sharply." (See chapter 4.)

However, the notion of directionality is manifestly the most conspicuous and characteristic feature of social evolutionism. Interestingly, most dynamics specialists who were social evolutionists acknowledged—as did the majority of textbook authors—the legitimacy of the cultural-anthropological criticisms directed at the notion of an invariant unlinear sequence of stages in different domains of culture or social institutions, though the language used varied considerably. For example, Ellwood (1927, 15) concedes that "the scientific study of the cultures of the world has left" the idea that "there was one typical line of concrete development in culture . . . without any standing." Lumley (1928, 448) notes that although many peoples had passed through the stages characteristic of the shift of human society generally to modernity, "it is an unproved and misleading assumption to say that all must do so." MacIver (1931c, 423) admits that if social evolution means "lineal" or linear evolution, and so involves "a sequence in which specific institutions of simpler peoples pass by similar processes into specific institutions of more advanced societies, . . . it is certainly to be rejected." Both Ogburn and Chapin acknowledge that the "inevitable series of stages in the development of social institutions has been disproven "or at least has not been proven (Ogburn [1922] 1950, 57; Chapin 1928, 202). And finally, Hankins (1928, 398) notes that the "critics of classical [social] evolutionism . . . [have] succeeded in showing that a simple, clean-cut series of stages was by no means universal." Presumably, then, their own theories make no claims to a uniform, invariant sequence of stages. (Only Bernard and Thomas and Znaniecki sidestep the issue of the tenability of invariancy in sequences of stages.)

Regarding the legacy of the notion of a uniform and invariable sequence of successive stages, three points must thus be noted before proceeding. First, even though this period reveals increasing concern with conceptual clarity and precision, only Howard Becker was preoccupied with a tenable notion of stages. Curiously, no one else shared his concern. Second, as just noted above, a majority of social evolutionary theorists of this period rejected the notion of a single, uniform, and invariable sequence of stages found in all empirical instances of a given kind of change. And third, the theories examined below are considered in terms of their increasing dissimilarity to or divergence from the conventional social evolutionism of the pre–World War I era. Thus, Ellwood, Bernard, and Lumley represent one position; MacIver a second; Ogburn and Chapin (in part) a third; Hankins a fourth; and Chapin (in part) and Thomas and Znaniecki a fifth.

VARIOUS FORMULATIONS OF STAGES IN SEQUENCE

Generalized Evolutionary (Linear) Schemes, Not Assuming Invariant Sequence

Ellwood, Bernard, and Lumley represent a position closest to that of their predecessors of the years before World War I. Their notions of directionality involve a combination of societal and institutional stages, or simply institutional stages.

Charles A. Ellwood. Of all the macrochange theories after World War I, Ellwood's version of cultural evolution as a series of sequential stages in both culture as a whole and in its chief subdivisions seems most closely to resemble its pre–World War I predecessors. Ellwood (1927) claimed—and this may seem to violate the immediately preceding statement—to argue for "many divergent evolutions in culture," "each concerning a different phase of the life process" developing "more or less independent of other traditions" (15, 78). So physical tools, food processes, clothing and bodily decoration, housing, fine arts, property, family, law and government, morality, religion, education, and knowledge have their own distinctive evolutionary series of stages. In some instances, such as food processes, clothing, housing, and the fine arts, the stages were more difficult to distinguish. Even in those realms in which stages could be demarked unambiguously, as in those of physical tools, family, morality, and religion, the number of stages varied. And Ellwood also proposes a series of societal stages.

Ellwood's effort to insist on the separateness of the divisions of culture, and yet on the organic character of any culture generally, seemed to lead him into inconsistency. So, he contended that modifications in any one tradition do not necessarily "keep step" with one another (78). But one page later, he urged that continuous cultural evolution in any one line of activity, "whether industrial, religious, or political is bound to react in time upon the development of other lines, such that the life of the group is, after all, interdependent in all of its parts," or organically one (79). Although the permissible variations are still very wide, the different traditions constituting the culture of a people do tend to have "a certain harmony and congruence" (79). Thus, the seeming contradiction alluded to above largely disappears.

Furthermore, Ellwood constantly resorted to a common parabolic curve (the parts of which derive from Lewis Henry Morgan's trichotomy of savagery, barbarism, and civilization) to represent the development of culture in general. Each realm of culture has its own distinctive stages, but these are superimposed on a parabola divided into four parts. The importance of this underlying conception becomes obvious in Ellwood's final chapter, where he contends that a long view of human cultural evolution can be taken and a line can be drawn to show the general direction of all of the separate curves in each realm of culture. The long line at the bottom of this horizontally placed parabola represents savagery. Barbarism is denoted by the rounded section of the line approaching the focus of the parabola. The similarly rounded line beyond the focus is what Ellwood terms "semicivilization." Finally, the projected future achievement of full civilization parallels the long curved line of savagery. The point at which savagery ends and barbarism is introduced is termed "the beginning of agriculture." Similarly, barbarism terminates and semicivilization begins with the "invention of writing," the point at the focus of the parabola. The culmination of the semicivilization of the present and the emergence of the full civilization of the future is represented by "universal literacy," which is a point exactly opposite the beginning of agriculture on the long curved line at the bottom of the parabola. This generalized curve of cultural evolution signifies human primal development from animality and our eventual emergence into full humanity.

The first half of the parabola may be construed as primarily an evolution of control over the physical. The second half, designated as the "invention of writing," entails an emergence and increasing control over the psychical. Together, both material and nonmaterial culture find their appropriate inclusion in the scheme. Clearly, this parabola envisages a directionality comprehensive of all humankind that, while broadly linear, conveys a judgment of the earlier or more primitive as being lower or inferior and the later, or more civilized and modern, as higher or superior. (The rising curve of the parabola, rather than the straight line, appears to be Ellwood's effort to interlink social evolution with progress.[1]

For Ellwood, the social and cultural evolution of humankind rest both on organic and psychic evolution. Ellwood seeks to explain the latter especially in terms of W. I. Thomas's theory in his earlier *Source Book for Social Origins* (1909). (See below.)

Viewed across the perspective of time, culture is a collective learning process in the group like the learning process in the life span of the individual, and stages may be similarly discerned as necessary steps in the learning process. In "the process of learning control over physical nature and over human behavior," certain stages are inevitable "because there are psychological stages in the process of learning" (Ellwood 1927, 15, 22).

L. L. Bernard. Like Ellwood, Bernard (1942) accepts a view of social evolution closely resembling that of his pre–World War I predecessors. Although he acknowledged the criticisms directed toward the stance, he refused to consider the attack. According to Bernard, social evolution involves a series of forms, types, or stages "beginning with the simpler . . . and ending with the most complex" (344). This growth in complexity (differentiation?) is accompanied by enhanced adaptability and increasing progress (346, 351). For Bernard, social evolution is orderly change involving a linear directionality on the part of humankind or human society as a whole.

Bernard's early chapters in his introductory textbook (Bernard 1942) testify to the centrality of an orderly sequence of stages in his conception of social evolution. Chapter 3 identifies the stages in the evolution of material artifacts: the Paleolithic, Neolithic, Copper, Bronze, and Iron ages. Chapter 4 expounds the evolution of human economies as a sequence of these stages: the direct appropriation economy, hunting and fishing, grazing or herding, agriculture, and industrialism. Chapter 5 reviews the evolution of family and marriage: maternal, paternal, patriarchal, and equalitarian families; group, monogamic, polygynous, and polyandrous marriages. Chapter 6 examines the evolution of social organization: from the sib (clans, gens) to the tribe, to confederation, to feudalism, and city-state, and the nation-state. Unfortunately, it is impossible to ascertain whether Bernard's conception of sequences of stages assumes that all societies universally will pass through the set or that each series represents only the general sequence for human societies as a whole, within which jumps or skips can occur in particular instances.

His schemes of social evolution are predicated on a notion of causal mechanisms drawn from organic evolution, such as the struggle for existence, survival of the fittest, selection (natural and cultural), and adaptation. He remarks that any culture trait can survive only if "it finds a place for itself through adaptation to the environment," either natural or cultural (751).

F. E. Lumley. For Lumley (1928), the third figure involved in this general stance, social evolution is the evolution of permanent human association, social relations, or society in the sense in which phenomena in general may be said to evolve. It means a process of naturalistic (nonmiraculous) change that involves continuity of the present with the past and the persistence of the past in the present (411–15). Whatever exists now is derived from the past and involves an identifiable continuation of that past (by a series of stages).

Lumley indicates his acceptance of a generalized sequence of developmental stages for particular institutions, such as the economy, in the first edition of his *Principles of Sociology* (1928). Thus, he refers to the collection, hunting and fishing, nomadic, agricultural, and manufacturing stages (449–52).

Interestingly, his second edition in 1935 entirely omits any reference to stages and shifts to a conception of evolution as differentiation, specialization, and cooperation, which he expressly borrowed from MacIver (Lumley [1928] 1935, 365). In addition, his second edition endeavors to accommodate a revolutionary with an evolutionary notion of social change. Social change may be both infinitesimal and gradual as well as vast and sudden (366–68).

Borrowing from Keller's *Societal Evolution*, Lumley (1928) supposes that social adaptations arise from individual variations (or deviations from standards), which are selected automatically (i.e., irrationally) or rationally by objective testing or empirical experimentation, and thus transmitted to the oncoming generation as an accepted item to constitute a new standard (430–43; Lumley [1928] 1935, 371–86). In his second edition, he proposes a set of distinctive stages through which revolutionary processes pass (Lumley [1928] 1935, 367–68).

Lumley's, Bernard's, and Ellwood's sequences of societal or institutional stages are, of course, only one kind of evolutionary series. MacIver's trichotomy of stages represents a second.

A Differentiation-and-Integration View of Social Evolution: R. M. MacIver

In contrast to Ellwood, MacIver (1931c) makes explicit in his scheme of evolutionary stages the fundamental assumption of differentiation and integration in the relation of the social and the cultural. He accepts a generalized abstract statement of the sequence of social stages as distinguished "not by the sheer presence or absence of social factors, but by their prominence, their relation to others, their organizing function" (430). His own trichotomy is presumably illustrative of what he intends. He thus proposes three basic evolutionary stages: a first of undifferentiated primitive communal customs, a second or intermediate stage of differentiated communal institutions, and a third or recent stage of differentiated (great) associations appearing concurrently with (past and present) civilizations. The first and third stages are conceived ideal-typically as "polar contrasts" (433). What typifies the first stage is not characteristic of the third stage.

In drawing this contrast, MacIver has followed the same procedure as his eminent evolutionary predecessors used. His earliest stage of human social existence is a characterization of (simpler) contemporary primitive societies that is also held to typify a conjectured undifferentiated social stage of a primordial human social existence. MacIver draws on the data of modern ethnography and the records of ancient history. The terminal point or, more accurately, the last, most recent, or third stage, is provided by the records of past and present civilizations.

Accordingly, MacIver contrasts the character of the first and third stages. Among primitive societies everyone is a member of a few groupings or categories, and membership in one tends to imply membership in a few others. But our own most recent stage of social existence involves "a vast multiplicity of organizations of such a nature that to belong to one has no implication . . . [for] belonging to the rest" (433). The "social unity to which we belong is conceived of as multiform" whereas that of the primitive is "uniform" (433). Our solidarity is complex, and our communities are differentiated. Their solidarity is simple, and their communities undifferentiated (435).

MacIver's second stage is thus intermediate. It is inferred as the outgrowth of divergent attitudes and interests of a differentiating mind behind a differentiating form.

MacIver offers considerable detail about each of the three stages. For instance, the (first) stage of (undifferentiated) communal customs, with its fusion of political, economic, familial, religious, and cultural usages, is characteristic of the functionally undifferentiated primitive society. Its main divisions of "families, clans, exogamous groups, totem groups . . . are segmentary or compartmental" (431). It often involves "a fairly elaborate system of ceremonial offices" and an extensive system of kin distinctions. Usually, the kin group is "predominant and inclusive" (431). Being a member of the kin groups mean sharing "the common and inclusive rights and obligations, the customs, the rituals, the standards, the beliefs of the whole" (431). The division of labor tends to be organized in accordance with age and gender criteria. Usually, secret societies, which are not specifically functional, are the only clearly associational groups. The communism characteristic of economic and property relations "typifies the simple solidarity of an undifferentiated community" (432). The mode of social life and the character of the social heritage preclude the public expression and formulation of any divergences of interests, aptitudes, and capacities "as endangering the solidarity of likemindedness, the only solidarity of which the group as a whole is yet capable" (433).

The stage of differentiated communal institutions is, as MacIver puts it, created out of the divergent attitudes and interests of the differentiating mind (434). Repeated deviations, whose suppression is impossible or inexpedient, may introduce a zone of indifference within older institutions or establish a new one. Specific modes of procedures, taboos, and approaches to the mysterious powers of nature or of the tribe, (i.e., new institutions) are developed. Hence, "the ways of the group are diversified without loss of unity" (434–35). At first only the growing variety of communal life, this diversity of institutions, conceals "the germ of a new order, but it takes ages to develop" (436).

The third stage of the (differentiated) great associations of past and present civilizations requires a more difficult unity, which the combination of difference with likeness creates. With the expansion of the scale of society and the reduction of the pressure of the common mores, "the diversification of interests [as] enlarged through the advance of knowledge and the specialization of . . . economic life," the right of free association can become effective. So also can the family "detach itself sufficiently from the social matrix to become an autonomous unit, dependent for its creation and for its dissolution on the will of the consenting parties." The uniformity of communal education is replaced by a variety of particular schools and other educational associations. And eventually the heretofore unified politico-religious system comes to acknowledge "the internal disharmonies of its enforced unity" and state and church become constituted as separate associations (435).

Put simply and succinctly, MacIver's (1937) conception of social evolution is the evolution of "society . . . from primitive types to developed civilizations," in which what he terms the "utilitarian orders" (or the systems of economy, technology, and polity) undergo differentiation and demarcation from one another and from the cultural order of (more or less common) ends (149). MacIver illustrated this fundamental process in terms of ancient Greece (especially Athens) from the Homeric age to the fourth century B.C. and in more recent Western European civilization of the medieval era (145–47, 148–51). Our own modern civilization has carried this demarcation of utility from cultural significance further than any previous one (143–44). What had earlier been a relatively all-inclusive unity has broken up into a number of partial semi-independent systems of diverse social range—economic systems such as capitalism in its various forms and with its necessary but insecure relations to political systems such as democracy; technological systems representing various stages of the one all-conquering system of industrial mechanization; cultural systems infinitely variable in many respects though cohering around certain foci of devotion and cerain symbols of loyalty; and ancillary systems, such as the educational, which perplexedly move in response to the divergent currents of change (145).

But MacIver leaves unspecified whether or not this phenomenon of differentiation and specialization (presumably with some degree of integration) is to be conceived as relatively unlimited (and thus indefinitely continuous) or limited (and thus finite and bounded at certain points). In other words, the basic question is whether the phenomenon involves not merely differentiation into a few semi-independent systems or the further unchecked proliferation of additional systems and subsystems.

With this "freedom of association," an "indefinite multiplicity of contingent forms" and innumerable modes of "interrelationship and independence" are possible. But they are still "based on the general foundations of a community life, the obligatory aspects of which are now safeguarded by the state" (436).

Although his chapter "Social Causation" is patently conceived as the culmination of the analysis of social change construed as social evolution in the last section of *Society*, no explanation of social evolution is undertaken. It follows three earlier chapters on evolutionary forces (Chaps. 23, 24, 25) and one entitled "The Reality of Social Evolution" (Chap. 22). At the end of the first section, "The Nature of the Problem," in the chapter "Social Causation," MacIver notes that the various aspects of structural differentiation "furnish the background for our study of social causation" (524). Yet, curiously, MacIver never shows, regarding the realm of the social, in which relationships are determined by and sustained in the mutual awarenesses of the participant personalities in given situations, how the convergent or divergent dynamic assessments have consequences that can be construed to be the structural differentiation of social evolution.

Within the broad comparative perspective of all of the schemes of stages examined in this chapter, MacIver's views differ only slightly from the prevailing pre–World War I ideas. But the conceptions involved in Ogburn's and Chapin's culture lag theories, with their emphases on material culture and technology, are further removed from the earlier dynamics theorists.

A Materialist, Technology-Based Scheme of Social Evolution: W. F. Ogburn and F. S. Chapin (in Part)

Undoubtedly, the most extensively discussed, popularly accepted, and distinctive theory of social change in the period was formulated by Ogburn in his *Social Change* (1922), substantially invoked by Chapin in his *Cultural Change* (1928), and reiterated essentially by Ogburn and Nimkoff in their *Sociology* (1940). As first stated by Ogburn, the theory conceived, on the one hand, the emergence of culture in terms of arguments about biopsychic human nature deriving from the premises of evolutionary naturalism and, on the other, changes in culture in terms of sociocultural evolutionism. In a word, then, the culture lag theory—as it came to be designated—resembled most of the other theories of the period in its fundamental indebtedness to major components of the older social evolutionism.

Major Points of Agreement between Ogburn and Chapin. First, emphatically naturalistic in their outlook and thus committed to regularity and continuity in phenomena of nature (including culture), both Ogburn and Chapin construed culture change, as the key to social change, as fundamentally entailing accumulation both in culture in general or "the main stream of culture" and in the cultures of particular or specific groups (e.g., societies). They both agree that culture accumulates because the number of new elements added in any given unit of time exceeds the number lost (Ogburn and Nimkoff 1940, 809; Chapin 1928, 203). Certainly, Ogburn would have concurred with Chapin's statement that the "process of cultural accumulation began long before the time of recorded history," that is, extended well back into the realm of human prehistory (Ogburn and Nimkoff 1940, 66–73; Chapin 1928, 24–30).

Second, whatever may be the antecedents of the distinction, culture is basically classifiable into the categories "material" and "nonmaterial." The term *material culture* seems to designate objects of human fabrication designed to facilitate adjustment to biophysical nature. This category includes tools, technology, machines, factories, houses, vehicles, boats, clothing, food, raw materials, manufactured products, and other material objects humanly produced (Ogburn [1922] 1950, 11–12, 202; Ogburn and Nimkoff 1940, 46). The term *nonmaterial culture* refers to non-physically-embodied culture, presumably to socially established responses in word and deed. It encompasses "ways of doing things, methods of making material objects, ways of reacting to nature and material culture . . . habits of organizing socially," and knowledge, art, philosophy, beliefs, customs, folkways, mores, morals, laws, and social institutions (Ogburn [1922] 1950, 12, 4, 60, 202; Ogburn and Nimkoff 1940, 46–67).

Chapin (1928), and many others, including Ellwood, also employed the material/nonmaterial dichotomy, with essentially the same meaning. However, Chapin also trichotomized culture into tools and implements, language, and social institutions and further classified material culture into the symbolic (e.g., icons, idols, flags) and the utilitarian (e.g., buildings, tools, factories) (20, 49). Indeed, Chapin's claim that utilitarian and symbolic culture traits "were once mental patterns and ideas" that have subsequently been expressed or embodied in "material substances" suggests the essentially non-material basis of material culture (20). Conversely, Ogburn further classifies nonmaterial culture into the subcategories "adaptive" and "nonadaptive" (Ogburn [1922] 1950, 202, 203, 271–72).

Third, because material culture is subject to criteria of utility, efficiency, and adaptiveness (i.e., one item can be objectively tested or compared with others) in relation to the conditions of existence, and nonmaterial culture is not, change in the two realms of culture occurs at differential rates at different times. Ogburn ([1922] 1950, 110) comments that the "rate of cultural growth as measured in terms of increased inventions is uneven, slow then rapid, then slow, and so on." Accumulation is selective, especially in the material domain. Ogburn is manifestly convinced that accumulation occurs in material culture, but he is hesitant about its occurence in the nonmaterial domain. Chapin (1928, 50–51, 202) regards all domains of culture as exhibiting accumulation, indeed at an ever-accelerating rate, although he acknowledged the differential between the rates in material and nonmaterial culture.

Ogburn and Chapin were the inheritors of a social evolutionism that argued that whatever new was added, whatever old persisted, whatever new was rejected, whatever of the old was discarded must ultimately hinge on facilitating the adaptation and survival of the society. Admittedly, they did not always directly use such terms as *selection, adaptation*, or *survival*. Sometimes they used somewhat more oblique terms such as *utility* or *efficiency*. Both seemed to regard material-culture items, or at least certain sub-varieties, as possessing a more patent significance for survival than the non-material. In particular, they both recognized that tools or machinery are subject to an "impersonal clean-cut and decisive" test of what they will do in the physical environment: Either they work or do not (Ogburn and Nimkoff 1940, 743; Chapin 1928, 402, 314).[2] (Interestingly, Chapin (1928, 42) regarded scientific method as a symbolic substitute in the modern world for the social and societal selection practiced among primitives.)

But it was Ogburn who designated the differential rates of change in the selective accumulation in different spheres of culture as involving "leads" and "lags." As the parts that are more prone to change, to change first, and to change faster, technology or material culture (in modern times) represents the independent variable and the cultural "lead." By contrast, customs and institutions are less prone to change, they change later, and they change more slowly. (See also Chapin 1928, 210, 313.) Their variation seems to depend on variation in material culture, to which, in the language of the organismic analogy, they are finally related, connected, and dependent, and behind which they lag. (See also Chapin 1928, 10, 314.) Accordingly, change in customs and institutions represent the dependent variable (Ogburn

[1922] 1950, 200; Ogburn and Nimkoff 1940, 886). This cultural-lag inter-pretation of social change became the most prominent feature of Ogburn's conception of cultural change and, indeed, eventually became a convenient designation for his whole theory.

And fourth, even though Ogburn concedes that the "inevitable series of stages in the development of social institutions has been disproven" or at least has not been proved, he and Chapin hold that a linear course of sociocultural change for humankind in general can be asserted. Ogburn's contention that material culture change occurs more rapidly, more commonly initiates change elsewhere, and accumulates selectively does imply directionality in culture change in general—because nonmaterial-culture lags must eventually come to terms with the material. His argument . . . involves a number of interesting assertions and admissions (Ogburn and Nimkoff 1940):

a.   An evolutionary sequence of material cultures (e.g., food gathering, hunting and trapping, agriculture, industry) in a series from early to late stages is factual and universally reliable (743).

b.   But efforts to construct a unilinear stages theory of the evolution of various social institutions have failed empirically, apparently, because diffusion tends to disturb endogenous development in any cultural area and because institutions tend to be interdependent (741–42).

c.   Although it might be thought that the "contemporaneity" of nineteenth-century Tasmanian stone-using culture and European power machinery would raise doubt about assertions of any universal time-sequence, Ogburn contends that "we are [still] able to infer that, for the world as a whole, the stone age preceded the age of metals and of steam power" (743).

d.   Because "the sequence in material culture is partly a matter of record and partly inferable," it may legitimately be used to classify "institu-tions and other parts of culture for which there are no discernible his-torical sequences, or where the sequences can be inferred only in very broad terms. The material culture thus becomes a standard of compari-son or a term of reference" (743–44).

e.   Finally, the proposal that an objective confirmation of utility, efficiency, and ultimately adaptation (and survival) of tools and machinery in mate-rial culture is possible, along with the necessary tendency of the nonma-terial culture ultimately to adjust to the material and thus catch up the "lags," entails a long-term linearity of direction in culture change.

Culture Lag and the Problems of Modern Social Life. In the views of Ogburn and Chapin, the sociocultural change characteristic of the modern era is the disproportionate accumulation in material culture, with which exponential and linear directionalities are associated. Admittedly, Ogburn did not explicitly deny, in either the original or the later versions of his theory, that nonmaterial culture accumulated in the past or in the present (Ogburn [1922] 1950, 273; Ogburn and Nimkoff 1940, 778). But—and Chapin agreed—accumulation is more frequent and obvious in material culture (Ogburn and Nimkoff 1940, 792; Chapin 1928, 313).

As suggested earlier, this disproportionate accumulation of material culture occurs both because material culture represents adaptation to objective conditions of the natural environment and because the superiority of a new technological instrument is easily and objectively demonstrable (Ogburn and Nimkoff 1940, 743; Chapin 1928, 314, 402). Hence, material culture tends to accumulate more rapidly from one generation to another in accordance with the criterion of increasing utility or efficiency, with the less useful or efficient items being discarded (Ogburn [1922] 1950, 76–77). In general, then, material culture comes to exercise a "logical or instrumental priority" in change (Ogburn and Nimkoff 1940, 743).

Not only does Ogburn claim that much social change in modern life is a consequence of change in material culture generally, but he insists that it is due specifically to changes in technology (Ogburn and Nimkoff 1940, 846). Still, he concedes that in the broad perspective of human development, it is impossible to generalize as to whether the mechanical or the social, the material or the nonmaterial, can be said to be the origin of change generally (866–67). Yet Ogburn seeks resolutely to avoid any minimizing of the significance of culture lag. So he asserts astoundingly that "[because] it appears easier to find illustrations of technology causing changes in social conditions, . . . we are inclined to favor the hypothesis of the greater importance of the sequence of technology causing social changes" (865). And Chapin agrees that material culture change tends to precede nonmaterial modifications in contemporary society, although he accepts Sorokin's warning that any such precedence is not inevitable or necessary (Chapin 1928, 209n).

Fundamentally, Ogburn claims that culture is an organic whole and that thus the differential rate of change must produce a strain. Accordingly, the related but less rapidly changing or responding nonmaterial culture, which lags behind the more rapidly changing or "leading" material culture, must inevitably find a more harmonious readjustment.

Thus, Ogburn argues that culture in the course of time will (must?) gradually reduce the lag by readjusting and reequilibrating the relationship of parts. He is confident that a new adjustment and a new equilibrium will naturally be effected if free experimentation in the use of new culture traits obtains (Ogburn and Nimkoff 1940, 881, 882). Yet Ogburn's appeal to what "most persons," a "majority of reasonable men," or "most observers" would consider clearly raises the specter of value judgments (cf. 887–88, 889). And

Ogburn's admission in his earlier *Social Change* (1922, 297) that one's notion of adjustment may depend somewhat "on one's attitude toward life, one's idea of progress, or one's religious beliefs" only emphasizes the valuational basis. Indeed, Ogburn is compelled to admit that "there is no known coefficient of correlation that measures the degree of correlation in the different parts of culture" (Ogburn and Nimkoff 1940, 886).

Still, Ogburn uses the "hypothesis" of culture lag to explain and propose the amelioration of various forms of social "maladjustment" or "disorganization" in modern society. It is employed in *Social Change* (Ogburn 1922, 203–52) to account for such phenomena as deforestation, industrial accidents, and loss of family functions, and in *Sociology* (Ogburn and Nimkoff 1940, 895–98) to account for unemployment, depression, poverty, ill-health, and the like.

Equally immmportant, Ogburn holds that such problems can be solved by the elimination of the lag. Logically, this result can be accomplished by any one or combination of several expedients:

a.   Retardation of the speed at which the lead or independent variable has been changing
b.   Acceleration of the speed at which the lagging or dependent variable has been changing, which is presumably "the most practicable" expedient (Ogburn and Nimkoff 1940, 900)
c.   A combination of deceleration of the rate of change in the leading variables and acceleration of the rate of change in the lagging variables

In effect, then, Ogburn's (and Chapin's) culture lag theory of change argues that all parts of culture must finally become adjusted to material culture, especially technology, because the latter represents an instrumentally effective adaptation to the natural conditions of existence. Thus, it proposed a sequence of stages of technology as an infrastructural evolutionary foundation to which other parts of culture must be finally related. Though subjected to extensive criticism, it remained a widely accepted theory of social change during the 1920s through the 1940s.[3] With its emphases on material culture and technology, it is substantially different from the conventional evolutionary conceptions of direction of the pre–World War I period, but not as different as the arborescent, multilinear notion of Hankins.

An Abrorescent, Cladogenetic, or Variational Notion of Social Evolution: F. H. Hankins

Acknowledging that the "critics of classical [social] evolutionism . . . [had] succeeded in showing that a simple, clean-cut series of stages was by no means universal [among all peoples]," Hankins (1928, 398) proposed not a total rejection of social evolution, but its reformulation in terms of what was later designated an "arborescent" or "branching" (cladogenetic) theory. This reformulation followed what Hankins then regarded as the newer conception of human organic evolution. "Instead of thinking of man as having evolved in a straight line from a monkey stage, through an ape stage, to homo sapiens, we now think of him as having evolved along a number of more or less diverse lines, like a many-branching tree" (398). Thus, social evolution was to be conceived as "much like the spreading branches of a great tree" (680). Presumably, it began with a common stem or trunk (i.e., unilinearly) and became diversified (i.e., multilinear and branching). Curiously, Hankins assumes a contradictory position at different points in his text on whether or not it entails a general shift from simplicity to complexity or from homogeneity to heterogeneity, with increasing differentiation, specialization, and integration (29 vs. 681–86).

Hankins believed that his new formulation retained "the doctrine of evolutionary stages in a more flexible form" made possible by a resort to "the idea of cultural parallels" (398). Whether viewed as a whole or as parts, social development is alleged to manifest successive phases that are "repeated in widely separated areas of the world" (398). For instance, "the feudalism of China and that of Europe a thousand years later had many similarities" (421) Significantly, Hankins denied that diffusion, or the "transfer of goods or ideas from one area to another," can account for such repetitions (398). Instead, he insisted that they "are due to the similarities of human needs and thought processes [i.e., the pyschic unity of mankind], and the uniformities and limitations of nature" (398–99).

Certainly he held that it was possible to identify broad general sequences of abstract stages in several institutional realms that are also characterized by striking historico-cultural differences and are not interdependent with one another (397–98, 680–81). Nevertheless, most, "if not all, the peoples who have reared great civilizations have passed" through "certain broad types of material culture" (487). So he accepted the sequence of material implements from the Paleolithic and Neolithic to the Copper, Bronze, and Iron Ages (399, 469–87). He also alleged that similar types or stages of economies developed: (1) the collectional stage; (2) the pastoral stage; (3) the horticultural stages; (4) the stage of settled agriculture, or of the village economy; and (5) the stage of commerce and industry, or of the urban economy (487–51). Later he qualified this assertion by claiming that although "Egyptians, Babylonians, Greeks, Romans, and Europeans have all passed through pastoral, agricultural, handicraft, and industrial stages and in that order, . . . the uniformities are general rather than specific and detailed" (421).

Hankins had considerably more difficulty in successfully delineating stages in the purported evolution of myth, magic, religion, and science, and in marriage and the family in chapters 12 and 13. His chapter 14, on the evolution of social organization and integration, contends that the differentiation of tribalism, feudalism, and nationalism as successive stages is "entirely within the range of observable facts . . . These are stages through which has passed the evolution of all those peoples who have achieved a high civilization" (681). (It appears that a contemporary critic might well claim that all Hankins has accomplished is to provide a distinctive name for a position that essentially resembled the qualifications of the successive stages of unilinear social evolutionism of most of his contemporaries. He had allowed only for empirical diversity without actually formulating multiple sequences of stages.)

Mixed Linear and Cyclical Formulations of Social Evolution

Finally, Chapin's and Thomas and Znaniecki's combination of (recti-) linear and cyclical theories seem to be farthest removed from conventional pre–World War I social evolutionism. Interestingly, both cyclical theories are predicated on a version of the Greek organismic notion of *physis* as an intrinsic tendency to change on the part of natural objects or objects in nature.

Chapin's Distinctive Combination of Linear and Cyclical Features. Although Chapin's (1928) emphasis on accumulation in the "main stream of culture" suggests his commitment to linear directionality, his most distinctive contribution to the theory of cultural change is to be found in his use of notions of cyclical change in the analysis of the emergence of specific inventions and their incorporation into their respective domains of culture (202, 203). Manifestly, he was impressed by the regularity of much of natural phenomena and its evident cyclical character, and, accordingly, he proposed the following hypotheses (208–12):

1. All cultural items have their laws of change, which are perhaps generalizable for certain types of social phenomena, are "probably cyclical" and possibly periodic in nature, and are expressible in quantitative terms.
2. The laws of such cycles or periods tend to fall into three phases: growth (and integration), maturity (equilibrium), and decay (disintegration).
3. The laws of such cycles (or periods) can be worked out for the components of material-culture, nonmaterial-culture, and national-culture

items, with the duration of the cycles being shortest for the material-culture items and longest for national-culture items.

4.   When "the cycles or periods of a number [a majority?] of cultural" items in the material and nonmaterial realms "are synchronous" (coincide at their zeniths), "the culture nation or group in which these culture traits are found" has attained a stage of maturity.

Of these four hypotheses, the first two occupied most of his attention. Indeed, he seems most concerned with documenting his view that each cultural item has a life cycle or growth curve resembling that of an organism. Two types of growth curves or frequency cycle curves are proposed: one plotting the rate at which improvements occur in a basic invention, and the other—which is not always carefully distinguished from the first—plotting the diffusion and acceptance of a given invention. He endeavored to show that the improvements of social inventions can be charted and graphically portrayed just as the inventions supplementing a basic invention can. Such curves tend to show first a phase of slow growth, second a phase of rapid growth, and third a phase of diminished growth. Presumably, the maximum number of improving inventions represents "a point of relatively perfect adaptation in meeting the situation for which" the invention was designed. Thereafter, the number of increments or supplemental inventions will diminish (382).

Another most important feature of Chapin's efforts to deal with social change involves his notion of a group (or societal) reaction pattern, with a sequence of stages, including more or less innovative endeavor and entailing adaptation to changing circumstances. Chapin defines the group (in terms of Gidding's views) as essentially a psychic phenomenon, that is as a "fluctuating equilibrium of interactions and interrelationships of individuals who are in contact" (225). At any point in time, their interactions and interrelationships are more or less definable and describable in terms of oral or written traditions (and, in modern societies, in terms of law) (225–26). Chapin suggests that a group's reaction to changing conditions can be described as a cycle with three phases: (1) An effort is made to compel conformity with traditional rules, or the enforcement of its mores, though this attempt soon fails to be effective, in the sense that maladjustment "is soon felt"; (2) efforts are made on a trial-and-error basis to make specific changes in the older social arrangements (e.g., a resort to particularistic uncoordinated laws); and (3) a comprehensive program is developed that integrates successful group practice as a set of more differentiated, specialized roles (228, 236–37). Undeniably, Chapin regards this pattern as associated especially with "social inventions" (e.g., poor relief in England, Massachusetts, Minnesota, and elsewhere) (229–37). It is an interesting commentary on Chapin's sociological assumptions that at the time he seems to have found considerable satisfaction in the apparent similarity between his social reaction pattern and "the learning process of an individual," which further indicates his commitment to social nominalism (228–29).

Manifestly, Chapin's resort to cyclical notions to characterize change in specific items of culture as involving three phases (growth, maturity, and decay) and a cycle of societal reaction patterns (compulsion of conformity, specific trial-and-error changes, and comprehensive modifications entailing role differentiation and specialization) reveals a further departure from the traditional unilinearism of modified social evolutionary formulations. But it is a departure that Thomas and Znaniecki also make, though in different form.

A Combined Evolutionary and Process (Linear and Cyclical) Notion of Social Change: Thomas and Znaniecki. Perhaps farthest—but certainly far—removed from the typical evolutionism of the first period, that of *The Polish Peasant in Europe and America* appears unobtrusively in a welter of empirical details at the outset of the second period. The term *social evolution* occurs infrequently, and *stage* or *stages* only by implication—for whatever reasons.[4] However, Thomas and Znaniecki do claim that a relatively general or pervasive change can be detected in the (linear) shift from primitive, savage, and peasant societies to modern urban civilized societies, which manifestly resembles the directionality of classical social evolutionism. But, in contrast, they also distinctively envisage this change as involving cycles of social organization, social disorganization, and social reorganization and reconstruction.

More precisely, Thomas and Znaniecki construe primitive, savage, and especially peasant societies as early social stages more or less approximating the primary group as an ideal type of social existence, with its unreflective and nonrational cooperation, and modern urban industrial society as a later stage more or less approximating the secondary group as an ideal type of social existence, with its reflective, rational cooperation. The general directionality of change is signified by the decreasing influence of the social organization of the first (primary) type and by the increasing influence of the second (secondary) type in the life of a people (i.e., the Polish peasantry).

In several articles and chapters a few years before appearance of *The Polish Peasant*, in that volume itself, and in publications soon afterward, Thomas employed the terms *primary group* and *secondary group* (as opposing types, perhaps influenced by Znaniecki). The six to eight contrasting features focus on the directness or indirectness and the personalized or impersonalized nature of relations, localized versus nonlocalized circumscription of membership, the place of sentiment versus reason in the solidarity of the group, general or common versus specialized or particular interests in the two, the place of informal versus formal controls in such groups, their isolation from or accessibility to other groups, and so on.[5] It must be conceded immediately that their remarks about primary and secondary groups are fragmentary, scattered, incidental, and unsystematic. Noteworthy, too, is the fact that they offer even fewer comments about modern civilized society, with the secondary group as its core, than they provide about primitive society and peasant society or community, with the primary group as its core.

The generalizations from empirical data in volumes 1 and 2 of *The Polish Peasant*—especially in the sections on marriage, family groups, the kinship system, the village, religious beliefs and practices of the parish, the commune, and the system of peasant agriculture—provide a foundation for their claim that Polish peasant social life substantially approximated a primary-group type of social existence (particularly before the mid nineteenth century). Volume 4 deals with the social disorganization of the peasantry in Poland, particularly family and community disorganization. Volume 5 is a study of the Polish peasant migrant to the United States, especially to metropolitan Chicago, which was the setting for a type of social organization and substantial social and personal disorganization.

The transition from a peasant social life based on a primary group organization to an urban industrial mode of life, with its differentiation and specialization of interests represented in secondary groups, tends to accentuate and aggravate the possibility of social disorganization—that is, deviation, the breaking of rules, and personal disorganization and demoralization. Existing rules of social behavior lose their influence, and instances of nonconformity increase. Social opinion is hesitant or divided, and thus the forms in which social solidarity formerly manifested itself are inadequately enforced. Indeed, solidarity itself may decay or virtually dissolve. In personality (or character) structure, the desire for new experience is awakened, and, in the new context of interaction, response and recognition do not necessarily and consistently support and reinforce one another. Still, the broader societal context itself has important consequences, and thus Thomas and Znaniecki separate out in their analysis the impact of change on those Polish peasants who remained in Poland versus those who migrated to urban America.

In construing the social changes in the Polish peasant communities toward modern urban life as typical of the direction of change generally, Thomas and Znaniecki were nevertheless sensitive to the character of the context of Polish society more generally. More importantly, the peasants were emancipated from their condition as serfs simultaneously with the beginnings of the industrialization and urbanization of Poland around the beginning of the last half of the nineteenth century. Though freed from duties and charges to the lords, the peasant were compelled to pay heavy taxes requiring orientation to a money system and to possible sources of monetary remuneration. As communications improved, peasant communities were drawn out of their isolation and into direct and continuous relation with the external world. The growth of large cities provided peasants with the possibility of selling the secondary products (i.e., foodstuffs) of their farming. But the rapid increase of the rural population required more substantial sources of additional income. The main source was hired seasonal work, which occurred first in the neighborhood, then in the more distant parts of the country (sometimes in cities), and on the landed estates of Germany (Prussia), and finally in America. Both the indirect communication with the outside world and the personal contacts gained through seasonal migration brought to the peasant an awareness of new standards and values of social life and work.

The more rapid changes from the outside society were introduced by two kinds of mediators, those from the outside who settled in peasant villages and those from the inside who had contact with the outside social world. In the former category were the Jewish shopkeepers and city workers and members of the lower middle class who became residents in the peasant community. In the latter category were younger members of the peasantry who worked in closely adjacent industrial or commercial centers, emigrants who returned from the United States, and especially the younger seasonal workers who had been employed on German (Prussian) estates. The latter were the most consequential source of social changes: Deriving from the same village or neighborhood, the migrants tended to have "common interests and memories," unifying them one with another and yet separating them from the rest of the community; the changes introduced on their return were a social rather than individual phenomena; and as younger persons they were able to influence other young people in the peasant community.

The changes introduced into the rules and rule structure of the family and community eventually became sufficiently substantial that Thomas and Znaniecki refer to family and community disorganization and to personal disorganization on the part of individuals so involved. In the case of family disorganization, the features included the use of new kinds of objects (e.g., food, drink, tobacco), modification of interpersonal relationships (e.g., sex before marriage, marriage outside of family arrangements or in disregard of dowry considerations, selection of a mate irrespective of family desires or exclusively in terms of personal preferences), and changes in basic attitudes of member personalities. Marriage may itself be evaluated economically or instrumentally. Notions of individual advantage may intrude into family land and property.

The disorganizing effects of the intrusion of individualism may be disclosed in conflicts between siblings over inheritance claims, dowries, the contributions of aging parents, or the claiming of hospitality from another family member. It may be seen in the desire for individual recognition as opposed to family standing in the community.

The young migrants returning from seasonal work in Germany became a substantial factor in community change and disorganization. They could attempt to gain sympathy from and to proselytize the rest of the youth in the community. They could appeal to the suppressed desire for new experience among the young who had remained in the community. Most importantly, the bloc of returned migrants could help other individuals to free themselves from the control of social opinion and could counter the conformist reactions of other family members.

Violations of the rules thus became widespread, with the undermining of informal social controls and social solidarity, and so constituted what Thomas and Znaniecki term "social disorganization." This became associated with personal disorganization, the replacement of "we-attitudes" by "I-attitudes," and the appearance of new values (individual values, individualism) appealing to the individual and not to the group. Nevertheless, Thomas and Znaniecki did not seriously anticipate disorganization to the extent of the dissolution of the peasant community. They believed that social reorganization and reconstruction were possible, though they did not point to specific instances of this third process.

In America, the Polish immigrants confronted a vastly different situation, a large metropolitan community, the social life of which was oriented to secondary group relations and with considerable preexisting social disorganization. The subcommunity that they established assumed, of necessity, the structure of a voluntary organization, linked with other such groups and subgroups. The new organization was more specific and weaker than the primary-group-oriented community in Poland. The influences of the old (Polish) rules were substantially reduced. Social disorganization was conducive to personal disorganization and demoralization in a variety of forms (economic, familial, age, and gender). Thomas and Znaniecki argue that the social and personal domains are always interconnected and interrelated, but the personal seems to be emphasized in the social context of the immigrant in the American city.

Undeniably, the more abstract, impersonal cycle of social organization, disorganization, and reorganization is linked with a personal one, which is, in turn, interconnected with the more basic linear shift from a more primary to a more secondary stage (or mode) of social organization. Admittedly, Thomas and Znaniecki's concern with a case study of social change imposes a much more limited scope and time span, so that their study is much less readily comparable to the others—in addition to employing a simpler, dichotomous scheme of (linear) directionality.

What is noteworthy in broad comparative perspective is that it is, indeed, difficult to say to what extent the alleged recognition of the anthropological critiques of social evolutionism have altered the various theorists' formulations of stages in sequence in different institutions. They do not appear to be significantly different from those of their pre–World War I predecessors. None of them specifically address the point—irrespective of whether their formulations closely resembled those of the first period (e.g., those of Ellwood, Bernard, or Lumley) or were far removed (such as those of Ogburn, Chapin, or Hankins). Both illuminating and distressing is the fact that none of them refer to the (English) Hobhouse, Wheeler, and Ginsberg study, *The Material Culture and Social Institutions of the Simpler Peoples* (1915).

SUMMARY ANALYSIS OF THE DIRECTIONAL IMPLICATIONS IN THE SOCIAL EVOLUTIONARY THEORIES OF THE PERIOD

Although it is true that many of the evolutionary theorists just examined developed their positions in relation to a conception of humankind as the subject, unit, or entity undergoing change, used some features of the comparative method, and stated views about the rate of change, but only a few drew on inferences from the organismic growth analogy, the central and critical feature of their theories involved a unilinear or rectilinear notion of directionality (with stages in sequence). Classical social evolutionism of the first period encompassed formulations of both general societal stages and stages in the development of institutions (or different institutional domains). And because the social was characteristically envisaged in relation to the cultural, analysis of sociocultural evolutionary theory in the second period began with those theories that most closely resembled classical social evolutionism and concluded with those least similar (but still evolutionary). Thus, study was initiated with theories involving both general societal stages and stages in the development of institutions (e.g., Ellwood, Bernard, Lumley), then considered those explicitly based on increasing social differentiation and integration (MacIver), an alleged basicness or priority of a stages sequence in one institutional domain (e.g., Ogburn), a version of multilinearity (e.g., Hankins), and a combination of linear and cyclical conceptions (Chapin, Thomas and Znaniecki).

However, it is still difficult to ascertain how these acknowledgments of the anthropological critiques apply to the stage-sequence formulations of the dynamics specialists themselves. If the sequence formulation for a particular institutional domain applies only to many or most societies, the question still arises as to what the bases of the exceptions are. Both Ellwood and Bernard invoke a generalized notion of a succession of stages both for a variety of cultural, subcultural, and institutional domains and for human society in general. (Admittedly, Ellwood's use of a parabolic rather than a simple linear representation of the sequence patterns of culture in general is distinctive, though it is based on Morgan's earlier trichotomy of societal stages.) Interestingly, Lumley directly commits himself only to a succession of economic stages. MacIver explicitly identifies evolutionary directionality with increasing differentiation and integration as exhibited allegedly in the three abstract stages of undifferentiated communal customs, differentiated communal institutions, and differentiated associations. Endeavoring to restrict the anthropological criticisms only to invariability of stages in different social institutions, Ogburn (1928, 398) argues for the tenability of a linear sequence of (substructural?) technological and economic stages, to which other (superstructural?) domains of culture must ultimately adaptively relate. Hankins proposes an arborescent (cladogenetic, multilinear) conception of the direction(s?) of sociocultural evolution as involving "stages in a more flexible form." But his analysis also invokes only a generalized, abstract sequence of stages for particular cultural and subcultural domains and institutional realms as well as for human society generally. His scheme, along with those of Ellwood and Bernard, shows resemblances to Clark Wissler's intellectual organization of universal cultural patterns.[6] Hankins never actually develops multiple patterns of development in different institutional realms. Thus, it appears that the arborescent, cladogenetic representation remains only an assertion about the diverse but allegedly parallel character of the actual empirical development of specific institutions and societies in time.[7]

Finally, Chapin and Thomas and Znaniecki, the farthest removed from classical social evolutionism, illustrate the combination of linear and cyclical features in social evolution. By assuming the legitimacy of a conception of a mainline development of culture (or culture in general as the aggregate of particular cultures), which he associates with Ogburn's culture lag thesis, Chapin seems committed to a linear version of evolutionary change. But he also contends that a concern for particular instances of social, institutional, and societal change are most accurately formulable in terms of organismic growth cycles. And perhaps seeking to avoid a public display of their intellectual differences, Thomas and Znaniecki never refer in *The Polish Peasant* to the problem represented by the anthropological criticisms of the invariability of the sequence of stages in different institutional domains. They propose only two comprehensive, abstract stages of societal evolution as exhibited in *The Polish Peasant:* a first entailing an earlier organization dominated by relations of a primary-group character, and a second entailing a latter organization dominated by relations of a secondary-group character. The transition from the first to the second stage is characterizable in terms of a repeated or repeatable cycle of social organization, disorganization, and reorganization.

As represented by the bulk of the theories (i.e., Ellwood, Bernard, Lumley, and Hankins), the more or less modified social evolutionisms of the second period have apparently achieved enhanced correspondence with the varying empirical social world, but at the price of a less determinate sequence of stages in given institutional domains. And the formulations of societal stages (as instanced by Ellwood, Bernard, MacIver, and Hankins) have become so differentiated or fragmented, and yet simplified and abstract, as to render their utility dubious.

CAUSAL CHARACTER OF EXPLANATIONS OF SOCIAL EVOLUTIONARY CHANGE

Although analysis of the causal mechanisms in as great detail as characterized the study of directionality (i.e., the formulation of stages and their sequences) may further illuminate social evolutionism generally, space limitations and the higher priority of another task preclude such an extensive undertaking. A more circumscribed approach to causal dynamics seems better fitted to account for the virtual disappearance of social evolutionism after 1930. But it does require, first, a brief résumé of the crucial characteristics of the causal accounts of social evolutionary change of the pre–World War I period.

In general, such first-period evolutionary theorists as Ward, Giddings, and Keller continued to ascribe to social evolution the same features as their European predecessors, Comte and Spencer, did. Human societies were regarded as objects in nature (or natural objects possessing a *physis*), and thus change was construed as being akin to organic growth, natural (or normal), necessary, continuous, and (unilinearly) directional (Nisbet 1969, 166–68; cf. Hinkle 1980, 192–213). Specifically, the causes were internal (to the social entity, i.e., society) and operated uniformly or constantly through time. As noted previously, these American theorists based their conceptions of social evolution primarily on the Darwinian-Spencerian notion of humankind as a particular species of organism still fundamentally involved in a struggle for existence within the broader domain of biophysical nature. All of them elaborated systems of arguments in which social change more or less necessarily, that is logically, derived from the Darwinian-Spencerian premises.

Ultimately, the most important set of causes was attributed to the internal nature of biopsychic human nature (involving the needs, wants, and desires of the social forces in conjunction with variably conceived reason) of individuals in the social aggregate. But within this constancy of human nature, individual differences operated in response to the external conditions of aggregate existence as given by biophysical nature, including shifts in the abundance and scarcity of resources. The variable individual responses were also oriented by or to the cumulative legacy of adaptive experience as transmitted to a given present generation.

From the vantage point of the more recent present, one of the more impressive blind spots of second-period social evolutionists in American sociology was their failure to recognize the basic implications of their anthropology-derived division of the sources of sociocultural change into those that are internal (independent inventions) and those that are external (entering via diffusion) to a given society or culture. Indeed, anthropologists in the second period emphasized that the bulk of items in a particular culture tended to be overwhelmingly the result of diffusion or borrowing as against the view of evolutionary theory. Classical evolutionism conceived of the sources of change as basically internal, intrinsic. or endogenous: as independent inventions devised by the human mind. Implicitly or explicitly, the doctrine of psychic unity—with varying emphases on trial and error or rationality in relation to the needs of biopsychic human nature and the problems for survival as presented by the environment—was thus presupposed.[8]

Curiously, too, most of the second period theorists simply remained silent about cultural anthropologists' critiques of the notion that social change was to be explained as being akin to the rational solution to an individual problem and that problems of a common environment can be met effectively only by one form of sociocultural response.

Typically, the textbook authors simply tended to present and discuss a vast array of different factors generally accounting for change. Hankins (1928) is illustrative. He explicitly acknowleges the role of habitat, the quantity and quality of the population, including race, along with the importance of the doctrine of psychic unity (the inclination of the human mind to respond similarly to like external circumstances, especially those of nature). He readily concedes the significance of prior stages of culture, its accumulation (the culture base), and the possibility of contact with other societies and their cultures (e.g., by war, migration, trade, travel, and communication), the occurrence of group crises, the possibility of cultural losses and disappearances, variable rates of cultural accumulation, the state of scientific knowledge, an atmosphere of intellectual freedom and toleration of the new, strange, or deviant, attachment to the idea of progress, and the (democratic) openness of the social system to talent irrespective of "social rank at birth" (437; cf. 413–39). Yet he seems to place special stress on the quality of the individual brain, on the unique initiative and talent of "creative genius."

Like others, Hankins fails to interrelate the factors in any consistent, systematic explanatory statement. The textbook format may in part explain the difficulty, but then it surely contributes to the lessened rigor of social evolutionary explanation.

Although Hankins regarded culture as first and foremost an adaptation to the conditions of social or collective existence, he apparently had become aware of the problem of acceptable criteria of adaptation. He even warned that "we cannot say with any degree of exactness that some elements of culture are adaptive in the sense that they tend to fit man for his particular habitat, while others are non-adaptive in the sense that they bear no relation to the habitat" (391). Thus, the whole notion of adaptation from the first period seems to lose explanatory significance.

Hankins fails, as do others, to account for the transition from one stage to another. He does not relate particular factors or causes to the specifics of a set of stages in their evolutionary scheme so that a second stage is generated from a first, a third generated from a second, and so on.

Furthermore, the fact that his and others' evolutionary explanations encompass a considerable range of intellectual positions is not necessarily to be regarded as a positive feature. They range from a predominant materialism (Keller, Lumley, Ogburn) to a balance between materialism and idealism (Bernard, Hankins, and Chapin) to a predominant idealism (Thomas and Znaniecki, Ellwood, MacIver). It might well be doubted that such explanatory heterogeneity enhances the acceptability of evolutionary formulations.

TOWARD AN ACCOUNT OF THE DECLINE AND DEMISE OF SOCIAL EVOLUTIONISM GENERALLY

At the outset, two preliminary comments seem warranted. First, the problem of the decline and demise of social evolutionism is not merely a problem of the tenability of its premises for its explanations of change, or even of the characteristic features of social evolutionary change, but of its theory (or theories) of origins and structure as well as of change. Second, any account of a decline and demise that involves a sudden "disappearance" or "absence" of a phenomenon (i.e., of social evolutionism after 1930) is likely to envoke charges of speculation, conjecture, or outright fabrication.

Now some additional points about the intellectual character of social evolutionism must be raised:

1. The substantial variation in the definitions and conceptions of social evolution could hardly prompt confidence in the tenability of the position. For Ellwood, (1925, 20) "social evolution is a scientific theory of social origins and all change or development of all sorts." Bernard (1942, 343) envisages social evolution as orderly social change and Lumley ([1928] 1935, 467) as "continuous, connected change in any direction." Young (1934, 99) viewed the phenomenon as the passage of societies and cultures "step-wise through more or less regular stages from simple to complex." Though Hank-

ins (1928, 29) regarded social evolution as entailing adaptation, its specific expressions in specific societies reveal that "organizations and institutions grow more complex for a long time and then fall into decay." MacIver (1931c, 402–5) conceived of social evolution as the actualization of potential forces internal to human society and involving gradually increasing differentiation, specialization, and integration of parts. Such diversity would not seem to augur favorably for continued acceptance of the theory in a period of increasing concern with general conceptual rigor.

2. It might be argued, similarly, that the continued evident centrality of the notion of stages, but prevalent disregard for its status as a concept, would hardly enhance the acceptability of the theory in the future. Only Becker was concerned with the character of "stages" as a concept.

3. In the above examination of the tenets of social evolution, the organismic analogy, especially the idea of growth, had virtually disappeared during the second period. Historically, the analogy had been critical in the intellectual genesis of ancient Greek philosophical naturalism (as *physis*), which was subsequently "linearized," first by St. Augustine and much later by Pascal. (Consult Nisbet 1970, 175–77; Nisbet 1969, 21–29.) Its virtual disappearance might well be taken as foreboding the demise of social evolutionism itself.

4. Although second-period social evolutionists' widespread denial that all societies would invariably undergo the same sequence of stages of development might seem to accommodate social evolutionism more adequately to the facts of cross-cultural inquiry, the accompanying failure to indicate positively what any asserted sequence of stages means can hardly be regarded as enhancing confidence in social evolutionism itself. Not one of the adherents of the stance addressed this problem in a period of heightening demand for empirical support of theories. If any stages-in-sequence theory is to represent an idealized version valid only for humankind as a whole, it still raises the problem of empirical support and confirmation. Such was, indeed, the problem of Condorcet's "rational fiction" in Comte and of Ogburn's (1950, 375n.) lament that anthropologists "abandoned the [evolutionary] explanation of culture [in general] for the attempt [nonevolutionarily?] to explain cultures [in particular]."

5. In addition, the dynamic process by which social evolution proceeded became less secure. True, the use of the term *adaptation* sometimes continued—sometimes with and sometimes without the earlier heritage of social Darwinist assumptions. Occasinally the term *adjustment* was also employed. Biologistic and eugenicist standards were no longer acceptable. Even demonstrable technological superiority might be recognized to have a relative value basis (e.g., efficiency). But generally criteria of adaptation or adjustment were not provided, and hence the meanings became ambiguous and variable.

6. Furthermore, certain assumptions about the process of change in social evolution were disputed. The naturalness of change was disputed by anthropogical inquiry, which suggested that inaccessible, isolated societies and cultures tended to be stable or static, if not also stagnant and resistant to change (see Faris [1937a] 1976, 26; and Becker, and discussed above). Manifestly, constant change was not necessarily a natural and normal state of affairs in any society, irrespective of its context (consult Faris [1937a] 1976, 26). In addition, the internalist assumption of normal change, which was adamantly maintained by insistence on the significance of independent invention and the role of biopsychic differences, especially genius, came into conflict with the anthropological emphasis on the place of diffusion in sociocultural change. Certainly, too, the apparent complexity of social and cultural conditions attaching to the phenomena of both invention and diffusion rendered suspect the assumption of any simple, natural uniformity of the change process in time (see Faris [1937a] 1976, 26–27; see chapter 7).

In turn, now, the question must be posed as to which interest group or groups (bloc or blocs) might have been inclined to look favorably upon, or accept, some or many of the anti-social-evolutionist views as just proposed, or similar ones. Apparently, the most likely bloc involved especially younger sociologists who were favorably disposed to the newer cultural (or culturalist) viewpoint stemming from cultural anthropology, and particularly views associated with Franz Boas. Many of them subsequently became associated with the field of cultural sociology during the early 1930s.

Most importantly, the stance did include sociologists who enjoyed considerable professional esteem, were "opinion leaders," and were in a position to act as gatekeepers to publications. One such person was Ellsworth Faris, who seems to have developed a critical attitude toward social evolutionism no later than the early 1920s. He had earlier had cross-cultural experience, followed the arguments in anthropology closely, and taught the course in "social evolution" in the Chicago department until the mid-1920s, when it was discontinued. Although not widely known at the time of its original publication, his chapter "Social Evolution" constituted the most trenchant criticism of classical social evolution by an American sociologist after World War I. (The chapter was later reprinted as part of his *The Nature of Human Nature* [1937a]. Certainly, he was in a position not only to influence graduate students at Chicago but also, as editor, to have a major impact on the contents of the *American Journal of Sociology* during the decades of the second period of theory.[9]

A second professional field that came to exercise considerable influence on the fate of social evolutionism in sociology was the field of research methodology. The major stance arising by the end of the 1920s involved a qualified empiricist epistemology and a neo-positivist quantitative methodology (as elaborated in chapter 2 above). Its protagonists were often early representatives from sociology on the Social Science Research Council, were active in funded research, entered the governmental agencies during the depression and World War II, and predominantly taught research courses in sociology departments.[10] Representatives of this position also included prestigious "opinion leaders" such as Ogburn, Chapin, Gillin, Gehlke, Rice, and Lundberg. Most significantly, many sociologists of this stance also became explicitly and actively a-, if not also anti-, theoretical, sometimes publicly and often privately. Many of them conceived of dominant theory of the first period, and its successor in the second, as their basic antagonist, as representing and illustrating what they strenuously opposed. And in most instances, that opposed stance was the social evolutionism of the first and second periods. They indicated such theory as not being empirically grounded, as involving secondary or indirectly acquired materials that were of dubious reliability, nonobjective, and generally deductively developed, conjectural, and abstruse.[11] In some cases, this indictment did not include all possible varieties of theory and, in a few cases, not all social evolutionary formulations.[12] But the opposition of many of the research methodologists to social evolutionism was surely a major obstacle to its continued acceptance.

Finally, the onset of the Great Depression apparently became an important factor in the demise of social evolutionism. It sharpened the issue of the rationale or justification for sociology as a discipline and profession. The depression demanded professional activity that was relatively immediately relevant and evidently useful. Social evolutionism could hardly remain relevant to sociologists working–or aspiring to work—in governmental bureaucracies under crisis circumstances.

Thus, it is not surprising that social evolutionism had no *new* proponents after the early 1930s, either in the textbooks or in change as a research field. True, the Ogburn and Nimkoff 1940 and Bernard 1942 volumes were social evolutionary in their stances, but that social evolutionism derived from positions assumed in the early to mid 1920s (i.e., Ogburn 1922; Bernard 1926a). MacIver and Page's *Society: An Introductory Analysis* (1949) adopts the position of MacIver 1931c.

Social evolutionism had persisted from the first period and, initially, substantially retained its foundational status in the second. But from the mid 1920s onward, it rapidly declined to become only a memory of a disparaged past. It had come to an end as a dominant theory—as a theory of social origins, structure, and change in the textbooks, and as a research field. Apparently, major intellectual problems developed within theory (albeit anthropology-inspired), as voiced by research methodologists and as engendered by the depression crisis.

But at least two other positions on the problem and explanation of social change remain to be examined. On the one hand, Park and his students (e.g., Reuter and Hart, Hiller, and Kimball Young) were adherents of what can be described as versions of larger- or smaller-scale cycles of social processes. On the other, Becker and Sorokin adopted what might be termed "directionally variable" or "reversible" schemes of social change. We turn to these next in chapter 6.

PART III: DISCONTINUITIES (IN RELATION TO FIRST PERIOD THEORY)

Chapter 6

Discontinuities Arising within American Sociology

Because social evolutionism was the only basic social ontological theory continuous with the substantive theory from the first period, the intellectual task now confronting inquiry is to locate, characterize, and explain substantially new or divergent theories. Potentially, such theories and components might arise in American sociology, in other disciplines in American academia, or in disciplines outside of American academia (e.g., European social science and social theory). Each one of these potential sources is now to be investigated. The present chapter will explore such discontinuities as potentially or actually arose in sociology itself. Succeeding chapters will be concerned with other sources. Chapter 7 will examine anthropology and history in the United States. Chapter 8 will consider psychiatry and psychology in the United States as sources. Chapter 9 will scrutinize a peculiar amalgam of disciplinary influences from philosophy, psychology, and sociology. Chapter 10 will consider European social science and social theory.

From within American sociology itself, several sources of theoretical innovation are evident in the second period. A first involves a vague movement to redefine and reconstruct the very nature of theory (as alluded to in

chapter 1). A second is represented in the work of Robert Park and his former students as a potential source of a general theory. A third is to be found
in the nonevolutionary theories of social change that arose in opposition to
the modified social evolutionisms as examined in the two previous chapters.

A MOVEMENT TO REDEFINE AND RECONSTRUCT THEORY

An aspect of the negative reaction to the kind of social and sociological theorizing represented by the first period, and especially social evolutionism and its aftermath in the second period, included a major effort to rethink
the nature of theory and the preparatory intellectual enterprise required for
the development and construction of a more tenable and defensible general
theory. Admittedly, the initial stimulus probably came from the empiricist-
positivist epistemological-methodological stance, but its idealist-interpretive
counterpart also became involved almost immediately. Bain, Chapin, and
Lundberg represented the former, and Becker, Parsons, and Merton the latter
(with Znaniecki's *The Method of Sociology* and MacIver's *Social Causation*
also linked with the latter).

Bain's (1929) chapter on sociological theory in Lundberg, Bain, and
Anderson's *Trends in American Sociology* is important not only for his
endeavor to redefine the nature of a "sound theory," but also for the evidence
it provides about the intellectual context of the movement. Bain's reconsideration of theory is manifestly predicated on a repudiation of the "over-simpli-
fication, premature generalization or . . . particularism" of earlier (especially
first-period) theory (80). In his indictment, he also includes theory that is
based on a metaphysical notion of society, involves a unilateral, chronological, mechanistic social evolution, presupposes social or other determinisms,
and accepts "isms" as adequate causes, means, and explanations of social
change (83). Most especially, he supports the attack on, and rejection of,
notions often associated with social evolution and evolution generally—natural selection, hereditariansim, instinctivism, racialisms, dysgenicisms, and
the social-forces doctrine—as entailing "the fallacy of explanation from
below" (86, 92, 93, 96, 100–102).

Bain provides a two-page account of his own view of the nature of
sound theory (73–74), proposing that such a theory is comprised of a body of
secure and confirmed generalizations, which are based on sense experience
and are logically consistent, critically analyzed, and pragmatically sanctioned.

Chapin and Lundberg also joined in the argument. Chapin (1936)
demanded that sound theory be based on operationally defined concepts,
depart from an explicitly stated frame of reference, involve a logical system
among concepts, postulates, and hypotheses, and be amenable to empirical

research testing. Lundberg's (1936b) article contained his (similar) views about the character of sound theory (esp. 708), which anticipated his position of his major textbook, *Foundations of Sociology* (1939b).

In his textbook, Lundberg (1939b) insisted that a defensible (i.e., scientific) theory will depart from a unified frame of reference, involve the major components of the sociological universe and unambiguously and operationally define concepts, which in turn can be interrelated as a set of postulates. From those postulates, a set of theorems can be deduced and, as hypotheses, be subjected to research and empirical confirmation or disconfirmation. (This notion of theory came to be known as "hypothetico-deductive" or "deductive-nomological," and it became the foundation of the theory construction movement in the years after 1950.)

From sociologists who were at least initially identified with an idealist-interpretive stance came somewhat similar ideas. Admittedly, Becker's views were more implicit than explicit in his *Systematic Sociology* (Becker 1932b). Though he did not explicitly define the nature of theory, for him it was clearly a closed system that is characteristically deductive but yet can accommodate empirical inductions. (See above, chapter 1.)

Parsons offered his own definition in *The Structure of Social Action* ([1937] 1968), emphasizing the importance of a body of interrelated generalized concepts of empirical reference that departs from a more or less unified frame of reference and can, in turn, yield consistently interrelated propositions (6, 24).

Merton's (1945) notion of theory signifies a necessary degree of generality and systematicity. It requires the development of a scheme of concepts that specify what is to be observed, as variables, successful disclosure of empirical relationships between such variables, (inductive, empirical) generalizations of these relationships, their formulation as propositions, and the logical interrelationship of propositions to comprise a system. (see also Merton [1945] 1968, 153, 155.)

Thus, theorists from all the major epistemological-methodological stances seemed to have achieved a basic agreement on the nature of theory. It resorted to both induction and deduction. It departed from a basic frame of reference and involved concepts that could be interrelated to comprise sets of statements or propositions, which in turn were oriented to, and confirmable or disconfirmable by, research in the empirical social world. But beyond this, these theorists could not agree.

PARK'S GENERAL SOCIOLOGICAL ORIENTATION

Park did not directly and explicitly become involved in the movement to renovate the notion of theory. Yet many of his student would likely have claimed that he was indeed, perhaps more than any other of his contemporaries in the 1920s and early 1930s, actually doing more than anyone else in the discipline to secure the kind of useful research-oriented theory that the movement sought.

Undeniably, Park left a valuable intellectual legacy to the discipline. Park and Burgess's *Introduction to the Science of Sociology* (1921) is a major intellectual achievement. It presents the major problems and topics, positions and concepts, and the most relevant literature, in sociology just before and after World War I. Park's many papers (most of which were republished in *Race and Culture, Human Communities*, and *Society* in the 1950s) comprise a series of essays on pertinent sociological concerns, involving careful conceptual analysis and illuminating data and engagingly presented within a more or less coherent, single intellectual perspective.

Certainly, Park had a distinctive sociological orientation that was predicated on both social epistemological-methodological and social ontological premises. For his epistemological-methodological views, he drew on Windelband's and Rickert's Neo-Kantian differentiation of the science-nomothetic disciplines from the history-idiographic disciplines (cf. chapter 2 above). He regarded sociology as part of the science-nomothetic disciplines. Interestingly, his substantive views involve a peculiar "double" dualism in which human societies are conceived to operate as they do because humankind is partially in nature (as living matter) and partially outside nature (as conscious beings) and because the social is sometimes alluded to as realistic and yet treated as nominalistic. In addition, Park also reflected the growing effort to develop a division of labor between anthropology and sociology by allocating the study of primitive, aboriginal, or nonliterate societies to the former and the inquiry into modern, civilized, or literate societies to the latter. He took no interest in generic social origins. But he was vitally concerned with the city or urban community as the central social unit in the emergence, persistence, and change of civilized societies. (See Hinkle 1980, 308–11.)

Although the social process formulation of social change was associated with several theorists before World War I (e.g., Small, Ross, and Cooley), it became distinctively identified with Park and his former students in the several decades thereafter. Certainly, major differences between the social-process and social evolutionary notions of social change can be instanced. Perhaps the most basic difference is the linear directionality of evolutionism and the cyclicity of the process conception. Nevertheless, Park's notion of the emergence of the realm of society (with social, moral, and cultural orders) from the realm of community (with its biotic and ecological orders), through the several social processes, has an affinity with evolutionism. Competition, which distributes plans and animals (including human beings) in terms of space and a natual economy, has a definite linkage, with impersonal struggle for existence and survival of the fittest with the other (more personal?) processes that yield social organization, personality, and culture at the distinctively human level. In effect, Park recast the ideas of Herbert Spencer in terms of those of the plant and animal ecologists.

Both Park and his students observed that competition in its pure form is opposition that is indirect, external, impersonal, and unconscious. Reuter and Hart (1933, 381), two of his former students, comment that "it results in the specialization of individuals, groups, and areas, and establishes among them a condition of balance and interdependence, an ecological order somewhat analogous to the natural order resulting from the struggle for life among the various biological forms." The human population becomes an occupationally differentiated unit within a geographically limited locale. This natural (and symbiotic) territorial and occupational arrangement, with an organic unity, is termed "community."

With the identification of individuals in competition, opposition between them becomes conscious and personal. Competition becomes conflict. But just as competition occasioned an economic order, so conflict gives rise to a political order.

For Park (1924, 509), accommodation tends to follow at the human level. Accommodation is the process by which individuals and groups "make the necessary internal adjustments to social situations . . . created by competition and conflict." Reuter and Hart (1933, 382) remark that "accommodation is a process of adjustment by means of which overt conflict is resolved and competition is restrained within fixed limits"; conscious and tentative forms of "subordination are evolved and behavior is defined and organized in terms of them." Conflict and accommodation elicit society, with social (organization) and moral orders.

Significantly, Park had insisted that humans cannot long continue to treat one another as mere utilities, as part of the flora and fauna of the habitat. Humans can and do communicate. Consequently, conflict or struggle does not generally tend to culminate in extermination, but rather is transformed into and succeeded by the processes of accommodation and assimilation. Whether this outcome is the result of mere communication per se, or of communication that elicits a common human nature sympathy, cannot be decisively argued. At some point, humans will endeavor to act collectively—presumably in relation to still other enemies or problems of the biophysical habitat.

Assimilation reconciles, consolidates, and fixes arrangements as defined and organized by accommodation. More importantly, assimilation is the more thoroughgoing transformation of persons and groups so that memories, sentiments, attitudes, and experiences are shared, with personality and a common cultural life resulting. Accommodation yields a social and moral order, whereas assimilation elicits personality and a cultural order. Understandings, with intent, design, purpose, and consensus, become manifest as the process of communication erects stable relationships that are customary, conventional, institutional, moral, and cultural. But viewed retrospectively, assimilation appears as part of a natural, serial (and evolutionary?) order of processes. It is part of a repeatable sequence or cycle of changes.

In some sense, all social phenomena are held to be invariably involved or enmeshed in these several social processes, whether they are personalities, groups, institutions, or societies. Indeed, these are the (natural) objects of sociology (as just indicated). Each has its own distinctive modes of change, requiring comparative study and identification.[1] Presumably, the most basic, generalized object with which sociology deals is society.

As the largest or most comprehensive social structures, societies are grounded in, based on, or localized (ecologically) through communities in space and in relation to (external) biophysical nature. Park certainly regarded communities as having a basic sociological significance. Presumably, it should have been possible to develop a systematic typology of communities, though Park really did not do so. At times, he alluded to smaller and larger communities, with the urban community apparently being prototypical of the latter. In turn, these demarcations were linked with the implications of Tön-nie's *Gemeinschaft und Gesellschaft* and Cooley's primary-nucleated dichotomy (as recast by Thomas into primary and secondary groups and societies, and about which Park was surely informed. Park also invoked a basic sacred/secular distinction (apparently derived from Tönnies and Durkheim and elaborted extensively by his student Howard P. Becker).

Park's interest in the study of the urban community is, of course, well known. However, his interest in the origins of urban society is infrequently cited. He was inclined to accept a professional division of labor, with anthropology assuming responsibility for the study of primitive and archaic societies and sociology investigating civilized and urban-centered societies. The origins of the city is central to the very emergence of civilization or civilized societies, which for Park was the distinctive realm for sociological inquiry.

Unfortunately, Park's ideas are scattered throughout a number of his papers. But his inquiry "The City and Civilization" (in Park 1952) is especially suggestive of his views on the origins of civilized societies, the contrast between ancient and modern civilizations (civilized societies), and the main features of modern civilizations.

Interestingly, Park conceived of civilization itself as a cyclical process. Each civilization begins with a new migration, extending humankind's intellectual horizons and broadening the area of competition and cooperation. Each civilization is accompanied by the rise of new cities. Prior to civilizations, social existence had been confined to wandering bands of herders and nomads and small settlements of peasants.

Park acknowledges two accounts of the transition to a civilized, urban mode of existence. In the first case, a clan or tribe, or some portion of it, settles at a spring where there is water for their flocks or at a ford or a crossroads where an opportunity for trade exists. Agriculture springs up where water and other conditions are favorable. With the establishment of a market, various workshops appear, and commodities of various sorts are imported to supply the demands of the market. In order to protect the settlements from marauding nomads, the villages federate and fortify themselves, and eventually a city develops.

In the second and perhaps more frequent case, the wandering nomads invade the settlements, conquer the sedentary people, establish themselves in a fortified position, and remain as rulers. Out of conquest, the state arises.

In both cases, the tribe is superseded by a territorial unit that acquires power superior to that of the tribe and clan, both of which are supplanted. The rule of a monarch is substituted for the authority of the elders. A provincial god supplants the tribal fetishes, and the primitive communism of the clan is displaced by an organization involving social stratification.

Thus, the origins of the state tend to coincide with the city. The first states were city-states; the terms *politics* and *political* are derived from the Greek word for city, *polis*, just as the words *city* and *civilization* are derived from the Latin word *civitas*. So politics, civilization, and the city have come into existence together.

Whatever the case, civilization is the triumph of humans over nature. Cities are the workshop of civilization and the natural habitat of the civilized person.

Ancient and modern civilizations do reveal major differences. Ancient civilizations tended to have one dominant center, whereas modern civilizations tend to have many metropolitan centers, and every commercial city is a world city. Ancient civilizations were limited in their scope; modern ones are worldwide. Although these cities are independent politically and administratively, they are commercially interdependent. Modern cities are much alike, showing integration and interpenetration of peoples and cultures.

Whether a part of ancient or modern civilizations, cities bring together people from the ends of the earth because they are useful and different. Cities are cosmopolitan; they are melting pots. They subject peoples from different races, cultures, and individual capacities to competition with one another, and thus older kinship and cultural groups are destroyed. On the one hand, individuals are sorted out and placed in positions and occupations (irrespective of their race or previous condition) where they are most likely to be efficient or make the largest contribution. Specialization is possible, and thus a greater contribution to the common fund of values is possible. On the other hand, such intermixtures of cultures tend to break the cake of custom and to free the individual from the routine and the control that tradition has imposed. He or she experiences release.

The city embodies characteristics of both organisms and artifacts, of community and society. The city is the result of both competitive and communicative processes. Its areas tend to become functionally differentiated and specialized and so are characterized as "natural areas" (Park 1952, 196). In turn, they become the sites of distinctive, unified cultural, moral, and meaningful features, and so in this sense can be characterized as "cultural areas" (201).

In spite of Park's basic interest in the modern city and its component groups, he nowhere developed a systematic account of their social structures. Indeed, Park's notion of social organization actually encompassed a duality or polarity between the individual and the group that precluded any definitive statement of the character of social organization. This difficulty appears in his consideration of Sumner's notion of folkways and mores apart from their connection with institutions. Park fails, therefore, to reckon with the "prescribed positions" or statuses defining the activities of institutionally involved persons through sets of relevant social norms (e.g., folkways, mores).[2] Similarly, Park fails to invoke social roles (i.e., socially defined roles) as his colleague Faris did.[3] Evidently for Park, the individual group member invariably possesses a modicum of personal freedom or choice (i.e., voluntarism), which Sumner, and perhaps also his colleague Faris, surely would have rejected.[4]

Park's failures to develop a general or comprehensive notion of social organization or a systematic account of the social structure of the modern urban community or urban-centered modern society can hardly have been an advantage to his successors.[5] The argument that social organization and morality are to be derived from the general process of accommodation was scarcely helpful to Reuter and Hart, Hiller, Young, or Sutherland and Woodward in their textbooks.[6] These theorists were especially involved in the effort to produce coherent accounts of in-groups versus out-groups, primary versus secondary groups, crowds and publics, types of community, and forms of social strata. (See chapter 3.) They could not and did not offer any general theory of social structure as an alternative to the adaptive notion of social evolutionism. Reuter and Hart (1933, 148–49) and Hiller (1933, 46) could only assert that people who have lived together over an extended period will profit from one another's experiences and develop consensus and usages that all will tend to share.

As indicated earlier, anthropology made a major impact on social change theory during the 1920s and 1930s. Park's students were compelled either to virtually ignore these newer developments or to explain them in only the briefest of terms. In some instances, the social processes were introduced apart from any connection with the problem and theory of social change (e.g., Hiller 1933, parts 2–5 vs. part 6; Young 1934, part 4; and Sutherland and Woodward [1937] 1940, part 5 vs. part 6).[7]

Certainly, Park's orientation as expounded by his students in their textbooks did not appear to have the more or less systematic unity that the social evolutionism of the first period had. Neither does it appear that the Park and Burgess text or any of the subsequent three Park volumes offers, or sought to offer, a rigorous, systematic, integrated, and unified conception of the field such that it could warrant the characterization of being a macro- or general theory. Although Blumer asserted that Park was pragmatically interested in analytical theory, that interest did not lead him to work out "the logical presuppositions of his concepts and propositions in the direction of developing systematic theories" (quoted in Rauschenbush 1979 125).

Perhaps it would be most accurate to characterize Park as having had a general sociological orientation in which the problem of social change was central and crucial. Becker, who was a graduate student under Park and later a member of the Smith and University of Wisconsin sociology departments, elaborated a generalized schema for the study of macrosocial change. Sorokin, who emigrated to the United States soon after the Communist revolution in Russia following World War I, joined the Department of Sociology at the University of Minnesota for a few years, and left to establish the department at Harvard in 1930, was similarly concerned with macrosocial dynamics and followed an approach roughly similar to Becker's (or vice versa).

NONEVOLUTIONARY MACROTHEORISTS AND THEIR THEORIES

Howard Becker

Although Becker's aim is not to provide an explanation or interpretation of the actual content of change in the total historical process (which he accepts as a legitimate problem), he rather proposes a method that will be appropriate to this objective. In Becker's work a notion of certain stages of sequence become a set of societal types in sequence. His chapter "Historical Sociology" (1934b) in the Bernard-edited *The Fields and Methods of Sociology* recognizes the liabilities of several types of stages theories.[8] But he does contend that stages can be acceptably formulated as constructed types, without the assumption of continuous, serial, successive development of one stage out of a prior stage (and, presumably, that one can thus avoid the postulate of genetic continuity). So, too, he believes the onus of rectilinearity and irreversibility of the earlier stages theory of social evolution can be avoided.

Indeed, he explicitly acknowledges the possibility and actual occurrence of the "skipping [of stages as types] and reversal" of direction of change (Becker 1957, 176).

Over the years, Becker developed a conceptualization of major societal types based on varying degrees of sacredness and secularity, characterizing these in terms of an inability, an unwillingness, or a reluctance to change versus an ability, a willingness, or an inclination to change.[9] More precisely, he insists that a continuum can be established from a maximum reluctance to change through a minimum reluctance to a minimum willingness to a maximum willingness to change.[10] He uses different kinds of norms, means-ends relationships, value systems, and the mode of relationship of the society to others in its ecological and sociocultural setting to construct types and subtypes.[11] The adjectival terms for such norms as proverbs, prescriptions, and principles provide the names for three of the four societal subtypes: a "proverbial" or "folk sacred society," a "prescriptive" or "prescribed sacred society," and a "principial" or "principled secular" society. To characterize the fourth, he invoked the term *pronormless* rather than the mere *normless*, because any society surviving as a society, whatever its instability, never quite reaches the ultimate of normlessness; it is never wholly without some normative structure (Becker 1957, 152–66). Initially, he employed Weber's typfication of means-ends relationships, though later he proposed his own terms. The value systems of the societal subtypes can be demarked in terms of varying degrees of implicitness or explicitness, noncodification or codification, and accreteness or discreteness. Finally, each societal subtype is associated with distinctive features of isolation or accessibility that can be further specified into vicinal, social, and mental varieties. Vicinal isolation of a society means the physical absence of, or separation, from other societies in the area of possible contact. Social isolation is basically an absence of effective communication. Societies may be vicinally accessible, yet remain socially isolated from one another because one or both are repelled by the social differences of the other. But even with relatively effective communication, one people may remain mentally (psychically) isolated from another (e.g., as blacks are from whites in American society).

Each subtype is in a sense pure, and empirical societies are only approximations to these. The proverbial sacred and the pronormless secular thus represent the extremes or polar points on a continuum on which the data of human history and social development may be arranged and generalized. As a continuum, it betrays both its unilinear antecedents and present character for representing possible change (from a first earlier point to a second later point in time) as movements toward one of two extremes—secularization or sacralization—even though the directionality is reversible. It is precisely this approximation (which is also simultaneously a departure) of an empirical instance from the ideal or constructed type that constitutes the beginning point (and return) for explanation and interpretation. (Becker would insist that not only the basic features of norms, the content and form of value systems, and the external relations of the society be considered, but that the possibilities of both endogenous and exogenous sources of change be reckoned with. See the elaborate subtypes and empirical instances in Becker 1950, 46–78, 264–80; Becker 1957, 166–76.)

Earlier designated as "folk," the proverbial subtype indicates the most stable, persistent, and change-resistant of the sacred varieties. It is dominated by tradition, which— in the absence of writing (literacy)—is orally transmitted across the generations. Age has prestige and authority. Ancestral wisdom is the basis of common sense, which is normatively incorporated and expressed in proverbs. Accustomed procedures are accepted unquestioningly. Use and wont are reinforced by bonds of kinship, ties of familiear locality, common language, and lore. Traditional nonrationality characterizes means-ends relationships. Value systems are "largely implicit in content and connection, primarily uncodified, and almost always accrete" (Becker 1957, 153). Empirical instances of this subtype are found in geographically remote, marginal, or inaccessible areas; they are both difficult to reach and difficult to leave (166).

Although some proverbial societies have not been marked by extreme vicinal isolation, their social and mental isolation adequately compensates for the absence of the vicinal variety. The rare stranger finds it almost impossible to act without violating sacred patterns, so outsiders tend to be stigmatized as unclean, immoral, hostile, or heathenish. In the virtual absence of social interaction with strangers, mental isolation is maintained, if not also intensified (166). Most frequently, proverbial societies thus evidence all three kinds of isolation to a pronounced extent and are notoriously difficult to change.

Although ordinarily larger and culturally more developed than the proverbial type and usually (but not always) associated with the advent of writing, prescriptive societies tend to preserve many of the same components as characterize their proverbial counterparts. As norms, prescriptions tend to be more definitely and explicitly formulated than the proverbs from which they may derive. Tradition has been brought up to date. So prescriptive law may supersede proverbial lore. The dominant means-ends relationship is sanctioned rationality. Ends thus forbid the use of certain means. Value systems are "explicit, codified, in some degree intentionally accrete, and are at least formally rational or even apparently deductive" (Becker 1957, 154). Still, prescriptive societies are characterized by substantial vicinal, social, and mental isolation. In the case of vicinal accessibility, cultural barriers may be erected. Governmental, ecclesiastic, educational, and similar organizations may aid in sustaining social isolation. This in turn facilitates mental isolation. (Admittedly, it is often difficult to ascertain whether mental or social isolation is first. But whichever one is first, it aids the other.) In modern terms, the social structure is prevailingly authoritarian—from the Egypt of Pharaoh's taskmasters, to the Genevan theocracy of Calvin, the Jesuit state of Paraguay, Fascist Italy, Nazi Germany, Communist Russia up to East Germany's Communist "people's democracy" (Becker 1950, 57; Becker 1957, 168).

Of the secular subtypes, the principial or principled is the more stable of the two. The term *principle* indicates that its prevailing rules involve adaptability, utility in new situations, and amenability to reasonable deduction (from components of proverbial or prescriptive types). Its means-ends relationships are a variant of expedient rationality. Its value system is explicit in content and connection, primarily codified, and of an accrete character.

Change is welcome, but by no means do "anything and everything go." Those changes threatening the core of the abstract principles will be resisted. First principles are sacred, but their abstractness "makes pursuant rationality [which is a variant of expedient rationality] widely applicable" (Becker 1957, 170). Normlessness does not necessarily follow drastic innovations if the latter accord with "principles abstractly sacred manifested in changes concretely secular" (170).

Vicinal, social, and mental accessibility are widely prevalent. Outsiders come and go without significant restrictions. They may even attain the rank of insider. In turn, social accessibility is linked with mental accessibility. (Becker refers to modern Britain as an example of a principial secular society [169–70].)

Though some instances of pronormless societies are essentially rural, a majority are urban—"Tobacco Road" versus "slum Liverpool, Saloniki, Algiers, Chicago's Near North Side, and Hamburg's Reeperbahn" (171–72). Their means-ends relationship is unmistakably affective nonrationality. Their values change so rapidly that identification of a system is difficult. They are explicit, but they are temporary and evanescent. As they become discrete, their connections tend to fluctuate rapidly or disappear, and even the semblance of codification may seem dubious.

Characteristically, strangers are present physically in large numbers and are often accepted with little question. Members of the society either travel freely themselves or by virtue of mass communications vicariously participate in travel and thus become aware of cultural contrasts, with attendant acceptance of relativism. Much actual or vicarious vicinal mobility exists.

Furthermore, social accessibility is extensive. Strangers are welcome both as sources of novel thrills and for the cash they contribute. All sorts of intermingling occurs. Social accessibility prevails among classes, castes, and like groupings. Stratification is undeniable, yet upward and downward mobility is rapid. Equalitarianism prevails, because discrimination among anonymous fragments of society is nearly impossible.

Easygoing open-mindedness, representing mental accessibility moving toward normlessness, is widely prevalent and is usually nonrational. Great leeway is granted to facile tolerance reflecting indifference to principle. Though many sacred formulas are in circulation, they do not effectively check comfortable and thrilling deviations. Science is even held worthwhile because it promises easy attainment of nonrational or even irrational ends.

But such societies are rarely of one piece. For many, perhaps a majority, normlessness is uncomfortable and even frightening. Intermixtures of irreconcilable value systems may flourish luxuriantly. Varied political, economic, moral, religious, and other gospels may be successfully cultivated by an extraordinary figure possessing charisma. A cult of regeneration may form and become a center of successful sacralization. Far-reaching secularization may engender intensified sacralization. The normative reaction to normlessness may not only brake ultra-rapid secularization but may also introduce or reinstate "reluctances to change that soon take on, or attempt to take on, the features of stabilizing value-systems" (Becker 1957, 174).

Pitirim Sorokin

In contrast to Becker, Sorokin's social dynamics (in his *Social and Cultural Dynamics*, 1937–41) focuses on change in the 2,500 years of Western European culture (from Greco-Roman to the modern era of the nation-state), which involves movement from one to another of the three possible "logico-meaningfully" integrated types of cultural supersystems.[12] Two of them, the ideational and the sensate, are logical opposites of one another, and the third, the idealistic, is a mixed type. Although it is true that Sorokin argues that multiple criteria are involved and include the nature of needs and ends to be satisfied, and the extent and mode of their satisfaction, the crucial criterion seems to have been the premises about knowledge, especially truth claims concerning reality (1:70–72). So for the ideational, reality "is perceived as nonsensate and nonmaterial, everlasting Being," whereas for the sensate it is "only that which is presented to the sense organs" (1:72–73). The idealistic envisages reality as "many-sided, with the aspects of everlasting Being and everchanging Becoming of the spiritual and material," but with ideational elements predominating (1:75). Each such supersystem consists of the five basic and functionally essential systems of language, religion, the arts, ethics, and science. In turn, each of these major systems may be divided into levels of subsystems that are also more or less logico-meaningfully integrated.

Sorokin contends that his historical inquiries reveal a pattern of orderly sequence (which he terms "rhythm with three phases") from the ideational to the idealistic to the sensate (and then from the sensate to the ideational) (4:425–737). This sequence has occurred twice (i.e., recurred) from the twelfth century B.C. to the end of the Middle Ages, and since the fifteenth century has entered the sensate phase for the third time (4:737).

It is important to note that Sorokin is interested in explaining empirical sociocultural systems in change. Presupposing the existence of prior meanings, Sorokin accepts as his first problem in change the genesis, formation, or creation of mental integration, or the synthesis of two or more meanings, hitherto unintegrated, into one logically interrelated, consistent system.[13] The second problem is the empirical objectification of this system of meanings by and into empirical vehicles through which and by which "it can be perceived by, conveyed to, and apprehended" by persons other than the creators or innovators (4:62). The third problem is to account for socialization, "the process by which the system finds its human agents and is accepted, used, and operated by others" (4:62). Significantly, Sorokin uses the organismic analogy to expand on the conception of the formation of the empirical sociocultural system.

Only in chapter 5 of volume 4 of *Social and Cultural Dynamics* does Sorokin examine the conditions underlying the genesis of mental integration. Three operative conditions are important. First, some (usually a few) individuals in the group possess a fortunate hereditary endowment (4:237). Second, there is an urgent need to create a new system for a given group in a given environment. Third, such favored individuals (who presumably also sense or experience the need for this) are exposed to "an intensive mobility, circulation, and cross-current of streams of different cultural values (systems of meanings and vehicles)" (4:237). The three aspects or stages of change may relatively coincide in time or may be separated by substantial intervals. But Sorokin emphasize that the order is sequential.

Once meanings have been linked with vehicles and vehicles with a plurality of human beings, they constitute an empirical sociocultural system. As Sorokin argued at length, meanings can become causally or functionally integrated, and human beings socially coordinated. Meanings, vehicles, and human beings or agents are all separable, and yet all three are interdependent. As a whole, they constitute a system, a peculiar kind of natural system or object, which has its own "nature" with its own distinctive internal or immanent tendency to change (or, as the ancient Greeks might have noted, its *physis*).

Sorokin advanced his own theory of social change by deriving two general implications from the general principle of immanent change. First is the principle of the immanent generation of consequences. Because the system is one in activity, the activity induces change in the system and change in its milieu. The latter will react on the system, and so the system must act differently (4:601). Second is the principle of the immanent self-determination of a system's destiny or existence career. At the moment when any sociocultural system emerges, it contains in itself "immanent potentialities" that unfold as a normal career or destiny (as in the course of growth).

Change as a normal, natural growth (or decline) of an empirical sociocultural system must by definition involve the aspects of meanings, vehicles, and human agents, and it may assume both quantitative and qualitative forms. Though Sorokin certainly does not ignore change in the vehicles and in the human agents, which he treats quantitatively, it is change in meanings, which is qualitatively analyzed, that clearly has the primary significance for Sorokin. Such qualitative change is change in the "logico-meaningful" integration of meanings. Yet Sorokin's presentation of his position does not make it entirely clear that this entails a distinctive combination of logic and teleology, on the assumption that the sociocultural realm is a peculiar domain of reason or, again to invoke Greek antecedents, *logos*. Change thus involves the intrinsic tendency for any sociocultural system interactively to elaborate its meanings as ends and its meanings as basic premises. Presumably, the former and latter occur conjointly. In its simplest form, change may be said to occur by the increasing (or decreasing) integration of meanings, by deductive elaboration, and by elimination of (unrelated) congeries. As inconsistencies are uncovered, the parts of a system of meaning can become more numerous, both more coordinated and super-subordinated, more dependent and interdependent (of parts with one another and with the whole, and the whole with them). (See especially 4:30, 31, 56, 67, 82–83, 85–86.) As the system of meanings becomes more consistent, the system becomes better integrated. Consistency and integration thus proceed apace. In the course of time, the system accepts and rejects selectively. "It selects what is compatible and rejects what is inconsistent with it" (4:76).

In addition to the principle that any empirical sociocultural system is a self-changing and self-directing unity, Sorokin also uses the principle of limits to explain change. In essence, change must remain change in something. If it becomes change of something into something else so that its original identity is lost, it ceases to exist. "Hence so long as a system lives, it has limits in its change" (4:702). Types of economic, political, religious, ethical, and legal organization are limited, as are types of society, cultural systems and supersystems, and sociocultural processes (4:704–7).

Basically, it is this principle of limits that accounts for recurrence in sociocultural change. Soroking argues that only three main (positive) forms of truth or reality exist (as stated dialectically): the supersensory (ideational), the sensory (sensate), and their positive combination (idealistic).[14] Accordingly, he argues that only three possibilities exist, and that cultural change must be recurrent if it persists beyond the realization of the first three phases (the ideational, idealistic, and sensate). For change to extend beyond this first rhythm—assuming only three possibilities exist—means recurrence or repetition.

Sorokin also uses a third argument for the occurrence of change in the three forms (ideational, idealistic, and sensate), to which no other American naturalistic or secular sociologist in that period would or could resort. It was essentially a metaphysical, or ontological, argument, holding that each phase is only a partial truth of (absolute?) reality, and thus also is partially false, and so all three phases are necessary to reflect reality adequately (4:741–43). Again, it seems significant that Sorokin employs an absolute rationalistic argument.

Finally, Sorokin does believe that a complete explanation or interpretation of empirical sociocultural change must also account for the actual sequence of ideational to idealistic to sensate (and back to ideational, etc.) phases.[15] Interestingly, he does insist that the order of succession indicated in *Social and Cultural Dynamics* is not one of universal occurrence, a point made several times in the four volumes. He even conceded that "it is probable that some other order of recurrence of these main forms can be found" if cultures other than the Graeco-Roman and Western ones are studied carefully (4:771). He acknowledges also that some other cultures," [like] the Brahmanic culture of India, have remained in the ideational phase far longer than either the Graeco-Roman or the Western cultures" (4:771). Furthermore, both "the tempo and the sharpness of the mutations from one type to another vary from culture to culture" (4:771).

But having made these points, Sorokin seems especially to be interested in why the idealistic follows the ideational but not the sensate in the sequence of the forms in Greco-Roman and Western cultures. Sorokin claims that he is interested only in a "consideration of . . . empirical nature," and yet he introduces metaphors, similies, and analogies that succeed one another in almost reckless abandon.

He begins with the botanical, immediately shifts to the organic (or, perhaps more accurately, the biopsychic), then a general equilibristic, and lastly a topographical model, which is said to suggest a mechanistic one. Initially, then, he remarks that sensate culture in its latest development has reached an "over-ripe stage," at which point "man becomes so 'wild' that he cannot—and does not want to—'tame himself.'" But the botanical metaphor immediately yields to the directly organismic (or biopsychic) one of the release of the animality of human nature. In turn, man is said to be like a "reckless driver" who "can be brought to his senses only by catastrophic tragedy and punishment, as immanent consequences of his 'folly.'" Sorokin immediately postulates that this stage of culture entails a sense of need for reequilibration by imposition of a totalitarian-like coercive "taming" that tends to predispose humans to the "strait-jacket of Ideational culture." He endeavors to reinforce his argument for the tendency to shift from the sensate to the ideational rather than the idealist by invoking a metaphor of travel and topography: "It is," he claims, "easier to descend from the heights of the Ideational snow peak to the beautiful plateau of Idealist reality than to ascent from the plane of over-ripe Sensate culture to the Idealistic plateau." This circumstance of "going down rather than up" may, indeed, only figuratively express E. Mach's mechanistic "principle of least resistance." Again, Sorokin insists that he has offered only a purely empirical argument and does not "imply any necessity for such a sequence [ideational–idealistic–sensate] to be universal in time or space." On this one page (4:772), Sorokin could hardly have offered a more graphic example of his deviation from the dominant stance of American sociology.

Comparison of Orientations to or Theories of Change: Park, Becker, and Sorokin

Initially, a comparison like the one we have been engaged in seems to indicate vast differences among the three sociologists. In broad perspective, Park appears to emphasize the universality of change through a cycle of processes conceived as abstract (Neo-Kantian) forms to which structure is subordinate and temporally and historically particularistic and variable, though the universal process is necessarily situated in a particular ecologically delimited habitat. Human aggregates are part of a larger biotic unit, and the basis of any distinctive unity (e.g., communicative, cultural, moral, personal) must arise from within the larger biotic unit.

By contrast, Becker and Sorokin regard humankind as preexisting differentiated structured sociocultural entities or unities, which—while set in a natural environment—become points of departure for sociological analysis of change. Sociocultural change tends primarily to be studied, explained, and interpreted at its own level.

Both Becker and Sorokin attempt to find and delimit more or less fundamental societal and cultural types, within or in terms of which change must be studied. Becker aspires to construct a set of (relatively) universally relevant societal types. In contrast, Sorokin restricts his problem to historical change in the cultural domain of Western European civilization, seemingly ignoring intrasocietal variations or external impingements of counterpart macrosociocultural entities.

But our understanding of the formulations of the three as so far presented is necessarily incomplete. An inquiry into and comparative analysis of the actual dynamic explanations, modus operandi, or mechanisms of each in relation to the other two (characterizable in terms of a materialism/idealism polarity) is required.

Chronologically the first, Park seems initially characterizable as having struck a relative balance between materialism and idealism in his social-process account of social change. Park held that humankind is one of the organic orders in the web of nature and thus fundamentally involved in the struggle for existence and, more broadly, in biotic competition. This view also included the basic argument of plant and animal ecologists so as to envisage competition as distributing and organizing human populations spatially into occupationally differentiated units within geographically limited locales. Park termed this natural (symbiotic) territorial and occupational arrangement, with an organic unity, a "community."

But Park also insisted that humankind's ability to communicate and to achieve a consensus can alter the outcome of conflict, accommodation, and assimilation, the other basic interactive social processes. Understanding, with intent, design, purpose, and consensus, becomes manifest as the process of communication creates stable relationships that can and do become customary, conventional, institutional, moral, and cultural. Thus, in addition to the ecological or community level of human association, which is essentially biophysical, or material, in nature, a moral-culture or societal level (essentially ideal) emerges. These arguments render Park's position manifestly and pervasively a social and sociological pluralism that draws on natural physical and organismic materialism and an artificial consensual or voluntaristic idealism; but see below.

In turning now to Becker, it is necessary to recall that his position emerged as part of a critical response to social evolutionism, with its social Darwinist emphasis on survival and adaptation, and in part to its internalist conception of the sources of change (individual variations in talent and innovativeness). Perhaps the most conspicuous feature of Becker's arguments are his allegations about the significance for social change of isolation, accessibility, and contact (vicinal, social, mental) in the external relation of one society to another. Certainly, he seems to emphasize study at the impersonal level of form and content in the sociocultural domain itself (norms, means-ends relations, values, value systems)—indeed, so much so that his position might appear, in the absence of further elaboration, to be a form of objective idealism. Yet such a stance would be susceptible to criticism as a form of "sociological determinism of cultural content, . . . a sociological variety of solipsism," which Becker surely wished to avoid (Becker 1950, 252). Conversely, while suggesting that he accepted the existence of an external world no matter how little may be known about it, he sought to avoid dualistic implications (282; also n. 2).

Unfortunately, our main exposition, earlier in this chapter, of Becker's sacred/secular theory of social change does not also reveal his insistence that favorable or unfavorable attitudes (as expressed in culturally specific terms) toward change must be related to the concrete personalities interacting or "sociating" (Becker's term) in situations conducive to social change. Becker's first chapter of his *Through Values to Social Interpretation* (1950) contains his own exposition of a theory of personality and self formation, derived from Cooley and Mead, which begins with "raw [organic] needs" of the human neonate that, while becoming socially processed, remain incontrovertibly significant for the emerging self or personality (6–7, but esp. 16–17 n. 19). Importantly, Becker insists on the utility of Mead's "I"—"to avoid a complete socio-cultural determinism" and to allow for "novelty, innovation, deviation, and similar breakaways" (19–20 n. 23). He notes—apparently approvingly—that the "I" may include "everything from biological deviation to individual variation in life-history patterns" (252 n. 10).

Interestingly, in everything from his doctoral dissertation to his late publications, Becker has always asserted that personality typology is relevant to the study of social change. Deriving especially from Thomas and Znaniecki's work, Becker's analysis of the charismatic-leader personality is abundantly revealing of his conception of the role of the unique individual in social change (Becker 1950, 64–65, 83, 263, 270, 273; Becker 1957, 174–75).

Clearly, then, the explanation or interpretation of the genesis of change cannot ignore possible genetic, organic variations of individuals, their peculiarities in socialization, or their subsequent life experiences as incorporated in their personalities, which will influence their interpretations as they interact in the broader background of social crises, population movements, and the prevailing rule structures, means-ends relationships, and values and value systems of their societies. In terms, then, of older distinctions (which Becker would presumably wish to avoid), he is not an ontological monist but a pluralist, with perhaps a dominant sociological idealism that qualifies an objectivism with a subjectivism.

As for Sorokin, the major features of his explanation seem to involve basically the premises of a social and sociological idealism. He construes the problem of sociocultural change as change in a logically meaningful integrated type of cultural supersystem (or systems). In general, a cultural supersystem involves meanings, which can and do acquire a "logico-meaningful" unity or integration, vehicles that can and do become causally or functionally integrated, and a plurality of persons by whom the integrated meanings and vehicles are accepted, used, and realized and who themselves become socially coordinated. Meanings, vehicles, and human beings singly and together are interdependent. As a whole, they constitute a system that has its own nature with its own distinctive internal or immanent tendency to change (a *physis*). (Because such cultural systems are socially shared and publicly represented and objectified, they would seem to indicate acceptance of an objective idealism—as opposed to a subjective idealism.)

However, it is important to notice that the synthesis of meanings in terms of which cultural systems and supersystems have their beginning depends on certain operative conditions: (1) "the possession of a fortunate hereditary endowment" by some (usually a few) individuals in the group (Sorokin 1937–41, 4:237); (2) an urgent need to create a new system for a given group in a given environment; and (3) exposure of such favored individuals (who presumably also sense or experience the need for this) to "an intensive mobility, circulation, and cross-current of different cultural values (systems of meanings and vehicles)" (4:237). Furthermore, once created, the synthesis of meanings must find "external vehicles" for appropriate externalization or objectification and by and through which it can be conveyed and communicated to others (4:64). Finally, the new meaning system with its appropriate vehicles must actually enter the sociocultural life of the society. It must become shared, transmitted, or disseminated, with "other individuals as its recipients, users, and bearers" (4:64).

It is also important to indicate the nature of the (impersonal) principles Sorokin adduces to account for change. They involve a peculiar combination of logic and teleology, on the assumption that the realm of the sociocultural is a peculiar domain of reason, *logos*. In its simplest form, first, change may be said to occur by immanent direction: by the increasing (or possibly decreasing) integration of meanings, by deductive elaboration, and by elimination of unrelated congeries. As inconsistencies are uncovered, the parts of a meaning system become more numerous, more coordinated and super-subordinated, more dependent and interdependent (with one another and with the whole, and the whole with them), and more consistent and integrated.

Second, change is also governed by the principle of limits. In essence change must remain change in or of something. But if it becomes change into something else, so that it loses its original identity, it ceases to exist. So long as it persists as an identifiable system, it has limits in its change. And it is this principle of limits that accounts for recurrence in sociocultural change, given Sorokin's argument that a cultural supersystem is basically determined by the character of truth or reality, of which only three forms exist (the ideational, the sensate, and their positive combination in idealism).

On the basis of his principles of change, it may be said that Sorokin's view is fundamentally an idealism and, given his basic reliance on Western logic, it may be further specified as a form of rationalistic and objective idealism.

―――――――――

However characterized, these efforts to renovate sociology and sociological theory seemed to appeal to few others than graduate students at Chicago, Wisconsin, and Harvard. Whatever the reasons may be—the urgency of problems in then-contemporary American society, the abstract or qualitative character of these formulations versus the increasing prestige of more specifically stated quantitative or statistical hypotheses, and so on—the further theoretical or research implications evoked little interest in the discipline at large.

But other possibilities for theoretical renovation existed outside of sociology. Attention must now turn to the intellectual developments in other disciplines, such as anthropology and history, the outcomes of which—perhaps curiously—contributed to allowing Park and his orientation to retain substantial intellectual prominence.

Chapter 7

Theory, Anthropology,
and History

Although some continuity can be discerned between pre- and post-World War I theory, its expression in general sociology in the 1920s and later reveals considerable dissatisfaction with, and in many ways outright rejection of, the earlier theories of social origins, social structure, and social change, especially social evolutionism. But by no means is such dissatisfaction or rejection the only indicator of the substantial negative post-World War I reaction to the intellectual legacy of the earlier years. All sorts of efforts were made to appropriate adaptations of orientations from outside the discipline in the United States and from major external figures in European social science. The former influences included anthropology and history, psychiatry and psychology, and a peculiar combination of (earlier) philosophy, psychology, and sociology. Indeed, it may well be that anthropology made the strongest impact on sociology.

CULTURAL ANTHROPOLOGY AND THE IMPACT OF CULTURE ON THEORY

The Diffusion of the Notion of Culture in Sociology

Among the most important intellectual changes that occurred in the second period, and that for some time seemed to augur the possibility of major theoretical alteration, was the introduction of the concept of culture. Its diffusion, from American anthropology, can be traced in articles, monographs, and textbooks in the period. It appeared first in Ellwood's "Theories of Cultural Evolution" in the *American Journal of Sociology* in 1918. Four years later (1922) Ogburn published his *Social Change,* which was substantially concerned with the phenomenon of culture (and which introduced the term *culture or cultural lag* into sociologists' vocabulary). In 1923, Willey was the junior author (with Herskovits, the anthropologist) of the article "The Cultural Approach to Sociology," also in *AJS.* Case's *Outlines of Introductory Sociology* (1924) was the first textbook to make culture an important focus of analysis. The following year (1925) Ellwood published *The Psychology of Human society* and a relevant article in the *Journal of Applied Sociology* (later *S&SR*). Hornell Hart and Adele Panzer's article "Have Subhuman Animals Culture?" in *AJS* (also in 1925) provided the first signs that the notion of culture was to become involved in controversy. In 1926, Bernard began the first of a series of pertinent articles in three of the four major journals. In part an answer to the earlier Hart and Panzer article, Case's "Culture as a Distinctive Human Trait" (*AJS,* 1927a) is indicative of an awareness of broader theoretical implications of the idea of culture. The very same year, Ellwood published his *Cultural Evolution,* and Willey was the author of "Society and Its Cultural Heritage" in *An Introduction to Sociology* (edited by Davis and Barnes). Hankins's *An Introduction to the Study of Society* (1928) contained the first separate chapter of analysis of culture ("The Cultural Factor in Social Life"), which was explored in the remaining five chapters of the section. By 1930, Stern's, Abel's, and Bernard's papers (in *SF* and *AJS*) were unmistakable evidence of the controversy that culture as a notion was evoking. By the outbreak of World War II, more than thirty articles and books had been published in which culture was a central or major concern.

Although a variety of notions during the first period of American sociology and sociological theory may be regarded as antecedents in sociology, the concept of culture was substantially an importation from American ethnology (or cultural anthropology, as it came to be more usually known).[1] True, the most frequently quoted definition of culture came from E. B. Tylor, one of the fathers of British anthropology. But the most frequently quoted researchers, analysts, and authorities were students of an American, Boas, in anthropology.[2]

As a discipline, anthropology was, of course, readily accessible to sociologists and sociology at this time. Sociologists and anthropologists were commonly a part of the same or joint departments. They participated in interdisciplinary ventures.[3] Anthropologists attended, and presented and discussed papers at, professional meetings of the American Sociological Society (later the ASA). Indeed, between the eves of World Wars I and II (i.e., 1915–1941), anthropologists published about fifty papers in the two major sociology journals (*AJS* and *SF*).

In addition, sociology was involved in intellectual controversies for which ethnology or cultural anthropology was decisively relevant during the period: biologism, racialism, and social evolutionism. In particular, culture as a concept was introduced to sociologists as they were induced, following World War I, to examine the critical works of American anthropologists (especially Boas and his students) in evaluating the tenability of social evolution as a theory of social change. Sociologists in general and social theorists in particular became convinced that social evolution was centrally dependent upon culture and cultural change. Sociologists' receptivity to arguments about the nature of culture was enhanced as a result of the disputes over instincts and racial differences in the 1920s. Organic hereditary, and biological arguments were subjected to considerable criticism, especially from an anthropological perspective, and cultural interpretations were often the theoretical beneficiaries of this negative critique. And, lastly, the role of individual genius in sociocultural change underwent substantial reexamination in the 1920s and 1930s.

Sociologists' Conceptions of Culture

A grasp of the arguments over the significance of culture in human social activity demands first an understanding of sociologists' conceptions of culture. Admittedly, the definitions, characterizations, demarcations, differentiations, analyses, and expositions of culture vary markedly from sociologist to sociologist. Some are very terse and cryptic. Others are detailed, extended, and elaborate. But the main interest lies not in the specific variations they disclose, but in what a comparative examination can reveal about the common, basic characteristics of culture as a general phenomenon.

First, culture in general (and any specific culture in particular) is held to have its origins as an adaptive instrumentality to the particular conditions of human social or aggregate existence. In a broad sense, culture is a device to adapt humankind, with its distinctive needs and impulses of a universal biopsychic human nature, to its conditions of existence, especially those involving the natural environment.[4]

Adaptation, of course, relates culture back to American sociologists' continued commitment to evolutionary naturalism during the second period. All nature, all life, including humankind with all of its distinctive features, was to be accounted for finally in terms of distinctive survival requirements. For humankind and its characteristics, the explanation was sought in the relationship between the needs, wants, appetites, desires, and other organic and psychic features of a common biopsychic human nature in relation to a habitat.

Culture is the common adaptive pattern worked out to provide for aggregate adaptation and survival in relation to a common human nature in a common environment. Accordingly, many sociologists of the period developed more or less elaborate catalogs of human nature constituents.[5] But it is the emphasis on adaptation and survival that led to a major preoccupation with behavior and material items of culture, though it ultimately encompassed the full range of items, including ideas and the ideal.

Second, culture is an attribute of human groups (or, more broadly, human societies). It is inextricably bound up with the social. It is acquired coadaptive behavior characteristic of, and established within or through, the group or society (Ellwood 1925, 11; Hankins 1928, 380; Ogburn and Nimkoff 1940, 24). It encompasses those activities "developed in association" between persons or learned from a group (Hiller 1933, 3) or the organized result of the experience of the group (Reuter and Hart 1933, 117). For Young (1934), it is the totality of common and accepted (learned) ways of thinking and acting in a group (xiii, 19; see also Lumley 1928, 182; Ogburn [1922] 1950, 3, 58.)

Third, culture possesses an inter- or transgenerational duration or temporality. It is the persistence of learned behavior or activity from one generation to another (Ogburn [1922] 1950, 6; Willey 1931b, 500; Ellwood 1925, 62, 324; Young 1934, 18). Reuter and Hart (1933, 119) indicate that culture is the organized experience of a group as received from a past generation and transmitted to a succeeding one. Bernard (1942, 728) for his part traces culture back to the specific inventions of given individuals who communicate them to others, both of their own and of subsequent generations.

Fourth, culture, therefore, exists in and through its transmission by communication in which language is of primary significance. But many sociologists of the period would probably have denied language a complete or exclusive role in cultural transmission, for they held that the rudiments of culture were evolutionarily present before language had made its complete and functionally significant appearance among humankind. (E.g., Bernard, Ellwood; presumably Ogburn, Reuter and Hart, and Hankins. All tend to include "man-made objects" in culture.) Nevertheless, they agree that language occupies a place of first importance in the transmission of culture.[6]

Some sociologists of the period began to use such terms as *gesture, sign, and symbol* in connection with the analysis of language, though in most instances the notions were not explicitly defined. Hankins (1928, 414), however, is distinctive in defining the symbol in relation to language, saying that it is "the conventionalization of a particular combination of sounds" to signify "a particular object, condition, or action." The second edition of Sutherland and

Woodward's *Introductory Sociology* ([1937] 1940) defines culture as including "anything that can be communicated from one generation to another" (19),
and thus its contents "can only be ideas or symbol-patterns" (21).

Fifth, any culture (and culture in general) is analyzable into parts that
in their aggregate comprise a structure. Sociologists reveal in this endeavor
their basic indebtedness to anthropology and anthropologists. They conspicuously resort to the cultural-anthropological concepts of the cultural trait,
complex, and pattern.[7]

It is also of significance that the concern with culture and its analysis
seems to have brought renewed attention to Sumner's conceptual differentiation of folkways, mores, and institutions.[8]

Sociologists' interest in, if not commitment to, generalizability and
generalization seems to be indicated conspicuously in their common acceptance of Clark Wissler's notion of "universal culture patterns."[9] No matter
how much specific, individual cultures might seem to diverge, they reveal
certain institutional commonalities in their adaptations of a common biopsychic human nature to their environments: speech, material traits (e.g., food
habits, shelter, transportation and travel, dress, utensils, tools, weapons,
occupations, industries); art (e.g., carving, paintings, drawing, music);
mythology and scientific knowledge; religious practices (ritualistic forms,
treatment of the sick and the dead); family and social systems (marriage,
reckoning of relationships, inheritance, social control, sports and games);
property (real and personal, standards of value, exchange, trade); government (political forms, judicial and legal procedure); and war.

Sixth, any particular culture is asserted to become more or less an integrated (interrelated, interconnected, and interdependent) whole, totality, or
system.[10]

Seventh, both culture in general and all particular cultures undergo
change (sometimes qualified and sometimes not). Indeed, it was precisely in
the study of social change that American sociologists, beginning especially
with Ellwood and Ogburn, most extensively employed the notion of culture.
Most sociologists held that slow, gradual, or accumulative change was distinctive of, if not intrinsic to, the very nature of culture. Each generation
begins with the legacy of the past, which it employs adaptively to resolve its
own problems and then transmits (with additions, variations, or other modifications) to the next generation.References to accumulation were virtually
universal.[11]

The impact of anthropology is evident in the resort to the notions of
invention and diffusion as sources of change.[12] It is present in all textbooks.

Other considerations and distinctions were raised, albeit less commonly. For instance, authors examined the nature and function of the culture
base for social change.[13] On the one hand, they considered the possibility of

resistance to change or inertia.[14] And on the other, they assessed the functions of isolation, contact, and crisis for sociocultural change.[15]

For the actual inclusion of culture as part of theories of sociocultural change, see above, chapters 4 and 5. It is abundantly clear that culture as a phenomenon had its most substantial and conspicuous impact in the study of change during the second period of American sociology.

Culture as a Domain or Level of Reality

Although the conceptions of the origins of culture held by American sociologists reveal the dualistic nature of culture, it is in the various kinds of items or contents designated "culture" that its dualism (involving materialism and idealism) becomes even more evident. Culture is alleged to involve all sorts of objects (e.g., tools and implements, houses, buildings, clothing, furniture, food and drink, technological devices, machines) contrived, refashioned, and used by group-related human beings. It also entails ways of doing things in relation to the natural environment (e.g., techniques, skills, practices, methods, technology, arts of various kinds). Clearly, too, it encompasses ways human beings act in relation to one another (e.g., customs, folkways, mores, rituals and ceremonies, and social institutions, such as family, religion and magic, education, government, and law). And certainly it involves ways of thinking and feeling—symbolization(language, ideas, ideals, beliefs, notions of beauty, the supernatural, morality, philosophy, knowledge, and science, etc.).

A variety of classifications were proposed. One was Folsom's six categories (Folsom 1928, 22ff): material; skills; the symbolic; beliefs, knowledge, and theories; social structures; and sentiments and social values. But probably the most commonly invoked and used scheme was the simple dichotomy between material and nonmaterial culture (e.g., Ogburn [1922] 1950, 4, 11–12, 60, 202; Ogburn and Nimkoff 1940, 46–47, Ellwood 1925, 9; Hankins 1928, 387; Reuter and Hart 1933, 166, 167; Lumley [1928] 1935, 343; Willey 1931b, 504; Young 1934, 22; Bernard 1942, 729). As a form of reality, culture in the second period of American sociology was prevailingly construed dualistically.

But such characterization does not recognize that the emphasis in the dualism may vary from a preponderant materialism to a predominant idealism. As perhaps the major figure in popularizing the material/nonmaterial dichotomy of culture, Ogburn nevertheless tended to stress the role of the material, particularly in modern urban industrial societies. This view is especially evident in connection with his lag thesis in his *Social Change* ([1922] 1950).Interestingly, he subdivides the nonmaterial domain into the adaptive and the nonadaptive. That portion of nonmaterial culture that is closely adjusted or thoroughly adapted to material culture, or to material conditions of existence, or to both, is termed "adaptive culture" (203, 271). It ranges from more narrow and isolated techniques and methods, such as ways of handling a tool, to "rather large usages and adjustments," such as customs, folkways, and social institutions, including government. Nonadaptive non-material culture refers to "ways of doing things valuable for their own ends and not particularly [i.e., indirectly, or partially] concerned with material conditions" (203, 271–2). Religion, art, ceremonies, and literature are illus-trative of this second subdivision. Manifestly, Ogburn's treatment empha-sizes the place of material culture and of adaptive nonmaterial culture.

By contrast, Ellwood (1925) stresses mind, consciousness, intelli-gence, reason, and choice. Humans have an original biopsychic nature of needs, wants, desires, and impulses that, concomitant with an expansion of intelligence and reason, permit the formation of habits, on the one hand, and articulate sounds or speech (the basis of language), on the other (296–97). Mind, consciousness, and purposiveness are also accompaniments of such intelligence, accentuated by interpersonal interstimulation and response, and rapid and complex adaptation (72–74, 78–80, 82). Intelligence and the power of articulate speech are necessary for abstract ideas or mental patterns that exist with, and are communicated by, language, "the first form of cul-ture," and the spoken word, "the first tool" (60–61, 80, 297). Such mental patterns, the basis of ideas, standards, and values, can control the formation and circulation of "coadaptive habits" in the group (324, 325). New ideas, new desires, new purposes can arise. Thus, the development of culture can scarcely be said merely to "satisfy original natural impulses" (297). Just as humankind has been able to control nature and build up an artificial physical environment through learning and intelligence, so also we are similarly able to control and modify our own nature and build upon an artificial social environment by learning and intelligence (323).

However, it is evident that the dualistic conception, if not dualistic assumptions, were troublesome to some of the sociologists as early as the beginnings of the controversy over culture. In referring to the Hart and Panzer (1925) exposition of culture in connection with Tylor's definition, Case (1927a) complains that the evidence offered does not seem to show that animal experi-ence can and does accumulate—which, he insists, could scarcely occur with-out symbols. However, he moves on quickly to insist that the basic difference resides not so much in how culture is transmitted, but in the very nature of what is being transmitted, that is, culture itself. He contends also that the argument of their paper is predicated on the assumption that the sum and substance of the culture process lies in the social transmission of behavior patterns (907, 908).

Turning then especially to Ellwood and Bernard, Case proceeds further with his critique. He claims that Ellwood's emphasis on "socially communicated mental patterns" has missed the central importance of tools and symbols in and of themselves (911). Case leaves the reader with the impression that he is also disappointedwith Bernard for having failed to see that the symbolic conditioning of inner behavior provides a means of external storage of ideas and action (911–12). He reiterates the significance of the possibility of external storage, and thus impersonal communication, of "the results of internal mental habit in the form of words and other symbols" (914). And he insists once more that an analysis of culture seems to reveal that it "consists essentially in the external storage, interchange, and transmission of an accumulating fund of personal and social experience by means of tools and symbols" (920). Yet his argument has failed to solve the dualism of culture as content versus means of communication, subject versus object, mind versus matter. He was struggling essentially with the nature of the public symbol in both language and tradition.

Thus, sociologists were beginning to grapple with the relationship between the symbol and culture from the later 1920s onward. Stern (1929), Lundberg (1939b), Sutherland and Woodward ([1937] 1940), and Bain (1942) are all illustrative. Stern (1929) argued that culture is "dependent on articulate language." Once in existence, language promotes and "heightens communication which facilitates individual and group interrelations" (267). By substitution of "sign words for highly complex images or association of images, speech enormously facilitates the formation of those associations which are the basis of cultural life" (267). In Stern's view, only articulate language "offers sufficient symbolic abstraction to permit conceptual projection beyond individual experience and substitution of symbol for behavior making possible the accumulative retention, transmission, and diffusion of culture" (267). Clearly, language and culture have a distinctive interrelationship, which Stern senses but does not formulate entirely clearly. He merely remarks that "with the inception of culture, human behaviors responds to artificial, external patterns; social behavior becomes culturally modified and variable" (267). He might have said: With the inception of culture in conjunction with language, human behavior can respond to nongenetically determined patterns that can be objectified and symbolized in language and communicated; social behavior becomes culturally modified and variable.

George Lundberg's exposition of culture uses the symbol as accommodated to habit and the conditioned response (within a behavioristic stance) as his point of departure in his *Foundations of Sociology* (1939b). He regards symbols as basically habits that correspond to some kind of "neural-muscular sets or covert neural behavior" in the human body or organism. Formed initially as the outcome of situational responses, they come subsequently to function "as substitute stimuli for these situations." If such symbols "correspond closely" or are adequate to the circumstances to which individuals "must adjust, they greatly facilitate [*sic*] . . . adjustments" (48).

It might appear that what Lundberg has actually described is the sign or signal, which is intrinsically tied to the thing symbolized and to a present situation, rather than the true or arbitrary symbol, which has no intrinsic connection whatsoever with the thing symbolized and can refer to situations in the past or future in the imagination. He does acknowledge that language symbols serve as (abstract?) stimuli not only for adjustments in present situations, but also for those in the "indefinite past . . . or . . . future" (178). But communication by genuine language entails more than a series of discrete signs or signals; it involves a system of interrelated arbitrary symbols in which meaning is signified by virtue of the system (Davis 1948, 42–43). Unfortunately, Lundberg never offers anything that might be regarded as an explanation of how the transition is made from the one kind of symbol (i.e., the sign or signal) to the other (the true or arbitrary symbol).

Habits, and especially the vocal habit or symbol (in the sense of substitute stimuli), are crucial for culture. The vocal habit or symbol is the basis of social adjustment patterns (folkways, traditions, customs, mores, and institutions) (Lundberg 1939b, 181–2). These patterns, along with related humanly fabricated products, in interaction with the actual (defined?) physico-organic surroundings, the human beings themselves, and their past products, comprise what (Lundberg claims) may be termed "culture" (228; cf. 179).

Interestingly, Lundberg avoids any detailed consideration of variability in folkways, traditions, customs, and mores. Nor is any of the institutions (e.g., family-sex-kinship, the economy, the state, religion, or recreation) ever systematically or comprehensively examined "either as found in some particular society at a particular time or as a general phenomena to be found in all groups" (412). His treatment of culture is distinguished by its brevity, if not also its ambiguity. (See below, chapter 8.)

Concentration of attention on selected basic and general features of the various institutional domains and avoidance of the specific particulars of folkways, customs, traditions, and mores tend, of course, to yield a characterization of the sociocultural domain much more in accord with the generic features those not bound by space and time, of physico-organic phenomena (and thus accords with his physico-organic materialistic social ontology; see below.) Admittedly, such avoidance also precludes confronting "overlapping boundaries" of the concepts (183).

Bain (1942) endeavored to formulate a conception of culture in terms of social symbols by an appropriation of Mead's notion of the significant symbol. A former behaviorist, Bain seemed to make both culture and group dependent on behavior mediated by social symbols. Though he doesn't precisely say so, a persisting group requires a continuing culture, and vice versa. The "minimum requirement for culture is the social symbol mediated *inter*action of a dyad" or two-member group (87). The two (or more members, if the group is larger) respond similarly to the same symbol because for them it refers to or stands for the same referent, which thus has a common or shared meaning for them. This circumstance is evident when "each responds to its own response to the symbol as it responds to the other's (or others') response(s) to the same symbol" (88). Thus, each is able to be both subject and object simultaneously. It means role-taking and communicative interchange of symbols so that other-oriented behavior is meaningful, that is, interaction. Curiously, though, Bain does not distinguish between signs and symbols or explicitly invoke verbal or linguistic symbols as the sine qua non of social symbols.

In any event, Bain contends that the distinction between material and nonmaterial culture is meaningless. Whether it is fabricated or not, neither inorganic nor organic objects can be said to constitute culture as such. Indeed, none of these objects can be asserted properly to "have" or "possess" culture. Such a claim can be made only for organisms like humans in groups (90, 91).

Significantly, Sutherland and Woodward ([1937] 1940) construe culture more comprehensively and completely in Meadian terms. They define culture as "anything that can be communicated from one generation to another" (19). The culture of a particular people "is their social heritage, a 'complex whole' which includes knowledge, belief, art, morals, law, techniques of tool fabrication and use, and modes of communication" (19). So it follows that if "culture exists only where there is communication, then the content of culture can only be ideas or symbol patterns. Culture is then an immaterial phenomenon entirely, a matter of thoughts and meanings and habits" (21). The gesture, especially the vocal gesture and the verbal or language symbol, are crucial to human communication and culture and must be learned in the course of socialization. It is important for the developing child that many gestures "take the form of partial or incomplete acts that stand for or symbolize the whole act and make its carrying through unnecessary" (203). The child's monosyllabic utterances may become for the adults symbolic vocal gestures that are eventually replaced by shared vocal symbols of his or her siblings and parents. As these are learned, the child also begins to acquire a grammar, "a technique of putting words together in socially meaningful combinations" (205). Eventually, the child has a "set of symbols and a way of using them" that permit communication and, simultaneously, the acquisition of culture. Curiously, the two authors never offer a rigorous specification of the gesture and the (verbal or language) symbol, though they do indicate how drastically the understanding of suggestion and imitation

must be altered in light of their conception of symbolization and the socialization of the child.

Of course, this notion of culture, to which communication and the language symbol are absolutely basic, raises the question of just how intellectually the tools, machinery, and broad classes of material objects created or
refashioned by humans and left for succeeding generations to use are to be
treated. The two authors propose the term *culture objects,* something closely
associated with culture but not a part of it. In turn, each such culture object
"will be represented in culture through (1) an associated technic of fabrication or manipulation (the art of building a bridge, printing a book, breeding a
new type of cat, mining an ore) and (2) a set of customs or usages governing
the object's utility and social significance" (21).

What this review of positions seems to indicate is that some professional disposition was being constituted to alter the materialistic idealistic
balance in the dualistic conception of culture. The nature and function of the
(arbitrary vocal) symbol in language was being grasped. So the relationship
of mind and matter, subject and object, internal and external, private and
public, disciplined sounds and word, word and idea, and patterned arrangement of words and meanings was gradually emerging. Some experts would
argue that the relation between material and ideal components was being
recast, others that the very meanings of *material* and *ideal* in relation to
symbols and to symbol system were being altered.

Yet the 1930s also witnessed the entrance of a European idealist
notion of culture in American sociology. Znaniecki (natural systems vs. cultural systems), MacIver (culture vs. civilization), and Sorokin (the cultural
system or supersystem) were primarily responsible for this introduction. But
it was anticipated and recognized by Park much earlier.[16]

Culture Accepted As a Concept but Rejected As a Theory

Certainly, the fact that the notion of culture had become widely diffused
and accepted throughout American sociology in general and in sociological
theory in particular in the mid to late 1930s, but never became the basis for the
development of a distinctive orientation or theory, may well seem to be a paradox. The question of why culture was accepted as a basic concept but rejected
as the foundation for a complete theory demands an answer.

Clues to an answer can most profitably be found in the dispute over
the acceptability of the notion of culture that arose in American sociology
from the mid 1920s to the mid 1930s and that so far we have not examined.
(Case, Stern, Willey, and Ellwood were generally the protagonists for acceptance, whereas Hart and Panzer, Abel, Bain, and Bernard were antagonistic
toward the notion.) The character of the arguments seems to indicate four

major reasons for the failure of a culturalist theory as such to develop in sociology during this second period.

First, it appears that the proponents of culture who might have been most likely to develop a full theory were subject to the stricture that they held a view of culture as a domain of phenomena separate and discontinuous from the rest of nature and so violated a basic premise of (evolutionary) naturalism. Case (1924, xxx), for example, had held that culture is a phenomenon "exclusively human and social," that animals have not been shown to possess it and humans even to be devoid of it, and that accordingly "a tremendous gulf separates man and the lower forms of life."

Two somewhat different lines of attack developed. One, as represented by Hart and Panzer ("Have Subhuman Animals Culture?," 1925) and Bain ("Culture of Canines: A Note on Subhuman Sociology," 1929a), tried to show that animals possess the rudiments of culture and that thus any sharp division between humans and lower life forms was untenable. A second line, represented by Bernard (1930a, 1930b), argued that culture is always a child of nature, is always to some extent connected with nature, supplements nature, and "has developed as an extension both of the natural environment and of the adjusting organism as an aid to further and more successful [evolutionary?] adjustment" (Bernard 1930a, 39). Bernard accused the protagonists of culture (which he sometimes termed "cultural interpretationists" and sometimes "cultural determinists") of having erected it "into an underived *ultra qua non* similar to the soul, the old time free will, the first cause, logos, etc., which are prone to be used as an axiomatic starting point in casuistical discourse and thus become the mothers of much error and more intolerance" (Bernard 1930b, 327). Bain (1925, 550), for his part, declared that both Case and Ellwood adhered to views implying a special place to humankind in the hierarchy of nature, as accepting discontinuity rather than continuity in nature, and as holding that humankind is somehow unique in the universe, "a little lower than the angels." Thus, the protagonists of culture were stigmatized as extremists and antinaturalists, as implicitly metaphysical or supernaturalist in their basic assumptions.

Secondly, the proponents of culture, as the ones most likely to develop a full-fledged theory, were unable to argue that the study of culture can provide a separate and distinctive domain so as to justify the independent intellectual existence of sociology. In his article "Is a Cultural Sociology Possible?" (1930), Abel drew on the arguments of his European heritage to contend that the entire domain of culture is divided among the various social (or cultural) sciences, with no residual remaining that could consitute an additional subject matter of inquiry for sociology. The sociologist who as a culturalist endeavors to make a distinctive approach through generalizing will have to use the materials of the special fields and thus become a synthesizer

(741). According to Abel (740), Willey's (1929, 205) position as a culturalist became vulnerable, because he had insisted that a synthetic approach is
defective. Indeed, Willey was compelled subsequently to concede the argument to Abel (Willey 1931a, 342n.), announcing that he now rejected the
"identification of sociology as the 'study of culture.'"

If sociology were seriously to commit itself to the study of cultures by
investigating particular modes of life in particular areas it would confront the
fact that American ethology or cultural anthropology had already preempted
the field. Admittedly, ethnology or cultural anthropology in the United
States continued characteristically to study the cultures of primitive peoples
in contrast to modern, civilized, urban industrial peoples. Still, some sociologists proposed the parallel development of a cultural sociology as a specialized field of the discipline. (See Leyburn 1933; Bernard 1933.)

Furthermore, American sociology had been historically committed to
the study of the human social—human association, the group, society, social
structure, and social change—and any effort to expand its primary focus of
inquiry to culture would probably only have evoked conflict. Clearly, sociologists (see esp. White 1940; Stern 1929; Bain 1942) had considerable difficulty in demarcating and separating the social and the cultural. Undeniably,
serious efforts to investigate the relationship of the nonsocial cultural with
the more directly social would likely have proved fruitful and illuminating.
The relative hiatus between sociologists' presentations of culture traits, complexes, and patterns and the Sumnerian folkways, mores, ethos, and institutions in their textbooks is itself suggestive of the classificatory and theoretical problems. True, such terms as *standard, rules,* and *norm* were sometimes
used, but no indigenous american sociologist actually endeavored rigorously
to define and conceptualize social rules or norms and differentiate them into
major varieties. The Scottish-born MacIver, who used the term *social heritage* but not *culture* in his textbooks ([1931] 1937), did provide a systematic
consideration of codes and rules, but his American colleagues scarcely
seemed appreciative of his contribution at the time. However, Davis's
Human Society (1948) was indebted to MacIver's work and to Linton's conceptualization of status and role in *The Study of Man* (1935). Certainly, the
pervasive indifference to the significance of such a classification was
scarcely conducive to a clarification of the relationships among the social,
the normative, and the broader cultural domain and to facilitating any theorization of culture in sociology.

Third, for sociological theory to have developed a theory of the cultures of modern civilized societies would have required a wrenching, if not
impossible, redirection of efforts. Manifestly, American sociology had
always been primarily preoccupied with the phenomena of American society

and culture. During the 1920s and 1930s, its instrumentalist proclivities were, if anything, deepened and strengthened. The past of American sociology had tied the discipline to social work and to social reform, in the United States. The onset of the depression in America only served to provide an additional dimension to the problematics of American society so as to link American sociology with its past concerns. In addition, the discipline was in the process of aligning itself even more strongly with a positivistic methodology that was especially American-oriented. Whether a positivist methodology could have been as readily adjusted to the study of other modern cultures in the 1920s and 1930s may well be questioned.

Conversely, sociology's adoption of the stance of American anthropology to the study of modern cultures would have required specific, particularistic, historically-oriented inquiries that would have been increasingly at odds with American sociology's devotion to a natural-science model of the discipline. Prominent American anthropologists during the 1920s and 1930s (Kroeber, Lowie, Wissler, and many others) had argued that the study of particular cultures had to be approached as detailed descriptions cast within specific space and time contexts. (Although primitive peoples were characteristically pre- or nonliterate and thus devoid of written histories, the character of their cultures as wholes had to be grasped in terms of reconstructed time sequences of contacts, conflicts, conquests, isolation, acculturation, etc.) The specific, particular, and concrete were emphasized, without assumptions of potentially large-scale generalizations or universals. The science of American sociology was oriented to the search for general, if not also universal, laws of social structure and sequence.

Finally, the most distinctive formulations of the cultural—which would seemingly have held the greatest potential for distinctive theorizing—also appeared to be the most antithetical to the basic assumptions of American sociology. The references to culture as an objective or self-existing entity, a phenomenon sui generis, which was superindividual, superpsychic, or superorganic,were readily associated with Durkheim, social realism, or an anti-individualistic (or antinominalistic) determinism, that is, with cultural determinism.

In his critique of the culturalist stance, Abel (1930, 749) notes that Durkheim was the first to attribute to cultural facts the character of a constraining and external mode of existence. Though expressed in modified terms, the culturalist conception of the superindividual is thus in effect a reiteration of Durkheim's point of view (749). It is significant, too, that frequent reference is made to the Durkheimian notion of collective representations.[17]

Even more crucial is the fact that Durkheim's fundamental intellectual assumptions are implied to be at variance with the basic outlook of American sociology. Durkheim and the notion of the superindividual are asserted by Abel (1930, 750) to introduce "the quandry of [social] realism and nominalism." Abel insists that, basically, a cultural fact cannot be said "to exist external to, or independent of, the individual" (751). Bernard (1942, 800) also denied the legitimacy of culture as "a thing in and of itself," as existing sui generis. Culture may be said to be only "the persisting more or less institutionalized product of the impact of an intelligent organism, seeking a necessary adjustment, upon its environment" (800).

Ellwood's 1945 article similarly protests against cultural determinism. Like many of his colleagues, he held that culture could only develop out of, and function on the basis of, a biopsychic "constitution" (or human nature) that makes human beings "organizing," "creative," "purposive," "selective," affectively motivated but potentially and at least rudimentarily rational (424–25, 425–30).

But the first sociologist to have explicitly explained, elaborated on, and then rejected the thesis of cultural determinism was Hankins (1928, 402–12). He denied the thesis because he claimed that ultimately culture can exist, function, and change only as a consequence of the activities of particular and unique individual minds (410). For Hankins, as for others of the time, inventive results received their distinctive character "in part from the special qualities of the creating genius" which derive in turn from rare organic combinations varying "from generation to generation" (411, 410). Cultural innovation stems finally from individual initiative and talent as based on organic, hereditary differences. Thus, cultural determinism must be rejected.

Culture as a notion could and did become widely accepted. But it could not and did not achieve an acceptable formulation as a theory in sociology during the second period.

HISTORY AND ITS INTELLECTUAL IMPACT ON THEORY

The Background

Although the volume of publications in sociological journals hardly suggests that history was as relevant for sociology as anthropology was, evidence shows that some sociologists regarded history as a potential source of both data and ideas for their discipline (see Barnes 1921; Ogburn 1921; Eliot 1922; McLaughlin 1927; Hertzler 1925, 1934; and Becker 1934, 1940). In spite of considerable animosity pervading past relations of the two fields, developments in both seemed to imply for a time the possibility of a "historical sociology" and perhaps even the rise of a historically-inspired theoretical stance in sociology during the 1930s and early 1940s.

The early methodological formulations in sociology during the 1920s and 1930s frequently alluded to a historical method in sociology. For instance, Case (1924) noted that each field or branch of the social sciences has both historical and analytical aspects and thus appropriately both a historical and an analytical method. (It is evident that this declaration includes the field of sociology too.) Case conceives of the historical method as seeking "to depict concrete reality in all of its concreteness," whereas the analytical (processual) method endeavors "to give an account in terms of abstract generalizations, mechanisms, processes, laws, and principles" (xvii). Ellwood (1925, 31) refers to the historical method as making a distinctive contribution "to the study of human social behavior." Yet his presentation merely asserts that the "study of human history enables us to compare social processes and social behavior at different points of time, and also to see the modifying effect exerted upon it by various conditions" (31–32). Presumably, the historical method is thus a version of the comparative method, which Ellwood has identified with the study of "uncivilized peoples" (31). Elsewhere, Lumley ([1928]) 1935, 35) paraphrases Ellwood's version of the historical method (as published in a journal article) as looking "back into the happenings among men during historic times" and drawing "conclusions from these events." For Hart (1921, 370), the historical method "uses documents," such as ancient manuscripts, autobiographies, and all sort of papers, all presumably from the past, as sources of information (cf. Lumley [1928] 1935, 35). Drawing apparently on Park, Reuter and Hart (1933) distinguished history and sociology in terms of a professional interest in the unique and nonrecurrent versus the general and the recurrent. Still, they do note that the practices and rules of social behavior and institutional norms and organization can be studied "genetically by tracing their origin, development, function and organization in a single group or, comparatively, by a parallel examination of many groups" (6). Curiously, they ignore the potential, and perhaps necessary, connection between the genetic and the historical, especially for modern peoples. It seems evident, though, that for the bulk of sociologists up to the mid 1930s, if not into the 1940s, sociology could and should make methodological use of the substantive findings of history. Hence, sociology and sociologists necessarily had some concern with history and what it had to offer.

Yet history as it was conventionally written up to the early part of the twentieth century was not likely to elicit positive interest from the sociologist. Many sociologists after World War I would have concurred with the indictment that Spencer had leveled at history in 1860 in his first chapter of his little volume *Education* (as quoted in Case 1924). He objected that history was oriented to the "biographies of monarchs," to "court intrigues, plots, usurpations, or the like, and with all the personalities accompanying them," the "squabbles for power that led to a pitched battle," the generals and their subordinates, the size of their forces, their changing fortunes, the outcome of the battles. The "great mass of historical facts . . . are facts from which no conclusions can be drawn—unorganizable facts; and therefore facts which can be of no service in establishing principles of conduct, which is the chief use of facts." What are wanted are "facts which help us to understand how a nation has grown and organized itself," that is, facts about developments in its major institutional domains and their consensus (as quoted in Case 1924, 6, 7, 8).

In 1912 James Harvey Robinson published a book entitled *The New History,* which Case (1924, 9) claimed showed "that the traditional catalog of military and political events was still parading itself as history seventy years after Spencer exposed its social worthlessness" and proposed a new conception of history. Robinson advocated a history so constituted as to allow us "to interrogate the past with a view to gaining light on great social, political, economic, religious, and educational questions in the manner in which we settle personal problems which face us" (as quoted in Case 1924, 12). He urged that history become useful and relevant by promoting progress through enlightening persons' understanding of the (past) processes that produced "existing conditions and opinions" (Case 1924, 13). It will be a history in which the past is employed to understand the present. Manifestly, it will "avail itself of all those discoveries that are being made about mankind by anthropologists, economists, psychologists, and sociologists—discoveries which during the past fifty years have served to revolutionize our ideas of the origin, progress, and prospects of our race" (Case 1924, 13). History must "alter its ideals and aims with the general progress of society and of the social sciences and . . . ultimately play an infinitely more important role in our intellectual life than it has hitherto done" (Robinson as quoted in Case 1924, 14).

It is of the utmost importance that this conception of history became the foundation for the development of a field of historical sociology, especially in the work of Harry Elmer Barnes in the 1920s, and facilitated the contributions of Howard Becker and others in the 1930s and later. Barnes, who received a Ph.D. in history at Columbia University in 1918, offered the first paper entitled "The Development of Historical Sociology" at the American sociological Society annual meeting in 1921. (Admittedly, many diverse features enter into "historical sociology," but it seems prevailingly to involve the study of social change using historical data—sometimes in opposition to ethnolographic data—to develop generalizations and propose change theories.) In 1927, Barnes and Jerome Davis (of Yale University) assumed editorial responsibility for the preparation and publication of *An Introduction to Sociology* and a companion *Readings in Sociology.* The influence of Robinson's "new history" was evident throughout Barnes's eight chapters on "the evolution of the great society" and was previewed succinctly in Barnes's first chapter, "The Genetic Viewpoint in Sociology: Its Abuses and Uses." Barnes ([1927] 1931, 5) remarks that the "present is intelligible only in the light of its genesis through the long ages of the past." However, he cautions that it is not possible to "find direct analogies between some distant historic situations and our present-day problems" (5). In envisaging the present in terms of the past, the modern time perspective has been vastly extended through science, especially astronomy and geology. For Barnes, all time is one and all human history is one, a continuity. However, he does conceive of the period since 1750, the era of the scientific and industrial revolutions, as having brought vast transformations of material culture and technology, which coexist "along with many ancient ideas and institutions" (11). In effect, Barnes accepted Ogburn's culture lag thesis. A body of historical material, if intelligently conceived and forcefully expounded, "should be able to disabuse our minds of . . . [a] fatal worship of [institutions] from an inadequate and archaic past, and thus give aid in lifting the weight of the 'dead hand' from the backs of our own and succeeding generations" (12). The "chief lesson of the newer history," then, is to disabuse us of "our reverence" for the past, "though not, of course, our interest in it" (13). Manifestly, then, history cannot merely be a narrative account. It must be approached interpretively in an effort to probe historical causation.

Barnes's writing contains a significant implication for the conception of sociology and sociological theory. True, Barnes—like Robinson—would have rejected any effort to construe sociology in a way that would have essentially detached it from the other social sciences. However, it does appear that he was advocating that sociology essentially focus on the study of the culture of modern, or civilized, society using the data of the newer (and modern) history as its foundation for generalization and theorizing. In effect, he was in agreement with Park (or Park with him) in the basic notion of the province of sociology, in contrast to emerging American ethnology or cultural anthropology, with its focus on the cultures of primitive peoples during the 1920s and 1930s. Barnes was required to forsake an academic career in 1930, but his subsequent occasional collaboration with Howard Becker continued to bring him to the attention of sociologists.

Still, the major developments in historical sociology, and their broader theoretical implications, were associated with historically-oriented sociologists who had been trained or located at the University of Chicago and a sociologically-oriented historian at the University of California, Berkeley. House and Becker were the sociologists who had been Park's students. The rather unique historian was Frederick Teggart, who was founder of the Department of Social Institutions at Berkeley and chaired it throughout most of the years of its existence. The three sociologists and the historian were involved in recurrent debates in the 1920s, 1930s, and early 1940s.

Teggart's Ideas

Although textbook references make it evident that sociologists were aware of many of Teggart's ideas in the 1920s,[18] the first direct exchange between them and Teggart came in 1928 and 1929, when House published his article "Social Change and Social Science" and Teggart responded with "Notes on House's 'Timeless' Sociology." In his article, House refers to the intellectual cleavage between those historians (and apparently also historically-oriented anthropologists and economists) who seek to make "social facts intelligible" by showing "how they have come to be as they are" (and Teggart is specifically cited) in terms of specifically dated and sited occurrences versus those social investigators who seek to do so by accounting for such social facts in terms of universal, timeless (i.e., unsited and undated) forces and processes in a natural or abstract science fashion (House 1928, 13). Clearly, House's sympathies and inclinations lie with the latter approach, and he cites three instances of such studies in sociology (including the University of Chicago inquiries in the "natural history" of the urban community) that tend to "establish generalizations . . . independent of historical setting and change" (14).

In examining Teggart's response to House's advocacy, it is necessary to point out that Teggart's case is a severe adumbration of his arguments as presented in his earlier *Prolegomena to History* (1916), *Processes of History* (1918), and *Theory of History* (1925). Teggart prefaced his objections to House's version of a natural science of sociology by observing that a resort to physiology, for instance, as a model of natural science entails the acceptance of an abstract conception of the human body having no relation to any concrete human organism and involving "timeless" processes representative of the "way things work" only "if nothing interferes" (Teggart 1929, 363). Indeed, "'natural' science, in general, is concerned with the investigation of the way things work, under controlled conditions, i.e., when they are not [externally] interfered with . . . It is this un-interfered-with working that is 'un-historical'" (363).

Teggart raises three specific objections to House's proposal. First, this conception in the social sciences in general, and in sociology in particular, stems from the ancient Greeks (especially Plato and Aristotle), who rigidly separated science from history or the scientific from the historical (equating the historical with the accidental). For the Greeks, the natural involves the domain of the *physis,* that which entails internal change, such as growth in the course of the life cycle of an organism. Accordingly, the Greeks employed the organismic analogy as a basis for the study of society. But such a notion is directly contradicted by the character of the actually existing social world in which people constantly influence one another and concrete human societies impact and intrude on one another. All are in a historical context in which intrusive or external change constantly occurs.[19] Such dated and sited occurrences (the stuff of history) cannot be ignored. To do so is to ignore empirical social reality.

Second, House's presentation does not commit itself to a comparison of the multitudinous instances of actual societies and their histories to discover actual processes at work. To do so requires study of actual human groups, "carrying on the actual affairs of life, and subjected frequently in their history to actual 'interferences'" (364). Use of an analogy as a point of departure, committing the investigator in advance to certain results (e.g., timeless findings), precludes comparison of actual societies and genuine "inductions" about "'the way things work' to produce the results [of] . . . the present" (364). Indeed, as represented by his *Processes of History* and his (later) *Rome and China* study, Teggart was, in effect, demanding that sociologists engage in a much more extended, detailed, and exacting comparative inquiry of civilized societies than they had ever contemplated and thus considerably postpone any claim to the instrumental utility of their studies.

Finally, he criticizes House for advocating background studies that do not methodologically require "an intimate acquaintance with the history of the guiding conceptions and preconceptions in the field . . . of special interest" (364–65). Yet the training of most sociologists during the period was scarcely such as to enable them to grasp the subtlety of his analyses of Aristotle, St. Augustine, Fontenelle, Perrault, Bossuet, Descartes, Condorcet, Turgot, Comte, and Darwin in his *Theory of History*.[20] Furthermore, the critical implications he drew about notions of science, social science, social change, progress, and evolution were, if understood, scarcely likely to win sociologists' acceptance, because they involved views that either already had achieved or were in the process of achieving dominance in sociology.

In addition, Teggart was in the curious position of being interpreted (if not misinterpreted) by sociologists who were committed to basic methodological notions that he rejected. Robert Park and Howard Becker, who referred to Teggart in their works more frequently than did any other sociologists, did so in a context of the contrast drawn between history and natural science (or between the idiographic and nomothetic disciplines) that the German philosopher-methodologists Windelband and Rickert had proposed and that Teggart rejected (Teggart 1925, 59–60 n. 16). Indeed, in the first chapter *Introduction to the Science of Sociology* (Park and Burgess 1921), Park had translated a portion of Windelband's famous inaugural address at the University of Strasbourg, which formulated the history/natural science distinction. (See chapter 2 above.)

This misconstruction is tellingly revealed in a 1929 paper (reproduced in Park 1952) in which Park quoted Teggart's distinction between science and history, the former as dealing "with objects, entities, things, and their relations," and the latter "with events" (178). Such events happen, whereas, things or objects "change . . . in orderly ways" (178). Continuing, Park remarks that a thing or object has a nature that is—and he footnotes Rickert—"the rule or law by which it changes." Such close juxtaposition of Teggart with Rickert might induce the unsuspecting and uninformed reader to assume that Teggart also subscribes to the view, which Park held, that sociology as a science has its own typical objects, each with its own typical (internal) tendency to change. Indeed, Park insists that such change involves a sequence of stages, each following the previous one in an orderly and irreversible way, as scientific (or naturalistic) inquiry into the various general objects of sociology (e.g., the gang, the plantation, the sect, the strike, the revolution, race relations, or any group or society) will divulge (224, 225).[21] However, such a conception of change was anathema to Teggart as an unquestioned assumption deriving from an analogy between social phenomena and natural objects that Greek philosophy had endowed with a *physis* or an internally contained growth-like tendency to change—and to which Teggart had objected only a few pages later in the same work Park had cited for the science/history dichotomy.[22]

Although Park's major interest in and contributions to the study of change, especially concerning the modern city or urban community, have been widely recognized, their basis in a general theory of social change and in a particular theory of modern or civilized societies, as types of "social objects," is much less commonly acknowledged. In Park's view, sociology was to investigate civilized, urban-centered societies, whereas anthropology was to assume responsibility for inquiry into primitive and archaic societies. Unfortunately, Park's ideas are scattered throughout a number of his papers.[23] His paper "The City and Civilization" (in Park 1952) is especially suggestive of his views on the origins of civilized societies, the contrast between ancient and modern civilizations (civilized societies), and the main features of modern civilization (chapter 6, above). However, Park was not particularly identified with efforts to develop a subfield of historical sociology.

The sociologist most conspicuously and substantially associated with an emerging field of historical sociology was Howard Becker, who had been a student of Park and was a member of the Department of Sociology at the University of Wisconsin from the fall of 1937 until his death in 1960. Certainly as conversant with Teggart's position as House was, Becker, in his review of two of Teggart's books in the *American Sociological Review*, reveals the same apparent inability or disinclination to recognize the basic points of Teggart's arguments. Becker insists, for his part, on the relativity of the separation of the "time-bound study of 'how things have come to be as they are' and the timeless study of the 'nature of things'" (Becker 1941b, 735). He avoided the whole issue of the analogically based argument involved in construing social phenomena as natural objects with intrinsic tendencies to change.

Becker's Historical Sociology

Becker's position appeared early and remained evident throughout his career. It is apparent in his doctoral dissertation at Chicago in 1930; in his chapter "Historical Sociology" in *The Fields and Methods of Sociology* (Bernard [1933] 1934); in a series of papers throughout most of the 1930s based on his doctoral dissertation; in *Social Thought from Lore to Science* (Barnes and Becker 1938); and in *Contemporary Social Theory* (Barnes, Becker, and Becker 1940), to mention only some of the relevant publications. However, the present analysis must be restricted to Becker's effort to develop the culture case study, which involves the use of historical date in conjunction with the ideal, or constructed, type for an effective inquiry into social change as a broad theoretical problem.

Becker's 1934 paper in *The Fields and Methods of Sociology* reveals that his own endeavors at developing a theory of social change began as a response to the difficulties diagnosed in unilinear stages theory of social evolution from the nineteenth and early twentieth centuries. Although Becker contended that a variety of legitimate objections might be raised against the older stages theory, he did not categorically reject all stages theorization. Stages can be acceptably formulated as constructed types, using historical data embodied in culture case studies, without the assumption of a continuous, successive development of one stage out of a prior one (i.e., if the postulate of genetic continuity is not assumed). And Becker surely does not reject stages because they are based on the premise of a generic, general trend of historical development.

Becker apparently advocated his dynamic analytic (i.e., sacred/secular) scheme because he believed that historical development is indeed unitary and unilinear (in conformity with the unilinear stages theory of social evolution) but may also entail reversibility (in contradiction to classical social evolutionism). His vigorous opposition to historical relativism, which is often associated with a pluralistic notion of history, stemmed from his conviction that there is a "total historical process" (Barnes, Becker, and Becker 1940, 517, 519). He proposed the use of constructive typology, or the ideal-typical method, as he first termed it, "to work out an acceptable theory of the general trend of historical development" (Barnes and Becker 1938, 789–90). As constructed types, sacred and secular societies are to be regarded as establishing the extremes of a continuum on which the data of human history and social development may be arranged and generalized. Becker's several types are construed as analogous to stages. In its formulation and use, his sacred/secular analysis contains, therefore, certain similarities to, if not continuities with, the abstract, general, and universal stages theory of social evolution, which it was presumably designed to replace. More importantly, it was to be employed with a methodology committed to a nomothetic conception of the purpose of science.

Becker's adoption of the constructed type was predicated on its utility for solving certain methodological difficulties in the study of change that the idiographic/nomothetic distinction of Windelband and Rickert suggested. Manifestly, the study of social change requires use of the data of history as an individualizing discipline. But sociology aims at the common, the general, and the recurrent, that is, the general or generalizing of social change. Through resort to the construction of appropriate types, sociology can abstract and generalize and so render historical data comparable. Thus, constructed types allow sociology to study change and to do so in conformity with the generalizing objective of science—as envisaged by Windelband and Rickert and Becker.

Although the type is designed to facilitate generalization and comparison, it tends initially to be relatively dated and localized. It stems from a specific problem, tends to beconstructed to aid in the proof or disproof of a definite hypothesis, and derives from the culture case study, the relevant data for which have been compiled from the selective observations required by the problem and hypothesis. The culture case study, which Becker described in detail only later in his career, is thus of crucial importance in the methodology of the constructed type.[24] It delineates the relatively unique on an explicitly selected basis. By focusing on such features as "promulgated beliefs, moral ideas, maxims of conduct, modes of action, and so on," the culture case study guarantees that whatever degree of generality the type has will not be in violation of the connections among the items in the historical context (Barnes, Becker, and Becker 1940, 528, 507–8).

Once constructed, types function to indicate what is comparable in the empirical world and what is susceptible of generalization (Barnes, Becker, and Becker 1940, 508–9; Becker 1950, 147–49). Because types vary initially in level of specificity or generality, the researcher may find that in some instances it may be advisable subsequently to construct more specific subtypes, and at other times it may be desirable to develop more generic, general, or universal types. Given the mandate of science, the sociologist should seek to reduce the dated and localized character of the constructed type. He or she can accomplish this end and at the same time expand the range and comparison and generalizability of the construct by careful examination of additional relevant cases. Presumably, her or his success in making types more general will condition how useful they are for transferring conclusions from one area and period to others. (In this respect, Becker appears to resemble, rather than to differ from, Teggart.)

Becker's studies of change among the ancient Greeks and within the German youth movement (and subsequently) involve distinctive use of the culture case study and constructed types as the logical extremes of a continuum. Problems of these two investigations were so construed that the relevant phenomena could be conceived as falling on a continuum between two extremes that represented logical and qualitative opposites, a quantitative gradation from minimum to maximum, and end points of an explicit or implicit temporal sequence (Becker 1932a; Becker 1950, 216–17). Sacred and secular societal types, which are based on cultural case studies, set the limits of the two extremes as opposites or polar types. Conceivably, any number of relevant similar case studies can be placed between the end points. If a sufficient number of instances were available, it is possible that an empirical continuum could be established. In the event that the number were very large, the differences between one case and another would become almost imperceptible, and the degree of change between any two instances would be minimal.

As indicated at the outset of this book, epistemological-methodological statements tend to yield, or become linked with, ontological positions. Such is certainly the case in this instance. The alleged continuum of constructed types that is supposed to eventually result from extended inquiry seems to reflect a series of temporal stages, each one preceded by and succeeded by another, behind which lies a natural entity or object tending to undergo organismic growth-like change that is never fully realized in the concrete social world of time and space because external interferences intermittently occur (as "accidents"). In this expanded intellectual perspective, then, Becker (along with Park and House) seems to diverge markedly from Teggart.

So Teggart's vision of a historically relativistic sociology—which entailed a reconstruction of the assumptions of both conventional history and social science, and which had intruded into the consciousness of sociology through the emergent field of historical sociology—was destined to remain unfulfilled on the periphery of sociology. Manifestly, Teggart's conception of such a sociology, with the distinctive forms of sociological theory that would have been entailed, was not in harmony with the major trends in sociology in the 1940s. Teggart's historical relativism is equally an antifoundationalism in contradistinction to the predominant foundationalism of American sociology. (Nevertheless, most of Teggart's students pursued doctoral dissertations distinctively relevant to sociological theory and predominantly pursued careers in departments of sociology.)[25]

It does seem doubtful that Teggart's views would have won acceptance in sociology even if Park, House, and Becker had interpreted him accurately and even if they had endorsed his position. Certainly, historical sociology as a field did not flourish. And even though Becker eventually was elected president of the American Sociological Association, that could scarcely be construed as an indicator of broad concurrence with and general recognition of the validity of his intellectual stance. Indeed, it might even be suggested that the predominance of the same mainline substantive and methodological views that precluded acceptance of Teggart's stance also militated against Becker's position. Any qualitative, historically-oriented theory would confront insurmountable intellectual barriers.

Even though neither anthropology nor history stimulated the development of a theory in sociology in this period, anthropology did contribute the notion of culture, which was not matched by any equivalent derivation from history.

SUMMARY AND CONCLUSIONS

Introduced both by actual direct personal contact with anthropologists, often in a joint department, and by impersonal contact through publication in periodicals of sociology, culture as primarily a derivative of anthropology was nevertheless subject to an accommodation with the intellectual legacy of sociology. First, the concept of culture was defined within the broad orientation of Darwinian evolutionary naturalism. It referred to a common or shared adaptive (behavioral) pattern that had been worked out to provide for aggregate adaptation and survival in relation to a common original human nature in a common environment. Because it was ultimately regarded as adaptive, it was in its most basic sense behavior or activity. Second, it was a learned attribute of human groups and especially human societies, acquired in association or interaction with other members. Third, it existed transgenerationally through time. Persistence in time is a distinctive feature. Fourth, its existence occurs in and through transmission by communication in which language is of primary significance. Fifth, it was held to be analyzable into parts. Sixth, in their aggregate, these parts are interconnected, interrelated, and interdependent and comprise a structure. Seventh, culture undergoes change, but the change bears a direct relationship to prior accumulation and can arise from within (as an invention) or from without (via diffusion).

Culture was, in addition, construed as a form of reality combining materialism and idealism. This combination was revealed in the various modes of classification, perhaps the most common of which was Ogburn's material/nonmaterial dichotomy. Although emphasis in Ogburn's classification was on the material component, in Ellwood's it was on the idealistic. Interestingly, the arguments over the nature of culture seemed to focus increasingly on communication, language, and the symbol (e.g., Stern, Sutherland and Woodward, and Bain). By the early 1940s, culture had become defined and conceptualized in terms of Mead's notion of the (significant, public) symbol.

However, the most important section of this analysis involves a failure: the failure of culture to become the basis for the elaboration of a theory in sociology. Three major obstacles seem to have prevented the formulation of a culturalistic sociological theory:

1.   The proponents of culture as a concept who were most likely to elaborate a full theory were subject to the stricture that their view of culture rendered it separate and discontinuous from the rest of nature. Thus, their conception violated the basic premise of evolutionary naturalism.

2.   These same proponents were also unable to argue, conversely, that culture could constitute a separate and distinctive domain justifying the autonomous intellectual existence of sociology as a discipline or field. (A variety of difficulties were suggested: e.g., that anthropology had already preempted the study of culture; that a partial use of any aspect of culture, such as norms or American culture as a type of modern culture, would only result in intellectual confusion or contradictions with dominant trends in the discipline.)

3.   Nor could the proponents readily invoke the Durkheimian conception of culture as a self-existing entity or a phenomenon sui generis (as superindividual, superpsychic, or superorganic) as the foundation of a theory, because it was committed to social realism. A Durkheimian based theory would thus have been at variance with the distincitve individualism, nominalism, and antideterminism of American sociology.

Accordingly, major intellectual obstacles prevented development of a culturalistic theory. Yet, henceforth, the broad acceptance of culture as a concept meant that any future generalized synthesis capable of becoming a general theory would have to deal with the implications of culture.

Regarding history as a potential source for a theoretical renovation of sociology, it becomes evident that the possibilities were considerably less promising. It is true that some sociologists had become increasingly concerned about the discipline's reliance on the data and theory of anthropology as a foundation for sociology, especially the study of social change. And it certainly was the case that, throughout much of the 1920s, sociologists included a "historical method" as one of their recognized methods (though it is less certain that historians would have accepted the sociological version). Furthermore, it is also correct that developments in history and among historians promised to make history and its practitioners more acceptable in sociological eyes (e.g., Robinson's *The New History*, Barnes's active participation in the American Sociological Society's annual meetings during the 1920s, and Teggart's impressive methodological sophistication regarding the relation between history and the social sciences in his *Prologomena to History, Theory of History,* and *Processes of History).*

Such sociologists as Case, Park, House, and Becker—and especially the latter three—referred to Teggart in their own publications. And Teggart came to the direct attention of sociologists in his 1929 response in *Social Forces* to House's 1928 article. In the exchange, it became evident, however, that Teggart's views were considerably at variance with those of most sociologists and thus unlikely to elicit a favorable response to a reconsideration of the basis of the earlier enmity between history and sociology.

1. Teggart denied that it is legitimate to construe the scientific study of the social world as entailing a "timeless" (abstract, general) process representing the "way things work if nothing intervenes." House's position—and presumably that of the many sociologists he represented—was based on the ancient Greek philosophical (especially Aristotelian) view of the social world as a domain of *physis,* in which only internal change, as typified by growth in the course of an organism's life cycle, was "natural" and "normal." This position violated the actual reality of modern societies, with their impact and intrusions on one another and, in effect, regarded external change as "accidental" and inconsequential.

2. Teggart cricitized House for failing to require the study of multitudinous instances of actual societies and their histories as the basis for the discovery of actual processes at work. Adoption of the Greek model of what is natural and normal biases the results in advance of research and precludes the discovery of genuine inductions about how the social world works. (But Teggart's view of adequate research would have demanded much more detailed and exacting inquiry than sociologists had ever contemplated and thus would have considerably postponed their claims to instrumental utility.)

3. Teggart insisted that House, along with most of his colleagues, presumably fails to understand that background studies must entail an intimate acquaintance with the history of methodological ideas (guiding concepts and preconceptions) in their fields. Yet the training of most

sociologists of the period scarcely equipped them to grasp the subtlety of Teggart's analyses of figures and ideas far removed from the present or, if they understood, to accept his (historical-relativistic) criticism of the views about science, social science, social change, progress, and evolution that either had achieved or were in the process of achieving dominance in sociology.

Teggart was in the very curious intellectual position of being presented and interpreted by sociologists who were committed to basic methodological notions that he rejected (e.g., the science/history dichotomy of the German Neo-Kantians Windelband and Rickert). These views were basic to the positions and arguments of Park, House, and Becker.

Indeed, Becker was involved in endeavoring to develop his own program and his own social change theory as a foundation of historical sociology. As indicated in chapter 4, Becker proposed an elaborate typology of sacred/secular societies, the methodological promises of which derive from the Neo-Kantianism of Windelband and Weber. The theory of social change he attempted to outline sought a compromise between the relatively ahistorical general and atemporal versus the relatively historical particular and temporal, between the sources of internal change and the sources of external change.

Unfortunately for both Teggart and Becker, the historical sociology that the former implied and the latter actually sketched certainly did not flourish, if indeed it was ever even established. Curiously, the same major characteristics of sociology that became substantively and methodologically ascendant and precluded acceptance of Teggart were the very ones that also blocked Becker (i.e., a statistically couched positivism and a presentist, utilitarian-justified model of research).[26]

Chapter 8

Theory, Psychiatry, and Psychology

Given the basic value of individualism in American society and culture, it may seem likely, if not also appropriate, that the developments in American psychiatry and psychology should have elicited considerable interest during the second period as significant sources for renovating the bases of sociological theory. Interest in psychiatry is evident as early as 1917 and, of course, in psychology substantially earlier. Indeed, some of the first generation or founding fathers of American sociology (e.g., Giddings) even construed sociology as essentially a branch of psychology. Certainly, no sociologist in the United States could envisage a sociology that did not involve assumptions about the nature of the human individual and that thus did not explicitly or implicitly invoked certain premises and features of psychology. And it is patently evident that sociology during the 1920s and 1930s especially resorted to psychology in this country as a model, both substantively and epistemologically-methodologically. But it is to psychiatry that we now turn our attention.

PSYCHOANALYTIC PSYCHIATRY

Background

Although G. Stanley Hall, who was instrumental in bringing Freud to Clark University in 1909 for its twentieth anniversary, was the first to describe the potentialities of Freudian discoveries for sociology (Hall 1913), it was not until 1917 that several articles, book reviews, and abstracts pertaining to Freudianism were published (G. Hinkle 1957, 577). Robert Gault's 1917 lecture appeared in the *American Journal of Sociology*. Though Ernest Groves's article in the May 1917 issue of *AJS* has some relevance for psychoanalysis, Groves's more general paper "Sociology and Psycho-Analytic Psychology: An Interpretation of the Freudian Hypothesis" in the July 1917 *AJS* may well be taken as the initial point of departure for Freud's impact on sociology. Groves also provided the first full-length book review that year, followed by others in the next two years.

Gault and Groves were the vanguard of the external and internal sources of the Freudian influence on sociology. In addition to Gault, William Healy, Carleton Parker, and Harold Lasswell were important external figures. And within sociology—in addition to Groves—Ogburn, Burgess, and Thomas were significant protagonists, at least initially. (Just how Freudian ideas impacted on the discipline generally is investigated in Burgess 1939; G. Hinkle 1951, 1957; Jones 1974.[1]

In the decade or so from 1917 on sixteen articles on Freudianism or pschoanalysis appeared in sociological periodicals.Seven were published in *AJS* (1917, 1918, 1920, 1926, 1928) and nine in *PASS* (1918, 1920, 1921, 1923, 1924, 1926, 1928). One was in the *Journal of Applied Sociology* and another in its successor, *S&SR*. Three were in journals outside of the discipline.

A number of sociologists (e.g. Groves, Ogburn, Burgess, Park, Thomas, Folsom, Weatherly, Chapin, Eliot) sought to apply or extend psychoanalytic ideas to explain social phenomena. Some (e.g., Krueger, Zorbaugh, Hayner, Shaw, and, from political science, Lasswell) endeavored to explore the Freudian-inspired case-study or life-history approaches and techniques to the study of various problems.

But major opposition to psychoanalytic ideas and assumptions became evident almost immediately. Faris's 1921 article "Are Instincts Data or Hypotheses?" includes Freud in its indictment. Bernard similarly raised objections to psychoanalysis in his "Instincts and the Psychoanalysts" (Bernard 1923, 350).

But some of the opposition to psychoanalysis in sociology seemed to have dissipated as the result of the development of a revisionist psychoanalysis, which included such major figures as Horney, Sullivan, Fromm, Adler, and Jung. Among its adherents, Sullivan, Alexander, Horney, Fromm, and Adler contributed papers to the two major sociological periodicals (*AJS* and *ASR*) from the mid 1920s to the mid 1940s.

The rise of the "culture-personality" school or orientation (which included such major figures as Kardiner, Linton, Benedict, Kluckhohn,

Leighton . . . and others who had been influenced by Freudian ideas) probably also contributed to the acceptance of psychoanalytic views in sociology,
especially between the years 1937 and 1945. Sapir, Dollard, Devereux, Dai,
Hallowell, M. Mead, and McKeel all published in sociological journals during this period.

In sociology itself, major figures from six basic fields evidence a substantial impact of psychoanalysis. These fields (with their representatives)
are:

1.   Sociology of the family (Burgess, E. R. Mowrer and H. Mowrer, K.
      Young, Groves, Brown, Eliot, Frazier, Nimkoff, Winch, Goode)
2.   Social psychiatry (Bain, Burgess, Dollard, Groves, Young, Park, Dun-
      ham)
3.   Social disorganization (Green, R. E. L. Faris, Dunham, H. Elkin, Dol-
      lard, A. Davis, W. L. Warner)
4.   Public opinion (esp. Laswell, Goldhamer, and associates)
5.   Race relations and prejudice (Dollard, A. Davis, A. Rose and C. Rose)
6.   Use of life history as such (Healy, Queen, Cavan, Krueger, Lasswell) and
      in conjunction with urban personality types (Zorbaugh, Hayner, Shaw).

Now it is quite evident that sociological theory was not one of the major
fields in which Freudian ideas had a substantial impact during the period. Certainly, no one endeavored to formulate a general sociological theory using
psychoanalytic concepts as its core. But two sociologists who became prominently associated with macrotheories of change did use Freudian ideas:
Ogburn and Thomas. Their views warrant comment and analysis.

Ogburn

Ogburn was introduced to Freud's ideas only one year after the latter
had lectured at Clark University. As a student at Columbia University in
1910, Ogburn had heard a seminar talk on Freud by anthropologist Franz
Boas, who not only had attended the Clark meeting, but had himself presented a paper there. At this same time, Ogburn was also a member of a
group that met weekly at the home of the anthropologist Alexander Goldenweiser. As a consequence of hearing Lewis Lorwin present a paper on one of
Freud's books, Ogburn was induced to read the volume and thus acquired
his first direct information about Freudian views. Subsequently he read other
works (e.g., by Bernard Hart, H. W. Frink, Edward J. Kempf, and others by
Freud himself) that contributed to his larger interest in the relationship of
mental phenomena and bodily states. Apparently, Ogburn was the first sociologist to be psychoanalyzed. (The analysis was performed by the social

psychiatrist Trigant Burrow, who later wrote on psychoanalytic subjects in sociological publication, and was carried out for scientific rather than therapeutic reasons about 1918 in Baltimore. See G. Hinkle 1951, 1957.)

Ogburn apparently followed the developments in psychoanalysis much more during the second decade of this century than his own publications would indicate. Before his 1918 analysis, he seems to have read everything on the subject available in English. Nevertheless, it was not until March 1919 that his first article using this knowledge was published. In this paper, Ogburn explained the paucity and unacceptability of economic interpretations of history in terms of the same psychic mechanisms that psychoanalysis had proposed. Like the sexual instinct in individual behavior, the economic motive was basically selfish and thus repressed into the forgotten past, the unconscious, and excluded from scholarly analysis. Ogburn declared that history is subject to distortion because persons as members of a social group omit or choose to forget certain "unpleasant events in history."

However, Ogburn's first major book (*Social Change*, 1922) offers a more extended analysis of his Freudian interpretations. He suggests that the distinctive innate (or instinctive) inclinations of original human nature were invariably limited by the demands of human social (i.e., associational) existence, both generally and particularly. Modern human beings inherited from their remote ancestors a set of instincts, which had "adaptive and survival value" for early humans just as surely as their muscles had. These innate biopsychic tendencies included sex, perhaps hunger, anxiety-fear-flight, anger, curiosity, desire for new experience and adventure, pugnacity, gregariousness, sociability, submissiveness, and selfishness and altruism. So Ogburn noted that the sex instinct created and perpetuated life and fear and pugnacity saved it—as did the increase in numbers resulting from sociability and gregariousness. (See Ogburn [1922] 1950, 272, 300, 302, 303, 191, 176, 182, 362.)

Although Ogburn wrote before the controversy over the instincts had developed, he seemed to sense impending problems in the notion of instinct. He regarded the "mechanism of instinct" as part of the original, hereditarily endowed equipment of humankind. Instinctive behavior is essentially a "reaction of the body or various parts of it to stimuli" and thus involves "a recognition of a stimulus, an accompanying emotion, and a motor reaction." However, the stimuli may be internally induced within the body or arise external to it. (Consult Ogburn [1922] 1950, 301–5.)

Ogburn suggests that permanent human association has introduced two major problems for the satisfaction of the instincts, one deriving from the consequences of the necessity of a moral code and the other from changes in culture. Association generally requires a moral code that demands conformity in conduct and a "repression of desires." Elsewhere, Ogburn notes that human beings are characterized by "desires to conform to social codes," which may be based on the "gregarious instinct, in sociability or in the instinct of self-assertion," but these desires conflict with "individual cravings and impulses." In addition, the culture of modern complex urban society does not allow the satisfaction of the instinctive proclivities, which were originally oriented toward survival under conditions of a much simpler life. (Put simply, modern human beings are organically the same as their ancestors in the ice age, but they are vastly different culturally.) Under the specialization of modern industry, certain wishes are never even stimulated (e.g., the monotony of a job doesn't allow for the expression of the desire for new experience.) Even worse is the stimulation of certain wishes along with the denial of an effective response (i.e., repression). The consequences are an increase in neurosis and in social problems of industry, labor, the family, immigration, and crime (Ogburn [1922] 1950, 352, 318, 286ff., 47, 312–35).

Efforts to rectify the conditions of modern society, Ogburn argued, met with a variety of impediments. In general, survivals, vested interests, tradition, social pressure, and habit tend to sustain the status quo. In addition, the extremism of conservatism and radicalism tends to find its explanation in the problems of personality formation. In reviewing the events of the past, conservatives, who are prone to forget the unpleasant, recalled only its glories and were hesitant and unwilling to exchange this security for a dark, unknown future. Contrarily, radicalism is often the response of persons who suffer from nonfulfillment of instinctive drives or who are under the pressure of intense mental conflicts (Ogburn [1922] 1950, 186, 192–93. This explanation seems very similar to Carleton Parker's theory of the causes leading to IWW membership before World War I.)

Clearly, Ogburn had invoked Freudian premises about the nature of original human nature, society, and modern culture to account for certain phenomena in conjunction with his general culture lag theory of social change. In addition, his account of obstacles to effective (i.e., gradual) social change also drew on theories having Freudian bases and assumptions. It is noteworthy that Ogburn seems to have abandoned these views in *Sociology* (Ogburn and Nimkoff 1940).

Thomas

Some "expert" commentators and analysts to the contrary notwithstanding (e.g., Barnes 1948, 800; cf. Janowitz 1966; xxii, xxxix–xl), Thomas's psychosocial theories of personality and society of the early 1920s do reveal the substantial impact of Freudian ideas. Admittedly, neither *The Polish Peasant in Europe and America* (Thomas and Znaniecki 1918–20) nor *The Unadjusted Girl* (Thomas 1923) explicitly declares indebtedness to Freud or conspicuously espouses the centrality of the libido or a structuring of the self in terms of id, ego, and superego. Clearly, then, the Freudian influnce is more indirect and covert than direct or overt. However, the connection drawn by Park and Burgess in *Introduction to the Science of Sociology* ([1921] 1924, 496) between Thomas's views about the four wishes and the wish of psychoanalysis in 1921 should have alerted sociologists. Indeed, Park and Burgess integrated the presentation of the four wishes into a total theory of personality development impressively similar to the Freudian theory of the evolution of the libido. The significance of the Park and Burgess interpretation may have been obscured because Thomas's own part in the composition of the work was substantially deemphasized and acknowledged only by brief references in the preface and the index. Still, Thomas's *The Unadjusted Girl* exhibits a number of Freudian affinities: (1) Its introduction was written by Mrs. Ethel Dummer, who had been closely associated with the work of Healy and Bronner on criminal misconduct and whose known adherence to a Freudian position is evidenced in her preliminary remarks; (2) Thomas makes direct favorable reference to psychoanalytic techniques of personality study and case records; and (3) Thomas makes frequent (but scattered and unsystematic) use of many Freudian concepts.

However, the important linkage between Thomas and Freud was revealed only when Gisela Hinkle contacted Florian Znaniecki (Thomas's collaborator on *The Polish Peasant*) in connection with the preparation of her doctoral dissertation (G. Hinkle 1951, to which the following analysis is indebted). Circa 1916–17, shortly before the publication of the first volume of *The Polish Peasant,* in which the classification of the four wishes was presented for the first time, Thomas read psychologist E. B. Holt's *The Freudian Wish and Its Place in Ethics* (1915). In a personal letter to Hinkle (3 April 1950), Znaniecki commented: "I remember that he [Thomas] was much interested in it [Holt's book] and afterwards wanted to use 'wish' instead of 'desire.'" (See also G. Hinkle 1957, 580–81). Thus, Znaniecki specified what it was that provoked Thomas's sudden interest in the "Freudian wish" (Znaniecki, 1948, 767). Apparently, early in the research and writing of the study of the Polish peasant, it became important to find some way to classify the variety of attitudes discerned in their data in relation to values. As part of this effort, Thomas came to rename "desires" as "wishes" in conjunction with the reading of Holt's book. Thus, a crucial but indirect connection between Freud and Thomas has been established.

However, the impact of Freud, psychoanalysis, and other psychoanalysts was certainly not limited to the mere naming of desires as "wishes." Beginning with the similarities between Holt and Thomas, the influence of Freudianism was more extensive.

The Nature and Functioning of the Wishes. Holt and Thomas agree that human behavior is subject to naturalistic causation through a dialectical process of conflicting wishes. Like Holt, Thomas conceived of wishes as basic units that impelled and directed human behavior but that required aspects of the environment for their satisfaction. Not only were the wishes in tension with the environment, but they were at variance with one another (Park and Burgess [1921] 1924, 439). In Thomas's case, two of the wishes were said to be on the individual, and two on the social, side of personal evolution. Thus, the former (individually oriented) wishes, for stability (or security) and new experiences, were in conflict with the (socially oriented) wishes for response and recognition. The evolution of the personality was a result of their interaction in the individual in relation to society. Abnormality might be manifested in an inhibited personal evolution or in the suppression of one of the basic wishes. The Polish peasants illustrate the former in that their primary-group mode of social existence developed the socially oriented wishes for response and recognition to excess and inhibited the individually oriented wish for new experience. In the event of a change in the social environment, the underevolved or inhibited wishes became the causes of inability to adjust to the new situation.

Thomas's notion of the four wishes as constantly in search of satisfaction was in accord with Holt's view that a constant interaction of the organism and the environment was required for steady adaptation of the individual to the world in which she or he lived. But the final outcome of the personality was also dependent on the nature of the society or social environment in which the wishes were gratified. Now, a culture might be adjudged good or evil in terms of the personalities that tended to be formed in it. To the extent that culture provided adequate satisfaction of wishes, it was good. But if, in the interest of the group, it inhibited or suppressed the expression of wishes, it was bad or evil, for repressed wishes would lead to expression in a social or antisocial behavior. Such is the case of the unadjusted girl whose wish for recognition was blocked by American culture. Only under wise counsel and guidance could her repressed wishes find socially acceptable outlets (via the mechanism that Freud had labeled "sublimation" and that he used to explain the rise of civilition).

The Particular Character of Two of Thomas's Four Wishes, the Wish for Response and the Wish for Recognition. Although Thomas notes that the desire for response manifests itself in the tendency to seek and give signs of interpersonally oriented appreciation and "is primarily related to the instinct of love," it certainly includes much of what Freud encompassed in sex (Thomas 1923, 17). Thomas remarks that "the desire for response between the two sexes in connection with mating is very powerful" (18). He also alludes to the "devotion of the mother to the child and the response of the child" (17).

In addition, the desire for mastery, which later became part of the wish for recognition, was derived directly from the writings of Nietzsche (see below), as is Freud's psychoanalytic theory of dreams as flashbacks to ontogenetic and phylogenetic childhoods (Brill 1938, 497). Analytically, the primitive character of the Freudian wish can, indeed, be traced back to Nietzsche's "will to power," just as can a part of Thomas's desire for recognition.

Briefly put, then, Thomas's desire for response includes much of what Freud had termed "sex"; and, in turn, both the general primordiality of the Freudian wish and a part of Thomas's desire for recognition stem from Nietzsche.

A Variety of Freudian Concepts of Psychic Processes. Admittedly, Thomas's "The Persistence of Primary Group Norms in Present–Day Society and Their Influence in Our Educational System" (1917) contains only references to "repression" and "suppression" (177, 186). Volume 3 of *The Polish Peasant* (1919) invokes "fixation," "suppression," and "sublimation" (37; 38, 39, 40; 42, 43, 44). But *The Unadjusted Girl* (1923) refers to "suppression," "repression," "sublimation," "fixation," "transference," "overdetermination", and "narcissism" (72; 71; 31, 98, 243, 250; 18; 21; 18; 250, 252, 254; 24).

Thomas's Professional Associates. Adolf Meyer was a contributor, as were Herbert Jennings and John B. Watson, to the volume in which Thomas's 1917 chapter appeared. As indicated above, Mrs. Ethel Dummer provided the foreward to Thomas's 1923 *The Unadjusted Girl,* which included an allusion to William Healy (35). Mrs. Dummer also authored the introduction to *The Unconscious: A Symposium* (1927) to which Thomas contributed a chapter, "The Configurations of Personality."

Clearly, then, Thomas had been substantially influenced by Freud and his American psychoanalytic apologists and expositors, though he may have become somewhat more critical of psychoanalysis in the late 1920s. Thomas was scarcely a doctrinaire disciple at any time, but Volkart (1951, 211n.) seems to convey more negativism about Thomas's views from about 1916 to 1925 than would seem to be warranted.

Criticism of Freudian Ideas

Most sociologists and most theorists in sociology continued to reject psychoanalytic ideas and techniques in the discipline. Five major, general objections can be distinguished:

1. Especially in its older, orthodox version, psychoanalysis overemphasized the role of sex in social life. Burgess (1939, 357) alluded to sex as an impediment to acceptance of Freudian ideas in American sociology. (Concurring were Groves 1917a, 113; Faris 1921, 188; Faris [1937a] 1976, 64–65; Bain 1936, 206, 208.)
2. But it was not simply emphasis on sex, but its instinctivist conception,

that was an obstacle to acceptance of Freudianism. Sociologists had become conversant with psychoanalysis just as the discipline had begun a general rejection of instinctivist doctrine as a basis of social behavior. Specifically, Faris's 1921 paper on instincts attributed the misuse of the instinct concept to a failure to differentiate hypotheses from data and to a disregard of information on the varied behaviors of primitive peoples. Bernard's *Instinct: A Study in Social Psychology*(1924) found a superabundant variety (5,759 types) of instincts, along with a usage that was too inaccurate, inconsistent, and uncritical to be scientifically acceptable and useful (200). Further, most of what was ascribed to instincts was the consequence of environmental conditioning. Sharing "in the popular fallacies regarding the instinctive control of human action," psychoanalysts are similarly subject to the criticisms of adherence to biological determinism, lack of precision, and construing instincts as though they were real data (Bernard 1923, 350).

3.   Conversely, psychoanalysis either fails entirely to recognize, or insufficiently recognizes, the place of culture in human behavior. (Concurring were Burgess 1939, 359; Bain 1936, 206, 208; Faris 1936a, 170; Faris [1937a] 1976, 156–58; Green 1946.)

4.   Freud's theories were particularistic and so violated the assumption of the multiple causation of social behavior. For sociologists, it was an obvious fact of experience that social phenomena and human behavior derive from the operation of many factors and conditions. Any explanation relying solely on one cause, such as sex, was prejudged as scientifically inadequate. (Concurring were Burgess 1939, 358–59; Faris 1921, 188; Faris [1937a] 1976, 64–65; Bain 1936, 215.)

5.   Many sociologists expressed reservations about the character of Freud's method. (Joining in this criticism were Burgess 1939, 358–59; Bain 1936, 208–9, 215; Kirkpatrick 1939, 327–28; and D. Young 1941, 878–79.)

It is noteworthy that sociologists who came to be identified with theory or who were associated with arguments in the theory domain were characteristically hostile to Freudian ideas—except, most notably, Parsons at the end of the period. Sorokin (1928), Znaniecki (1936), Faris ([1937a] 1976), and MacIver ([1942] 1964) had objections.

Sorokin (1928), for instance, alleges that the manifold problems of Freudian theory are exemplified in the notion of the libido, which has been ascribed a variety of meanings—"sometimes quite narrow, sometimes unlimitedly broad," indeed, so much so that it "is identical to the conception of life" (607). Under such circumstances, no clear correlation, causal relation, or other definite relationship between phenomena can be established. It is impossible to know what is being correlated with what, and "we wander in the forest of undefined phenomena and shadows of phenomena" (607). To be so lost intellectually, "as factually the Freudian theorizers are, . . . is only natural. In brief, the theory is utterly inadequate and unsatisfactory" (607).

In particular, Faris ([1937a] 1976), Znaniecki (1936), and MacIver ([1942] 1964) develop extensive arguments against Freud and psychoanalysis:

1. In Faris's ([1937a] 1976) view, perhaps the basic objection to Freudian interpretation is that it assumes the existence of invariant universal psychological elements at the basis of personality and human conduct. Along with innate ideas, acquired ideas, faculties, sensations and feelings, reflexes, and cognitive forms, instincts or instinctive desires are examples of such elements. But intellectuals cannot agree on these elements—asserts Faris—because "they do not exist" (159). To assume immutable units"of origin or stable elements" that combine in "personality" and in turn influence or structure social order "is to reverse the order of development" (161).

2. Znaniecki (1936) is especially adamant that an inquiry into the active experience of the individual to find something "more real, more essential, more valid than this experience itself" is unacceptable (23). Unless "we have empirical evidence to the contrary, we must assume that" actual, overt action is the expression or "realization of its tendency" (23). But otherwise, tendency is to be interpreted in terms of the action as actually and empirically given, "just as we define a physical force by its empirically given results" (24). To ascribe an "empirical connection between the past action and the present action to the persistence of certain complexes and wishes in the unconscious" is to ascribe it to something "inaccessible to our observation" (28). MacIver ([1942] 1964) similarly objects to the resort to "hidden, disguised, or 'unconscious' motives" (213). At best the researcher can "discover, examine, and organize" evidence suggesting "the presence of particular motives" and so reveal the basis "for an inference that can be no more than highly probable" (213). Faris ([1937a] 1976) claims that the "central doctrine of the Unconscious [impressively capitalized] appears to be a hypostatization of the notion of the subliminal which is at least three hundred years old and has received recognition ever since" (156).

3. MacIver ([1942] 1964) declares that Freudians are vulnerable to the charge of unjustified "certainty" and of treating as established fact that which is only an inference (214). All too frequently, psychoanalytic literature discloses "the contentment with the congenial guess, the acceptance of analogy as proof, the daring leap into the dark—the *salto mortale* of faith" (214).

4.   In their three usages of the term *unconscious motives*, the psychoana-
      lytically committed constantly and confusingly pass from the level of
      the conscious to that of the unconscious. In MacIver's ([1942] 1964)
      view, organic tensions and strivings should not be cast in language that
      imputes "unconscious motives." He contends, second, that in designat-
      ing as "motives" that which "the agent is fitfully or dimly aware but
      without realizing their full significance" is "to employ a mode of
      speech that plays havoc with any distinction whatever between the
      conscious and the unconscious." Third, characterizing certain motives
      that have been unexamined by the subject, are inexplicable to her or
      him, and have bases that are incomprehensible to her or him does not
      entitle one "to call these motives themselves 'unconscious' or to call
      'motives' the unconscious factors that may determine them" (215,
      216).

5.   MacIver further argues that Freudian interpretation reduces the com-
      plex to the simple, leaving the complex "still unexplained." The reduc-
      tion has been based on an "act of faith" that has accepted "the original
      hypothesis as the major premise from which the conclusion is derived"
      (218).

6.   MacIver also insists that Freudians, in often ignoring the most unlike
      conditions, tend to postulate the specific incentive a priori rather than
      infer it from historical evidence. The "other considerations and needs,
      economic, social, and cultural, that accompany sexual desire, blend
      with it, follow after it," are subordinated "without warrant" (221).

7.   Faris ([1937a] 1976) warns that Freud, Jung, LeBon, and Kropotkin
      exhibit a similar fallacy in their conception of human nature. Though
      they do not agree on what it is, they "reduce it to a single instinctive
      principle" (64–65).

8.   Further, according to Faris, Freudian psychoanalysis has no physiolog-
      ical underpinnings. Not a neuron can be found. Built upon the experi-
      ences of the individual person, the whole system is "concerned with
      wishes, images, anxieties, fears, and dreams. It is a sort of antithesis
      and counterpart to behaviorism" (133–34).

9.   Attention is, Faris argues, largely confined to "conflict in the 'soul.'"
      Because its "incestuous and selfish desires are assumed to be primary
      and elemental," it is "in tragic and perpetual conflict with social
      requirements" (155).

10.   Faris insists that Freud's efforts to "explain social origins by psycho-
      logical principles . . . is no longer acceptable." Freud's account of
      totem and taboo "which enables him to explain the culture of African
      natives on the basis of the dreams of neurotic Austrian women is as
      simple and naive as it is unsound" (215–16). MacIver ([1942] 1964)

notes, "All traits of civilized man are phylogenetically determined"; personal development and social change are rendered superficial (217, 216).

11.   In their specificity and universality, Freudian psychological arguments invite cultural refutation. Faris ([1937a] 1976) notes that among the Forest Bantu the father "is not a tyrant and never punishes his children." Although the "maternal uncle has a special status and function," the notion of authority doesn't seem "applicable"; indeed, he "is indulgent to the point of being imposed upon" (246).

12.   Faris accuses Freud of being persistently in error in accounting for "cultural forms and social disorder by a theory of individual infantile experience" (246).

13.   In classical psychoanalysis, the expression of need is erroneously treated as absolute rather than situationally relative. By contrast, MacIver ([1942] 1964) argues—and surely Znaniecki and Faris would agree—that sexual "need finds expression" in accordance with "the cultural setting" and "the restrictions and permissions of the mores" (223).

14.   Finally, MacIver insists that the Freudian interpretation of society "ignores totality—ignores environment," "history," "genuinely social products," and "anthropology" as it is professionally known and practiced. Total situations or even total personalities are unconfronted. In the Freudian construction, the whole, the personality, is not analyzed in "its specific aspect relative to the situation, but only through the agency of the designated complex." And that "complex is insulated in the whole—or from it . . . But this methodology does not do justice to the integrative and selective self." Only the "parthenogenetic products of the complex" are provided, "not the products of the relation of the self and the environment." Freudian causality is devoid of the "process of interaction, interadaptation" (MacIver [1942] 1964, 220).

As a group, theoretically oriented sociologists were unfavorably disposed to Freudian psychoanalysis. Only Ogburn and Thomas (and apparently Bain, at one point) were positively inclined to the use of Freudian ideas. But the majority, as illustrated by the positions of Sorokin, Faris, MacIver, and Znaniecki, were overwhelmingly negative in their response to the central premises of Freudianism as a basis for general social theory. As just noted, they rejected its universalism and absolutism, its conjecturalism, its reduction of the complex to the simple, its dubious psychological principles for explaining social origins, and its general neglect of history and culture in accounting for diversity in human conduct. Still, psychiatry was not the discipline sociologists associated characteristically with the study of human nature. During the second period this "other" discipline presented new conceptions to which many theorists in sociology reacted vigorously.

PSYCHOLOGY

Stimulated especially by the works of such psychologists as Pavlov, Watson, Weiss, Hull, and Tolman, several sociologists endeavored to reconstitute general sociological theory under the inspiration of a behaviorism typically associated with positivism. In the history of American sociology, the proponents of the one tended to be the advocates of the other, and, conversely, the opponents of the one were the antagonists of the other, with the controversy reaching a climax from the late 1920s to the mid 1930s. Although the terms are sometimes used interchangeably, they are not identical. *Positivism,* as noted above, is characteristically and decisively a methodological term, whereas *behaviorism,* though it is often used in a methodological sense, does convey ontological implications. As an intellectual stance, behaviorism seems especially to have been generated as one response to the increasing disrepute of the doctrine of instincts and the increasing environmentalism in the 1920s.

However, the first obvious reference to behaviorism as a potential stance is to be found in Ellwood's 1916 article "Objectivism in Sociology." Ellwood claims that a new school of "objectivists" in psychology and sociology has arisen, asserting that the old standards of objectivity were not adequate to produce "objective" science in these fields, that is, that the description of processes should be investigated so that any scientific investigation can verify them, and that elimination of the personal equation (or subjectivity) is insufficient to produce science. For the adherent of this school, a scientific fact is "not 'anything in experience,'" but only that which "can be observed" (externally) and can "be described without reference to individual psychic processes." In psychology, such persons are external behaviorists and in sociology those "who would describe everything in social life in terms of habit ('folkway' or 'custom') and environment" (289).

Bernard responded to Ellwood's views, at first partly agreeing and partly disagreeing with those views, but eventually he supported a "moderate" behaviorism. In "The Objective Viewpoint in Sociology" (1919), Bernard clearly wished to avoid being identified with "an extreme form of the behaviorist school in psychology" (304; cf. 302–3). Similarly, he apparently repudiated objectivist terminology cast in narrowly or exclusively neurological or mechanistic vocabulary, though he didn't take the efforts of the Russian Zeliony as seriously and ominously as did Ellwood. Conversely, it is evident that Bernard applauded the trend toward objectivism in the sense of the "definiteness of measurement in sociological method," which can be associated with positivism and which was preceded by similar trends earlier in psychology and the biological sciences (302–3, 305).

By the time *An Introduction to Social Psychology* (1926b) was published, Bernard had come to regard himself as a behaviorist. Perhaps the designation *moderate behaviorist* is accurate, for he indicates that he thinks of himself as "a behaviorist," but in contrast to some of the "ultra behaviorists" (42; cf. 45–48, 74–89, 118–22, 142–56). It is also very evident that he still substantially retained this earlier position some sixteen years later (1942) when *An Introduction to Sociology* was published.[2]

Several other sociologists in the years between World Wars I and II became associated with Bernard in subscribing to some form of behaviorism. The position is evident in Hankins's *An Introduction to the Study of Society* (1928), in articles by Read Bain, Stuart Rice, and George Lundberg, and especially the latter's famous *Foundations of Sociology* (1939b).[3] But only the later volumes by Bernard and Lundberg suggest what might be expected in a relatively fully developed sociological behaviorism (in its ontological sense and in conjunction with a positivistic methodology).

The three general theory texts of Hankins, Bernard, and Lundberg reveal many likenesses and some differences. All of them envisage human sociocultural behavior as essentially constituted of habits as adjustive or adaptive mechanisms. But Hankins's and Bernard's notions manifestly connect these adjustive or adaptive forms of behavior (via habit) with a broadly construed hierarchy of evolutionary processes—physical, organic, psychic, and sociocultural. In contrast, Lundberg, who received his doctorate after World War I rather than before, referred only to adjustment in situations without relationship to an explicit hierarchy of evolutionary processes. But it appears that Lundberg did accept evolution, though its psychic and sociocultural forms were substantially suppressed. Lundberg wrote his *Foundations* after the controversy over sociocultural evolutionism but he made no reference to that controversy.

Hankins and Bernard

Manifestly, Hankins and Bernard regarded human societies as entailing adaptive behaviors that reflected the kind of organisms humankind had become in the course of an extended period of organic and psychic evolution. In turn, human organisms were dependent on the general conditions of life (as required of all organisms) in relation to the conditions of existence that stemmed from the physical evolution of the earth and its attendant characteristics. Therefore, both Hankins's and Bernard's books examine the earth and the conditions it provides for life in general and human life in particular (e.g., its relation to the sun and moon, its revolution and angle of declination, its varying topography, climates, flora, and fauna). They consider the general requirements of life itself: organic variation, heredity, environment, fecundity, struggle for existence, and natural selection. (At the human level, Bernard proposed natural, cultural, and artificial selection.) Both authors provide an interpretation of the fossil finds in the physical evolution of humankind and some account of the emergence and characteristics of human races. Developing out of organic evolution, and yet distinctive from it, is the third level or domain, that of the psychic or consciousness, which characterizes complex, "higher" organisms and especially human beings. Both of them treat in this context the elementary random and uncoordinated movements of the organism, tropisms, instincts (proper), reflexes (simple, unconditioned, and inherited vs. simple, conditioned, or learned) as the basis of habits, along with intelligence and consciousness. Interestingly, even Lundberg also offers this same account of evolutionary levels culminating in the possibility of conditioning and habit formation.

What is noteworthy for both Hankins and Bernard is that their presentations offer an essentially dualistic conception of the basis of human sociocultural reality, that is, a conception that encompasses both (reflective) mind or consciousness and (routinized, unreflective) organismic materiality. Within this domain of the sociocultural, human societies, for Hankins and Bernard, also manifest distinctive evolutionary developments in different institutional spheres, such as economy and technology, marriage and the family, religion, and social organization.

Perhaps most significant in the present context is the fact that the moderate behaviorism of Hankins and Bernard endeavors to allow for some modicum of consciousness in the reality of human sociocultural activity. Clearly, the sociocultural domain is one in which learning or acquired adjustive activity is characteristic and thus is predicated on conditioning (i.e., the conditioned response is taken to be the basic unit in the formation of habits). But some place remains for consciousness, though its relation to habit may or may not be directly and clearly worked out. In Hankins's case, the relationship between the two remains ambiguous and inferential, whereas in Bernard's exposition, it is directly confronted and an effort made to account for it.

For Hankins (1928), culture consists of modes of responses, or behavior patterns, of a group that have become habitual, stem from experiences of earlier generations, are "more or less" adapted to the conditions of the environment, and are transmitted to the next generation (380). Habit is thus conceived to be the foundational unit of culture, the basis of the folkways, mores, and institutions. Indeed, a gradation of habits can be discerned, from the ordinary or "commonplace," through those having the vaguely defined "status of custom," to customs termed "mores" because they are regarded as involving the welfare of the group, and finally to those mores that are designated as "institutions" because society has established "rules and agencies for their support and advancement" (450).

But in addition Hankins also holds that mind and consciousness are attributes of the complex nervous structures of higher organisms (especially humans), who in contrast to lower organisms possess a capacity to react in a greater variety of ways to a "greater diversity of external situations" (320, 321). Certainly, consciousness is not a "separable entity, or . . . a mysterious, indwelling potency" (321). It does involve the individual's awareness "of himself and his experiences," a capacity to introspect or to observe the operations of one's own mind (320). Certainly, consciousness is associated with reflection and with thought, the chief medium of which is language (416). Yet Hankins does not explain the relationship of conventional or verbal symbols as the crux of language to the process of thought. Hankins's readers are unfortunately left to speculate at just what point or points mind and consciousness intervene in human sociocultural activity.

Bernard (1942) also develops his position in terms of an exposition of the conditioned response. But he distinguishes between two "behavior levels" at which such conditioning of response occurs, such that the old body/mind dichotomy is encompassed. One is the overt or "neuro-muscular," and the other is the covert or "neuro-psychic" or symbolic (601). Conditioning on the overt level predominates in lower animals throughout their lives and in a large portion of the period of human childhood. But humans are peculiarly characterized by the predominance of conditioning on a symbolic level, which has already significantly occurred in childhood. Activity on the first level is overt, objective (or externally observable), muscular. Activity on the second is covert, subjective (not externally observable), psychic or mental. Or, put more precisely, the external muscular response is so reduced or truncated that it stands for the completed overt act, as in the case of a gesture, a vocalized expression (or symbol) "produced by the throat and mouth muscles" (604, 601).

In neuropsychic behavior, the behavior impulse is not fully transmitted to the muscles to produce a complete overt response. By virtue of an unfamiliar or unusual environment, the response that the organism would ordinarily make is inhibited or is in conflict with another stimulus. The unsuitableness of the behavior pattern is signaled and intercepted as it is being transmitted "through the ganglionic centers" (604). The unusual pattern is thus not actualized in full activity, but is revealed only as symbolized "in a gesture, in muscular twitchings, or in a vocal or . . . substitute gesture" (604).

Furthermore, such inhibition of response tends to be accompanied by a subjective, emotional, or feeling consciousness merely indicating to the organism that something is awry or unusual, but without specifying what is amiss or has disrupted its adjustment (605). Gradually, this emotional and subjective consciousness is supplemented by an intellectual recognition of the causes of the disruption of adjustment and of the processes by which the disruption has occurred (606). For Bernard, both the feeling and the intellectual recognition of these occurrences are the registers by which external and environmental events are recorded "within the consciousness of the organism" (606). As the human powers of intellectual perception and analysis are enhanced by the aid of language, the individual can increasingly refine "analyses of his environment" and assess its influence both on "his subjective behavior, or consciousness, in terms of pleasure and pain," and also on "his conduct as a whole" (606).

With symbolic conditioning, adjustment through overt trial and error is replaced by anticipatory or covert (i.e., symbolic) trial and error. Humans can think out, plan, or consciously envisage adjustments in advance of actual behavior "instead of working them out by means of unintelligent overt responses." To think is to engage in symbolic response (601). It is important that symbols are subject to conditioning in precisely the same way as are overt movements and stimuli—"that is, by means of associating one symbol with another" (601).

Clearly, it is necessary to understand Bernard's conception of habit and the genesis of habits through the mechanism of the conditioned response (as based on Pavlov's "conditioned reflex" and as aggregatable and selectable through a process akin to Locke's "association of ideas"). Bernard explains habits in human beings as the building blocks of acquired behavior, "as learned adjustment patterns, such as random movements, reflexes, instincts, tropisms, or previously formed habits of a simpler character" (581). In Bernard's view, habits are necessarily more complex than any of the antecedent behavior patterns, both because they are constructed or constructable out of the several response types and because they can arise in relation to more complex conditions of the natural environment and varying or new sociocultural situations (582). It is most important that, especially among human beings, new habits or habit responses can be constructed upon previous behavior patterns by a process of further conditioning.

Bernard indicates two ways in which such an extension of conditioning may occur. The first is "the substitution of stimuli (including the aggregation of stimuli)" (583). The second is "the selection of responses" (583). He acknowledges that the first was what John Locke had termed the "association of ideas" and Pavlov the "conditioned reflex." Because the sociologist is ordinarily concerned with behavior patterns that are more complex than reflexes, Bernard opts for the term *conditioned response* rather than Pavlov's *conditioned reflex.* He rejects Locke's association of ideas because the behavior patterns deriving from the conditioning of responses are not restricted to ones on the symbolic or ideational level. Indeed, they ordinarily consist of behavior patterns exclusively on the neuromuscular level (583).

Pavlov's experimentation with a dog readily illustrates the simplicity of the principle of substitution and aggregation of stimuli. Because in successive instances the experimenter rang a bell at the same time as the dog was shown the meat, the two stimuli were eventually so closely associated in the dog's experience that the flow of saliva would start at the sound of the bell alone. After the two stimuli had become associated in the behavior pattern, the secondary stimulus (the ringing of the bell) "came to be substituted for or aggregated to the primary stimulus (sight of the meat)." Bernard cautions that two explanatory inferences are possible: It may be supposed that the dog's response to the primary stimulus has derived from "an inherited behavior pattern, while his response to the secondary stimulus was the result of conditioning"; or it may be supposed that "his responses to both stimuli were the result of acquired behavior" (583–84).

As suggested earlier, Bernard's conception of habit is the key to his explanation for the transmission and inculcation, and also the expansion and elaboration, of human culture. Conditioning can occur through indefinitely extensible substitution or aggregation of stimuli—a secondary stimulus can be associated with a tertiary, and a tertiary with a fourth, and so on. But because one cannot respond to all of the stimuli in a situation, only some responses will be selected: those producing an effective adjustment to the environmental situation in relation to the organism's needs. (In this way, Bernard preserves continuity with an adaptive or adjustive theory of social and cultural evolution.) In addition, habits can be built up into increasingly elaborate chains or constellations of responses (598–601).

It is significant that Bernard regards symbols and language as based on the same mechanisms. Language is founded on the gesture, which may be of the foreshortened or inhibited type, the abstract substitute or arbitrary type (612). For the latter, the pointing gesture, which came to be accompanied by vocalization, has crucial significance. Later the vocalization "became detached from the gesture and was used alone as a substitute intellectual response or symbol" (622). Interestingly, Bernard regards the earliest symbol as the noun or name, arising as "an abstract or symbolic method of designating environmental objects (622). In effect, the symbol thus has an important function in facilitating (or impeding) adjustment or adaptation to the environment.

Symbols are also expandable through substitution and aggregation. One symbol is associated with another, and so it calls "into action other symbols to which it is conditioned" (601). For Bernard, thinking is therefore a "stringing together of conditioned symbols into a chain . . . (as the words in a sentence)," or their constellation "into an aggregation (as in a display advertisement)." Either a neuromuscular (or overt behavioral) response or a neuropsychic (symbolic) response may be indicated. If the chain of conditioned symbols "is logically integrated into meaning," it can be story, narrative, argument, principle, formula, or law. If formulas, laws, or principles are combined, they become a "philosophic or scientific theory or system" (601).

In brief, then, Hankins's and Bernard's moderate behaviorism constitutes an ontological pluralism in which the conditioned response is the distinctive key to the roles of both consciousness and the (nonconscious) materiality of the body in explaining human individual and multi-individual behavior and conduct. For Bernard especially, the conditioned response operates at both the overt, or neuromuscular, and the symbolic, or neuropsychic, levels. It is the key to the rise of the gesture and symbol, and to the combination of symbols into ever-larger chains of response.

Lundberg

Although Lundberg resembled Hankins and Bernard (and also Bain, who has not been examined here) in making the conditioned response and habit the core of his behaviorism, he was markedly different in subscribing to a social ontology that tended to be virtually (i.e., almost exclusively) materialist. (After all, the others had endeavored to provide a place for consciousness.) Lundberg insisted that he did not ignore consciousness; he proposed to include what might be objectively confirmed or demonstrated from consciousness in his behaviorism. So presumably consciousness was to be translated (or transformed?) into behaviorism, and apparently into a physico-organic materialism.

Even though Lundberg (1939b) claims that assertions about ultimate reality are "unverifiable hypotheses and hence outside the sphere of science" (9), he accepts a tentative, or working definition of reality that in some contexts seems physicalist and in others organicist. Not surprisingly, he claims that the naturalistic basis of reality is "matter," which has an (intrinsic) "structure." In turn, that structure is alleged to be a "function of its electron-proton configuration," which can be as variegated as human sensory discriminations of differences have become "refined" (differentiated, specialized, standardized, or measurable?). Whatever the "elementary hypothetical entities" may be, they permit the construction of systems of virtually unlimited degrees of complexity—inorganic, organic, from atoms to galaxies, including plants, animals, and humankind in varying degrees and kinds of organization (204). Indeed, the entire universe can be conceived as a "continuum of such systems" (209).

In turn, the various sciences can be classified in accordance with the "level of behavior-configuration" that is of interest. Each level is regarded as a closed system for purposes of inquiry (204). Furthermore, the mere fact that any chosen level is comprised of units from other levels does not render it "less real" for inquiry than its constituent systems, such as the individual and the group (204; cf. 172).

In the case of the social sciences, "the behaviors of those electron-proton configurations [that are] . . . principally human groups" are of basic concern (204). Although the behavior mechanisms of different systems or levels of electron-proton configuration may be designated by different words, certain basic concepts such as motion, energy, force, and equilibrium are equally applicable to all behavior (204). Lundberg's willingness to follow and to quote Child in differentiating mere physical equilibrium from a physiological or dynamic equilibrium is symptomatic of Lundberg's acceptance of, and involvement in, what might be termed an "organicist" or "organismic" materialism.

Indeed, in approaching the realm of the social, which he disarmingly terms "social or interhuman behavior," Lundberg does more frequently seem to invoke organicist or organismic materialism. The frame of reference in terms of which the basic factors in his scientific theory of social behavior are defined and interrelated is cast fundamentally from the assumptions of such a materialism. It is a materialism revealed in the inclination to envisage human beings in an adjustment situation as organisms in an environment, in relation to a physiological or dynamic equilibrium, tensions in organisms, and the behavior mechanisms of organisms, and especially conditioning and habit as the fundamental background for Lundberg's notion of the components of a scientific theory of interhuman behavior. Each of these notions, from organism in an environment to behavior mechanisms, is examined in chapter 6, "Dynamics of Behavior—General," of his *Foundations of Sociology* (1939b).

However, it is the category of behavior mechanisms (e.g., tropisms, reflexes) that brings conditioning and habit into focus for social ontological examination. Habits, he notes, are differentiable from reflexes, because their basis in conditioning behavior is comparatively well known and, accordingly, is subject to teaching and learning, in contrast to inborn or hereditary features (177). Among organisms with nervous systems, the technique of conditioning has become highly developed and permits the development of behavior patterns of unparalleled complexity (177).

For Lundberg, habits arise in those circumstances in which such inherited behavior patterns as tropisms and reflexes do not adequately serve the adjustive (adaptive or survival?) needs of organisms. In their most simple forms, habits are probably developed from overt behavioral trial-and-error adjustments (or adaptations?) that are repeated by virtue of their successes (in securing survival?). Without any further elaboration, Lundberg merely observes that this process becomes more complex once symbolic behavior has developed. He argues that initially animal outcries that are associated with certain types of emotion, such as fear, come to serve as a substitute stimulus to other animals of that species who have acquired "the habit of responding in a certain way to a particular sound." This sound arouses the same emotional response (e.g., fear) among the other animals, who are not immediately exposed to or in direct experience with the specific situation evoking the emotional response. Lundberg subsequently raises the account to another level by noting that when "this primitive method of communication is supplemented [or supplanted?] by speech [the nature of which he does not indicate], the variety, kinds, and degree of substitute stimuli and responses are greatly accentuated" (178).

Lundberg suggests that the human species has a distinctive "capacity to acquire linguistic and symbolic mechanisms" that are in fact habits (178). Because such symbolic habits or patterns come to "represent and largely overlay" (i.e., reorganize and dominate) all other mechanisms, their consideration is substantially sufficient to account "for human groups" (178). Habits in this symbolic form are critical to such basic "group patterns of behavior . . . [as] folkways, public opinion, traditions, customs, mores, and institutions" (178). Lundberg has offered a severely schematic or truncated social evolutionary account, but without acknowledging evolutionism.

Yet the full materialistic implications of Lundberg's behaviorism can be gauged only if attention is directed to Lundberg's inclination to use the epistemology on which his positivistic methodology is based as a criterion of social reality. In the early 1930s Lundberg recognized that his positivism and/or behaviorism involved a qualified empiricist epistemology. So he claimed that "only natural, objective, and verifiable data gained through sense experience are proper subject matter for science"—any science, including a developing natural science of sociology. But Lundberg's claim clearly raises the issue of what the relationship is between the data of "sense" or "sensory experience" and the domain of consciousness. Manifestly, it was Lundberg's objective to show that the latter was definitely assimilable to the former. And he did so by contending that "we secure knowledge of social phenomena" only by means of "sense experience conceptualized and organized into the patterns determined by the reactions of our neuro-muscular system to the culture in which we have lived, and now live." In an aside, Lundberg remarked that the "desperate attempt . . . to reserve culture and social phenomena as the unique and peculiar attribute of man and human society" is essentially an effort to save the domain of mind "from a naturalistic attack" (Lundberg 1933, 300–301, 304).

However, the continued severity of the attacks on behaviorism indicated that Lundberg's opponents were unconvinced by his arguments. The effects of Lundberg's redoubled efforts are evident in his attempt in his *Foundations of Sociology* (1939b) to conceive of words and their meanings as stimuli evoking responses in accordance with prior conditionings and thus as standing for some kind of "behavior" (18). By virtue of the fact "that numbers of individuals use the same word to designate similar behavior (i.e., to the extent that numbers of individuals behave in a given way in a given situation)" (18), it might be conjectured that the word designates a way of responding that has been "corroborated by others" and is thus objective, that is, stands for an objective response (though Lundberg does not phrase the matter this way). Furthermore, Lundberg notes that he takes the prevalently acknowledged view that "all thinking involves symbols" and that only objects and behavior so symbolized have meaning (23). On the basis of this reasoning, it might be concluded that all behavior mediated by symbols or in association with symbols can be said to be objective, and thus that language, thinking, and consciousness will have been assimilated to external behavior.

Indeed, such is the conclusion to which Lundberg is compelled to come in conjunction with his reference to an iron fence and a taboo, both of which will deter persons "from touching an object or going to a certain place" (21). But this illustration raises the problem of the "objectivity" of a shared or cultural definition versus the "objectivity" of scientific knowledge (or the knowledge of the participants versus that of the "scientific" observer), which Lundberg endeavors to avoid by alluding to greater and lesser "objectivity". So he avers that the taboo will have a prohibitory effect only upon the behavior of those "conditioned to a certain culture," whereas "the fence may have [*sic!*] the same effect on all men." Accordingly, it may be claimed that for *"men in general,"* a "greater objectivity is ascribed properly to the fence." But to those "conditioned by the given culture, the taboo has the same degree of objectivity," the test for which in either case is "the observed behavior of . . . men" (21–22).

What the illustration reveals is the awkward position in which Lundberg is placed vis-a-vis the definition of reality of the participant (an observer) versus the detached (or "scientific") observer. The word *iron* subtly introduces a naturalistic definition of reality as allegedly certified by the sensory experience of any qualified (scientific) observer versus the definition by "taboo" of the participant ("observer") as yielded in "consciousness." But the latter is clearly a problem for the former. Earlier, Lundberg had remarked that the more undeveloped the techniques of objectifying certain experiences (e.g., the "subjective" and "spiritual"), the more difficult the task of communicating them [for whom? presumably the scientist] "so that they can be verified (the test of objectivity)" (10). Lundberg is evidently

convinced that a basic justification of science is to determine whether or not
our "verbal mechanisms and symbols" of everyday sociocultural life "correspond closely to the conditions to which we must adjust" and thus "facilitate
our adjustments" or vary from the conditions and thus impede adjustments
(48). Clearly, it is understandable why Lundberg claims that because "numbers of individuals use the same word to designate similar behavior phenomena . . . it is conventional to designate" not their behavioral response as
"objective" but "the phenomena to which they respond as objective" (18).

But the important point to make is that Lundberg can thus contend that
behaviorism does not ignore the features of consciousness. Instead, he insists
that consciousness, the subjective, the mental, can enter into sociology as a
natural science to the extent that the sociologist can discern "sensory evidence of the imaginings, thoughts, and other phenomena of 'consciousness'"
(20). But these are presently inaccessible to objective study because an
objective terminology (e.g., operational definitions) and instruments (e.g.,
scales) with which to observe and describe experience have not yet been
developed, and so experience remains "very inadequately communicable or
subject to verification" (20). (Here Lundberg must have had as his concern
the scientist as observer rather than the participants).

But it is also manifest that Lundberg is convinced that much in the
domain of consciousness is imaginary and without any apparent verification
and verifiability. Whatever remains after long-term sociological study will
thus be adjustment, or akin to adjustment, to the biophysical conditions of
existence. If not, any concern with them will have to be abandoned. So many
terms currently used in sociology will probably have to be totally eliminated
as bereft of legitimate "content when the behavior phenomena to which they
once referred has been more adequately described by other terms" (10).
Clearly, Lundberg believes that any concern with the theological, metaphysical, occult, esoteric, or nonnaturalistic warrants rejection. Indeed, he even
insists that terms entailing or substantially associated with mind or the subjective, such as *thought, experience, feeling, judgment, choice, will, value,
emotion,* and so on, "are the phlogiston of the social sciences" (11). It is his
view that sociologists will sooner or later conclude that issue of subjectivity,
and that it and other "metaphysical questions of 'existence,' 'reality,' . . .
and 'tangibility'" can all take their place "with the question of how many
angels can stand on the point of a needle and other profound issues that agi-
tated learned men of other ages" (21). Yet, ironically, the naturalism (as
opposed to supernaturalism) to which the working definition of social and
cultural reality is reduced (as the implications of the taboo and iron fence
example finally reveal) is essentially a physicalist, or a physico-organic,
materialism.

Perhaps better than anyone else in sociology during the second period,

Lundberg exemplified the interconnectedness of behaviorism (with a prevailingly materialist notion of social reality) and a qualified empiricist-positivist
epistemology-methodology. And certainly, he was an important figure in the
discipline in the predominance that quantitative positivism eventually
achieved. Yet it is also noteworthy that behaviorism did not carry the field in
providing the fundamental social psychological foundations of the discipline.
Behaviorism elicited a vigorous intellectual opposition, one manifestation of
which was the attempt to develop other psychological or social psychological
stances, such as Case's advocacy of gestaltism.

Case

Manifestly, the attempt to develop a gestaltist sociology was directly
patterned after the efforts in psychology, and, as in psychology, the endeavor
was elicited substantially as an antagonistic response to behaviorism. Admittedly, relatively few gestaltist proposals in sociology achieved published
form. A forum "Gestalt and the Case Study" appeared in the June 1931 issue
of *Social Forces* (vol. 9, no. 4), with five contributors—two social workers
and three sociologists. Rice's article, "Units and Their Definition in Social
Science," adopted a decisively negative stance. Queen's "Some Problems of
the Situational Approach" was somewhat equivocal. MacIver's "Is Statistical Methodology Applicable to the Study of the Situation?" was favorable to
a "situational" or case study approach that was equatable to a holist or
gestaltist stance. Waller's later article "Insight and Scientific Method"
(1934), was an effort to develop an argument about social causation based
on the gestaltist notion of the configuration of perceptions versus the percep-
tual atomism of empiricism. But it was Case's paper, "Toward a Gestalt
Sociology" (1930), that most fully developed an argument for a gestaltist
position in sociology.

Case's article begins with contemporary exponents of emergentism
and holism in philosophy and the biophysical sciences (vs. reductionism and
atomism). It is both social ontological and methodological, and inferentially
epistemological, in its stance. As against Floyd Allport's position on the
nature of the group, Case argues that society is a situational unity or context,
"a Gestalt or configuration, an actual and vitally functioning whole." It must
be understood accordingly, at its own level, and as undeniably emergent,
without the encumbrance of disciplines, such as psychology, committed to
reductionism. Thus, attempts to use psychological phenomena, such as
reflexes, are impotent guides to foretell what social and cultural forms will
be assumed in any given social situation. To the extent that the life of the
culture-group represents a real emergent, the effort to substitute psychological explanations of individuals for groups as wholes become useless and

irrelevant (11–12). Although Case rejects the Lowie-Kroeber position that any component or feature of culture stems from prior culture as an overstatement, he concedes that it has exerted a stimulating and significant influence in the social sciences (13).

Accordingly, Case takes a more moderate point of departure from Wolfgang Kohler's *Gestalt Psychology*, with its central contention that the "organism reacts to an actual constellation of stimuli by a total process which, as a functional whole, is the response to the whole situation" (Case 1930, 13). He notes that Kohler indicts behaviorism for claiming that direct (or conscious) experience is not to be acknowledged as scientifically legitimate but only reflexes and conditioned reflexes. He also refers to Kohler's critique of Fechner as having assumed that measurement alone would make psychology a science (20).

Case objects to preoccupation with measurement—whether in psychology or in sociology—as emphasizing only physical or external aspects of personal activity "because they alone are spatial." In contrast, Case contends that the distinctive reality of individual and group life lies in experience (presumably akin to German *erleben*). In the course of time a living being experiences events that are accumulated in memory and consciously developed "into personal purposes and social values." The central fact of individual, personal, and group life is thus meaning as subjective, conscious, and purposive. Meaning and significance so construed reside in the time dimension and not in the external spatial dimension subject to measurement (23).

The methodological corollary of such a declaration is that the sociologist must impartially trust all kinds of experience, including subjective experience (23). Case advocates the personal group history method to deal with the total situation, from which neither the person nor the group nor the culture can be abstracted (14). Presumably, it will potentially involve the participant observer and the observing participant, the former of whom will surely resort to Cooley's "sympathetic imagination" (25). Certainly it will entail the study of experience as involving subjective conscious meanings and values, with both analysis and even more synthesis in the end (25, 27). For Case, such is the methodological corollary of the ontological recognition that the life of human culture-groups is a new and relatively independent level of phenomena (27).

Case was unique in his effort to develop an argument for the use of Gestalt psychology as a model for sociology. However, the character of his social ontological and methodological views were not unique, for they also entailed a rejection of behaviorism, in which several other sociologists joined.

Major Critics and Critiques of Behaviorism

It should come as no surprise that the articulation of major arguments against behaviorism should have been associated with sociologists and social psychologists who espoused competing theoretical stances, both social onto-logically and social epistemologically-methodologically. Indeed, the ontological and epistemological tend to be associated: Parsons, MacIver, Becker, and Znaniecki were proponents of both a neo-idealist (or Neo-Kantian) epistemology-methodology and an idealist social ontology (i.e., of social action). Case, Sorokin, and Faris were also involved. Case positively endorsed the only gestaltist version of the basis of a social and sociological theory that had resemblances to the idealist social action stance. Faris's basic symbolic interactionism also had major similarities with the social action perspective. Sorokin seems to have been the only basically objective idealist in terms of his theory.

Social Action and Cognate Critiques. Interestingly, it was the social actionists plus Case and Sorokin who developed the basic social ontological arguments against behaviorism. It was they who contended, for instance, that behaviorism as an ontological stance was simply a version of reductivist materialism, which could either be argued on its own or be regarded as the companion or correlative ontological stance of an empiricist-positivist epistemological-methodological viewpoint.

In *Social Actions* (1936), Znaniecki claimed that by virtue of its opposition to a return to any form of idealism, behaviorism in effect represented a version of materialism. Ultimately, human beings are viewed as bodies in movement, as forms of matter-in-motion, the activities of which are occasioned by animal needs, wants, drives, and so on in relation to external objects and persist or recur because such learned activity (as conditioned through trial and error) affords gratifications, adaptation, and survival in the environment (7).

Parsons noted in *The Structure of Social Action* ([1937] 1968) that behaviorism was thus also an environmentally oriented form of social Darwinism (as opposed to instinctivism as hereditarily oriented). Behaviorism, Parsons remarked, "is simply the Darwinism of individual behavior." It postulates a set of random movements varying around a few hereditary tendencies, a few unconditioned or prepotent reflexes. "These random movements are subject to a process of environmental conditioning, by which some that meet the functional needs of the organism in its adaptation to the environment are perpetuated by conditioning and become conditioned reflexes or habits and others, which do not meet such needs, are eliminated." These random movements of the individual (according to behaviorism) correspond to the random variations of (whole) organisms in the species (according to Darwin). The process of conditioning is only a potential form of environmentally induced adaptation, which the fit with the conditions of existence confirms by natural selection (115–16).

In effect, then, behaviorism argues that the only legitimate explanation of human behavior is in terms of what it has in common with other forms of organic or animal behavior and not in terms of what is distinctive. Basically, then, the opponents indict behaviorism for refusing to accept any view of human inter- or multipersonal activity recognizing the distinctiveness of activity in the human real (consciousness, meanings, values, culture, etc.).

Case (1930) adopts a cautious emergentist position, contending that to the extent that the culture (-group or group-culture) is a real emergent, the resort to a psychological account centering on the individual becomes useless and irrelevant (12). And he also, in effect, indicts and rejects behaviorism as an intellectual continuation of the abstractionism and atomism of an earlier "sensationalist and associational psychology" (13).

Znaniecki (1936, 13) criticizes behaviorism more specifically for rejecting any resort to the agent's active or conscious experience in order to avoid any possible reintroduction of earlier metaphysical or theological notions, such as "the old 'mind' or 'soul.'" Case (1930, 13) agrees and similarly objects to its neglect of "conscious experience."

MacIver (1931c, 530) claims that behaviorism rejects the subjectivity of experience and thus denies any difference between "a paper flying in the wind and a man flying from a pursuing crowd." Parsons ([1937] 1968, 117) concurs, declaring that behaviorism renders the subjective "epiphenomenal."

Becker (1950, 194) insists that a social analyst who restricts himself "to the use of sense data directly given in the immediate situation," without invoking a model of motivation, will be "unable to render predictions of any kind."

Finally, Sorokin (1947, 47–51), who appears to be an emergentist and to adopt an objective idealism, holds that any behavioristic treatment of human phenomena must necessarily require exclusion of what are most distinctive: meaningfulness, values, and norms. Human phenomena are reduced to a biophysical level.

Another major, fundamental objection to behaviorism focused on its implications for social epistemology-methodology. Clearly, behaviorism accepted only the data of sensory experience, or perception, as given to an external observer. And so it was indicted, for instance, by Znaniecki (1936, 14) as rejecting any evidence from experience claiming meaningfulness, nonmateriality of content, and irreducibility to sensory perception. All reference to subjective categories must be excluded initially, and thus behaviorism methodologically leads to objectivism, positivism, acausalism, and probability statistics (see, e.g., Parsons [1937] 1968, 117).

Manifestly, the opponents of behaviorism disagreed with its basic assumptions. They objected to its fundamental ontological premises and to the related epistemological-methodological stance. Clearly, one might become a behaviorist ontologically and then adopt the related epistemological-methodological position, or begin with the latter and then adopt the former. The opponents of one tended to be the opponents of the other.

Faris's Meadian Critique. It is obvious that much, perhaps all, of what the antagonists of behaviorism argued was also fundamental to Faris's position. However, Faris, with his background in philosophy, psychology, and sociology, was in a unique position to provide a detailed critique of the conditioned response, which was the central notion of behaviorism. As represented by his various statements in *The Nature of Human Nature* ([1937a] 1976), his objections were far-ranging, extending over behaviorism's failure to recognize the disjunctive, intermittent character of human activity, its exclusive concern with the externals of activity, its ignoring of the structure and temporality of activity, its avoidance of the significance of reflective (as opposed to automatic, mechanical) action, and its inability to recognize the correlative character of stimulus and response.

According to Faris, the conditioned-reflex notion of human interpersonal activity as behavior fails to recognize that such activity is disjunctive, intermittent, or periodic. Activity consists of separate acts, between which silence, nonactivity, calm, or rest occurs. Not only are there beginnings and endings, but there are also middle or mediating phases, which are vitally significant (118).

The conditioned-reflex notion, Faris argues, tends to focus inaccurately on the overt or objective, on external movement (in space) or behavior, and to exclude as unimportant or nonexistent the covert, subjective, internal, or conscious. It reduces experience to sheer (physical) sensation. Although experience includes movement and actions, "it includes more." Much happens to human individuals "which no one can see." Admittedly, experience "is not wholly inner or subjective," but it also "does not wholly yield itself to external scientific record." Yet an act without the inner phase is no more an act than one without an outer. Both the internal (e.g., consciousness, especially purpose) and the external (e.g., movement) are required. What Faris is in effect arguing is that although some acts are automatic and mechanical, the more important for humans is the reflective, planned, or rational class of acts (203).

The conditioned-reflex notion of human interpersonal activity as behavior thus also ignores the structure, form, configuration, or organization of that activity. More completely, therefore, an act tends to be a series of overt movements oriented by some end or purpose in view that in some sense initiates and in some sense terminates activity. As Faris comments, movements "are integrated into acts by the fact that there is an imagined end and a felt unity" (118).

Accordingly, Faris argues, this notion of human interpersonal activity is silent about the temporal or durational character of such activity. In some sense, human activity always arises in the past and is in some sense oriented to a future, although it terminates in the present. Any discussion of an act must take account of "the past and the future as well as the present." Any act will have been preceded by certain conditions and be succeeded by "residual effects," one of which is an attitude or attitudes toward future action (120).

The notion of interpersonal activity as conditioned response fails to account adequately for change in the activity or for the middle phase of the act. Faris contends that in a changing and contingent world not every situation can be foreseen or every emergency provided for by means of drill and training. New problems for which an adequate response does not already exist are encountered. Reflection, deliberation, planning, reasoning, or thinking out a means of meeting the exigency are required when the situation is contingent and means are not at hand to enable the action to go on to completion. Both within and without, internally and externally, uncertainty exists. "If the unknown is pressing and insistent and sufficiently strange, there may be utter confusion and total disorganization [or crisis?]. There is neither habit, mechanism, object, stimulus nor response. Internally, there is disorganization and search for response; externally there is vagueness and search for stimulus." Put otherwise, "instead of a stimulus there is an ambiguity or vagueness toward which we would like to act, while instead of a response there is an urge or tension which we do not know how to release." It is, of course, in the effort to solve problems by means of reflection that the role of the significant symbol and the phenomena of imagination, meaning, desires, wishes appear. If and when the problem is solved, stimulus and response can emerge and organization can succeed disorganization (206, 119).

Indeed, Faris argues that the entire conception of stimulus and response must be altered:

> [The] response then, may be said to constitute the stimulus, for a stimulus is such because we respond to it. An article is food because we eat it, and we make it into a food by eating it . . . [Thus,] the familiar and over-simplified behavioristic doctrine [must be completely restated,] for in human experience are involved imagination, tentative ways of conceiving, various attempted definitions of object [using significant symbols], and the final selection of some concep-

tion that will harmonize and organize this particular moment. (Faris [1937a] 1976, 206)

Moreover, response and stimulus thus do not stand in an effect-and-cause relationship. Instead, they "occur simultaneously" and thus are "correlative." Sociologically speaking, then, our associates are those who exist for us "as images of possible movements." To describe them in terms of muscles, bones, and glands is to misconstrue reality. They are rather the imagined responses of which one thinks (207).

Faris does hold that attitudes as tendencies to act (in relation to objects) are intellectually indispensable. Although an attitude may be the beginning of an act, it cannot be the act. It is a certain proclivity, or bias, to a certain type of activity. But it exists in relation to symbolized objects, and so indeed attitudes and objects are correlatives. They arise simultaneously in experience. When one changes, the other does. The externalized aspect of the organization of experience is the object or value, whereas the internal or the subjective tendency toward it is the attitude. Presumably left after the experience, the attitude remains to be activated once more (121–23).

Finally, Faris insists that the notion of the reflex as conditioned and the conditioning process must be drastically altered, if not abandoned. For Faris, a "conditioned reflex is a movement which remains unmodified." The conditioning "consists in producing this movement by simultaneous association with the stimulus of another and irrelevant one." If the reflex is altered, "the problem of the modification should receive attention . . . A 'reflex' or response' is often said to be 'conditioned' when it is really modified or changed, that is, when it disappears' (133).

He argues that the

> the conditioning of a reflex is the arousal of an inherited movement by a stimulus not originally capable of such an effect; conditioning [thus] offers no interpretation of the growth and development of new and complicated habits and attitudes. The reflexes and other less definite movements must enter into combination for which conditioning is an inadequate explanation.

In brief, Faris indicted behaviorism for the untenability of the implications of the core notion of the conditioned response as a conception of personal and interpersonal activity. He argued that such activity has a disjunctive, intermittent character (ignored by the behaviorist stance), is more than mere observable externality, has structure and temporality, and is more frequently reflective than simply automatic and mechanical, and that its core notions of stimulus and response are reciprocally correlative rather than cause-effect sequential and fail to indicate how new and more complicated habits and attitudes arise. Apparently, too, he is in essential agreement with the more encompassing arguments advanced by the social actionists that behaviorism (falsely) assumes an abstractive and atomistic social ontology of reductive materialism, is actually an environmentally oriented individualistic form of social Darwinism, disregards the subject's own active experience (as a basis of social knowledge), and also ignores the distinctiveness of meanings, values, and norms in human activity.

SUMMARY IMPLICATIONS

This chapter and chapter 7 have attempted to assess the impact of potential (disjunctive) influences external to sociology and its general theory—anthropology and history, on the one hand, and psychoanalytic psychiatry and behavioristic psychology, on the other. Manifestly, anthropology's contribution of the notion of culture, though not elaborated into an independent theory, has had the most significant impact of the four disciplines studied. And its influence has been exercised at the macro level, which is the level of the concern of this monograph.

Although it is true that one might have assumed a priori that psychiatry and psychology would likely have an impact at the microlevel, the decision was made to allow for the possibility of influences on the macrolevel from less-than-likely sources. The results of actual study do conform to the a priori presumption. Freudian psychiatry was invoked to account for the nature of personal and interpersonal activity, in both Ogburn's and Thomas's cases. Freudian ideas were appropriated to develop certain aspects of a theory of original human nature and to "explain" the relationship between certain personalities and others in certain interpersonal situations. Ogburn implicated Freud to account for acertain lag between human nature and circumstances. Thomas included Freudian premises in the nature and operation of the four wishes in personalities in certain interpersonal circumstances. In both instances, a certain residual hereditarianism is presupposed.

By contrast, the adoption of psychological behaviorism represents an expression and affirmation of the impact of notions of environmentalism, nurture, and learning (as opposed to notions of hereditarianism, nature, and instinct or instinctivism). In spite of the evident environmentalism, behaviorism appeared to have only slightly more impact than Freudian psychiatry in the reconstruction of the theory of the nature of human nature and its operation. Only Hankins, Bernard, and Lundberg (plus perhaps Bain and Chapin) were adherents. Theorists in sociology were overwhelmingly negative toward Freudian psychiatry. And certainly a substantial branch of theorists also rejected psychological behaviorism. Neither psychoanalysis nor behaviorism became the foundation for any reconstruction of macrotheory at the level of social structure or social change. (See chapters 3–5.)

One more possibility remains to be examined from disciplines outside of sociology (but still within an American academic setting). This last represents a peculiar combination of philosophy (pragmatism), psychology (behaviorism), and sociology itself (idealist and other strands) and involves the development of symbolic interactionism as a major theoretic stance in American sociology, to which the next chapter turns.

Chapter 9

Philosophy, Psychology, Sociology, and Symbolic Interactionism

Although symbolic interactionism has been predominantly associated with sociology in its more recent past, its formulation as an intellectual orientation is also substantially indebted to pragmatist philosophy and a modified behaviorist psychology. The term *symbolic interactionism* was coined by Herbert Blumer (1937) a sociologist who received his Ph.D. in sociology from the University of Chicago in 1929 and taught there until 1952. Blumer was the chief protagonist of the stance, but acknowledged that George Herbert Mead, the philosopher, was the main figure in the development of the orientation. Mead's involvement in pragmatist philosophy and in (modified) behaviorist psychology throughout his career at Chicago, was self-acknowledged, well known, and extensively documented.[1] Blumer's doctoral dissertation was directed by Ellsworth Faris, who received his doctorate in psychology from Chicago in 1914, with a committee including Mead, and was a member of the sociology department from 1918 until his retirement in 1939.[2] Blumer also indicated his intellectual indebtedness to W. I. Thomas and Charles H. Cooley. Thomas also had received his doctorate from the Chicago department, in 1896, and was a member of that department from

1897 until 1918.[3] Cooley was awarded his University of Michigan doctorate in 1894 and was a prominent Ann Arbor sociologist from 1899 until his death in 1929. All of their professional careers substantially overlapped, except for Blumer and Cooley and only minimally for Blumer and Mead.

The following preliminary comments may prevent misunderstandings about the character of this chapter.

First, although it is argued here that philosophy in the form of pragmatism and psychology in the form of behaviorism and a sociology entailing a qualified idealism contribute the main intellectual foundations of symbolic interactionism, the basic objective of this chapter is not to offer a systematic analysis of the five figures in terms of the three disciplinary orientations. Probably most investigators would concede the central relevance of the stances from the three disciplines. (Mead and Faris have intellectual orientations most readily displaying the impact of the three disciplinary orientations, but occasional, albeit not systematic, references will indicate the relevance of the orientations in the case of Thomas and Cooley, on the one hand, and Blumer, on the other.) Instead, the main objective is to provide a concise exposition of the central features of their individual contributions to what becomes identified as symbolic interactionism in (sociological) social psychology vis-a-vis what Blumer selects and emphasizes. Intellectual dissimilarities and divergencies demonstrably exist among the several figures and require acknowledgment—as do similarities and convergences.

Second, no claim is made that the five figures indicated are the only persons who have been influential in the rise of symbolic interactionism. But the five do seem to have exercised a central, indeed a preponderant role. (Consult Lewis and Smith 1980, chaps. 1–6.) Over the years, symbolic interactionism has acquired a complex and elaborate history. The problem in this particular chapter is to confine the exposition within limits that are compatible with the other earlier analyses.

Third, in spite of the fact that the present volume is concerned with general, or macrosociological, theory, its continuities and discontinuities, in the period 1915-45, the intellectual specialization and field differentiation that are apparent at the end of the period may not be invoked to disregard or demean the status of general theory at the beginning of the period. Otherwise put, the formation and rise of symbolic interactionism is itself a manifestation of the differentiation of social psychology out of, and understandable in terms of, general sociology and sociological theory. Furthermore, and very significantly, even if symbolic interactionism is prevailingly identified with the differentiation of social psychology out of general sociology and sociological theory and thus more basically a micro- than a macrotheory, its proponents have insisted and continued to insist on its macropotentialities.

And even if it is now argued to belong more properly to microtheory, its antecedents link it to a period and a context in which premises and concepts intimately associated with earlier evolutionary naturalism were being contested vigorously. Humankind was envisaged as undergoing evolution—organically, psychically, and socioculturally. The nature of original human nature (e.g., the social forces) as given in the human organism was being controverted. (See chapter 3.) The rise of symbolic interactionism and the related conceptions of social psychology that were involved is associated with a series of controversies over biologism, hereditarianism and instinctivism, the social forces, learning, behaviorism, socialization, character-, personality-, and self-formation, and the like, some of which were prefigured before World War I but assumed major significance in the 1920s and 1930s. Clearly, these controversies as manifested in general theory in the 1920s were not endogenously developed. (See chapter 2.) The analyses in chapters 7 and 8 would not be complete without a consideration of the peculiarly joint influence on sociology of ideas from pragmatist philosophy and behaviorist psychology.

W. I. THOMAS

Blumer's implicit and explicit references to Thomas in his early chapter on symbolic interactionist social psychology in 1937 are few, hardly extensive, and relatively inconspicuous. He claims that, in the symbolic interactionist explanation of the formation of social conduct in individuals in their associations with others, two mechanisms are of importance. First, the elders recurrently provide *satisfactions* of the unorganized and undefined impulses of young children in accordance with the prescriptions of the culture. An impulse tends to become organized around, or in terms of, a goal or object. An image of the requisite satisfaction is developed and the impulse becomes a wish (Blumer 1937,164). The second mechanism apparently may occur concurrently. The others who provide satisfactions also do so in terms of a (common or shared?) *definition of the situation.* The child becomes aware of how he or she is supposed to act or view a situation in the course of learning the symbols or meanings to guide his or her conduct. The child's actions become oriented to the expectations and understandings of the group (Blumer 1937, 165). Thomas's name is not actually noted, but Thomas is explicitly acknowledged as the source of the notion of the four wishes as a scheme of motivation (Blumer 1937, 185–86).

Thomas's (1917, 1918–20, 1923) views of adult interpersonal action are considerably more complex. Such conduct must always be explained in terms of the immediate situational context. Action can occur only as each person defines the situation, which tends to pose problems to be resolved (more or less consciously and voluntarily) by individual or interindividual action (Thomas and Znaniecki 1918–20, 1:68–69, 26–27; 3:26). For Thomas, such *personal* definitions may or may not coincide with social or *collective* definitions as signified by commonly supported social rules. Indeed, the individual and society are always in some degree antagonistic. Still, any individual phenomenon must always be explained causally in relation both to another individual phenomenon and a social phenomenon.

In their most comprehensive significance, definitions always entail *attitudes* in relation to *objects* in the external world, that is, socioculturally specified *values*. Attitudes as (internal) subjective tendencies to act are always oriented to (external) objects or values (Thomas 1923, 233). Thus, attitudes and values exist reciprocally (Thomas and Znaniecki 1918–20, 1:25). An attitude always presupposes a value or values, and a value an attitude or attitudes. Apparently, most values are actually social values and are thus clearly a part of the domain of the sociocultural as opposed to the biophysical natural (1:22, 28).

In turn, the nature of an individual's attitudes must be sought in the formation or genesis of his or her personality, which begins in an inherited organic base centered on a few instinctive appetites and emotions that constitute *temperament*. Unlike many of his first-generation colleagues in American sociology, Thomas did not attempt to provide a more or less complete statement of the major features of the nature of original human nature. He referred only to the neonate organism as mobilized by the appetites of food-hunger and sex-hunger, along with the basic emotions of anger and fear. Thus, temperament is constituted of a fundamental original set of attitudes—essentially instinctive, independent of social influences, devoid of reflective consciousness—that impel behavior (3:18, 19, 20).

However, the primary groups of which the child is a part (especially the family) tend to require that the (unconscious) temperamental attitudes (with their bases in organic wants) be expressed and/or satisfied in conformity with appropriate group definitions of objects (as social values; 3:22–23). The child is consciously taught to share these values. He or she is induced or constrained (consciously) to regulate his or her behavior, and thus *temperamental attitudes* are transformed into *character attitudes*(3:20, 25). The child is taught to behave consciously or reflectively—that is, to act. He or she must thus develop a set of general schemes—instrumentally effective techniques or *strategies*—or *rules* for definite situations, which together comprise what are termed the individual's "life-organization."

At a more comprehensive level, Thomas proposes four types of attitudes or wishes: the desires for new experience, security, response, and recognition.[4] They constitute the basic desires, ends, or goals of humankind. They are the "forces which impel to action," the "motor element, the starting point of activity," the basic sources of human motivation (Thomas 1923, 4, 40). Like the social forces, with which they were associated by Park and Burgess ([1921] 1924, 442–43), they are regarded as based on or derived from instincts. (Involving "inherited" emotions, they stem from, if they are not a part of, temperamental attitudes.) All individuals must be able to find some satisfaction for all the wishes, and all societies must provide some avenues for their satisfaction, albeit with dramatically varying avenues or means of gratification (cf. Thomas 1923, 39).

The classification of the wishes into *individual* and *social* reflects Thomas's view of the antagonistic relation of the individual and society. In the former category (i.e., on the personal side) are the desires for new experience and security. The latter (i.e., on the social side) involve the desires for response and recognition. (Indeed, conflict may arise not only between the two sets of wishes but between the two in a given set.) This division between the individually and the socially oriented wishes reflects Thomas's notion of the conflict between the individual and society. He notes, thus, that "personal evolution is always a struggle between individual and society—a struggle for self-expression on the part of the individual, for his subjection on the part of society" (Thomas and Znaniecki 1918–20, 3:35–36; see also Thomas 1923, 42).

Perhaps most important of all, the exposition of the four wishes in *The Polish Peasant* and especially in *The Unadjusted Girl* documents Thomas's involvement in and commitment to the doctrine of evolutionary naturalism, especially organic and psychic evolution.[5] (Thomas thus became vulnerable to critiques of instinctivism, the social forces, and parallelistic evolutionism, which have been largely overlooked, forgotten, or ignored in the 1990s.[6]

Out of the four wishes and the development of appropriate behavioral strategies or rules for their satisfaction, Thomas claimed to detect the *lines of genesis* or formation of three basic personality types, the *philistine* (rigidly disposed to stability), *bohemian* (uninhibitedly disposed to change), and *creative* (discriminatingly disposed to rational change) (Thomas and Znaniecki 1918–20, 3:31, 27–30). Still, the limits on accessible social values for any individual mean that sociocultural structure (especially the crucial or predominantly primary and secondary groups) retains a critical function in the maintenance or alteration of the dominant personality type or types in a given society. Thus, for Thomas, the character of the wishes in the dominant personality type in the group was always in dynamic tension with the rules, values, and character of the (primary or secondary) group in accounting for the concrete action among members (in the group and in relation to other groups).

CHARLES HORTON COOLEY

In Cooley's case, as in Thomas's, Blumer used his predecessor's ideas selectively to construct his own symbolic interactionist notion of the formation of personality and self. Blumer was especially influenced by Cooley's views about a derived, associationally formed human nature, the significance of sympathy in its development, sentiments as its major constituents, and the emotionally tinctured experiences within the primary group as the basis of its emergence (Blumer 1937, 167–69). In this instance, too, Blumer's efforts can be genuinely assessed only in the context of Cooley's more encompassing views and general orientation.[7] All of Cooley's major works are relevant (e.g., *Human Nature and the Social Order* ([1902, [1922] 1964), *Social Organization* ([1909], 1962), and the *Social Process* ([1918], 1966).

For Cooley, as for Thomas, human social life is constituted of persistent interpersonal contacts and relations in a concrete situation. Distinctively, Cooley ([1918] 1966) claimed that social life is itself analyzable into the subsystems of personality, group, and culture (or idea systems) (4, 6–7, 27–29). Each plays an important part in studying social life.

Cooley holds that the interaction of adult or mature persons or personalities within a group entails the dynamic of the social process. It tends to involve opposition in some degree, is resolvable by compromise and valuational selection, and culminates in a more or less new synthesis or reorganization of ideas, values, and activity, affording a new basis of cooperation (xxviii–xxxiv).

For such an outcome of interaction to occur, the adult individuals must have become socially responsive and responsible personalities. They must have acquired a genuine and distinctive human nature, as opposed to mere animal nature, with a self that is both social and moral—capable of engaging in reasoning about right and wrong. Cooley certainly acknowledged that both humankind and animalkind have heredities transmitted by the germ plasm. But the two differ in the kinds of traits transmitted. Animal heredity is definite and fixed. That of human beings is not—it is indefinite, plastic, substantially modifiable and teachable. But its bases are certain hereditary feelings, emotions, or dispositions (to anger, fear, sexual love, and self-assertion) appearing early in the child's life (Cooley [1902] 1964, 25, 7, 18–22; Cooley [1909] 1962, 36).[8] Cooley insists that "such passions" as well as others "are not, distinctively, human nature at all, but animal nature" (Cooley [1909] 1962, 36). It is the tutelage, sympathy, imagination, the subtle approvals and disapprovals (concomitant with the learning of language), and eventual identification with the other persons in the course of experience in the *primary group* (especially the family) that are so crucial in the reconstruction of (human) animal nature and the transition to and formation of a universal (socially induced) human nature as characteristically constituted of personal and social sentiments. Most importantly, Cooley does not construe (original) human nature as implying a socially resistant egoism and inclination to atomism as Thomas did (Cooley [1902, 1922] 1964, 43–48; Cooley [1909] 1962, 109).[9]

In the *primary group* (e.g., family, neighborhood, play group) the number of members is small; their persistent and durable contacts are face-to-face, generalized, and inclusive of the full range of their personalities. The group structure is simple and undifferentiated, unspecialized. Because everyone knows everyone else, relations are direct, intimate, personalized, emotionally warm, authentic. Communication is full, relatively unrestricted, and marked by easy give-and-take. Members can ordinarily find common ground, have communion, enter into and share each other's minds, ideas, and sentiments (Cooley [1909] 1962, 54, 23, 24, 27, 30, 33; see also R. Hinkle 1980, 158–61).

Out of such positively emotionalized experience involving the operation of imagination and sympathy, the developing child acquires a (socially induced) *human nature.* (For Cooley, sympathy is not to be conceived in the narrow sense of pity or compassion, but as the unique human ability to project oneself imaginatively into the place or role of another.) Accordingly, the individual comes to conceive of him- or herself as others do and so voluntarily disciplines the emotionally explosive discharge of passions. He or she eventually acquires a human nature, which is essentially composed of impulses and especially sentiments that are human in "being superior" to affective features of lower animals and in belonging to humankind as a whole rather than to any particular portion, race, society, or epoch (Cooley [1909] 1962, 28). *Sentiment* is "socialized feeling," which thought and intercourse have raised out of a hereditary base to become properly human (177). So "love is a sentiment, while lust is not" (177).[10] In addition to sentiments, primary social ideals and basic values are also inculcated in children as they include in their imagination each other person as a point of reference for thought and action and to discipline themselves voluntarily in relation to the "we" of the whole (32–56).

Clearly, Cooley's notion of the stages in self-development also parallels these changes.[11] The *sensuous self,* which corresponds to a rudimentary self of human nature, becomes the *social self.* Indeed, it is also evident that the "looking-glass self" must be expanded. The one or ones about whom the child is concerned in his or her imagination, the one or ones whom the child imagines to be judging him or her, and the one or ones in relation to whose judgment the child senses or experiences some sort of self-feeling, such as pride or mortification, must be expanded to include the group as a whole (Cooley [1902] 1964, 183–84). Cooley notes that not only are imaginings about the thoughts and feelings of particular others from the primary group a part of the self, but so also is the "group as a whole" a part of the self and "self-feeling" identified with it (Cooley [1909] 1962, 33). Surely, Cooley had arrived at the equivalent of Mead's notion of taking of the role of the generalized other.

Because the individual thus envisages him- or herself in relation to the whole and judges him- or herself in terms of what it approves and disapproves, its standards of right and wrong (Cooley [1909] 1964, 34), his or her *personal conscience* cannot be other than socially developed and identified with the *social conscience*. Thus, the social self must also be a *moral self,* with an ability to engage in moral judgment and reasoning about right and wrong, and to make moral decisions or syntheses by extended sympathy and comparison of the rules and values in different institutional domains under new circumstances (Cooley [1902] 1964, 359–60, 363, 365–66, 371). The third stage, then, of Cooley's conception of the self is the moral stage. Blumer is strangely silent about this stage.

Overall, it would hardly seem likely that Blumer's reactions to, and uses of, Thomas's and Cooley's ideas were developed entirely on his own apart from the positions of Mead and Faris, his two most immediate predecessors. As attention turns to the two Chicagoans, concern thus will be directed not only to their own sociological and social psychological views, but also to their attitudes toward Thomas and Cooley. Presumably, they will take positions on evolutionary naturalism, human nature (as distinctively innate or acquired), the relationship between reason and affect in human conduct, the possibility of individual/society antagonism, and the impact of the group on the formation of personality and self.

GEORGE HERBERT MEAD

Like the two sociologists previously examined, Mead held that the conduct of human beings is to be envisaged as the interrelated and organized acts of members of groups that are themselves part of or constitute (human) societies. Their interrelated and interconnected acts constitute cooperative social acts through which (adaptive) control is exercised over their situations (habitats). Also like many other sociologists and intellectuals of the years before and after World War I, Mead conceived of human conduct as explicable in terms of the premises of evolutionary naturalism, pragmatist philosophy, and his distinctive stance termed "social behaviorism."

At least in part, the qualifying adjective *social* in *social behaviorism* indicates Mead's rejection of the common "individualistic" behaviorism in psychology (e.g., Watson). For Mead (1934), "the conduct of the individual [is to be explained] in terms of the organized conduct of the social group, rather than . . . the organized conduct of the social group in terms of the conduct of the separate individuals belonging to it" (7). In his conception of social psychology, "the whole (society) is prior to the part (the individual), not the part to the whole; and the part is explained in terms of the whole, not the whole in terms of the part or parts" (7). Mead clearly objects to the notion that societies have arisen by an act of deliberate voluntary consent of prior existing individuals, as in a social contract (233). In certain respects, Mead's position approximate Durkheim's (associational) social realism as opposed to any variety of social nominalism. (See also 222–23 and 223 n. 25)

Evolutionary Naturalism, Animal Societies, and Human Society

As an evolutionist, Mead endeavors to account for the distinctive characteristics of human societies in terms of evolutionary naturalism, that is, in relation to earlier and simpler forms of associations of organisms. Such an endeavor involves a statement of similarities and dissimilarities between human societies and earlier, simpler forms of social life (among both invertebrates and vertebrates).

Turning first to the similarities: Mead declares that *all* organisms (including also the monocellular?) are endowed with certain impulses and needs that indicate a common, basic social aspect in all of their behavior. Hunger and sex (nutrition and reproduction) are social in character or in implication, because "They involve or require social situations and relations for their satisfaction by any given individual organism"—no matter how simple, crude, rudimentary or complex, highly organized, or well-developed (288). Because of these impulses and needs, the "experience and behavior of any individual organism are always components of a larger social whole or process of experience" (228).

Among the fundamental organic impulses and needs basic to the behavior and organization of all species of organisms, the most important one at the human level is the sex or reproductive impulse. Mead concedes that certain related others are scarcely less important: "the parental impulse or attitude, which is of course closely connected or associated with the sex impulse, and the impulse or attitude of neighborliness, which is a kind of generalization of the parental impulse or attitude and upon which all cooperative social behavior is more or less dependent" (228–29). Accordingly, he tends to view all the larger units or forms of human organization, such as the clan or the state, as "ultimately based upon, and (whether directly or indirectly)" as "developments from or extensions of the family," which is the fundamental unit of reproduction and maintenance of the species (229).

Rather than endeavoring to offer a comprehensive account, or even a mere delineation, of a gradation of a series of societal forms from simplicity to complexity, Mead next compares and contrasts the characteristics of invertebrate societies, on the one hand, and of vertebrate proto- or quasi societies, on the other, with human societies.

Invertebrate societies (especially those of insects, such as ants and bees) are characterized by individual organic differentiation by which the functions of the whole are carried out (230). The individual becomes an organ in the social whole (231).

By contrast, human societies exhibit only minimal organic differentiation, such as sex-gender and age-maturational (immature child vs. mature parent), among members. Conversely, insect societies do not reveal any transmission of experience across generations.

In the *vertebrate social forms* (e.g., schools of fish, flocks of birds, herds of cattle), no physiological, anatomical differentiation exists, and the equivalents or rudiments of the family are detectable (e.g., period of infancy with parent-childrelationships, and possibilities of relatively permanent relationships between the sexes). However, no larger organization based solely on the family exists. Such larger groups seem to have no discernible function beyond physical protection and a tendency to sustain themselves. Mead concludes that such social forms are relatively insignificant, associationally (238–39).

Relationships in the primitive human group can perhaps include "attitudes of mutual defense and attack" (239). Some sort of cooperative activity involving different individuals exists. That cooperation, Mead is convinced, provides the necessary basis "in which the gesture of the individual may become a stimulus to himself of the same type as the stimulus" to another and so provide for conversation of gestures and situations out of which vocal gestures, symbols, the self, mind, and the differentiated organization of roles characteristic of human societies today can develop (239–40).

Basically, these features of human social life in society in turn stipulate the nature that original human nature must possess. Obviously, this nature must itself have arisen in the course of organic evolution of the mammalian forms out of which proto-organic forms of human beings emerged, though Mead does not himself enter into any such inquiry.

Original Human Nature

From what was just noted above, it is evident that Mead assumes that original human nature is endowed with the same impulses and needs that more or less impel all organisms in general to associate. He presupposes that human nature involves hunger and sex impulses or needs, along with a closely related "parental impulse or attitude, which is closely connected or associated with the sex impulse, and the impulse or attitude of neighborliness, which is a kind of generalization of the parental impulse or attitude and upon which all cooperative social behavior is more or less dependent" (228–29). (Mead also offers a more extended list; see 348–49.)

Manifestly, Mead thus asserts the existence in the human organism of certain vague hereditary needs or urges varying in the specificity of the objects in terms of which they can be satisfied. He recognizes that some analysts have applied the term *instincts* to humankind; but he objects to any assumption that instincts as they are found "in the lower animals" can "be identified in man" (349). Instincts involve sets of unreflectively fixed and inseparably complex activities (*hereditary* as an adjective is not inserted here). In contrast, (human) impulses entail sets of complex activities that are susceptible to reflective analysis, decomposition, and recombination (362).

Broadly speaking, then, original human nature has virtually the same plasticity and teachability that it had in Cooley's view. It must allow for the capacity to learn complex cooperative activity through the verbal symbols characteristic of linguistic communication. Vocal gestures, symbols, significant symbols that signify the acquisition of social or shared meanings, inhibited or delayed responses, thought, reflexion, and rationality in confronting problems of environmental adjustment are all presupposed. But these latter are also premised on the organism's ability freely to explore and manipulate tactily objects that are somewhat removed in its immediate environment so that it can make appropriate adjustments preparatory to its satisfaction of needs (as above). Thus, the following features of human nature are also involved (234–37):

a.   The possession of genuine hands (which presumably can be effectively used only if upright posture, bipedal locomotion, and binocular vision are assumed

b.   A brain and cortex characteristic of humankind

c.   A complex central nervous system

d.   Complex organs of speech and hearing so that speakers can simultaneously hear what they are saying just as can the others to whom they direct their speaking.

Presumably, these features of human nature, along with the basic impulses and needs listed above, will mean that primordial human beings in a state of association will display the coordinated activity of the social act in all of its stages. They will at least exhibit a conversation of gestures.

Behavioral-Gesture and Vocal Gesture

As an evolutionist, Mead is concerned to indicate the genesis of the vocal gesture out of the matrix of the social act which must also be present for any gesture (including the nonvocal) to arise. The earliest origins lie in an unconscious conversation of truncated acts, such as those that might occur in a dogfight. The act of each dog becomes a stimulus to the other in its response. And between the two a relationship exists. As the second dog responds to the first, it changes. The readiness of the first to attack becomes a stimulus to the other to change its position or attitude. No sooner has it done this than the change of attitude in the second causes the first to change its attitude. A conversation of gestures has developed.

In contrast, the vocal gesture conveys, to both the one who vocalizes and the other who responds, a definite meaning as indicating the resultant of the social act it initiates and in which both are involved. The existence of meaning depends on "the fact that the adjustive response of the second organism is directed toward the result of the given social act as initiated and indicated by the gesture of the first" (80).

Under such circumstances, the vocal gesture becomes a symbol, and meaning becomes shared and conscious. The conversation of vocal gestures or symbols involves significance because it is conscious (80, 81). Presumably, language becomes a system of such significant symbols. Concomitant with the emergence of symbols is the emergence of consciousness of self (and others, role-playing, and moral judgment) and of mind (and of thought, reflection, and instrumental reason), both of which imply delayed or inhibited response as asubstitute for manipulation in the stages of the act.

In contrasting the two types of gestures, Mead used the dogfight as the basic example or paradigm of the nonhuman or mammalian vertebrate gesture, in which a gesture is the activity of the total organism, of each and in which change occurs as the other intervenes or is about to intervene. Mead (364, 378–79) alludes to the distinctiveness of the second or human type of gesture as occurring with the use of "the finger" (or fingers, vs. the whole hand, and the whole hand vs. the hand and arm?), an "attitude of the body" (movement of the body), "by direction of head and eyes" (movement of head and/or eyes); "but as a rule by means of the vocal gesture" (unconscious vocalization vs. conscious, disciplined vocalization). However, the word *but* has a major significance, because it retains and reinforces "the vocal gesture" as the distinctively human gesture. In fine, Mead distinguishes gestures as either (human) conscious and significant (involving intended, shared meaning) or as (nonhuman) unconscious (unaware, unintended) and nonsignificant (nonshared but concomitant with the stimulus behavior of another individual of the same species). For Mead, meaning can be meaning only if it is shared, held in common, and communicated by members of the same group.

Indeed, the fact that Mead construed gestures as necessarily implicated in a social act may have some interesting consequences. In his original account of the (human) act, Mead (1938, 3–25) demarked the four phases of impulse, perception, manipulation, and consummation. Animal behavior (up to and including mammals) tends to collapse activity into an undifferentiated or continuous whole from beginning to end (impulse to consummation). But for Mead, human organic evolution was distinguished by the emergence (presumably along with upright posture) of hands, whose activity (i.e., manipulation of external objects) preliminary to consummation facilitated adjustment or adaptation to the environment. To indicate that activity is prior to consummation is to acknowledge that acts can be interrupted, that typically the human act is characterized by delay, disruption, or inhibition, so that impulse and perception are separated from consummation. Manipulation has certain important functions:

a.   Manipulation provides a last sensory test of the consumability or utility of exterior objects for direct consumption and the bodily satisfaction of organic need (as consummation). "The fruit we can have is a thing we can handle" (Mead 1934, 248).

b.   Through past direct-contact experience in connection with manipulation, our perceptions (at a distance) include the imagery of contacts that vision or other distance sense anticipates. "We see things as hard or soft, rough or smooth, big or little in measurement with ourselves, hot or cold, and wet or dry" (363).

c.   Experience from manipulation of objects expands the stimuli to which the organism can respond and thus expands the range of possible responses (and the eventual field of choices). Manual contacts offer a "multitude of different stimuli to a multitude of different ways of doing things" (363).

d.   In its testing of objects, manipulation provides the possibility that some objects not directly consumable may be useful as instruments or means to the satisfaction of ends, consumption, consummation. Things in the environment are not simply goals of movement but "means at our disposal" (248, 249).

e.   Manipulable objects may also be frangible: They may be broken into minute parts and thus reveal further potentialities for use (249). Most significantly, Mead construes this potential frangibility (and decomposability) of some objects as the physical counterpart of the logical analysis that the use of language symbols can entail, along with the subsequent possibility of synthesis or recomposition.

f.   The use of fingers in manipulation in conjunction with vision allows for an indicative function among human individuals in the social act. They can "point out" to one another "what is of importance in cooperative activity" in a situation (Mead 1936, 378–79). By specifying the situation as the setting of the social act, the problematicity for evolutionary adaptation or adjustment is disclosed. The hand is useful to indicate physically or locationally what is consequential for possible survival of the whole in the environment. Indication is thus part of what must be present to select out, interrelate, and organize those stimuli most appropriate for (adaptive) action in the situation. True, Mead tends to connect the digital-manual indication, along with eye, head, and total body movement, with the vocal gesture. But such would scarcely mean that all would be equally present in the course of biosocial evolution. At least the possibility exists for an intermediate stage between mere animal gesture and the full human (vocal) gesture.

At this juncture, it is also necessary to note that not only does Mead equate the emergence of the vocal gesture, the language gesture, and the language symbol, but he also seems to assume that with any one instance a full system arises; that is, that a vocal gesture implies the emergence of language as a system.[12]

Finally, Mead holds that the advent of vocal gestures as significant symbols is explicable as an emergent because only members of the species *Homo sapiens* can produce disciplined sounds (or speak) and simultaneously hear these sounds; have a large brain, cortex, and complex central nervous system; have descended from ancestral forms already in a permanent social state (by virtue of sex, hunger, parental impulses); and have dependent offspring who are readily teachable. Given the nature of original human nature as delineated above, with permanent association and the ability to engage in a conversation of gestures, and the shift to fully developed vocal gestures and significant symbols, distinctively human society is a necessary concomitant for Mead and is so explicable as an emergent.

Human Social Organization: Institutions, Conventions, Manners

Presupposing thus the possibility of communication by language symbols, Mead's next major intellectual undertaking is the development of his conception of social organization or structure in relation to language symbols. Mead introduces the notion of organization or structure to contrast the behavior of subhuman and human organisms. At the human level, he regards organization or organized activity as direct joint or multiple person-to-person cooperation involving linguistic communication and role-taking. Curiously, the social division of labor is not directly or problematically considered.

More revealing of Mead's approach is his resort to the notion of social institution, which he conceived within a social evolutionary perspective in very much the same way as early American sociology. Impulses or needs were regarded as akin to the social forces (e.g., sex and hunger) and their effective satisfaction through adjustive or adaptive behavior under the conditions of social or group existence. Thus, the family (the sex, reproduction, and parental impulses), the economy (hunger, nutrition, exchange), religion (extended neighborliness, sharing), state and government, and so on, are illustrative (Mead 1934, 229, 241, 281–303).

More specifically, institutions as shared adjustments are the habits of individuals that involve their interrelations with one another and that are handed down from one generation to another (Mead 1936, 366, 377). They are habitually organized forms of group or social activity—so organized that individual members "can act adequately and socially by taking the attitudes of others" (as the generalized other) toward their activities (Mead 1934, 261–62). They require socially responsible patterns of individual conduct, but only in a broad and general sense, and so afford scope for originality, flexibility, and variety (262).

Individual members of a community (or society), having acquired linguistic symbols, a self, and a sense of the generalized other, and continuing to interact with other members, will have a standard in terms of which they can continually evaluate their own conduct, engage in self-criticism, and so have their conduct subject to (social) control.[13] Mead also insists that individuals retain some modicum of freedom so that they can critically reassess the standards in relation to emerging problems and propose a new (initially deviant) definition of conduct, which eventually other members may accept. "The process of conversation is one in which the individual has not only the right but the duty of talking to the community of which he is a part, and bringing about those changes which take place through the interaction of individuals" (168). The order of things can be reformed; "we can insist on making the community standards better standards" (168; cf. 214–22).

Conversely, Mead also recognizes the possibilities of what were later termed "deviations" in modern civilized societies. He acknowledges that membership in gangs or cliques may well entail a more circumscribed or narrowed generalized other (265). Interests among persons may be divergent rather than convergent. The size of the group or community may be such as to preclude identification of individuals with one another (326). In the exercise of differentiated functions, individuals may not be able to "take the attitude of those whom they affect" (327).

Less central and significant are manners and conventions in the life of the group or society. Manners are simply the expressions of courtesy of individuals to one another (e.g., ways of greeting) and as such may be quite arbitrary (263). Conventions are "isolated social responses which would not come into, or go to make up," the essential character of the nature of the group, are not organically related to one another, and may be arbitrary (263).

Mead also alludes to "organized custom," which is assumed to represent "what we call morality" (168).

Finally, the possibility of Mead's entertaining a structural conception of role must be raised. However, such would seem to be precluded. When Mead refers to an adult taking a role, it is in the sense of taking the role of the generalized other (as the attitude or perspective of the social whole or the accepted standards of that whole). He does not *focus* on the adult as having internalized sets of behaviors or activities as, or sets of such relevant rules for, "mother,' "teacher," "policeman," (baseball) "pitcher," though such seems to be presupposed (cf. 150–51). Rather, he emphasizes that adult membership in any group requires the symbolic learning of "the logic," or sense, of its "game," so that any one participant has a conception of the whole and the parts in that conception, with an attitude or predisposition to respond (*reflectively* and *reflexively* in a complementary or reciprocal fashion in relationship to one or more such parts. (E. T. Krueger—who was one of Mead's and Faris's students—in conjunction with W. C. Reckless in their *Social Psychology* [1931, 331–32] was the first sociologist to envisage a [structured] role as the named, designated activity in a group that is part of the division of labor and may involve manners, dress, characteristic attitudes, sentiments, and ideals as fixed by tradition and social opinion.)

In broad perspective, then, Mead's analytical scheme includes only a minimal basis for structural differentiation in institutions, manners, and conventions, which seem to occupy only a background intellectual position. As will become evident, roles as role-taking assume a much more prominent place in Mead's analysis of ongoing person-to-person interaction and in the formation of personality, especially the self and mind.

Acquisition of the Self

In Mead's account, for a self and mind to form, there must be an original human nature that endows each neonate with certain impulses or needs, a central nervous system, brain, and cortex, developed forelimbs constituted as hands (with opposable thumb and fingers), and vocalizing and auditory organs. Given also a preexistent group into which the neonate is born, this organic equipment permits *Homo sapiens* to expand the (behavioral) gestures characteristic of mammals into vocal gestures, symbols, and significant symbols. By virtue of the acquisition and manipulation of symbols, mind (as typified in thinking and reflection) can arise, and the self can emerge as individuals can become objects in their own thinking and for their own responses—just as they are for the thinking and acting of other persons.

Prerequisites and Stages of Role-Taking. Mead uses the notion of gesture in relation to the young child's involvement in social acts with others (especially parents and older siblings) to indicate how the biological individual (impelled by certain impulses) becomes socialized initially, takes the roles of separate, related others as part of organized games, and finally can take the role of the generalized other in relation to his or her various activities with particular others so that the human individual comes to possess a mind and self as crucial parts of his or her personality. By virtue of the "long period of infancy," the child is dependent on the social conduct of the family group for satisfaction of its needs (which are implied in the various human nature impulses). Need and impulse satisfaction of the infant thus involves it in social acts with other members of the family. Such acts are typically accompanied by extensive vocalizations or vocal gestures that were actually preceded by (full bodily) gestures (Mead 1934, 145–46). The gestures, in turn, "serve to adjust the attitudes of the different individuals within the whole act to each other's attitudes and actions" (374). Thus, for instance, the "child's cry directs the attention of the mother toward the location of the child and the character of his need. The mother's response directs the child toward the mother and the assistance he is prepared to accept" (374). What is most important, of course, is the response of the older others to the child, their approvals and disapprovals (e.g., "prohibitions," "taboos") regarding (impulsive) actions toward certain objects in certain situations (375). Eventually, as the child begins to act in the situation, he or she takes over the attitude of the parent toward the object. The "child repeats the prohibition in the role of the parent" (375). The attitude of the parent is incorporated into the oncoming act, and as the child vocalizes appropriately, the vocal gesture permits an associated "imagery of the results of the actions" to be anticipated (373). Accordingly, the impulsive action is checked. The child who has started to do something finds him- or herself objecting. Such is the rudimentary beginning of consciousness, thought, reflection, mind, and self (366).

Thus, Mead has arrived at the first of the three basic stages in the process of role taking. The child in this first stage is able to assume the role of another without being aware of the role of itself (375). The child takes over the responses associated with the roles of others in the immediate social environment, and they become incorporated as vocal gestures that also convey an attitude. The biological individual, the developing subject, again replies to this attitude and its gesture, "but his replay is to the self, while the responses of the self are not directed toward the subject but toward the social situation involved in the attitude which has called it out" (372).

This stage culminates in play, play at something. It is peculiarly anticipatory and partial play of self and other in which one is reciprocally linked with the other. She or he plays that he or she is a storekeeper and then buys something; she plays that she has a letter and then takes it away as the mailcarrier; he assumes that he is a police officer and then arrests himself; she addresses herself as parent and then takes her own role as child. (See 150–51.) As Mead observes:

> The child says something in one character and responds in another character, and then his responding in one character is a stimulus to himself in the first character, and so the conversation goes on. A certain organized structure arises in him and in his gestures which replies to it, and these carry on the conversation of gestures between themselves. (151)

The second stage involves participation in organized games. In contrast to the first stage, the child must be ready to take the roles and attitudes of everyone else who is involved in the game and must be aware of the definite relationships of these different roles to each other (151). By this second stage, the child has developed these responses, in some degree, in his or her own thinking. In the organized game, a set of responses is so organized in the individual that the attitude of one calls out the appropriate attitudes of the other (151). This organization is embodied in the form of rules of the game, which are actually sets of responses a particular attitude calls forth (152). Participation in the organized game entails a dialectical experience in that, in taking a certain attitude, an individual can demand a certain response in others. In turn, the assumption of the attitude of the other players in the game and their organization into some sort of unity allows the participant's own responses to be controlled. Indeed, the game requires the development of an "organized other" structuring the activity in the child's own nature and "controlling the particular responses which gives unity, and . . . builds up his own self" (160).

Mead regards involvement in organized games as a preparation for membership and participation in adult society. Participation in games enlists the child's enthusiasm and commits him vitally to a social whole. "The child passes into the game [from play] and the game expresses a social situation in which he can completely enter" (160). In turn, the child moves from games into a variety of groups and organizations, some of which "are fairly lasting, some temporary" (160), playing a "sort of social game in them" (160). During this period "in which he likes 'to belong,'" the child "becomes a something which can function in the organized whole, and thus tends to determine himself in his relationship with the group to which he belongs" (160). Thus, the child can become a "self-conscious member of the community" (169).

Certainly, Mead suggests that no sharp lines can be drawn between the taking of the roles of others in playing (more or less complex) games and the ability to take the role of the generalized other characteristic of the fully developed self, the third stage in the process. To acquire a unity of self, the individual must be able to adopt the attitude of the organized community or group, which constitutes a "generalized other." Indeed, successful participation in the (more or less complex) organized game requires "an organized other, a generalized other," which is taken over and incorporated in the "organized activity in the child's own nature controlling the particular response which gives unity, and which builds up his own self" (160). The self must develop beyond "an organization of . . . particular individual attitudes" (158). The individual must bring his or her own field of directly experienced social or group attitudes and he or she will do so "by means of further organizing, and then generalizing, the attitudes of particular other individuals in terms of their organized social bearing and implications" (158). Mead's statement of an emergentistic perspective is somewhat ambiguous and uncertain. He almost suggests that the acquisition of the perspective or attitude of the whole is a mere logical progression from an inductive generalization of the perspectives and attitudes of particular individuals. The self "reaches its full development by organizing these individual attitudes of others into the organized social or group attitudes, and by thus becoming an individual reflection of the general systematic pattern of social or group behavior in which it and the others are all involved" (158). For Mead, becoming a full self means becoming a part (a self-conscious part) of an organized social whole, a group or community. One must be able to put oneself "in the place of the generalized other, which represents the organized responses of all the members of the group" (162). Through the generalized other, the social process influences the behavior of the individuals involved (155).

To become a self is, of course, to become self-conscious. *Consciousness* refers to the entire field of experience, whereas *self-consciousness* refers to the ability to call out in ourselves a set of definite responses that are shared with other group members (163). Self-consciousness is "a recognition or appearance of a self as an object" (169). This development arises in "the social process of influencing others in a social act" and in taking the attitude of others, including especially the attitude of the generalized other, aroused by the stimulus and then reacting in turn to this response (171).

Mead insists that conceiving of oneself as an object in one's experience is a form of thought and not of emotion. It is a cognitive, and not an affective, phenomenon. The essence of the self lies "in the internalized conversation of gestures which constitutes thinking, or in terms of which thought or reflection proceeds" (173). Mead contrasts his own position with—and rejects the views of—Cooley and James, who find the basis of the self in experience involving self-feeling (173). Mead takes an explicitly cognitivist or rationalist stance on the nature and rise of the self. (In so doing, Mead emphasizes the interconnection between self and mind.)

The "I" and the "Me." The fully developed self is constituted of two phases, the "I" and the "me." Mead defines the "I" as the response of the individual to the attitudes of others, and the "me" as "the organized set of attitudes of the others which he himself assumes" (175). Neither the "I" nor the "me" exists in the conversation of gestures until the whole social act is completed, though the preparation takes place in the field of gestures (175). Because individuals are able to arouse in themselves the attitudes of others, they develop an organized group of responses that constitute their self-consciousness. "The taking of all those organized sets of attitudes gives him his 'me' (i.e., the self he is aware of)" (175). The "I" responds to the "me" in a creative, uncertain way, because the "I" represents an actor's action over against the social situation within which one's own conduct occurs; and it gets into one's experience only after one has completed an act. Then the individual becomes aware of it (175). The "me" arises in an individual's immediate experience in response to what is expected by others: The actor perceives the others' attitudes, which call for a response to the situation—and this (more or less uncertain) response is the "I" (176). The "I" in its relation of the "I" and "me" responds to a social situation that lies within the individual's experience (177). The "I" represents the individual's answer to the others' attitudes toward one when one assumes an attitude toward them (177). One's attitudes toward the others are present in one's own experience, but one's "I" response to them will contain a novel, unpredictable element. "The "I" allows for freedom and initiative in social interaction and is the basis for social change (177, 217). By contrast, the "me" is conventional and customary (199). The individual is aware of her-/himself and of what the situation is, but exactly how she/he will act does not enter the individual's experience until after the action occurs (177–78). The response simply happens and then becomes incorporated into experience (178). The "I" calls forth the "me" and responds to it. Together, they constitute a self as it appears in social experience.

The self is essentially a social process going on with these two distinguishable phases (178). Without both phases, there could be neither conscious responsibility nor novel experience (178). The "I" and "me" exist in the process of thinking and indicate its give-and-take character (182). Constituted of the two phases, the self "represents an eddy in the social current" and remains part of the current. "It is a process in which the individual is continually adjusting himself in advance to the situation to which he belongs, and [dialectically] reacting back on it" (182). The self is able to experience social control through its "I" phase (individual response to others' attitudes) and its "me" phase (individual's assumed organized sets of others' attitudes), which enable the individual to interact effectively in cooperative ventures (210).

Mind

To say that the two phases of the self exist in thinking is to insist that mind coexists with the self. Thinking exists in terms of symbols, which means that the activities of individuals can be, and are, organized not only with reference to one another but also with reference to the biophysical environment. Symbols make possible mentally controlled or intelligent activity, and it is such thoughtful, reflective, or deliberative action that constitutes mind for Mead. Mind begins to emerge as the child is able to interrupt his/her impulses to act by taking the attitude of the parent toward his/her own tendency to act. Manipulation of symbols "is a way of indicating characters of things which control responses, and which have various values" to members of the community or society, so that "such characters will engage the attention" of the member individual and "bring about a desired result" (119–20). Symbols allow a selection of "particular characteristics of the situation so that the response to them can be present in the experience of the individual" (120). In Mead's view, "the response to a symbol does and must involve consciousness" (122n.). It involves consciousness of meanings (as appropriatable from the past of the group), consciousness of the problematics as represented by the situation in the environment, and a consciousness of self as a reflexive reference to self, that is, "an indication to the individual of the significance which his actions or gestures have for other individuals" (122n.). Possessing symbols, only "the human animal is able to indicate to itself and to others what the characters are in the environment which call out . . . complex, highly organized responses, and by such indication is able to control [and select] the responses" (132).

Summary

Mead developed a distinctive theory of the self. It was noteworthy not only in and of itself but also for the basic assumptions and conceptions on which it was predicated. It presupposed an evolutionary naturalism markedly akin to that of early American sociology. It also reflected a version of the dominant pragmatism of American philosophy. And it offered a substantially altered view of behaviorist psychology.

In accordance with evolutionary naturalism, Mead argued that human beings had always existed in a social condition, which had its antecedents in earlier animal societies. However, human social existence was distinctive in that its social acts were based crucially on a peculiar (vocal) form of the gesture involving multiple participants. Unlike the conception of society endorsed by most American sociologists of the era, Mead's notion was decisively antinominalistic and pro- (social) realist.

In the book review and major paper in which he sought to summarize Mead's position for sociologists, Faris alluded to Mead's notion of the human social. He declared that Mead took "associated life as a . . . datum," or given (Faris 1937b, 396). In his review of *Mind, Self, and Society,* he commented that for Mead "acts are always within a society, and [its] . . . pre-existent organization" (Faris 1936c, 810). The acts of an immature member of society are social because others respond to them as (gestures or) part of a larger whole, the meaning of which "arises in the experience of response" (Faris 1936c, 810). Significantly, too, Faris remarked that Mead "made large use of, and considered of the highest importance, those collective phenomena which are not only never intended by any individual but which are unknown to those who participate in the experience," such as changes in language (Faris 1937b, 393, 392). Nevertheless, Faris failed to invoke any appropriate terminology to specify the implications of these remarks for Mead's position on the nature of society, social organization, and culture.

Faris's paper is the only synoptic account of the relevance of Mead for sociology and social psychology. Unfortunately, Faris omits any direct consideration of Mead's views on the nature of original human nature. He does review most of Mead's major concepts, such as the act, those of the delayed or reflective act, the gesture, the vocal gesture, the significant symbol, meaning, self-stimulation, self-response, role-taking as the basis for the development of the self (though Faris does not specify its phases except for the generalized other), and the "I" and the "me," along with Mead's modifications of the notions of imagination, perception, attitude, and redintegration. (Faris ignored the relation of the rise of the self and mind.)

Faris is important in his own right and thus now warrants consideration.

ELLSWORTH FARIS

Faris has exercised a more influential role in the development of social psychology and the rise of symbolic interactionism in sociology at the University of Chicago than has sometimes been recognized. He was Blumer's doctoral dissertation advisor and chairman of the department after Small's resignation in the mid 1920s. During Faris's own earlier years as a graduate student, he enrolled in Mead's courses, and Mead was his dissertation advisor (in psychology). Soon after Faris joined the sociology department as Thomas's successor, Mead asked him to introduce a basic course in social psychology, which he did. And, as chairman, Faris surely played a role in Blumer's being asked to assume responsibility for Mead's course in advanced social psychology (which was then shifted from philosophy to sociology). (See Lewis and Smith 1980 170; R. E. L. Faris 1967, xvii, xxii; E. Faris 1937b, 391–93.)

As revealed in his *The Nature of Human Nature* (1937a), Faris's own stance in social psychology reflects a number of intellectual influences: His conceptions of group and culture derive from the French school of sociology (associates and followers of Durkheim) and American ethnology; his notion of imagination, human nature, and the primary group stem from Cooley; his ideas about the nature and development of the self and the act had their origins in Mead; and his view of attitude is owed, at least in part, to Thomas. The works of James and Dewey were also important in forming the background for his psychology.

His chapters from the section "Conduct and Attitudes" in *The Nature of Human Nature* provide an illuminating intellectual context for viewing the major historical polemics out of which social psychology, and especially sociological social psychology at Chicago, emerged during the 1920s and 1930s. Faris conceived of the social psychology of the past quarter century as the study of how the immature member of society becomes a developed person with his/her own individuality and character. So envisaged, it has been an interstitial domain, on the borders of, and influenced by, sociology, psychology, psychiatry, and ethnology (Faris [1937a] 1976, 140–41). Faris's chapters include succinct reviews (and often critiques) of the doctrines of associationism, suggestion or imitation, instinctivism, behaviorism, psychoanalysis, and gestaltism. Representing the general point of view of Cooley, Dewey, Mead, Thomas, Park (and himself), the book emphasizes "the social group, or matrix, in which the personality takes shape" and thus "the social nature of individual personality" (134).

Society and Culture

Faris is unique among both social psychologists in particular and sociologists in general for his adoption of a realist notion of human society and culture. He was especially influenced by what he had termed the "French school" of sociology and by American ethnology (and his own experience in the former Belgian Congo). Like Mead, he had concluded that human life is always "an associated life" (Faris 1937b, 396). For Faris also, human activity always occurs "within a society, and the ongoing social process with its habits, customs, language, and institutions is a pre–existent organization into which every child is born" (Faris 1936c, 810).

Faris had argued explicitly that the nature of the group is not the result of the mere addition of individuals. Nor is the group only a name for an aggregation. It has a distinctive character as a whole "when it acts as a whole" (Faris 1937a, 99). As temporally prior to particular individuals, the group constitutes or makes its members (Faris 1937a, 100; Faris [1937a] 1976, 39). It can act as a whole only in and through communication, interaction, in concert, and with more or less consensus (Faris [1937a] 1976, 38–39). Its features are revealed in what Faris had termed (with evident French indebtedness) "group consciousness" (which is apparently especially facilitated by a common name), "group morale," and "esprit de corps," a more or less distinctive group terminology for distinguishing and communicating the experiences of the group (presumably as signified by collective representations), a certain allocation of the group's activities among members in accordance with certain recognized roles involving certain rights and duties, characteristic and appropriate social norms (e.g., customs, folkways, mores) and distinguishable social integration requiring more or less conformity as secured through forms or modes of social control, both informal and formal (Faris [1937a] 1976, 199, 277; 100, 199; 129; 283–84; 176ff., 284; 171, 198; Faris 1937a, 99, 100, 101).

In addition, society and its groups are important in the culture that they mediate and transmit, and that the child internalizes as he or she becomes a personality. Curiously, Faris never explicitly defines, comprehensively and systematically formulates, or extensively illustrates his own notion of culture. Among other things, it seems to be the residue of collective experience that is transmitted across the generations. Faris declares that it is a phenomenon of nature, a separate domain of reality, that is collective, impersonal, and traditional, is temporally and existentially prior to particular individual members of the group, persists across generations, has its more subjective and objective manifestations, tends to be static rather than dynamic in a state of isolation or inaccessibility, and in its expression as social norms (e.g., customs, folkways, mores, institutions) is probably of most significance to the sociologist.

An Original Organic Human Nature and a Socially Acquired Human Nature

To be compatible with the above views of society and culture, the original organic human nature would have to be pervasively plastic and teachable, especially in and through linguistic communication. Still, it is curious that Faris, with his considerable knowledge of the biology, psychology, and anthropology of his day, simply never endeavored to set forth any of the hereditary organic features of the human organism that afforded such plasticity and teachability.[14] Given his considerable intellectual kinship with Mead, it might be assumed that he adopted Mead's position as he had summarized it (Faris 1937b, 394, 393). It is noteworthy that Krueger and Reckless, students of Faris, were also somewhat ambiguous about original organic human nature in their *Social Psychology* (1931, 33)—except to note that such "native equipment" is assumed as will enable and facilitate "the acquisition of traits in social interaction and experience." Later (45), they note such organs of speech ("vocal cords, larynx, soft palate, uvula, teeth, tongue") as will allow the infant later to make combined sounds of vowels and consonants, and such organismic bases of gestures as the ability of the baby to "turn its head, wink, frown, smile, move his hands and so on."

Faris only cryptically acknowledges indebtedness to Cooley for his notions of imagination, sympathetic introspection, and (a socially derived) human nature. Many years earlier, Cooley had shown that personality and human nature are acquired within "the first groups, the primary groups, in which . . . [the individual] is received" (Faris [1937a] 1976, 17). Two sentences later Faris commented that the individual becomes a person (and acquires personality and human nature) "when he reaches that period, not always exactly datable, when the power of imagination enables him to reconstruct the past and build an image of himself and others" (17–18). In particular, Faris recognized that his notion of human nature "always requires the ability to take the role of another in imagination and to discover in this manner qualities that we recognize in ourselves" (9). Such role taking always requires an empathic imagination oriented by, and focused inward on, one's own experience (by introspection) (10).

Primary Group(s)

Human nature, personality, and self are all formed in the course of communicative interaction within what Cooley termed "primary groups." Faris is certainly one of the first of his generation to devote a complete paper or chapter to the primary group (Faris [1937a] 1976, 36–45), which is essentially a critique of its major characteristics. Ultimately, he insists that it is a peculiar kind of feeling, the "we-feeling" as a sense of the whole, to which he adds "face-to-face association and cooperation," and then the "free-flowing informality of personal relations," "looseness of organization, absence of set regulations or formulas, the possibility of doing more or less as one pleases . . . the spontaneity and interpenetration of its character—as crucial to its being the "matrix in which human nature takes form" (41, 174, 195, 43).

Personality and Self

Clearly, a learning of the language is crucial to taking the role of the other in self and personality formation. Faris ([1937a] 1976) distinguishes a prelinguistic stage (up to about three years) from a later, linguistic stage "in which articulate speech gives the power to reason easily and makes a consciousness of self possible" (196). In learning to talk and in "his talking with himself," the child "acquires a conception of his own and other personalities" (197). Furthermore, the treatment of the child with respect and mutuality as intrinsic to the primary relation is important in his or her acquiring "a feeling of dignity and self-respect" (197). And it is "as a member of the primary group that virtues [Cooley's sentiments?] appear and become conscious" in the individual (193). Certainly, too, primary groups are crucial to the formation of individual conscience in relation to a devotion or commitment to the whole, judgment in terms of its standards, and responsiveness to a personal reputation in relation to informal controls. It "is from the members of the primary group that attitudes are taken over" (173).

Attitudes are important, of course, in the formation of the personality and the self, though Faris denied that they could be construed "as elements out of which personality is constituted" (159). Interestingly, Faris apparently held that they "result from the particular selection and variation [i.e., individualization] made by each individual person on the folkways and mores he encounters" in the group and internalizes (159). Personality is then the more or less integrated consequence of playing roles in the script society provides in the form of rules, folkways, mores, and institutions (161).

Arising, then, in interaction, communication, and the learning and assumption of roles, personality "is the result of conduct which takes place in the presence of others and in contacts with friends and enemies, allies and opponents" (161). It "is mobile, self-developing, self-organizing" (161). But the prior existent groups stimulate, arouse, excite, approve, and disapprove of the activity of the developing child.

Act and Attitude

Oriented to the psychological controversies of his era, Faris was of necessity involved in the arguments about the continuity or discontinuity of human and animal behavior. The concepts of act and attitude are reflective of these polemics. Act and attitude are an important pair of concepts in arguments for the distinctiveness of human activity and against the position of behaviorism.

Most importantly, the act involves activity on the part of the human organism, part of which is non-overt or covert and part of which is overt and observable. The attitude is a part of the covert or non-overt phase and is technically an inclination or predisposition to act in a certain way.

Although Faris does not actually employ Mead's identification of impulse, perception, manipulation, and consummation as the typical features or phases of the act, what he does provide as the characteristics of significant acts are broadly consistent with Mead's views:

1. Significant acts exist in and through time. They have a duration in

that they are more than merely instantaneous. The adjective *significant* is of major consequence, for it rules out automatic and mechanical acts or movements, such as certain reflexes and "certain learned activities which are evoked by an appropriate stimulus" (119). "Significant acts" are acts involving reflection, and they occur over measurable time spans of greatly varying intervals (from seconds to years).

2. Each such significant act will tend to have three interrelated phases.

a. For the beginning phase, such words as *intent, purpose,* and *motive* are indicative (118–19). Manifestly, these terms allude to features that are not themselves directly observable. They are subjective or covert rather than objective and overt. But the completed significant or reflective act includes both subjective purpose and objective activity or movement.

b. The middle, mediating, or reflective phase involves "deliberation, planning, reasoning, thinking out a means of meeting the exigency. These acts occur when the situation is contingent and there is no immediate means at hand to enable the action to go on to completion or consummation." Accordingly, uncertainty is characteristic of the organism both within and without, both internally and externally (119). Clearly, then, a stimulus-response formulation of behaviorism is unacceptable (119).

It is in the attempt to solve problems by means of reflection that the social psychologist must introduce the notions of deliberation, imagination, and selection or choice to achieve realization of purpose or intention. Faris assumes that, because actors have internalized their culture, they will be inclined to resort to its resources and to devise appropriate means, techniques, or strategies to achieve the end or goal in view. The presence of folkways and mores suggests that rules or norms will be invoked to make an appropriate choice or decision in the selection of means to ends and so forth.

c. Finally, in the third phase, the significant or reflective act will come to a termination as a consequence of the achievement of the end (118). (Interestingly, Faris raises only indirectly the possibility that reflection, deliberation, or the putative devising of means to ends may be only partially successful or even result in failure.)

3. The interrelated phases of the act mean that it has a (meaningful) structure, organization, or configuration. It has a unity through time. The beginning, middle, and end phases are more or less interrelated, so that the observable physical movements are integrated by the imagined end and presumably by achievement or satisfaction, more or less, of that end. A sensed unity of the past, present, and future exists (120).

4. Most importantly, the termination or consummation of the act has a major consequence for the personality of the actor. He or she has had an experience in relation to the reflective act (120). So, Faris contends, "Some deposit remains, not only in experience, but also in behavior" (120). An atti-

tude (positive or negative, e.g., a bias or prejudice) results in relation to the object or objects of the act or action. Thus, completed acts leave an experiential deposit, in the form of an attitude or attitudes, that will affect future action.

In turn, human activities, whether individual or collective, personal or social, are, for Faris, actions rather than merely behavior, and human rather than merely animalistic, because they are so typically associated with the phenomenon of attitudes. Thus, Faris's notion of attitude demands attention.

Satisfactory definition of an attitude requires its demarcation from a number of related notions, such as impulse, instinct, habit, reflex. Still, Faris concurred in the use of 'attitude' as a general notion to describe the tendency to perform actions of a describable and identifiable sort" (99). In his view, the introduction of the term into social psychology signified a "change of emphasis from sensation to behavior, from receptivity to spontaneity," from innate to acquired motor tendencies, and "from a timeless principle or force to a concrete event" (99,100). His own analysis of attitude centered around several controversies:

The changeable versus the unchangeable (dynamic vs. static, particular versus the universal). Faris clearly adopted the former as against the latter position, especially seen in his attack against the doctrine of instincts.

The subjective versus the objective. Again, Faris opted for the former as against the latter in his battle against behaviorism. *Attitude* designates a certain proclivity, bent, bias, predisposition, aptitude, or inclination as the beginning of an act (121). Admittedly, these are inferential, but they must be assumed to exist between the times of actual (overt) activity or behavior.

Experience versus an (inner) idealist or (outer) materialist definition of human reality. But it is necessary to immediately concede that such a set of alternatives in a dichotomy is both unjust to, and inaccurate regarding, Faris's position. In a discussion of Thomas's notion of the causality of attitudes and values, Faris notes that the relation is not causal or sequential. Rather, it is "the double aspect of one phenomenon" (101). The subject/object dualism is in a sense a false one. An attitude is always toward something (i.e., a value or an object), and a value or an object is, "in some sense, the externalization of the attitude. Neither causes the other, either with or without help. They appear together in experience" (101–2, 110–11). One is the correlative or counterpart of the other. Value and attitude, or attitude and value, "are two aspects of the same experience" (111).

Unfortunately, Faris is not as explicit about his notion of experience as might now seem intellectually desirable. He acknowledges that experience has both its inner and outer aspects. The act does involve movement in space with physical (sensory?) contact with an object or objects. But the inner or subjective—involving both thoughts and ideas and feelings and sentiments—

is involved (207, 208). So an act is initiated by an attitude or intent, interrupted by reflection (in some form), and terminated with an emotional component such as satisfaction and joy or disappointment and disillusionment. If the emotional residue is positive or favorable, the experience will likely maintain the attitude in relation to a value; if it is not, and especially if it involves an emotionally heightened experience, crisis may ensue, and the relation between attitude and value may be redefined (111).

The individual versus the social versus the group (or collective). Although Faris seems to adhere to a social realist notion of the group, he may still argue (as Durkheim did) that the social or the group can have no existence anywhere except in individuals. Thus, social and group attitudes must also be located in individuals. "Social" attitudes for Faris are acquired or learned from others, interpersonally, and they are but "specific instances in individuals of . . . collective" or cultural phenomena (106). A "group" attitude is one that is shared with others as typical or characteristic of the group as a whole and is apparently more or less obligatory of membership in the whole. In this sense, group attitudes are collective in that they "are not mere summations" of individuals (100). (Interestingly, Krueger and Reckless's *Social Psychology* (1931, 258) further differentiates group from cultural attitudes.)

Attitudes versus wishes. Faris rejected both Park's and Thomas's notions of the wishes. In regard to the former, he rejected wishes as smaller or simpler elements composing the attitudes (102). And Faris's hostility to instincts means that he objected to Thomas's notion of instinctively based wishes. For Faris, the wish is a part of the act rather than of the attitude. It is an "impulse together with an image of the object of satisfaction" (123, 157). Faris clearly allows for the possibility that a wish may not be realized, so that "the act is left incomplete" (123).

Summary Implications

In summary, first, Faris is the only social psychologist and sociologist of the period to adopt a social realist notion of the nature of the group. It resembles that of Mead, though no reference is made to Mead. Second, Faris's account of how the individual is inducted into human society, through his or her membership in primary groups, and acquires a distinctive human nature, personality, and self definitely entails an emotional or affective dimension (empathic imagination) as opposed to Mead's exclusive reliance on a cognitive or rational argument. Third, Faris's account of the act and attitude, while compatible and linkable with social realism, also permits a much more individualist or nominalist and voluntarist interpretation. Again, it can be made congruent with Mead's position, but direct references to Mead as such are missing. Indeed, if the saying among (former) graduate students that "if you have taken one course from Faris, you have taken all and all about Mead" (Lewis and Smith 1980, 315, n. 29) has any merit, it is strange that so little on Mead is revealed in *The Nature of Human Nature*. Even Kimball Young noted in his review of Faris's book that Faris had actually not made "much use of . . . [Mead's] detailed analysis . . . of the rise and development of the social self" (Young 1938, 649.) Still, little if any exception can be taken to Faris's review of *Mind, Self, and Society* (1936c) or to his article "The Social Psychology of George Mead" (1937b).

HERBERT BLUMER

For four of the six decades since Mead's death, in 1931, Herbert Blumer has been regarded both as the chief protagonist of symbolic interactionism and the major contemporary exponent of Mead in sociology. Presumably, major intellectual continuities can be identified between Mead and Blumer. But initially, it is important to allude to another kind of similarity in the dearth of published expositions by the two. During the period studied here, Blumer published only a textbook chapter on his own conception of social psychology (Blumer 1937). Fortunately, reliable student notes on Blumer's advanced social psychology course from 1951 at Chicago do exist, and one set has been accessible as the basis of the following analysis (Blumer 1951).

Like Faris, Blumer begins his social psychological presentation of the nature and characteristics of human action or social conduct with a sketch of the historical background of social psychology in German and French thought. Like both Mead and Faris, he rapidly enters into a critique of what were then more contemporary conceptions of, and dominant orientations in, the field. In Blumer's case this critique entails assessment of the basic assumptions of instinctivism, stimulus-response behaviorism, gestalt psychology, and cultural determinism (which he alleges to be illustrated by Durkheim's social realist structural sociology (Blumer 1937; notes).[15]

For Blumer (1951), the predominant focus of social psychology (at the time of his course offering) was "the individual"—how individuals are affected by participation in group life, on the one hand, and how they affect group life by their participation, on the other. These concerns are epitomized in the concept of personality.

Three major areas of interest can be designated: (1) the nature of group life itself as a setting inside which the individual carries on conduct, (2) the analysis of the individual himself as a participating agent, and (3) the nature of interaction between the individual and other individuals. Still, these three areas are not sufficiently specific to deal with the complexities of the field.

Thus, his exposition is divided into six sections: (1) the nature of the group setting, (2) the nature of original human nature, (3) a socially acquired (and primarily affective) human nature, (4) interaction among individuals, (5) the origins and role of the self, and (6) act, self, and designation or indication.

The Nature of the Group Setting

Blumer (1937, 154) acknowledged what sociologists have generally claimed: "Every human infant is born into a human group. Its survival during the early stages of infancy depends on aid, protection, and care at the hands of some older human beings, either its parents or others. In this sense, the group is prior to the child." Note the word *child,* but not *individual.*

To the symbolic interactionist, group life consists of cooperative activities (of member individuals) arising from and "made possible by the sharing of common symbols, understandings, or expectations" (159).

In his course lectures, Blumer (1951) argued—claiming that he was following Mead—that a group exists if individual lines of conduct converge, are interrelated, are fitted together, and entail adjustment so that they are organized to pursue a common objective. The group process finds its prototype in a dyad in which a second individual imaginatively projects the implications of the activity of the first and thus comes to have the meaning of the action of the first. The second will also have an understanding or sense of what the first intends to do. Each person is able to form a judgment, an understanding of the way others are acting, and on that basis adjust his or her action so that it fits in with the actions of others. The effort to understand leads to attempts to define the situation. Hence, cooperative (group) activity can occur (cf. Blumer 1937, 159).

Three comments are in order. First, according to Blumer the mechanism involved in the foregoing is substantially the process of role taking, in which Mead's views are assumed. But in such circumstances Mead would argue that the individuals would be taking not only the role of the other or another but also that of the generalized other. Blumer has shifted the problem from one of accounting for public, shared, objective meanings of significant symbols to interpreting or conjecturing meaning of private or subjective intentions in symbols.

Second, in spite of Blumer's presumed effort to invoke Mead as a basis for his conception of the group (in e.g., interpersonal cooperation, individuals fitting into one another),[16] a reader who is also aware of the state of the sociological literature in the late 1930s and during the 1940s will be amazed that Blumer so cavalierly ignores the complexities in characterizing the basic nature of the group, such as primary/secondary and in-group/outgroup distinctions.

Third, Blumer's objections to the determinism of the contemporary cultural approach as exemplified by Durkheim's (associational) social realism (which were more combative than his earlier discussion of Levy-Bruhl in Blumer 1937), seem designed to anticipate a more voluntarist and nominalistic conception of the group as interpersonally and interactionally purposive and dynamic (cf. Lewis and Smith 1980), 173).

The Nature of Original Human Nature

Blumer's conception of the group is underpinned by an appropriate notion of the nature of original human nature. Put simply, the neonate has an unformed, unorganized, and amorphous nature. It is manifestly helpless, unable to carry out concerted actions, and utterly dependent on older human beings for satisfaction of its needs, and so for survival. In general, its behavior is random and unorganized (Blumer 1937, 152–53). Accordingly, the child's impulses and feelings are regarded as similarly vague and unorganized. Very active, its impulses occasion distress and impel activity. However, these impulses are plastic and unchannelized, without any specific goals. Impulses gain expression in the child's emotional behavior and random activity. Thus, "the development of the infant into childhood and adulthood is fundamentally a matter of forming organized or concerted activity in place of its previous random activity and of channelizing its impulses, and giving them goals or objectives" (153).

Although Blumer has not explicitly adopted Mead's specific features of human original nature, his views are congruent with, if not actually derived from, those of Mead.

A Socially Derived Human Nature

Blumer (1937, 1945–51) appears to accept Cooley's conception of a socially acquired, basically affective core human nature that is developed out of intimate interpersonal experiences in primary groups. Impulses and feelings are sympathetically disciplined and transformed into sentiments (Blumer 1937, 167–69). Occurring in all cultures and societies, these primary groups—into which children are born and where they experience intimate, personal, and sentimental relations—induce these young members sympathetically and imaginatively to take the roles of the elders and to incorporate, quoting Cooley, such sentiments as "love, resentment, ambition, vanity, hero-worship, and feelings of social right and wrong" (167).

Cooley is thus the basis for supplementing Mead's exclusive (and thus inadequate) reliance on the cognitive or rational potentialities of role taking in human nature. Blumer insists that full role taking must involve affectivity or emotionality. Indeed, for Blumer (1945–51), human nature consists essentially of urges, feelings, and sentiments that must find their expression in interpersonal acts and relations. (Blumer also refers approvingly to the French scholar Blondel, whose book and articles contend that all groups have a nomenclature to designate or identify the feelings of their members; see Blumer 1937, 157.)

Interaction

In turning to interaction (whose beginnings in the primary group are substantially ignored), Blumer's (1951) account is almost as notable for what is not said as for what is said. As in his chapter, so in the student lecture notes he declines to specify why he selected the term *symbolic interaction* to designate his position.[17] He cited Mead, Cooley, Thomas, Dewey, Williams, and Baldwin as predecessors in the development of the stance. Even though Cooley was of major importance in conceiving of a socially derived affective human nature, Cooley's "looking-glass self" contribution was not specifically acknowledged. Although the notes declare that "the heart and core of social psychology" reside in the answer to the question of "what leads an individual to interpret the situation as he does," Thomas's definition of the situation is cited only in Blumer 1937 (164–65), not in the notes. True, Blumer does insist that, in contrast to the stimulus-response view of the human organism as simply reactive, the interactionist view contends that it is active: It acts. (Only in the 1937 chapter, p. 172, does he characterize interaction as a "shuttling process" in which each successive participant begins by seeking to judge the meanings or intentions of the preceding and/or succeeding actions.) But he does not explicitly introduce Mead's notion of the social act, though again Blumer portrays the individual as recurrently in situations with others whose intentions are relevant for his or her own achievement of purposes.

Blumer's (1951) own point of departure is the claim that the human being must and does act in situations (or more broadly, a world) constituted of objects. Only through the actions of (other, older?) individuals do objects become defined, designated, and meaningful. The meaning of an object arises as a social attribution deriving from the perspective of the group. Meaning is thus shared or common.

For Blumer, interpersonal activity, or the acts of one person that directly impinge on and affect others—and in terms of which objects are constructed or defined—is actually interaction. Such is the case because human interpersonal activity is essentially mediated by an interchange, or conversation, of gestures or symbols (the adjective *significant* is missing), in which each actor's entrance into the ongoing conversation is cast or oriented in terms of the perspective of the others or others whom he or she is responding to or addressing.

Apparently, three modes of ascertaining meaning are available: (1) by the imaginative projection of the act of one person by another, (2) by an interpretation of that which has been said and done, and (3) by emergent definitional construction. Unfortunately, no explicit narrative elaboration is provided.

However, each of the three is illustrated. Mode 1 occurs in instances in which A begins to act toward B, and B attaches a meaning to that act that is a projection of the intentions attributed (cf. Blumer 1937, 171–72). Mode 2 refers to the expansion or elaboration of the inferences that B draws from A's acts and verbalizations. A also attaches a meaning to the act as A begins it. Insofar as the meaning A assigns to the initial act is the same as B assigns to it, the oncoming activity (-verbalization?) has a shared meaning. Mode 3 is left imprecise. It is not clear whether it designates the problem that the meaning of A's act is unclear and/or incomplete and so B must respond ambiguously and await further action from A or a clarifying response from C. Mode 3 suggests the potential fluidity, incompleteness, and changeability of meaning at different stages of acts or verbalizations.

At this point, it is necessary to caution that any apparent continuity between meaning as analyzed by Mead and by Blumer may be suspect. In Mead's case, the importance of the adjective *significant* as modifying symbol must be noted. A significant symbol is a verbal or language symbol whose meaningfulness exists prior to any particular speech exchange between A and B. The meaning is not merely shared between A and B; it is common to the (language) community and in this sense comprises a universal. It is public and standardized. But Blumer raises the possibility of a nonuniversal, private, and variable meaning (which is at best only partially communicated), that is, a personal intention, end, or goal. A and B are envisaged as having the possibility of privately bargaining with or accommodating with one another—as separate from, and possibly in contravention to, the meaning or common standard of the community, the generalized other (cf. Lewis and Smith 1980, 174–76).

But in any event, Blumer holds that when A acts in relation to B, A's action will have been preceded by A's taking of the role of the other (i.e., B) in order presumably to gauge what meaning B is likely to ascribe to A's action and how B may respond. Blumer does assume some sharedness of meaning as deriving from the formation of A and B as selves. He turns now to Mead's explanation of role taking and the origin of the self in interaction. (In the 1937 chapter (179–80), Blumer first explains personality in relation to attitudes, which are related in turn to the meanings of objects).

The Origin and Role of the Self

Role-taking and the Self. Blumer observes that the human being differs from animals in having a self, which means that he or she is able to act socially toward the self and the self toward others. The individual becomes an object of his or her own activity. He or she is sensitive as an object of the approval and disapproval of others.

As Mead argued earlier, the self comes into existence as the individual is able to view himself or herself from the outside. Both some degree of organic maturation and of sensitiveness and responsiveness to others are required. He or she acquires this external perspective as the individual plays (takes?) the roles of other persons around him or her. Blumer's (1951) account of the first two of the three stages approximates Mead's views.[18]

In the play stage, the child "plays" individual parts and addresses itself from each of the roles it takes. The child acts toward itself from the viewpoint of discrete roles. Such a self is unsettled, changeable, unorganized.

In the game stage, the child is required to assume several different roles simultaneously. He/she has to view his/her self from what is common to a number of different roles. Indeed, the child must incorporate into itself the positions of others. In playing baseball, the individual has to "take the role of the group" (cf. Blumer 1937, 182). To maintain the continuity of action, one has to address oneself from an abstract, generalized role (cf. Blumer 1937, 183). (Mead referred to this phenomenon as the development of an "organized other," structuring the activity of the child's own nature and "controlling the particular responses which give unity and build up his own self" [Mead 1934, 160.)

By virtue of abstraction from specific roles and specific situations, as Blumer (1951) puts the matter, the individual has developed a self that is emancipated from given situations but is oriented to what both Mead and Blumer term "the generalized other," as the third stage. This acquisition of the role of the generalized other means, in effect, that the individual has incorporated (the perspective of the) group or community. Whether Blumer regards the generalized other as an emergent unity from the self's having taken the perspectives of many others or simply as the summation "of the views and expectations of others" as concrete members is difficult to establish decisively. Blumer does comment that to the extent that the views and expectations of such specific (individual) member others "are organized or are organized by the individual, the individual has incorporated the group. In this sense, the group has come inside the individual."

Most importantly, Blumer contends that membership in a variety of groups, especially with divergent values, will mean that the individual will be required to work out a compromise or synthesis of some kind of role out of the divergent and conflicting roles. This synthesis can provide the basis for innovation, for introducing new or novel actions into a group or groups. The individual can become an innovator, a creator, a changer. In a broad sense, association or interaction can stimulate or evoke change. Individuals can bring their own unique syntheses (involving significant symbols) back into the group. Such a possibility involves an account of the "I" and "me" as aspects of the self.

The "I" and the "Me". Just as Blumer invoked Mead's delineation of the stages in the development of the self as stages in taking roles, so Blumer also adopts Mead's notion of the "I"/"me" distinction as (internal) phases of the self. The "me" arises a the response to the initial impulse (or composite of impulses) of the "I," as the impulse under control, as an object in relation to a subject, as the incorporation of the public, shared, group, or community as opposed to the private, personal, or idiosyncratic. What is especially significant is that Blumer finally explicitly acknowledges that the "me" represents the internalized moral definitions, standards, or principles of the group or society. In contrast to Mead, Blumer virtually ignores the place that morality occupies in taking the role of the other as it comes to implicate the generalized other in interaction. (Note that in the characterization of the generalized other, Blumer has endeavored to avoid any intimation of a holistic good that seems to be other than the goods of one or more individuals.

The Act, Self, and Designation-Indication

Still, it is the act that claims the primary attention of both Blumer and Mead. And like Mead, Blumer (1951) envisages virtually all human activity as falling within the domain of the act. The very idea of the act presupposes that the human organism engages in an effort to satisfy its impulses. The act, then, is that span of activity beginning with the impulse and ending with its satisfaction (or consummation; cf. Blumer 1937, 192). (Curiously, Blumer never directly refers to Mead's four stages of impulse, perception, manipulation, and consummation.) Human activity at any specific moment is an aspect or phase of the attempt to achieve some goal, whether fully explicit or only dimly sensed.

However, the impulse itself occurs before overt activity. As it apparently rises into consciousness, it evokes imagery. The image defines or gives direction to the impulse (Blumer 1937, 192). Past experience builds up a stock of images, relevant ones of which are evoked in present experience. Admittedly, images may be congruent or incongruent with the impulses. Congruent imagery serves to sustain, invigorate, or intensify the impulse. Incongruent imagery tends to negate or counteract the impulse (Blumer 1951).

Thus, a covert stage precedes the overt stage of activity in which inter-action occurs between the impulse and images. Clearly, the internal covert process is preparatory to overt action. At least two different aspects can be distinguished in approaching this inside process. The first involves an inter-play between the "I" and the "me" as just noted. The interplay between the two is what makes the act social (Blumer 1951).

The second aspect of this internal process is to a considerable extent understandable as the operation of what Blumer termed (the process of) "designation." Individuals point out things to themselves as important to achieving their goals. The overt act is a construction predicated on prior choices, decisions, selections (Blumer 1951).

In this context, too, Blumer has followed, at least in part, Mead's process of indication, the use of which Blumer resumed in his chapter "Soci-ety as Symbolic Interaction" (Blumer 1962, 183). In Mead's original usage, indication is the distinctive pointing-out and selecting-out process of humans—whether by use of the fingers, hands, eyes, head or body move-ment or inclination, or by vocal gestures or significant symbols (Mead 1934, 92, 94, 96; Mead 1936, 376–77, 378, 402–3; also Mead 1982, 137, 139, 143, 149, 161).

In its most comprehensive sense, designation is part of the interper-sonal orientedness or directionality of acts interrelated with the exchanges of symbols. The emerging act of one person is oriented or directed specifically to another or others in relation to certain social, physical, or abstract objects. Undeniably, designation is social—interpersonal, symbolic, and meaningful (Blumer 1951). Blumer's formulation makes explicit certain possibilities that remain implicit in Mead's indication.

However, differences do exist between two intellectuals' the concepts. A major difference concerns the place of morality. Although Mead did not always explicitly emphasize the moral dimension, taking the role of another was ordinarily presumed also to involve the generalized other, which clearly entailed moral standards of the whole to be observed in what was indicated as important (Lewis and Smith 1980, 174).

In contrast, Blumer's (1951) *designation* (which became *indication* later) was virtually devoid of moral implications as such. The self has essen-tially become a cosmopolitan self whose creative syntheses of role and value conflicts of different groups involve abstraction and personal detachment. In the urban world, vast numbers of groups intersect. Considerable conflict, dif-ficulty, and misunderstanding ensue. Secondary relations involve the prob-lem of "fronts," of deliberate deception. Thus, the self must reckon with deceit, deception, manipulation, and the use of the social context for achievement of its goals. Put otherwise, an interpersonal setting has devel-oped conducive to the rise of a relatively autonomous self whose indications are oriented to the conscious, calculating pursuit of its own ends (as revealed in Blumer 1962).

Accordingly, the objects of indication (in Blumer 1962) are extricated from their settings, held apart, and construed in relation to the self's disposition to act and in accordance with its goals (182; Blumer 1969, 80). Indication itself is a process preparatory to (or in interrupted) action that defines goals, specifies task steps in accomplishment, reckons with (physical?) conditions (and selects appropriate means), judges social approval and disapproval, and develops effective adjustments (Strategies) in relation to such approvals or disapprovals (Blumer 1962, 183; Blumer 1969, 1).

The autonomy of such self-indication is strikingly asserted in the declaration that "it cannot be accounted for by factors preceding the act." It "exists in its own right and must be accepted and studied as such" (Blumer 1962, 183; Blumer 1969, 82; cf. Lewis and Smith 1980, 178–79). As the self indicates, so the self is for Blumer. Certainly, it is instrumentally and voluntaristically oriented (cf. Lewis and Smith 1980, 176–77).

BLUMER'S "SYMBOLIC INTERACTIONISM" AND ITS ANTECEDENTS

Finally, it has become possible to engage in a comparative analysis of the social psychological stance of Blumer vis-a-vis those of Faris, Mead, Cooley, and Thomas. It should become possible to detect genuine similarities, continuities, and convergences from those that are only apparent or professed and thus conceal actual dissimilarities, discontinuities, and divergences.

A major and fundamental difficulty must be acknowledged at the very outset. Blumer tends to state relations with possible predecessors in such a fashion as to demand acceptance and to imply that the "facts" as represented cannot be otherwise. He quoted only one predecessor, Cooley, in his 1937 chapter and referred only to the title of the volume without citing a specific page or pages. The 1951 student notes do not indicate any quotations, and in the rare case of an allusion to a title, a definite page reference is not provided. His 1969 *Symbolic Interactionism* offers no references or page citations in the first five chapters that are relevant for the present study. His relative indifference to documentation does not facilitate detection of intellectual indebtedness, such as the present effort.

1. Blumer differs from Faris, Mead, Cooley, and Thomas in his disinterest in the problem of evolutionary origins. He assumes a thoroughly "modern" attitude toward questions of genesis. Thus, he has completely ignored the intellectual setting of Mead's problem of the origin and rise of

permanent human association, on the one hand, and of the self, on the other, in evolutionary naturalism. He adopts a presentistic or presentistic-futuristic stance.

2. By ignoring Mead's and Faris's interest in and commitment to evolutionary naturalism, Blumer presumably found it easier to ignore arguments about the genetic priority of human association or society in relation to the individual member and to avoid having to confront Mead's and Faris's patently divergent notions of the group or society. As indicated above, they adopted what may be termed a "social realist" (as opposed to a nominalist) position (see chapter 11). Blumer's conception of the group as a mere setting for individuals' actions is apparently designed to reduce structure to a minimum congruent with the maximal exercise of individual consciousness and choice (i.e., with an individualistic or nominalistic-voluntaristic notion of the group). He can and does avoid offending academic proprieties (as would be involved in a public disagreement with Mead and Faris as his academic mentors) by attacking the most famous modern apologist of social realism, Durkheim, for his (related, alleged) cultural determinism. This tactic also avoids Faris's (and apparently Mead's) acknowledged acceptance of the basic significance of culture in interpersonal or social orderliness.

3. Blumer's insistence that the social attribution of meaning is crucial to inter- and multipersonal interaction, and accords with Mead's position, is only terminologically correct. Blumer and Mead actually disagree over the notion of meaning and its relation to language. For Mead, the foundation of the meaning of significant (or language) symbols resides in their being shared or held in common and existent prior to any particular activation in speech. The meanings of language symbols do not have to be interpreted. Although Blumer uses *symbol* as a term, he omits the adjective *significant*. Symbols have meanings that are sometimes said to be shared and to involve intentions, but both sharedness and intentionality are claimed to require interpretation in the course of conversational interaction.

4. Although Mead uses the words *intent* and *intention* in a few instances, the contexts scarcely permit a direct appropriation of the kind of meaning Blumer attributes to the terms.[19] Conceivably, such might occur if Mead is basically reread in terms of the individualism and voluntarism to which James, Dewey, and Thomas subscribed. But it is more likely that *intention* derives from the components of Faris's notion of the significant act.

According to Faris, each significant act has a beginning phase for which such words as *intent, purpose,* and *motive* are indicative (Faris [1937a] 1976, 119). A middle, mediating, or reflective phase involves deliberation, reasoning, thinking out a means of meeting the exigency, of devising appropriate techniques or a strategy to achieve the end or goal (118). A third or overt phase entails observable activity to achieve the end or goal

(118). Manifestly, Faris's notion of the significant act does basically entail a means-ends or instrument-intention conception, which Blumer might have used and included in his formulation of his concept of designation (in the 1951 lectures) and in his later concept of indication (Blumer 1962).

5. The lecture notes indicate that Blumer suggested three modes of inferring meaning. Imaginative projection is the only one of these that is connected with the predecessors of symbolic interactionism, and it may well have had its source in Cooley. (However, use of this first mode is apparently discontinued in the publications of the later 1950s and thereafter.) Interpretation and construction-development as modes of inferring meaning seem to have no evident originators among the predecessors. Mead rarely used the terms *interpret* or *interpretation* and apparently not in conjunction with *intent*. (Admittedly, the remote possibility exists that Blumer may have acquired the term *interpretation* through knowledge of Wirth's study and translations of Weber in the 1930s and 1940s.)

6. Blumer's insistence that the participants in interaction always intervene by taking the role of the other or another derives from Mead. However, other aspects diverge substantially from Mead. Blumer rejects Mead's exclusive cognitivism-rationalism, insisting instead that normal role taking requires an emotive, nonrational aspect (which apparently stems from Cooley). His references to taking the role of another frequently ignore the generalized other and its representation of moral norms, standards, and principles. Often, too, taking the role of another appears to be used as part of the phenomenon of interpretation to assess how another person may respond to a putative possible line of conduct. As against Mead's usage, Blumer apparently regards taking the role of another as a potentially instrumental or manipulative use.

7. Although the term *designation,* which is replaced by *indication* later, apparently originated in Mead's use of the term *indication*, it seems to acquire in Blumer's usage a substantially expanded meaning and implies a different philosophical stance. Mead employed the term objectively as a behavioral or verbal pointing to or designation of something residing in the situation in which two or more persons are. Curiously, the term appears innocently in Blumer 1937 in conjunction with an exposition of Thomas's definition of the situation (165). Put directly and without excessive argumentation, Blumer's "self-indication" seems to expand to include Thomas's personal definition of the situation. In effect, Blumer has subjectified Mead's "indication" so that it comes to include the contents of any actor's personal consciousness as he or she reflectively deals with problems in achieving a goal or intention in an interpersonal or a multipersonal situation.

8. Although Blumer follows Mead in asserting that the genesis of the self requires the learning of language symbols, communication, interaction

with others, and taking of the roles of others, Blumer—unlike Mead—seems to imply that the mature self has become relatively autonomous, substantially or even primarily oriented to gaining advantage in achieving his own intentions, goals, ends. Self-indication reveals a willingness to be manipulative, calculating. As the self indicates to itself, so the self is.

———————

Undeniably, Blumer proved himself to be an able exponent, indeed an articulate apologist, for symbolic interactionism (as his version of the Meadian legacy for sociology). Although it did not develop into a general theory, it surely appeared to be a major candidate for self and personality theory in any future synthesis. However, a vindication of the claim must await an examination of the appeal of alternatives from the social sciences from Europe, which is to be undertaken in chapter 10.

Chapter 10

Possible European Influences on
American Theory

Renovation of American sociological theory was influenced not only by other disciplines in American academia but also by earlier European predecessors in sociology. True, sociological theory in the United States before World War I also had important European progenitors. But only three (Marx, Simmel, and Durkheim) of the seven influential European figures after the war had some influence earlier in American sociology and sociological theory.[1] Although some European inspiration was apparent before the mid 1920s, it was substantially registered only thereafter.

Publications are very revealing. Fifteen relevant articles were published in sociological periodicals from 1926 to 1936. Five were in the *Publications of the American sociological Society,* seven in *Social Forces,* two in the *American Journal of Sociology,* and one in *Sociology and Social Research.* Four concerned sociology in Germany, three in England, and one each in Russia, Italy, France, Czechoslovakia, and Argentina. Two also involved comparisons and contrasts between European and American sociology. One assessed American sociologists' judgments of the significance of European sociologists. Another compiled autobiographical statements from

258 American sociologists, which often yielded judgments about important European sociologists. (Baker, Long, and Quensel 1973 summarized the results.)

Several books at the end of the 1920s examined important European sociologists. They included Sorokin's *Contemporary Sociological Theories* (1928), House's *The Range of Social Theory* (1929), and Abel's *Systematic Sociology in Germany* (1929).

In 1930 the multivolume *Encyclopaedia of the Social Sciences* began to come from the presses, with entries on a vast array of topics, issues, ideas, and personages by internationally recognized experts from across the globe. This herculean undertaking is an invaluable, though presently a relatively infrequently recognized, intellectual source on the state of the post-World War I social sciences.[2]

Comprehensive assessments of sociology were undertaken in the late 1930s and 1940s. Among them were House's *Development of Sociology* (1936), Becker and Barnes's *Social Though from Lore to Science* (1938), Barnes, Becker, and Becker's sequel, *Contemporary Social Theory* (1940), Gurvitch and Moore's *Twentieth Century Sociology* (1945), and Barnes's *An Introduction to the History of Sociology* (1948).

The articles and books analyzed the contributions and relevance especially of such major theorists as Durkheim, Pareto, Marx, Simmel, Tönnies, Mannheim, and Max Weber. In certain instances, the interest was continuous from the pre-World War I period (e.g., Durkheim, Marx, and Simmel), though the character of the interest often changed. But in other instances, the interest of the second period (1915–45) was new, without any earlier counterpart (e.g., Pareto, Tönnies, Mannheim, and Weber). In each case discussed below, the inquiry begins with a consideration of the volume of response of American sociologists in general to the particular European and then examines his influence on the renewal of general theory in American sociology during the years 1915–45.

EMILE DURKHEIM

Although American sociologists's interest in Durkheim after World War I was continuous with that before, it seems to have increased substantially during the 1920s and 1930s.[3] It is evident in articles, books, translations, reviews, and dissertations.

Fourteen articles appeared on Durkheim from 1921 to 1939. Eight were published in the *American Journal of Sociology* (1921–28, 1934–39), two in *Social Forces* (1934, 1939), three in *Sociology and Social Research*

(1933–34, 1938), and one in the *American Sociological Review* (1937). (Consult Hinkle [1960] 1964.)

Books are important evidence, too. Durkheim was (negatively) consequential in the methodological stance adopted by Thomas and Znaniecki in their famous "Methodological Note" (1918–20, 1:44n). Park's articles on "Sociology and the Social Sciences" (1921), which also constitute the introductory chapter of Park and Burgess ([1921] 1924) textbook provide the first extensive, lucid, perceptive, and sympathetic interpretation of Durkheim up to that point in the history of American sociological theory. Sorokin's 1928 volume contains a substantial section of a chapter on Durkheim (463–80). Becker 1932b deals with Durkheim in a portion of a chapter (in part 4, "Historical Postscript," 703–5). Elliott and Merrill 1934 includes a major chapter entitled "Social Disorganization in Contemporary French Thought," which emphasizes the tradition of Durkheim. House examined Durkheim in his 1936 work (204–9, 264–65). With its four chapters on Durkheim, Parson's *The Structure of Social Action* ([1937] 1968) became a major contribution to the exposition and analysis of the Frenchman's sociological views. Barnes and Becker's treatise (1938, 828–39) and its sequel (Barnes, Becker, and Becker 1940, 66–72, 85–88, 628–30, 644–46, 810–13, 838–41) document the continuing interest in Durkheim.

Translations of two of Durkheim's major works were undertaken during this period. George Simpson translated Durkheim's volume on the social division of labor into English as *The Division of Labor in Society* (Durkheim [1893] 1933). At the end of the decade, Sarah A. Solovay's and John H. Mueller's English translation of Durkheim's *The Rules of Sociological Method* (Durkheim [1895] 1938) appeared.

Six reviews of several of Durkheim's books are contained in sociological periodicals. Two appeared in the *American Journal of Sociology* (1924, 1934), one in *Social Forces* (1926), one in *Sociology and Social Research* (1924), and two in the *American Sociological Review* (1938, 1940).

Interest in Durkheim is also revealed in the theses and dissertations of the period. Two were completed in 1915 (at Columbia and Harvard Universities), one in the mid 1930s (apparently at Northwestern), and three at the end of the 1930s (at Harvard in 1938 and at Columbia and the University of California, Berkeley, in 1939).

But just what this substantial interest in Durkheim means for his influence in American sociology is not simply or easily determined. Considerable opposition existed to fundamental features of Durkheim's sociology, which apparently was registered either by ignoring him altogether or by direct objection or attack. For instance, Durkheim seems to have exerted no perceptible impact on the newer movement in empirical research at Chicago, as is evident in the series of monographs published by its press. Cavan's *Suicide* (1928), for instance, cites Durkheim's research on the subject only once and entirely ignores his theoretical argument. Ellwood's (1923, 104) apparent protest at Lichtenberger's neglect of Durkheim in the latter's *The Development of Social Theory* (1923) does not mitigate the fact that he was widely neglected. Indeed, Durkheim's lowly position (twenty-seventh) in the rating of social thinkers by Hornell Hart 1927 and his fourth rank in L. L. Bernard's autobiographical study (Baker Long, and Quenzel 1973) may well have been an accurate index of Durkheim's imagined minor relevance to American sociologists then.

Perhaps the primary opposition was directed against Durkheim's social realism, which was at variance with the pervasive voluntaristic nominalism of American sociology. This objection is manifest in Gehlke's (1915, 94–101) explicit arguments and implicitly in Bristol's (1915, 146, 148–49) views. It appears as the basis for Thomas and Znaniecki's (1918–20, 1:44n.) insistence that the cause of an individual or social phenomenon is always a combination of the two, and never only one or the other. Other sociologists objected to Durkheim's social realism because it appeared to be metaphysical or mystical (e.g., Simpson 1933). Others indicted him for particularism, premature generalization, or oversimplification. Furthermore, his very insistence on research that is conceived strategically in terms of theory could well have had paradoxical consequences: Before World War I, some sociologists might well have taken exception to his emphasis on research; but in the decade following, given the prominence of an a- or antitheoretical empiricism, others may well have objected to his stress on theory.[4]

However, the intellectual changes during the decade after World War I seemed to prepare the way for and facilitate the reorientation and reevaluation of Durkheim that arose in the 1930s. These modifications stemmed—directly or indirectly—from disputes concerning methodology, in the course of which sociologists were led toward, rather than away from, Durkheim's methodological views. Although American sociologists affirmed their adherence to a pluralistic approach, as opposed to what they believed to be his particularistic (or monistic) conviction, they redefined and restricted the range of variables that they conceived to be directly and immediately relevant to the explanation of behavior. Their ideas tended to converge with those of Durkheim as they came to reject Lamarckianism and instinctivism; to accept the organic plasticity of humankind, the acquired character of social behavior, and the notion of culture from cultural anthropology (which such sociologists as Gary and Faris readily recognized as congruent with Durkheim); to understand George Herbert Mead's notion of the role of the significant symbol (with its considerable similarity to Durkheim's collective representation); and to insist on inductive, objective research (which appears congruent with Durkheim's rules of method, his research on suicide, and his rejection of a normative or evaluative approach). (Consult Hinkle [1960] 1964, 277–79.)

Certainly, too, the unprecedented attention paid to Durkheim is, in part, to be related to the impact of the larger social context, the problem of social order under the twin crises of depression and war. Having made social order his fundamental theoretical problem, Durkheim's works were germane to the major concerns of American sociologists then. Elliott and Merrill referred in their *Social Disorganization* (1934, 735) to French sociologists, inspired largely by Durkheim, as the only European intellectuals "consistently interested in the theoretical aspects of social disorganization" (735). But actual exploration of the possibilities of Durkheim's theory of social disorganization did not begin until 1938, when Merton's analytical essay "Social Structure and Anomie" was first published (this was later republished in Merton 1968).

Though Durkheim was apparently becoming more acceptable to American sociologists, objection and reservation remained. The criticisms in Merton's (1934) review of *The Division of Labor in Society* and in Alpert's *Emile Durkheim and His Sociology* (1939a) are illustrative of the range and depth of the strictures still directed to Durkheim:[5]

1. In Durkheim's work, such basic methodological notions as those of thing, fact, mechanical, objective, natural, individual, and constraint have varied or ambiguous meanings.
2. Positivism requires that Durkheim ignore the fact that the concept of causation, more markedly perhaps in the social sciences than in the physical, is an epistemological assumption and not of observation.
3. Durkheim fails to recognize the role of the *capta* (that is, indirectly, the investigator) and is exclusively preoccupied with the data (the object investigated).
4. His method of deriving definitions ignores the a priori assumptions of the inquirer and fails to offer criteria for deciding how a class (or category) should be defined.
5. He does not distinguish properly between his abstract conceptions, which are ideal constructions, and the concrete, empirical situations in all their variety.
6. He employs concepts as they have been defined in polemics, so that he is compelled to accept the terms set by his opponents.
7. His indexes are deficient in systematic rationales and narrowly limited by his principle of the objectivity of data.
8. The resort to the method of elimination is methodologically fallacious.
9. He adheres to an unverified conception of unilinear social evolution.

10.   His scheme of analysis is defective, because it omits a *verstehen* and means-ends type of inquiry.

However, these criticisms, unlike those of the earlier period,were accompanied by a recognition of Durkheim's accomplishments. Emergence of a favorable disposition seems to have been a concomitant of four developments in the treatment of Durkheim.

First, his methodological canons—despite acknowledged defects—were sympathetically explored. After the vigorous disputes over methods in the late 1920s and early 1930s, Durkheim's statement became more meaningful. Alpert (1939a) devoted about one-fifth of his volume to elucidating Durkheim's procedure for making scientific inquiries and giving scientific explanations. In his account of Durkheim's conception of sociology, he adverts to Durkheim's conviction that sociology can prosper only as it confronts specific problems, accumulates relevant facts, and uses "the methods of accurate observation, logical validation and systematic generalization that are characteristic of the scientific approach" (80). Alpert provides a concise, lucid exposition of Durkheim's schema of analysis (86–108).

Second, a critical review and redefinition of Durkheim's position on the group, the individual, human nature, and psychology helped to elicit a more positive reaction. Earlier sociologists were repelled by what they regarded as his social realism and his antipsychological animus. Alpert's designation of Durkheim's realism as a "relational or associational realism," which he differentiates from both social nominalism and substantialist social realism, did mitigate, if it did not entirely remove, the onus of the "group mind" label (156–57). Durkheim does not hypostatize society. Collective representations and consciousness can "exist nowhere else than in individual minds and individual consciousness" (161). In effect, Alpert's analysis of Durkheim also suggests that the earlier charges of the alleged anti-individualistic and antipsychological orientation in his sociology were exaggerated. Durkheim does not ignore "the biological basis of human nature," and he does not reduce "the individual to a mere automation impassively receiving and conforming to his social heritage" (Alpert 1939b, 70).

Third, Durkheim's acceptability was substantially increased by a theoretical association with the voluntarism of American sociology. Alpert's study only implies that Durkheim, near the end of his career, moved vaguely in that direction; but Parsons cites Durkheim—one of the four contributors to his social action theory—as adhering to notions of constraint and the functioning of ritual that presuppose a discernible voluntarism. Constraint is eventually conceived, so Parsons argues, as the voluntary acceptance or self-imposition of the moral obligation to obey a norm. The function of ritual demands the exercise of "what is generally called will or effort" (Parsons

[1937] 1968, 440). Thus, Parsons has achieved a strategic accommodation of Durkheim to the pervasive voluntarism of American sociology.

Fourth, the emergence of functionalist theory during the 1940s provided another basis for a more favorable evaluation of Durkheim. Alpert's article "Durkheim's Functional Theory of Ritual" (1938a) seems to have been the first study to link Durkheim prominently with functionalism. By the mid 1940s, Parsons was expanding (and modifying) his action theory by incorporating functionalism to account for social action systems. In 1945, he cited the work of Durkheim and his followers as important antecedents of modern functionalism, averring also that in the course of Durkheim's career "a genuine structural-functional treatment of the social system . . . gained increasingly in strength" (Parsons [1945] 1949, p. 31). In his essay on "Manifest and Latent Functions" (in Merton 1968), Merton refers to Durkheim and to Radcliffe-Brown, who had been inspired by Durkheim. Indeed, Merton came to regard his earlier inquiry, "Social Structure and Anomie" (in Merton 1968), which combines the means-ends-norms action schema of his mentor Parsons with Durkheim's notion of anomie, as providing a functionalist approach to the study of social change (115–17).

Nevertheless, in spite of some utilization of Durkheimian notions in American sociology, resistance to certain basic premises of Durkheim remained. No general sociological theory based on Durkheim was developed in the second period.

VILFREDO PARETO

The interest in and influence of Pareto in American sociology and sociological theory differ from that of many other European figures in their cross-disciplinary character and restricted duration. House (1935, 78) remarked that "so many expressions of admiration" for Pareto's *Treatise*—"most of them written by other than recognized sociologists—have found their way into print that members of the sociological fraternity are being constrained to take account of Pareto, and to define for themselves and for others the relation of his work to their own and to that of their acknowledged predecessors." At Harvard University, the physiologist Lawrence J. Henderson became the acknowledged leader of a multidisciplinary "Pareto Circle" at Harvard (see Heyl 1968, 316–40). Other figures in the informal group included Bernard DeVoto (literature), Crane Brinton (history), Elton Mayo (industrial relations), Joseph Schumpeter (economics), Charles P. Curtis, Jr. (law), and (from sociology) George C. Homans and Talcott Parsons.

In sociological periodicals, eleven articles appeared on Pareto during the 1930s. Three were published in the *American Journal of Sociology*

(1930, 1936, 1940), three in *Sociology and Social Research* (1932, 1935–36), one each in the *American Sociological Review* (1948), *Social Forces* (1930), the *Southwestern Review* (1941), and two in the *Journal of Social Philosophy* (1935–36).

Books further document the interest. Sorokin (1928, 37–62) offered an extended treatment of Pareto. Handman (1931, 139–53) wrote about Pareto in *Methods in Social Science,* edited by Rice. Homans and Curtis's *An Introduction to Pareto: His Sociology* was printed in 1934. Parsons was the author of the entry on Pareto in the *Encyclopaedia of the Social Sciences* (Parsons 1933). House's 1936 textbook contained a lengthy chapter on Pareto. Ellwood 1938, Barnes and Becker 1938, Furfey 1942, and Crawford 1948 also contained relevant chapters or major portions of chapters. DeGre's *Society and Ideology* (1943) similarly deserves mention.

Pareto's *Trattato di sociologia generale* (1916) was published in English as *The Mind and Society* in 1935. Reviews followed immediately: three in 1935 (in *Social Forces,* the *American Economics Review,* and the *Yale Review*) and one in 1936 (in the *American Sociological Review*).

Of all the sociologists with a major interest in Pareto, Parsons surely wrote most voluminously and in greatest detail. In addition to his entry on Pareto in the *Encyclopaedia of the Social Sciences* (1933), Parsons was reviewer of the English translation of Pareto's *Treatise* in the *American Economics Review* (Parsons 1935a) and the *American Sociological Review* (Parsons 1936b), author of a major article on Pareto in the *Journal of Social Philosophy* in 1936 (Parsons 1936a), and of three chapters on Pareto in *The Structure of Social Action* (Parsons 1937, chaps. 5, 6, 7). Like most other students who dealt with Pareto in the sociological literature of the period, Parsons also offered a summary analysis of the main features and ideas of Pareto's general system of sociology. And in that endeavor he was critical of the interpretations of some of his predecessors (e.g., Handman and Sorokin; see Parsons [1937] 1968, 199, 212 n., 225). He remained basically appreciative of Pareto's acceptance of a mathematicized methodological conception of analytical mechanics as a model for social science, with its system of simultaneous differential equations. He seems much more inclined than many others to ignore or forgive Pareto's apparent hereditarianism and the many terminological issues associated with his use of residues, "derivations," and "sentiments." Unfortunately, the sharpest criticism of Pareto was issued in the *American Journal of Sociology* in 1936—at about the time the final drafts of *The Structure of Social Action* must have been being prepared.

However, the basic stance of American sociology, including theory, seems to have been prevailingly negative toward Pareto. The views of the Moores, Handman, and Faris reveal substantial objections to the Italian economist and sociologist:

1. The massiveness of Pareto's treatise precludes its being readily understood. Moore and Moore (1935, 298) comment that it would have gained in clarity and readability if it had "been stated more succinctly."

2. Handman (1931), Moore and Moore (1935), and Faris ([1936a] 1937) concur that Pareto fails to conform to his promise to remain faithful to the logico-experimental method and to prove his propositions by experience and observation. His treatment of materials "disclose personal sentiments, residues, and derivations" that are favorable to certain, and unfavorable to other, value stances (e.g., aristocracy over democracy; Handman 1931, 152, 153; Moore and Moore 1935, 298; Faris 1937a, 192).

3. In spite of his promise, Pareto fails to pay meticulous attention to rigorous and exact definitions of terms. The Moores (1935, 299) are somewhat restrained in their criticism, whereas Faris (1937a, 196) asserts categorically that Pareto offers no definitions of the residues, sentiments, or manifested instincts.

4. Both the Moores (1935, 298) and Handman (1931, 140) insist that Pareto's charge against other works and their authors that they are metaphysics and metaphysicians is equally applicable to him. Handman (1931, 140) remarks that Pareto is unfair in postulating "the existence of something" that someone else is asked to explain.

5. Faris (1937a, 193) accuses Pareto of simultaneously desiring a mathematical sociology but conceding that "mathematical treatment is not possible." Indeed, it is clear, Faris says, that Pareto does not know of the statistical work of modern sociologists.

6. Faris (1937a, 194) claims that in spite of Pareto's interest in the deeds of men, the reasons for such actions, and the underlying motives, he actually abandons such interests. His "attitude toward the strange customs of other times and lands is that of the untutored ethnocentric."

7. Handman (1931, 148) objects to Pareto's discussion of sentiments and instincts because it is too "vague and formalistic," deriving from his "logical rather than his psychological approach." Thus, an alleged common factor lying behind the apparent dissimilarity of different sentiments and instincts is conceived "in a classificatory fashion" such that the "similarities between the two situations" remain wholly external.

8. The Moores (1935, 298) argue that the question of validity must be confronted if "derivations coming from a given residue may assume different and even opposite forms." In fact, Handman (1931, 149, 150) asserts that the problem of ascertaining "what residues will select what derivations as expressions of themselves . . . is insoluble because it

depends on too many accidental factors." In failing to point "out in detail what forms of derivations represent the appropriate residues at specific times and places," Pareto compels the reader to accept his word. Other analysts may come to different conclusions. Pareto's approach reveals the same difficulty as the language of Freudian symbolism. So the Moores (1935, 299) observe that "his technique of tracing residues through derivations" is subject to attack.

9. Both Moores the (1935, 299) and Faris (1937a, 198) complain that Pareto's classifications are labored, "long-drawn out," and "singularly sterile."

10. Devastatingly critical, Faris (1937a) alleges that Pareto was confused because he invented his problem. "The sentiments, the emotional aspects of the attitudes, are powerful and non-logical, but they are the effects of social participation, not of innate constants" (197). Pareto mistakes "that which is collectively originated and socially transmitted for a unitary and inherited individual tendency" (198). What Pareto regarded as a psychological problem was rather a sociological one (199).

11. Handman (1931, 152) denies that Pareto can seek only experimental uniformities in the field of social behavior. Instead such "uniformities are made and not found." Both he (152) and the Moores (1935, 294) argue that in the resort to historical data from fairly remote times, selection is required and occurs unconsciously in terms of the "folk background" of the historian or social researcher. In fact, the "immense mass of material presented [in the *Trattato*] will be culled differently by persons who approach it with different conceptions" (or, perhaps better, preconceptions) (Handman 1931, 153).

By 1945, Parsons himself had come largely to a negative verdict about Pareto's effort to construct a system of general sociology. He concedes that Pareto's three (isolated) variables are "very heterogeneous relative to one another." These "three referred immediately to elements of the motivation or orientation of the action of individuals," whereas the fourth, social heterogeneity, involves a shift to an altogether different level, "an aspect of the structure of a system of social relationships." He concludes that what Pareto provides as "detailed analytical tools in detailed research" has "signally failed to work." It is "too vague and general. The gaps have to be filled by arbitrary ad hoc constructions and classifications or by the introduction of structural categories which are merely tolerated, not systematically developed." Rather than employing analytical mechanics as a model in the study of structured or institutionalized social action, Parsons concludes that structural functionalism is the only viable alternative (Parsons [1945] 1949, 30).

Thus, the major figure on whom the possibility of a relatively thorough Paretian sociological theory rested now disavowed precisely that possibility. No exemplar of a Paretian sociological theory thus appeared in the second period of American sociological theory, 1915–45.

Finally, it appears that the character of American sociology in the 1930s was logically incompatible with Pareto's views. His conceptions were heavily hereditarian at a time when American sociology was pervasively inclined to construe social conduct as learned or acquired. His sociology seemed to be substantially psychological and individualistic, whereas American sociology was endeavoring to demark the personal and the social, the individual and the collective.

And perhaps most importantly of all, American sociology had come to a recognition that social conduct was based on custom and tradition as acquired "irrationally, uncritically, and even sub-consciously . . . by the masses of the people of a society" (House 1936, 87). It had developed a notion of "culture," in part from the German ethnologists and folk psychologists beginning with Lazarus, Steinthal, and Wundt, in part from Bagehot's *Physics and Politics* and such works of Sir Henry Maine as *Ancient Law,* and the notions of folkways and mores as elaborated by Sumner (House 1936, 87–88). House acknowledges that the research and writings of the small but active group of cultural anthropologists under Franz Boas's leadership had served to reinforce this conception of culture (87). In a word, American sociologists have developed a theory of human behavior abundantly recognizing its largely nonrational character in substantial (if not total) independence of Pareto.

In contrast, American sociologists of the period had a more or less persisting interest in other European, especially German, predecessors and contemporaries. They included Karl Marx, Georg Simmel, Ferdinand Tönnies, Karl Mannheim, and Max Weber. (Undeniably, the magnitude of the interest varied considerably.)

KARL MARX

Although a number of textbooks in social and sociological theory included consideration of Marx and Marxism, Marx remained of only minimal or marginal interest to mainstream American sociologists through the 1920s, 1930s, and 1940s. Marx was cited only twice as a significant influence among the 52 American sociologists mentioning a European sociologist as an important factor in their intellectual outlooks in the autobiographical statements (from 258 American sociologists) that L. L. Bernard had collected in 1927.[6] And he was eighteenth in a list of ninety-three figures in Hornell Hart's study of American sociologists' opinions in the history of social thought, also in 1927. (Ten relevant papers had been published in the sociology journals of the period: seven in the *American Journal of Sociology* [1916, 1920, 1925, 1930, 1931, 1947, 1948], and one each in the *American Sociological Review* [1937], *Social Forces* [1941], and *Sociology and Social Research* [1937].)

Even the advent of the depression did not radically alter matters. Certainly, the structure of American society and academia and their basic value-premises were markedly hostile to Marx and Marxism. Bernhard J. Stern seems to have been the only senior sociologist with a Marxist orientation at a major university (Columbia; Page 1982, 28). Of the younger generation just beginning a career in sociology at the outset of World War II, only C. Wright Mills displayed an unmistakably positive stance toward Marx and Marxism.

It is also important to note that, in 1934, members of the (German) Frankfurt Institute of Social Research settled in New York City, only a few doors from the Columbia University Department of Sociology. Beginning in 1936, Horkheimer, Lowenthal, and others offered lectures and seminars in the Extension Division of Columbia.[7] Certainly, some of the more theoretically inclined graduate students in Columbia's Department of Sociology availed themselves of these opportunities. But if Page's own reactions were at all typical, it would appear that the impact of this Marxism-based emerging critical theory on fledgling sociologists was negligable in the years before the war (Page 1982, 30–31; cf. Jay 1973, 38–40, 289). No indigenous Marxist sociological theory emerged during the second period.

GEORG SIMMEL

Of all the German sociologists who had an impact on American sociology, Simmel's influence was the most persistent and continuous throughout the several periods of the history of the discipline in this country, in spite of some fluctuations.[8] Fortunately, Levine, Carter, and Gorman have provided a relatively accessible account in "Simmel's Influence on American Sociology" (1976).

Certainly, Simmel was the only German sociologist to have exercised any substantial influence on the discipline or its practitioners here during the 1920s. He was the third most frequently cited European sociologist (exceeded only by Spencer and Tarde) in Bernard's 1927 study of autobiographical statements of American sociologists (as indicated in Baker, Long, and Quensel 1973). By contrast, he was only twenty-seventh out of ninety-three figures in Hornell Hart's inquiry, also in 1927.) Clearly, it was important that Park was Simmel's champion at the University of Chicago. Furthermore, the ten selections on Simmel in Park and Burgess's text ([1921] 1924) were many more than were drawn from any other figure. The selections from chapters 4 through 7 indicate just how individuals move from isolation into contact and then interaction. Social distance is conceptualized both laterally and vertically. The remaining sections in chapter 8 through 11 examine the four major interaction processes of competition, conflict, accommodation, and assimilation. Still, Park displays some ambiguity about Simmel's basic conception of society. In some contexts, especially his earlier writings, he follows Simmel in equating society with human interaction. But, particularly in his later study, Park was inclined to invoke the "more conventional identification of the social with the moral order, which he contrasted with the ecological order derived from the mere pursuit of individual self-interest" (Levine, Carter, and Gorman 1976, 825).

Manifestly, a number of persons were interested in Simmel over the several decades of the second period, admittedly critically in several instances. In 1925 the University of Chicago Press published Nicholas J. Spykman's *The Social Theory of Georg Simmel*. It systematically summarized Simmel's basic notions and so facilitated acquaintance with ideas in works not yet translated. Sorokin's textbook (1928, 502n.) paid considerable attention to Simmel but basically rejected his contributions as misguided in aim, flawed in execution, based on speculation and metaphysics, and devoid of scientific method. Simmel was the first of four German sociologists analyzed in Abel's *Systematic Sociology in Germany* (1929). Abel criticized Simmel for propounding an approach to sociology that was not congruent with his actual substantive analyses, therein being unable to make "valuable contributions to sociology." In *Social Thought from Lore to Science* (Becker and Barnes 1952) Becker alluded to the many defects of Simmel's sociology, "chief of which are its unsystematic character, its use of an illustrative rather than truly comparative method, and its lack of emphasis" (2:891). Finally, Floyd House's *Development of Sociology* (1936) devotes more than half a chapter to Simmel (as part of a study of his and Wiese's formal sociology). House did note that critics of his formal sociology contended that Simmel does "not distinguish between form and content of social interaction as his methodological propositions demand" (389). But he also defends Simmel by arguing that "there is much that is suggestive and revealing" in "Simmel's treatment of various topics" and by insisting that the form/content distinction "expresses a principle that the social science of the future will have to take into account" (390).

Certainly, any inquiry such as this one would be derelict in its obligations if it failed to note Simmel's impact on research into the "marginal man" (Park, Stonequist, Wood), social distance (Park, Bogardus), the city and urbanism (Park, Wirth), and small groups (Becker, Useem). (Consult Levine, Carter, and Gorman 1976, 1115ff.)

Simmel also apparently had macrotheoretical impact on the formulation of general introductory sociologies of two of Park's students. Hiller's 1933 and K. Young's 1934 textbooks seem conspicuously indebted to Simmel's form/content distinction in their reliance on social process analysis. Otherwise, Simmel did not provide a major impetus to efforts seeking to renew macrosociological theory in the United States during the 1930s or 1940s.

FERDINAND TÖNNIES

Tönnies was a third German sociologist who exercised some influence on American sociology in the years 1915–45, though he certainly was known among the founding fathers of the discipline in this country.[9] Park and Burgess's text ([1921] 1924) included a section from Tönnies' *Die Sitte* (The Mores). As Cahnman and Heberle remark in their "Introduction" to the translation of Tönnies' *On Sociology: Pure, Applied and Empirical* (Tönnies 1971), "Park's dichotomy of 'family' versus 'marketplace' clearly is an adaptation from Tönnies, turning what had been an ideal type into a real type—a very Parkian procedure" (xvii). In his 1931 article "The Problem of Cultural Differences" (reprinted in Park 1950), Park acknowledges that his dichotomy of "sacred" versus "secular" societies derives from Tönnies's notions of *Gemeinschaft und Gesellschaft* (Park 1950, 12n.). Howard Becker and Robert Redfield, two of Park's students, developed this dichotomy and that of "folk" versus "urban." However, the first major article, "The Sociology of Ferdinand Tönnies," was the work of Louis Wirth (1926). Presumably, Wirth's paper "Urbanism as a Way of Life" (1938) was also indebted to Tönnies's ideas, though explicit acknowledgement is lacking. (See Wirth 1956.) But Cahnman and Heberle suggest that Tönnies's influence became subterranean: He was used both with and without quotation, yet not read (Tönnies 1971, xvii). True, the texts by Sorokin, House, Barnes and the Beckers, and Barnes on social and sociological theory and the history of sociology included chapters, or sections of chapters, on Tönnies. However, only two relevant articles were published in the periodical literature of the period (in the *American Journal of Sociology,* 1926, and the *American Sociological Review,* 1937).

Parsons 1937 included an essay entitled "Note on *Gemeinschaft und Gesellschaft.*" Three years later, Charles P. Loomis translated *Gemeinschaft und Gesellschaft* into English under the title *Fundamental Concepts of Sociology* (1940). (Loomis's translation was reviewed in the *American Sociological Review* and in *Social Forces* in 1941.) Arndt and Folse translated a selection from Tönnies into English as "The Concept of Law and Human Progress" in *Social Forces* in 1940 (Tönnies 1940). Eight years later, Tönnies's son-in-law, Rudolf Heberle (1948), published the authoritative "The Sociological System of Ferdinand Tönnies: 'Community' and 'Society.'" In the perspective of the relevant literature, it must noted that Tönnies did not become the inspiration for any general American sociological theory.

KARL MANNHEIM

Apparently, Karl Mannheim was of interest to American sociology late in the second period, especially by virtue of his work in the sociology of knowledge.[10] Wirth and Shils' English translation appeared under the title of *Ideology and Utopia* in 1936 (Mannheim 1936). That same year the original German version was reviewed in the *American Sociological Review,* and two years later the English translation was reviewed in the same periodical. Interestingly, the four relevant articles in sociology journals (from 1937, 1939, 1940, and 1941) were reprinted in Merton ([1945] 1968, chaps. 14, 15) and in Horowitz's collection of Mills's papers (Mills [1936] 1967, part 4). And Dahlke's "The Sociology of Knowledge" (1940) was based in part on Mannheim.

American sociology was also exposed to other dimensions of Mannheim's intellect. *Man and Society in an Age of Reconstruction* was reviewed in the *American Sociological Review,* 1940. (The original German text was reviewed in the same journal in 1936.) *The Diagnosis of Our Time* was examined in the *American Sociological Review* and *Social Forces* in 1944.

As in the case of Tönnies, no American endeavored to construct a general sociological theory along Mannheimian lines.

MAX WEBER

But by far the greatest European and German influence in the renewal and reorientation of American sociological theory was provided by Max Weber. Although he is cited in the Park and Burgess ([1921] 1924) text, is referred to with varying degrees of prominence in the general articles on German sociology just after the mid 1920s, and is accorded a substantial part of a chapter in Sorokin's 1928 theory text and an entire chapter in Abel's 1929 volume, his major impact is not evident until actual articles in 1934 and 1935.[11] Including those two, a total of fifteen articles on Weber were published in the sociological literature up to 1949. Four appeared in the *American Journal of Sociology* (1939, 1944–48), four in the *American Sociological Review* (1938, 1947), one in *Social Forces* (1934), five in *Social Research* (1934, 1935, 1944, 1949), and one in the *Review of Politics* (1942).

Books afford further documentation of the interest in Weber. A major portion of chapter 25 of House 1936 was devoted to Weber. Hans Speier's entry on "Max Weber" in the *Encyclopaedia of the Social Sciences,* and Parsons's *The Structure of Social Action,* with its several chapters on Weber, were published in 1937.[12] Barnes and Becker 1938 *Social Thought from Lore to Science* included an analysis of Weber (768–73, 894–901). Parsons (1948a) also published a chapter on Weber.

Just after the mid 1940s and the end of World War II, three English translations of Weber were published. Gerth and Mill's selected translations *From Max Weber: Essays in Sociology* (with three introductory chapters) appeared in 1946 (Weber 1946); Henderson and Parsons's translations *Max Weber: The Theory of Social and Economic Organization* (including five introductory chapters) in 1947 (Weber 1947) and Shils and Finch's translation of *The Methodology of the Social Sciences* (with Shils's foreword) in 1949 (Weber 1949).

These translations were reviewed in chronological sequence. Reviews of the first appeared in the *American Sociological Review* and the *American Journal of Sociology* in 1947 and in *Social Forces* in 1948. Those of the second were published in the *American Sociological Review* and *Social Forces* in 1948. And those of the third were in the 1950 volumes of the *American Sociological Review* and *Social Forces.*

Important too is the fact that the (two) Gerths published a bibliography on Weber in *Social Research* (1949).

Finally, for an understanding of American sociological interest in Weber, two circumstances may have some importance. First, refugee intellectuals from Germany (e.g., Gerth, Salomon, Speier, Honigsheim, Delatour, and Bendix) were prominent in the Weber Scholarship. Furthermore, Weber's acceptance in the United States surely benefited from the intellectual activity of such emigre figures as Arendt, K. Wolff, S. Riemer, Lowe, Lederer, and C. Meyer. Only Benoit-Smullyan and Levi-Strauss can be cited as playing a similar role in the case of Durkheim. Clearly, Weber seemed to have the advantage in the support of his exiled countrymen in America.

A second condition bears mentioning, though its significance may be disputable. Major articles on Durkheim frequently took issue with many of his major epistemological-methodological and/or social ontological views, whereas those on Weber seemed more generally to be presented in straightforward fashion without either positive or negative judgments being intruded.[13] Certain aspects, features, and ideas of Durkheim were adopted, but no American theorist ever tried to construct a general theory based fundamentally on Durkheimian premises or a Durkheimian frame of reference. However, four figures in American sociology developed their own versions of a social action frame of reference—which seems to have a substantial indebtedness to Weber—as a foundation of their own general theoretical orientations. The four were Talcott Parsons (American-born but with a German Dr. Phil.), Robert M. MacIver (Scottish-born and educated, who came to Columbia in 1927 after about a decade at the University of Toronto), Howard P. Becker (American-born and American-educated but with many German intellectual connections), and Florian Znaniecki (Polish-born and educated, with periodic stays in the United States and permanent residence after 1941).[14]

Although Parsons refers to Weber's purposive rationality in "'Capitalism' in Recent German Literature" (Parsons 1929, 32n. 27), his espousal of an action of orientation seems to be signaled first in his "Sociological Elements in Economic Thought" (Parsons 1935b, 414–53, 646–67). He uses the expressions *human action, human action in general,* and *human conduct in general* (e.g., 452, 660), notes that action is distinct from "behavior" and must "be analyzed in terms of some form of the scheme of the relation of means and ends" (421, and in footnote 7 on page 656 alludes to Weber's distinction of *wertrationales Handeln* from *zweckrationales Handeln* in *Wirtschaft und Gesellschaft,* chapter I. His commitment to a social action orientation is evident in *The Structure of Social Action* (Parsons [1937] 1968, 43–51), with an extended analysis of Weber's notions of action and social action (641–58 esp.).

Admittedly, MacIver's reliance on Weber seems considerably less conspicuous. Weber is the second most cited figure in his *Society* (1931c), although the references are predominantly to his work in the sociology of religion. Only one is to his *Gesammelte Aufsatze zur Wissenschaftslehre.* In his chapter on sociology in England, France, Italy, Germany, and the United States (MacIver 1931d), he ascribes considerable importance to German views, with one page allotted to Max Weber and another to Alfred Weber. Max Weber was the most frequently cited author in his *Social Causation* ([1942] 1964). Of the utmost significance is MacIver's English rendering of a passage ([1942] 1964, 174) that derives from *Wirtschaft und Gesellschaft,* chapter 1, section 1, and that explicitly refers to "social action . . . understandable in terms of typical motives and typical meaningful intentions of the acting individuals." The passage and its context would seem to make it highly likely that MacIver must have known and understood Weber's typology of social actions and Weber's general methodological stance. *Social Causation* also contains MacIver's own social action formulation (330–31).

Howard P. Becker was thoroughly conversant with Max Weber's intellectual stance from at least the time of his early career as a doctoral student at the University of Chicago. Both his preliminary extensive draft of his doctoral dissertation and his more narrowly drawn and accepted version directly refer to Weber's ideal type as an important methodological foundation of his own inquiry.[15] His *Systematic Sociology* (Becker 1932b) contains his own English translations of Weber's definition of action and social action, and his "Culture Case Study and Ideal-Typical Method, with Special Reference to Max Weber" (Becker 1934a, 399–405) was the first full article on Weber in American sociological periodicals. With his 1945 chapter "Interpretative Sociology and Constructive Typology," his commitment to a substantially Weberian social action orientation seems relatively indisputable. Admittedly, the conceptual components of Becker's own scheme are eclectically derived.

Of all of the exponents of the social action orientation, Znaniecki is the least informative about the sources of his views and the only one on whom a Weberian influence cannot be documented. His 1927 article contains his first reference to the social action stance—apparently also the first reference generally in American sociology—but it is virtually devoid of documentation. His *The Method of Sociology* (1934), a substantial expansion of the 1927 article, alludes only once specifically to Weber and his sociology of religion (206). *Social Actions* (1936), which provides a full development of all of the components of his social action orientation, includes three references to Weber (673, 713, 715), but not one is to *Wirtschaft und Gesellschaft* or to *Gesammelte Aufsatze zur Wissenschaftslehre*.

However, Znaniecki's basic views and concepts in his *The Method of Sociology* (1934) suggest that he had a relatively intimate and detailed grasp of late-nineteenth-century German neo-idealism and Neo-Kantianism in general and of Dilthey, Windelband, and Rickert in particular—all significant as antecedents of Weber's theoretical stance. Znaniecki (1934) asserts the following:

1. Concrete reality is illimitable or inexhaustible, in the sense that a complete representation can never be given (8-11), as Weber also insisted.
2. Knowledge in the social realm may be oriented toward the nomothetic-generalizing or to the idiographic-individualizing (or historical), as Windelband and Rickert had proposed (21–26; cf. 130) and as Weber also accepted.
3. Cultural data and systems are to be distinguished from natural data and systems (36–37), as many late-nineteenth-century German neo-idealists (e.g., Dilthey) would have held.
4. Such cultural data and systems are distinctive because they exist only as, and in, somebody's "active experience." (Clearly, this conception resembles, if it is not identical with, Dilthey's notion of *Erlebnis*—*erleben* is its verb form—implying the "dynamic" or "lived experience" of the cultural realm.)
5. One of the major modes of access to such "active experience" of indi-

viduals and groups is what Znaniecki terms "vicarious experience," the active re-creation and reexperiencing of someone else's activity in one's own imagination. (But see the seeming paradox discussed above in chapter 2.)

In summary, then, analysis reveals that three of the four theorists who are often classified as social action theorists were significantly indebted to or influenced by Max Weber. Indeed, the evidence strongly suggests that they were aware of and understood Weber's social action orientation as presented in his *Wirtschaft und Gesellschaft*. In the case of Znaniecki, analysis indicates his indebtedness to German neo-idealism (Dilthey) and Neo-Kantianism (Windelband and Rickert), an intellectual indebtedness shared by Weber in his formulation of his own position.

WEBER AND AN AMERICAN SOCIAL ACTION ORIENTATION

Obviously, it is one thing to show Weber or his major intellectual antecedents to be associated with the emergence and adoption of an American position that can be termed "social action" theory, but another thing to indicate that the content of such social action theory is, indeed, essentially the same as Weber espoused. Consequently, it becomes necessary to examine the individual views of Parsons, MacIver, Znaniecki, and Becker to ascertain just what the basic commonalities of the American social action orientation are. Eight such major, common features can be identified.

Consciousness

Deriving its philosophic antecedents most directly from subjective idealism, the social action orientation holds that human activities are distinguished by their issuance from consciousness. Action is more than mere behavior. Human beings do not merely behave or react as objects in nature: They act with some awareness of what they are doing. To use MacIver's ([1942] 1964) expression, people are part of the realm of conscious being (272). They are "in some degree aware of what they are doing and . . . are in some sense purposive in doing it" (15).[16] By contrast, Parsons avoids the use of the term *consciousness* as such, but it seems to be implied. He notes that his action frame of reference is subjective in the sense that phenomena are dealt with as "they appear from the point of view of the actor" (Parsons 1937; Parsons [1937] 1968, 46, 733). Most importantly, the actor, as opposed to being a mere object in nature, is an ego, a self, and has a mind (Parsons [1937] 1968, 47). In Znaniecki's case, the "humanistic coefficient" is the crucial notion. It signifies that human beings are characteristically "conscious and active beings," developing a domain of active (not passive) experience (Znaniecki 1936, 38, 36–37, 71). Lastly, Becker—like Parsons—is also indirect in reference to consciousness. But he does remark that the action orientation requires that the investigator impute to the actor a "certain 'state of mind'" (Becker 1950, 196), which is to be understood as a naturalistic product (196n.). Becker's appropriation of Mead's notion of the significant symbol and the latter's conception of the acquisition of the self through role taking and role playing suggests, of course, the concomitant development of mind and consciousness as Mead envisaged (Becker 1950, 11–17 and footnotes).

Subject/Object Distinction

This consciousness or awareness involves a subject/object distinction. Human beings as subjects are aware of initiating activity in relation to certain (external) desired or valued objects in the immediate environment or situation.[17] In addition, some of these objects in the situation of action are, of course, other persons. Thus fully analyzed (i.e., envisaged reciprocally), any human being is both a subject and an object of activity in a genuine social situation, that is, a situation involving a plurality of individuals. So MacIver (1931c) notes that each individual sees the others as part of the total environment (527). But their relationship is distinctively social only because each conducts himself or herself toward the other in mutual awareness, that is, in "ways determined by their recognition of one another" as subjects or potential subjects of action (6–7, 26, 43). This (social) subject/(social) object differentiation is also unmistakably evident in Znaniecki's (1936) distinction of the (social) agent (actor, or subject) and the (social) object whose response or reaction is necessary to the attainment of the end of the (social) agent (77–85, 105–110). Most importantly, Znaniecki had earlier argued that "social" has its ultimate grounding in the agent's or subject's experience that "the object of an action is himself as a conscious and active subject" (48). In Becker's (1950) view, any actor is a valuing subject who may value another as object as well as be a valued object to that other, or alter (6–17). Irrespective of the terms used, subject and object are never separated in actual experience, and, accordingly, any reference to one must necessarily imply a correlative reference to the other (e.g., MacIver 1931c, 533).

Purpose or Intention

Associated with these states of consciousness of self, other(s), and the external situation is the development of intention or the formation of purpose. All four sociologists more or less concur. Parsons ([1937] 1968) proposes the concept of end as a future state of affairs that the actor regards as desirable and seeks to attain by his or her purposive intervention or nonintervention in the situation (44, 49, 731). Generally, an end entails an intentional effort to bring about a state of affairs differing from the initial state of the situation, but it may also mean a conscious effort to maintain the present situation (44, 75). MacIver ([1942] 1964) prefers the notions of objective and motive to separate out different aspects of interaction. The former signifies a goal objectively as the outcome of an anticipated modification in the situation exterior to the agent, whereas the latter refers to an end subjectively in terms of internal satisfactions to the ego (16–17, 195–96, 202–3, 230–31). Although Znaniecki does not formally and explicitly define an end or purpose, he implies its existence as the outcome of the successful influencing of the action of others. For instance, Znaniecki notes that the "agent may at first define the expected reaction rather vaguely and, as he become more clearly conscious of his aim, redefine the object, change instruments, readapt the method" (Znaniecki 1936, 106). Becker also fails to define ends or purposes, though he clearly presupposes their existence in action. (Note his classificatory use of Thomas's doctrine of the four wishes in this context; Becker 1950, 35.)

Means or Instrumentality

Because a purpose can ordinarily be realized only with some modification in the external situation, social action theory must necessarily introduce some notion of means or instrumentality. Insofar as a particular subject or actor is concerned, the situation contains, or potentially contains, both aids and agencies as well as obstacles and hindrances to the achievement of purpose. For Parsons ([1937] 1968), the means are those aspects or components of the situation over which the actor has control and that he can (and presumable does) use to gain his end (44, 49, 732–30). Emphasizing objectively tested and confirmed utility, MacIver's ([1942] 19364) notion of means involves a "set of techniques or controls, derived from the apparatus of a particular civilization, and applied to . . . specific objectives" (331). More precisely, means are differentiable into technique, procedure, and instrument. As "a specific formula [involving both a mode of procedure and an appropriate instrument or instruments] for obtaining a specific result," a technique is a part of the technological order, which depends particularly on the various relations of external biophysical nature (283). Znaniecki (1936) introduces the two notions of "social instrument" and "social method." The former is a vehicle for influencing the social object, whereas the latter is "the particular way in which a social instrument or complex of instruments" is used to influence the social object (73). As noted earlier, Becker is eclectic. He accepts Znaniecki's differentiation of "social instrument" and "social method." But he also endeavors to classify means in terms of economy of effort, efficiency, and absence of undesirable consequences, as dictated by the end, as governed by tradition, and as fused with ends (as is signified in Weber's expedient rationality, sanctioned rationality, traditional nonrationality, and affective nonrationality, i.e., Becker's rendition of Weber; Becker 1950, 22–32).

Conditions

However, certain aspects or components of the situation, the conditions, are taken as given or unchangeable. In accordance with his perspectivism, Parsons ([1937] 1968) defines the conditions as those aspects of the situation that the actor or subject believes she/he must accept as given and unmodifiable (44, 47). (Ordinarily, the biophysical environment is to be taken as a set of given conditions, i.e., unmodifiable from the point of view of the actor. But in late-twentieth-century culture, with its technology of mechanized earth-moving equipment and explosives, a mountain or a river may indeed be alterable. Furthermore, the external features of the physiognomy of an individual may not necessarily be taken as given, with the possibility of plastic surgery and available financial resources.) MacIver ([1942] 1964) seems less relativistic, for he refers to a "set of biophysical conditions, as relevant to and prerequisite for the particular action" (331). But subsequently he seems to acknowledge that such conditions are what they are only within the consciousness of the dynamic assessments of particular actors in a social situation, given the character of a particular culture with a certain kind or level of technology. Accordingly, he remarks that "even the biophysical conditions do nothing by themselves to create the social phenomenon" (331). For Znaniecki (1936), "conditions" refers more simply and broadly to the preexisting reality, the variety of objective features in the external situation in which action occurs (55). Yet, in view of what Znaniecki suggests later, what is taken as given also depends on the consciousness of the acting persons, which can vary with time and place. Becker avoids concern with "conditions."

Moral Norms or Rules

In genuinely social action, human beings are more or less regulated in their selection of means to ends, and of one end in relation to another, in a social situation, by moral rules, norms, standards, or principles. Parsons precisely, emphatically, and elaborately develops the nature of the normative component in his conceptualization of the action scheme, but MacIver and Znaniecki also point rather unmistakably in the same direction. In Parson's ([1937] 1968) analysis, a norm is a selective standard (in relation to means to ends or one end in relation to others) that is ideal in several senses (377, 396). Its reality is not exhausted by its mere existence: It refers simultaneously to a desirable future state of empirical affairs—outside of itself—and to the present subjective state of the actor, such that he or she regards himself or herself as obliged to act in order to realize the desirable future state of affairs (396). Realization of what the norm entails is contingent both on the individual's effort and on the conditions in which she or he acts (396). It is the individual's decision and will as reflected in an effort to overcome resistances or obstacles that constitute the creative or voluntaristic component of action (396). Although MacIver ([1942] 1964) refers directly to a "set of social relations" as part of the social action orientation, that set contains the social rules or norms (274n.). In his earlier *Society* (1931c), he was extensively preoccupied with the nature of social codes and the variety of rules involved. The considerable variation in empirical social circumstances means that individuals must select a rule from the normative code, interpret, and apply it (299). Thus, invocation of a rule occurs in relation to consciousness and choice, that is, dynamic assessment (329–30). Although Znaniecki (1934) analytically separates the study of social action from inquiry into social relations (which necessarily entails moral rules), investigation of persisting or recurrent social action does require consideration of moral rules. Social relations can be orderly only if the actors involved reciprocally recognize and accept certain duties that are specified in a set of norms or rules (114). In his *Social Actions* (1936, 633) Znaniecki obliquely acknowledges the relevance of rules for social actions by conceding that a concrete social action may deviate from a pattern prescribed by "the socially sanctioned norms."

In his *Through Values to Social Interpretation* (1950, 18–21), Becker notes simply that "conduct is always normative," though his many references to approvals and disapprovals do not involve specific, concrete rules as such. However, his efforts to differentiate his "sacred/secular" typology of societies in the 1950s invokes norms as a fundamental consideration. (See chapter 6.)

Choice

All of the prior constituents of social actions can lead to bona fide social action only if they are integrated by the operation of choice. A coherent line of activity relating means to ends, rules, and the conditions of the situation demands of any ego the exercise of a modicum of will, evaluation, or assessment. Without the inclusion of choice, action would be mere behavior.

Although Parsons ([1937] 1968) does not stress the role of choice in his frame of reference as he does the other components, it is unmistakably and indispensably present. So he alludes to the "choice of alternative means to the end," the "choice of ends," and the "choice of either ends or of means" (44, 61, 51). And, most importantly, the resort to social rules or norms manifestly presupposes "choice" or "selection" (77, 731, 48). Although it is true that Parsons emphasizes will in the sense of "effort," "resolve," or "determination" (in attempting to overcome or surmount the obstacles or resistances in achieving an end) as "voluntaristic," he also acknowledges will in the sense of "choice" or "selection" as a component of voluntarism (44).

Like Parsons, Znaniecki (1936) also refrains from making choice an explicit component of social action, though he also clearly assumes its role. He refers to the "agent . . . choosing the social object," the "choice of instrument," "choice of method," "choice . . . of social instruments and methods," all of which are calculated as nearly as possible (i.e., "chosen") to elicit a desired reaction or response from the social object (106, 74, 106 [cf. variants, 74, 75, 104]; 83).

Of all the action theorists, MacIver is the most explicit and extensive in his analysis of the role of choice, which he terms "dynamic assessment." Social conduct is willed activity consciously oriented to the presence of others. It involves freedom so long as restraint is not total, so long as the actor can select among some alternatives. MacIver ([1942] 1964) cautions that freedom is the "choice between alternatives, not the choice of what the alternatives shall be" (241). Choice is, of course, exercised within a means-ends relationship in the situation. What is sought is partly a reflection of society's value system and in part that of the actor's in relation to her or his own distinctive being as an organism, personality, (social) actor, and bearer of culture (see 241, 296). The alternatives he envisages and reviews are "those that have some weight with him" and some relevance to his wants or desires in relation to a "preview of their respective consequences" (240–41). The actual process of decision (i.e., the dynamic assessment) involves an anticipation of a future state of affairs as based on two alternatives: (1) the course of events occurring external to his own activity and existing, enduring, or emerging if he does not intervene, and (2) the change to be introduced by his own activity. Accordingly, the dynamic assessment involves a predictive judgment entailing a double contingency: "If this is done, this consequence will (or is likely to) follow and if this is not done or if this other thing is done, this other consequence will (or is likely to) follow" (297).

Once the decision is made, certain aspects of the external situation are transformed from mere externality into subjective relevancies as means, vehicles, accessories, obstacles, conditions, limitations, and costs in the attainment of the dominant desire or values (297, 293). Indeed, all of the

components of social action are such only as "they are subjectively apprehended and [differentially] assessed" and thus weighed and weighted (332).

Interestingly, Becker was the only one of the four theorists who
resisted the acknowledgment of choice as an indispensable feature of the
social action orientation. Indeed, his preference for Znaniecki's "definition
of the situation" as opposed to MacIver's "dynamic assessment" may have
been based on the former's apparent neutrality on the issue of choice
(Becker 1950, 195n.). Interestingly, he does cite MacIver's presentation of
the "free will versus determinism" controversy (MacIver [1942] 1964,
240–41).

The Methodological Indispensability of Subjective Motivational Imputation

Clearly, Parsons, MacIver, Znaniecki, and Becker envisage the study
of action and social action as requiring a distinctive methodological access,
which has been termed *Verstehen* in German traditions. Unfortunately, not
all of them are entirely explicit about their positions. Parsons ([1937] 1968),
for instance, declares that the sciences of action require a combination both
of *Verstehen* and the "observation of 'behavior'" (764–65, 765n), but he
does so after having raised major opposition to Weber's position (748–53).
Without further elaboration, which Parsons does not provide, the reader is
unable to be sure what Parsons means. In MacIver's ([1942] 1964) view,
"imaginative reconstruction" follows external observation and the resort to
statistical analysis and other methods common to all of the sciences. Using
direct testimony and other than direct evidence, it requires the researcher to
project him- or herself into the situation "as assessed by others" (39; also
264, 174–67). Znaniecki's (1934) "vicarious experience is active personal
experience" in which an agent recreates or reproduces in her or his imagination the activity of another person as it and its results appear to that other
person (167–68). It, too, may involve putting oneself in the place of another
(169). In Becker's (1950) "interpretation," the interpreter puts himself "in
the place of the actor as best he can" and, based on increasingly refined
models of motivation (which extend beyond the "sense data directly given in
the immediate situation"), attempts to infer the outcome of conduct (191–94,
197, 198).

Significantly, three of the four allude to the necessity of the inquirer's
"putting himself in the place of the other" or subject. The resemblance to
Dilthey's *Hineinversetzen* is evident, for references to Dilthey otherwise are
provided (but none to Cooley). In such other methodological respects as
concern for causal adequacy (or adequate causation) and objective possibility, Becker seems to approximate Weber's stance most closely (Becker
1950, 110ff; 97, 108, 172–74, esp. 195n.92, 262–62, 282).

RETROSPECTIVE

Undeniably, Max Weber exercised a preeminent influence in the emergence and rise of an action and social action frame of reference or orientation in American sociological theory in the late 1930s and throughout the 1940s. References, acknowledgments, citations, and basic premises adopted suggest that for Becker, MacIver, and Parsons the ideas of Max Weber were fundamental. In Znaniecki's case, the views of Dilthey, Windelband, and Rickert—significant predecessors and contemporaries of Weber—were important. Interestingly, only Becker invoked Weber's four types of social action as part of his sociological point of departure. Admittedly, the actual concepts and vocabulary of each of the four figures varied extensively. But basically the major ideas were all accurately characterizable in terms of consciousness, a (social) subject/object dichotomy, means, ends, conditions, norms, voluntarism (choice), and the (methodological) indispensability of subjective motivational imputation.

SUMMARY OF PART III

As indicated above, Weber was only one of the European figures whom the literature in American sociology construed as a potentially important source for the intellectual renovation of American sociology and sociological theory. Periodicals (*AJS, PASS, SF*), textbooks, monographs, and histories of the discipline (e.g., Sorokin's *Contemporary Sociological Theories,* House's *The Range of Social Theory,* Abel's *Systematic Sociology in Germany, Encyclopaedia of the Social Sciences,* Barnes and Becker's *Social Thought from Lore to Science,* Barnes, Becker, and Becker's *Contemporary Social Theory,* Gurvitch and Moore's *Twentieth Century Sociology,* and Barnes's *Introduction to the History of Sociology*) displayed a major interest in European social scientists and sociologists. They included Durkheim, Pareto, Marx, Tönnies, Simmel, Mannheim, and Weber. Of the seven, the predominant interest lay in Durkheim and Weber. But in neither case can it be said that any American sociologist developed a full-fledged Durkheimian or Weberian general sociological theory. Still, Weber did seem to provide the primary inspiration for a domestic version of an action or social action frame of reference (for Becker, MacIver, and Parsons).

Significantly, Blumer's symbolic interactionist social psychology (of chapter 9) exhibits some startling similarities with the social action frame of reference. Though Blumer's stance emerged ostensibly from pragmatist philosophy, it revealed a pronounced subjective- idealist bent. Its concern resided in the consciousness of the individual actor. It conveyed a strong means- ends orientation. And it was emphatically voluntaristic and, as against the then- current positivism, it insisted on an independent or autonomous methodological stance. Still, Blumer was never able to transform his social psychological orientation into a general sociological theory.

Manifestly, too, Freudian, behaviorist, and gestaltist orientations from psychiatry and psychology never were able to achieve satisfactory formulation as general sociological theories. Thomas and Ogburn employed certain notions from psychoanalysis. Bernard and Lundberg extensively resorted to behaviorism. But general theorists resisted and rejected their efforts.

Apparently, the intellectual impact of culture from cultural anthropology had the most far- reaching effects of any of the external academic disciplines on sociology. It substantially weakened the influence of biology and psychology and effectively undercut hereditarian and eugenicist claims. Still, a thoroughgoing culturalism was resisted. No sociologist ever developed a comprehensive macrocultural or culturological theory (though Ogburn and Willey were suspected of having such sympathies). Interestingly, history was far less influential, in spite of the special efforts of Howard P. Becker to create a historical sociology, if not to develop a historical sociological theory.

Demonstrably, then, potential external, and thus discontinuous, influences never were able to achieve actualization in theory. Indeed, the same conclusion can be drawn for the potentialities within sociology itself. Park did develop a distinctive dualistic (ecological- moral) stance essentially predicated on a cyclical process theory of social change. It won adherence from a number of his students, but its formulation was insufficiently rigorous and systematic to warrant characterization as a general theory. On the other hand, Becker and Sorokin elaborated what might be termed "directionally variable" or "reversible" analytical schemes for the macro- or general study of social change. Clearly they aimed to offer alternatives to the variant evolutionary notions of social change. But they failed to win major support from their colleagues. Their failure, and the failure of other potential stances, to win any substantial number of adherents and to be formulable as general theory allowed the influence of Park and his students (who developed a quasi- theory or a sociological orientation rather than a full- fledged theory) to remain more or less dominant throughout the period.

Now, finally, it is appropriate to confront more comprehensively than earlier the alleged foundationalism in American sociology and social and sociological theory. Part I had concluded that social evolutionism suffered its demise only in part by virtue of immediate intellectual defects, such as the assumption of instincts as basic to the doctrine of social forces that were crucial to the theory of social origins, the conceptual elasticity of adaptation as an argument for social structure, and the invariance claim of a unilinear sequence of stages of change.

Presently under review, part II sheds additional light on foundationalism. First, it reveals that although a general theory of culture was never satisfactorily developed, culture was defined and ascribed characteristics thoroughly compatible with foundationalism. Henceforth, culture would become an indispensable component of any future synthesis. During the 1930s and 1940s, it was construed as a necessary adaptation in relation to the (relatively constant) needs of a (common) biophysic human nature vis- a- vis the biophysical conditions of existence of any human aggregate. Though variable, it is characteristic of entire societies. Its major divisions or categories arise from the invariant character of a common human nature (of humankind, e.g., the popularity of Wissler's universal culture patterns). Each culture has its particular and specific time- and space- bound features, but sociologists (including theorists) conceived of culture generically in terms of asserted generalized, abstract, universal characteristics. (See chapter 7.)

Second, the potentiality for a renewal of interest in modern history as a source of data for modern societies was never achieved, because the most likely protagonist from history,Teggart, was misrepresented by sociologists and disputed the features and bases of foundationalism in sociologists's assumptions about the nature of social change. He could and did show that each of the major assumptions of sociologists' macrotheory of change had its origins in (and carried with it certain metaphysical baggage from) Western intellectual thought. In effect, he rejected the foundationalism underlying the concepts of social dynamics and thus was himself subject to rejection. (See chapter 7.)

Third and finally, the psychological candidates for foundationalism—freudianism, behaviorism, gestaltism, and symbolic interactionism—all failed to become sufficiently intellectually comprehensive to provide a foundation for general theory.[18] The grounds of rejection suggest many of the criteria of sociological foundationalism. In an even broader sense, the several stances represent actual examples of the continuing effort to use different types of reconstructed conceptions of human nature to develop the bases of a general theory. The rejection of psychoanalysis, and especially behaviorism, and the acceptance of symbolic interaction (and the formulation of a social action frame of reference) testify to the significance of voluntaristic nominalism as foundational in any future generalized synthesis. Presumably, therefore, the analysis of the next chapter, dealing with the assumptions entering into the concept of the group in the second period, should be very revealing!

PART IV: SUMMARY RETROSPECTIVE AND PROSPECTIVE

Chapter 11

The Concept of the Group:
An Analytical Summary

Although American sociologists before World War I made considerable use of the notion of the group, the term was not a central or prominent feature of their sociologies.[1] For their successors after World War I, the reverse became the case. The group increasingly moved into a central and often conspicuous position in their sociologies. Indeed, the group frequently was their sociological point of departure.

Unfortunately, two major difficulties obstruct easy inquiry into the concept of the group after 1915. On the one hand, antagonism to personal systems of theory apparently reduced the number of acknowledged general systems published. On the other, the shift from general sociologies to introductory expositions of the field meant that many subjects, especially the more abstract and abstruse, were treated more schematically, fragmentarily, or incompletely.

Nevertheless, a determined attempt will be made below to summarize the results of the study of the group in terms of the same analytical classificatory scheme as was used in *Founding Theory of American Sociology* (Hinkle 1980; see chapter 1 above). The actual point of departure is the conception of the (known) social as inter- and/or multipersonal relations and activities that persist and become structured (i.e., a group; see chapter 1).

In addition, it must be understood that the classificatory endeavor below is undertaken in full recognition of an intellectual context in which the group was more or less distinguished from other "near social" phenomena, such as the plurality, category, or aggregate, by the late 1930s. That context involved a shifting range of arguments of evolutionary naturalism to ascertain what demarked human association from various levels and kinds of animal association. Although the formulations varied considerably, they tended, in the mid to late 1930s, to gravitate to the view that for the human group to be fully and typically a group, that is, to have organization or structure as considered in chapter 3, certain minimum requirements, such as the following, would have to be satisfied:

1.   It would have to be based on a collection, plurality, or aggregate of human individuals (at least some of whom are) in immediate, spatial contact, juxtaposition, or proximity.
2.   It would have to possess a basic means of communication (i.e., language).
3.   It would have to have transmitted a (past) fund of experience (i.e., culture) from an earlier, older generation to a current, younger generation.

CRITERIA FOR CLASSIFYING OR CHARACTERIZING THE GROUP

Two sets of criteria are crucial in the nature of the group: (1) the social as a form of reality as, or as not, an extension of other forms of reality (materialism vs. idealism); and (2) the nature of the relation of part to part and to the whole in the social as an (aggregative) derivative or (holistic) emergent (nominalism vs. realism; the analytical classificatory scheme in chapter 1).

Materialism and Idealism as Characterizing Terms in the Nature of the Group

In a monistic social or sociologically materialistic conception of the group, the group's basic components, elements, factors, conditions, or causes are essentially explicable, directly or by extension, in terms of matter, matter in motion, or energy, as something physical or chemical (e.g., electrical impulses, gland secretions, organic needs, instincts, reflexes in relation to the biophysical environment, struggle, survival, adaptation). (On the basis of what is included in this general definition of materialism, a further division into physical (chemical) and organic (or organismic) types can be undertaken. In turn, this division permits further intellectual refinements but also creates certain problems.)

In direct opposition, a monistic social or sociological idealism asserts that the basic components, factors, or causes of the group are essentially accountable or interpretable, directly or by extension, in terms of mind, consciousness, feeling, will, ideas, intentions, symbols, meanings, values, communication, consensus/dissensus, etc. (In turn, idealism can be divided into rational and nonrational [or romanticist], as well as subjective and objective, types.)

However, the ontological positions of American sociological theory have not ordinarily been cast in monistic terms. Instead, they are dualisms, involving a combination of the main features of materialism and idealism, or pluralisms, involving one or more subdivisions of the other of the two main realms. Because virtually all sociologists of the second period either explicitly or implicitly accepted a division between the physical- chemical and life or the organismic domains, along with differentiations among the personality- self, social- societal, and the cultural domains, the predominant social ontological positions were pluralisms. In terms of emphasis, cruciality, or centrality of the causes or factors, three positions seem to result: predominantly materialist, relatively balanced materialist- idealist, and predominantly idealist. (See section C.1. of the classificatory periodizing scheme in the Appendix; also Hinkle 1980, 62.)

Nominalism and Realism in the Nature of the Group

In addition, it is important to acknowledge the dispute over the question of the reality of the parts in relation to one another and to the whole as a whole. Nominalism, which derived from medieval philosophy, had argued that the concept, category, or logical universal (*universalia*) had no reality apart from the (composite summary of the) characteristics or properties of the particulars (or *singuli*) to which it refers. Reality resides in the particular (or *singuli*). As applied to the notion of the group—that is, as social nominalism—it signifies either that the group as a whole has no reality in itself or that whatever reality it does possess is acquired derivatively on the basis of the features of the particulars (or individuals) that are conceived to form the aggregate.[2] (In founding sociological theory, the group was prevailingly conceived of according to some variant of social nominalism.)

Conversely, realism had argued that the concept, category, or logical universal represents something different from, and organizes the properties or characteristics of, the particulars to which it refers. Reality resides in the universal, the idea, ideal, the logical whole. As applied to the group—that is, as social realism—it signifies that the group as a whole has a reality different from, if not more than or greater than, the sum of the particulars of which it is composed. The whole exists as an emergent of association or interaction and possesses a reality in and of itself (e.g., Durkheim). (See section C.2. of the classificatory scheme in the Appendix; also Hinkle 1980, 62.)[3]

A PROPOSED CLASSIFICATION OR CHARACTERIZATION OF THE GROUP

A Predominant (Social or Sociological) Materialism

As noted above, no theorist can be argued to be an ontological monist. Indeed, the most extreme (pluralist) position that can be identified is a predominant (social or sociological) materialism (or its opposite, an idealism). Lundberg and Ogburn articulate views that seem to be identifiable as predominantly materialist, albeit for different reasons. Both strongly emphasize the reality of (external) behavior and deemphasize or significantly reduce the role of consciousness. Admittedly, both adopt relatively vague conceptions of the group. One seems, in effect, to endorse a social nominalism, and the other a social realism.

For Lundberg, the human group involves a plural number of human beings who behave as a whole, or collectively, and toward whom others so behave, as opposed to the single units of which it is composed. The constituent units exhibit certain specific likenesses (and differences) as a class or category, one of which is their spatial proximity (or aggregation). Finally, as a group it displays observable interaction, though Lundberg also alludes to social behavior or interhuman behavior.

Most importantly, this whole or collectivity is such objectively, in terms of externally observable behaviors by which it is adapted or adjusted to its situation, habitat, or environment. Habit is the crucial behavioral unit. As aggregatable among a plurality of human beings, habit is the basis of such sociocultural phenomena as customs, folkways, mores, and institutions.

But in a very fundamental sense all social behaviors, all groups, are actually forms of physical materiality: They are electron- proton systems or types of energy transformation that are constantly rearranging themselves on various levels or in various behavior configurations (Lundberg 1939b, 203, 204, 210). What this notion thus assumes is that the group is reducible to an aggregate of organisms whose behaviors depend on the physical and chemical nature of the nervous system.

(Parenthetically, Lundberg does acknowledge the "existence" of consciousness, presumably arising as a concomitant of the human development of speech- language symbol systems. He suggests that entities claimed to exist through consciousness are to be made objectively verifiable and verified by social science, especially sociology. If they cannot be so demonstrated, they deserve consignment to oblivion.)

In a more immediate sense, social phenomena consist of forms of behavior which adapt a group or aggregate of individuals to its environment just as individual forms of behavior adapt an individual to his/her environment. The specific organism adapting to its environment is thus the immediate model for the human group or aggregate, and thus, in effect, an organismic materialism is presupposed. (The habit as the result of a conditioned response, or reflex, presupposes a certain kind of life with a nervous system.)

Notwithstanding the analysis just offered, Lundberg rejects the nominalist notion of the group in which the whole becomes merely a summary aggregate of individuals (Lundberg 1939b, 163–73). For him, group and individual are equally real or equally figurative (155, 174). Indeed, his declaration that the group as an organization of (interrelated) individual behaviors is as susceptible of observation and description in its own terms and at its own level as is the behavior of an individual (as an organization of cells and organs) may seem tantamount to realism (174). However, he also denies validity to epigrammatic statements about the (social) whole's being something more than and different from the sum of its parts (195). At best, he is a reticent, perhaps "closet," social realist.

In his *Sociology* text (coauthored with Nimkoff) Ogburn advances a notion of the group with the same kind of ambiguity as that of Lundberg. He conceives of a group as "two or more individuals who come together and influence one another" (Ogburn and Nimkoff 1940, 250). But it is also evident that Ogburn presupposes that any such group (and certainly any in the expanded sense of a society) will possess a culture. Interestingly, this prior existence of culture and its characteristics virtually implicates a sociocultural realism and a prevailing (behavioral) materialism for the position taken in *Social Change.*

In *Sociology,* Ogburn has dichotomized culture into two domains: one of material culture involving humanly fabricated objects designed to facilitate adjustment to biophysical nature, and another of nonmaterial culture referring to socially established methods, techniques, responses, beliefs, and ideas (of various kinds, including those typically associated with "consciousness"). True, Ogburn argued that the two realms were necessarily ultimately interconnected, interrelated, and interdependent. But the former domain had a priority over the latter (as is required by the notion of "culture lag"). Manifestly, it is technique (as a form of behavior) in relation to material objects (which are frequently linked with adaptation to the conditions of existence and thus survival of the group) that provides the emphasis on objective materiality versus subjective ideality.

But it is also evident in his virtual impersonal determinism involved in the character of the structure and change of culture that also confirms that this domain of reality operates as does biophysical nature. Ogburn disavows the conception of culture as immediately and directly adaptive to geographical conditions or as reflective of a rational, purposive, or calculated adjustment. He rejects the role of the great man, with its assumption of exceptional hereditary endowments, as a vast exaggeration. Rather, he holds that present and future changes in a culture depend upon past development and accumulations. Once a particular stage of accumulation has been reached, "certain inventions if not inevitable are certainly to a high degree probable, given a certain [persisting] level of mental ability" (Ogburn [1922] 1950, 343). Social structure and change thus are crucially influenced by the material culture and the related adaptive nonmaterial culture, all of which tend to occur by an impersonal process akin to the impersonal regularities of biophysical nature and to entail Ogburn's version of social evolutionism.[4]

A More Balanced Materialism- Idealism

For Bernard, Hankins, and Chapin, (human) groups and societies are themselves the outcome of sociocultural evolution, which is in turn a derivative of a general evolutionary process in nature. These three theorists have been characterized as being committed to a "moderate" behaviorism that acknowledges the role of consciousness as being of some importance and that can, therefore, be said to represent a more or less balanced materialism-idealism. Admittedly, their conceptions of group (and/or society) are only rudimentarily elaborated.

Bernard defines a group as "people who respond to the same stimuli, either uniformly or diversely, in such a way as to cause their responses to supplement each other" (Bernard 1931, 467). A society is apparently a total aggregate group, that is, a group of smaller and/or larger groups (Bernard 1942, 853).

Although Hankins ignored the group as a basic concept, he defined a society in effect as the most permanent and comprehensive group in which individuals have membership. A society provides for organic reproducibility and maintenance. It is characterized by common territory, kinship relations, economic interdependence, political and cultural unity, and a pervasive consciousness of kind.

Chapin (1928) defines a group (apparently following Giddings's later views) as essentially a psychic phenomenon, as a "fluctuating equilibrium of interactions and interrelationships of individuals who are in contact" (225).

At any point in time, their interactions and interrelationships are more or less definable and describable in terms of oral or written traditions and, in modern societies, in terms of law (1928, 225–26). As conditions change, society undergoes a typical reaction pattern, which apparently includes conscious innovation by talented individuals. Interestingly, Chapin seems to have found considerable satisfaction in the apparent similarity between the societal reaction pattern and "the learning process of the individual" (228–29). That similarity may well be a further clue to his inclination to a social nominalism.

All of these theorists apparently envisage sociocultural evolution—out of which specific groups and societies emerge—as the outcome of (human) biopsychic evolution (of the human organism and a human nature entailing consciousness), which has occurred within the limits and possibilities of certain physical and chemical conditions. All three accepted the importance of habit (as the adaptive behavioral unit), the doctrine of psychic unity (i.e., the tendency of the human mind to respond similarly to certain external circumstances, especially biophysical nature), race, the quality and quantity of the human population, and the character of its physical, organic habitat.

Adaptation was a generally effective process operating at the sociocultural, psychic, and organic levels. Failure to adapt or the ineffectiveness of a change meant eventual elimination rather than survival (and selection). Bernard (1942, 450) especially emphasized selection, differentiating among natural, artificial, and cultural selections. Hankins (1928, 310–16) differentiated between societal and group selection. And as committed evolutionary naturalists, both rejected any notion of culture as autonomous and explicable in and of itself (Bernard 1942, 800; Hankins 1928, 402, 409–11).

Unlike Ogburn, Bernard, Hankins, and Chapin attributed major significance, within the broad range of individual differences, to the biogenetic characteristics of the exceptional person, his or her unique gifts, talents, or endowments in the production of sociocultural change. Critical in those endowments is the quality of consciousness as expressed in the mode of adaptive behavior that is transmitted and recurs as habit to become the foundational unit of culture.

In a broad sense, it must appear, therefore, that the quality of the whole, of the group, of the society and its culture, must depend on the quality of its parts or individuals—or the ratio of the exceptional to the ordinary and the mediocre. Thus, a kind of social nominalism seems to be presupposed.

In addition, such nonsocial evolutionists as Park and his students (e.g., Reuter and Hart and Hiler) also seem to be includable among those who had struck something of a balance between materialism and idealism.

Park and his students insist that the study of social phenomena must proceed by analysis of and equal attention to the two levels of the more or less unconscious ecological and the more or less conscious moral. It means, in effect, that humankind is to be understood as being both inside and outside of biophysical nature, as involved in physical organismic matter (materialism) and mind or consciousness (idealism).

Emeshed in the web of nature and implicated in struggle or conflict and competition (as envisaged by Spencer), human individuals are part of a natural order and economy. Thus, they find their proper niche within a competitive territorial or spatial distribution, along with other plants and animals of the habitat or geographical locale.

But persistent relationships among an aggregate of *Homo sapiens* will also reveal another facet of human nature: sympathy or altruism as opposed to an egocentric survival preoccupation. A conscious level of orderliness emerges. It is definable in Comte's terms and is organized through communication and consensus, rather than conflict and competition. Significantly, Park chose the term *accommodation* as an intermediate process—between conflict and assimilation—because it meant "acquired adjustments [of human beings] that are socially" rather than "biologically transmitted" (as is the case for adaptations; Park and Burgess [1921] 1924, 663–64). Out of communicative interaction, consensus develops, corporate action can result, and over time a common experience is transmitted; that is, a cultural or societal level can be identified. (Consult also Hinkle 1980, 308–11.)

It is of the utmost importance that Park, especially by the late 1920s, and his students tended to conceive of groups (including societies) as prevailingly operating at the conscious level, achieving consensus, and thus being able to engage in corporate action. The consensus that Park and his students envisage hardly seems possible without more or less conscious and deliberate choice on the part of the participants in the group. Accordingly, Park would seem to be oriented sociologically to a voluntaristic nominalism in which the social whole is what it is by virtue of the specific choices and decisions of the individual participants in the group. However, Park apparently conceived of himself as a social realist and endeavored to expound the contesting positions of (social) nominalism and (social) realism in considerable detail. Others joined in the debate later. The dichotomy was discussed and used by Park (Park and Burgess [1921] 1924, 36–41), Karpf (1932, 109), Wirth 1939b; but see Wirth 1956, 21–22), Sutherland and Woodward ([1937] 1940, 296–97), and Burgess (1945, 20–21).

The Ascent of Social Realism?

In contrast to social nominalism, social realism conceives the group to be a whole in and of itself—different from, sometimes more than, the mere summative characteristics of its individual members (Warriner 1956; Adler 1964). Modern social realism is less likely to be substantialist in character than its medieval predecessor. In modern terms (e.g., Durkheim), the group has no ultimately real substance that is not also in its individual members. But it is the association or interaction of its members that generates and maintains the group as a relatively transpersonal and impersonal category. Although the position was associated with idealism in medieval philosophy, it may also conceivably be oriented in the modern world to materialism and to either a humanistic or a positivistic methodology. The group tends to be envisaged as prior in time to any one individual whose outlook is molded by the historical experience of the whole. Although choice may not be denied, it is more likely to be conceived to have a more limited scope than in nominalism. Social realism is inclined to be holistic, collectivist, and at times deterministic.

Park is by no means entirely explicit about his own position in the conflict between social nominalism and realism. He writes that the "controversy between the realists and the nominalists reduces itself apparently to this question of the objectivity of [the social process and] social tradition and of public opinion" (Park and Burgess [1921] 1924, 39). As indicated above, Park does conceive of any concrete group as implicated in the social process, which is constituted of several subprocesses, some of which are explicable in terms of the sociological tradition typified by Spencer, and others in terms of that typified by Comte. If, indeed, Park regards himself as a realist, his effort to reinterpret Comte's notion of consensus through Dewey's conception of communication, as well as to use the latter to explain Durkheim's collective representations, is beset with difficulties.

Although he correctly refers to Comte's notion of social consensus in his early exposition (Park and Burgess [1921] 1924, 24–25), Park never explains—if he knows—that it refers to an impersonal, objective quality of the relation of one part of a coexisting social structure with another. Such consensus has nothing immediately to do with the achievement of personal understanding and consent among an aggregate of communicating individuals.[5] Accordingly, confusion arises when Park later introduces Dewey's notion of communication to argue that it involves not merely transmission of experience from one individual to another but also the creation of a common experience (36–37). Through communication, "experiences that are individual and private" can become (engender) "an experience that is common and public" (37). In turn, such a

> common experience becomes the basis for a common and public existence in which every individual, to a greater or less extent, participates and is himself a part. Furthermore, as a part of this common life, there

grows up a body of custom, convention, tradition, ceremonial, language, social ritual, public opinion . . . all that ethnologists include under the term "culture." (37)

Most particularly, Park misconstrues the basis of Durkheim's social realism by asserting that the communicative interactive process of Dewey is a "description of the process by which . . . [Durkheim's] collective representations come into existence" (38). Yet he is aware that collective representations are characterized by externality and constraint, which is, in turn, a manifestation of the distinctiveness of the domain of social or collective existence (39; as based on a quotation from Gehlke's translation). On a prior page (p. 34) Park refers to the "fermentation which association breeds" (i.e., collective ferment or effervescence), but he fails to indicate awareness of the fact that in Durkheim's later career the term *collective effervescence* signified a peculiarly heightened or intensified association or interaction elicited by unusual circumstances of crisis, shock, or upheaval.

The degree of objectivity and externality involved in Dewey's communication (38) is hardly comparable to that which arises in connection with collective effervescence. It is out of this unusual state of interaction that individual representations are synthesized and transformed into collective representations, because a collective experience or existence is created (or re- created) and appropriately symbolized. A collective consciousness and a collective conscience (entailing social norms or morality) also arise. This state of heightened interaction is indispensable for morality, because it is of such intensity and completeness that all minds are monopolized "to the more or less complete exclusion of egoism and the commonplace" (Durkheim 1953, 92). To forget oneself "for the common end" is to accept an impersonal or common good—one that is disinterested. It cannot be the good of a single individual or the mere aggregate of single individual goods (Durkheim 1953, 91). Such an emergent is not consistent with Dewey's (mere) communicative interaction or the public discussion of, and "consensus" arising from, individual ends or purposes. Park hardly envisaged his position in these terms, and thus he can scarcely be said to be a (Durkheimian) social realist.[6]

Interestingly, Faris (Park's Chicago colleague) might seem more appropriately to warrant the social realist designation. Faris (1937a) noted that, reminiscent of Durkheim's ideas, individual and social facts can be distinguished, but social facts are not obtained by mere addition. *Group* is not a name for an aggregation (98). Groups exist because they are experienced: Men recognize groups, they love groups, they lay down their lives for groups. "The group is not only a reality," but "a prior reality." It has its own level of existence, which it transmits as culture, especially in and through language. Like language, our mannerisms, customs, moral codes, folkways, mores, fashions, religious conceptions and practices, and public opinion are all collective phenomena. Society is a type of whole with new distinctive qualities appearing "when it acts as a whole" (97–101; for the social realism in Faris's conception of the group, see chapter 9). Curiously, Faris (with his considerable knowledge of philosophy) never used the terms *nominalism* or *realism*, but his choice of sociological vocabulary otherwise and the nature of his arguments seem to suggest an identification with social realism. Furthermore, he does not refer to Durkheim in the contexts containing the most explicit acknowledgment of many features of social realism.

It is, moreover, of some significance that the two textbooks most completely elaborating the features of groups during the second period (Krueger and Reckless 1931; Reuter and Hart 1933) do reject—either explicitly or implicitly—social nominalism. But they also fail to endorse social realism. For instance, Krueger and Reckless directly reject the notion that groups are only nominal collections of individuals, but also deny the validity of the "theory of the social mind" and the "organic analogy" (often associated with social realism), and though they acknowledge that "group relationships do bring control over the behavior of individuals" (Park is explicitly footnoted), they note that it only states the "function or effect of group contacts and does not reveal concretely the actual relations of individuals to groups" (Kreuger and Reckless, 1931, 79–81).

Admittedly, Reuter and Hart (1953) do assert that "society is something more than an aggregate of individuals" and their "sum," claiming that it is a "real, objective reality" (131). They also deny the claim that society and the group are illusions corresponding "to nothing real" and the nominalist declaration that the "only realities are individuals and relations of individuals" (131). Conversely, they declare that the unity of the social group is the same as that of all entities in nature: It is a bounded unity in organization and relationship of parts (132). In the case of human society, that unity in organization and relationship of parts is distinctively "based on consensus arrived at through communication" (133). That essentially repeats Park's use of Dewey to restate or reformulate Durkheim. But nowhere do they explicitly commit themselves to a social realism as such or provide integrated statements of characteristics of groups that signify an unquestionable social realism.

Unfortunately, most of the other textbook characterizations or inquiries into the nature of the group or the relationship of individual to group—excepting those examined earlier in this section—are so terse or cryptic that only conjecture can result. Nor are their expositions about commitment to general theoretical stances or positions on nominalism and realism especially illuminating.

But by the end of the 1930s, sociologists seemed inclined either to reject the relevance of the realist/nominalist distinction or to find a middle ground. In his "The Individual and the Group" in the symposium on that topic in May 1939 issue of the *American Journal of Sociology*, Wirth included a brief survey of the controversy over nominalism and realism in ancient and medieval philosophy and in modern sociological theory (Wirth 1939b; also Wirth 1956, 21–22). Wirth himself took the position that "the mainstream of sociological and social- psychological thought had forgotten" (rejected or ignored?) this issue "as to whether the individual or the group is the ultimate unit in terms of which social life" is to be analyzed (22). Rather, he claims that the focus of interest now lies in social interaction—though in the immediately preceding sentence he alluded to "social phenomena as complexes of meaningfully oriented actions of persons reciprocally related to one another" (22). Thus, Wirth opts for the first position as indicated in the first sentence of this paragraph (and adopts Weber's social action).

Sutherland and Woodward (1940) declared for the second position. They insisted that a "sociologist can find a fairly satisfactory middle-ground" that denies that a society is a 'real' group person having a 'group-mind'" or is "solely an aggregate of individual behavior" (297). One can pay attention to the "collective aspects of human behavior," but still not ignore "that in the last analysis group life can only be perpetuated through the behavior of individuals" (297). Cooley's position that the "individual and society are but different aspects of the same thing" is endorsed. "The person and the group are not identical but they are coexistent and interrelated" (297).

Nevertheless, Burgess 1945 involves social realism and nominalism. If the position is taken that society is a reality, that is, is organic (or a whole in itself) and "exists in interaction and the interests and intercommunication of its members" (i.e., in such social processes as "communication, collective representation and social control"), it represents social realism. Its illustrations are Comte with his notion of social consensus, Durkheim and collective representations, Simmel and the social forms of interaction, Weber and ideal types, Sumner with folkways and mores, Small and the group, Cooley and sympathetic introspection, and Park and collective behavior.

Conversely, if society is merely an aggregate or collection of individuals (who alone are real and) whose behavior and mental processes are constitutive of the group, the position is social nominalism. Burgess's examples are Aristotle, who posited a social instinct, Tarde and imitation, Giddings with his consciousness of kind, and (Floyd) Allport and his "prepotent reflexes."

Yet intellectual developments in sociological theory in the late 1930s and even later seem to suggest that the conceptions of realism and certainly nominalism inherited from the earlier years might, indeed, be too simplistic. The emergence of the social action orientation is relevant here.

Social Action, Symbolic Interaction, and Voluntaristic Nominalism:
A Predominant Idealism

Along with Thomas and Znaniecki, Ellwood (1925) anticipates the development of the predominant idealist stance in the mid 1930s. Although for Ellwood "the whole network of interaction and interrelations between individuals and groups of individuals" are of concern, it is the group or particularly the concrete group "rather than abstract society that is fundamental to sociological theory" (14, vi). Undeniably involving "interdependence of activity," the human group is especially distinguished by conscious relations, mental interaction, or interstimulation and response, "reciprocal consciousness on the part of the individuals in the group" (7, 8). Most important, such interaction is prevailingly coadaptive and entails the conscious pursuit of purposes or ends, in which the exercise of choice is apparently presupposed (73, 76–77).

Between the years 1930 and 1945—the period of the depression and World War II—interest in general theory revived and was especially expressed in the social action orientation (or frame of reference). This revival of concern with theory involved both (social) epistemological-methodological and ontological divisions. Within the former, both empirical- positivist and idealist- interpretive stances were present. Developments in social ontology were pluralistic, with some being predominantly behaviorist- materialist and others actionist- idealist. (See also Hinkle 1980, 311–12.)

Certainly, the interest in, and availability of, translations of European theorists (e.g., Durkheim, Pareto, Freud, Tönnies, Simmel, Mannheim, and M. Weber) were of considerable consequence. So, too, was the relocation of many refugee intellectuals and professors who were themselves theoretically trained and concerned (e.g., Gerth, Speier, von Hentig, Heberle). In addition, the increased importance of prestigious Columbia and Harvard Universities as centers of graduate training, each with theorists of major statue, played a role.

Although advocates of general theory can be found among the empiricist- positivists and behavioristic materialists (e.g., Lundberg), the major elaboration of theory came from the idealist- interpretivists. The articles of Columbia's Robert MacIver on social causation in the late 1920s are the first contribution. Others, such as Talcott Parsons (Harvard University), Howard P. Becker (University of Wisconsin), and Florian Znaniecki (later at the University of Illinois), also joined in the advocacy of the orientation, as explained in the previous chapter. Undeniably, some differences in commitment and terminology exist among the four, but they do tend to concur in the basic assumptions of the social action orientation or, more precisely, frame of reference (see chapter 10 above).

In envisaging the application of the social action orientation to a conception of the group, a number of implications emerge. But two are especially important. First, fundamentally, all adherents to the orientation also accept a pluralistic notion of social reality. Although all human beings as social actors are more or less conscious beings, they not only are conscious organisms in a world of other organisms, but their distinctive form of matter is also constrained by the laws or regularities of the larger physical universe. Certainly, this pluralism is evident in MacIver's exposition of the physical, organic, and conscious domains in his *Social Causation* ([1924], 1964, 24, 11–26) and in Parsons's *The Structure of Social Action* ([1937], 1968, 762ff.). Such notions are also implied in the arguments of Becker and Znaniecki. The realms of the physical and organic clearly are involved in the concrete objects of means and ends as conceived by all four theorists. Still, it is apparent that the domain of human actors is one of conscious subjects and objects whose interactions are symbolically mediated and interpreted as group members, the reality of which is defined substantially in the terms of idealism. But in its fullest sense that reality is pluralistic.

Second, perhaps even more crucial is the assumption that actors can and do make choices, evaluate, assess, select, et cetera, so that eventually consensus and common purpose are achieved with some degree of voluntarism. Obviously, choice is hedged, restrained, and circumscribed by all sorts of considerations and limitations, but some modicum is still operative. Each member is actually or potentially in possession of some minimum of choice as interactions occur in the course of defining, specifying, qualifying, and attaining some social end. Thus, the functioning of the group is peculiarly and creatively dependent on the individual members' choices, on consent or assent, on some actual or implied concurrence, agreement, or consensus. The conception of the group as a reality and a whole thus crucially depends on individual choices. It involves a peculiar nominalism, a voluntaristic nominalism.[7]

It is of major importance that symbolic interactionism reveals substantial congruence with the voluntaristic nominalism of the social action schema. Admittedly, Mead's comprehensive views seemed to involve a social realism, but Blumer's elaboration diverged. (Howard Becker's social action formulation also revealed, independently of Blumer, how Meadian views could be incorporated in an action schema.) In specifying intent or purpose, deliberation and planning to devise an appropriate means, and actual achievement of a goal as the phases of the act, Faris had provided clues for Blumer's alteration of Mead's own notions of its phases (as impulse, perception, manipulation, and consummation). Most importantly, Blumer followed Thomas in making meaning in action dependent on personal intention rather than on Mead's public, objective language symbols.

(And even when Blumer did use the term *symbol,* he tended to omit *significant* as a qualifying adjective.) Indeed, he in effect adopted Thomas's (individualistic "personal") "definition of the situation," which Blumer termed "interpretation." By the late 1950s, Blumer also recast Mead's "indication" to signify a process preparatory to, or an interruption of, action involving definition of goals, specification of task steps, determination of conditions, selection of means, and assessment of social approval or disapproval (Blumer 1962, 182, 183; Blumer 1969, 80, 81). Accordingly, Blumer had achieved a substantial congruence with the action orientation, with perhaps an even great individualistic- nominalistic emphasis.

Illuminating, both social action theorists and the primary exponent of symbolic interaction acknowledged Thomas as a common precursor. Blumer referred to and implicated Thomas's ideas significantly in his own position. MacIver ([1942], 1964, 37n.) cited Thomas and Znaniecki's "definition of the situation" as being the "closest" approximation to his own formulation of "dynamic assessment." In the decade or so following publication of *The Structure of Social Action* (1937), Parsons recognized the relevance of Thomas's 'definition of the situation" for his own schema (Parsons [1945] 1948, 37). Znaniecki was certainly aware of the linkage between his own action formulation and Thomas's and his own contribution in *The Polish Peasant in Europe and America.* Finally, Becker's own eclectic action scheme explicitly included components derived from Thomas.

In Thomas and Znaniecki's (1918–20) analytic schema, human activity typically involves a plurality of individuals in a situation that constitutes a problem to be resolved by subsequent individual or corporate action. But prior to such action, a "definition of the situation" must arise. This definition must be made consciously and more or less voluntaristically (i.e., must entail choice), for two basic reasons:

1. An indefinite plurality of actions is possible under given conditions and sets of attitudes. Thus, conditions must be selected, interpreted, and combined and one set of attitudes must predominate over the others so only one action is possible (1:68).
2. Each social situation is always concretely somewhat different and thus more or less new (combining human activities differently). Hence, the individual must consciously define it as basically similar to or dissimilar from past situations (1:69).

Definitions of the situation may be personal or social and are constituted of (internal) attitudes in relation to (external) objects (or socioculturally defined values). Personal and social definitions are likely to be in tension and actual conflict. Each individual's attitudes reflect his or her unique genetic, organic, psychic, and experiential circumstances and differ from those of others. Some attitudes include goals, ends, aims (e.g., the four wishes). Some values are, or can be, means. Attitudes begin (organically, hereditarily) in temperament and are necessarily subsequently consciously reconstituted as character components. In addition, the individual acquires or devises strategies or rules, which in their socially accepted forms regulate access to objects or values. Thomas's scheme emphasizes the possibilities of individual- to- individual conflict in the group and of the divergence of personal and social definitions of the situation. Its components anticipate in many respects the later social action orientation, with perhaps an even greater individualistic- nominalistic emphasis.

Blumer recognized the relevance of Cooley for explaining the development of the self, but neither he nor any of the social action theorists were apparently conscious of the action implications of Cooley's process of valuation as developed in the (relatively ignored) *Social Process* ([1918] 1966). Cooley's notion of the process identifies a subject oriented to an object or objects in a situation (283–85). Using a scale or hierarchy of values, the subject compares, weighs, organizes, integrates, and chooses among the objects to solve a problem (283, 289–91, 311, 312, 331, 332, 338). What works or seems to fit or integrate the situation is the basic criterion of choice (284; Cooley [1909] 1962, 121).

Valuation seems to imply consciousness, reflection, choice, and purposive or ends- oriented conduct. Admittedly, the process must be conceived within the context of Cooley's analysis of suggestion, choice, and moral judgment (Cooley [1902] 1964, 51–80, 358–69). He certainly recognizes the nature and function of principles, rules, or standards in social conduct (Cooley [1922] 1964, 287–88, 295, 382). Though he explicitly invoked the notion of ends, he only infrequently used means- ends as such (Cooley [1909] 1962, 261).

The significance of voluntarism (and, more fully, the voluntaristic nominalism) of the social action orientation is most decidedly not peculiar to the second period of sociological theory in American sociology. Analysis of the social theory of the previous founding period of American sociology revealed that it was also a characteristic and distinguishing feature of the years 1881–1915 (Hinkle 1980, 290). For early American theorists in sociology, both the structure of the group and the introduction and dissemination of the new in social change are held to be "crucially a matter of multi- and/or inter- individual choice, will, decision, or volition" (Hinkle 1980, 291). Unfortunately, the fragmentary and incomplete character of many of the expositions of the textbooks used in the present study meant that the authors failed to speak to the issue at all or did so ambiguously (e.g., Park, Reuter and Hart, and Hiller in relation to "consensus"). True, Max Weber was a crucial figure for at least three of the four social action theorists. Accordingly, essential concordance, if not lineal continuity, exists in a major assumptional strand of theory between the first and second periods in American sociology. (Indeed, technically, the fact that Cooley did not die until 1929 and Thomas until 1947 means that a voluntaristic nominalistic conception of the group persisted uninterruptedly from the first through the second period.)

A COMPARATIVE SUMMARY: THE NOTION OF THE GROUP
IN THE FIRST AND SECOND PERIODS

Any endeavor to assess the continuities and discontinuities, similarities and dissimilarities, in the notion of the group in the sociological theory of the first and second periods must begin with a recognition of the basic problems as presented in chapter 1. During the 1920s, theory and theorization were subject to substantial disapprobation. Few sociologists, wanted to be labeled "theorists." Furthermore, works in general theory (then equated with general sociology) were undergoing a transformation, a simplification, into introductory textbooks with varying degrees of systematization. Accordingly, the works immediately after World War I often lack the detailed exposition and elaboration of those before the war. Hence, the notion of the group is sometimes only fragmentarily and incompletely presented.

Nevertheless, it has been possible to employ the same ontological designation (e.g., *materialism- idealism, nominalism- realism*) to characterize the different positions on the nature of the group in the two periods, though not in all instances or with the same degree of confidence in the second as in the first. *Founding Theory of American Sociology 1881–1915* (Hinkle 1980) delineated a predominant materialism, a more balanced materialism- idealism, and a prevalent idealism. Sumner and Keller represented the first, a predominant materialism. Ward, Giddings, and perhaps Ross are exemplars of the second, a more balanced materialism- idealism. Cooley is perhaps the most unambiguous protagonist of the third, a predominant idealism, though Small may seem at times a close approximation (Hinkle 1980, 271, 272–80).

In addition, the group for early American theorists was prevailingly conceived nominalistically—even in Cooley's case (Hinkle 1980, 281–90). But it is a nominalism that is inextricably joined with voluntarism (290–95), though Ross's and Cooley's views suggest departures from a strictly nominalistic voluntarism (Hinkle 1980, 293–95). Nevertheless, no early American theorist deviates so markedly as to warrant the designation "social realist" in the full Durkheimian sense (Hinkle 1980, 295–96).

Second- period theory as examined in the present study also admits of similar characterization. Ogburn and Lundberg articulate views that seem to be identifiable as predominantly materialist, but for different reasons. (Though not examined above, Bain's acceptance of behaviorism and an adapted Freudianism in the late 1920s to the mid 1930s might also suggest a type of materialism. Indeed, though an "ontological" behaviorism never appears to have been a majority position in theory, the support achieved may well suggest that materialism had won proportionately more adherents in the second than it did in the first period.)

The more balanced materialist- idealist position apparently enjoyed a majority of supporters in the second period as in the first. Bernard, Hankins, Chapin, Park, Reuter, Hart, and Hiller (the last three were students of Park) are exemplars of the stance.

Certainly, the explicit consideration of the social nominalist- realist dichotomy and controversy by Park and his students (and in effect by Faris and some of his students) differentiates the second from the first period of theory. But the extent to which social realism was actually adopted by theorists is itself open to debate. If, indeed, Park regarded himself as a social realist, his effort to reinterpret Comte's notion of consensus through Dewey's conception of communication, the latter's conception to explain Durkheim's collective representations, and Park's own failure to understand Durkheim's process of collective ferment or effervescence seem to be inconsistent with a realist claim.

In actuality, Park's colleague Faris appears more appropriately to warrant the "social realist" designation. He is precise about the group as being a prior reality (to the individual) with its own level of existence. It has new distinctive qualities appearing "when it acts as a whole." It can act as a whole only in and through communication, interaction, in concert, and with more or less consensus. Though Faris never alluded to social nominalism or realism or to Durkheim in the appropriate context, he was in effect a social realist.

Interestingly, two of Faris's and two of Park's former students might also seem eligible for the designation "social realist." Krueger and Reckless and Reuter and Hart reject—either implicitly or explicitly—a social nominalist notion of the nature of the group. As in the case of Faris, neither pair of authors explicitly claims to be, but both actually are, social realists.

By the end of the 1930s, sociologists seemed inclined either to reject the relevance of the nominalist/realist distinction and dispute or to find a middle ground. Clearly, to the extent that the social realist stance intrudes into sociological theory of the second period, it differs significantly from that of the first.

Finally, a predominant idealist stance can be identified in the second period—a stance that also entails a voluntarist nominalism. It was prefigured by Thomas and Znaniecki, Cooley, and Ellwood. But its major development involves two different traditions: one from a more European tradition and the other from more American roots. The first is an American version of Weber's social action. MacIver's, Becker's, and Parson's writings all testify to Weberian influence, though Znaniecki's reveal only congruence. Blumer's version of symbolic interactionism (which stems from Mead, Faris, Cooley, and Thomas) represents a somewhat more directly American-derived stance. Both the social action and the symbolic interaction positions are committed to a voluntaristic nominalism (as is also Cooley's process of valuation). Thus, the predominantly idealist stance in the second period is to be explicitly identified with the social actionist and symbolic interactionist orientations.

Clearly, the second period entails counterparts of the first period: predominantly materialist, balanced materialist- idealist, and predominantly idealist standpoints. The second period is also characterized by an explicit consideration of the social nominalist /realist controversy and by some apparent adherence to social realism in contrast to the first period. Given the vigorous commitment to it that continued from the first into the second period, voluntaristic nominalism might well be expected to appear as one of the foundational components in any subsequent formulation of a general theory. Its foundational character was evident in, and thus supported by, the conceptions of the group in the second period.

Chapter 12

An Overview in Context:
Past, Present, and Future

As chapter 1 endeavored to indicate, this inquiry into the nature of social and sociological theory during a particular, limited timespan in American sociology adopts the same basic objective and the same primary focus on ideas (as opposed to "famous persons"), and similarly accepts the indispensability of periodization and employs same analytic classificatory-periodizing scheme as did its predecessor *Founding Theory of American Sociology* (Hinkle 1980). But it does, of course, involve a different time interval, broadly encompassing the years from World War I through the Great Depression and World War II, during much of which general or macrotheory was not held in especially high esteem in the discipline. Thus, the approach to the study of theory is applied to an interval of time markedly different from the founding period.

True, the study aspires, as did its predecessor, to contribute to explaining or accounting for how contemporary sociological theory has come to be as it is—to adapt a phrase from the work of F. J. Teggart. But this objective is to be reached only by a series of studies of successive periods of time that will link the earliest years to the present in American sociological theory.

Thus, the undertaking can contribute only *in part* to a much more extended chain of inquiries.

Moreover, this study, like the prior one, is predicated on the premise that the desired results can be obtained only if the undertaking is genuinely historical, that is can tap the sociohistorical and intellectual context in considerable depth and detail, as a mere single linkage of "great persons" in chronological sequence cannot do. Full opportunity must be provided to explore the rise and fall, acceptance and rejection, integration and disintegration, of constellations of ideas in an interval of time.

The approach must entail periodization, which is accomplished in terms of the major features of types of sociological theories, some of which may become dominant and others minor. For such purposes, the comprehensive analytic classificatory periodizing scheme has been useful. It has facilitated the establishment of dated boundaries of the period (beginning 1915–18 and ending 1945–50) and the determination of the character of the included theory.

It is crucial to caution here that the use of the scheme must not be mechanical. It must be adjusted to the peculiarities of the time context. A review of the literature (i.e., resources) of the time period has revealed that although interest in theory is apparently continuous, the kind of documents present in the previous period—that is fully expanded personal statements of theoretical commitments—are not available in the years under consideration. But careful study also revealed that the textbooks of "general sociology," which was explicitly equated with "general theory," are available. Roughly, a dozen such texts—temporally distributed from about the mid 1920s through the early 1940s—have been scrutinized. They were particularly useful in the effort to assess intellectual continuities between the founding years and the present, second period. They were less useful in indicating discontinuities (e.g., intrusions of theoretical stances from other disciplines in American academia).

To determine the discontinuities, it has been necessary to examine the content of the professional literature (i.e., journals and monographs). Such examination can yield evidence of the influence of theoretical positions from other disciplines in the United States and of the views of European figures.

But before summarizing the main substantive findings of this inquiry, it is necessary to refer to a reversal of the first- period relationship between the social epistemological- methodological and social ontological divisions of theory that occurred in the second period. In the years 1881–1915, the concern with social ontological theory was primary. During the years 1915–18 and 1945–50, social epistemological- methodological concerns became predominant and, indeed, defining of the character of second- period theory. The emergence of the three stances and the controversies as analyzed in chapter 2—the dominant statistically focused, qualified empiricist, and neo- positivist versus the minority American counterparts of German neo-idealism and Neo- Kantianism—reflect this shift from the first to the second periods.

However, this study is mainly concerned with the nature of social ontological theory during the second period. This concern is reflected in two forms, or under two rubrics: (1) persistence of, and continuities in, the major stances from the first period, and (2) internally generated idiosyncracies and external intrusions or discontinuities in relation to the first period. Of course, this analysis is delimited by certain temporal boundaries. Accordingly, the main findings are presented under three topics: "Continuities," "Discontinuities," and "Temporal- Historical Context and Periodization."

REVIEW OF THE MAIN FINDINGS

Continuities (in Social Evolutionism)

Predicated on evolutionary naturalism, social evolutionism as the dominant social ontological theory of the first period persisted into the second. Ellwood, Lumley, Bernard, MacIver, Hankins, and Ogburn were its exponents during the 1920s and early 1930s. However, its formulation tended to be far more oblique, truncated, fragmentary, and diffuse than was the case before World War I. Its decline and demise occurred in all three subdomains—origins, structure, and change—subsequent to the early 1930s.

Social and cultural origins. During the second period, the relatively equal adherence to the pre- and post- organic theories of social origins, which had prevailed earlier, changed substantially. Opinion shifted in favor of the pre- organic stance: that permanent human association, social relations, or society had emerged before rather than after our prehuman ancestors became organically human. But the few remaining supporters of the post-organic view also based their position on the doctrine of social forces, as had been the case during the first period.

The arguments raised denied evolutionary theories of origins such as had prevailed during the first period. First, publication of research on our nonhuman primate relatives by such experts as Kohler, Yerkes, and Zuckerman tended initially to shift opinion toward the pre- organic stance. Subsequently, the effect was to reduce interest in and controversy about the problem of origins generally.

Second, the criticisms of the doctrine of social forces, and in turn the instincts, undermined the tenability of social evolution. During this period, instincts as applied to humans were substantially disputed and the doctrine of social forces subjected to basic critique. One of Faris's graduate students, E. N. Simpson (1926), indicted the social forces for their definitional flaws (confusing causes of the social with social causes having social effects), for methodological and empirical defects, for redundant abstractionism, for the assumption that they can account for the facts of social diversity, and for presupposing that individual and collective behavior has certain normal, natural, and universal ends (23–61).

Third, a shift to an interest in cultural origins, which was accounted for in terms of a parallel physico- biopsychic and sociocultural evolutionism, led in turn to an examination of the assumptions in this conception. They were also criticized:

a.   Inductive generalizations on the basis of the newer anthropology or paleontology were shown to be incompatible with the basic assumptions of parallel evolutionism: for instance, the thesis that similar environments produce similar human types producing in turn similar cultures was denied.

b.   The effort to argue that features of a culture derive from components of biopsychic human nature, which have altered in response to change in the physical environment or organism, is untenable. For instance, if it alleged that instincts produce customs on the human level, and different tribes have different customs, it must follow that the different tribes have different instincts, and thus the human race must disappear as a single organic whole or species.

c.   Furthermore, the evolutionary effort to derive cultural origins from contemporary primitive peoples is beset by major problems. For example, it is not possible to hold that contemporary primitives may be regarded as representatives of the earlier stages of the life we are now living.

Clearly, then, the major bases of an evolutionary theory of social origins had been attacked. Even the problem of origins became suspect.

Social Structure. Now, manifestly, it is impossible to develop a theory of social origins without some notion of social structure. Of necessity, structure or organization involves the nature of (human) society and its constituent groups or, perhaps more appropriately, the group one of whose varieties is society. Organization means that the relations and interactions of individuals have become defined, regularized, reciprocally ordered, and predictable. It means order and orderliness. It means that the group is a whole or unity of parts, which are interrelated, coordinated, or coadapted to one another and to the external world.

More precisely, five of the six characteristics of organization during the first period are relevant in the second (e.g., a social identity; acceptance of common ends or purposes; stability, complementarity, differentiation, specialization, and coordination of activities; normative regulations; the effective operation of social controls to secure compliance and integration and deter deviation and disintegration.

However, major concern resides primarily in the nature of the theory or theories of social structure. Only Hankins, Bernard, Lumley, and Ellwood advance evolutionary explanations. Furthermore, their accounts were offered only in the most vague, general terms, such as *selection, survival,* and *adaptation,* without details or specifications.

Most importantly, the sociologists who developed differentiated structural typologies (e.g., in- and out- groups, primary and secondary groups, different community types) were not evolutionists. Indeed, they offered no comprehensive structural theories at all.

Thus, both origins as a problem and parallel physico- biopsychic and sociocultural evolutionism became intellectually untenable. And apparently, too, social evolutionism as a theory of structure could not readily be accommodated with the increasingly complex typologies of the group.

Social Change. It is noteworthy that even before the mid 1920s certain former students of the anthropologist Boas (e.g., Lowie, Goldenweiser, Herskovits, and Wallis) published articles in sociology journals controverting virtually all of the basic tenets of social evolutionism as a change theory. The sociologist Faris also joined in the critique, and still later Sorokin and Becker also contributed indictments of social evolutionism.

Surprisingly, however, sociologists during the 1920s, with only one notable exception (Faris), seemed to be largely unmoved by these objections. They remained virtually unanimous in the view that the ultimate social unit undergoing change was human society, society, humankind, or the human species. Only a few objected to the organismic growth analogy (but perhaps more were either ignorant of or ignored the importance of the analogy in the total structure of evolutionism). Some did qualify the prevalent notion of rate to hold that change among primitive peoples was relatively slow and gradual but becomes increasingly rapid among civilized and especially modern (industrial?) societies. But it was the notion of invariant unilinear (successive) stages through which all societies must go that provoked most widespread rejection among both the research specialists and the textbook writers.

Still, the great majority of sociologists who espoused some theory of change adhered to some modified version of social evolutionism. The positions of the various authors range from those who fundamentally resembled the earlier conventional social evolutionism to those who substantially diverged from it. Ellwood, Bernard, and Lumley accepted some variant of a generalized evolutionary scheme (but not one committed to invariant sequence). MacIver developed his own differentiation- integration view of social evolution, entailing a first stage of undifferentiated communal customs, a second of differentiated communal institutions, and a third of differentiated great associations. Ogburn (and in part, Chapin) propounded a culture lag theory of social change based on a sequence of stages of the technology and economy (which was retained in the Ogburn and Nimkoff textbook). Hankins offered an arborescent, cladogenetic, or variational (quasi-multilinear) notion of social evolution. Finally, Chapin (in part) and Thomas and Znaniecki (as a whole) are protagonists of mixed linear and cyclical formulations of social evolution. The latter two advocated an evolutionary primary- to- secondary- group- dominated societal sequence combined with an organization- disorganization- reorganization cycle. (Interestingly, each one of these was initially formulated just before or during the 1920s—including apparently those of Bernard and perhaps even MacIver.

In their exposition of causal mechanisms, second- period social evolutionists appear more simplistic than their first- period counterparts (perhaps, of course, because they were endeavoring to communicate with students.) Yet their inclusion of both endogenous (e.g., invention) and exogenous (e.g., diffusion) factors introduces a basic, and, for many, unrecognized, contradiction.

Social evolutionary theory thus persisted in all of its subdivisions (origins, structure, and change) throughout the 1920s. Clearly, continuity between founding theory and the theory of the 1920s can be substantially claimed, but not thereafter. Nonevolutionary change theories did appear in the 1930s and 1940s, but they never seemed to have achieved the following that their earlier evolutionary counterparts had won.

Discontinuities

Interestingly, all identifiable actual or potential intellectual stances failed to achieve formulation as general theories or to acquire dominance after the early 1930s. This failure is evident within American sociology, in instances of ideas introduced from other disciplines in American academia, and in the fate of ideas of major figures from European social science.

A Potential Stance from within Sociology: Park, Becker, and Sorokin. Park's own development of a distinctive sociological orientation (along with contributions of his students, Reuter and Hart, Hiller, K. Young, and R. L. Sutherland) is presented as a potential discontinuity because it arose from within American sociology but from antecedents in European philosophy and social and natural science substantially different from those of first-period theorists. Ostensibly, it involves a complex dualism including both biotic- ecological and sociocultural (moral) levels. But in actuality it is predicated on a cyclical social process formulation of social change (i.e., competition, conflict, accommodation, and assimilation), which his former students also invoked. (Park's own failure to provide a sufficiently rigorous and systematic formulation of his ideas seems to preclude its characterization as a general theory, but its designation as a general sociological orientation is warranted.)

Two other social change analytic schemes (or quasi- theories) also deserve consideration at this point. One was propounded by a former student of Park but the second was not. Howard P. Becker, author of the first, envisaged social change as formulable within a series of sacred and secular societal types (the proverbial sacred, the prescriptive sacred, the principled secular, and the pronormless secular), with reversible directionality. Sorokin conceives of social change as movement from one to another of three possible logico- meaningfully integrated types of cultural supersystem (ideational, idealistic, and sensate).

Whatever the merits of the several formulations may have been, they did not win any substantial adoption beyond a succeeding generation of graduate students at the respective institutions of the three sociologists.

Possible Stances Stemming from the Influence of Other Disciplines in American Academia.

Anthropology and the influence of the concept of culture. Important as it was in repelling instinctivism, hereditarianism, racialism, and biologism generally throughout the 1920s and 1930s, the concept of culture never became the basis for the elaboration of a general theory in sociology. (Admittedly, certain portions of Ogburn's works might seem to have confirmed the charge of cultural determinism.) In general, three major obstacles seem to have prevented the formulation of a culturalist sociological theory:

1.   The proponents of culture as a concept who were most likely to elaborate a full theory were subject to the stricture that their view of culture rendered it separate and discontinuous from the rest of nature. Thus, their conception violated the basic premise of evolutionary naturalism.
2.   These same proponents were also unable to argue, conversely, that culture could constitute a separate and distinctive domain justifying

the autonomous intellectual existence of sociology as a discipline or field. A variety of difficulties were suggested, such that anthropology had already preempted the study of culture; that a partial use of any aspect of culture (such as norms or American culture as a type of modern culture) would only result in intellectual confusions or contradictions with dominant trends in the discipline.

3. Nor could the proponents readily invoke the Durkheimian conception of culture as a self- existing entity or a phenomenon sui generis (as superindividual, superpsychic, or superorganic) as the foundation of a theory, because it was committed to social realism. A Durkheimian-based theory would thus have been at variance with the distinctive individualism, nominalism, and antideterminism of American sociology.

History as a source of data and critique. Perhaps the historian most amply equipped to encourage a rapprochement between history and sociology, and to promote the development of a historical sociological theory, was Teggart, from Berkeley. However, the exchange of ideas with House in *Social Forces,* and Park's and Becker's misinterpretation of his views, rendered unlikely any such role for him.

Teggart denied that it is legitimate to construe the scientific study of the social world as entailing a "timeless" (abstract, general) process representing the "way things work if nothing intervenes." House's position—and presumably that of many sociologists—was based on the ancient Greek philosophical (especially Aristotelian) view of the social world as a domain of *physis,* in which only internal change, as typified by growth in the course of an organism's life cycle, was "natural" and "normal." Teggart insisted that that view violated the actual reality of modern societies, with their impact and intrusions on one another, and in effect regarded external change as " accidental" and inconsequential.

Teggart criticized House for failing to require that the study of multitudinous instances of actual societies and their histories be the basis for the discovery of actual processes at work. Adoption of the Greek model of what is natural and normal biases the results in advance of research and precludes the discovery of genuine inductions about how the social world works. Further, Teggart's view of adequate research would have demanded much more detailed and exacting inquiry than sociologists had even contemplated and thus considerably delay or postpone any claim of instrumental utility.

Teggart insisted that House—and presumably most of his colleagues—failed to understand that background studies must entail an intimate acquaintance with the history of methodological ideas (guiding concepts and preconceptions) in their fields. Yet the training of most sociologists of the period scarcely equipped them to grasp the subtlety of Teggart's analyses of figures and ideas far removed from the present; on the other hand, those who understood Teggart's analyses were hardly equipped to accept his criticisms of views about science, social science, social change, progress, and evolution that either had achieved or were in the process of achieving dominance in sociology.

Freudian psychiatry. Although both Ogburn and Thomas—each closely associated with theory—used Freudian concepts and ideas in their work (the former in *Social Change* and the latter in *The Polish Peasant in Europe and America* and especially *The Unadjusted Girl*), they were, unlike many of their colleagues, interested in theory. Among those interested in theory (e.g., Sorokin, Faris, MacIver, and Znaniecki), the majority apparently assumed a markedly negative view toward Freudian assumptions and concepts.

Among other things, they objected to (1) its assumption of certain instincts or instinctive desires as universal psychological elements; (2) the dubious effort to go beyond (or beneath) the actual active level of individual experience (e.g., the unconscious); (3) the inadequacy of its methods; (4) a constant and confusing shift from the conscious to the unconscious; (5) the reduction of the complex to the simple, but still leaving the former unexplained; (6) the unwarranted assertion of the universality of sexual desire; (7) the absence of any physiological underpinning for its system of ideas; (8) its view that incestuous and selfish desires are primary and elemental and thus in perpetual conflict with social requirements; (9) an unacceptable psychological explanation of social origins; and (10) an erroneous use of a theory of infantile experience to explain cultural forms and social disorders.

Behavioristic psychology. Hankins's, Bernard's, and Lundberg's textbooks all espouse forms of behaviorism. Hankins and Bernard can be designated as "moderate behaviorists" because even though they argue that learning or acquired adjustive activity is primarily based on the conditioned response as the basis of habit, they both allow some role for consciousness. Importantly, too, the two interrelate their "moderate" behaviorisms with their basic social evolutionary positions. Accordingly, their espousal of behaviorism does not occasion a distinctive theoretical stance.

In contrast, Lundberg remains silent about any connection of behaviorism with (earlier) social evolutionism. More consequentially, he seeks to undermine any role of consciousness by conferring recognition only to the extent that it can be confirmed or verified in the terms of the criteria of behaviorism. He thus becomes a "radical" behaviorist (and, as argued elsewhere, predominantly materialist).

For such theoretically prominent sociologists as Case, Sorokin, Faris,

MacIver, Znaniecki, Becker, and Parsons, any version of behaviorism contained major difficulties. They contended that it is simply a version of reductive materialism, an atomistic and environmentally oriented form of social Darwinism, which accepts only the data of sensory experience as given to an outside observer and rejects those distinctive of the participant in the human sociocultural realm (e.g., consciousness, meanings, norms, and values).

With his background in philosophy, psychology, and sociology, Faris was in a unique position to provide a detailed critique of the conditioned response as the central notion of behaviorism. He objected to its failure to acknowledge the disjunctive, intermittent character of human interpersonal activity, its exclusive concern with the externals of conduct, its ignoring of the structure and temporality of activity, its avoidance of the significance of reflective (as opposed to automatic, mechanical) action, and its inability to recognize the correlative character of stimulus and response. Like Freudianism from psychiatry, behaviorism from psychology was essentially rejected as a potential source of a general theory.

An amalgam of behavioristic psychology, pragmatic philosophy, and idealistic strains of ideas from sociology. As crystallized in Blumer's formulation, symbolic interactionism may be said to have its antecedents in responses to behavioristic psychology (Mead, Faris), pragmatic philosophy (Mead, Faris), and certain idealistic strains in American sociology (Thomas, Cooley, Faris). Blumer's formulation is perhaps predominantly an interpretive accommodation of Mead to Thomas. Nevertheless, the focus lies on the self.

As seems obvious, his formulation involves a social psychological focus on the self arising in the context of a group or groups. But the group is construed to be considerably less structural than Mead's or Faris's realism might suggest. According to Blumer, the group is an inter- and multipersonal setting within which each adult is constantly taking the role of the other (or others) so that he or she can act effectively adjust his or her conduct so that it "fits in" with that of others and cooperative activity can result.

In Blumer's view, Mead's notion of the acquisition of the self is excessively rational. Accordingly, Blumer invokes Cooley's primary group, one of whose functions is to elicit the formation of the social sentiments in the individual and thus to provide an emotive grounding of the self. Blumer does follow Mead's delineation of the three stages in the development of the self in role-playing.

Most importantly, Blumer conceives of each adult's activity in relation to those of others as assuming the form of an act beginning in impulse and culminating in satisfaction or achievement of a more or less specific end. By the late 1940s, Blumer was emphasizing the internal intervening process of designation. A decade or so later he had returned to Mad's term *indication,*

but with a meaning more or less approximating Thomas's (personal) definition of the situation and decisively individualistic, voluntaristic, and instrumentalist (i.e., means- ends oriented) in character.

Certainly, Blumer had a self- acquisition theory in the late 1940s, but
excessive intellectual generosity would seem to be required to designate his
conception of adult inter- and multipersonal acts, action, and interaction a
bona fide general theory.

*Possible Stances from European Social Philosophy and Social Science
and Scientists.* Beginning in the 1920s and persisting up into and through
World War II, the conceptions and theories of Durkheim, Pareto, Marx, Tönnies, Simmel, Manheim, and Max Weber undeniably influenced American
sociology. However, in no case can it be said that the influence of any one of
these European figures had become a direct model for the construction of a
general theory. Probably the impacts of Durkheim and Weber were greatest.

However, it would surely be inaccurate to infer that because no one of
them became the basis for the creation of a full- fledged general theory, no
one of them influenced general theory in the United States. Evidence was
presented revealing that Max Weber was the primary stimulus and source of
ideas entering into the development of a social action orientation (or, perhaps more accurately, a social action frame of reference) of at least three
American sociologists: MacIver, Parsons, and Becker. And it also appears
that European neo- idealism and/or Neo- Kantianism was important in the
development of Znaniecki's stance.

In spite of differences in personal formulation, the following ideas are
fundamental to this social action frame of reference. Interpersonal activity is
typically or prevailingly oriented by consciousness and involves awareness
of self and others, some level of purpose, some form of means- instrumentality, some unchangeable or unmodifiable aspects or conditions in the situation, the regulation of activity by moral rules, and the exercise of at least a
modicum of choice; and its study is predicated on resort to understanding (or
verstehen), interpretation, imaginative reconstruction, or vicarious experience
of the actors involved.

Implications

Although correct and appropriate in themselves, the designations *continuities* and *discontinuities* do not tell the full story of the changing character of the period. The term *continuities* indicates the persistence from the
earlier, first period of social evolutionism. *Discontinuities* indicates the various sources of major diversity and disruption of such theory. The former
term is oriented to the past. The latter looks forward to future sources of

renewal and reorientation. Not only do they involve alternatives to social evolutionism, but they were often linked to a basic reconsideration of the notion of theory itself.

They included (or were associated with) a major effort to rethink the nature of theory and the preparatory intellectual enterprise required for the development and construction of a more tenable and defensible (or "sound") theory. Bain (1929b, 13–16), Chapin (1936), and Lundberg (1936b, 708) represented what might be termed "neo- empiricism- positivism." Becker (1932b, 61–62, 39), Parsons (1937, 1968, 6, 24), and perhaps also Merton (1945, 462–73; Merton [1945] 1968, esp. 153, 155) wrote from a more idealist- interpretive stance. It is important that representatives of both stances concurred in the necessity that empirical research be regarded as a necessary component of sound theory. But paradoxically, the ultimate consequence of this concurrence in the nature of "sound" theory and the indispensability of empirical research was a renewed appreciation for the role of deductive reasoning of the kind associated with the first period.

One of the agreed-upon constituents of this "newer" conception of theory was the frame of reference, one idealist version of which was the action or social action frame of reference. As presented above, this frame of reference represents a "discontinuity," and yet it also fundamentally predicates or is based on (and thus is intellectually continuous with) the voluntaristic nominalism of early American sociology. Significantly, the same presupposition undergirds Reuter and Hart's and Hiller's emphasis (and perhaps also that of Park) on the required achievement of consensus for collective or group action. It is also involved in the complex of meanings associated with the expanded notion of "indication" in Blumer's symbolic interactionism of the 1950s. Hence, it might be said that, paradoxically, three apparent "discontinuities" actually involve continuity with pre- World War I theory!

TEMPORAL-HISTORICAL CONTEXT AND PERIODIZATION

Interestingly, the years signifying the temporal boundaries of the second period, its beginnings (1915–18) and its ending (1945–50), involve the aftermath of the large societal upheavals and crises of World Wars I and II. These crises significantly impacted on the profession and discipline, in both periods, so that relatively rapid expansion and generational succession in the profession were associated with fundamental intellectual changes in the discipline and in theory.

In the aftermath of World War I, the control of the founding generation was displaced, and the discipline became firmly committed to empirical research. Social epistemological-methodological preoccupations assumed predominance over social substantive (ontological) concerns. Indeed, the defining difference between the first and the second period in theory lies in the reversal of the relationship between social epistemological-methodological theory and social ontological theory. (The latter was predominant during the founding period, the former during the second period.) What is important is that during the second period major and minor contending epistemological-methodological stances (i.e., a statistically couched qualified empiricism-neo-positivism for the former, and American counterparts of German neo-idealism and Neo-Kantianism for the latter) agreed on the indispensability of research but seemed to collide particularly over quantitative (statistics) versus qualitative (case study) methods, though much more is really involved.

During the second period (and especially the last fifteen years), theory seemed to have a peculiar intermediary function between the discipline and the larger society. In part, that function involved the justification of the discipline in relation to the larger society and its changing problems. Initially, it was expressed in terms of the earlier ideology of progress (i.e., "developing" knowledge as contributing to the intellectual and moral betterment and advancement of society, etc.). Eventually, sociologists' recognition of cultural-value diversity or relativity compelled them to deal forthrightly with their own commitment to science as a value (supreme value?) versus the values of society itself as change occurred. Thus, the actual response to such changes become significant.

For instance, the 1935 annual meeting of the American Sociological Society had as its general theme (the depression-relevant) "Social Theory and Social Planning." Chapin's (1936) presidential address was entitled "Social Theory and Social Action." The Division on Social Theory had the immediately related topic "The Practical Application of Sociological Theory," which included papers by (E. A.) Ross and Sorokin.[1]

In 1940, the society had a general session entitled "The Challenge of the Times to the Sociologist." Two theorists presented papers. Sorokin's was entitled "The Nature of the Challenge" and Becker's was "Sociologists and the Supreme Values of our Times" (Becker 1941c, 155–72).

In 1943 the Social Theory session was devoted to "Some Contributions of Social Theory to Post-World War Organization." North (Ohio State University), Moore (University of Texas), Hertzler, (University of Neb.), and LaPiere (Stanford University) were the participants.

In 1945 the Social Theory session concerned "The Social Responsibilities of Sociological Science," with Parsons as its chairman. Wirth presented one of the two major papers.

It is significant that the arguments of Max Weber played a prominent role in American theorists' efforts to adopt a position accommodating science as a value of sociologists in relation to the changing values of their own society. Becker's "Sociologists and the Supreme Values of Our Times" is illustrative, as is his own more comprehensive (but concise) exposition in the Becker and Barnes ([1952] 1961, 3:896–98).

The intellectual situation in relation to the broader societal and political context is even more complex in the years constituting the ending boundary of the second period than it was at its beginning. Baldly stated, a new, different graduate department (Harvard) became ascendant in theory, the prominent members of which had backgrounds and interests substantially at variance with those of an older generation, were able to place their graduate students in other major graduate departments, and did so at a time of rapid (post-World War II) expansion in the discipline and profession, such that potential opposition from older members of the profession could be mounted less effectively.

The failure of the Chicago, Columbia, and Wisconsin departments to produce a significant number of graduate students interested in and committed to general theory in the years 1936–45 was to the advantage of the Harvard department. There Sorokin initially had an almost exclusive role in the training of graduate students, but somewhat later Parsons came to play an increasing major part. Though Sorokin and Parsons became antagonists and differences in their orientations emerged, both had intellectual backgrounds that were characteristically European and not American. (In three long papers developing arguments for his early conception of a structural-functional theory in 1945, 1948, and 1950, Parsons cites Thomas alone once in one paper and again in the company of Sumner, Cooley, and Park in a different paper.[2] These are his only references to American sociologists.) Parsonsian theory in general and his structural functionalism in particular claimed their origins in earlier European, as distinct from earlier American, theory.

Clearly, Parsons was intellectually persuasive with a number of graduate students. Furthermore, their placement in department at Columbia, Princeton, Cornell, Wisconsin, Indiana, and Berkeley was a singular accomplishment during the 1940s and 1950s.

Many were productive. Kingsley Davis's *Human Society* (1948), Robert Merton's *Social Theory and Social Structure* (1949), and Robin Williams's *American Society* (1950) provided major anticipatory, complementary, and expository statements of Parson's own (later) *The Social System* (1951), *Toward a General Theory of Action* (1951), and *Working Papers in a Theory of Action* (1953). They were, or were soon, in a position to exercise major intellectual influence in academia and the discipline.

Theory from the earlier generation in American sociology had no effective protagonists. Parsons and his functionalist allies (generally former students) could virtually ignore most of the earlier heritage of the first and

second periods, without effective protest, as the number of sociology graduate students and faculty appointments and membership in the ASA rose. The
history of American sociology and sociological theory was substantially and
effectively displaced and re-Europeanized to begin with the predecessors of
action and structural functional theory.[3]

Nevertheless, the perceptiveness of sociological genius is scarcely
required now to discern the "resonance"—as Gouldner might say—or even
counterparts of Parsons's early structural-functionalism and later social evolutionism with, or in, certain notions in the displaced, suppressed, ignored,
or forgotten history of the second, or even first, period in the history of
American sociological theory. For a simple beginning, the notions of the
organismic analogy or model of a social system, in equilibrium [equilibra-
tion] or adaptation in relation to its larger environment, and exhibiting a
sequence of social stages akin to organismic growth are sufficient.

Viewed retrospectively, the rapid increase in graduate students in the
discipline in the late 1940s, the rise in membership in the American Sociological Society from 1,651 in 1946 to 3,241 in 1950, and the expansion of
the number of papers presented at its annual meetings over the same years
may well be viewed as serving to buffer, insulate, dampen, diffuse, and mitigate any residual intellectual antagonism from the past. By roughly 1950 the
ascendance of structural functionalism seemed to be assured. The second
period in the history of American sociological theory had come to a close.

RELEVANCE: THE PAST AND PRESENT OF THEORY JUXTAPOSED

Until recently, sociologists were ordinarily disinclined to attribute any
substantial relevance to history generally or to historical inquiry in their own
professional specialties (perhaps, even including theory). Given sociology's
past strong attachment to a natural science (or natural-science-like) model,
this past disinclination may itself be derived from an earlier identification
with science in the science/history antagonism, in which many social sciences shared.[4] Put a slightly differently, the past adoption of the science side
of the argument is itself tantamount to a foundational claim in accordance
with the arguments of postmodernism in current theory.

To the potential or actual "So what?" challenge of the sociological presentist raised after a perusal of the previous chapters, a two-pronged defense
may be posed. Specifically, two courses are available to make the case for
current relevancy of second-period theory: (1) development of an argument
drawn from a present stance that both illuminates the past and extends implications of the present, and (2) development of an argument showing how a
past (second-period) stance in its anticipation of present features of theory

also enhances an understanding of the present. The next two sections of this chapter endeavor to employ both strategies in the sequence just stated.

The Past in the Perspective of the Present: The Relevance of the Foundations and Foundationalism of Postmodernism

The objective of this section is to provide a summary verdict on the basic assumptions that were retained or introduced (either explicitly or implicitly) as part of the legacy of second-period theory. As indicated in the very first chapter, assumptions are to be viewed in accordance with the notions of the foundations and foundationalism from the current theoretical stance of postmodernism.[5] Applied to sociology, a foundation is a basic general or generic assumption that may be either social epistemological-methodological or social ontological in nature. Even more specifically, a foundation is thus a logically generic assertion or premise "beyond which we need not go" and that is thus assumed to be indubitable, necessary, fixed, enduring, ultimate, and universal. Foundationalism is the assumption that it is necessary and/or desirable that the discipline be made to possess—if it does not already possess—a single, consistent set (or system) of foundational, generic, elemental, constitutive (or first-order) assumptions about the domain of sociocultural phenomena—how it should be conceived and studied.

Viewed within the perspective of sociology's history between World Wars I and II, theory was implicated in a series of controversies. The immediate problem is to analyze just how basic assumptions were affected in turn.

Analysis of Possible Foundations. Although the partisans of the emerging dominant epistemological-methodological stance attacked the content of social evolution only indirectly in public (though directly in private) as the chief exemplar of the defects of theory early in the second period, they never explicitly controverted the idea of a general sociology or general theory that provided its supporting framework. In part, the idea of a general discipline or theory derived from a much earlier notion of science as the study of the common, general, recurrent, invariant, or universal in phenomena (Teggart [1941] 1977). In part, and more immediately, it stems from Giddings's and Small's applications of the idea to sociology—that is, that a general sociology or general theory is the result of the study of the basic components, general elements, and first principles of what is found to be essential to social life—the common, general, invariant, or universal in societies everywhere and always.[6] For second-period theorists, it made no fundamental difference whether sociology as a subject was defined as inquiry into social relationships, processes, or the group in its origins, development, functioning, or structuring—so long as the focus was on studying the general, the generic, the universal, unlimited by time or space. Thus, the very basic conception of what was to be studied (or derived from inquiry) was, in effect, foundational.

Like their predecessors, second-period sociologists, with but few exceptions, regarded social phenomena as natural, as part of nature, as constituting a separate domain in nature with its own natural regularities. In turn, this view was part of a much more encompassing notion of nature as a chain or hierarchy of domains, each studied by a distinctive science. Put more broadly, it was envisaged as part of the general conception of evolutionary naturalism, which also was foundational (at least for these first 2 tenets).

However, the emphasis in the notion of science seemed to shift in the second period from the aim of what was to be studied to the method of study. Certain particular methods and techniques eventually became exclusively identified as a natural science model. In its broadest implications, it represented—and may be characterized as—a statistically couched, qualified empiricism and neo-positivism. By the late 1930s to mid 1940s, it had achieved a foundational status in sociology as a whole. (Admittedly, its exclusivist claims were rejected by some theorists of the period.)

In accordance with the general acceptance of evolutionary naturalism and as confirmed by the strong preoccupation with various psychological or social psychological stances (none of which gained wide acceptance), theorists, as well as sociologists generally, continued to hold that some version of biopsychic human nature was indispensable to sociology and general theory.

Certainly the notion of a common human nature (plus monogenism) was basic to the conception that all specific concrete societies were generalizable and categorizable as part of a comprehensive, generic human society. (This view ultimately stemmed from universal Judeo-Christian religious assumptions.) It remained the ultimate subject of a naturalistic, secular sociology.

Yet the rejection of instincts (as applied to human beings) proved disastrous to the idea of a human nature anchored in or derived from social forces. If the social forces had a foundational status, it was undermined. In addition, the legitimacy of a concern with social origins as a basic intellectual problem sphere for ontological social theory was questioned, henceforth, in sociology.

Furthermore, the same needs, appetites, and so on continued to be construed as foci around which at first adaptation and later merely adjustive behavior of an aggregate of human beings necessarily emerged and persisted as folkways, mores, and institutions—so long as they afforded satisfaction in relation to surrounding circumstances (a weakened version of the older "conditions of existence"). A notion of adjustment was the basis of social structure, whereas persistent nonsatisfaction of needs, or maladjustment, became the basis for change. Yet the failure to articulate any rigorous criteria of adjustment predestined theoretical vacuousness and a nontheory status.

Theorists' consideration of Freudian psychiatry, behaviorist psychology, and the amalgam represented by symbolic interactionism seems to imply a recognition (along with the weakening of biological hereditarianism) that some version of human nature is still required. It is needed, on the one hand, to account for the transmission and instillation of culture (as shared learned experience) and, on the other, for the structuring or organizing of individual experience in relation to norms so as to constitute personality and self.

Certainly, the several chapters on culture, the implied focus on personality in connection with Freudian psychiatry, behaviorist psychology, and the amalgam represented by symbolic interactionism, and the group (with its norms) seem to suggest, in their totality, their common prerequisite status for formulation of any new theoretical synthesis as the basis of a new general theory by the end of the 1930s. (And so it would appear that essentially culture, personality and self), and the group and society were becoming or had become foundational, both for sociology generally and for theory specifically.)

Because none of the potential sources of new theory were actualized, and because Park's successors especially failed to systematically develop his orientation into a bona fide general theory, an "opening" or possibility was created and eventually filled by Parson's synthesis.[7]

Although the demise of social evolutionism essentially brought an end to concern with theories of social origins as problematic, the interest in theories of social structure and social change did not terminate. Considerable energy was devoted to conceptualizing important aspects of social structure (chapter 3 and 10), which would be significant for the development of later theory. Obviously, activity in (macro-) social change did not cease with the debacle of social evolution. Ogburn's so-called culture lag theory continued to have supporters long after social evolutionism as such had passed. (Indeed, its relation to social evolutionism was either unknown or ignored, though Ogburn recalled the relation in the 1950 edition of *Social Change*.) In spite of their inability to elicit an interest comparable to that in social evolution earlier, Becker and Sorokin did consequential social change theorizing. Through their work, a basis for articulating the abstract features of a linear change theory was retained. But it would seem well nigh impossible that the foundational character of rectilinear change theory could have been reinvigorated through their theories. Certainly, the universal invariant irreversibility of a sequence of stages was rejected.

Finally, the character of the rejection of Freudian psychiatry and behaviorist psychology, with the appeal of symbolic interactionism and the social action frame of reference, together with the pervasive assumption of concert or consensus in the actualized conduct of the group (chapters 7–11) seem to testify to the continuing foundational character of voluntaristic nominalism in American social and sociological theory. Given this significance, it might even be said more broadly that American theory centers crucially on the subject (which French structualism and poststructuralism sought to banish by what they termed a "de-centering").

Put very simply, the history of theory during the second period (between World Wars I and II) might be characterized as a story of contested foundations, some of which were reaffirmed and persisted, and uncontested foundationalism in the sense that the tenability of a persisting search for a set or system of foundations was itself not contested. (The inability or unwillingness seriously to consider Teggart's historical relativism is itself illuminating.)

The Present in the Perspective of the Past

The objective of this section is to provide an estimate of the relevance of the past for understanding the present. But in order to deal with the complex heterogeneity of theory in the 1990s, some delimitation or restriction on the diversity of the present will have to be accepted. (Otherwise, another book rather than an additional section is demanded.) More narrowly and precisely, a summary of second-period social action-interactionism is to be examined as an antecedent or partial anticipation of the more recent expanding interest in the emerging variant branches of interpretive theory (including hermeneutics).[8]

Certainly, any juxtaposition of past (second-period) theory with a segment of current theory presents some rather formidable problems. The temporal distantiation of forty to fifty years and the differences in intellectual and social contexts are considerable, if not vast. Indeed, the undertaking may seem to require a transcending of a primary requisite of genuinely historico-intellectual analysis, that is, deployment of analysis within a given delimited, but meaningfully interrelated, span of time; namely, a period and periodization. And actually not one but two periods must be considered in this undertaking: (a) the (third) period, entailing domination of structural functionalism from the early 1950s into the 1970s, and (b) a (fourth or) current period of theory beginning sometime in the 1980s and continuing into the present.

Surely, the possibility of having to confront two additional periods should prompt further concern with the criteria of periodization, commencing possibly with further scrutiny of what seems to be involved in typing or classifying theory—for instance, macrotheory verses "middle-range" (or meso-) theory verses micro theory, and the implications of various mixes for given periods. Furthermore, the hesitancy to distinguish the epistemological-methodological domain from a substantive (ontological) domain should be confronted directly.

The Two Periods. Undeniably, the structural functionalism of Parsons, Merton, and colleagues achieved considerable preeminence, coupled with a continued domination of the statistical natural science model of epistemology-methodology. Conflict theory appeared on the scene, as did critical theory, phenomenology, ethnomethodology, and a continuing symbolic interactionism. Manifestly, both macro- and microlevels of theory were represented. (Using the terms *modernity, modernism, modernization* in relation to the "postmodern" controversy, the particular span of years are those of "high," "mature," or "full-fledged" modernity in sociology and sociological theory, corresponding to what Rhoades and the two Turners have termed the "Golden Era" of sociology.[9] Interestingly, structural functionalism as a general theory began as a distinctively ahistorical venture devoid of major diachronic or sequentialist claims. But by 1965, it had been substantially modified to account for social change by inclusion of a revived social evolutionism.

Somewhere between the mid seventies and mid eighties, the dominant structural functionalism (and the neo-positivism) encountered additional major challenges from a variety of other theoretical stances, one of the last of which was postmodernism.[10] What was most distinctive about the ending of the hegemony of structural functionalism and the advent of a heteronomous condition of theory—the ending of the third period and the beginning of the fourth, as opposed to the ending of the second and the beginning of the third, in the history of American sociological theory—is that none of the contesting stances was displaced. The dissident (marginal) stances emerging during the sixties and seventies have persisted relatively continuously up into the present period. In many, if not most, instances they have explicit European antecedents (e.g., phenomenology, ethnomethodology, critical theory, a renewed Marxism, exchangism, rational choice theory, action theory, hermeneutics, a linguistically derived French structuralism with semiological and semiotic varieties, deconstructionism, feminist theory, and now postmodernism itself). Although some orientations seem to have only a fringe existence, theory in American sociology has never encompassed such a range of diversity as it has in the early 1990s.

Just how these current positions interconnect and ultimately contribute to this context of intellectual heterogeneity in which postmodernism can at least find a hearing is just being preliminary explored. Certainly, the post–1965 social evolutionism can hardly be said to have been critically examined with respect to its earlier predecessor in the second period. Furthermore, several of the recent positions can be claimed to together contribute to or to constitute a broadly interpretive theoretical-methodological stance (e.g., phenomenology, ethnomethodology, symbolic interactionism, a renewed social actionism, and especially hermeneutics).

The Past As Prospective or Precursor of the Present. It is at this point that the older, second-period social action theory is to be considered as antecedent, or anticipatory of this newer, more general stance. But perhaps the most critical figure to be used as a comparative point of departure is the German theorist Dilthey, who had a close counterpart in the somewhat young later American sociologist, Cooley. Chapter 2 analyzed the similarities between Dilthey and Cooley and differentiated two somewhat similar American epistemological-methodological orientations, ones involving Cooley and MacIver, akin to neo-idealism, and the other, involving Park, Becker, Znaniecki, and possibly Parsons, akin to Neo-Kantianism.

Though these American sociologists differ, as must be acknowledged, they display overall similarities with Dilthey. Several similarities (which, however, do not apply to Cooley and Park) deserve comment:

Like Dilthey, the American theorists were pervasively opposed to positivism (as were many symbolic interactionists). Admittedly, the time periods and contexts were different (Dilthey, 1965–1910, in a German academic intellectual context; the Americans, late 1920s and through the 1940s, in U.S. academia.)

Like Dilthey, the action theorists held that the study of human sociocultural life requires a distinctive set of categories and apparently a distinctive epistemology-methodology. Dilthey sharply distinguished the mental, or human, sciences (*Geisteswissenschaften*) from the natural sciences (*Naturwissenschaften*). MacIver envisaged the human sociocultural phenomena as a part of the domain of "conscious being" as opposed to the biophysical domains. Znaniecki differentiated a realm of cultural sciences as opposed to natural sciences, and Parsons the analytical sciences of action and culture versus the analytical sciences of nature. Becker regarded sociology as an interpretive (but nomothetic) science as opposed to the positivistic sciences of nature.

Like Dilthey, they envisaged (human) interpersonal activity as a form of action (i.e., social action). Although only MacIver seems to regard action as a type of expression of lived social experience as Dilthey did, all of the American theorists accepted a notion of action very similar to the views of Dilthey. All of the features of the action and social action frame of reference (see chapter 10, esp. components 1 through 8) are basically congruent with, if not derivable from, Dilthey's tentative formulation of categories (cf. Rickman 1976, 231–45). In addition, two very important congruities between social actionism and symbolic interactionism warrant comment. Recall that, as we saw at the end of our analysis of his designation-indication, Blumer was fundamentally committed to an ego-centered, means-ends, or instrumentally oriented, calculating view of the self akin to Weber's *Zweckrationalitat* (purposive or instrumentally oriented rational action; see chapter 9). Conversely, Becker, who was committed to social action (and the only action theorist with a University of Chicago doctorate), reveals an arresting accommodation of Weber and Mead in presenting his analysis of the formation of personality or self in his *Through Values to Social Interpretation* (1950, 6–17). Thus, a main figure from symbolic interactionism and another from social actionism provide at least partial transitions to the other position.

Like Dilthey, American action theorists argued that the study of human sociocultural life requires a distinctive methodology centering on understanding or interpretation, in two senses: (a) For Dilthey, a system of signs or symbols standing for or representing the experience of a historically and culturally developed sphere of "objective spirit," in which the members of a community (or group) participate, is a prerequisite and especially emphasized in his later writings (Plantinga 1980, 92, 119; Ermarth 1978, 225–29, cf. 256–60). Such common meaning can exist only "if it springs from and presupposes something common and shared among members," such as a tradition or constellation of meanings like a common language (Plantinga 1980, 92). Parsons ([1937] 1968, 484–85) explicitly acknowledges Dilthey's notion, and other action theorists subscribed to similar views, albeit more schematically or cryptically (MacIver [1942], 1964, 264; MacIver 1931c, 259; Becker 1950, 211; Znaniecki 1934, 176).

(b) Like Dilthey, the American action theorists also envisaged understanding as entailing a personalized dimension of motivational imputation through empathic identification. Dilthey had especially used the notions of a reliving of experience, putting oneself in the place of another, feeling as another does, and reproducing or reconstructing the context or situation of another. American theorists employed similar notions. Becker (1950, 191) notes that the "interpreter puts himself in the place of the actor as best he can and . . .views the situation" as the actor does. MacIver (1964) proposes imaginative or sympathetic reconstruction as appropriate to the role of mind and purposiveness in social phenomena. These latter two require that the covert systems of thoughts, attitudes, desires, motivations, and relevant background experiences be made consciously available for interpreting and reconstructing the meanings of symbols used in communication (262–65, 294, 332–33n., 388–92). Parsons ([1937] 1968) uses only *understanding* (or *Verstehen*) itself, in two senses: The first refers to action as requiring an interpretation of words and deeds as expressions of motives (1968, 583) which are not "evident in particular concrete observation and [so] remain problematical" (636); and the second to an understanding of atemporal complexes of meaning as such, or culture (637). (Interestingly, Znaniecki denies that reproduction or reconstruction of experience in the cultural domain is epistemologically different from experience in the natural domain.) And now one last comment on the general concern of this paragraph: Certainly "taking the role of the other" in symbolic interactionism might well be construed as "understanding-interpretation."

Like Dilthey, the Americans held that the sociocultural world is especially constituted by the interrelationship of the particular-individual and the general-social, which is characteristic of the province of understanding. The type is a basic significant notion for Dilthey and for MacIver, Becker, and Znaniecki, though Weber may be equally as important (or more so) for MacIver and Becker. (See chapter 2 above.)   *& Schutz*

Finally and most critically, for Dilthey and apparently also for MacIver, the notion of *Verstehen* or *understanding* (explicitly for the former and implicitly for the latter) entails what has come to be designated as hermeneutics," the centerpiece of which is the hermeneutical circle. In his study of Dilthey, Ermarth (1978, 252–53) has provided an apt characterization. The hermeneutical circle has "neither an absolute beginning nor ending . . . is neither purely inductive nor deductive, but both at once, for it involves a to-and-fro movement from part to whole and back to part again"; it entails no simple, atomistic elements or "indubitable starting points." Indeed, any particular understanding "depends upon a vast fund of prior understanding[s] . . . which remain in the twilight of consciousness and past experience," but which come into play at each stage of inquiry. Put very simply, interpretation "begins with a provisional or shiftable hypothesis," which is alterable in the interplay (shuttling back and forth) as further data and questions arise in inquiry. Context is of the utmost importance. Initially, written or printed texts were basic data (or "capta") of hermeneutics.

None of the American theorists explicitly adopts a hermeneutical approach. But MacIver in effect espouses it (as does Becker) in his emphasis on part-whole considerations and in his interpretive analysis of part in relationship to part, and to whole, in varying contexts. For MacIver ([1942] 1964), the basic methodological notion is sympathetic or imaginative reconstruction, which certainly is congruent with Dilthey, if not inspired by the latter, and seems to imply a hermeneutical procedure. Using various types of available evidence as aids, the researcher must project himself into the situation as it is defined and evaluated by others (391). At all places and all times, some meaningful unity and coherence exists in and surrounds the life of the individual, beyond him or her in the life of the group, and beyond the group in the life of the society as a whole. Each presumably interrelates with the others. Each social phenomenon must be understood as an expression of a meaningful system, which must be inferred, interpreted, or dynamically reconstructed (392). (The evocation of an "expression" of a meaningful system is characteristically Diltheyan.) What individuals and groups do must be related to a scheme of values, each of which more or less upholds and yet is constantly reconstructed in the course of adjusting means to ends and ends to means through all the hazards of the experiences of life (393). Although not unambiguously acknowledged as the shuttling to-and-fro of part to whole and whole to part, the interpretive or reconstructive process of dynamic assessment as presented by MacIver (and as partially extracted) seems to conform substantially to what Dilthey and others would have termed "hermeneutics," with the hermeneutical circle. (Although the evidence is not as detailed, Becker appears also to invoke the hermeneutical circle.[11]

Regrettably, this skeletal account of second-period theory's anticipation of a current expanded interpretive theory must now be concluded, though it is severely truncated and at best only suggestive. Among its implications is the caution that exclusive reliance on any one second-period theorist (e.g., Parsons) will ignore other important evidence (from Blumer, Becker, and MacIver). If the account had been carried through the third period, the significance of phenomenology and ethnomethodology would have become apparent.[12] And on the contemporary scene, one branch of critical theory can be shown to be congruent with the current expanded interpretive stance.[13]

Thus, the issue of relevance has been approached by juxtaposing past and present alternatively. On the one hand, the relevance of present-day or current theory (i.e., the foundations and foundationalism opposed by post-modernism) for second-period theory has been examined and indicated. On the other, the relevance of second-period theory (especially action-interactionism) as anticipatory of the character of the current expanded interpretive stance has been preliminarily explored and suggested.

And now, finally, a more technical aspect of relevance must be considered.

THIS ACCOUNT OF HISTORY AND THE FUTURE HISTORY OF AMERICAN SOCIOLOGICAL THEORY

To constitute the history of a period of theory in American sociology, an analytical classificatory-periodizing scheme, which was devised two decades ago and used for the first time more recently, has been invoked. In effect, this scheme conceives of theory as a (more or less) coherent set of explanatory and interpretive statements focusing on fundamental questions (or problematics) and answers (or stances), which are susceptible of increasingly more particular and specific formulations. Such theory is, at least potentially, both comprehensive and generic in scope, that is, a general theory. In addition, it includes both social epistemological-methodological and social ontological divisions, each having implications for the other, whether formally and explicitly interrelated or not.

Nevertheless, this conception can be applied to inquiry of delimited time intervals so that detailed, specific expositions can result. (Indeed, the scheme itself can become the basis for periodization.) It was applied earlier to the first period of American sociological theory (1881–1915) and now to the second period of theory (1915–/18–1945/50).

By virtue of the fact that (obviously) the second period immediately follows the first, two problems are immediately present. One concerns the continuity and discontinuity of the basic epistemological-methodological stances, and the other the continuity and discontinuity of the basic social ontological stance or stances.

Chapter 2 indicated the emergence of a substantially altered view of science as entailing particular kinds of methods or techniques that presuppose a particular type of epistemology and implementing methodology. That which emerged (and indeed became dominant) may be characterized as a statistically couched, qualified empiricist, and neo-positivist epistemology-methodology. (In fact, its hegemonic position in the discipline resulted in social ontological theory's eventually having a vastly inferior status to that in the first period.)

Chapters 3–5 revealed that social evolutionism (as the dominant social ontological stance, with social origins, structure, and change as primary problematics) was continuous up to the early 1930s, when essentially new additions suddenly ceased. Although accounts of the decline and demise of social evolutionism in its origins, structure, and change divisions have been offered, they cannot be argued to be complete in all respects. Certainly, research on the unpublished papers of such "gatekeepers" as Ellsworth Faris might prove extremely rewarding.

Chapter 7–10 indicated that new general theory did not develop around the stances from other disciplines: anthropology (culture), history (either as modern data or as critique of past ideas), psychiatry (Freudianism), psychology (behaviorism, gestaltism), the amalgam of behavioral psychology, (pragmatist) philosophy, and (idealist) sociology, and the (especially Weberian-derived) social action frame of reference. (Analytically, the classificatory scheme was deficient in failing to provide more than basic outlines for the disciplines examined in these chapters. Indeed, it was necessary to offer an ad hoc mini-scheme.)

Although it is true that the closest approximation to a relatively widely respected and accepted theory was that of Park and his students (chapter 6); even that languished by World War II. Accordingly, an argument might be made that no extensively accepted genuine general social ontological theory existed in American sociology after the early 1930s. But recognition of this argument would not necessarily mean that theoretically relevant activity had ceased. The critical evaluations involved in the just-preceding paragraph belie any such inference. Furthermore, the analysis offered in connection with foundations and foundationalism (above) even suggests that unintentional preparatory developments occurred favorable to Parsonsian functionalism.

So the question must now be raised at the abstract analytical level. Can the analytical classificatory scheme used here be of any serious use in a comprehensive, systematic endeavor to deal with the rise and fall of the several branches of structural functionalism in the next period of theory and, indeed, in determining the duration of the next period? Considerable work has already been undertaken, but much remains to be done. Even if the primary problem continues to be explanation within the American academic setting, it probably will not be intellectually prudent so to limit it. Structural functionalism had an international (certainly, a European) impact. A comparative study of reactions, especially of sociologists and social scientists in France, Germany, and Great Britain, is almost certainly warranted—even to learn what may be peculiarly American! The role of the analytical scheme in all of this? Only if the future (here conceived as possibility) becomes actuality (the present) can the answer be known.

Appendix

ESSENTIALS OF A SCHEME FOR CLASSIFYING AND PERIODIZING
(GENERAL OR MACRO-) THEORIES IN THE HISTORY OF
AMERICAN SOCIOLOGY

I.   Criteria for the analytical classification and periodization of sociological theory
    A.   The nature of theory in sociological theory (implying an expanded concern with social epistemological-methodological theory)
    B.   The nature of the social in sociological theory (implying an expanded concern with social ontological theory)
II. Theory about knowing and studying the social (social epistemology-methodology)
    A.   Bases of knowing the social (social knowledge)
        1.   Sensation (empiricism) vs. reason (rationalism)
        2.   Feeling, empathy, *nacherleben*
    B.   Methods for studying the social
        1.   Similarity and dissimilarity of methods for studying the social with respect to the biophysical sciences: positivism (as similar) vs. humanism (as dissimilar)
        2.   Focus of methods on parts (as methodological atomism or individualism) vs. wholes (as methodological holism or collectivism)
    C.   Epistemological-methodological implementation in formulating theory as:
        1.   Explanation (positivist, objectivist): physical model, deductive-nomological, universal
        2.   Interpretation (humanistic, intersubjectivist): language-communication basis; ethnomethodologically-phenomenologically-hermeneutically-construed; meaningfully limited
III. Theory about the (known) social (social ontology)
    A.   Conceptions of the social (as):

1. (Interpersonal and/or multipersonal) Relation(s) or relationships
2. (Interpersonal and/or multipersonal) Activity or activities
    a. The character of the activity: "behavior," "action," "inter-action," "sociation" (association-dissociation)
    b. Forms of activity: (process of) cooperation, competition, conflict, accommodation, assimilation, etc.
3. (Persisting, structured) Group
    a. Basis: interpersonal and/or multipersonal relations and activities that persist and become structured
    b. Kinds: dyads to society

B. Relations of the social to other phenomena and/or realities
    1. The social as a domain, realm, or system
        a. As a type of object (or object-like) entity in nature (as constituted of distinctive forces, for instance)
        b. As a distinctive whole possessing some autonomy from biophysical nature
    2. Relations of the non- and near-social to social phenomena
        a. Nonhuman biophysical
        b.Human: (1) organic, (2) psychic, (3) cultural, (4) near-social: Plurals, categories, aggregates

C. Nature of the social
    1. As a form of reality
        a. Preponderantly "pure" forms (monisms): social and sociological "materialisms" vs. social and sociological "idealisms"
        b. Substantially "mixed" forms (dualisms or pluralisms, etc., of types and subtypes of social "materialisms" and social "idealisms")
    2. In relation to the (Logical-ontological) part/whole or whole/part controversy ("universals-particulars," "holism-atomism")
        a. Social nominalism (and neo-nominalism)/social atomism
        b. Social realism (and neo-realism)/social holism

D. Major problems and their interrelations in the study of the social
    1. *Genesis* (origins, emergence)
    2. *Stasis* (statics, stability, persistence, structure)
    3. *Dynamis* (dynamics, instability, change, variation, transformation)

Source: Taken from, by permission of the author and copyright holder, Roscoe C. Hinkle, *Founding Theory of American Sociology 1881–1915,* (Boston: Routledge & Kegan Paul, 1980). For further elaboration, consult pp. 63–4 and note #2 (of the same work), p. 331.

Notes

CHAPTER 1

1. Certainly, a crucial problem for contemporary *scholarship* in sociology today is the nature of the historical process by which "classical masters" and their texts are established. Clearly, Weber's rise to fame as a classical master in American sociology is associated with major theoretical shifts in American sociology, such as the emergence of a social action orientation, anticipations of structural functionalism, and (an accommodation with?) a neo-positivist quantitative stance in the 1930s. Conversely, within the last decade, a few representatives of an older German generation of historical scholarship have vigorously protested their younger contemporaries' uncritical acceptance of the dominant American interpretation of Max Weber and the (American) English translations of the latter's major works. Friedrich Tenbruck and Wilhelm Hennis have been major spokesmen for this older generation. See Tenbruck's chapter on Max Weber and Eduard Meyer (Tenbruck 1987, 241, 263 n. 40); Wilhelm Hennis's *Max Weber: Essays in Reconstruction* (1988, 59, 60, 108, 200–201 n. 14, 205 n. 91); Tribe 1988, 1, 7, 8). See also Oakes's reference to a "positivist reading of Weber's methodology" and to its "virtual stranglehold in Weberian studies," especially in the United States, Oakes 1988, 15b n. 20, 159–62 n.1.

2. It is illuminating that Alvin Gouldner could have attempted to account for the rise of Parsonsian structural functionalism (e.g., his Period IV; Gouldner 1970, 138–57) without ever even suspecting that the character of American sociology and sociological theory during the 1930s and 1940s might be part of that account. He was apparently unaware that Parsons's (and his followers') own intellectual success was contingent on reorienting American sociology and sociological theory from one set of traditions to another (or "discrediting" of one in behalf of another?). See Kivisto and Swatos 1990, 150, 151–52, 153–54. A major objective of the present inquiry is to indicate what the character of this pre-Parsonsian theory was.

3. In the years 1915–19, 14.5 percent of the articles are classified as "Theory and History" (and so it is the third largest class); in the period 1920–24, the percentage is 35.9 (and so it is the first or most numerous); but in the years 1925–29, it drops to only 15.1 percent (still remaining in first place but only by 0.4 percent). However, it declines to 5.3 percent (or eighth place) in the years 1930–34 and rises to 7.1 percent (or sixth place) in 1935–39 and increases to 8.5 percent (but still sixth largest) in 1940–44.

4. Only six can be so discovered in the *AJS* for the years 1915–44 (i.e., two in 1918, one in 1920, two in 1938, and one in 1940).

5. One relevant article occurs in 1936, one in 1938, one in 1939, one in 1940, three in 1941, two in 1942 and in 1943, and one in 1945.

6. Of the seven in *S&SR,* two occur in 1927, one in 1933, two in 1937, and one each in 1938 and 1942. Of the three in *SF* one occurred in 1927 and two in 1940.

7. A substantially different meaning of *social theory* has emerged in the 1990s. See the articles by Seidman and Lemert in *Sociological Theory* (Fall 1991).

8. In his *Systematic Sociology,* Becker does not define what theory is, though it is manifestly a closed system (61) that is characteristically deductive (62) yet can accommodate induction. It presumably involves a set of basic postulates or frame of reference (39). The frame of reference must be comprehensive and generic and yet distinctive of the phenomena to be studied and also nonevaluative in nature (39). What is to be investigated must be identified and defined and arranged (classificatorily) in terms of major and minor categories. Deduction and induction must be perpetually cross-corrected (62). (Although Becker explicitly acknowledges indebtedness to von Wiese's *Allgemeine Soziologie,* his own *Systematic Sociology* is far more than a mere translation. The adaptation, extensions, elaborations, and additions are so numerous and extensive that the work is substantially his own.)

9. Bain conceives of theory as a summarization of sense experience. *Law* and *principle* is a term for a verified hypothesis. Sociological theory comprises the body of generalizations that sociologists have formulated after a more intensive and extensive study of human group phenomena than that obtaining from commonsense generalization. It must stand the tests of logical consistency,"critical analysis, and pragmatic sanction" (Bain 1929b, 73).

10. Consult Hinkle and Hinkle, *The Development of Modern Sociology* 1954, 18–19, 44; Rhoades 1981, 11, 33, 42, 74–76.

11. See tables of the 4th, 5th, and 6th editions of the compendium on

American Universities and Colleges, ed. Clarence Stephen Marsh, A. J. Brumbaugh, and Mary Irwin, in 1940, 1948, 1952 respectively Washington D.C.: American Council on Education.

12. *American Universities and Colleges,* 1952, 50, 59.

13. *American Universities and Colleges,* 1940, Tables I–X, pp. 70–89; same work but 1952, Table 4, pp. 54–57.

14. The author is indebted to (Prof. Emer.) John H. Useem for the specifics of the formulations of the first four characteristics (personal communication on 24 April 1992).

15. Baker, Ferrell, and Quensel 1975. Manifestly, considerable variation existed among universities in attaining departmental independence and recognition. At Chicago, sociology became almost immediately a joint department with anthropology and was so designated in the 1890s. The discipline was represented at Columbia as a single department in the 1890s. Sociologists at Wisconsin remained a part of the Department of Political Economy (or Economics) until 1930, when a Department of Sociology was officially constituted. Interestingly, the same pattern was repeated at about the same dates for sociology at Michigan (Ann Arbor). Minnesota became an independent department in 1910. At Ohio State, sociology was recognized at the turn of the century as a joint department with economics. It achieved separate departmental status in 1922.

For Chicago, see R. E. L. Faris 1967; Bulmer 1984. For Columbia, see Lipset 1955; Page 1982. For Wisconsin, see Gillin n.d. For Michigan, information kindly supplied by Prof. Werner S. Landecker. For Minnesota, see Fine and Severence 1985. For Ohio State, see Hagerty n.d.

16. Senior faculty are defined as full-time (full) professors and associate professors of sociology. Faculty in anthropology, social work, or in other disciplines (jointly) in departments of sociology were excluded, as were sociologists of lesser rank.

The sources cited in previous note 15 were used to compile the data for the Departments of Sociology at the University of Chicago, Columbia University (graduate), the University of Wisconsin, and the University of Minnesota by mid years of four decades (1915, 1925, 1935, and 1945). Specific individuals were identified for each department for each of the four years specified. A similar procedure was followed for senior faculty in the Department of Sociology at Ohio State University using *The Ohio State University Bulletin,* vols. 19, 29 (Oct.), 39 (May) and 50 (Nov., i.e., the "University Directory" section) for the same four years.

A total of 83 senior faculty were identified for the years 1915, 1925, 1935, and 1945 in the departments at the five universities. Columbia and

Chicago had the largest numbers across the four intradecade years (Columbia, 19, and Chicago, 18). Minnesota had 17, Ohio State 16, and Wisconsin 13.

Interestingly, both the Chicago and the Columbia senior sociology staffs were larger in 1935 than in 1945, though only by one person in each case (i.e., 6 for Chicago in 1935 as against 5 in 1945, and 7 for Columbia as against 6 in 1945). Conversely, the Wisconsin and Minnesota senior sociology staffs were larger in 1945 than in 1935, though by only one person in one case and by two in the other (i.e., 5 for Wisconsin as opposed to 4, and 6 for Minnesota as opposed to 4). Ohio state had 5 senior sociologists in 1925, 1935, and 1945.

At Chicago, the 1935 senior sociologists consisted of E. Faris, E. Burgess, W. Ogburn, S. Stouffer, L. Wirth, and H. Blumer. At Columbia the 1935 senior sociologists were R. MacIver, R. Lynd, A. Lindsay, R. Chaddock, A. Tenney, and T. Abel.

At Wisconsin, the 1945 senior sociologists consisted of J. Gillin, T. McCormick, H. P. Becker, H. Gerth, and S. Riemer. At Minnesota, the 1945 senior sociologists were F. S. Chapin, C. Kirkpatrick, G. Vold, E. Monachesi, L. Nelson, and R. Sletto. At Ohio State (also in 1945), the senior sociologists were P. Denune, C. North, W. Reckless, L. Cook, and J. Cuber.

17. Hughes 1975; Committee on Graduate Instruction, American Council of Education 1934.

The list includes seventeen presidents of the ASS who had been faculty members or former graduate students in the Department of Sociology at the University of Chicago. Sixteen of the list came from Bulmer 1984, 43. The seventeenth is E. C. Hayes, who is included by virtue of extending the time period backward to 1920. Ogburn is, of course, found on both the Chicago and the Columbia lists. Columbia is second but with only seven of the presidents.

18. For early sections, see Rhoades 1981, 15. On the formation of regional associations, see Hinkle and Hinkle 1954, 45; Turner and Turner 1990, 155–57; also Hetrick, Pease, and Mathers 1978, 87–93; Pease and Hetrick 1977b, 9–10; Pease and Hetrick 1977a, 42, 47).

19. For ISRR, see Turner and Turner 1990, 41–45, 53, 58, 68, 76–77, 101, 109). For the LCRC, see also Turner and Turner 1990, 45–47, 51; and Bulmer 1984, an entire chapter so entitled.

20. Turner and Turner 1990, 51.

21. See Hinkle and Hinkle 1954, 44; Foster and Standing n.d.

22. Consult Hinkle 1980, 59–74; Hinkle 1975; Hinkle 1978.

23. Other volumes in the tracing of leads about the meanings of socio-

logical theory included Timasheff 1957; Sorokin 1966; Martindale 1960; Martindale 1965; Teggart 1941.

The question of what makes sociological theory distinctively "sociological" and "theoretical" (i.e., a theory) led back logically first to a consideration of *sociology* as the noun form of the adjective *sociological*, that is, to the notion of a discipline and profession characteristically endeavoring to know and to study the social (L. *socius*) in its most comprehensive sense. The implications of theory (as the Greek *theoria*) were pursued epistemologically and ontologically.

Of all the theorists of this period, only Howard P. Becker alluded to the ancient Greek origins of *theoria*. See his chapter on "Historical Sociology" in the Barnes, Becker, and Becker 1940, 541, also Becker 1950, 188. For a brief historical reconstruction of the details, consult Lobkowicz 1967, 3–8; McCarthy 1978, 57–58.

24. It is surely appropriate, if not also necessary, to identify the nature of the intellectual undertaking suggested with other similar ventures in sociology. Alvin Gouldner's *The Coming Crisis of Western Sociology* (1970) refers to "background assumptions" of various kinds, some more global and overarching (even metaphysical) and some more limited in scope, termed "domain assumptions" (29–31), such as those of the sociocultural. These latter might involve popular assumptions of the "man on the street" about human nature and society (31), those of the intellectual practitioners in the social sciences generally, and those more narrowly limited to particular social sciences, such as sociology, American sociology, or American sociological theory. See Hinkle 1971.

Conceived in the broad terms of even more recent theoretical arguments deriving from postmodernism, the assumptions involved here might be said to entail those basic or foundational to (i.e., the foundations of) general theory in sociology between World Wars I and II. Clearly, the term foundation has not been used precisely in the way here proposed by either Lyotard or his proponents, critics, or interpretors. But such figures as Bernstein and Kellner in philosophy (Bernstein 1985, 9–18, 23, 73, 155; Kellner 1988, 248–57) and Lemert in sociology (Lemert 1990, esp. 237) provide the basis for legitimating the usage here advanced. Certainly, Lyotard's illustrations suggest that foundations have been a critical concern of philosophy, especially epistemology (and perhaps methodology?). Furthermore, allusions to progress and Marxism also signify the possibility for more substantive or social ontological formulations of foundations. In either case, it is the logically generic bases or premises that constitute—to paraphrase Derrida— "that beyond which we need not go," that is the foundations (Culler 1982, 92). In Bernstein's words, they have the characteristics of that which is "supposed to be fixed, eternal, ultimate, necessary, or indubitable" and universal (Bernstein 1985, 9). Accordingly, it seems appropriate to refer to the foundational assumptions in both the social epistemological-methodological and social ontological domains of social and sociological theory.

CHAPTER 2

1. Consult Ellwood 1925, 31–34; Lumley 1928, 536–39; Reuter and Hart 1933, 18–20.

2. See Odum's *American Sociology* for summary statements of the views of Ogburn, Bernard, Chapin, and Lundberg (Odum 1951, 147–52, 161–65, 172–76, 205–12). Consult also Bierstedt 1981, 349–88, for an analysis of Lundberg; Duncan 1964, vii–xxii, and Bannister 1987, chaps. 8–12, on Bernard, Chapin, and Ogburn.

3. See Odum 1951 for summary statements of the views of Cooley, Ellwood, Park, E. Faris, and MacIver (109–12, 128–31, 131–35, 180–86, 194–97). Consult also Bierstedt 1981 for analyses of Cooley, Znaniecki, MacIver, and Sorokin (89–130, 185–242, 243–98, 299–348).

4. Interestingly, at least six of the nine features of the statistically oriented, qualified empiricist, neo-positivist stance, to be elucidated in the following sections, are derivable from arguments in Pearson 1900. See Pearson's arguments that science is not limited to any one set of materials, that it is beginning to emerge in the domain of social facts, and that it is uniformly characterizable in terms of natural laws (Pearson 1900, 12, 16, 77ff); the repeated references to the "world of phenomena," "objective reality," "reality of things," the "external universe" (66–67, 51, 60, 95); Pearson's emphasis on "sensation," "sensory experience," "sense-impressions" (e.g., 53, 66); the declaration that the unity of science resides in its (common) method (12); his claim of the necessary deducibility of conceptions in science from sensory experience; his contention that all (natural) science involves the formulation of (natural) laws, along with the possibility of sociology's emergence as a science; his allusion to "progress in formulating natural laws" (96–100); and his apparent acknowledgment of quantifiable units, measurement, and statistical analysis in physics and biology which were then the most advanced branches of science (last several chapters in his book). For an analysis of the linkage between Pearson and Giddings, see Ross 1991, 156–57, 227–28, 326–27, 369.

5. Chapin (1920, 6) alludes to the scientist's "problem". Ogburn (1929, 9, 10) refers to the sociologist choosing problems. For Meroney (1925, 100, 101) note the phrase "problem at hand".

6. Chapin 1920, 6; Chapin 1922, 169, 172–74; Lundberg 1929b, 4–5, 90, 94, Lundberg ([1929b] 1942, 10; Meroney 1925, 100, 101; Ogburn 1922, vi; Ogburn 1929, 10; also Hankins 1928, 163; Reuter and Hart 1933, 16–17; Lumley 1928, 7–19).

7. Lundberg 1929b, 4, 82, 83, 90; Lundberg [1929b] 1942, 9; Chapin 1920, 6; Chapin 1922, 169, 172; Meroney 1925, 101–4; Ogburn 1922, vi, vii; also Hankins 1928, 163; Reuter and Hart 1933, 17; Lumley 1928, 10–11).

8. (E.g., Chapin 1920, 7; Chapin 1922, 170–1; Meroney 1925, 101–4; ellwood 1925, 28). Both Chapin (1920, 78) and Meroney (1925, 106–7) seem to regard a law as being causally stated and as a potential basis for prediction (Chapin 1920, 7; Meroney 1925, 107). See also Hankins 1928, 164–65. By 1929, Ogburn had come to regard statistics as increasingly important (Ogburn 1929, 6–7). Because Lundberg (1929b) envisages the ideal form of such generalization as the mathematical formula, it is presumably to be formulated with the aid of statistical procedures (5). Clearly, the intervention of statistics is to occur at some point after step two or three and up to step four.

9. Unfortunately, the details and implications of this recasting of Comte by Pearson and its transmission through Giddings are not entirely clear (cf. S. Turner 1991, 108). But S. Turner notes that Giddings's resort to Pearson had "two curious implications" for theory (Turner 1991, 109). On the one hand, it justified the use of speculative social theory as potential claimants for confirmation through observation and eventual metricization. On the other, it precluded acceptance of deductive theory as an ideal. By construing statistical correlations as "uncontrolled experiments," it would become possible to discover "which variables and which relations are important in many settings" (111). They would become the equivalent for sociology of the constants of the natural sciences (111).

Admittedly, Giddings's *Inductive Sociology* is the most complete example of his adherence to Pearson's views, though his *The Principles of Sociology* and *Studies in the Theory of Human Society* are also indicative. Perhaps the most succinct statement of Giddings's views are to be found in the latter volume in connection with his notion of the inductive method in sociology: (1) accurate firsthand observations must be made in great number and carefully checked; (2) these observations must be painstakingly recorded and intelligently classified; and (3) "the data so obtained and prepared must be subject to statistical analysis for the purpose of discovering ratios, modalities, coefficients of variation and correlation" (300). A more extended account is provided in chapter 3 ("Inductive Method," Book I, 11–27).

So Giddings set the course for an empirical, inductive, quantitative sociology, which his students developed and elaborated. Notwithstanding his inclinations to use such notions as explanation and cause, his support of general theory seems to have been much less consequential for his followers. For early comments of the present author, see Hinkle 1980, 86, 92, 96–97.

10. Becker 1940 argued from the conception of causation in terms of necessary-sufficient conditions and directed it explicitly at Lundberg. Becker claims that a reduction of all experienced things conceptually to "forms of energy-transformation in a field of force" (or to "electron-proton configurations"), as Lundberg in effect recommends, is not scientifically or predictively useful. Physical and organic types of configurations are "the necessary conditions of social configurations," but they are not their sufficient conditions (Becker 1940, 11). A reduction of phenomena to their necessary conditions has no predictive value. The distinctive and efficacious factors of social phenomena are lost. It is these sufficient conditions that must be known and that involve the distinctive human capacity for speech (and presumably culture) that Lundberg in effect ignores in the reduction.

In spite of Lundberg's claim that as a sociologist he is interested in the special kind of interaction occurring through communication by means of symbolic behavior, he constantly ignores the possibility of a difference in the definition of the situation as held by the human subjects and as held by the inquiring observer. There "is often no readily determinable relation between 'stimuli' as the physicist would define them and the human 'responses' to these 'stimuli.' The same physical units may call forth widely differing varieties of conduct" (Becker 1940, 12). If the sociologist is serious about dealing with "that discrepancy between 'stimulus' and 'response' that so frequently appears, he must take as his unit those aspects of phenomena that the subject selectively defines and makes effective as elements in the structure of *his* actions" (Becker 1940, 13). But Lundberg obscures and confuses this problem "by treating units and aspects merely as convenient configurations imposed by man [but which man? observer? subject?] upon the data for a given purpose." In effect, claims Becker (1940, 14), Lundberg "reduces a situation to elements or units as defined by himself as observer, and because 'stimulus', 'response', and 'conditions' are units of this observer-defined character, the internal consistency of . . . [his behavioristic-materialistic] postulation system, again observer-created, permits no troublesome stimulus-response discrepancies to appear." Accordingly, the "basic sociological problem is 'solved' by failing to recognize it as a problem" (Becker 1940, 14). To equate Thomas and Znaniecki's "situation" with the physicist's field of force is to reduce it and to ignore its sufficient conditions. "Thomas and Znaniecki do not talk about situations as *they* define them, but as specific *subjects* define them" (Becker 1940, 15). Human beings must be understood in terms of "what they live by" (that is, their language and culture) and by the observer's interpretatively, empathically putting himself in their place.

Unfortunately, Becker must have discovered that Lundberg (1939b, 121) had declared that "all behavior is relative to the behaver's definition of the situation" and, accordingly, he never published the review in this form. However, Lundberg (1939b, 21–22) did encounter the problem Becker specified in accounting for the effectiveness of a taboo (as given in one culture) versus an iron fence (other*s*) in "preventing" movement or touching of an object. His effort to resolve the explicative dilemma by arguing for "lesser" and "greater" objectivity (*sic*), with the former referring to the definition of men in one culture and the latter for "men in general," discloses that Becker had actually revealed a genuine problem of Lundberg's "behavioristic-materialism," though it could not be presented as simply as Becker had initially believed. (See also chapter 8.)

11. Except for Cooley, all of the Americans involved had been British- or European-born or educated or had extensive Continental (and more precisely, German) contacts (the latter in the case of Becker). Cooley's linkage with Dilthey must remain wholly inferential; he makes no explicit references to Dilthey in any of his published works. Admittedly, finding such relevant references in his journals (in the University of Michigan libraries in Ann Arbor) may still remain a possibility. Scottish-born and -educated, MacIver published a chapter on contemporary developments in sociology (MacIver 1931c), revealing his substantial awareness of the main feature of German philosophy, social science, and sociology (70–80, with particularly important references on pp. 72 and 75, but without disclosure of any personal indebtedness).

In some instances (e.g., Park and Becker), the documentary evidence of connections with Windelband and Rickert as the major spokesmen of German Neo-Kantianism is easily accessible and already widely known. For more about Park, see below. Becker's linkages are readily evident in Barnes and Becker 1938; Barnes, Becker, and Becker 1940; Becker 1950. Becker was, of course, also substantially indebted to Max Weber, whose concurrence with Rickert is extensively known. This latter comment is also applicable to Parsons, especially his *The Structure of Social Action* ([1937] 1968, 500–696). (For references to Dilthey, Windelband, and Rickert, see Parsons [1937] 1968 476, 490, 484; 476; 476, 580, 595, 636.)

Interestingly, Znaniecki's connection with German (and especially Neo-Kantian) sources is least evident documentarily. Such may be the case primarily because Znaniecki provides far fewer footnotes, for instance, in his important *The Method of Sociology* (1934) than do many of his colleagues in their major works. Nevertheless, his *Cultural Reality* (1919) cites Windelband and

Rickert as taking a position similar to his (or vice versa? viii). His *The Method of Sociology* refers to Dilthey once (33) and to Windelband and Rickert twice (21, 33), but the structure of Znaniecki's argument suggests that Rickert is far more important than these two citations indicate.

Nevertheless, the difficulties of providing documented indebtedness (as opposed to intellectual similarities or congruencies) have prompted the author to refer to "American counterparts of" (or "congruencies with") German neo-idealism and Neo-Kantianism in the text above.

12. See Cooley's "The Roots of Social Knowledge" (1926), the "Case Study of Small institutions as a Method of Research" (1928), and "The Life Study Method as Applied to Rural Social Research" (1929). All three papers are in Cooley 1930. (See also Hinkle 1980, 88–89, 97–101.)

13. Dilthey, *Einleitung in die Geisteswissenschaften,* 1883. This major work has never been translated in its entirety into English. Numerous passages were translated in H. A. Hodges's *Wilhelm Dilthey, An Introduction* (1944). The readily accessible compendium *W. Dilthey: Selected Writings* was edited, translated, and introduced by H. P. Rickman (1976). For expositions, see Ermarth 1978 and Plantinga 1980. Given American sociologists' interest in late-nineteenth-century German philosophy, social thought, and sociology, Dilthey is not known nearly as well in the United States as he should be.

14. Park completed his doctoral dissertation under Windelband in 1903 after the latter had moved to Heidelberg. It was Park who first introduced Windelband's ideas (and thus the Neo-Kantian orientation) to American sociology, in the course of a paper he presented to the American Sociological Society (Park 1913, 167–68). He referred to the German philosopher's notion of history in conjunction with the history/science dichotomy. Subsequently, Park elaborated more fully on both parts of the dichotomy (with selected translated quotations) in an extended paper that was published in the *American Journal of Sociology* (Park 1921) and appeared again as part of the first chapter of Park and Burgess 1921 (8–10), and once more in Park 1955, 194–96. The full text of Windelband's address (in German) is printed in volume 2 of his *Praeludien* (5th ed., 1924, 136–60). It was translated into English by Guy Oakes in *History and Theory* (Windelband [1984] 1980).

15. The original German title of Rickert's first work was *Die Grenzen der naturwissenschaftlichen Begriffsbildung,* the first three chapters of which were published in 1896 and the entire work in 1902. The German title of his second volume was *Kulturwissenschaft und Naturwissenschaft,* which is literally "Cultural Science and Natural Science" and was published in 1899. It was translated into English under the (misleading) title *Science and*

History by George Reisman (and edited by Arthur Goddard) and published in 1962. The first work on *The Limits* was translated into English (in part and edited) by Guy Oakes under the English title as indicated above in 1986.

16. Becker 1950, 124, may suggest a shift in position: If perceptions are to be communicated, they require articulate or inarticulate concepts.

17. Parsons regards his "action scheme as analogous to the space-time framework of physics which is 'necessary' for the comparison of every physical phenomenon—precisely as Kant claimed it to be" (Bershady 1973, 68).

18. Becker (1950) equates the study of the general with the study of recurrence, and the latter with the possibility of prediction. The "ultimate criterion of scientific generalization in sociology is . . . prediction of the recurrence of social phenomena" (101). The sociologist will claim that, "given such and such circumstances, these [other] circumstances will follow" (161).

19. Having an excellent command of written and spoken German, and being widely read in German philosophy and social science, Becker must have known about Rickert's more complex fourfold classification of types of fields of knowledge as based both on type of method and on subject matter. So two extreme polar types can be discerned: at one end, a natural-science (generalizing) method with a natural-science subject matter (a kind of natural object), such as physics, and at the other, a cultural-historical (individualizing) method with a cultural-historical subject matter (a type of value), such as history. But two intermediate types are also identifiable, one with a natural-science method and a cultural-historical subject matter (e.g., sociology) and another with a cultural-historical method and a natural-scientific subject matter (e.g., evolutionary biology). Although Becker explicitly ignored the differentiations, his conception of sociology as a generalizing science entailing interpretation or understanding (*verstehen*) implicitly invokes one of the intermediate fields. (See Ricker [1899] 1962, 104–12.)

20. Behind, or basic to, the two types of systems, natural and cultural, are (natural) objects or things (which exist independently of human experience) and values (which can exist only in the active experience of some particular people). See Znaniecki 1934, 34–43; also with Znaniecki and Thomas 1918, 1:21, 29.)

21. Subjectivity and *verstehen* are indispensable to the character of action (theoretical) systems. See Parsons (1937) 1968, 764–65.

22. One of the papers was originally published in 1924 and later reprinted in 1950; the other was unpublished until it was printed in a collection

on race that was compiled by Thompson and Hughes, two of Park's students. In neither case was Dilthey cited. In Park's 1924 paper as republished in *Race and Culture* (1950), he explicitly contrasts explanation and interpretation (understanding). An attitude (or motive?) of another person can be understood if the observer can "reproduce the circumstances under which it arose so completely" that he or she "can enter imaginatively into the situation and the experience of which the attitude [of the other] is a part" (154). Park (1958, 462–64) explicitly refers to "re-living" (or "re-experiencing").

23. For Becker, human action is meaningful basically both because it is "understandable" motivationally in a means-ends motivational sense and because it is predicated on communicatively shared linguistic symbols. Either way, human action is meaningful, and it is understandable because it is meaningful. And either way, it must be understood or interpreted in context.

24. Znaniecki (1934, 207) holds that social reality is constituted of specific, objectively observable, distinct systems, the elements of which are objectively given values. He claims that each possesses a structure "having an objective order of its own, though it is neither an order of ends and means . . . nor an order of deductive construction."

25. Finally, it is no longer possible or desirable to avoid the obvious: This chapter involves an illuminating case study for testing the possibilities of further development of the epistemological-methodological sections of the classificatory periodizing scheme (Appendix, II.A.1, 2; B.1, 2; C.1, 2). Manifestly, the positivism of the second period displays some differences/discontinuities with that of the earlier period, such as the concern with statistical procedures, the resort basically to a physicalist model, and the insistence on utility. Hence, the specification of "neo-positivism" (or instrumentalist positivism). It has continued to employ an empiricist epistemology (i.e., sensory experience), albeit with some qualifications or reservations. Earlier positivism was committed to generalized causal explanations, whereas that of the second period restricted itself to statistical correlation and probability logic.

Neo-idealism is another term for humanism (Appendix, II.B.1), with such knowledge involving especially a peculiar feeling for another or others, that is, empathy, *nacherleben,* etc. (as Cooley, Dilthey, and MacIver have argued). Its objective is not explanation but understanding.

Compared with the two previous positions, Neo-Kantianism is distinctive. Its original German version emphasizes the rational or logical organization of knowledge (which only Znaniecki seems to have closely approximated). The antithetical "generalizing" and "individualizing" tendencies derive from the interest in or methods of (natural) science and history (historical disciplines). But it also acknowledges a dichotomy of subject matter of natural objects (or things) and (human) values. The stance can embrace both (individualizing) subjectivist *verstehen* or understanding and (restricted generalizing) objectivist value interpretation.

However, a major caution must be introduced in the apparent equation of "generalizing," "nomothetic," and "natural science." Neo-Kantianism retains the assumption of the active intervention of mind in knowledge. It rejects the view that mind is wholly or primarily subordinate to the impact (via sensation) of the external world and thus merely photographically reproduces the "external world" as data given to it. But, unawares, American (positivistic) social scientists are, accordingly, frequently misled into assuming that (the German Neo-Kantian) "nomothetic disciplines" or "natural sciences" are conceived to be empiricist epistemologically as are their "own natural sciences." (A Neo-Kantian would contend that mind has an active "interest" in the external world, albeit a "generalizing" one). An insistence on the use of the term *nomothetic* may have some advantage, but it doesn't insure that an epistemological error may not be made. Hence, it becomes absolutely imperative that both epistemological and methodological criteria be kept in "mind" in distinguishing the domains of the sciences as fields of knowledge.

26. By the end of World War II, the protagonists of a natural-science, statistically oriented sociology were substantially successful in defining normal sociology in terms of their views (i.e., a statistically oriented, qualified empiricist, and neo-positivist epistemology-methodology). Their success was the outcome of a series of complex developments extending over more than two decades, including membership on the early Committee on Standardization of Research (of the ASS), the influence of the SSRC, extra-academic funding of research (especially by the foundations, such as Rockefeller and Carnegie, by way of, for instance, the Institute for Social and Religious Research and the SSRC), the kinds of persons and projects to be awarded graduate or professional fellowships, the kinds of professional skills leading to inclusion in special research projects (e.g., the study of American Black-White [race] relations as published in *An American Dilemma*), formation and maintenance of research bureaus and institutes (e.g., University of North Carolina's Institute for Social Research and Columbia University's Bureau of Applied Social Research), and in participation in research under the auspices of the federal government (as noted above). (Consult Turner and Turner 1990, chaps. 2 and 3 as relevant. Also Bulmer 1984, chaps. 8, 9, and 10). Paradoxically, their success was reflected in their unwillingness to engage in polemics with their opponents after the early 1940s (Turner and Turner 1990, 110–11). Their dominant views were expected to be mirrored in the responses of graduate students in masters' and doctoral examinations.

Their notions had increasingly gained ascendancy as the criteria of satisfactory, acceptable journal articles, and, indeed, as hallmarks of professional prestige generally.

CHAPTER 3

1. For the relevance of the analytical classificatory periodizing scheme to evolutionary naturalism, see the full version of the scheme in Hinkle 1980, chap. 3, pp. 61–62, III.C and III.B.1.a) and 2.a), b); also pp. 68–71, 103–29.

2. In comparison, MacIver's *Society* is not explicitly committed to evolutionary naturalism, though his chapter "Social Causation" leads to such implications in its linkage with his views in *Social Causation* ([1942] 1964). In this latter work, MacIver alludes to the three dynamic realms of physical, organic, and conscious being in nature, each with its distinctive coherence, its own dynamic quality and mode of causality, which is naturalistic rather than supernaturalistic.

Although Lumley (1928) does not offer any exposition of the various domains or realms of existence as so many spheres in which distinctive laws prevail, he does note that evolution denies "the unnaturally caused" (presumably in favor of the naturally caused). The logic of his position is that social phenomena are a domain of the naturally caused.

Lumley also alludes to continuity in all evolution in such fashion as to imply genetic filiation. To talk "of the evolution of organisms or the earth or society" is to "mean that there is continuity in everlasting change" (412). Because there is continuity at so many points in nature, evolutionists "have no reason to believe that man is an exception" (412). Continuous with "all organic life," man is derived "from so-called lower forms of animal life" (412).

3. Ellwood's chapter 2 also includes sections entitled "The Origins of Group Live Among Animals" and "The Nature of Primitive Human Social Life"; Hankins's chapter 8, the sections "Human Associative Tendency Rooted in the Struggle for Existence" and "Gregariousness, Consciousness of Kind, and Group Formation"; and Reuter and Hart's chapter 5, a section "The Universality of Group Life."

4. Social forces are confined to the human realm, generally to human nature, and especially to the psychic. They are consciously felt desires of human beings, impelling or attracting them to act for or against other persons. Basically, they are "organic-affective in nature and constitute the true dynamic agents of society" (Hinkle 1980, 70). At the psychic level (as

desires), they "are conscious, telic, volitional, and motivational" (70). Most significantly for this analysis, they were believed to interconnect directly the organic and the psychic within human nature. They embraced a broad range from instincts, innate appetites, needs, wants, cravings, and impulses to inclinations, feelings, sentiments, desires, and wishes (69).

The notion of social forces as part of human nature has ancient origins in Western philosophical and scientific traditions, deriving from *natura* as the Roman-Latin rendition (mistranslation?) of the Greek *physis* (especially in Aristotle's formulation). In his *Social Change and History,* Nisbet (1969) explains what Aristotle's notion of *physis* involved, with its implications for humankind and (human) society as objects in nature (21–29; also Nisbet 1970, 151–52, 175–76).

As a distinctive type of object in nature, society has its own internal principle of motion, growth or, more accurately, (gradual) growth as a model of change. The social forces doctrine may be said to reflect at least two of the several meanings of *physis* as it applies to society (but construed in terms of late-nineteenth and early-twentieth-century social evolutionism). First, *physis* refers to certain constituents of human nature,—seedlike, elemental, or atomlike components or entities, such as instinctive needs, that provide society's internal dynamic or intrinsically activate it. *Physis* also signifies an original state, condition, or stage that society exhibits in the association generated from the constituents of human nature (i.e., primitive society). In the broadest sense, *physis* is revealed in the patterned tendency of society to change as exhibited in a life-cycle series of stages representative of, or akin to, growth as based on the components of an original human nature. It was the objective of nineteenth-century evolutionary science to *abstract* out that general pattern (that which exists for the most part, generally, etc.) as opposed to the (historically) accidental, variant, or unique.

5. For a relevant bibliography, see Bernard 1926b, 597–600; and Bernard's selection "Instincts" in the *Encyclopaedia of the Social Sciences,* 1930.

6. Ellwood, who was chairman of the above session at the American Sociological Society meeting and the author of several papers, summarized his position in his *The Psychology of Human Society* [1925] 1929, esp. 81–104, 275–309.

Bernard was a discussant in the above session, contributed several relevant articles, and was the author of the major book *Instinct* (1924) and the definitive selection on "Instincts" in the *Encyclopaedia of the Social Sciences.* His position is conveniently summarized in his *Introduction to Social Psychology* (1926b, 114–41).

Hankins, whose section "Elements of Behavior" in his chapter on "The

Psychological Basis of Social Life" in Hankins 1928 (327–45) is especially discerning and illuminating in this period.

Ellsworth Faris published a series of relevant articles and chapters on the instincts throughout the 1920s. Most of them are included in his *The Nature of Human Nature* ([1937a] 1976).

7. Ogburn and Nimkoff (1940, 27–45) adduce like data and arguments. Bernard adopts a similar stance in his chapters on the physical and early cultural history of humans in *An Introduction to Sociology* (1942, chaps. 2 and 3). Hankins 1928 also includes chapters entitled "The Evolution of Material Culture" (i.e., of technology and economy), "Myth, Magic, Religion, and Science," "Marriage and the Family," and "The Evolution of Social Organization and Integration.")

8. Among sociologists, Ellsworth Faris wrote most extensively on the sociocultural evolutionary explanation of sociocultural origins. See his *The Nature of Human Nature* ([1937a] 1976), especially his papers "Social Evolution" (esp. 255–60), "The Mental Capacity of Preliterates," "Ethnological Light on Psychological Problems," "The Origin of Punishment," and "The Sect and the Sectarian." Although he rejected the generic problem of sociocultural origins as insoluble, he held that the origins of certain more specific sociocultural forms and features, such the modern isolated sect are accessible in history (46). Graduate students at Chicago and elsewhere largely ignored his statement and suggested recommendation.

CHAPTER 4

1. Park claimed that he rejected the social evolutionisms of Comte and Spencer because they resulted in a "philosophy of history, [and] not a natural science of society" (Park and Burgess [1921] 1924, 210). More particularly in the case of Spencer, Park also remarked that the then-current trend of sociology was "toward the study of societies rather than [human] society" as a whole, as it was in Spencer's time (210).

Nevertheless, Park manifestly accepted human involvement as an organism in organic evolution. But human social change differs from human organic change and requires, therefore, a different term, one differentiating what is or was socially acquired and transmitted from what arises from organic individual variation and is hereditarily transmitted. Accordingly, Park followed Baldwin's proposed use of the term *accommodation* for the former and *adaptation* for the latter (663). Adaptation is an effect of competition, and accommodation is the result of conflict (as Park construes the two). The products of accommodation are acquired adjustments (e.g., "social heritages, traditions, sentiments, culture, technique") that are socially rather than organically-genetically transmitted. They "are not part of the racial inheritance of the individual, but acquired by the person in social experience" (664).

2. See Appendix, section III.D.2. See also Hinkle 1980, 63, 192–212, and esp. 344 n. 4. Keller is of particular interest as a theorist, for even though he lived and published throughout the first and second periods of American sociology, he is entirely associated with the theoretical interests and stance (i.e., social evolution) of the first. As a change theorist, his position differs substantially from that of Sumner. For details of the basic differences between Keller and Sumner, see Smith and Hinkle 1979, 41–48, esp. 41–42 nn. 3–6. A comparison of the views of the two Yale sociologists indicates disagreement on at least five of the six major features of social evolutionism and possibly also on the organismic growth analogy regarding Sumner after 1899 (42–47). It is, therefore, inappropriate to term Sumner a "social evolutionist" but entirely valid so to designate Keller.

Furthermore, Keller's social evolutionism appeared in his publications during the first period and, importantly, the social evolutionism of *The Science of Society* (Sumner and Keller 1927) is entirely Keller's. Accordingly, Hinkle 1980 considered Keller as a first-period social dynamics theorist, and he is so regarded in the present work. Keller simply continued a typical social evolutionism of the first period into the second. Even though *The Science of Society* was published in 1927, its adoption of an unqualified and unquestioned social evolutionism is typical of the first rather than the second period.

3. Much of Faris's chapter on social evolution is substantially critical. In its original version of 1924 (but not in its later republication in 1937 and 1976), it contained a series of illuminating headings and subheadings, the major one of which is "Older Theories of Social Evolution" (twelve pages of a total of thirty-two). Yet criticisms are to be found throughout the chapter. Curiously, Faris implies that social evolution as a notion differs from social progress, "to which it is indeed closely related," but he never actually specifies the difference or differences as such except for the claim that the former is factual-objective and the latter evaluative-subjective (Faris [1937a] 1976, 249, 252, 254). Nevertheless, Faris's exposition of social evolution in the chapter includes all of the basic features, save the comparative method (which he treats elsewhere in *The Nature of Human Nature*).

4. Like the classical social evolutionists, Ogburn and Chapin adopted the organic or organismic analogy or, more exactly (because change is at issue), the organismic growth analogy. The term *growth* was often employed virtually interchangeably with *change*. Ogburn also invoked a mechanistic

analogy, that a society or its culture is constituted of parts like a machine and, so, interrelated.

Both sociologists use the organismic growth analogy to develop several implications of the change process. First, they claim that change is like growth in the sense that it has a directionality in expansion (or increase in the number of units) and in differentiation and specialization. Such change does, of course, entail additions that exceed losses over time and does involve both continuity and accumulation through time. The implication of a set of stages of growth as in the life cycle of an organism is a difficult issue for both of them. Both deny the legitimacy of a unilinear sequence of specific, determinate, and inevitable stages so characteristics of the older social evolutionism. Nevertheless, both of them are committed to the notion of a general directionality in a "main stream" of human culture (or human society). Chapin (1928) is distinctive in holding that the various sociocultural forms have their distinctive life cycles, each with its own "cyclical law of growth, maturity, and decay" (215, 214).

Second, both Ogburn and Chapin regard the parts of a society and its culture as an organic or organismic system and as thus possessing some minimal intercorrelation, interdependence, equilibrium, or integration of parts. For instance, Ogburn remarks in his *Social Change* ([1922] 1950) that the culture of a group is usually marked by "a fairly close integration or intercorrelation," "interdependence," or a "certain equilibrium or balance" among its parts, like that of an "elaborate" or "complicated machine" (138, 200–201, 16; note qualifications, 164, 211, 267). His later *Sociology* (Ogburn and Nimkoff 1940) also claims that the parts of culture are interlocked "in varying degrees of closeness" (47). They "are all related to one another and do not function separately" and thus resemble "a machine or organism with all its parts interlinked" (47, 48; see also 745, 878). Chapin (1928) uses the word *integration* in the sense that the new part or parts become coordinated, organized, or unified with the old so that they can all function or work as a whole (351).

Third, Ogburn and Chapin both continue to construe the parts of society and its culture as evolutionarily engaged (like an organism) in endeavors to survive through adaptive innovation to changing conditions of existence. (Admittedly, Ogburn sometimes equivocates by merely claiming that culture is useful. And both he and Chapin are aware of the sociological problems in employing social Darwinian notions such as "struggle for existence" and "survival of the fittest.") But the phenomenon of culture lag in the modern world is meaningful only if it entails the requirement that at some point in time objectively determinable adjustment or adaptation must occur. Both sociologists concur that accumulation is selective. But only Chapin's (1928) analysis retains an extended inquiry into the mechanisms of social and societal selection that, he argues, are adaptive (387–401). Interestingly, Chapin construes the scientific method as a device for selection (402ff.).

CHAPTER 5

1. Ellwood's (1927) commitment to progress (which he confuses with social evolution) is the basis of a generalized unilinear directionality in change (254, 260–61, vs. 19, 258). Admittedly, short-term change does assume a "zig-zag," sympodial character, as in Ward's first-period formulation (Ellwood 1927, 51).

2. For his own era, Ogburn had a relatively complex notion of the process of invention and the acceptance and rejection of invention. See, for instance, his presentation of cross-fertilization in Ogburn and Nimkoff 1940. He also delineates the objective sources helping or hindering the acceptance and dissemination of innovations and inventions. They include the utility and efficiency of operation of the invention, its compatability or incompatability with other sectors of the culture, the presence of survivals serving the same function, the advantageousness or disadvantageousness of cost, and the existence of vested interests (Ogburn [1922] 1950, 166–69; Ogburn and Nimkoff 1940, 827–32). In addition, he acknowledges the role of such subjective factors as habit and hostile attitudes (e.g,. fear of the new, traditionalism, conservatism, fear of disapproval for nonconformity, devotion to things as they are, reverence for the past (Ogburn 1950, 146–59, 166–93; Ogburn and Nimkoff 1940, 833–38; also Chapin 1928, 386).

Furthermore, Ogburn provides a relatively systematic and extended account of the impediments or obstacles to the diffusion of cultural items from one society or culture to another. They involve accessibility or isolation by virtue of geographical location, availability or nonavailability of transportation technology, significance and magnitude of differences between the two cultures (i.e., the potential donor and recipient cultures), presence or absence or lack of preparation to understand or use a particular item, and the extent of the readjustment (or reequilibration) demanded from other parts of the society or culture if borrowed materials or ideas are to be extensively and satisfactorily used (Ogburn 1950, 162–64; Ogburn and Nimkoff 1940, 784–85, 800, 802).

3. The controversy includes S. C. Gilfillan, *The Sociology of Invention* (Chicago: Follett, 1935), 43–46, 151–52; W. D. Wallis, "The Concept of Lag," *S&SR* 19 (1935): 403–5; James W. Woodward, "Critical Notes on the Culture Lag Concept," *SF* 12 (1934): 388–98; James W. Woodward "A New Classification of Culture and a Restatement of the Culture Lag Theory," *ASR*

1 (1936): 89–102; Michael Choukas, "The Concept of Culture Lag Re-examined," *ASR* 1 (1936): 752–60; Abbott P. Herman, "An Answer to Criticisms of the Lag Concept," *AJS* 43 (1937): 440–51; John H. Mueller, "Present Status of the Cultural Lag Hypothesis," *ASR* 3 (1938): 320–27; Joseph Schneider, "Culture Lag: What Is It?" *ASR* 10 (1945): 786–91; Hornell Hart, "Technological Acceleration and Cultural Lag Are Crucial," *ASR* 13 (1948): 487–89; Hornell Hart, "The Pre-War Upsurge in Social Science," *ASR* 14 (1949): 599–607.

4. Consult chapter 4.

5. See Thomas and Znaniecki 1918–20, 5:242–43; 3:263–65 241–42, 57, 47–48, 55, 59–60; Thomas 1923, 49–50, and 70–71. Documentation from other sources could also be introduced.

6. Hankins (1928, 391) cites Wissler's notion of a universal cultural pattern. See Teggart's criticisms in *Theory and Processes of History,* 1941, 213–17.

7. Hankins (1928, 398) does not deal with the variations of stage sequences in particular institutional domains. Rather, he suggests generally the factors of "differences of place, of contacts, group crises, racial temperament, and historical accident."

8. And as Goldman noted: "If cultural and social features move across the world and are borrowed by simpler peoples from more advanced peoples, then, of course, sequences as well as processes will not be uniform, argue as one may that society will borrow only what it is prepared to accept" [*Victorian Studies,* 1959, p. 67].

9. Others subject to a gatekeeper–opinion leader may extend his influence so that some phenomenon, such as social evolution or derivative culture lag, is defined preemptorily as outdated, passé, irrelevant, and unworthy of further intellectual consideration. So a particular paper submitted may be simply rejected as neither "news nor newsworthy" by an associate editor of one of the two major journals, such as the *AJS* or *ASR*.

10. See chapter 2.

11. See chapter 2.

12. For instance, Bernard simply chose to ignore the specific criticisms directed against social evolutionism. By contrast, Ogburn (1950, 374–93) acknowledged the seriousness of specific criticisms lodged against social evolutionism, but expressed the hope that a tenable general social evolutionism was still possible and, indeed, that he had achieved it.

CHAPTER 6

1. Park suggested that it should be possible to work out an intrinsic change pattern or natural history (or *physis*) for each type of natural object. (He offered many illustrations, e.g., a plantation, a gang, a sect, a strike, a revolution, a race-relations cycle. Yet he never did offer a rigorous and systematically developed exemplification.) Presumably, one stage would tend naturally to follow or succeed another in an orderly and irreversible way (Park 1952, 224, 225). But in 1936, he seems to have qualified his conception of all social objects as having a distinctive cycle of change by designating as "succession" only recurrent changes falling into a temporal series such that "the effect of each succeeding increment of change reinforces or carries forward the effect of the preceding" (229). Two years later (1938), Park remarks that a sequence of change may "take or seem destined to take if sufficiently prolonged, the form of a cycle which *may and often does repeat itself*" (235, italics added).

2. Sumner, *Folkways,* 1907, 53, 54, 55, 345. For those who know the theoretical foundations of *Folkways*, Park's two partial papers on Sumner that have been reproduced in *Society* (Park 1955, 243–52, 284–91) will scarcely prove illuminating.

3. See Faris 1937a, 100; Faris [1937a] 1976, 171ff.; Krueger and Reckless 1931, 331–33.

4. See Park 1955, 285, where Park refers to the *role* persons "*seek* to play in the communities and social groups in which they live" and defines status as the recognition conferred on the individual (286). Role and status are accorded an individualistic, social psychological definition (Park 1952, 176–77, 175–76).

5. Even those contemporary sociologists who are knowledgeable about the mode and level of analysis of the first and second periods of American sociology may not be impressed by Park's 1942 characterization of "modern society" in terms of size, complexity, speed, mechanism, and freedom (Park 1955, 322–41).

6. Significantly, of all of Park's students who were involved in writing textbooks, only Reuter and Hart contributed major analyses of each of the six features of social organization as originally developed during the first period.

7. The specific chapters involved in the separation of the treatment of the social processes from sociocultural change are these: Reuter and Hart

1933, chaps. 10–14 vs. 5 and 6; Hiller 1933, chaps. 13, 14, 17–20, vs. 21 and 12 (on sources of culture change and culture borrowing), 23 and 24 (on assimilation); chaps. 17–25 vs. s, 3, and 29; and Sutherland and Woodward (1937) 1940, chaps. 22–25 vs. 4 (on cultural accumulation) and 26–30 (on social change, disorganization, and reorganization). Furthermore, the exposition of the sources of culture change (e.g., invention and diffusion) is not ordinarily interconnected with that on change in social norms.

8. Consult Becker 1934b, 28–29; also Becker and Barnes 1952, 777–79; H. Becker 1940b, 525–27; Becker 1950, 169–71.

9. His interest in the sacred and secular extends from his doctoral dissertation (Becker 1930) and his *Systematic Sociology* (1932b) to his last major publication in the 1950s. In view of the stated time boundaries of the present study (ending 1945–50), some explanation or justification of the inclusion of Becker's publications after 1950 is required. To ignore what seems to be a refinement or elaboration of his basic ideas in, for instance, his "Current Sacred and Secular Theory" (Becker 1957), would likely lead to a charge of arbitrariness or capriciousness. However, an analysis of the elaborate sacred/secular attitudinal terminology (from the "holy" sacred through "thrilling secularity") has not been included, on the grounds of its apparent emulation of the Parsonsian pattern-variables. Interested readers can, of course, examine his 1957 essay for themselves.

10. Without unduly involving the reader in the intricacies of the argument, it is evident that Becker's desire to incorporate elements from German idealism and American positivism in his own epistemological-methodological position, as manifest at different times in his sacred/secular conceptualization, involves contradictions. For instance, in a 1950 article in *Social Forces* (see Becker 1950, 252–53), he indicated that inference of a sacred or secular characterization was to be based on the unwillingness/inability or willingness/ability to respond to the culturally new, as the new is defined by members of a society in terms of its existing culture, whereas in his 1957 essay he suggests that it is the scientific investigator who makes the final judgment (Becker 1957, 140, 141–42, 152, 153). (Of course, the problem can be raised as to whether sacredness/secularity can be assessed as a whole or will have to be inferred in terms of different institutional domains, etc.)

11. See chapter 3 for a statement on Becker's method for constructing types.

12. Sorokin's theoretical interest in social change dates at least from his a "Survey of the Cyclical Conceptions of Social and Historical Process" (1927).

13. At one point in *Social and Cultural Dynamics* (1937–41, 1:58n.), Sorokin refers to two modes for sociologically interpreting meaning. He terms one "psychological" or "subjective." The second, which he endorses and uses, is sociologico-phenomenological (or presumably "objective"). He remarks that he used "the term phenomenological in a sense congenial with E. Husserl's term, indicating by it the socially 'objective' existence of meaning, regardless of whether it coincides with the psychological meaning." As sources, he cites E. Husserl's *Ideas* (trans. Gibson, 1931) and *Logische Untersuchungen* (3 vols., Halle, 1922).

14. Sorokin concedes two other negative forms: (1) that truth-reality is unknown or unknowable, and (2) that reality is known only in its phenomenal aspect, whereas its transcendental aspect, if it has such an aspect, is unknowable. But Sorokin excludes such possibilities for basic forms of cultural integration because they are negative.

15. Sorokin's examination of the considerations involved in an abstract analysis of sociocultural change is illuminating and provocative. Consult Sorokin 1937–41, 1:153–89. See especially his distinction between linear and cyclical recurrence as they relate to the problem of directionality (181–89), including his representation of the varieties of linear process—unilinear, oscillating, spiral, branching (184).

His representation of change from the ideational to the idealistic and to the sensate and then back to the ideational, and so on, is a much more complex problem for Sorokin than for his colleagues in the study of social change. To many of them, the sequence would have appeared to be unilinear. But two arguments rule out linearity for Sorokin. First, recurrence includes some deviation from the main trend, and thus unilinearity is precluded (1:183). Second, the transitions from ideational to idealistic, etc., mean sections, steps, or phases. They mean variations or punctuations in the processes, which signal changes in direction. (A "succession of qualitative states essentially different from one another" is neither linear nor nonlinear (1:182). Interestingly, too, Sorokin rules out a cyclical representation. He cannot claim that one cycle is entirely qualitatively the same as another or that the time periods in each are identical. Apparently, he classifies the representation of the directionality he proposes as a form of the variably recurrent, the third type of directionality. This type has three features, which he argues are present in his own particular characterization of directionality: (1) It allows for "ever new variations of the old themes," but with recurrence or repetition emphasized; (2) it stresses the existence of limits in the direction of most social processes (in contrast to linear and cyclical notions); and (3) it involves the principle of immanent causation or self-regulation of sociocultural processes (187–88). Sorokin thus tends to connect his notion of direction with two features (i.e., [2] and [3]) that basically concern the modus operandi or explanation and interpretation of sociocultural change.

CHAPTER 7

1. Clearly, early (pre-World War I) American sociological theory employed ideas and concepts that closely approximated the term *culture* as it was introduced and used in the second period. The terms *social heritage* and *tradition* are, for instance, encountered commonly in the literature of the first period. Some theorists then also had their own distinctive terms (e.g., Ward's *social achievement,* Ross's *social heredity,* and Cooley's *social intelligence*).

House is probably correct in asserting the more distant importance of more Germanic influences, but manifestly anthropology's impact was more significant and directly influential in the actual introduction of the concept of culture into American sociology and sociological theory in the second period. See House 1936, 259–72; also chapter 10 below.

2. They include Alexander Goldenweiser, Melville Herskovits, Alfred Kroeber, Robert Lowie, Margaret Mead, Edward Sapir, and Clark Wissler. Wilson Wallis, Ralph Linton, Robert Redfield, William Christie MacLeod, Bronislaw Malinowski, and Richard Thurnwald also became known to American sociologists as contributors to their journals during this period.

3. E.g., Harry Elmer Barnes (ed.), *The History and Prospects of the Social Sciences,* 1925; E. C. Hayes (ed.), *Recent Developments in the Social Sciences,* 1927; and W. F. Ogburn and A. A. Goldenweiser (eds.), *The Social Sciences and Their Interrelations,* 1927; plus, of course, the *Encyclopaedia of the Social Sciences,* 1930 and later.

4. Consult Ellwood 1925, 296, 297; Reuter and Hart 1933, 350; Bernard 1942, 728; Bernard 1930a, 42; Young 1934, 35, 37; cf. importance of Ogburn's material and adaptive nonmaterial culture.

5. See Ellwood 1925, 111–15; Reuter and Hart 1933, 103–7, 350; Bernard 1942, 728. See chapter 3 above. Ogburn ([1922] 1950) provides elaborate details of his notion of original and acquired human nature (50–51, 283–331).

6. Consult Ellwood 1925, 62, cf. 341, 345; Ogburn and Nimkoff 1940, 26; Reuter and Hart 1933, 268; Hankins 1928, 416; Hiller 1933, pt. 2.

7. See Willey 1931b, 516–25, 528–37; Hankins 1928, 385–90; Lumley

(1928) 1935, 335–39, Young 1934, 20–21; Ogburn (1922) 1950, 28–29; Ogburn and Nimkoff 1940, 63, 48–49; Sutherland and Woodward (1937) 1940, 32–39; Bernard 1942, 755–60.

8. Consult Ellwood 1925, 90–91; Willey 1931b, 498–500; Hiller 1933, 46–51; Reuter and Hart 1933, 147; Ogburn and Nimkoff 1940, 53–60; Young 1934, 18–19; Sutherland and Woodward (1937) 1940, 22–32.

9. See Willey 1931b, 529–31; Hankins 1928, 390–91; Reuter and Hart 1933, 164; Ogburn and Nimkoff 1940, 53–60; Young 1934, 18–19; Sutherland and Woodward (1937) 1940, 22–32.

10. Documentation is provided in the views of Ogburn (1922) 1950, 138, 164, 200–201; Ogburn and Nimkoff 1940, 47, 745, 787; Lumley (1928) 1935, 342; Ellwood 1925, 144–50, 162–77; Willey 1931b, 533–35; Hankins 1928, 402, 403; Reuter and Hart 1933, 165,149; and Bernard 1942, 750.

11. See Ogburn (1922) 1950, 73, 69, 273; Ogburn and Nimkoff 1940, 74; 743, 778, 780, 792; Case 1924, xxxiii, 482; Chapin 1928, 50–51, 55; Ellwood 1925, 328ff., 103, 323–24; Willey 1931b, 558–60; 1929, 208–9; Hankins 1928, 432–36; MacIver 1931c, 401; Hiller 1933, 343, 342, 101–3; Reuter and Hart, 1933, 165, 31–32; Lumley (1928) 1935, 357; Young 1934, 51–52; Sutherland and Woodward (1937) 1940, 69–101; and Bernard 1942, 633–34, 716, 731–33.

12. Consult Ogburn (1922) 1950, 89, 88, 162–63; Ogburn and Nimkoff 1940, 780, 781, 784–85, 800, 802; Ellwood 1925, 103–4, 323–29; Willey 1931b, 565–69; Chapin 1928, 203–4, 345–46; Hankins 1928, 346–51, 357–51, 357–68, 401–2, 406–9; Hiller 1933, 340–46, 346–53, 357–73; Reuter and Hart 1933, 118–19; Young 1934, 35–44; Sutherland and Woodward (1937) 1940, 719–26; and Bernard 1942, 674ff., 728–29, 808ff.

13. See Ogburn (1922) 1950, 82, 342–43; Ogburn and Nimkoff 1940, 780, 815–19, 867–68; Hankins 1928, 406; Willey 1931b, 561–62, 571; Hiller 1933, 343; and Sutherland and Woodward (1937) 1940, 718–20.

14. Consult Ogburn (1922) 1950, 149–99; Hankins 1928, 421; Hiller 1933, 11ff.; Reuter and Hart 1933, 118; Sutherland and Woodward (1937) 1940, 764ff.

15. See Chapin 1928, 352–53; Hankins 1928, 421–23; Hiller 1933, 341–42; and Reuter and Hart 1933, 216, 166.

16. Even though the Park and Burgess *Introduction to the Science of Sociology* (1921) was published prior to the major impact of the notion of culture, the inclusion of the term in that text provides an important historical benchmark. Park's use of the word *culture* reflects both his experience with

the German intellectual scene and some initial appreciation of the notion as conceived by American cultural anthropology. His references to the cultural processes as functioning "to shape and define the social forms and the social patterns which every preceding generation imposes upon its successors"—illustrated by the preexisting "objective systems, the more or less complex sets of schemes" of Thomas and Znaniecki's *The Polish Peasant in Europe and America* (1918–21, 3:34)—seem to bespeak both the German notion of culture (*Kultur*) as "objective mind" or "spirit" (*objectiver Geist*) and its transmission as a formative process (*Bildungsprozess*) (Park and Burgess [1921] 1924, 52). Elsewhere (Park and Burgess [1921] 1924, 71), Park alludes to seven types of social heritage, one of which is "culture" (as distinguished from technique, formal organization, and machinery). In so doing, Park seems to invoke the German differentiation of "culture" (*Kultur*), as a basic domain of ends and values, from "civilization" (*Civilisation*), as a domain of means, techniques, and such (71; see also MacIver 1931c, 225–36.)

Still, the consideration of conflict and fusion of cultures, as part of the chapter on assimilation, in conjunction with the bibliography on acculturation, suggests some familiarity with the anthropological notion of culture. Included in that bibliography are Boas's *The Mind of Primitive Man* and articles by Lowie and Goldenweiser (Park and Burgess 1921, 776–77). In the bibliographies of other chapters are citations to Tylor's *Primitive Culture,* Sumner's *Folkways,* Westermarck's *The Origin and Development of Moral Ideas*, Levy-Bruhl's *Primitive Mentality,* Ratzel's *History of Mankind,* Lippert's *Kulturgeschichte der Menschheit in ihrem organischen Aufbau,* and Frazer's *The Golden Bough* (151).

For Park, culture is a type of social heritage. The "culture of a group is the sum total and organization of the social heritages which have acquired a social meaning because of racial temperament and of the historical life of the group" (Park and Burgess [1921] 1924, 72). Although he acknowledges that the social heritage is transmitted both by tradition (as from generation to generation) and by acculturation (as from group to group), and more specifically by "imitation" and "inculcation," he concedes a significance to racial temperament as "an active selective agency, determining interest and the direction of attention," which American anthropology (certainly the prevailing Boasian school) had rejected.

17. See Case 1924, 267; Ellwood 1925, 315; Park and Burgess (1921) 1924, 33–38; Hankins 1928, 387; Lumley 1928, 79; Stern 1929, 264n.; Hiller 1933, 119; Reuter and Hart 1933, 135–36; Faris 1937a, 28–29; Sutherland and Woodward (1937) 1940, 296–97.

18. Certainly, Teggart was known to many sociologists on the Pacific

Coast (e.g., Case) and to many who had been trained at the major graduate departments in the Midwest and East (e.g., Chicago and Columbia; in addition to Park, House, and Becker, see also, Hiller 1933, 16, 116, 127; Sutherland and Woodward (1937) 1940, 793; MacIver (1942) 1964, 257; and Hankins 1928, 164, 206.

On Teggart, see Hodgen 1968; Nisbet 1978–79; Lyman 1978, and Ross 1991, 446–48.

It is important to note that Barnes, who continued to be interested in the relationship between history and the social sciences, recurrently referred to Teggart in laudatory terms (e.g., see Barnes 1940, 568–69, Barnes 1952, 258; and Barnes 1948, 70–71.

More important in the context of the exchange being examined here is the fact that Case, whose views on history and science were cited above and who was a member of the Department of Sociology at the University of Southern California, published an extensive essay review of Teggart's *Theory of History* and his *Processes of History* under the title of "Method in the Social Sciences" (Case 1927b). (The first six pages are a fair and judicious summary analysis, but the last five, concerning Teggart's own methodological proposals, warrant other adjectives.) Noteworthy also is House's review of Teggart's earlier work (House 1926, 131–32). Fairness also requires that House's subsequent assessment of Teggart (House 1936, 301, 308–9) be noted.

19. Teggart 1941 noted that the study of the social change had been obstructed by a set of assumptions about the nature of history (the historical, specific, and concrete events) and science (the natural, abstract, universal processes) that derive from Greek philosophy, especially Aristotle. He regarded science as knowledge of the universal and history as knowledge of the particular, and more especially the former as the study of the natural or normal taking place of itself and the latter as the study of the accidental, chance, or unintended (85). The distinction appeared in post-Renaissance Europe, as manifested in the contrast between the facts that recur versus the nonrecurrent, the typical in the manifold versus the manifold separated from the typical, the realm of necessity versus freedom, the systematic and classificatory versus the individualized and narrative, the abstract and conceptual versus the actual and concrete (57, 58). Science is held to deal with objects, entities, things and their relations, which undergo change, and history with events, occurrences, the unusual, uncommon, the unique (77).

20. Teggart examines the basic assumptions and focal intellectual controversies of the seventeenth century as an indispensable background for the central views of Comte about the positive sciences in general, more particularly biology, and especially sociology, and most crucially social change as

developmental and progressive. Teggart points to the later years of the seventeenth century, with its famous quarrel over the relative merits of the ancients and moderns (in literature), as providing a set of influential ideas in the subsequent study of man. One of the most important is the analogy between the incremental learning of the individual in the course of his life cycle and the advance of the species or humankind (e.g., Pascal). A second is the notion, deriving earlier from St. Augustine and more recently from Bossuet, that the historical course of (human) change falls into a series of epochs under providential design. (Bossuet's work became a model for the generalized histories of culture of Turgot, Concorcet, and Comte.) A third entails the Cartesian view that the natural universe involves an established order that is manifest in a body of laws characterized by stability, regularity, permanence, immutability, and a favorable disposition to human welfare and progress. Fourth, it involved the belief that the scientific study of man was modeled after physiology, focusing thus on what is natural or normal in the body social and excluding the abnormal and accidental. Accordingly, science endeavors to determine the natural or normal course of development as abstracted from the accidental interferences or hindrances of historical events (Teggart 1944, 91). Finally, the comparison of conditions of things, which the quarrel introduced into the study of literature, was extended to the study of man as a comparison between the social conditions of existing savages and those in the earliest historical records of civilized peoples (93–94).

Teggart is thus in a position to ascertain Comte's intellectual indebtednesses and to assess continuities with his predecessors, especially in sociology's division of social dynamics. He shows convincingly that Comte invokes the analogy between the learning of the individual throughout his life cycle and the advance of humankind (Pascal), the Cartesian conception of the natural universe and its laws as applicable to the domain of the social, a physiology-derived model of the scientific study of the social as an inquiry into what is natural and normal (for the most part), the comparative method (in two phases, including a resort to Condorcet's rational fiction of a unique people to which all consecutive social modifications are referrable), and Condorcet's progressivist stages' (secularized) adaptations of Bossuet's thesis of a unilinear sequence of change. Thus, Teggart claims that Comte conceives of social change as natural and normal, slow, gradual, continuous, with a fixed and determined order (universally) entailing a law of advance or progress. Comte's view of sociology retains and sustains (especially through his peculiar, ahistorical method) the separation of natural science (as the study of the abstract, unsited and undated) from history (as the study of concrete events, the sited and dated) to the continued obstruction of a comprehensive and unified study of social change.

Because Teggart limited his study to sociology as represented by Comte, its founder, and ignored (some would claim superciliously) its earlier and later representatives in the United States, his critics (e.g., Case and House in their reviews) in the discipline contended that American sociology was otherwise. Subsequently, Bock, one of Teggart's last students, published his *The Acceptance of Histories* (1956), in which he indicated that by no means could it be argued that American sociology was exempt from Teggart's critique (34–35, 93–95; see also Hinkle 1980, 336 n. 6, 89–91).

21. Of course, House had intimated that the Parkian-Chicago enterprise of the study of urban community was predicated on the view that any group (such as a community or total society) is a natural object with an internal tendency to change—that is, from an aggregate in which competition prevails, to one of overt conflict, then accommodation, and finally assimilation and unity.

22. I.e., *Theory of History* (1925), 71 vs. 90–91; republished in *Theory and Processes of History* (1941), 77 vs. 86–87.

23. For instance, in "The City and Civilization," republished in *Human Communities* (1952); in "Culture and Civilization," republished in *Race and Culture* (1950); and in "Modern Society," (in Park 1952) republished in *Society* (1955).

24. Although Becker's (1934a) early paper on Weber concerned the culture case study, Becker did not provide a detailed analysis of this technique until his article on "Culture Case Study and Greek History" (1958).

25. Students (with their doctoral dissertations) who subsequently affiliated with sociology departments included Gladys Bryson, "The Scottish Moral Philosophers" (1928), Smith Col.; Joseph Schneider, "Genius and the Origins of Fame" (1933), U. of Minn. and Indiana Univ.; Harry Frost, "Maxweiler and the Solovay Institute" (1939), Univ. of Utah; John H. Foskett, "Emile Durkheim and the Problem of Social Order" (1939), Univ. of Oregon; Robert Nisbet, "The Group in French Social Thought," (1939), Univ. of Calif., Berkeley and Riverside. Univ. of Arizona, Columbia Univ. In addition, Edward Rose, who received his B.A. and M.A. under Teggart but his Ph.D. at Stanford, has taught at the University of Colorado, and Kenneth Bock, who received his B.A. and M.A. under Teggart but completed his Ph.D. at Berkeley after Teggart's retirement, continued as a member of the Berkeley department. Only a very few of Teggart's students have been associated with fields outside of sociology (e.g., George Hildebrand, economics, Cornell Univ., and Katherine B. Oaks, history, N. Illinois Univ.).

26. The alert reader may have noticed that this chapter has involved an organization of contents vastly different from that of the chapters of part 2 and thus requries resort to a different section of the classificatory analytical scheme. The same follows for the other chapters of part 3. The earlier chapters of part II derived their structure from continuity with the previous period and from the relevance of a subsection on macrochange from the analytical-classificatory scheme. But interest in theories from disciplines outside of sociology (e.g., anthropology, history, psychiatry, psychology, and philosophy in the United States as well as from European social science) implies discontinuity, along with the possible relevance of a section of the analytical-classificatory scheme dealing with relations of the non- and near-social to social phenomena (e.g., the human organic, psychic [or human biopsychic as human nature], and the cultural of Hinkle 1980, sec. III.B.2.b., p. 62). Unfortunately, no appropriate further differentiation of the scheme has been developed, and thus the reader may find the following ad hoc generalized framework of analysis useful in anticipating the organization of contents of subsequent chapters:

1.   A consideration of evidence of the impact of a stance or orientation from another discipline (e.g., Freudian psychiatry or behaviorist psychology) on sociology and social and sociological theory
2.   A brief examination of the main features of the stance from that discipline and its potential relevance for, or actual use in, social sociological theory;
3.   An assessment of the reception (acceptance and rejection) of the main ideas of the stance by social and sociological theorists, along with any possible attempts to construct or reconstruct general theory accordingly

CHAPTER 8

1. This analysis of Freudianism and psychoanalysis is pervasively indebted to the research G. J. Hinkle undertook in her doctoral dissertation (1952) and its later extension (1957).

2. See Bannister's (1987) comments about Bernard's behaviorism (117–18, 127, 128, 129, 132–33, 137–43, 144, 198).

3. Consult Bannister (1987, 156–57, 164–65) on Chapin's and Ogburn's behaviorism. See also Bain 1933.

CHAPTER 9

1. For a general orientation, consult Rucker 1969; Lewis and Smith 1980; Joas 1985; Charles W. Morrison's introduction to Mead 1934; Anselm Strauss's introduction to Mead 1964; also David L. Miller, *George Herbert Mead* (1973); and David L. Miller ed., of Mead 1982.

2. See below, this chapter.

3. Thomas's departure from the University of Chicago faculty has occasioned extensive comment in subsequent years. See Ross 1991, 310.

4. See especially Thomas's second (or revised) formulation of the four wishes (Thomas 1923, 12, 17–18, 31, 32). The desire for new experience is "emotionally related to anger, which tends to invite death, and expresses itself in courage, advance, attack, pursuit" (12). It implies, therefore, "motion, change, danger, instability, social irresponsibility. The individual dominated by it shows a tendency to disregard prevailing standards and group interests" (12). By contrast, the desire for security "is based on fear, which tends to avoid death and expresses itself in timidity, avoidance, and flight. The individual dominated by it is cautious, conservative, and apprehensive, tending also to regular habits, systematic work, and the accumulation of property" (12). Primarily "related to the instinct of love," the desire for response "shows itself in the tendency to seek and give signs of appreciation in connection with other individuals" (e.g., devotion of mother to child and response of child; mating, marriage, etc.; 17–18). Although the desire for response is termed by Thomas "the most social of the wishes," he notes that it both "makes selfish claims" and "is the main source of altruism" (31). It contains "both a sexual and a gregarious element" (31).

Apparently, the wish for recognition has a primarily social basis. But because this wish also includes distinction sought on the basis of "skillful and hazardous activities" deriving from the wish for mastery or will to power, it involves an element "allied to the emotion of anger" and thus does entail a more primitive (e.g., mammalian) biopsychic linkage. It is reflected in "the general struggle of men for position in their social group, in devices for securing a recognized, enviable, and advantageous status" 931). And it finds expression in vanity and ambition (32).

For the Freudian impact on the four wishes, see above, chapter 8.

5. Interestingly, it is in the analysis of the desire for new experience that Thomas most pointedly displays his commitment to evolutionary naturalism, which stipulates the continuity or filiation of the realms of the social and psychic with, and their genesis out of, the organic domain. He argues for the rise

of a psychic disposition from the organic, that is, the origin of curiosity from anger and an interest in the new as a development of curiosity (Thomas and Znaniecki 1918–20, 3:33; Thomas 1923, 4, 9). Furthermore, he suggests illuminatingly that the series of biopsychic transformations from anger to the development of a generalized desire for new experience is the consequence of an ability among "the higher animals, and above all man," to inhibit a response to an "earlier stimulation" that "may have had painful consequences" (Thomas 1923, 41). In addition, this ability or power is also "dependent on the fact that the nervous system [especially of man] carries memories or records of past experience [racial memory or unconscious?]" (41).

6. This circumstance seems to be exemplified in Wiley 1986. Although Wiley places Thomas and Znaniecki's stance in *The Polish Peasant* within the context of the controversy over the instincts generally, he displays no awareness of the specific content of that dispute in sociology in his article as such. (See chapter 3 above.)

Curiously, he seems to be unaware that his effort to link his analysis with a hierarchy of levels of phenomena by resort to Edel (Wiley 1986, 23) is entirely unnecessary because Thomas was committed to the general stance of evolutionary naturalism, including the second tenet of genetic filiation of phenomena. (See note 5, this chapter.)

Most importantly, Wiley advances a series of claims that are entirely at variance with the arguments and supporting documentation just offered in the text above. Those claims are the following:

a.   Thomas and Znaniecki cut off the "biological tail" from the notion of attitude, "producing a concept that was completely supra-biological" (Wiley 1986, 22; but surely the quoted evidence above is to the contrary).
b.   "The *Polish Peasant* replaced instinct theory largely by not mentioning it" (23); but "largely" is not entirely. Moreover, the role of instincts is very obvious in Thomas's *The Unadjusted Girl* (1923).
c.   The "four wishes . . . can be interpreted as purely interactional" (23)— but to do so violates Thomas's own basic commitments.
d.   "The *Polish Peasant* . . . was sociology's most effective and decisive break with biology and [the] enunciation of a disciplinary point of view" (23). This statement fails to reckon with the work of Faris and his students, including Blumer. Note particularly Faris's objection to the instinctivism in the four wishes as stated in Karpf 1932 and quoted above in chapter 3.

Finally, Wiley (1986, 30) seems to have missed the point in the potentially differentiable meanings between the individual, private, idiosyncratic attitude in the personal definition of the situation (vis-a-vis a personal value), on the one hand, and the shared, public, rule-regulated social attitude in the social definition of the situation (vis-a-vis social values), on the other. See chapter 11.

7. For a detailed exposition of Cooley's basic sociological orientation, see Hinkle 1966. It is explained there as a form of romantic or affective idealism. See also Hinkle 1967. For Cooley's view of the "social," consult Hinkle 1980, 278–79.

8. Note the similarity with Thomas's statement (this chapter, above). For the broader features of human nature, see Cooley (1902) 1964, 7, 18, 22. Importantly, Cooley was inclined to deny that human beings possess instincts as applied to behavior, i.e., in the sense of a certain behavior fixed or "predetermined by a hereditary mechanism," or a "system of fixed hereditary responses to fixed stimuli" (24; Cooley [1918] 1966, 198, 199, 200).

9. Cooley rejected any conception of separate individuals as originating social phenomena through their independent acts, any view of a causal separation of power between society and individual, any division of human nature into individualistic and social faculties (Cooley [1902] 1964, 35–50). In Cooley's view, humans did not become anatomically and physiologically distinct (as a species first) and only later come to associate permanently. Rather, humankind had descended from an ancestral genetic line in which relatively permanent association had already existed (Cooley [1909] 1962, 109); and thus he was committed to a pre-organic rather than a post-organic theory of social origins (Hinkle 1980, 110–11, 128). In the most comprehensive sense, he held that the individual and the group, the one and the many, the singular and the plural are presently joint, equal, simultaneous, complementary, and interrelated forms of reality (e.g., Cooley [1909] 1962, 5; Cooley [1902] 1964, 37, 38).

10. Resentment is a sentiment, "but not rage; the fear of disgrace or ridicule, but not animal terror and so on" (Cooley [1918] 1966, 177). Pity, grief, gratitude, generosity, respect, mortification, ambition, vanity, and hero worship are further illustrations of sentiments. Gratitude illustrates that these sentiments do not describe an aspect of either ego or alter but a relationship between them, and "so with all personal sentiments" (Cooley [1902] 1964, 128).

11. These stages, including their designations, were developed some years ago in an unpublished paper by Gisela J. Hinkle.

12. The consequence of this association has apparently prompted some subsequent sympathetic analysts to charge that Mead was a "verbal atomist" who failed to recognize that meaning is not only in (separate) words but

even more in the interrelation of words, as in phrases, sentences, and so on. The relevance to meaning of grammar, syntax, and such, even discourse itself, has been ignored.

13. See Gisela J. Hinkle on "universal attitudes and institutions" in (Hinkle 1992, 327–28).

14. In his review of Faris's *The Nature of Human Nature* (1937a), Kimball Young objected to Faris's "complete neglect of the place of constitutional and maturational factors as at least partial determinants of behavior," on the one hand, and his "view that culture is all important in determining behavior," on the other (Young 1938, 650).

15. Blumer 1937 includes analysis and criticism of instinctivism (147–51); stimulus-response, or conditioned response (151–61, 157–58, 161–63, 170–71, 178–79, 185, 187–91); and cultural determinism (154–57).

16. Note Mead 1934, 321–23, 55–56; Mead 1982, 152, 150.

17. See Blumer 1962, 180 ([1962] 1969, 78–79), for the first apparent explicit definition of "symbolic interaction."

18. It is noteworthy that Blumer's 1937 chapter contains a curious characterization of Mead's three stages: (1) a stage of "meaningless imitative acts" (181); (2) the play-stage, or playing of separate roles, which is directly connected with the child's (imaginative) taking of a number of roles in organized games (181–82); and (3) taking the role of the "generalized other" (182–83).

19. For instance, Mead (1982) insists that an act "is purposive and teleological" (108). But the act is not peculiarly human; it is rather characteristic of organisms, living forms in general, and tends thus to sustain life. Again, he declares that such "purposiveness is independent of any mind" (108). Admittedly, Mead claims that the (human) "act cannot be carried out unless there is intention" (161). However, he ordinarily and normally associates such intentions with group attitudes and group purposes (161; but see also Mead 1934, 322–23).

CHAPTER 10

1. For the European impact during the first period of American sociological theory (1881–1915), see Hinkle 1980, 50–53. Shils's comments on the impact of European sociology in the 1920s and 1930s are to be found in his *The Calling of Sociology and other Essays on the Pursuit of Learning,* 1980, 46, 106–8, 153.

2. For instance, volume 1 contains a section "War and Reconstruction" on each of the social sciences; subsection 5, "Sociology and Social Work," (204–10), treats in some detail developments in Germany, Italy, United States, and France. Part 2 of the introduction includes an overview of the state of sociology in France (251), Germany (261, 263), Austria (267), Russia (284), Scandinavia (292–93), Spain (297–98), Latin America (307–11, 315, 316–17), and Japan (321–22).

3. This summary of the impact of Durkheim on American sociology and sociological theory is drawn from Hinkle (1960) 1964. Note Shils's comments on the American response to Durkheim during this period (Shils 1980, 7, 205–6).

4. See Hinkle (1960) 1964, 275, 292 nn. 54 and 55.

5. Ibid., 283, 284, 295 n. 95.

6. As summarized by Baker, Long, and Quensel 1973. See also Gurney 1981; Calhoun 1950. See Shils's comments on American sociology's response to Marx and Marxism during this period (Shils 1980, 7, 46, 110, 133, 372–73).

At this point a caveat must be issued. Exclusive reliance on publications as an index of an intellectual's influence may be undependable in certain instances. For example, Page 1982 reveals Marx as exercising a major, though subterranean, role as one of the "three theoretical masters" of the depression-wartime generation of graduate students at Columbia teaching at, or recruited from, CCNY (99, 69–99).

7. See also Shils's (1980) comments on Horkheimer (190–91).

8. Simmel was the second most commonly mentioned influential foreign sociologist in the Bernard data as summarized in Baker, Long, and Quensel 1973. Consult Shils 1980, 122, 202–23, for Shils's remarks about American sociology's response to Simmel during this period.

9. In actuality, "some influence" is only a modicum of influence. For Ross's effort to avoid the accusation of borrowing his "community-society" dichotomy from Tönnies, see Ross (1901) 1969, 432. Not one of the American sociologists in the Bernard study indicated Tönnies as exercising any influence (Baker, Long, and Quensel 1973, 9–10). See also Hinkle 1980, 162, and Shils 1980, 203.

10. For Shils's comments about Mannheim and American sociology during this period, see Shils 1980, 177–78, 188–90, 373–74.

11. Note that in this context interest lies especially in references to Weber's general theory and methodology and not in those to his work in the

sociology of religion. For Shils's remarks about American sociology's interest in and response to Weber during this period, see Shils 1980, 131, 177, 179, 199–200, 272. Consult also Gerth 1982 (chaps. 16, 17); Roth and Bendix 1959.

It is noteworthy that Parsons's English translation of Weber's *Die Protestantische Ethik und der Geist des Kapitalismus* in 1930 (as *The Protestant Ethic and the Spirit of Capitalism*) was not reviewed in any of the extant American sociological periodicals (i.e., *AJS, SF,* or *S&SR*). Presumably, the book review editors still regarded Weber as a German and an economist and Parsons as a young and unknown economist, and both as having no special relevance to sociology. The same fate befell Frank Knight's earlier translation of Weber's *General Economic History.*

12. Parsons 1937 was reviewed in the *American Sociological Review* and *Social Forces* in 1939 and in the *American Journal of Sociology* in 1950.

13. Manifestly, Bendix's 1946 paper, with its inclusion of major objections to and criticisms of Weber, was an exception. Bierstedt's 1938 article is unqualifiedly critical, but it is focused directly and primarily on Parsons and only secondarily and derivatively on Weber.

14. Others perhaps should be included. Wirth 1937 (485) and Wirth 1938 (involving Wirth's own English translation of passages from Weber's *Wirtschaft und Gesselschaft* vol. 1, chap. 1) suggest that Wirth also may have been substantially preoccupied with the analysis of Weber in the mid to late 1930s. Note also that Wirth offered and gave a course entitled "The Sociology of Max Weber" in 1937 and one entitled "Modern German Sociology" at Chicago in 1937 and 1927–28 and 1934 (Harvey 1987, 275, 276). See also R. E. L. Faris's (1967, 110) own notes about knowledge of Weber at Chicago.

15. Becker's preliminary extensive draft of his doctoral dissertation (entitled "Movement in Relation to Mobility and to Social Change") directly refers to Weber's ideal type as an important methodological foundation of his own inquiry (Becker n.d., 3). This indebtedness is retained in his more narrowly drawn and accepted doctoral dissertation (Becker 1930, 2–3). It is, of course, possible that his interest in Weber began with a contact with Honigsheim at Cologne in 1926 (Gerth 1960, 743).

16. Presumably, this realm of conscious being is related to what MacIver (1931c) had earlier termed an "inner" versus an "outer" order. The "inner" order is a complex of desires, motivations, and attitudes, which are definite states or qualities of consciousness involving tendencies to act in characteristic ways whenever an appropriately stimulating object or occasion is presented (532–33, 43.)

17. Note Parsons's (1968) demarcation of the "actor-situation" (46, 46n., 47, 49, 49 n. 3), MacIver's (1931c) "inner" and "outer orders" and "attitude-interest" classifications (48–49, 532–33), and Znaniecki's "attitude-value" conceptualization (Znaniecki 1934, 60–63; Znaniecki 1936, 44).

18. Consult chapter 8 and 9; also above, this chapter.

CHAPTER 11

1. See, for instance, Ward's "group sense of safety" (Ward [1903] 1970, 134); Sumner's "in-group" and "out-group" (Sumner [1907] 1959, 12–13); Small and Vincent's "rural groups" and "primary social group" Small and Vincent [1894] 1971, 112ff. 182); Cooley's "primary group" and "nucleated group" (Cooley [1909] 1962, 23ff.; Cooley [1918] 1966, 252ff.).

2. To assume, without any further questioning, that "parts" in relation to a social whole or group means "individuals" is to permit the introduction of possible bias—toward nominalism. In terms of more recent structural conceptions in sociology, "roles" might well be considered to be the "parts" of the social whole.

3. Unfortunately, this analysis cannot include the elaboration of the interconnection of inter- and multipersonal relations, relationships, and activities so as to yield the persistent structured quality of a group. The definitions of the group in the textbooks are too incomplete or fragmentary. Only in the case of Park has it been possible to approximate the summary analyses of the first period as provided in Hinkle 1980, 270–89.

4. Sumner's disciple Keller is also classifiable under the rubric of a "predominant materialism." See Hinkle 1980, 272–74.

5. Unfortunately, chapter 5, "Social Statics," of Comte's book 6, on Social Physics—as represented by Martineau's English translation (Comte 1893, vol. 2)—treats only certain components of social organization rather than the ideas of social order, consensus, or concurrence. Instead chapter 3, on the application of his positive method to social phenomena, contains a few hints about Comte's views on the action and reaction of the different parts of the social system, their spontaneous harmony, and the universal consensus of the social body. They provide the bases for Levy-Bruhl's (1913) contention that the idea of social consensus dominates the whole of Comte's exposition of social statics. The diverse parts of the social system act and react on one another. But instead of being viewed as separate or in isolation, each part should be conceived in relation to all of the others, with which it is interdependent. In effect, Levy-Bruhl seems to claim that Comte's social

consensus is an early anticipation of functionalism involving the interconnectedness, interrelatedness, and interdependence of the parts as an equilibrium, harmony, or concord of the whole, which has the character of an
ensemble and must be so conceived (288–89). Comte's consensus is not
directed to any possible "voluntary order," but to the "natural and involun-
tary order to which all human society tends" (Comte 1893, 2:666). Park thus
can scarcely be regarded as having correctly conceived of Comte's "social
consensus." (See also Cynthia Eagle Russett's relevant analysis of the double equilibrium, both external and internal, of Comte's social organism and
its ever-changing or dynamic character (Russett 1966, 29–36).

6. See also Hinkle 1980, 307–11.

7. See also Hinkle 1980, 290–91. The necessity that additional components be added to the social action scheme in order to produce anything like
a general theory for all four of its protagonists is an interesting revelation of
its sociological limitations. Parsons eventually added the social, cultural,
personality, behavioral, and organism systems; Becker elaborated a typology
of norms and values culminating in his sacred/secular analytical schema;
Znaniecki included the theories of social relations, social persons, and social
groups in addition to that of social actions; and MacIver differentiated cultural, technological, and social orders.

CHAPTER 12

1. Sorokin's paper appeared in the *American Sociological Review*
(1936): 12–25.

2. The three papers were Parsons (1945) 1949, Parsons 1948, and Parsons 1950. The first reference to Thomas occurs in Parsons (1945) 1949, 37,
and the second in Parsons 1950, 4.

3. Two references are relevant, one to a declaration in Kivisto and
Swatos 1990, and the other to a certain silence of Gouldner in his *The Coming Crisis of Western Sociology,* 1970.
Illuminatingly, Kivisto and Swatos insist that Parson's achievement of
hegemony in theory could be accomplished only by discrediting the Chicago
School. His tactic was to act as though it did not exist—by benign disregard
or inattention (Kivisto and Swatos 1990, 158, 150).
Conversely, Gouldner's exposition of the success of Parsonsian structural functionalism in relation to the social structure of American society is
curiously devoid of any detailed consideration of the actual (then contemporary) situation in American sociology as a profession and discipline. See
Gouldner 1970, 138–57.

4. Consult Teggart's arguments as summarized in notes 19 and 20 of chapter 7 above and as elaborated in part 2 of his *Theory and Processes of History* [1941] 1977).

5. On the critique of foundationalism, see Featherstone 1988; Kellner 1988, 240–41, 249, 251–57, 262–66; Fraser and Nicholson 1988, 379–91; Caravetta 1988, 395–96; C. Turner 1990, 112; Culler 1982, 92, 151–54. For opposing views, consult Lash 1988, 311–12; Lash 1990, 63, 71; also Rose 1988, 367–68.

6. See Hinkle 1980, 54–56, 267, for the original statement. For background, consult Teggart 1977, part 2 and S. Turner 1991.

7. At Chicago, Wirth's work fell particularly into what Merton would subsequently term "middle-range theory." In 1949–50, Shils participated in Parsons's seminar out of which came the joint editorship of *Toward a General Theory of Action* (1951), v–vi).

8. The value of Merton's differentiation of "rediscoveries," "prediscoveries," and "adumbrations" (Merton 1968, 13, 9–27) is reduced because such similar terms as *antecedents* and *precursors* are not considered. In the inquiry at hand, concern lies with the continuation of ideas, their elaboration, and the eventual recognition of a kinship with similar strains or complexes of ideas. Social action theory is taken as the point of departure. But after 1950 Parsons becomes its chief exemplar as his importance is enhanced by identification with structural functionalism and as that of Becker, MacIver, and Znaniecki seems to wane in comparison.

9. At the 1989 American Sociological Association annual meeting in San Francisco, Bryan Turner organized a special session on the theories of modernity and postmodernity. See B. Turner 1990. In addition, refer to "Golden Era" in Rhoades 1981, chaps. 7 and 8; also Turner and Turner 1990, chaps. 3 and 4.

10. See, for instance, Antonio 1990, Lemert 1990, and Kellner 1990. Consult also the series of articles "Symposium on Postmodernism" in *Sociological Theory*, vol. 9, no. 2 (Fall 1991), which includes articles by Steven Seidman, Charles Lemert, Laurel Richardson, and Robert J. Antonio. See also Turner 1991.

Lemert 1990 analyzes the intellectual development of French structuralisms, one of which is postmodernism, and simultaneously reveals the nature of the resistances of current conventional American sociology and sociological theory to postmodernism. See especially pp. 120–46.

11. Like the hermeneuticists, Becker argues (reciprocally) that any social "situation is a whole within the context of at least one larger whole"

and any "more inclusive social framework impinges on social situations in the narrower sense" (Becker 1950, 203–4). Social actions occur within clusters and each cluster is "functionally bound up with many other clusters," at the apex of which is society with its overarching and comprehensive systems of value (5). The implications of a "to-and-fro" analysis as in hermeneutics are clear.

12. Schutz (1967) 1977; Leiter 1980, 50; Fine 1990, 128–29, 139, 141–42; Boden 1990, 186–200; J. Turner 1986.

13. See the special series of articles on "Habermas, Pragmatism, and Critical Theory" (Shalin 1992), with articles by Dmitri Shalin, Hans Joas, Robert Antonio and Douglas Kellner, David Sciulli, Gisela Hinkle, and Eugene Halton.

Selected Reference List

Abel, Theodore. 1929. *Systematic Sociology in Germany.* Studies in History, Economics, and Public Law, no. 310. New York: Columbia University. 2d. ed., Octagon Books, New York, 1965.

———. 1930. "Is a Cultural Sociology Possible?" *American Journal of Sociology* 35 (March): 739–52.

Adler, Franz. 1964. "Social Nominalism, Social Realism." *A Dictionary of the Social Sciences,* ed. Julius Gould and William L. Kolb, 658–59, 665–66. New York: Free Press.

Alpert, Harry. 1938a. "Durkheim's Functional Theory of Ritual." *Sociology and Social Research* 23 (November-December): 103–8.

———. 1938b. "Operational Definitions in Sociology." *American Sociological Review* 3 (December): 855–61.

———. 1939a. *Emile Durkheim and His Sociology.* New York: Columbia University Press. Republished by Russell & Russell, New York, 1967.

———. 1939b. "Emile Durkheim and Sociologismic Psychology." *American Journal of Sociology* 45 (July): 64–70.

Antonio, Robert J. 1990. "The Decline of the Grand Narrative of Emancipatory Modernity: Crisis or Renewal in Neo-Marxian Theory?" In *Frontiers of Social Theory,* ed. George Ritzer, 88–116. New York: Columbia University Press.

———. 1991. "Postmodern Storytelling Versus Pragmatic Truth-Seeking: The Discursive Basis of Social Theory." *Sociological Theory* 9 (Fall): 154–63.

Antonio, Robert J. and Douglas Kellner. 1992. "Communication, Modernity, and Democracy in Habermas and Rorty." *Symbolic Interaction* 15 (Fall): 277–97.

Bain, Read. 1926. "The Scientific Viewpoint in Sociology." *Sociology and Social Research* 11 (September-October): 38–49.

———. 1928. "An Attitude on Attitude Research." *American Journal of Sociology* 33 (May): 940–57.

———. 1929a. "Culture of Canines: A Note on Subhuman Sociology." *Sociology and Social Research* 13 (July-August): 545–56.

———. 1929b. "Trends in American Sociological Theory." *Trends in American Sociology,* ed. by G. A. Lundberg, R. Bain, N. Anderson, 72–114. New York: Harper & Bros.

———. 1929–30. "The Concept of Complexity in Sociology." Parts 1, 2. *Social Forces* 8 (December, March): 222–31, 369–7.

———. 1931. "The Concept of Social Process." *Publications of the American Sociological Society* 26:10–18.

———. 1933. "Die Behavioristische Einstellung in der Soziologie." (The Behavioristic Perspective in Sociology). *Sociologus* 9 (March): 28–44.

———. 1935. "Measurement in Sociology." *American Journal of Sociology* 40 (January): 481–88.

———. 1936. "Sociology and Psychoanalysis." *American Sociological Review* 1 (February): 203–16.

———. 1942. "A Definition of Culture." *Sociology and Social Research* 27 (November-December): 87–94.

Baker, Paul J., Mary Z. Ferrell, and Susan Quensel. 1975. "Departmentalization of Sociology in the United States, 1880–1928." Paper presented at the American Sociological Association annual meeting, San Francisco.

Baker, Paul, Martha P. Long, and Susan L. Quensel. 1973. "The Pioneers of American Sociology: An Empirical Study." (Study of L. L. Bernard's compilation of sociologists' autobiographies). Paper presented at the American Sociological Association annual meeting, New York.

Bannister, Robert C. 1987. *Sociology and Scientism.* Chapel Hill: University of North Carolina Press.

Barnes, Harry Elmer. 1920. Comment on "The Future of Sociology" by Albion W. Small. *Publications of the American Sociological Society* 15:194–8.

———. 1921. "The Development of Historical Sociology." *Publications of the American Sociological Society* 16:17–49.

———. 1924. *Sociology and Political Theory.* New York: Alfred Knopf.

———. ed. 1925. *The History and Prospects of the Social Sciences.* New York: Alfred Knopf.

———. 1927. "The Evolution of the Great Society." *An Introduction to Sociology,* ed. Jerome Davis and Harry Elmer Barnes, 3–190. Boston: D. C. Heath. 2d. ed. 1931.

———. 1940. "The New History, Archaeology, and Cultural Evolution." In *Contemporary Social Theory,* ed. Harry Elmer Barnes, Howard Becker, and Frances B. Becker, 543–97. New York: D. Appleton-Century.

———. 1948. *Historical Sociology.* New York: Philosophical Library.

———. ed. 1948. *An Introduction to the History of Sociology.* Chicago: University of Chicago Press.

———. 1952. "Historical Sociology." *Contemporary Sociology,* ed. Joseph S. Roucek, 238–69. New York: Philosophical Library.

Barnes, Harry Elmer and Howard Becker. 1938. *Social Thought from Lore to Science.* 2 vols. Boston: D. C. Heath. For later editions, see Becker, Howard and Harry Elmer Barnes.

Barnes, Harry Elmer, Howard Becker, and Frances B. Becker (eds.) 1940. *Contemporary Social Theory.* New York: D. Appleton-Century. Republished by Russell & Russell, New York, 1971.

Becker, Howard. c. 1928. "Movement in Relation to Mobility and Social Change." Wisconsin State Historical Society, Madison, Wisconsin. Manuscript, c. 1928.

———. 1930. "Ionia and Athens: Studies in Secularization." Ph.D. diss., Department of Sociology, University of Chicago.

———. 1932a. "Processes of Secularization: An Ideal-typical Analysis with Special Reference to Personality Change as Affected by Population Movement." Part 1. *Sociological Review* (Britain) 24 (April-July): 135–54.

———. 1932b. *Systematic Sociology.* New York: John Wiley & Sons. Wisconsin edition re-issued in 1950 by Norman Paul Press, Gary, Ind. See also *Allgemeine Soziologie,* Parts 1, 2 by Leopold von Wiese 1924 and 1929.

———. 1934a. "Culture Case Study and Ideal-Typical Method: With Special Reference to Max Weber." *Social Forces* 12 (March): 399–405.

———. 1934b. "Historical Sociology." In *The Fields and Methods of Sociology,* ed. L. L. Bernard, 18–34. New York: Farrar & Rinehart.

———. 1940a. "The Creed of Physics and Definitions of the Situation, or How Firm the Foundations?" Paper presented at the 35th Annual Meeting of the American Sociological Society.

———. 1940b. "Historical Sociology." In *Contemporary Social Theory,* ed. Harry

Elmer Barnes, Howard Becker, Frances B. Becker, 491–542. New York: D. Appleton-Century.

———. 1941a. "The Limits of Sociological Positivism." *Journal of Social Philosophy* 6 (July): 362–70.

———. 1941b. Review of *Prolegomena to History* and *Theory and Processes of History* by F. J. Teggart. *American Sociological Review* 6 (October): 731–36.

———. 1941c. "Supreme Values and the Sociologist." *American Sociological Review* 6 (April): 155–72. Amplified in 1950 in *Through Values to Social Interpretation* (below).

———. 1945. "Interpretive Sociology and Constructive Typology." In *Twentieth Century Sociology,* ed. Georges Gurvitch and Wilbert E. Moore, 70–85. New York: Philosophical Library.

———. 1950. *Through Values to Social Interpretation.* Durham, N.C.: Duke University Press.

———. 1957. "Current Sacred-Secular Theory and Its Development." *Modern Sociological Theory in Continuity and Change,* ed. Howard Becker and Alvin Boskoff, 133–85. New York: Dryden Press.

———. 1958. "Culture Case Study and Greek History." *American Sociological Review* 23 (October): 489–504.

———. 1960. "Normative Reactions to Normlessness." *American Sociological Review* 25 (December): 803–10.

Becker, Howard and Harry Elmer Barnes. 1952. *Social Thought from Lore to Science.* 2 vols. 2d. ed., Herren Press, Washington, D.C. 3d ed., Dover, 1961.

Bendix, Reinhard. 1946. "Max Weber's Interpretation of Conduct and History." *American Journal of Sociology* 51 (May): 518–26.

Bernard, L. L. 1909. "The Teaching of Sociology in the United States." *American Journal of Sociology* 15 (September): 164–213.

———. 1919. "The Objective Viewpoint in Sociology." *American Journal of Sociology* 25 (November): 298–325.

———. 1921. "The Misuse of Instinct in the Social Sciences." *Psychological Review* 28 (March): 96–119.

———. 1923. "Instincts and the Psychoanalysts." *Journal of Abnormal and Social Psychology* 17 (January-March): 345–55.

———. 1924. *Instinct: A Study in Social Psychology.* New York: Henry Holt.

———. 1926a. "The Interdependence of Factors Basic to the Evolution of Culture." *American Journal of Sociology* 32 (September): 177–205.

———. 1926b. *An Introduction to Social Psychology.* New York: Henry Holt.

———. 1928. "The Development of Methods in Sociology." *Monist* 38 (April): 292–320.

———. 1930a. "Culture and Environment: The Continuity of Nature and Culture." *Social Forces* 9 (October): 39–48.

———. 1930b. "Culture and Environment: The Unity of the Environment." *Social Forces* 8 (March): 327–34.

———. 1931. "The Psychological Foundations of Society." *An Introduction to Sociology.* Rev. ed., Jerome Davis and Harry Elmer Barnes, 397–494. Boston: D. C. Heath.

———. 1933. "The Sources and Methods of Cultural and Folk Sociology." In *The Fields and Methods of Sociology,* ed. L. L.Bernard, 346–65. New York: Farrar & Rinehart.

———. 1942. *An Introduction to Sociology.* New York: Thomas Y. Crowell.

Bernstein, Richard. 1985. *Beyond Objectivism and Relativism.* Philadelphia: University of Pennsylvania Press.

Bershady, Harold J. 1973. *Ideology and Social Knowledge.* New York: John Wiley & Sons.

Bierstedt, Robert. 1938. "The Means-Ends Schema in Sociological Theory." *American Sociological Review* 3 (October): 665–71.

———. 1975. *Power and Progress.* New York: McGraw-Hill.

———. 1981. *American Sociological Theory.* New York: Academic Press.

Blackmar, Frank W., and John Lewis Gillin. 1915. *Outlines of Sociology.* New York: Macmillan. 2d ed. 1923; 3d ed. 1930.

Blumer, Herbert. 1931. "Science Without Concepts." *American Journal of Sociology* 36 (January): 515–33.

———. 1937. "Social Psychology." In *Man and Society,* ed. Emerson P. Schmidt, 144–98. New York: Prentice-Hall.

———. 1940. "The Problem of the Concept in Social Psychology." *American Journal of Sociology* 45 (March): 707–19.

———. 1942. Rejoinder to "Operational Definitions in the Social Sciences," by George A. Lundberg. *American Journal of Sociology* 47 (March): 743–45.

————. 1951. Notes to Blumer's course in Advanced Social Psychology, University of Chicago, as taken by E. L. Quarantelli.

————. 1962. "Society as Symbolic Interaction." In *Human Behavior and Social Processes,* ed. Arnold M. Rose, 179–92. Boston: Houghton-Mifflin. Reprinted in *Symbolic Interactionism,* 80–82. See Blumer 1969.

————. 1969. *Symbolic Interactionism.* Englewood Cliffs, N.J.: Prentice-Hall.

Bock, Kenneth E. 1956. *The Acceptance of Histories.* Berkeley: University of California Press.

Boden, Deidre. 1990. "The World as It Happens: Ethnomethodology and Conversation Analysis." In *Frontiers of Social Theory,* ed. George Ritzer, 185–213. New York: Columbia University Press.

Bogardus, Emory S. 1922. *A History of Social Thought.* Los Angeles: University of Southern California Press.

Bridgman, Percy. 1932. *The Logic of Modern Physics.* New York: Macmillan.

Brill, A. A., ed. and trans. 1938. *The Basic Writings of Sigmund Freud.* New York: Random House, Modern Library.

Bristol, Lucius Moody. 1915. *Social Adaptation.* Harvard Economic Studies, vol. 14. Cambridge: Harvard University Press.

Brumbaugh, A. J., ed. 1948. *American Universities and Colleges.* 5th ed. Washington, D.C.: American Council of Education.

Bryant, Christopher G. A. 1985. *Positivism in Social Theory and Research.* New York: St. Martin's Press.

Bulmer, Martin. 1984. *The Chicago School of Sociology.* Chicago: University of Chicago Press.

Burgess, E. W. 1927. "Statistics and Case Studies as Methods of Sociological Research." *Sociology and Social Research* 12 (November-December): 104–20.

————. 1939. "The Influence of Sigmund Freud upon Sociology in the United States." *American Journal of Sociology* 45 (November): 356–74.

————. 1945. "Research Methods in Sociology." In *Twentieth Century Sociology,* ed. Georges Gurvitch and Wilbert E. Moore, 20–41. New York: Philosophical Library.

Calhoun, Donald W. 1950. "The Reception of Marxian Sociological Theory by American Academic Sociologists." Ph.D. diss., Department of Sociology, University of Chicago.

Caravetta, Peter. 1988. "On Gianni Vattimo's Postmodern Hermeneutics." *Theory, Culture, and Society* (June): 395–97.

Case, C. M. 1924. *Outlines of Introductory Sociology.* New York: Harcourt, Brace.

——. 1927a. "Culture as a Distinctive Human Trait." *American Journal of Sociology* 32 (May): 906–20.

——. 1927b. "Method in the Social Sciences." *Sociology and Social Research* 11 (January-February): 255–65.

——. 1930. "Toward a Gestalt Sociology." *Sociology and Social Research* 15 (September-October): 3–27.

Cavan, Ruth S. 1928. *Suicide.* Chicago: University of Chicago Press.

Chapin, F. Stuart. 1913. *An Introduction to the Study of Social Evolution.* New York: Century.

——. 1914. "The Elements of the Scientific Method in Sociology." *American Journal of Sociology* 20 (September): 371–91.

——. 1917. "The Experimental Method and Sociology." *Scientific Monthly* 4:133–44, 238–47.

——. 1920. *Field Work and Social Research.* New York: Century.

——. 1922. "Methods of Conducting Research Courses for College Students." *Publications of the American Sociological Society* 17:168–77.

——. 1928. *Cultural Change.* New York: Century.

——. 1929. "The Meaning of Measurement." *Publications of the American Sociological Society* 24:83–94.

——. 1935. "Measurement in Sociology." *American Journal of Sociology* 40 (January): 476–80.

——. 1936. "Social Theory and Social Action." *American Sociological Review* 1 (February): 1–11.

Committee on Conceptual Integration, American Sociological Society, Subcommittee on Definition of Definition. (Hornell Hart, Chairman). 1943. "Some Methods for Improving Sociological Definitions." Abridged Report. *American Sociological Review* 8 (June): 333–42.

Committee on Graduate Instruction, American Council of Education. 1934. *Report of the Committee on Graduate Instruction.* Washington, D.C.: American Council of Education.

Comte, Auguste. 1893. *The Positive Philosophy of Auguste Comte.* Trans. Harriet Martineau. London: Kegan Paul, Trench, Trubner.

Cooley, Charles H. 1902. *Human Nature and the Social Order.* New York: Charles Scribners Sons. Rev. ed. 1922. Reprinted in 1964 by Shocken Books, New York.

———. 1909. *Social Organization.* New York: Charles Scribners Sons. 2d ed. 1937. Reprinted in 1962 by Schocken Books, New York.

———. 1918. *Social Process.* New York: Charles Scribners Sons.Reprinted in 1966 by Southern Illinois University Press, Carbondale.

———. 1926. "The Roots of Social Knowledge." *American Journal of Sociology* 32 (July): 59–79.

———. 1927. *Life and the Student.* New York: Alfred A. Knopf.

———. 1928. "Case Study of Small Institutions as a Method of Research." *Publications of the American Sociological Society* 22:23–32.

———. 1929. "The Life Study Method as Applied to Rural Social Research." *Publications of the American Sociological Society* 23:248–54.

———. 1930. *Sociological Theory and Social Research.* New York: Henry Holt. 2d. ed., Augustus M. Kelley, New York, 1969.

Crawford, W. Rex. 1948. "Representative Italian Contributions to Sociology: Pareto, Loria, Vaccaro, Gini, Sighele." In *An Introduction to the History of Sociology,* ed. Harry Elmer Barnes, 553–84. Chicago: University of Chicago Press.

Culler, Jonathan. 1982. *On Deconstruction.* Ithaca: Cornell University Press.

Dahlke, H. Otto. 1940. "The Sociology of Knowledge." In *Contemporary Social Theory,* ed. Harry Elmer Barnes, Howard Becker, and Frances Bennet Becker, 64–92. New York: D. Appleton-Century.

Davis, Kingsley. 1948. *Human Society.* New York: Macmillan. 2d ed. 1949.

DeGre, Gerard L. 1943. *Society and Ideology.* New York: Columbia University Book Store.

Dewey, John. 1922. *Human Nature and Conduct.* New York: Henry Holt.

Dilthey, Wilhelm. 1883. *Einleitung in die Geisteswissenschaften* in *Gesammelte Schriften.* Vol. 1. Stuttgart: B. G. Teubner Verlagsgesellschaft and Gottingen; Vandenhoeck and Ruprecht; 2d and 3d ed., 1959, 1962.

Duncan, Otis Dudley. 1964. Introduction to *William F. Ogburn on Culture and*

Social Change, ed. Otis Dudley Duncan, vii–xxii. Chicago: University of Chicago Press, Phoenix Books.

Durkheim, Emile. 1893. *De la Division du travail social.* Paris F. Alcan, 2d ed. Published in English in 1933 as *The Division of Labor in Society.* Trans. George Simpson. New York: Macmillan. Reprinted in 1947 and 1949 by the Free Press, Glencoe, Ill.

———. 1894. *Les Regles de la methode sociologique.* Paris: E. Alcan, 8th ed. Published in English in 1938 as *The Rules of Sociological Method.* Trans. Sarah A. Solovay and John H. Mueller, George E. G. Catlin. Chicago: University of Chicago Press. Reprinted in 1950 by the Free Press, Glencoe, Ill.

———. 1953. *Sociology and Philosophy.* Trans. D. F. Pocock. Glencoe, Ill.: Free Press.

Eaves, Lucille. 1917. A Resolution Authorizing Continuation of a Committee on Research by the American Sociological Society at the Business Meeting of Its 12th annual meeting on 29 December 1917. *Publications of the American Sociological Society* 12:248.

Elliott, Mabel A., and Francis E. Merrill. 1934. *Social Disorganization.* New York: Harper & Bros.

Ellwood, Charles A. 1912. *Sociology in Its Psychological Aspects.* New York: D. Appleton.

———. 1916. "Objectivism in Sociology." *American Journal of Sociology* 22 (November): 289–305.

———. 1917. *Introduction to Social Psychology.* New York: D. Appleton.

———. 1918. "Theories of Cultural Evolution." *American Journal of Sociology* 23 (May): 779–800.

———. 1923. Review of *Development of Social Theory,* by James P. Lichtenberger. *American Journal of Sociology* 29 (July): 104.

———. 1925. *The Psychology of Human Society.* New York: D. Appleton. 2d ed. 1929.

———. 1927. *Cultural Evolution.* New York: Century.

———. 1938. *A History of Social Philosophy.* New York: Prentice-Hall.

———. 1945. "The Psychological Basis of Culture." *Sociology and Social Research* 29 (July-August): 423–30.

Ermarth, Michael. 1978. *Wilhelm Dilthey: The Critique of Historical Reason.* Chicago: University of Chicago Press.

400   *Selected Reference List*

Faris, Ellsworth. 1921. "Are Instincts Data or Hypotheses?" *American Journal of Sociology* 27 (July): 184–96.

———. 1924. "Social Evolution." In *Contributions of Science to Religion,* ed. Shailer Mathews, 211–42. New York: D. Appleton.

———. 1936a. "An Estimate of Pareto." *American Journal of Sociology* 41 (March): 657–68. Reprinted as chapter 16 of *The Nature of Human Nature.* See Faris 1937a.

———. 1936b. "On Psychological Elements." *American Journal of Sociology* 42 (September): 159–76.

———. 1936c. Review of *Mind, Self, and Society,* by G. H. Mead. *American Journal of Sociology* 41 (May): 809–13.

———. 1937a. *The Nature of Human Nature.* New York: McGraw-Hill. Reprinted in abridged ed. in 1976 by the University of Chicago Press, Midway Reprint, Chicago.

———. 1937b. "The Social Psychology of George Herbert Mead." *American Journal of Sociology* 43 (November): 391–403.

Faris, Robert E. L. 1967. *Chicago Sociology, 1920–1932.* San Francisco: Chandler.

Featherstone, Mike. 1988. "In the Pursuit of the Postmodern: An Introduction." *Theory, Culture, and Society* 5 (June): 195–215.

Fine, Gary Alan, and Janet E. Severence. 1985. "Great Men and hard Times—Sociology at the University of Minnesota." *Sociological Quarterly* 26 (April): 117–34.

———. 1990. "Symbolic Interactionism in the Post-Blumerian Age." In *Frontiers of Social Theory,* ed. George Ritzer, 117–57. New York: Columbia University Press.

Folsom, Joseph K. 1928. *Culture and Social Progress.* New York: Longmans, Green.

Foster, Arnold, and Theodore Standing. n.d. Untitled study of about 110 sociologists and anthropologists working for the federal government during the New Deal era.

Fraser, Nancy, and Linda Nicholson. 1988. "Social Criticism without Philosophy: An Encounter between Feminism and Postmodernism." *Theory, Culture, and Society* 5 (June): 373–94.

Furfey, Paul Hanly. 1942. *A History of Social Thought.* New York: Macmillan.

Gault, Robert H. 1917. "Psychology in Social Relations." *American Journal of Sociology* 22 (May): 734–48.

Gehlke, Charles Elmer. 1915. *Emile Durkheim's Contributions to Sociological Theory.* Studies in History, Economics, and Public Law, vol. 63, no. 1. New York: Columbia University.

———. 1926. "The Use and Limitations of Statistics in Sociological Research." *Publications of the American Sociological Society* 21:141–48.

Gerth, Hans H. 1960. "Howard Becker, 1899–1960." Obituary. *American Sociological Review* 25 (October): 743–45.

———. 1982. *Politics, Character, and Culture,* ed. Joseph Bensman, Arthur J. Vidich, and Nabuko Gerth. Westport, Conn.: Greenwood Press.

Gerth, Hans H., and Hedwig Ida Gerth. 1949. "Bibliography on Max Weber." *Social Research* 16 (March): 70–89.

Giddings, Franklin H. 1986. *The Principles of Sociology.* New York: Macmillan.

———. 1901. *Inductive Sociology.* New York: Macmillan.

———. 1924. *The Scientific Study of Human Society.* Chapel Hill, N.C.

Giddens, Anthony. 1977. "Positivism and Its Critics." *A History of Sociological Analysis,* ed. Tom Bottomore and Robert Nisbet, 279–98. New York: Basic Books.

Gillin, John L. 1919. "Report of the Committee on the Standardization of Research." *Publications of the American Sociological Society* 14:252–59.

———. 1920. "Report on the Committee on the Standardization of Research." *Publications of the American Sociological Society* 15:231–41.

———. 1921. "Report of the Research Committee of the American Sociological Society." *Publications of the American Sociological Society* 16:243–48.

———. 1923. "Report of the Research Committee." *Publications of the American Sociological Society* 18:155–58.

———. [probable author]. n.d. "History of the Department of Sociology, University of Wisconsin." Mimeograph, c. 1948.

Goldenweiser, Alexander. 1916. "Culture and Environment." *American Journal of Sociology* 21 (March): 628–33.

———. 1921. "Four Phases of Anthropological Thought: An Outline." *Publications of the American Sociological Society* 16:50–69.

———. 1925a. "Cultural Anthropology." *The History and Prospects of the Social Sciences,* ed. Harry Elmer Barnes. New York: Knopf.

———. 1925b. "Diffusion and the American School of Historical Ethnology." *American Journal of Sociology* 31 (July): 19–38.

Goldman, Irving. 1959. "Evolution and Anthropology." *Victorian Studies* 3 (September): 55–75.

Gouldner, Alvin. 1970. *The Coming Crisis of Western Sociology.* New York: Basic Books.

Green, Arnold. 1936. "Sociological Analysis of Horney and Fromm." *American Journal of Sociology* 51 (May): 533–37.

Groves, Ernest, R. 1917a. Sociology and Psycho-analytic Psychology: An Interpretation of the Freudian Hypothesis." *American Journal of Sociology* 23 (July): 107–16.

———. 1917b. "An Unsocial Element in Religion." *American Journal of Sociology* 22 (May): 657–62.

Gurney, Patrick J. 1981. "Historical Origins of Ideological Denial: The Case of Marx in American Sociology." *American Sociologist* 16 (August): 196–201.

Gurvitch, Georges, and Wilbert Moore, eds. 1945. *Twentieth Century Sociology.* New York: Philosophical Library.

Hagerty, James E. n.d. "History of Sociology at Ohio State University." Typescript, c. 1932–36, copy in this author's possession.

Hagood, Margaret Jarman. 1941. *Statistics for Sociologists.* New York: Henry Holt.

Hall, G. Stanley. 1913. "Social Phases of Psychology." *Publications of the American Sociological Society* 7:38–46.

Halton, Eugene. 1992. "Habermas and Rorty: Between Scylla and Charybdis." *Symbolic Interaction* 15 (Fall): 333–58.

Handman, Max S. 1931. "The Sociological Methods of Vilfredo Pareto." In *Methods in Social Science,* ed. Stuart A. Rice, 139–53. Chicago: University of Chicago Press.

Hankins, Frank H. 1928. *An Introduction to the Study of Society.* New York: Macmillan.

Hart, Hornell. 1921. "Science and Sociology." *American Journal of Sociology* 27 (November): 364–83.

———. 1927. "The History of Social Thought: A Consensus of American Opinion." *Social Forces* 6 (December): 190–96.

Hart, Hornell, and Adele Panzer. 1925. "Have Subhuman Animals Culture?" *American Journal of Sociology* 30 (May): 703–79.

Harvey, Lee. 1987. *Myths of the Chicago School of Sociology.* Aldershot, England: Avebury.

Hayes, E. C., ed. 1927. *Recent Developments in the Social Sciences.* Philadelphia: Lippincott.

Heberle, Rudolf. 1948. "The Sociological System of Ferdinand Tonnies: 'Community' and 'Society.'" In *An Introduction to the History of Sociology,* ed. Harry Elmer Barnes, 227–48. Chicago: University of Chicago Press.

Henderson, Lawrence J. 1935. *Pareto's General Sociology: A Physiologist's Interpretation.* Cambridge: Harvard University Press.

Hennis, Wilhelm. 1988. *Max Weber: Essays in Reconstruction.* Trans. Keith Tribe. London: Allen & Unwin.

Herskovits, Melville J., and Malcolm W. Wiley. 1923. "The Cultural Approach to Sociology." *American Journal of Sociology* 29 (September): 188–99.

Hertzler, Joyce Oramel. 1925. "The Sociological Uses of History." *American Journal of Sociology* 31 (September): 173–98.

———. 1934. "The Sources and Methods of Historical Sociology." In *The Fields and Methods of Sociology,* ed. L. L. Bernard, 260–73. New York: Farrar Rinehart.

Heterick, Barbara, John Pease, and Richard A. Mathers. 1978. "Historical Notes on the First Regional Sociological Society." *Sociological Forum* 1 (Fall): 87–93.

Heyl, Barbara S. 1968. "The Harvard 'Pareto Circle.'" *Journal of the History of Behavioral Science* 4 (October): 316–34.

Hiller, E. T. 1933. *Principles of Sociology.* New York: Harper & Bros.

Hinkle, Gisela J. 1951. "The Role of Freudianism in American Sociology." Ph.D. diss., Department of Sociology, University of Wisconsin.

———. 1957. "Sociology and Psychoanalysis." In *Modern Sociological Theory in Continuity and Change,* ed. Howard Becker and Alvin Boskoff, 574–603. New York: Dryden Press.

———. 1992. "Habermas, Mead, and Rationality." *Symbolic Interaction* 15 (Fall): 315–31.

Hinkle, Roscoe C. 1960. "Durkheim in American Sociology." In *Emile Durkheim 1858–1917,* ed. Kurt H. Wolff, 267–95. Columbus: Ohio State University Press. Reprinted in 1964 in *Essays on Sociology and Philosophy,* ed. Kurt H. Wolff. New York: Harper Torchbooks.

———. 1966. Introduction to *Social Process.* See Cooley [1918] 1966.

———. 1967. "Charles Horton Cooley's General Sociological Orientation." *Sociological Quarterly* 8 (Winter): 5–20.

———. 1971. Review of *The Coming Crisis of Western Sociology,* by A. Gouldner. *Social Forces* 49 (March): 497–99.

———. 1975. "Basic Orientation of the Founding Fathers of American Sociology." *Journal of the History of Behavior Sciences* 11 (April): 107–22.

———. 1978. "Toward Periodicization of the History of Sociological Theory." *Journal of the History of Sociology* 1 (Fall): 68–89.

———. 1980. *Founding Theory of American Sociology 1881–1915* Boston: Routledge & Kegan Paul.

Hinkle, Roscoe, and Gisela J. Hinkle. 1954. *The Development of Modern Sociology.* New York: Random House.

Hobhouse, Leonard T., G. C. Wheeler, and Morris Ginsberg. 1915. *The Material Culture and Social Institutions of the Simpler Peoples.* London: Chapman & Hall.

Hodgen, Margaret T. 1968. "Frederick John Teggart." In *The International Encyclopedia of the Social Sciences,* ed. David Sills, 15:598–99. New York: Macmillan.

Hodges, H. A. 1944. *Wilhelm Dilthey: An Introduction.* New York: Oxford University Press.

Holt, E. B. 1915. *The Freudian Wish and Its Place in Ethics.* New York: Henry Holt.

Homans, George C., and Charles P. Curtis, Jr. 1934. *An Introduction to Pareto: His Sociology.* New York: Alfred Knopf.

House, Floyd N. 1926. Review of *Theory of History* by Frederick J. Teggart. *American Journal of Sociology* 32 (July): 131–32.

———. 1928. "Social Change and Social Science." *Social Forces* 7 (October): 11–17.

———. 1929. *The Range of Social Theory.* New York: Henry Holt.

———. 1935. "Pareto in the Development of Modern Sociology." *Journal of Social Philosophy* 1 (October): 78–89.

———. 1936. *Development of Sociology.* New York: McGraw-Hill.

Hughes, R. M. 1925. *A Study of the Graduate Schools of America.* Oxford, Ohio: Miami University.

Hull, Clark L. 1935. "The Conflicting Psychologies of Learning—a Way Out." *Psychological Review* 42 (November): 491–516.

———. 1943. *Principles of Behavior.* New York: D. Appleton-Century.

Irwin, Mary, ed. 1952. *American Universities and Colleges.* 6th ed. Washington, D.C.: American Council of Education.

Janowitz, Morris, ed. 1966. *W. I. Thomas On Social Organization and Social Personality: Selected Papers,* by W. I. Thomas. Chicago: University of Chicago Press.

Jay, Martin. 1973. *The Dialectical Imagination.* Boston: Litle, Brown.

Joas, Hans. 1985. *G. H. Mead: A Contemporary Re-examination of his Thought.* Trans. Raymond Meyer. Cambridge: MIT Press.

———. 1992. "An Underestimated Alternative: America and the Limits of 'Critical Theory.'" *Symbolic Interaction* 15 (Fall): 261–75.

Jocher, Katherine. 1928. "The Case Method in Social Research." *Social Forces* 7 (December): 203–11.

Jones, Robert Alun. 1974. "Freud and American Sociology, 1909–1949." *Journal of the History of Behavioral Sciences* 10 (January): 21–39.

Karpf, Fay Berger. 1932. *American Social Psychology.* New York: McGraw-Hill.

Kellner, Douglas. 1988. "Postmodernism as Social Theory." *Theory, Culture, and Society* 5 (June): 239–71.

———. 1990. "The Postmodern Turn: Positions, Problems, and Prospects." In *Frontiers of Social Theory,* ed. George Ritzer, 255–86. New York: Columbia University Press.

Kellogg, W. N., and L. A. Kellogg. 1933. *The Ape and the Child.* New York: McGraw-Hill, Whittlesey House.

Kirkpatrick, Clifford. 1939. "A Methodological Analysis of Feminism in Relation to Marital Adjustment." *American Sociological Review* 4 (June): 325–44.

Kivisto, Peter, and William H. Swatos, Jr. 1990. "Weber and Interpretive Sociology in America." *Sociological Quarterly* 31 (1): 149–63.

Kohler, Wolfgang. 1926. *The Mentality of Apes.* New York: Harcourt, Brace.

Kolakowski, Lezak. 1968. *The Alienation of Reason: A History of Positivist Thought.* Trans. Norman Guterman. Garden City, N.Y.: Doubleday.

Krueger, E. T., and Walter C. Reckless. 1931. *Social Psychology.* New York: Longmans, Green.

Lash, Scott. 1988. "Discourse or Figure? Postmodernism as a 'Regime of Signification." *Theory, Culture, and Society* 5 (June): 311–36.

———. 1990. "Postmodernism as Humanism? Urban Space and Social Theory." *Theories of Modernity and Postmodernity,* ed. Bryan S. Turner, 62–74. Newbury Park, Calif.

Leiter, Kenneth. 1980. *A Primer on Ethnomethodology.* New York: Oxford University Press.

Lemert, Charles C. 1990. "The Uses of French Structuralism in Sociology." In *Frontiers of Social Theory,* ed. George Ritzer, 230–54. New York: Columbia University Press.

———. 1991. "The End of Ideology, Really." *Sociological Theory* 9 (Fall): 164–72.

Levine, Donald N., Ellwood B. Carter, and Eleanor Miller Gorman. 1976. "Simmel's Influence on American Sociology." *American Journal of Sociology* 81 (January, March): 813–44, 1112–32.

Levy-Bruhl, Lucien. 1913. *La Philosophie d'Auguste Comte.* 3d rev. ed. Paris: Librarie Felix Alcan.

Lewis, J. David, and Richard L. Smith. 1980. *American Sociology and Pragmatism.* Chicago: University of Chicago Press.

Leyburn, James G. 1933. "The Fields and Problems of Cultural and Folk Sociology." In *The Fields and Methods of Sociology,* ed. L. L. Bernard, 110–18. New York: Farrar & Rinehart. 2d ed. 1934.

Lichtenberger, James P. 1923. *The Development of Social Theory.* New York: D. Appleton-Century.

Linton, Ralph. 1935. *The Study of Man.* New York: D. Appleton-Century.

Lipset, S. M. 1955. "The Department of Sociology." In *A History of the Faculty of Political Science, Columbia University,* ed. R. Gordon Hoxie, 290–97. New York: Columbia University Press.

Lobkowicz, Nicholas. 1967. *Theory and Practice.* Notre Dame, Ind.: University of Notre Dame Press.

Lowie, Robert H. 1914. "Social Organization." *American Journal of Sociology* 20 (July): 68–97.

Lumley, F. E. 1928. *Principles of Sociology.* New York: McGraw-Hill. 2d ed. 1935.

Lundberg, George A. 1929a. "The Logic of Sociology and Social Research." In *Trends in American Sociology,* ed. George A. Lundberg, Read Bain, and Nels Anderson, 389–420. New York: Harper & Bros.

———. 1929b. *Social Research.* New York: Longmans, Green.

———. 1933. "Is Sociology Too Scientific?" *Sociologus* 9 (September): 298–320.

———. 1936a. "Quantitative Methods in Social Psychology." *American Sociological Review* 1 (February): 38–54.

———. 1936b. "The Thoughtways of Contemporary Sociology." *American Sociological Review* 1 (October): 703–23.

———. 1939a. "Contemporary Positivism in Sociology." *American Sociological Review* 4 (February): 42–55.

———. 1939b. *Foundations of Sociology.* New York: Macmillan.

———. 1942. "Operational Definitions in the Social Sciences." *American Journal of Sociology* 47 (March): 727–43.

———. 1945. "The Proximate Future of American Sociology: The Growth of Scientific Method." *American Journal of Sociology* 50 (May): 502–13.

———. 1947. *Can Science Save Us?* New York: Longmans, Green.

Lyman, Stanford M. 1978. "The Acceptance, Rejection, and Reconstruction of Histories." In *Structure, Consciousness, and History,* ed. Richard Harvey Brown and Stanford M. Lyman, 64–79. New York: Cambridge University Press.

Lynd, Robert S. 1939. *Knowledge for What?* Princeton: Princeton University Press.

MacIver, Robert M. 1930. "Is Sociology a Natural Science?" *Publications of the American Sociological Society* 25:25–35.

———. 1931a. "Is Statistical Methodology Applicable to the Study of the Situation?" *Social Forces* 9 (June): 479.

———. 1931b. "Social Causation." *Publications of the American Sociological Society* 26:28–35.

———. 1931c. *Society.* New York: Ray Long & Richard R. Smith. 2d ed., Farrar & Rinehart, 1937.

———. 1931d. "Sociology." In *A Quarter Century of Learning, 1904–1929,* ed. Dixon Ryan Fox, 62–91. New York: Columbia University Press.

———. 1937. "The Historical Pattern of Social Change." In *Authority and the Individual,* 126–53. Cambridge: Harvard University Press.

———. 1940. "The Imputation of Motives." *American Journal of Sociology* 46 (July): 1–12.

——. 1942. *Social Causation.* New York: Ginn. 2d ed. 1964.

MacIver, Robert M., and Charles H. Page. 1949. *Society: An Introductory Analysis.* New York: Rinehart.

Mannheim, Karl. 1936. *Ideology and Utopia.* Trans. Louis Wirth and Edward Shils. New York: Harcourt, Brace, & World.

——. 1940. *Man and Society in an Age of Reconstruction.* New York: Harcourt, Brace.

——. 1944. *Diagnosis of Our Time.* New York: Oxford University Press.

Marsh, Clarence Stephen, ed. 1940. *American Universities and Colleges.* 4th ed. Washington, D.C.: American Council on Education.

Martindale, Don. 1960. *The Nature and Types of Sociological Theory.* Boston: Houghton-Mifflin.

——. 1965. "Limits and Alternatives to Functionalism in Sociology." In *Functionalism in the Social Sciences,* Monograph 5, ed. Don Martindale, 144–62. Philadelphia: American Academy of Political and Social Science.

McCarthy, Thomas. 1978. *The Critical Theory of Jürgen Habermas.* Cambridge: MIT Press.

McCormick, Thomas C. 1941. *Elementary Social Statistics.* New York: McGraw-Hill.

McLaughlin, Isabella. 1927. "History and Sociology: A Comparison of Their Methods." *American Journal of Sociology* 32 (November): 379–95.

Mead, George Herbert. 1934. *Mind, Self, and Society,* ed. Charles W. Morris. Chicago: University of Chicago Press.

——. 1936. *Movements of Thought in the Nineteenth Century,* ed. Merritt H. Moore. Chicago: University of Chicago Press.

——. 1938. *The Philosophy of the Act,* ed. Charles W. Morris. Chicago: University of Chicago Press.

——. 1964. *George Herbert Mead on Social Psychology. Selected Papers.* Ed. Anselm Strauss. Chicago: University of Chicago Press, Phoenix Books.

——. 1982. *The Individual and the Social Self: Unpublished Work of George Herbert Mead,* ed. David L. Miller. Chicago: University of Chicago Press.

Meroney, W. P. 1925. "The Meaning and Method of Science." *Southwestern Political and Social Science Quarterly* 6 (September): 83–111.

Merton, Robert K. 1934. "Durkheim's Division of Labor in Society." *American Journal of Sociology* 40 (November): 319–28.

———. 1945. "Sociological Theory." *American Journal of Sociology* 50 (May): 462–73. Republished as chapter 4 of *Social Theory and Social Structure*. See Merton 1968.

———. 1968. *Social Theory and Social Structure*. 2d ed. New York: Macmillan, Free Press.

Mills, C. Wright. 1963. *Power, Politics, and People,* ed. Irving Louis Horowitz. New York: Oxford University Press. 2d ed. 1967.

Moore, Harry E., and Bernice M. Moore. 1935. "Folk Implications in Pareto's Sociology." *Social Forces* 14 (December): 293–300.

Nisbet, Robert A. 1969. *Social Change and History*. New York: Oxford University Press.

———. 1970. "Developmentalism: A Critical Analysis." In *Theoretical Sociology: Perspectives and Developments,* ed. John C. McKinney and Edward A. Tiryakian, 167–204. New York: Appleton-Century-Crofts.

———. 1978–79. "Teggart of Berkeley." *American Scholar* 48 (Winter): 71–80.

Oakes, Guy. 1988. *Weber and Rickert: Concept Formation in the Cultural Sciences.* Cambridge: MIT Press.

Odum, Howard W. 1951. *American Sociology*. New York: Longmans, Green.

Ogburn, William Fielding. 1919. "The Psychological Basis for the Economic Interpretation of History." *American Economic Review* 9 (supplement, March): 291–308.

———. 1921. "The Historical Method in the Analysis of Social Phenomena." *Publications of the American Sociological Society* 16: 70–83.

———. 1922. *Social Change*. New York: B. W. Huebsch; Viking Press, 1950.

———. 1927. "Sociology and Statistics." In *The Social Sciences and Their Interrelations,* ed. William Fielding Ogburn and Alexander Goldenweiser, 161–77. Boston: Houghton-Mifflin.

———. 1929. "The Folkways of a Scientific Sociology." *Publications of the American Sociological Society* 24:1–11.

Ogburn, William Fielding and Alexander Goldenweiser, eds. 1927. *The Social Sciences and Their Interrelations*. Boston: Houghton-Mifflin.

Ogburn, William Fielding, and Meyer F. Nimkoff. 1940. *Sociology.* Boston: Houghton-Mifflin.

Ohio State University. 1915, 1925, 1935, 1945. *The Ohio State University Bulletin.* Vols. 19, 29 (October), 39 (May), and 50 (November, "University Directory"). Columbus: Ohio State University.

Page, Charles H. 1982. *Fifty Years in the Sociological Enterprise.* Amherst: University of Massachusetts Press.

Pareto, Vilfredo. 1916. *Trattato di sociologia generale.* Florence: G. Barbera. Ed. Arthur Livingston. Published in English in 1935 as *The Mind and Society,* trans. Andrew Bongiorno and Arthur Livingston, 4 vols., by Harcourt, Brace, New York.

Park, Robert E. 1913. Comment at "Informal Conference." *Publications of the American Sociological Society* 8:167–68.

———. 1921. "Sociology and the Social Sciences." *American Journal of Sociology* 26 (January): 401–24; 27 (July, September): 1–23, 169–83. Republished as chapter 1 of *Introduction to the Science of Sociology* by Park and Burgess, 1921, 1924, and as chapter 16 of *Society* by Park, 1955.

———. 1950. *Race and Culture.* Glencoe, Ill.: Free Press.

———. 1952. *Human Communities.* Glencoe, Ill.: Free Press.

———. 1955. *Society.* Glencoe, Ill.: Free Press.

———. 1958. "Human Nature as Elemental Communication." In *Race: Individual and Collective Behavior,* ed. Edgar T. Thompson and Everett C. Hughes, 462–64. Glencoe, Ill.: Free Press.

Park, Robert E., and E. W. Burgess. 1921. *Introduction to the Science of Sociology.* Chicago: University of Chicago Press. 2d ed. 1924.

Parsons, Talcott. 1929. "'Capitalism' in Recent German Literature." *Journal of Political Economy* 37 (February): 31–51.

———. 1933. "Pareto, Vilfredo." *Encyclopaedia of the Social Sciences* 11:576–78.

———. 1935a. Review of *The Mind and Society,* by Vilfredo Pareto. *American Economics Review* 25 (September): 502–8.

———. 1935b. "Sociological Elements in Economic Thought." *Quarterly Journal of Economics* 49 (May, August): 414–53, 647–67.

———. 1936a. "Pareto's Central Analytical Scheme." *Journal of Social Philosophy* 1 (April): 244–62.

———. 1936b. Review of *The Mind and Society,* by Vilfredo Pareto. *American Sociological Review* 1 (February): 139–48.

———. 1937. *The Structure of Social Action.* New York: McGraw-Hill, Free Press. 2d ed. 1968.

———. 1945. "The Present Position and Prospects of Systematic Theory in Sociology." In *Twentieth Century Sociology,* ed. Georges Gurvitch and Wilbert E. Moore, 42–68. New York: Philosophical Library. Reprinted in 1949 in *Essays in Sociological Theory: Pure and Applied,* 17–41, by the Free Press, Glencoe, Ill.

———. 1948a. "Max Weber's Sociological Analysis of Capitalism and Modern Social Institutions." In *An Introduction to the History of Sociology,* ed. Harry Elmer Barnes, 297–308. Chicago: University of Chicago Press.

———. 1948b. "The Position of Sociological Theory." *American Sociological Review* 13 (April): 156–64.

———. 1950. "The Prospects of Sociological Theory." *American Sociological Review* 15 (February): 3–16. Republished in 1954 in *Essays in Sociological Theory,* idem, rev. ed., by the Free Press, New York.

Pearson, Karl. 1900. *The Grammar of Science.* 2d ed. London: A. & C. Black.

Pease, John, and Barbara Hetrick. 1977a. "Associations for Whom? The Regionals and the American Sociological Association." *American Sociologist* 12 (February): 42–47.

———. 1977b. "An Historical Sketch of the Relationship between the Regional Sociological Societies and the American Sociological Association, 1934–1977." *ASA Footnotes* (May): 9–10.

Plantinga, Theodore. 1980. *Historical Understanding in the Thought of Wilhelm Dilthey.* Toronto: University of Toronto Press.

Queen, Stuart A. 1931. "Some Problems of the Situational Approach." *Social Forces* 9 (June): 480–18.

Radnitzky, Gerard. 1968. *Contemporary Schools of Metascience.* Chicago: Henry Regnery. 2d ed. 1970. 3d ed. 1973.

Raushenbush, Winifred. 1979. *Robert E. Park: Biography of a Sociologist.* Durham: Duke University Press.

Reuter, E. B., and C. W. Hart. 1933. *Introduction to Sociology.* New York: McGraw-Hill.

Rhoades, Lawrence J. 1981. *A History of the American Sociological Association 1904–1980.* Washington, D.C.: American Sociological Association.

Rice, Stuart a. 1928a. *Quantitative Methods in Politics.* New York: Alfred A. Knopf.

———. 1928b. "A Viewpoint Concerning Scientific Social Science." *Social Science* 3 (February-March): 169–72.

———. 1931. "Units and Their Definition in Social Science." *Social Forces* 9 (June): 475–85.

———. 1932. "What Is Sociology?" *Social Forces* 10 (March): 319–26.

Richardson, Laurel. 1991. "Postmodern Social Theory: Representational Practices." *Sociological Theory* (Fall): 173–79.

Rickert, Heinrich. 1899. *Kulturwissenschaft und Naturwissenschaft.* Tubingen: J. C. B. Mohr. 2d ed. 1926. Published in English in 1962 as *Science and History,* trans. George Reisman and ed. Arthur Goddard, by D. Van Nostrand, Princeton, N.J.

———. 1902. *Die Grenzen der naturwissenschaftlichen Begriffsbildung.* Tubingen: J. C. B. Mohr. First 3 chaps. published 1896. Published in English in 1986 as *The Limits of Concept Formation in Natural Science,* ed. and trans. Guy Oakes, by the Cambridge University Press.

Rickman, H. P. 1976. *W. Dilthey: Selected Writings.* Cambridge and New York: Cambridge University Press.

Robinson, James Harvey. 1918. *The New History.* New York: Macmillan.

Rose, Gillian. 1988. "Architecture to Philosophy: The Postmodern Complicity." *Theory, Culture, and Society* 5 (June): 357–71.

Ross, Dorothy. 1991. *The Origins of American Social Science.* New York: Cambridge University Press.

Ross, Edward Alsworth. 1901. *Social Control.* New York: Macmillan. 2d ed. 1929. Reprinted in 1969 by Case Western Reserve University Press, Cleveland, Ohio.

Roth, Gunter, and Reinhard Bendix. 1959. "Max Webers Einfluss auf die amerikanischen Soziologie." *Kolner Zeitschrift fur Soziologie und Sozialpsychologie* 2 (1):38–53.

Rucker, Darnell. 1969. *The Chicago Pragmatists.* Minneapolis: University of Minnesota Press.

Russett, Cynthia Eagle. 1966. *The Concept of Equilibrium in American Social Thought.* New Haven: Yale University Press.

Schutz, Alfred. 1967. "Concept and Theory Formation in the Social Sciences." In *Understanding and Social Inquiry,* ed. Fred R. Dallmayr and Thomas A.

McCarthy, 225–39. Notre Dame, Ind.: University of Notre Dame Press. 2d ed. 1977.

Sciulli, David. 1992. "Habermas, Critical Theory, and the Relativistic Predicament." *Symbolic Interaction* 15 (Fall): 299–313.

Seidman, Steven. 1991a. "The End of Sociological Theory: The Postmodern Hope." *Sociological Theory* 9 (Fall): 131–46.

———. 1991b. "Postmodern Anxiety: The Politics of Epistemology." *Sociological Theory* 9 (Fall): 180–90.

Shalin, Dmitri, ed. 1992a. "Symposium on Habermas, Pragmatism, and Critical Theory." *Symbolic Interaction* 15 (Fall): 251–358

Shalin, Dmitri N. 1992b. "Introduction: Habermas, Pragmatism, Interactionism." *Symbolic Interaction* 15 (Fall): 251–59.

Shanas, Ethel. 1945. "The *American Journal of Sociology* Through Fifty Years." *American Journal of Sociology* 50 (May): 522–33.

Shaw, Clifford. 1927. "Case Study Method." *Publications of the American Sociological Society* 21:149–51.

Shils, Edward A. 1980. *The Calling of Sociology and Other Essays on the Pursuit of Learning.* Chicago: University of Chicago Press.

Simpson, Eyler Newton. 1926. "Wishes: A Study in Social Psychology." Ph.D. diss., Department of Sociology, University ofChicago.

Simpson, George. 1933. "Emile Durkheim's Social Realism." *Sociology and Social Research* 18 (September-October): 3–11.

Small, Albion W. 1905. *General Sociology.* Chicago: University of Chicago Press.

———. 1912. "General Sociology." *American Journal of Sociology* 18 (September): 200–14.

Small, Albion W., and Vincent, George E. 1894. *An Introduction to the Study of Society.* New York: American Book Co. Reprinted in 1971 by Brown Reprints, Dubuque, Iowa.

Smith, Norman E., and Roscoe C. Hinkle. 1979. "Sumner versus Keller and the Social Evolutionism of Early American Sociology." *Sociological Inquiry* 49 (1): 41–48.

Sorokin, Pitirim A. 1927. "A Survey of the Cyclical Conceptions of Social and Historical Process." *Social Forces* 6 (September): 57–62.

———. 1928. *Contemporary Sociological Theories.* New York: Harper & Bros.

——. 1931. "The Principle of Limits Applied to Problems of Causal or Functional Relationship between Societal Variables and of the Direction of Social Processes." *Publications of the American Sociological Society* 26:20–27.

——. 1936. "Is Accurate Social Planning Possible?" *American Sociological Review* 1 (February): 12–25.

——. 1937–41. *Social and Cultural Dynamics.* 4 vols. New York: American Book Co.

——. 1945. "Sociocultural Dynamics and Evolutionism." In *Twentieth Century Sociology,* ed. Georges Gurvitch and Wilbert E. Moore, 96–120. New York: Philosophical Library.

——. 1947. *Society, Culture, and Personality.* New York: Harper & Bros.

——. 1966. *Sociological Theories of Today.* New York: Harper & Row.

Speier, Hans. 1937. "Weber, Max." *Encyclopaedia of the Social Sciences* 15:386–88.

Spykman, N. J. 1925. *The Social Theory of Georg Simmel.* Chicago: University of Chicago Press.

Stern, Bernard J. 1929. "Concerning the Distinction between the Social and Cultural." *Social Forces* 8 (December): 264–73.

Sumner, William Graham. 1881. "Sociology." *Princeton Review* (ser. 4) 9 (November): 303–23. Republished in 1963 in *Social Darwinism: Selected Essays of William Graham Sumner,* ed. Stow Persons, Prentice-Hall, Englewood Cliffs, N.J.

——. 1907. *Folkways.* Boston: Ginn. Reprinted in 1959 by Dover, New York.

Sumner, William G., and Keller, Albert G. 1927. *The Science of Society.* 4 vols. New Haven: Yale University Press.

Sutherland, Robert L., and Julian L. Woodward. 1937. *Introductory Sociology.* Philadelphia: J. B. Lippincott. 2d ed. 1940.

Symposium on Postmodernism 1991. In *Sociological Theory* 9 (Fall): 131–90.

Teggart, Frederick John. 1916. *Prolegomena to History.* Berkeley: University of California Press.

——. 1918. *Processes of History.* New Haven: Yale University Press.

——. 1925. *Theory of History.* New Haven: Yale University Press.

——. 1929. "Notes on House's 'Timeless' Sociology." *Social Forces* 7 (March): 362–65.

———. 1941. *Theory and Processes of History*   Berkeley: University of California Press. 2d ed. 1977.

———. 1949. *The Idea of Progress: A Collection of Readings.* Rev. ed. Berkeley: University of California Press.]

Tenbruck, Friedrich H. 1987. "Max Weber and Eduard Meyer." In *Max Weber and His Contemporaries,* ed. Wolfgang J. Mommsen and Jurgen Osterhamel, 234–67. London: Allen & Unwin.

Thomas, W. I. 1909. *Source Book for Social Origins.* Chicago: University of Chicago Press.

———. 1917. "The Persistence of Primary Group Norms in Present-Day Society and Their Influence in Our Educational System." In *Suggestions of Modern Science Concerning Education* by Herbert S. Jennings, John G. Watson, Adolf Meyer, and W. I. Thomas, 159–97. New York: Macmillan.

———. 1923. *The Unadjusted Girl.* Boston: Little, Brown.

———. 1927. "Configurations of Personality." In *The Unconscious: A Symposium,* by C. M. Child, Kurt Koffka, John E. Anderson, John B. Watson, Edward Sapir, W. I. Thomas, Marion E. Kenworth, F. L. Wells, and William A. White, 143–77. New York: Alfred Knopf.

———. and Florian Znaniecki. 1918–20. *The Polish Peasant in Europe and America.* 5 vols. Boston: Richard G. Badger. Vols. 1 and 2 originally published by the University of Chicago Press, 1918; Vols. 3 (1919), 4 and 5 (1920) originally published by Badger. 2d ed., 2 vols., Alfred Knopf.

Timasheff, Nicholas S. 1957. *Sociological Theory: Its Nature and Growth.* New York: Random House.

Tönnies, Ferdinand. 1887. *Gemeinschaft und Gesellschaft.* Published in English in 1940 as *Fundamental Concepts of Sociology.* Trans. (and supplemented by) Charles P. Loomis. New York: American Book. Republished in 1957 as *Community and Society* by Michigan State University Press, East Lansing. Reprinted in 1963 as a Harper Torchbook by Harper and Row, New York.

———. 1940. "The Concept and Law of Human Progress" (translated from the German by Karl J. Arndt and C. L. Folse). *Social Forces* 19 (October): 23–9.

———. 1971. *On Sociology: Pure, Applied, and Empirical, Selected Writings.* Trans. and ed. Werner J. Cahnman and Rudolf Heberle. Chicago: University of Chicago Press.

Tribe, Keith. 1988. Translator's Introduction to *Max Weber: Essays in Reconstruction* by Wilhelm Hennis. London: Allen & Unwin.

Turner, Bryan S., ed. 1990. *Theories of Modernity and Postmodernity.* Newbury Park, Calif.: Sage.

Turner, Charles. 1990. "Lyotard and Weber." *Theories of Modernity and Postmodernity,* ed. Bryan S. Turner, 108–116. Newbury Park, Calif.: Sage.

Turner, Jonathan. 1986. "The Mechanics of Social Interaction: Toward a Composite Model of Signaling and Interpreting." *Sociological Theory* 4 (Spring): 95–105.

Turner, Stephen. 1991. "The Strange Life and Hard Times of the Concept of General Theory in Sociology: A Short History of Hope." In *Postmodernism and Social Theory,* ed. Steven Seidman and David Wagner, 101–33. Cambridge, Mass.: Blackwell.

Turner, Stephen, and Jonathan H. Turner. 1990. *The Impossible Science.* Newbury Park, Calif.: Sage.

Volkart, Edmund H., ed. 1951. *Social Behavior and Personality: Contributions of W. I. Thomas to Theory and Social Research.* New York: Social Science Research Council.

Waller, Willard. 1934. "Insight and the Scientific Method." *American Journal of Sociology* 40 (November): 285–97.

Wallis, Wilson D. 1926. "Geographical Environment and Culture." *Social Forces* 4 (June): 702–8.

Ward, Lester F. 1883. *Dynamic Sociology.* 2 vols. New York: Appleton. Reprinted by Greenwood, New York, 1968.

———. 1903. *Pure Sociology.* New York: The Macmillan Co. Reprinted by Augustus M. Kelly, New York, 1970.

———. 1906. *Applied Sociology.* Boston: Ginn and Co.

Warriner, Charles K. 1956. "Groups Are Real: A Reaffirmation." *American Sociological Review* 21 (October): 549–554.

Weber, Max. 1930, 1958. *The Protestant Ethic and the Spirit of Capitalism.* Trans. Talcott Parsons. New York: Charles Scribners Sons. 2d ed. 1958.

———. 1946. *From Max Weber: Essays in Sociology,* trans. and ed. H. H. Gerth and C. Wright Mills. New York: Oxford University Press. Reprinted as a Galaxy Book, Oxford University Press, New York, 1958.

———. 1947. *Max Weber: The Theory of Social and Economic Organization.* Part 1 of *Wirthschaft und Gesellschaft* from vol. 3 of *Grundriss der Sozialökonomik* by Max Weber. Tübingen: J. C. B. Mohr (Paul Siebeck), 1922. Trans. A. M.

Henderson and Talcott Parsons, ed. Talcott Parsons. New York: Oxford University Press.

———. 1949. *The Methodology of the Social Sciences.* Trans. Edward A. Shils and Henry A. Finch. Glencoe, Ill.: Free Press.

White, Leslie A. 1940. "The Symbol: The Origin and Basis of Human Behavior." *Philosophy of Science* 7 (October): 451–63.

Wiese, Leopold (von). 1924. *Allgemeine Soziologie als Lehr von der Beziehungen und Beziehungsgebilden der Menschen.* Part 1: *Beziehungslehre.* Munich and Leipzig: Duncker and Humblott.

———. 1929. *Allgemeine Soziologie als Lehr von der Beziehungen und Beziehungsgebilden der Menschen.* Part 2: *Gebildelehre.* Munich and Leipzig: Duncker and Humblott.

Wiley, Norbert. 1986. "Early American Sociology and the *Polish Peasant.*" *Sociological Theory* 4 (Spring): 20–40.

Willey, Malcolm W. 1929. "Validity of Cultural Concepts." *American Journal of Sociology* 35 (September): 204–19.

———. 1931a. "A Proposed Reorganization of the Introductory Sociology Course." *Social Forces* 9 (March): 338–43.

———. 1931b. "Society and Its Cultural Heritage." In *An Introduction to Sociology,* rev. ed., ed. Jerome Davis and Harry Elmer Barnes, 495–592. Boston: D. C. Heath.

Windelband, Wilhelm. 1984. "Geschichte und Naturwissenschaft." Republished in 1924 in (author's) *Praeludien,* vol. 2 by J. C. B. Mohr, Tübingen. Published in English as "History and Natural Science," trans. Guy Oakes, in *History and Theory* 19, No. 2 (1980): 169–185.

Wirth, Louis. 1926. "The Sociology of Ferdinand Tonnies."*American Journal of Sociology* 32 (November): 412–22.

———. 1937. Review of *Permanence and Change* by Kenneth Burke. *American Journal of Sociology* 43 (November): 483–86.

———. 1938. "Urbanism as a Way of Life." *American Journal of Sociology* 44 (July): 1–24. Reprinted in *Community Life and Social Policy.* See Wirth 1956.

———. 1939a. Translated excerpts from Weber's *Wirtschaft und Gesellschaft,* vol. 1, chap. 1. In *Critiques of Research in the Social Sciences,* vol. 1, pt. 2, *Appraisal of Thomas and Znaniecki's The Polish Peasant in Europe and America,* ed. Herbert Blumer, 119–20. New York: Social Science Research Council.

——. 1939b. "Social Interaction: The Problem of the Individual and the Group." *American Journal of Sociology* 44 (May): 965–79. Reprinted in *Community Life and Social Policy.* See Wirth 1956.

——. 1956. *Community Life and Social Policy.* Chicago: University of Chicago Press.

Yerkes, R. M. 1925. *Almost Human.* New York: Century.

Yerkes, R. M. and A. W. Yerkes. 1929. *The Great Apes.* New Haven: Yale University Press.

Young, Donald. 1941. "A Memorandum on Suggestions for Research in the Field of Social Adjustment." *American Journal of Sociology* 46 (December): 873–86.

Young, Kimball. 1934. *An Introductory Sociology.* New York: American Book.

——. 1938. Review of *The Nature of Human Nature* by Ellsworth Faris. *American Journal of Sociology* 43 (January): 648–50.

——. 1942. *Sociology: A Study of Society and Culture.* New York: American Book.

Znaniecki, Florian. 1919. *Cultural Reality.* Chicago: University of Chicago Press.

——. 1927. "The Object Matter of Sociology." *American Journal of Sociology* 32 (January): 529–84.

——. 1931. "The Analysis of Social Processes." *Publications of the American Sociological Society* 26:37–43.

——. 1934. *The Method of Sociology.* New York: Farrar & Rinehart.

——. 1936. *Social Actions.* New York: Farrar & Rinehart.

——. 1948. "W. I. Thomas as a Collaborator." *Sociology and Social Research* 32 (March-April): 765–67.

Zuckerman, S. 1932. *The Social Life of Monkeys and Apes.* New York: Harcourt, Brace.

Index

A

Abel, Theodore: as author, 10, 285, 287; notion of culture, 173, 183–184, 186; relation to Willey, 184

Adler, A.: 201

Adler, F.: 311

AJS (*American Journal of Sociology*): 5, 6, 9, 10, 16, 173, 201, 274, 279, 287

Alpert, H.: 44, 277–278, 279

Allport, F.: 77, 223

Anthropology, anthropologists, cultural: 105–107, 173–174. See also Boas, Goldenweiser, Herskovits, Kroeber, Linton, Lowie, Wallis, L. White, Wissler, and E. B. Tylor

Arendt, H.: 288

Aristotle: 190, 377 n20, 314

Arndt, K. J. and Folse, C. L.: 286

ASA (American Sociological Association, see also ASS): 5, 174

ASR (*American Sociological Review*): 6, 16, 275, 284, 287

ASS (American Sociological Society, now ASA): 5, 7, 8, 12, 14, 16, 90, 93, 173

B

Bain, Read: behaviorism, 213; conception of culture, 179, 181, 197; explanation by reduction rejected, 78, 152; Freudianism, 202, 208; qualified empiricist and neo-positivist, 34, 35,

37, 38, 40, 58; revival of theory, 152; rudiments of culture at animal level, 183; social versus cultural, 184; theory defined, 7, 11, 152, 352 n9

Bagehot, Walter: 283

Baker, P. J., Long, M. P., and Quensel, S. L.: 276, 283, 284

Barnes, H. E.: academic data, 188; collaborator, 188, 189; invoked anthropological arguments against social evolutionism, 105, 106, 107, 110, 113, 116; history relevant to sociology, 186, 188–189; implied "pre-organic" social origins theory, 72

Becker, Howard: academic data, 289, 159; collaborator, 188, 189; compared with Teggart, 196, 198, 199; with Sorokin, 167; critiques of comparative method, 112, 114; of historical relativism; 194; of social evolution, 100, 108, 159–160, 168; of neo-positivism, especially Lundberg's, 357–358 n10; constructive typology a means for historically generalizing culture-case studies or achieving a historical sociology, 193–195; involved in revival of theory, 10, 152; misconstrued basic points of Teggart's position, 191, 192–193; proponent of Neo-Kantian epistemology-methodology, 49, 52, 53, 54, 56, 58, 199; proposed a sacred-secular theory of social change, 160–163, 169; social ontologically, an idealist, with balanced

objectivism and subjectivism, 169;
theory defined, 100, 11, 152; types to
replace stages in change theory, 160.
See also action-social action theory
Becker, Howard and Useem, R. H.: 285
Behaviorism: historical background,
212–213; moderate or qualified form,
214–218; radical or unqualified form,
218–223; critiques of, 225–230. See
Hankins, Bernard, and Lundberg
Bendix, Reinhard: 288
Benoit-Smullyan, E.: 288
Bernard, L. L.: academic data, 35; selection of author's text justified, 17, 18;
contents of text analyzed, 20, 21, 22; a
balanced materialist-idealist, 308,
309, 320; like pre-World War I predecessors in social change theory,
123–124; statistically-oriented, qualified empiricist, neo-positi- 34, 37, 48,
58; unpublished study of sociologists'
autobiographies, 276, 283, 284. See
also behaviorism, evolutionary theory
of social change, instinct controversy,
notion of culture, parallel evolution
Bierstedt, Robert: 46, 47
Blackmar, Frank W. and J. L. Gillin: 69,
70, 71, 81, 84, 90
Blumer, Herbert: academic data, 232,
233; comparison with and contrast to
Faris, Mead, Cooley, and Thomas,
235, 269–272; major contemporary
expositor of symbolic interactionism,
262–269; objected to quantification
and measurement, 47; opposed to sta-
tistics, empiricism, and neo-posi-
tivism, 46; references to Thomas, 234
Boas, Franz: 105, 106
Bogardus, Emory S.: 77, 285
Bossuet, Bishop: 191, 377 n20
Bougle, Celeste: 71
Bridgman, P. W.: 38, 44
Brill, A. A.: 207
Brinton, Crane: 279
Bristol, L. M.: 6, 9, 276
Bryant, Christopher: 35, 45–46

Burgess, E. W.: 34, 48, 49, 207, 314
Burrows, Trigant: 203

C

Cahnmann, W. and Heberle, R.: 286
Case, C. M.: arguments about nature of
culture, 173, 178–179, 183; proposed
a gestaltist sociology, 223–224;
quoted Spencer and Robinson,
187–188; reference to, and critique of
Teggart, 198, 377 n18; selection of
author's text justified, 17, 18
Case-study: 48–49. See Cooley,
MacIver, Park, Becker, and Znaniecki
Cavan, R. S.: 202, 276
Census of Current Research Projects: 6
Change, social, evolutionary theory of
(social evolution, -ism): characteristics of first period, 100–104; cultural
anthropological critique, 105–107;
second period sociologists' own views
of first period features, 108–116; their
own second period formulations,
119–140; decline and demise of this
theory, 144–148; summary, 140–143
Chapin, F. S.: academic data, 35, 98,
354 n16; balanced materialist-idealist,
308–309, 320; distinctive views about
culture, 109, 116, 119, 140; linear and
cyclical change theories combined,
99, 127–132, 134–135; statistically-
oriented, qualified empiricist, and
neo-positivist, 34, 35, 38–44 passim;
theory defined, 11, 152–153. See also
evolutionary theory of social change
Classificatory-periodizing scheme: purpose, 23, 24–25; precedents, 23; stems
from two basic problems, 23–24; used
to classify theories of first and second
periods and to demark periods themselves, 25–27. See Appendix,
349–350
Committee on Conceptual Integration
(of ASS): 44

Committee on Social and Religious Surveys: 14

Comte, Auguste: early American sociologists' views on, 32, 112; law of three stages of knowledge, 41; classical social evolutionist, 142; reference to Condorcet, 145; Teggart on, 191, 377 n20; Levy-Bruhl on Comtean consensus, 386 n5; Park on Comte's consensus, 310, 311; on his social realism, 314, 320

Condorcet, Marquis de: 145, 191, 377 n20

Cooley, C. H.: academic data, 233; unlike other early American sociologists, 30, 31; on instincts, 77; anti-positivist, 61; neo-idealist, 49–50, 51, 59, 60; precursor of symbolic interactionism, 232, 237–239; notion of individual–society relationship, 314; social process, valuation, and action implied, 318–319; "pre-organic" social origins theory accepted, 70

Culture, notion of: borrowed (diffused) from cultural anthropology, 173–174; characteristics of, among sociological theorists in second period, 174–177; domain of reality, 178–182; rejected as a theory in sociology, 182–186, summary, 196–198

Curtis, C. P.: 279

D

Dahlke, H. O.: 287

Darwin, Charles: 68, 85, 91, 103, 142, 191

Darwinism, social: 68, 85, 91, 103, 104, 124, 309

Davis, Kingsley: 184

Delatour, G. S.: 288

Descartes, R.: 30, 191, 277 n20

DeVoto, Bernard: 279

Dewey, John: 82, 311, 313, 320

Dilthey, Wilhelm: 15, 48, 49, 50–51, 52, 56, 58, 59, 60, 61

Dodd, Stuart A.: 11

Dummer, Ethel: 205, 207

Durkheim, Emile: Park's notion of his social realism, 311–312; culture conceived as akin to social realism, 185–186, 306; Faris's notion of the group close approximation to his social realism, 312–313, 320; indications of American sociologists' interest in, 274, 275; responses to his views, 275–279; theses and dissertations on, 275; translations and reviews of translations, 275

E

Eaves, Lucille: 32

Eliot, Thomas: 186, 201

Elliott, Mabel and Merrill, Francis E.: 275, 277

Ellwood, Charles A.: academic data, 17; selection of author's text justified, 16, 17, 18; contents of text analyzed, 18, 19, 20, 21, 22; except for parabolic depiction, directional trend in change theory resembles that of his predecessors, 121–123; opposed behaviorism, 212; predominantly an idealist, 144, 183, 197; specialist in change theory and research, 94. See also evolutionary theory of social change, social forces, social origins theory, parallel evolution

Empiricism: a major basis of social knowledge, 23, 24, 35; ordinarily joined with reason–rationalism, 24; qualified, 37–38; first period, 30–31; second period, 37–38. See Appendix, 349

Epistemology, social; social epistemological theories: defined, 23–24; possible bases of social knowledge, 24; ordinarily linked with (social) methodology, 23–24; first period, 30–31; second period, 35–57. See

Appendix, 349; also Materialism;
Empiricism; Individualism, methodological; Scientific Method, common;
Generalizations and laws; Positivism;
Statistics; Operationalized terminology; Neo-idealism; Neo-Kantianism;
also Chapin, Ogburn, Rice, Lundberg,
Bernard, Bain
Ermarth, M.: 343, 344
Evolution, -ism, parallel (physical-
organic-psychic-socio-cultural):
defined, 87; sociological objections,
87–89

F

Faris, Ellsworth: academic data, 232, 69,
146; critiques of behaviorism,
227–230; of classical social evolution,
108, 110, 112, 114; of cultural origins
theories, 88–89, 92, 115; of Freudian
ideas, 201, 207, 208, 210, 211; of
instincts, 88, 92; of Pareto's views,
281–282; of Thomas's four wishes,
81; his orientation in sociology and
social psychology an amalgam of
pragmatist philosophy, (Meadian)
modified behaviorist psychology, and
several strands of thought in sociology, 133, 253–261; involved in
instinct controversy, 77, 79–80, 81,
91; social ontologically predominantly an idealist, 144, 183, 197;
social origins problem unsolvable, 89,
92–93
Faris, Robert E. L.: 202, 353 n15
Fink, H. W.: 203
Folsom, Joseph Kirk: 177
Fontenelle, B.: 191
Forces, social: 70–71
Foundation(s), -alism: 147, 299–300,
337–340, 355 n24
Freud, Sigmund: 210
Freudianism, Freudian – psychoanalytic
psychiatry: 201–211. See Ogburn,

Thomas, Bain, Bernard, Burgess,
Faris, MacIver, Znaniecki
Fromm, Eric: 201

G

Gary, D. P.: 276
Gault, Robert: 201, 202
Gehlke, C. E.: academic data, 9; definition of theory, 9; notion of research,
33; opposed to Durkheim's social
realism, 276; statistically-oriented,
qualified empiricist, neo-positivist,
34, 37, 42, 147
Gerth, Hans H. and Ilse Gerth: 288
Gerth, Hans and C. Wright Mills: 288
Gestaltism (gestalt sociology): 223–224
Giddens, Anthony: 35
Giddings, F. H.: most complete exposition of elementary statistics in 1920s,
34; general sociology and theory, 16,
10; founder and mediator of statistically-oriented, qualified empiricism,
neo-positivism, 34, 38, 42, 49; mediating role in transmitting Pearson's
ideas, 41; theory defined systematically, 16
Gillin, J. L.: 32, 33, 35, 58
Goldenweiser, Alexander: critic of
social evolutionism before and after
World War I, 106, 107; discussant of
ASS's session on instincts in early
1920s, 77; provided evidence to deny
parallel evolution, 87, 92; meetings on
psychoanalysis held at his home
before World War I, 202; one of several cultural anthropologists influential in sociology in 1920s and later,
105
Gouldner, Alvin: 336, 351 n2, 355 n24,
387 n3
Green, Arnold: 208
Group, nature of the: See social reality
Groves, E.: 201, 202, 208
Gumplowicz, Ludwig: 4

H

Hagood, Margaret J.: 42
Hall, G. Stanley: 201
Handman, Max: 280, 281
Hankins, Frank H.: academic data, 17;
    selection of (author's) text justified,
    16, 17; contents (of text) analyzed, 19,
    20, 21, 22; ape-human similarities, 76;
    balanced materialist-idealist, 144,
    308–309; branching multilinear direc-
    tion claimed for social evolution,
    132–133. See also behaviorism, evo-
    lutionary naturalism, evolutionary the-
    ory of social change, instinct contro-
    versy, notion of culture, social struc-
    ture, social origins theories
Hart, Bernard: 203
Hart, Hornell: 187, 276, 283, 284
Hart, Hornell and Panzer, Adele: 173,
    178, 183
Harvey, L.: 69
Hayner, N. S.: 201
Healy, W.: 201
Healy, W. and Bronner, A.: 205
Heberle, Rudolf: 287
Henderson, Lawrence J.: 279
Hennis, Wilhelm: 351 n1
Herskovits, M. J.: 105, 326
Herskovits, M. J. and Willey, M.: 106,
    107, 173
Hertzler, J. O.: 186
Heyl, Barbara: 279
Hiller, E. T.: 17, 21, 22, 23, 148
Hinkle, Gisela J.: 202, 203, 205
Hinkle, Roscoe C.: characteristics of
    first period social structure, 73–74;
    change and organismic growth, 142;
    classificatory-periodizing scheme, 24,
    95, 303, 305; criteria for periodizing,
    25; evolutionary naturalism, 69; first
    period social ontological stances, 319;
    social forces, 70; social ontology,
    315; voluntaristic nominalism, 318
Hobhouse, L.T., Wheeler, M., Ginsburg,
    M.: 140

Holt, E. B.: 205, 206
Homans, George: 280
Honigsheim, Paul: 288
Horkheimer, Max: 284
Horney, Karen: 201
Horowitz, L.: 287
House, F. N.: 8, 9, 190–191, 279, 283
Howe, F.: 10
Hughes, R. M.
Hull, C.: 38, 212

I

Individualism (atomism), methodologi-
    cal: defined, characterized and illus-
    trated, 38. See Appendix, 349
Induction: 39; 56–57
Interchurch World Movement: 14
Instinct controversy: 77–81
ISRR (Institute for Social and Religious
    Research): 14

J

Janowitz, M.: 204
Jay, M.: 284
Jennings, H. S.: 207
Jocher, K.: 34, 48
Jones, Robert A.: 201
Jung, Carl: 201, 210

K

Kant, Immanuel: 53
Kantor, J. R.: 77
Karpf, Fay B.: 310, 311
Keller, A. G.: 100, 362 n2, 124, 142,
    144. See also evolutionary theory of
    social change and notion of culture
Kellogg, W. N. and Kellogg, L. A.: 76
Kempf, E. J.: 203
Kirkpatrick, C.: 43, 208
Kolakowski, L.: 35

Kohler, Wolfgang: 76, 77, 91, 224
Kroeber, Alfred: 105, 185
Kropotkin, A.: 210
Krueger, E. T.: 201, 202
Krueger, E. T. and Reckless, W. C.: 313, 320

L

Lamarck, J. B.: 92, 104
Lasswell, Harold: 201
Lazarus, M.: 283
LCRC (Local Community Research Committee at University of Chicago): 14, 15
LeBon, G.: 210
Lederer, E.: 288
Levine, D., Carter, E., Gorman, E.: 284, 285
Levi-Strauss, Claude: 288
Lewis, J. D. and Smith, R. L.: 233
Leyburn, J. G.: 184
Lichtenberger, J. P.: 6, 9, 276
Linton, R.: 184
Locke, John: 216, 217
Logos: 165
Loomis, Charles P.: 286
Lowie, Robert: 105, 185
Lowe, A.: 288
Lowenthal, Leo: 284
Lumley, F. E.: academic data, 17; resembles first period social evolutionist, 124, 140. See also evolutionary theory of social change, notion of culture, social forces, social origins theories, social structure
Lundberg, George A.: academic data, 17, 10; selection of author's text justified, 17, 18; text contents analyzed, 19, 20, 21, 22; committed to a radical or ultra-behaviorism, 218–222; epistemology-methodology stated comprehensively as statistically oriented, qualified empiricism, neo-positivism, 29, 34, 137–46 passim; neo-posi-
tivism compared with neo-idealism and neo-Kantianism, 59, 60, 61, 62; opposed social evolutionary type theory, 147; predominantly a behavioristic materialist, 315, 320; research defined, 33; reticent or "closet" social realist, 306–307
Lynd, Robert S.: 14

M

MacIver, Robert M.: academic data, 17; selection of author's text justified, 16–17; contents of text analyzed, 18, 19, 22; critique of behaviorism, 226; of Freudianism, 209, 210–211; of empiricism and positivism, 46–47, 58; crux of evolutionary directionality is differentiation-integration process in three stages, 124–127; groups, types of , 75; neo-idealism supported, 49, 50, 51, 60–62 passim; renewal of theory, 10; social ontological position, predominantly idealist, 144, 315, 317. See also action-social action theory and evolutionary theory of social change
MacIver, R. M. and Page, C. H.: 147
McCormick, T. C.: 35, 42
McDougall, William: 77
McLaughlin, I.: 186
Maine, Sir Henry: 283
Mannheim, Karl: 287
Marx, Karl: 283–284
Mathews, S.: 93, 108
Mayo-Smith, R.: 35, 42
Mead, George Herbert: academic data, 232, 233; major features of what came to be known as his symbolic interactionism, 239–253
Mead, Margaret: 202
Meroney, W. P.: 33
Merton, Robert K.: 7, 153, 333, 335
Method, scientific, common: basic characteristics, 39; versus levels of scien-

tific inquiry, 40. See Ogburn, Chapin, and Lundberg

Methodology, social, theories of: linked with social epistemology, 23, 24; first period, 30–32; second period, 34–57. See also Epiricism, Methodological individualism, Common Scientific Method, Sociological Methods, Positivism, Generalizations and Laws, Statistics, Operationalized Terminology, neo-idealism and Neo-Kantianism

Methods, sociological: specified and discussed, 33–34

Meyer, Carl: 288

Mill, John Stuart: 38

Mills, C. Wright: 284

Moore, Harry E. and Moore, Bernice M.: 280, 281

Morgan, Lewis Henry: 105, 141

N

Naturalism, evolutionary: 66–69

Natural science generalizations and laws possible in sociology: 40–41

Neo-idealism: 49, 50–51

Neo-Kantian, -ism: 52, 53–55, 362 n25

Nimkoff, Meyer: 201

Nietzsche, Frederick: 207

Nisbet, Robert: 142, 145, 376 n18

Nominalism, social: group defined, 305, 314, 316; illustrated, 309, 310, 311, 314, 316–317, 318, 319; first period, 319, versus second period, 321. See Appendix, 350, notions of social reality

O

Ogburn, W. F.: academic data, 35, 42, 95; culture lag theory of social change, 127–132; denies parallel evolution as a basis of cultural change, 87–88; discussant at ASS session on instincts, 77; form of theory represented by social evolution later rejected, 147; predominantly a materialist, 307–308; psychoanalysis, 201, 202–204; refused to emphasize the role of individual differences in genesis of innovation, 309; statistically-oriented, qualified empiricist, and neo-positivist, 34, 35, 38, 147. See also evolutionary theory of social change and notion of culture

Ogburn and Goldenweiser: 34, 35

Ogburn, W. F. and Nimkoff, M.: second author's academic data, 17; selection of authors' text justified, 17; contents of text analyzed, 20, 21, 22, 23; substantial interest in types of groups, 75; technology as the prime mover in social change, 131; tools subject to decisive test of workability-efficiency, 129; ways to reduce lag, 132. See evolutionary theory of social change, notion of culture

Ontology, ontological, social, theory (theories) of: See notion of social reality and social origins and social change theories

OPA (Office of Price Administration): 15

Operation(al)ism, -ization of terms: 43, 44. See Chapin, Lundberg, Alpert

Origins, social, evolutionary theories of: 70, 324–325

OSS (Office of Strategic Services, became Central Intelligence Agency): 15

P

Page, Charles: 284

Pareto, Vilfredo: 27, 279–283

Park, Robert E.: academic data, 17, 95; concern with urban community-urban society, 156; epistemology-methodology, Neo-Kantian, 53, 54, 55–56, 57;

interest in origins of civilized, urban
societies and characteristics, 152, 292,
378 n23; interpretation of Comte's
social consensus, 311; interpretation
of Durkheim's social realism, 312;
misconstrued Teggart's intellectual
stance, 191–192; nomothetic/idio-
graphic division of knowledge
accepted, 90, 154; notion of culture
reflects German training, 373 n16;
social ontological position, balanced
materialism-idealism, 168, 309–310;
social phenomena as natural objects,
54, 156, 192; social process formulation of social change, 148, 155–156;
social realism, conception of, 311,
312, 320; sociology and anthropology
have different foci of problems, 154;
specialist in change theory and
research, 94; students of Park, 90;
translator of portions of Windelband's
rectoral address, 54; universality of
change through cycle of (abstract)
processes, 167
Park, Robert E. and Ernest W. Burgess:
17, 19, 20, 21, 29, 81
Parker, Carleton C.: 201
Parsons, Talcott: critique of behaviorism, 225–226; early articles on M.
Weber, 289; evidence of interest in
theory after 1935, 16; exemplifies
interest in M. Weber, 288, 321; favorably disposed to Neo-Kantian epistemology-methodology, 53, 55, 56, 57;
in renewal of theory, 10, 315; indicative of closing years of second period
of theory, 26, 335–336; influenced by
European arguments, 34; reflects an
ontological pluralism, 316; Thomas
and Znaniecki's definition of the situation, 317; Weber as major influence
in Parson's formulation, 332. See also
action-social action theory
Pascal, B.: 101, 145, 377 n20
Pavlov, I. P.: 216, 217
PASS *(Publications of the American
Sociological Society)*: 33, 201, 273

Pearson, Karl: 35, 37, 39, 41, 52
Perrault, C.: 191
Periodization (of theory): 24–27,
333–346; 337–345. See Appendix,
349–350
Physis: 142–143, 164, 192, 364 n4
Plantinga, T.: 343
Plato: 190
Positivism: notion of in sociology, 35;
versus philosophy, 35; for second
period, "neo-", 35, 362 n25; major
historical figures in sociology, 35, 41,
356 n4; major exponents in second
period, 35, antagonists of social evolutionary theory, 147; opposition to,
46–47. See Appendix, 349
Process, -ualism, social: non-evolutionary theory of social change, 153–156

Q

Queen, Stuart A.: 223

R

Radnitzky, G.: 23
Realism, social: group defined,
305–306, 310–311; illustrated for the
second period, 307, 311–313, 314,
319, 320, 321. See Appendix, 350
Reality, social, notion of: nature of the
"social," including the group, 303,
304; minimum requirements for a
group and structure, 304; criteria for
classifying-characterizing the group
as based on reality generally (the
materialism-idealism polarity),
304–305; the part-whole and whole-
part relationship (the nominalist-real-
ist dichotomy), 305–306; group in the
second period of theory, 306–319,
144; notion of group compared in first
and second periods, 319–321. See
Appendix, 350, and references to
social nominalism and social realism

Redfield, Robert: 286
Research movement, social, rise of:
32–33
Reuter, E. B. and Hart, C.: academic
data, 17, 90; influenced by Neo-Kantianism, 90; selection of authors' text
justified, 17; contents of text analyzed, 19, 20–21, 22, 23; social
process conception of social change,
148, 155, also 159, 371 n7; social
realism, 309–310, 313, 318, 320;
socio-cultural change non-evolutionary, organic change evolutionary,
89–90; sociology defined, 67; used
Thomas's four wishes as social forces,
81, 90. See also notion of culture,
social origins theory, social structure
Rice, S. A.: bias and prejudice affect
operation of the senses, 37–38; hostile
to a holistic or gestaltist perspective,
223; social and natural phenomena
have heretofore unnoted resemblances, 36; statistically-oriented,
qualified empiricist, and neo-positivist
stance, 34, 37, 58, 146–147
Rickert, H.: 48, 49, 51, 57, 90, 192
Rickman, H. P.: 342
Riemer, Svend: 288
Robinson, J. H.: 188, 189, 198
Ross, Dorothy: 41, 376 n18
Ross, E. A.: 30, 31, 70, 71, 373 n1

S

Saint Augustine: 145, 191
Salomon, A.: 288
Schumpeter, J.: 279
SF (*Social Forces*): 6, 10, 16, 173, 174,
273, 274, 279, 284, 287
Shanas, Ethel: 6, 7
Shaw, Clifford: 48, 201
Shils, E. A.: 287, 288, 385 nn6, 8, 9, 10;
386 nn11, 14
Simmel, Georg: 4, 284–286, 314
Simpson, E. N.: 81–82
Simpson, George: 275

Small, Albion: 9, 16, 71
Smith, Norman E. and Hinkle, Roscoe
C.: 100
Society, American, World War I – II: 12
Sociology, American, World War I – II:
12–15
S&SR (*Sociology and Social Research*):
6, 10, 173, 201, 273, 274, 279, 284
Solovay, S. A. and Mueller, J. H.: 275
Sorokin, Pitirim A.: academic data, 95;
conceives of sociology as a generalizing science (as Rickert), 55; comparison with Becker and Park, 167,
169–170; comprehensive systematic
theory, 29; contributions to classification of sociological theories, 23; critique of behaviorism, 226; of Freudian
assumptions, 208, 211; of major theories of social change, including social
evolutionism, 99–100, 108; espoused
case-study and qualitative research,
34; mind, reason, or logos as model of
social change, 110; organismic growth
as a model of social change, 110; Neo-
Kantian epistemologically, 58; rate or
tempo as notion not applicable to
social change, 113, 116; specialist in
change theory and research, 94; theory
of social change, 109, 148, 163–167
Speier, Hans: 288
Spencer, Herbert: classical European
theorist, 4; conception of conflict and
competition, 310; features of social
evolution, 142; his legacy, 103; objections to history, 187–188; his Social
Darwinism, 91; view of organic evolution, 68, 85
Spykman, N. J.: 6, 285
SSRC (Social Science Research Council): 14
Statistics: 41, 42
Stern, Bernhard J.: 173, 179, 183, 184,
197, 284
Steinthal, H.: 283
Stouffer, Samuel: 35
Structure or organization, social, theories of: 73–74

Sullivan, Harry S.: 201
Sumner, William Graham: 10, 73, 184, 319
Sumner, W. G. and Keller, A. G.: 101, 104
Sutherland, Robert E. L. and Woodward, Julian: academic data, 17; selection of authors' text justified, 17; text contents analyzed, 21, 22, 23; social process conception of social change, 148, but see also, 159, 371 n7; social nominalist/social realist distinction, 310; cf. 314. See also notion of culture
Symbolic interactionism: 232–234. See also Thomas, Cooley, Mead, Faris, Blumer

T

Tarde, Gabriel: 104
Teggart, F. J.: 111, 190–191, 300, 337
Terminology, social change: 96–97
Theory, action – social action (means-ends scheme): indebtedness to Weber, 288–290, or to Neo-Kantianism, 290–291; major assumptions-concepts, 291–297; second period exponents, 288–289
Theory, sociological: defined, 23–24, 354–355 n23; assumptions, background, domain, foundational, 255 n24; problematics of a historiographic study World War I – II, 3–5; classical masters in, 351 n1; indications of interest in, second period, 5–7, notions of, in second period, 7–10; sources of data and criteria of inclusion in present study, 17–18; structure of books in general sociological theory of second period, 19–21. See classificatory-periodizing scheme; Appendix, 349–350; also social ontological and epistemological -methodological theories
Thomas, W. I.: academic data, 232–233, 69; advocate of case study, 49;

Blumer's self-indication and (his) personal definition of the situation, 271, 316–318; contributions to symbolic interactionism, 234–236; earliest social psychological stance, 123; evidence of Freudian influence on, 204–207; four wishes, 71, and as used by others, 80–81; four wishes criticized by Faris, 81, 91; protagonist of Freudian influence in sociology, 201; subscribed to individualism and voluntarism, 270, 316–318, 320–321
Thomas, W. I. and Znaniecki, Florian: definition of social theory, 8; intellectual disagreements over nature of social change, 98, 100; mixed cyclical and linear theory of social change, 136–139; direction from predominantly primary-group oriented to secondary-group oriented, 136–139; position on social causation negatively influenced by Durkheim, 275; social ontological stance, 98, 100; predominantly idealist, 144; specialists in change theory and research, 94; temporal beginning boundary of this study set by their book, which marks beginning of concern with research and research methods in American sociology, 25
Tocqueville, A.: 10
Tolman, E. C.: 212
Tönnies, Ferdinand: 286–287
Turner, Jonathan: 41
Turner, Steven: 41
Tylor, E. B.: 173, 178

V

Volkart, Edmund: 207

W

Waller, Willard: 223
Wallis, Wilson: 87, 92, 105, 107

Ward, L. F.: 142, 319, 374 n1
Watson, John B.: 212
Weatherly, U. G.: 201
Weber, Max: Becker's typology came from, 199; crucial figure for majority of American social action theorists, 318–319, 332; mediated Dilthey's *verstehen,* 61; Neo-Kantian commitment, 48, 49; "new" classical master, 4; innovative stimuli to American theory, 27; Parsons rejected his ideal-types, 57; translations important, 315; voluntaristic nominalism derives from American version of his social action conception, 321; Wirth accepts Weber's social action notion, 314
White, Leslie: 184
Willey, M. M.: See notion of culture
Windelband, Wilhelm: 48, 49, 50, 59
Wirth, Louis: 285, 286
Wissler, Clark: 105, 141, 176, 185
Wolff, Kurt H.: 288
Wood, M.: 285
WPA (Works Project Administration): 15
Wundt, W.: 283

Y

Yerkes, R. M.: 76, 77, 91
Yerkes, R. M. and Yerkes, A. W.: 76

Young, Donald: 208
Young, Kimball: academic data, 17; selection of author's text justified, 17; contents of text analyzed, 19, 20, 21, 22, 23; apes display basic forms of human social relations, 76, 77; commented on Faris's use of Mead's analysis of rise and development of self, 261; indebted to Simmel, 286; social process theory of social change, 148. See also culture and social structure

Z

Zorbaugh, H. W.: 201
Znaniecki, Florian: case-study and qualitative research advocated, 34; critique of Freudian ideas, 208, 209, 211; European idealist notion of culture, 182; in revival of theory, 10; Neo-Kantian epistemology-methodology, 49, 52, 53, 54–55, 56, 57; rejected empiricism and positivism, 46, 47
Zuckerman, Sol: 76, 77, 91